The March of World History

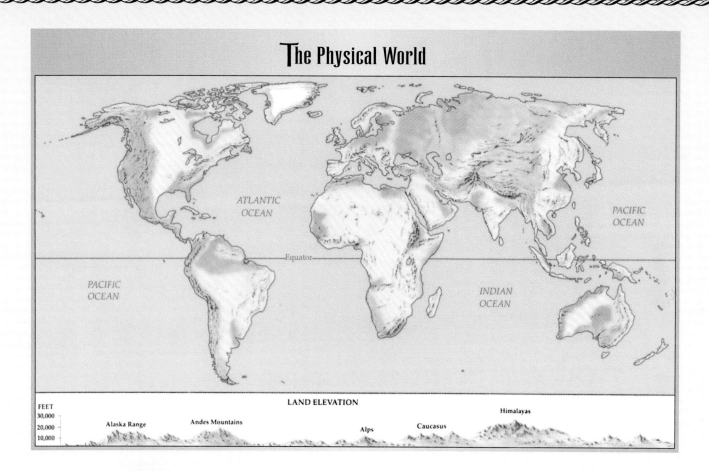

The Physical World

T he topographical features of the world, its mountains, plains, deserts, rivers, and the seas, have profoundly affected history. The Himalayas cut China off from India, preventing potential conquest but also eliminating lucrative trade prospects. The terrain to the north and west is more open; this invited commercial connections with the civilizations far to the west, but made China vulnerable to invasion by the nearby steppe nomads; hence the need for the Great Wall.

The history of Europe also provides examples of the effects of topography. In Greece, for instance, the combination of mountainous terrain and a long, jagged coastline divided the inhabitants into little isolated pockets. This made political unity difficult—there were hundreds of city-states in an area smaller than the U.S. state of Michigan—and stimulated Greeks to turn to the sea for trade and communication.

Modern technology, however, has diminished or even eliminated the importance of topographic features. Currently, ballistic missiles have made mountains and seas largely irrelevant as protective barriers.

West Asia and Africa	South and East Asia	Europe
7000 B.C.E.	7000 B.C.E.	7000 B.C.E.
Neolithic revolution in the Fertile Crescent	Neolithic period in China	Earliest agricultural villages (in Greece)
Agriculture in the Nile Valley	Neolithic period in India	
	Chinese culture heroes	
	Cultivation of silkworms in China	
Bronze metallurgy in West Asia	Urban civilization in the Indus Valley	
King Menes unifies Egypt	Mythical Hsia dynasty in China	Megalithic construction begins at Stonehenge
Great pyramids at Giza		
2000	2000	2000
Hammurabi's code	T'ang the Successful establishes the Shang dynasty	Indo-Europeans arrive in Balkan Peninsula
Hyksos domination in Egypt		
Akhenaton and Nefertiti rule in Egypt	Aryans destroy Indus civilization	Height of Minoan civilization on Crete
Introduction of chariot warfare by the Hittites	Earliest extant Chinese writing	
		Eruption of Thera
Judaism: Moses	Anyang, capial of Shang China	
	Kings Wen and Wu	Trojan War
	Duke of Chou	Collapse of Mycenaean civilization
1000 King David	1000 *Books of Poetry, History, Rites, Change, Rig-Veda*	1000
First Temple at Jerusalem		Spread of iron metallurgy
Kushite kingdom in Nile Valley		
	Eastern Chou	
750 Zoroaster in Persia	750	750
Nebuchadnezzar builds the Hanging Gardens in Babylon	Spring and Autumn era	Greeks adopt Phoenician alphabet
	Early *Upanishads*	Homer, *Iliad* and *Odyssey*
Solon's reforms at Athens		
Persian royal road network		
The Babylonian captivity	Buddha	
Conquests of King Cyrus	Mahavira	
	Confucius	
	The *Lao Tzu*	Beginning of the Roman Republic
	Iron weapons, crossbow, metal tools, and coins	
500	500	500

Major States and Cultures, c. 500 B.C.E.

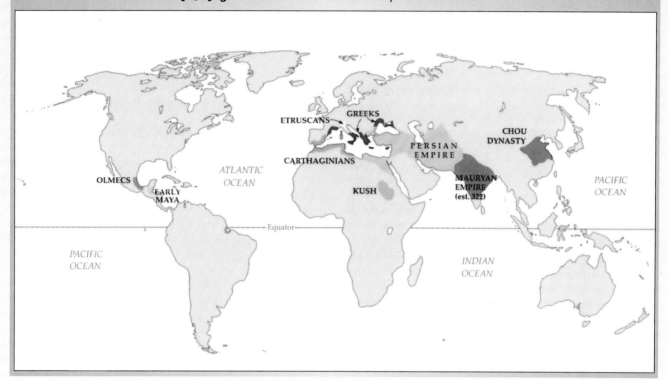

About 500 B.C.E., civilizations were scattered across a narrow, temperate band of the Northern Hemisphere. The rest of the world was either uninhabited or occupied by various Paleolithic or Neolithic peoples.

The early civilizations in the Fertile Crescent and Egypt had now been absorbed by the expanding Persian Empire, which controlled its many subject peoples through a centralized bureaucracy and an extensive road network. The Greeks and Carthaginians were trading throughout the Mediterranean Sea and colonizing its shores.

China's first era, that of the Bronze Age Shang and feudal Chou dynasties, was now in decline; the following period of disorder would bring forth Confucianism. In India, the Indus Valley culture had long disappeared; Hinduism was well developed. Buddhism and the first extensive Indian state, the Mauryan Empire, were on the horizon.

Up the Nile, the African state of Kush, strongly influenced by Egyptian culture, held sway. In the Western Hemisphere, the Olmec culture was producing the Mesoamerican calendar, based on sophisticated astronomical and mathematical knowledge.

West Asia and Africa	South and East Asia	Europe	Western Hemisphere
500 B.C.E.	500 B.C.E.	500 B.C.E.	500 B.C.E.
First five books of Tanakh codified	Gautama Buddha, *Tripitaka* Confucius's *Spring and Autumn* and *Analects* Chandragupta Maurya Kautilya, *Arthasastra* Mencius, *The Mencius* Shang Yang, *Book of Lord Shang* Alexander the Great invades India	Greek-Persian Wars The Parthenon Sophocles, *Oedipus the King* Pericles Peloponnesian War Trial and death of Socrates Plato, *Republic* Aristotle Demosthenes Alexander the Great	Calendar, writing, and numerical system in Mesoamerica Olmec civilization flourishes at La Venta Later era of Chavin cult civilization in Peru
300	300	300	300
	The *Mahabharata* and *Ramayana* Emperor Asoka: Third Buddhist Council Shih Huang-ti: The Great Wall Indians sail to Southeast Asia Han Kao-tsu founds the Han dynasty Emperor Wu: Confucianism the state ideology in China	Euclid's *Elements* Stoicism and Epicureanism Scipio defeats Hannibal at Zama	Preclassic Maya civilization
Roman Empire expands into West Asia and North Africa			
100	100	100	100
Extensive trade along the Silk Road linking western and eastern Asia Cleopatra Kingdom of Axum Christianity: Crucifixion of Jesus Nok in western Africa; iron tools and weapons	Buddhism spreads to China Ajanta and other cave excavations begun Ssu-ma Ch'ien, *Records of the Historian*	Cicero Assassination of Julius Caesar Emperor Augustus	Obsidian trade in Mesoamerica Maya center at Tres Zapotes
100 C.E.	100 C.E.	100 C.E.	100 C.E.
The Gospels Bantu migrations in Africa		Plotinus and Neoplatonism	Moche succeeds Chavin civilization in Peru Rise of classic Maya civilization at Tikal
300	300	300	300
Christianity in Ethiopia Compilation of the Talmud	Gandharan and Mathuran art styles Paper invented Gupta dynasty Cave temples in China	Emperor Constantine Augustine, *City of God* Last emperor of Rome	Teotihuacán begins era of full flowering in Mesoamerica Maya calendar fully formulated
500	500	500	500

Major States and Cultures, c. 200 C.E.

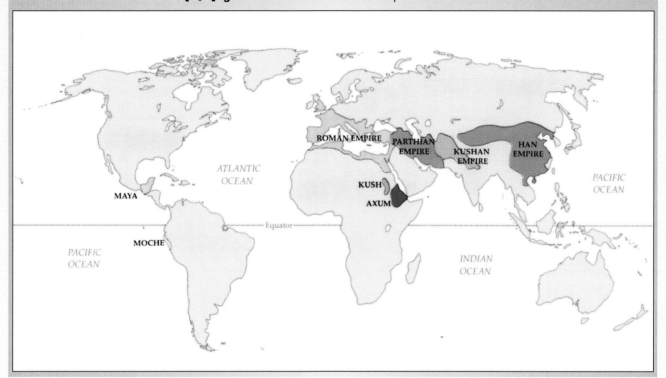

The Roman Empire and China under Han rule constituted the most powerful civilizations in 200 C.E. Rome, now at its height, had carried civilization into western Europe and, in the eastern Mediterranean region, had superseded the Hellenistic kingdoms spawned by the conquests of Alexander the Great. Rome, which possessed its own gift for technological innovation and efficient administration, had inherited the rich cultural legacy of Greece.

The Han Empire matched Rome in technological innovation, military strength, and bureaucratic efficiency. Although in decline by 200 C.E., the Han era had witnessed great economic prosperity and cultural splendor. The Parthians, successors to the Persian Empire, halted Rome's eastward expansion.

In Africa the state of Kush was now rivaled by Axum, which was well protected in the Ethiopian highlands. In the Western Hemisphere, Mesoamerican civilization centered in the Maya city states. The Moche culture was one of a series of advanced civilizations in ancient Peru.

West Asia and Africa	South and East Asia	Europe	Western Hemisphere
500	500	500	500
	China reunified; Grand Canal built	Justinian I	
		Hagia Sophia	
	Prince Shotoku's regency in Japan		
	Chinese trade in Southeast Asia		
600	600	600	600
Islam: Muhammad	T'ang Tai-tsung		Tiahuanaco-Huari era in Peru
The Qur'an	Harsha rules in India		
Umayyad caliphate: battle of Yarmuk	Hsuan-tsang goes to India	Byzantines use "Greek fire"	
Ethiopian Coptic church established			
700 Shi'i-Sunni split	700 Muslims invade Sind	700	700
Abbasid caliphate	T'ang Ming-huang: golden age of Chinese poetry		Maya civilization at its height: Copán
Umayyad predominance in Spain	Borobodur built		
800 Spread of Islam in North and East Africa, to Indus River in east, and Iberian Peninsula in west	800 Silla unifies Korea	800 Charlemagne and the Carolingian Renaissance	800
900 Arab scientists flourish	900 Printing becomes widespread	Photios, patriarch of Constantinople	900 Toltec Empire centered at Tula
Fatimids in Cairo	Angkor Wat built	900	
al-Azhar University	Northern Sung dynasty	Olga, princess of Kiev	
	Feudal Japan; code of bushido	*Epic of Digenes Akritas*	
	Neo-Confucianism in China		
	Chinese examination system developed		
1000 Ibn Sina (Avicenna)	1000 Turkish Muslims conquer North India; Rajput resistance	1000 Vernacular literatures begin in Europe	1000
Rabbi Musa bin Maymun		Romanesque architecture	
Ibn Rushd (Averroës)	Lady Murasaki, *The Tale of Genji*		
Rise of the Seljuk Turks			
Byzantine Empire declines		al-Cid	
1100 Crusader conquest	1100 Shogunate in Japan	1100 Gothic architectural style begins	1100 Postclassic Maya civilization: Chichén Itzá
European-Asian trade increases	Southern Sung dynasty		
1200 Salah ed-Din	1200 Rise of Genghis Khan	1200	Appearance of the 1200 Inka in the Peruvian highlands
Kingdoms of salt and gold in West Africa			
East African city-states			
Stone complexes in Zimbabwe			

Major States and Cultures, c. 800

B y 800 the T'ang era in China witnessed the economic and military expansion of a cosmopolitan, religiously pluralistic society. In India, Hindu and Buddhist cultures had thrived under the Guptas and Harsha. The Khmer civilization was flourishing and the Japanese culture, heavily derivative of China, had made its appearance. The Roman Empire had been succeeded by the rival Christian Carolingian and Byzantine Empires. One of Byzantium's rivals was the Bulgarian Empire, but its main enemies were the Muslims, who had swept out of the Arabian Peninsula in the seventh century. The Islamic world of the rival Abbasid and Umayyad caliphates marked a great age of literature and science.

In northeastern Africa, the beleaguered Coptic Christian state of Axum continued to hold on. In West Africa, Ghana was the first of the "kingdoms of gold and salt" that controled a prosperous trade network across the Sahara to the Mediterranean.

Amerindian cultures continued to evolve. The Maya focused on an elaborate system of religious ceremonies and sacrifices based on their astronomical calendar. The Peruvian cultural matrix expanded away from the coast and south into the highlands of the Andes.

West Asia and Africa	South and East Asia	Europe	Western Hemisphere
1200	1200	1200	1200
Mamluks rule in Egypt and Syria	Mongols conquer Russia, eastern Europe Kubilai Khan conquers the Southern Sung Marco Polo in China	The *Magna Carta* Thomas Aquinas, *Summa Theologica*	Aztecs enter the basin of Mexico
1300	1300	1300	1300
Ottomans conquer Anatolia *The Rubaiyat of Omar Khayyam* Mansa Kankan Musa, leader of Mali Timbuktu at its zenith; University of Timbuktu	Ashikaga shogunate in Japan Mongols replaced by Ming in China	Philip IV, "the Fair" Dante Alighieri, *The Divine Comedy* Francesco Petrarca The Black Death	Beginning of Inka conquests
1400	1400	1400	1400
Timurlane's conquests Predominance of the Benin kingdom in West Africa Portuguese arrive in West Africa Songhai Empire peaks under Muhammad the Great	Ming capital established at Peking Chinese naval expeditions to South and Southeast Asia	Ottomans capture Constantinople Johannes Gutenberg's printing press Ferdinand and Isabella end Muslim rule in Spain	Expansion of Aztec rule: Tenochtitlán Inka conquests throughout the Andes: Pachacuti Columbus arrives in the Carribbean
1500	1500	1500	1500
Beginnings of the Safavid Empire Afonso I, king of the Kongo Ottoman Turks conquer Arab territories Slave trade in Africa Suleiman the Magnificent Suleimaniye complex by Sinan in Istanbul Shah Abbas the Great	Portuguese trade empire in Southeast Asia Guru Nanak founds Sikhism Moghul conquest of India Portuguese introduce Christianity and firearms to Japan Spanish rule in the Philippines English East India Company formed Dutch trade empire in the East Indies	Copernicus, *On the Revolutions of the Heavenly Spheres* Leonardo da Vinci Desiderius Erasmus Martin Luther's Ninety-five Theses Roman Catholic Reformation Queen Elizabeth I William Shakespeare Miguel de Cervantes, *Don Quixote*	Moctezuma II becomes Aztec ruler Voyages of Magellan Spanish conquests of Aztecs and Inka Spanish conquest of the Maya begins Centralized Spanish administration of South American colonies
1600	1600	1600	1600
"King" Nzinga in Angola Ashanti kingdom in West Africa Dutch settlement in South Africa	Tokugawa shogunate in Japan Jesuit missionaries in China Japan expels foreigners Neo-Confucianism in Japan Ch'ing (Manchu) dynasty in China Taj Mahal built in India	Romanov dynasty in Russia René Descartes Louis XIV, the "Sun King" Newton, *Mathematical Principles of Natural Philosophy* The "Glorious Revolution" in England	British and French begin to colonize North America de la Vega, *Royal Commentaries of the Incas* Harvard University founded The poetry of Sor Juana Inés de la Cruz
1700	1700	1700	1700

Major States and Cultures, c. 1500

Major States and Cultures, c. 1500

RUSSIA
ENGLAND
FRANCE
PORTUGAL **SPAIN** **OTTOMAN EMPIRE**
SAFAVID DYNASTY
MING DYNASTY
JAPAN
ATLANTIC OCEAN
MAYA **SONGHAI**
MAMLUK EMPIRE
MOGHUL EMPIRE [ca. 1600]
PACIFIC OCEAN
AZTEC EMPIRE **BENIN**
ETHIOPIA
Equator
KONGO
PACIFIC OCEAN
INKA EMPIRE
INDIAN OCEAN

In Europe about 1500, power was shifting to the technologically advanced national states of the western part of the continent. To the northeast, the Slavic state of Russia was taking shape.

In the Muslim world, the Mamluks in Egypt and the Safavids in Persia revitalized Arabic and Persian culture. The dynamic Ottoman Empire conquered the remnants of the Byzantine Empire and spread into the Balkans. The Ottomans would soon conquer the Mamluks, most of North Africa, the Fertile Crescent, and part of Arabia.

Shortly after 1500, the Muslim Moghul dynasty would arise in northern India, bringing about a cultural renaissance. In China, the Ming dynasty brought economic prosperity and cultural innovation.

In Africa, Christian Ethiopia resisted Muslim pressure. Songhai exploited the lucrative trade of West Africa. Meanwhile, Benin, Kongo, and Lunda emerged on or near the Atlantic coast.

The Western Hemisphere was dominated by two rapidly emerging empires. The Aztecs continued the tradition of Mesoamerican culture, while the Inka in the Andean highlands created a unique culture that fused centralized authority with an elaborate state socialism.

West Asia and Africa	South and East Asia	Europe	Western Hemisphere
1700	1700	1700	1700
West African kingdoms		Peter the Great begins Westernization of Russia	European nations compete for colonies
East African city-states		Daniel Defoe, *Robinson Crusoe*	Western Hemisphere linked with global economy
Dutch settlements in South Africa		Johann Sebastian Bach	
1725	1725	1725	1725
		The philosophes	Vitus Bering finds straits between Asia and Western Hemisphere
			Heavy migration into British North American colonies
		Frederick the Great	
1750 Slave trade between Africa and Western Hemisphere	1750 Ts'ao Hsueh-chin, *The Dream of the Red Chamber*	1750 Voltaire, *Candide*	1750 Benjamin Franklin's scientific investigations
	Battle of Plassey		
	Effective Moghul rule ends in India		Great Britain destroys French Empire in North America: battle of Quebec
	Christian missionaries end activity in China	James Watt's steam engine	
			Great Britain tightens control on North American colonies
Declining Ottoman power	Captain James Cook	Catherine the Great of Russia	Bourbon reforms in Spanish colonies
Russian advances around the Black Sea			
1775	1775	1775	1775 Rebellion in British North America
		Adam Smith, *The Wealth of Nations*	Declaration of Independence
		Destruction of Poland	Amerindian revolt in the Andes: Túpac Amaru
	The British colonize Australia	Joseph II of Austria	
	British embassy to China	Wolfgang Amadeus Mozart	U.S. Constitution and Bill of Rights
	Great Britain conquers Ceylon and East Indies from Netherlands	The French Revolution: Maximilien Robespierre	Black slave revolt frees Haiti
			The cotton gin
1800	1800	1800	1800
Muhammad Ali in Egypt		Napoleon Bonaparte	Robert Fulton's *Clermont*, first steamboat
		Ludwig van Beethoven	Thomas Jefferson
King Shaka's Zulu kingdom in South Africa	Great Britain returns East Indies to Netherlands	Battle of Waterloo	Latin American independence movements: Bolívar and San Martín
		Congress of Vienna	
		Greek War of Independence	
	Great Britain obtains Singapore	Romantic poetry: William Wordsworth	Brazil gains independence
1825	1825	1825	1825

The World, c. 1800

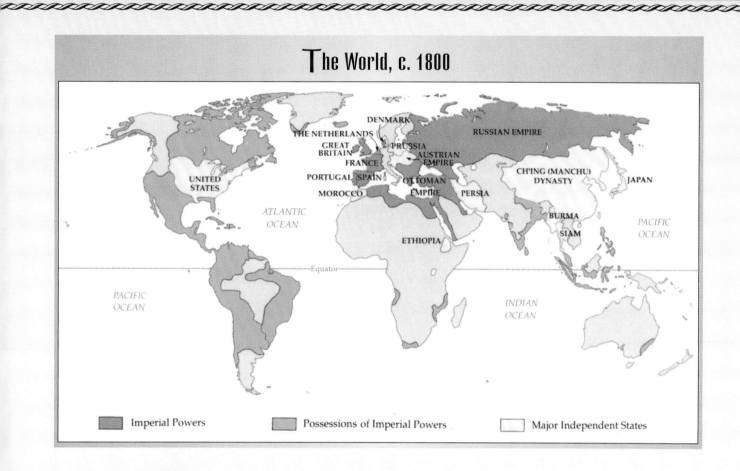

Imperial Powers   Possessions of Imperial Powers   Major Independent States

Before 1500 the states and cultures of the world were separate entities scattered across the globe; by 1800 Europeans had overrun the world and had confronted indigenous people on five continents.

By 1800 Russia had expanded east across Siberia into Alaska and west into central Europe. The nations of western Europe had turned the Western Hemisphere into a vast European colonial holding. The United States and Haiti, however, had become independent, and most of the mainland would soon follow suit.

The British were conquering India and had a foothold in Australia, while the Dutch were expanding in Indonesia. The traditional powers of Asia were less formidable. The Ottoman Empire was now in decline. The Moghul Empire was disintegrating, and Persia and Japan were relatively feeble. Only the Manchu dynasty in China seemed strong enough to fend off the Europeans.

Africa had largely escaped European takeover, although the Dutch and the Portuguese had major holdings on the coast. Nonetheless, Africa had suffered enormously. Millions of black Africans had been shipped to the Western Hemisphere as slaves.

West Asia and Africa	South and East Asia	Europe	Western Hemisphere
1825	1825	1825	1825
Abd al-Kadir in Algeria	Decline of Ch'ing dynasty	The Great Reform Act in Britain	McCormick reaper Tales and poems of Edgar Allan Poe
	Great Britain defeats China; unequal treaties	Revolutions of 1848 Marx and Engels, *The Communist Manifesto*	Samuel Morse and the telegraph
1850	1850	1850	1850
Christian missionary movement in Africa Ottoman Tanzimat reforms	United States opens Japan Gret Britain ends Moghul dynasty Direct British rule over India established	Second French Empire: Napoleon III Charles Darwin, *On the Origin of Species*	Henry David Thoreau, *Walden*
The Mahdi in Sudan al-Afghani: Pan-Islam		Italian nationalism: Camilio di Cavour, Giuseppe Garibaldi	Undersea telegraph cable link to Europe
Opening of the Suez Canal		Charles Dickens Eugène Delacroix Leo Tolstoy, *War and Peace*	Transcontinental railroad completed across the United States
	Meiji restoration	Unification of Germany: Otto von Bismarck	
	Japanese begin industrialization	Paris Commune	
1875	1875	1875	1875 Alexander Graham Bell and the telephone
Europeans partition Africa		Impressionist painting: Monet Gladstone/Disraeli era Louis Pasteur and germ theory	Thomas Edison and electric light Latin American revolutionary poetry: José Martí
		Tsar Alexander III	Rise of industrial monopolies: John D. Rockefeller Internal combustion engine
	Stories and poems of Rudyard Kipling		U. S. domination in the Caribbean begins: Spanish-American War
Boer War	Boxer Rebellion		
1900	1900 United States proposes "Open Door" policy in China	1900	1900
African resistance movements: Herero revolts	Russo-Japanese War	Freud, *The Interpretation of Dreams* Curie receives Nobel Prize in Physics	Wright brothers' flight at Kitty Hawk Euclides da Cunha, *Rebellion in the Backlands*
Rise of Turkish and Arab nationalism		Einstein's theory of relativity V. I. Lenin and Bolshevism	Ford Model T introduced; assembly-line production
	Japan annexes Korea	Arms stockpiling and war plans	Women's suffrage movement
South African Native National Congress	Chinese republic: Sun Yat-sen	Internal combustion engine	Mexican Revolution begins
1915	1915	1915 Women's suffrage movement	1915 Panama Canal

The World in 1914

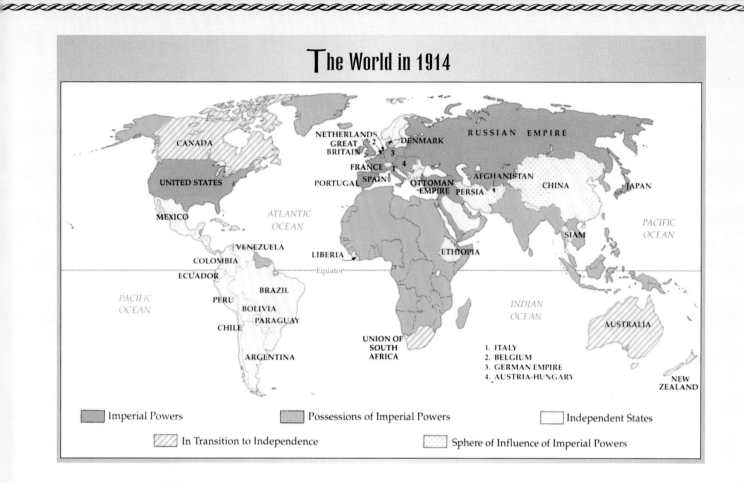

NETHERLANDS
GREAT
BRITAIN
DENMARK
RUSSIAN EMPIRE
FRANCE
PORTUGAL SPAIN
OTTOMAN EMPIRE PERSIA
AFGHANISTAN
CHINA
JAPAN
CANADA
UNITED STATES
MEXICO
ATLANTIC OCEAN
VENEZUELA
LIBERIA
Equator
ETHIOPIA
PACIFIC OCEAN
COLOMBIA
ECUADOR
PERU
BRAZIL
BOLIVIA
PARAGUAY
CHILE
PACIFIC OCEAN
UNION OF SOUTH AFRICA
INDIAN OCEAN
SIAM
PACIFIC OCEAN
AUSTRALIA
NEW ZEALAND
ARGENTINA

1. ITALY
2. BELGIUM
3. GERMAN EMPIRE
4. AUSTRIA-HUNGARY

Imperial Powers   Possessions of Imperial Powers   Independent States

In Transition to Independence   Sphere of Influence of Imperial Powers

By 1914 the world showed the effects of the outburst of imperialism that began in the 1870s. Europeans had divided up Africa, leaving only Liberia and Ethiopia independent. Their power continued to grow in Asia, joined—and challenged—by the United States and Japan. India and Indonesia had been completely conquered, and imperial powers took over Burma, Malaya, Ceylon, Laos, Cambodia, Vietnam, Korea, Taiwan, and part of the Arabian Peninsula. Much of what remained in Asia, including most of China, had fallen under the indirect control of the imperial powers. Meanwhile, Russia expanded into central Asia, and Austria-Hungary moved further into the Balkans.

Most of the former colonies of Europe in the Western Hemisphere had become independent. Canada, Australia, and New Zealand had attained autonomy, and European holdings were now reduced to Caribbean islands and a few mainland enclaves. Imperialism was not dead, however; many of the new Latin American nations around the Caribbean had fallen under the economic, military, and political control of the United States, which regarded the area as its sphere of influence.

West Asia and Africa	South and East Asia	Europe	Western Hemisphere
1914	**1914**	**1914**	**1914**
Conflicting interests of Arabs and Zionists	Indian nationalism: Gandhi, Mohammed Ali Jinnah	World War I	U. S. in World War I Motion pictures
Pan-Africanism		Russian Revolution	
Atatürk modernizes Turkey		Versailles Treaty, League of Nations	"Roaring Twenties" Great Depression
Reza Khan Westernizes Iran	Vietnamese and Indonesian nationalism: Ho Chi Minh, Sukarno	Mussolini	
Afrikaner domination in South Africa		Stalin: 5-Year Plan	
		Modernism in art: Picasso, Moore	
1930 Négritude movement	**1930** Japanese militarism: "Manchurian incident"	**1930** Hitler	**1930** The New Deal Cárdenas in Mexico
Mussolini invades Ethiopia		Spanish Civil War	
	Sino-Japanese War	Munich Agreement	
	Japan attacks Pearl Harbor and Western colonies in Asia	World War II	
		Existentialism: Sartre	A-bomb developed
		The Holocaust	
		United Nations	
1945	**1945**	**1945**	**1945**
Creation of Israel	Atomic bombing of Hiroshima and Nagasaki	Truman Doctrine and Marshall Plan	
Algerian revolution			
Suez crisis		NATO/Warsaw Pact	Juan and Evita Perón
	Independence in India: Nehru		Television age begins
		COMECON/EEC	Rock and roll music
	Chinese Communist victory: Mao Zedong	USSR launches Sputnik	Cuban revolution: Fidel Castro
African independence			
	Korean War		
	Bandung Conference: neutralist movement		
1960 "Six-Day War"	**1960**	**1960** Berlin Wall	**1960** Cuban missile crisis
			King: U.S. civil rights crusade
OPEC becomes global force	U.S. in Vietnam		Man on the moon
			Women's liberation movement, United States
Independence struggles in South and East Africa			
1975	**1975** "Pacific Rim" economic boom	**1975** Gorbachev promotes *glasnost* and *perestroika*	**1975**
Iranian Revolution			
Continuing struggle against apartheid in South Africa	Bhutto in Pakistan	Green movement	Allende government overthrown in Chile
		Collapse of Communism in eastern Europe	Marxist insurgencies in Central America
Iran-Iraq War	Revolution in the Philippines		The computer age
1980 Persian Gulf crises		Dismantling of the Berlin Wall	Movement toward democracies in South America
Intifada			
1990 Mandela released	**1990** Chinese Communists retain power	**1990** Reunification of Germany	**1990**
Israeli-Palestinian agreements		Collapse of USSR	
		Boris Yeltsin	
		Ethnic disputes in Bosnia	
Universal suffrage in South Africa			
1995			

The World in 1930

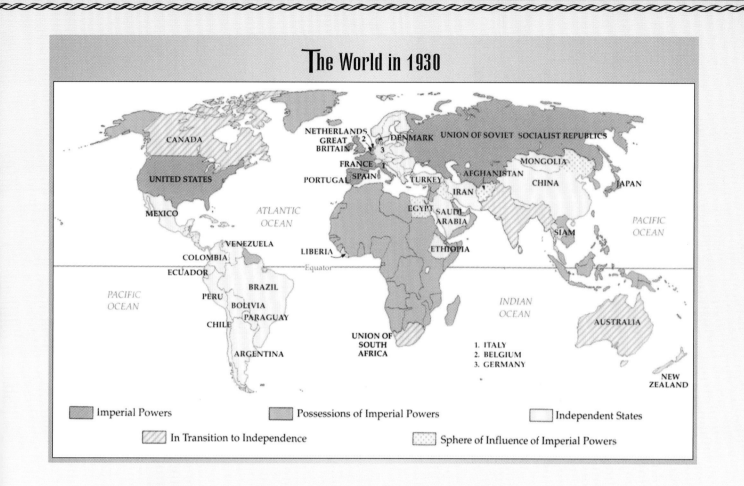

Imperial Powers   **Possessions of Imperial Powers**   **Independent States**

In Transition to Independence   **Sphere of Influence of Imperial Powers**

(Within map:)
NETHERLANDS
GREAT BRITAIN
DENMARK
UNION OF SOVIET SOCIALIST REPUBLICS
CANADA
FRANCE
MONGOLIA
UNITED STATES
PORTUGAL SPAIN
TURKEY
AFGHANISTAN
CHINA
JAPAN
IRAN
MEXICO
ATLANTIC OCEAN
EGYPT SAUDI ARABIA
PACIFIC OCEAN
VENEZUELA
LIBERIA
ETHIOPIA
SIAM
COLOMBIA
ECUADOR
Equator
BRAZIL
PACIFIC OCEAN
PERU
BOLIVIA
PARAGUAY
INDIAN OCEAN
AUSTRALIA
CHILE
UNION OF SOUTH AFRICA
1. ITALY
2. BELGIUM
3. GERMANY
ARGENTINA
NEW ZEALAND

The map of the world in 1930 shows a mixture of imperialist advances and retreats, but on the whole the colonizing powers kept a firm hold on their possessions. Germany's colonies had been parceled out to other imperial powers by the League of Nations. The defeat of the Ottoman Empire in World War I brought on the last round of Western imperial acquisition, as much of the Middle East came under British and French control. Elsewhere, Japan was ready to consolidate its grip on Manchuria.

There were a few signs that imperialism was on the wane. The Soviet Union, Austria-Hungary, Germany, and Great Britain had lost control over many of their ethnic minorities. Some of these groups, such as the Poles and the Irish, formed independent states. The new Chinese republic was beginning to extricate itself from European controls, although pressure from Japan was increasing. The United States, under the Good Neighbor policy, would soon bring to a close four decades of intervention in the Caribbean. Under the pressure of Indian nationalists, Great Britain set India on the road to independence, as it had done for Canada, Australia, New Zealand, and South Africa.

The World Now

1. JAMAICA	6. DENMARK	12. AUSTRIA	18. CROATIA	23. GREECE	29. AZERBAIJAN	35. TURKMENISTAN
2. BAHAMAS	7. NETHERLANDS	13. CZECH REPUBLIC	19. BOSNIA AND	24. BULGARIA	30. ARMENIA	36. KYRGYZSTAN
3. HAITI	8. BELGIUM	14. SLOVAKIA	HERZEGOVINA	25. ROMANIA	31. CYPRUS	37. TAJIKISTAN
4. DOMINICAN	9. LUXEMBOURG	15. HUNGARY	20. YUGOSLAVIA	26. MOLDOVA	32. LEBANON	
REPUBLIC	10. GERMANY	16. ITALY	21. ALBANIA	27. POLAND	33. ISRAEL	
5. PUERTO RICO (U.S.)	11. SWITZERLAND	17. SLOVENIA	22. MACEDONIA	28. GEORGIA	34. UZBEKISTAN	

The large number of new independent states seen on this map reflects the tumultuous nature of world events since the 1930s. After World War II Italy and Japan were forced to give up their imperial possessions, but the war drained even the victorious European nations of the resources and will to counter growing demands for independence.

In Asia and Africa the imperial powers often departed without a fight, but subject peoples sometimes took up arms to achieve independence. For example, the British left Sri Lanka and Nigeria peacefully, but it required protracted warfare to force Western powers out of Algeria and Vietnam.

The relaxation of totalitarian controls in the Soviet Union after 1989 encouraged nationalism within the fifteen federated republics. By the end of 1991 they had gained independence, and the once-mighty Soviet Union had ceased to exist. East Germany reunited with West Germany in 1990. The reemergence of ethnic animosities broke up Czechoslovakia and Yugoslavia.

Globally, the imperial holdings have now been reduced to scattered islands and a few mainland enclaves. Current membership in the United Nations approaches 200, most nations having achieved independence after 1957.

WORLD HISTORY

THIRD EDITION

WORLD HISTORY

VOLUME I

Before 1600: The Development of Early Civilizations

JIU-HWA L. UPSHUR
Eastern Michigan University

JANICE J. TERRY
Eastern Michigan University

JAMES P. HOLOKA
Eastern Michigan University

RICHARD D. GOFF
Eastern Michigan University

GEORGE H. CASSAR
Eastern Michigan University

WEST/WADSWORTH
I(T)P® An International Thomson Publishing Company

Belmont, CA • Albany, NY • Boston • Cincinnati • Johannesburg
London • Madrid • Melbourne • Mexico City • New York
Pacific Grove, CA • Scottsdale, AZ • Singapore • Tokyo • Toronto

History Editor Clark Baxter
Senior Development Editor Sharon Adams Poore
Editorial Assistant Melissa Gleason
Marketing Manager Jay Hu
Print Buyer Barbara Britton
Permissions Editor Robert Kauser
Production Hal Lockwood, Penmarin Books
Cover and Text Designer Diane Beasely
Copy Editor Pat Lewis
Cover Image Great Temple, Abu Simbel, Egypt (David Austen/FPG International)
Compositor Thompson Type
Printer World Color

Printed in the United States of America
1 2 3 4 5 6 7 8 9 10

For more information, contact Wadsworth Publishing Company, 10 Davis Drive, Belmont, CA 94002,
or electronically at http://www.wadsworth.com

International Thomson Publishing Europe
Berkshire House
168-173 High Holborn
London, WC1V 7AA, United Kingdom

International Thomson Editores
Seneca, 53
Col. Polanco
11560 México D.F. México

Nelson ITP, Australia
102 Dodds Street
South Melbourne
Victoria 3205 Australia

International Thomson Publishing Asia
60 Albert Street
#15-01 Albert Complex
Singapore 189969

Nelson Canada
1120 Birchmount Road
Scarborough, Ontario
Canada M1K 5G4

International Thomson Publishing Japan
Hirakawa-cho Kyowa Building, 3F
2-2-1 Hirakawa-cho Chiyoda-ku
Tokyo 102 Japan

International Thomson Publishing South Africa
Building 18, Constantia Park
138 Sixteenth Road, P. O. Box 2459
Halfway House, 1685 South Africa

ISBN 0-534-55035-5

About the Authors

JIU-HWA L. UPSHUR received her B.A. at the University of Sydney in Australia and Ph.D. in history at the University of Michigan. She is the author of two catalogs on Chinese art and many articles on Chinese history and has lived and traveled extensively in China, Taiwan, and other parts of Asia. She is co-author of *The Twentieth Century: A Brief Global History* (5th edition, 1994) and co-editor of *Lives and Times: Readings in World History* (1994). Since 1993 she has been a member of the world history committee of the College Board.

JANICE J. TERRY is a graduate of the School of Oriental and African Studies, University of London. She is author of *The Wafd, 1919–1952: Cornerstone of Egyptian Political Power, Mistaken Identity: Arab Stereotypes in Popular Writing,* and numerous articles on contemporary events in western Asia. Dr. Terry has lived and traveled extensively throughout western Asia and Africa. She is co-author of *The Twentieth Century: A Brief Global History* (5th ed., 1994). In 1990, she received an award for excellence in teaching from the state of Michigan.

JAMES P. HOLOKA received his B.A. from the University of Rochester, his M.A. from SUNY, Binghamton, and his Ph.D. from the University of Michigan, where he was a Rackham Prize Fellow. He has taught Greek and Latin, classical humanities, and ancient history since 1974; he received a teaching excellence award in 1980 and a scholarly recognition award in 1991. He is a published translator and the author of three textbooks and over sixty scholarly articles and reviews in such journals as *American Historical Review, Classical World, Classical and Modern Literature,* and *Transactions of the American Philological Association.*

RICHARD D. GOFF received his A.B. from Duke University, his M.A. from Cornell University, and his Ph.D. from Duke University. He has taught courses in western civilization and specializes in teaching twentieth-century world history. He is the author of *Confederate Supply* and encyclopedia articles on southern history and culture. In 1983 he received a distinguished faculty service award. He is co-author of *The Twentieth Century: A Brief Global History* (5th ed., 1994).

GEORGE H. CASSAR received his B.A and M.A. from the University of New Brunswick and his Ph.D. from McGill University. He is presently Professor of History at Eastern Michigan University, where he has taught European and military history since 1968. His output is extensive and includes half a dozen books on various aspects of the First World War as well as co-authorship of *A Survey of Western Civilization* (1987). In 1985 he received the prestigious Faculty Award for Research and Publication from Eastern Michigan University. He is currently working on a book related to British strategy during the Great War.

Brief Contents

Contents

Maps

Preface

Modern communications and transportation have linked the world's regions closer together and made them more integrated politically, economically, and culturally than ever before. Our technological society is predicated on a world economy and depends on a precarious ecological balance; these facts make events in the forests of Brazil or the deserts of Africa and Asia vitally important to people all around the globe.

Many institutions of higher learning have come to realize that students need insights into the historical backgrounds of other cultures in order to respond effectively to the currents that are making us all citizens of a global village. As a result, many are now emphasizing world history as an essential part of the basic undergraduate curriculum, rather than traditional courses in Western civilization.

In response to the need for a truly global and well-balanced world history text, in 1987 we assembled a team of five authors with expertise in different regions and periods of history, including specialists in the classics and Greco-Roman history, modern Europe, military history, the Western Hemisphere, the Islamic world, American history, and South and East Asia. The authors are conversant in more than a half-dozen ancient and modern languages. Each has more than twenty-five years' experience teaching college survey courses of Western and world history and advanced courses in special subjects. All have extensive experience in writing successful textbooks and editing primary source materials in world history and Western civilization. The result is a smooth integration of diverse materials.

Our first edition, widely adopted across the United States and Canada, was a success. Our second, revised edition was even more successful. We have now made additional improvements to further enhance the textbook.

In our view, human civilizations have produced too rich a tapestry of experience to limit our examination of them to any single theme. Our consistent goal has been not only to show students the diversity and distinctive qualities of the various civilizations, but to trace their social, cultural, and economic influences and interactions. Furthermore, we point out the many dimensions of the lives of individual men and women across cultures, religions, social classes, and times.

Several distinctive features about our book, some new in this edition, bear enumeration.

First, we have divided world history into seventeen chapters, each highlighting a major trend (emergence of civilization, early empires, invasion and disruption, and so on) during a distinct chronological era. The subsections of each chapter are devoted to the areas of the world affected by this trend. This effective organization has been continued from previous editions, with revisions based on the latest discoveries and advances in scholarship. Chapter 17, for example, has been carefully reworked to incorporate recent events.

Second, we have placed twelve comparative essays at strategic points in the book. These lay the groundwork for the historical concepts examined in detail in subsequent chapter sections. For example, the essay "Characteristics of Empires," which discusses the dynamics of large states, precedes Chapter Four, which covers the roughly contemporary Hellenistic, Roman, Mauryan, and Han Empires. For this edition, we have added quotations from original sources at the opening of each essay to demonstrate the pertinence of such material and to heighten the essays' interest and relevance.

Third, we have included many charts and maps. Each chapter begins with a timeline of important events that occurred during the period covered by that chapter, an important learning aid for students. Each chapter also features helpful maps to accentuate the geographical contexts of historical events.

Fourth, we have chosen numerous attractive illustrations, often in color, to bring to life events, individuals, and locations of historical interest. As the old adage says, a picture is worth a thousand words. This books abounds with good pictures, some never before published. About a quarter of the illustrations in this edition are new, and many are unique.

Fifth, we have inserted several boxes into each chapter that mostly consist of quotations from primary sources. Students, reviewers, and professors have praised this engaging and useful enhancement of the text.

Sixth, expanding on a successful feature, we have added more than thirty inserts of a new, more comparative type. Entitled "Lives and Times Across Cultures," these informative, often offbeat, and entertaining pieces present facts and details of life not found in traditional textbooks.

Seventh, for this edition, we have modified the chapter summaries, retitled "Summary and Comparisons," to stress the comparative aspect of historical study. Since each chapter contains much information about diverse regions of the world, this added emphasis on comparison ensures a better integration of the various materials of a given chapter and a clearer overall view of world events.

Eighth, at the end of each chapter we have compiled a list of sources to guide interested students to well-written monographs, fiction, dramas, films, and television programs that provide historical perspective. For this edition, we have added a selection of appropriate and exciting Internet resources.

Ninth, the publisher has put together an invaluable package of ancillary materials. These include aids for instructors:

- **Instructor's Manual/Test Bank**. Prepared by James Holoka, one of the text authors, this manual includes chapter outlines, recommended readings, paper topics, identification questions, multiple-choice questions, short-essay questions, and, new to this edition, Internet resources. One comprehensive volume.
- **World-Class Testing Tools**. This is a fully integrated collection of management tools for the creation and delivery of tests and for classroom management that utilizes all the test items featured in the Instructor's Manual. The package includes World-Class Test, Test Online, and World-Class Manager software. Available in both Windows and Macintosh formats.
- **Full-Color Transparency Acetates.** The acetates contain maps from the text and other sources as well as commentary on each map. The commentary, by James Harrison of Siena College, includes not only the text caption but additional points of interest about the map, what it shows, and its relevance to the study of world history. Possible discussion questions for student involvement are included.
- **Powerpoint.** Acetate map images delivered in the Powerpoint format. Available in both Windows and Macintosh formats.
- **Sights and Sounds of History Videodisk.** Short, focused video clips, photos, artwork, animations, music, and dramatic readings are used to bring life to historical topics and events that are most difficult for students to appreciate from a textbook alone. For example, students will experience the grandeur of Versailles and the defeat felt by a German soldier at Stalingrad. The video segments (averaging 4 minutes long) are available on VHS, and they make excellent lecture launchers.

- **CNN World History.** This compelling video features footage from CNN's archives. The twelve 2- to 5-minute segments are easy to integrate into classroom discussions or to use as lecture launchers. Topics range from India's caste system to Pearl Harbor.
- **History Video Library.** Select from videos covering a variety of periods and topics. List available on the bulletin board. Adopters must qualify.

The following aids for students are also available:

- **Study Guide.** Prepared by James Holoka, one of the text authors, it contains chapter outlines, identifications, true/false questions, study questions, and suggestions for further reading.
- **Map Exercise Workbooks.** Prepared by Cynthia Kosso of Northern Arizona University, the workbooks feature approximately thirty map exercises in each volume. Designed to help students feel comfortable with maps by having them work with different kinds of maps and to identify places to improve their geographic understanding of world history. Available in two volumes.
- **Document Exercise Workbooks.** These workbooks, written by Donna Van Raaphorst of Cuyahoga Community College, provide a collection of exercises based on primary sources in history. Available in two volumes.
- *Lives and Times: A World History Reader.* Assembled by two of the text authors, James Holoka and Jiu-Hwa Upshur, the reader includes 150 short and lively selections, usually biographical in nature.
- *Journey of Civilization CD-ROM* for Windows. This CD-ROM takes the student on eighteen interactive journeys through history. Enhanced with QuickTime movies, animations, sound clips, maps, and more, the journeys allow students to engage in history as active participants rather than as readers of past events.
- *Internet Guide for History* by Daniel Kurland and John Soares. Section One introduces students to the Internet, including tips for searching on the Web. Section Two introduces students to how history research can be done and lists URL sites by topic.
- *Hammond Historical Atlas.* Available shrink-wrapped to the text.
- *InfoTrac, College Edition.* This online library allows students to study and learn about history at any time of the day or night. The online database gives students access to full-length articles from more than 700 schol-

arly and popular periodicals, updated daily, and dating back as far as three years. Periodicals include *Historian, Smithsonian,* and *Harper's* magazines.

- **Web Page.** Visit Historic Times, the Wadsworth History Resource Center at http://history.wadsworth. com. From this full-service site, instructors and students can access many selections, such as a career center, lessons on surfing the Web, and links to great history-related Web sites. Students can also take advantage of the on-line *Student Guide to InfoTrac, College Edition,* featuring lists of article titles with discussion and critical-thinking questions linked to the articles to invite deeper examination of the material. Instructors can visit book-specific sites to learn more about our texts and supplements, and students can access chapter-by-chapter resources for the book, interactive quizzes, and a lively "Join the Forum" online bulletin board.

In sum, we have striven to make this book not only accurate and informative, but also exciting to use for all students, whether they are majoring in history or simply fulfilling a basic requirement for graduation. Our textbook combines key characteristics to work effectively in various learning situations. It offers a clear narrative focusing on major historical forces and concepts, uncluttered by minute detail. This third edition increases the proportion of social, economic, and cultural history in order to provide a more complete and vital account of human experience.

We have kept our book relatively short, making it suitable for courses at most colleges. Instructors may assign supplementary readings without fear of overwhelming their students.

To provide a true world perspective, rather than a Western-oriented one, we have adopted several special conventions. First, because the text will be used mostly in North American colleges, we have based our general chronology on the traditional Christian/Western calendar; however, we have designated year dates as B.C.E. (Before the Common Era) instead of B.C. (Before Christ) and C.E. (Common Era) instead of A.D. (Anno Domini). Next, wherever possible we have eliminated Eurocentric geographical terms such as Far East, Levant, New World,

and the like. Finally, we have generally transliterated (rather than Latinized or Anglicized) names and terms from their original language; thus, *Qur'an* instead of *Koran, Tanakh* instead of *Old Testament,* and (post-1949) *Mao Zedong* instead of *Mao Tse-tung* and *Beijing* instead of *Peking* (see also "Romanizing Chinese Words" at the end of this volume). However, we have made exceptions of such familiar Westernized spellings as Confucius, Averroës, Christopher Columbus, and Aztec.

An enterprise of this magnitude and complexity succeeds only through the dedicated efforts of many people. Wadsworth Publishing secured the services of reviewers whose insights and information materially strengthened this and the previous two editions. The list follows this preface.

We wish to thank our colleagues at Eastern Michigan University—in particular, Ronald Delph and Joseph Engwenyu for their assistance at several stages in the writing—and Gersham Nelson, head of the History Department, for his constant support and encouragement. Nancy Snyder and her assistants were stalwart helpers in handling innumerable practical and technological chores. Raymond Craib at Yale University supplied information and text on women's history and Mexican history. From the outset of this project, Sally Marks in Providence, Rhode Island, has been exceptionally helpful in suggesting improvements. We also wish to thank Margot Duley of Eastern Michigan University and Richard Edwards of the University of Michigan for making available to us photographs of historical interest from their personal collections. We are grateful to John Nystuen of the University of Michigan for photographing some of the artifacts illustrated in this edition. The authors' spouses furnished copious practical and moral support and showed a high tolerance for hectic writing and production schedules. A final word of thanks goes to Clark Baxter, Sharon Adams Poore, Amy Guastello, and other members of the Wadsworth Publishing team for their patient attention to all manner of details. Their collective skills have once again transformed our project into an attractive textbook.

THE AUTHORS

Reviewers

Charles F. Ames, Jr.
Salem State College

Jay Pascal Anglin
University of Southern Mississippi

Gary Dean Best
University of Hawaii at Hilo

Edward L. Bond
Alabama Agricultural and Mechanical University

Patricia Bradley
Auburn University at Montgomery

Cynthia Brokaw
University of Oregon

Antoinette Burton
Indiana State University

Antonio Calabria
University of Texas

Daniel P. Connerton
North Adams State College

Lane Earns
University of Wisconsin at Oshkosh

Edward L. Farmer
University of Minnesota

William Wayne Farris
University of Tennessee

Gary R. Freeze
Erskine College

Ronald Fritze
Lamar University

Ray C. Gerhardt
Texas Lutheran College

Marc Jason Gilbert
North Georgia College

Steven A. Glazer
Graceland College

Joseph M. Gowaskie
Rider College

Zoltan Kramar
Central Washington University

Susie Ling
Pasadena City College

Craig A. Lockard
University of Wisconsin at Green Bay

Raymond M. Lorantas
Drexel University

Susan Maneck
Murray State University

Delores Nason McBroome
Humboldt State University

Robroy Meyers
El Camino College

Terry Morris
Shorter College

Henry Myers
James Madison University

Cecil C. Orchard
Eastern Kentucky University

James L. Owens
Lynchburg College

Oliver B. Pollak
University of Nebraska at Omaha

Dennis Reinhartz
University of Texas at Arlington

Cynthia Schwenk
Georgia State University

Wendy Singer
Kenyon College

Paul D. Steeves
Stetson University

Cheryl Thurber
Shippensburg University

Hubert van Tuyll
Augusta State University

Introduction

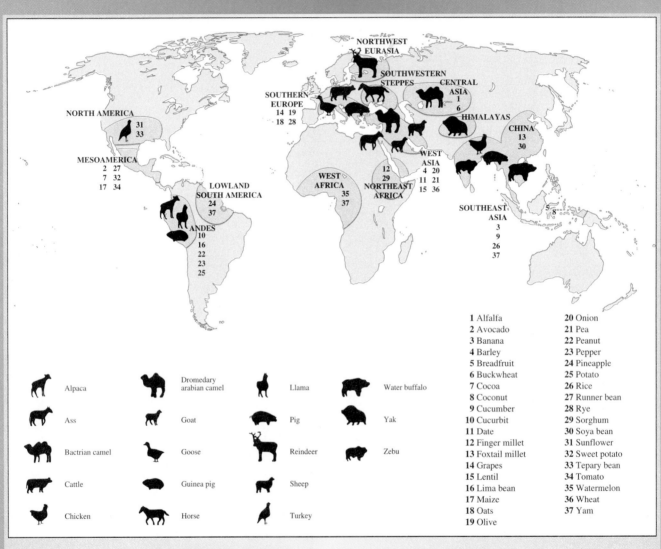

The Origins of Agricultural Crops and of Domestic Animals

Animals

Alpaca	Dromedary arabian camel	Llama	Water buffalo
Ass	Goat	Pig	Yak
Bactrian camel	Goose	Reindeer	Zebu
Cattle	Guinea pig	Sheep	
Chicken	Horse	Turkey	

Crops

1 Alfalfa	20 Onion
2 Avocado	21 Pea
3 Banana	22 Peanut
4 Barley	23 Pepper
5 Breadfruit	24 Pineapple
6 Buckwheat	25 Potato
7 Cocoa	26 Rice
8 Coconut	27 Runner bean
9 Cucumber	28 Rye
10 Cucurbit	29 Sorghum
11 Date	30 Soya bean
12 Finger millet	31 Sunflower
13 Foxtail millet	32 Sweet potato
14 Grapes	33 Tepary bean
15 Lentil	34 Tomato
16 Lima bean	35 Watermelon
17 Maize	36 Wheat
18 Oats	37 Yam
19 Olive	

Precivilization: Paleolithic and Neolithic Cultures Around the World

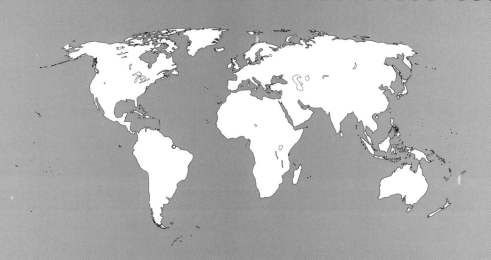

What are we? To the biologist we are . . . Homo sapiens sapiens. . . . But what is particularly interesting about our species? For a start, we walk upright on our hindlegs at all times, which is an extremely unusual way of getting around for a mammal. There are also several unusual features about our head, not least of which is the very large brain it contains. . . . Unlike the apes, we are not covered by a coat of thick hair. . . . Very probably this has something to do with [the fact that] the skin is richly covered with millions of microscopic sweat glands. . . . Our forelimbs, being freed from helping us to get about, possess a very high degree of manipulative skill. . . . No other animal manipulates the world in the extensive and arbitrary way that humans do. . . . Unlike any other animal, we have a spoken language which is characterized by a huge vocabulary and a complex grammatical structure. . . .

All [these] . . . are characteristics of a very intelligent creature, but humans are more than just intelligent. Our sense of justice, our need for aesthetic pleasure, our imaginative flights and our penetrating self-awareness, all combine to create an indefinable spirit which I believe is the "soul."*

*Richard E. Leakey, The Making of Mankind (New York: Dutton, 1981), pp. 18, 20.

This passage by anthropologist Richard Leakey expresses the dual nature of human beings—physical and spiritual. Students of history are particularly concerned to identify how these various distinguishing traits have found expression in the accomplishments of humankind. Such historical study records advances in production of food, in technology, in the building of social groups and their habitations, and in the more efficient control of the environment in general. It also seeks to define what it is to be human. This means that historians also study the ways human beings have viewed the world around them, that is, how people have understood its working through science, contemplated unfathomable questions through religion, and expressed their thoughts in art, literature, and philosophy.

Through such investigation, students of history have ascertained that initially humans survived precariously through hunting and gathering. Eventually, after hundreds of thousands of years, humans living in several continents created first the agricultural and then the urban revolution, thereby bringing about civilized life in both the Eastern and Western Hemispheres. This section of *World History* surveys these initial advances of humankind. It first discusses what modern researchers have reconstructed about the emergence of the human species and about life in the hunter-gatherer era around the world. It then takes up the dramatic material changes brought by the invention of agriculture.

Human Development in the Old Stone Age

The story of humanity's achievement begins with the Paleolithic or Old Stone Age sometime around 2,000,000 B.C.E., probably in East Africa, as the famous finds in the Olduvai Gorge show. (The labeling of ages as "Stone," "Bronze," and "Iron" refers to the materials used in the making of tools at a given stage in history.) After 1,000,000 B.C.E., hominids of the *Homo erectus* type moved out of East Africa into West Asia, Europe, East Asia, and Indonesia. This vast stretch of time cannot be described with great confidence or detail because there are no written records to illuminate it. Instead, we have had to rely on the conclusions and conjectures that modern scientists have drawn from materials obtained from archaeological excavations.

In response to changes in the natural environment, Old Stone Age people made physical and cultural adaptations that were fundamental for subsequent human development. Crucial physiological refinements included the ability to stand and walk easily in an upright position, changes in the position and size of teeth (especially the canines) in response to changing diet, the evolution and increasing dexterity of an opposable thumb, and changes in the size and configuration of the skull. Particularly dramatic was the doubling of brain size. This gave men and women mental superiority over other species, demonstrated in the creation of artifacts, particularly tools. Humans could both expand and perfect their cultural equipment and transmit knowledge of how to use that

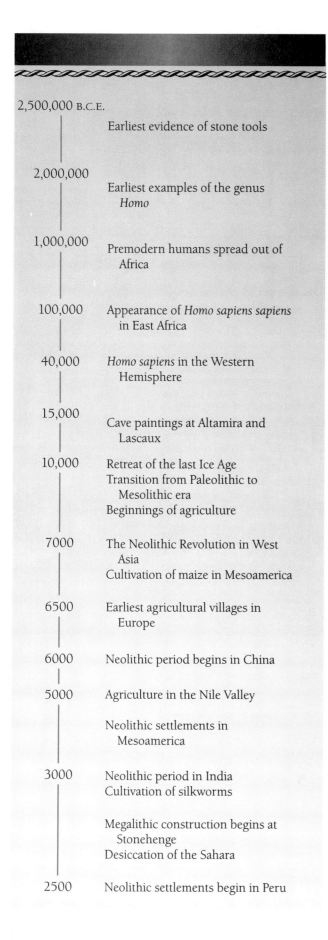

2,500,000 B.C.E.	
	Earliest evidence of stone tools
2,000,000	
	Earliest examples of the genus *Homo*
1,000,000	
	Premodern humans spread out of Africa
100,000	
	Appearance of *Homo sapiens sapiens* in East Africa
40,000	
	Homo sapiens in the Western Hemisphere
15,000	
	Cave paintings at Altamira and Lascaux
10,000	
	Retreat of the last Ice Age
	Transition from Paleolithic to Mesolithic era
	Beginnings of agriculture
7000	
	The Neolithic Revolution in West Asia
	Cultivation of maize in Mesoamerica
6500	
	Earliest agricultural villages in Europe
6000	
	Neolithic period begins in China
5000	
	Agriculture in the Nile Valley
	Neolithic settlements in Mesoamerica
3000	
	Neolithic period in India
	Cultivation of silkworms
	Megalithic construction begins at Stonehenge
	Desiccation of the Sahara
2500	
	Neolithic settlements begin in Peru

equipment through language, the most flexible and finely calibrated tool of all.

A series of four major ice ages, marked by the movement of ice sheets hundreds of feet thick over vast areas of the earth, stimulated human development. The glaciation changed land formations, sea levels, and plant and animal life and habitats. To survive, people had to be innovative and able to modify their patterns of living. Many animals, solely dependent on physical equipment for their survival, were unable to adjust to the changing environmental conditions and became extinct.

By 100,000 B.C.E., modern humans (*Homo sapiens sapiens*) had evolved in Africa. By 40,000 B.C.E., they had occupied the areas originally settled by *Homo erectus;* subsequently, they began to spread into northern Eurasia and into Australia. The South Pacific was settled much later, between 1100 B.C.E and 1300 C.E.

Modern *Homo sapiens* also migrated through Siberia, across to Alaska, and then east and south throughout North America. Most scholars think that, as in Australia, the majority of these movements occurred during the last ice ages when glaciers locked up some of the world's water, lowering sea levels and exposing land bridges.

As elsewhere in the world at this time, these *Homo sapiens* migrants were still hunters and gatherers, fire-users with chipped stone tools, whose relics in the Western Hemisphere date from about 40,000 B.C.E. By 20,000 B.C.E., humans had arrived in Middle America (the southern two-thirds of Mexico and parts of current Central America south to Panama). It appears that they soon spread thereafter throughout South America, although isolated archaeological finds hinting at settlements even as early as 30,000 B.C.E. may require a revision of our chronology.

The Arctic zone of North America, though it was on the migration route from Asia, was in fact the last part of the continent to be settled. The earliest Paleolithic culture of the Eskimo dates to about 7000 B.C.E. in the region of the Bering Strait. Succeeding cultures known as Pre-Dorset and Dorset combined influences from East Asia and from regions to the south in North America. They were characterized by hunting of caribou, rabbits, and birds, with a gradual shift to fishing and the hunting of polar bears and marine creatures such as walrus and seals. By the first millennium B.C.E., these Eskimo cultures were prevalent in the Arctic from Alaska in the west through northern Canada to Greenland in the east.

By the late Paleolithic era, human beings around the world had (1) manufactured a range of stone or bone implements (knives, scrapers, borers) and weapons (blades, bows and arrows, spears and spear throwers); (2) controlled fire for cooking and for giving heat and light; (3) developed spoken language in addition to the nonverbal gestures used by all primates; (4) formulated an artistic tradition, seen for example in the famous cave

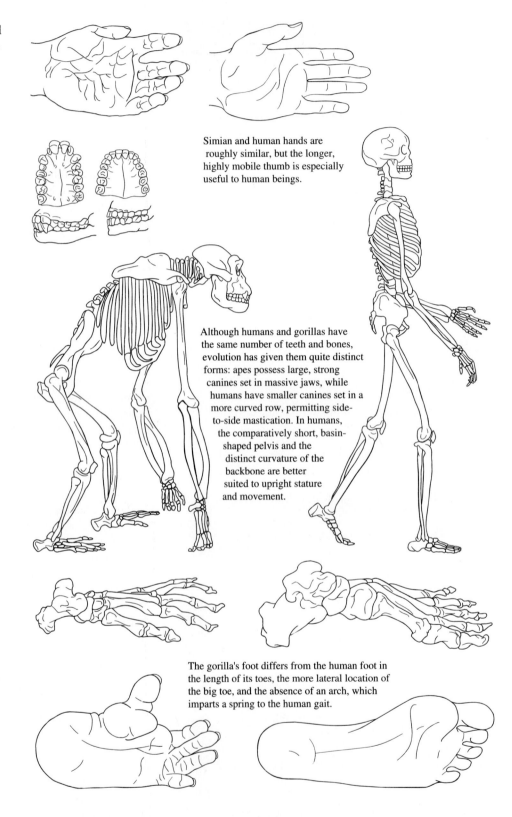

Comparisons of the Skeletal Structures of Humans and Apes.

Simian and human hands are roughly similar, but the longer, highly mobile thumb is especially useful to human beings.

Although humans and gorillas have the same number of teeth and bones, evolution has given them quite distinct forms: apes possess large, strong canines set in massive jaws, while humans have smaller canines set in a more curved row, permitting side-to-side mastication. In humans, the comparatively short, basin-shaped pelvis and the distinct curvature of the backbone are better suited to upright stature and movement.

The gorilla's foot differs from the human foot in the length of its toes, the more lateral location of the big toe, and the absence of an arch, which imparts a spring to the human gait.

The Ascent of Mankind

Fossil skulls have been found in Southern Africa . . . which establish the characteristic structure of the head when it began to be man-like. . . . A historic skull, found [in 1924] . . . at a place called Taung, by . . . Raymond Dart . . . is [that of] a baby, five to six years old. . . . Dart called this creature *Australopithecus* [Southern Ape]. . . . For me the little *Australopithecus* baby has a personal history. In 1950, . . . I was asked to do a piece of mathematics. Could I combine a measure of the size of the Taung child's teeth with their shape, so as to discriminate them from the teeth of apes? I had never held a fossil skull in my hands, and I was by no means an expert on teeth. But it worked pretty well; and it transmitted to me a sense of excitement which I remember at this instant. I, at over forty, having spent a lifetime in doing abstract mathematics about the shape of things, suddenly saw my knowledge reach back two million years and shine a searchlight into the history of man. . . . I do not know how the Taung baby began life, but to me it still remains the primordial infant from which the whole adventure of man began.*

Thus Jacob Bronowski described the excitement he felt as he looked at a bit of evidence of ancient human life on our planet. The title of his book, *The Ascent of Man,* is an allusion to Charles Darwin's famous book *The Descent of Man*, published a century earlier, which advanced evidence for the hypothesis that humans had evolved from more primitive life-forms. Darwin's claim with its challenge to the traditional belief in the biblical story of Creation aroused a torrent of controversy, but it also stimulated the sciences of physical anthropology and archaeology. Researchers have made stunning discoveries about the ancestry of our species through excavations at sites such as the Olduvai Gorge in East Africa and Hsihoutu in Shansi province in China. Their work has yielded insights into the earliest achievements that brought humanity from primitive origins to civilized life, from crude stone implements to spacecraft, from the rudiments of spoken language to the art of poetry, from nomadic hunting and gathering to the complex socioeconomic and political structures of city life.

*Jacob Bronowski, *The Ascent of Man* (Boston: Little Brown, 1973), pp. 28–30.

---

paintings at Lascaux in France and Altamira in Spain; (5) created ritual practices connected chiefly with fertility and with burial of the dead; and (6) organized themselves into social groups for more efficient collection and sharing of food.

Also by late Paleolithic times, human beings had probably acquired the superficial physical traits conventionally known as racial. Differences in skin, hair, and eye color, in size and shape of the nostrils, and perhaps in stature and cranial shape likely resulted from adaptation to environmental conditions in various parts of the world.

The Neolithic Food-Producing Revolution in West Asia

Because Paleolithic humans lived by hunting animals and by gathering wild fruits, nuts, and grains, they needed a relatively large space to support even a single family. This severely restricted the size of human communities and made settled life in one area impossible, since the group had to follow its food supply and move in conjunction with animal migrations and vegetation cycles. Only when people shifted from the random collection of food to its regular cultivation did they overcome such limitations. In the Neolithic or New Stone Age, humans assured themselves of a regular food supply by developing agricultural techniques and domesticating food-producing animals. Stable food supplies in turn led to a rapid increase in population and the founding of permanent settlements, which later became the basis for the more complex social structures and more dynamic technologies of urban civilization. These characteristics of the Neolithic Revolution varied from region to region and emerged much earlier in some parts of the world than in others. Indeed, to speak of a "revolution" is somewhat misleading, since the transformation in most areas was very gradual. Still, in terms of the vast time frame of human evolution, the change was comparatively quick. In 10,000 B.C.E., 100 percent of the world's population of some 10 million were hunters and gatherers; by 1500 C.E., only 1 percent of the world's 350 million people were hunters and gatherers; today, less than 0.001 percent of the world's population—for example, Eskimo, African !Kung San people, and the aborigines of Australia—still live in pre-Neolithic conditions.

With the retreat of the last ice age, beginning around 10,000 B.C.E., climatic conditions in that part of West Asia

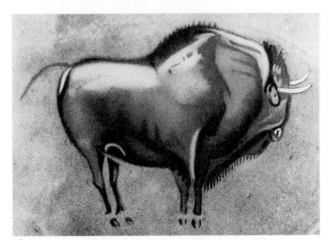

✦ Altamira Wall Painting. A section of the famous Paleolithic wall paintings in the caves of Altamira, Spain. Similar paintings and carvings, found in caves throughout Europe from southern Spain and France in the west to the Ural Mountains in the east, testify to the wide dispersion of Paleolithic culture.   Corbis-Bettman

called the Fertile Crescent became well suited to raising grain and domesticating animals. The valleys and foothills of this region were home to the wild ancestors of domesticable plants (barley, wheat, millet, and the like) and animals (for example, goats and donkeys). During a transitional period, the Mesolithic or Middle Stone Age (10,000–7000 B.C.E.), at places like Mount Carmel in Palestine, humans made tentative efforts to move from hunting-gathering subsistence methods to the systematic harvesting of grain.

By 7000 B.C.E. the residents of West Asia had developed the true farming villages that typify the Neolithic era. These centers consisted of at most a few thousand inhabitants engaged in the cultivation of wheat, barley, peas, beans, and lentils and the raising of goats, sheep, pigs, and cattle. These early farmers continued to supplement their diet with wild fruits, nuts, and grains. They lived in caves, pit houses, or huts made of mud, reeds, logs, or stones, grouped in small open communities or in larger fortified towns like Jericho in the Jordan Valley near the Dead Sea or Çatal Hüyük in the Anatolian Peninsula (modern Turkey). The point of such communities was to concentrate labor both for agricultural work—plowing, sowing, harvesting—and for the protection of the farmland on which the community's survival now depended.

Early farmers also devised techniques for making porridge, bread, and beer and developed ovens for cooking and, later, for firing pottery. (Pottery in particular is a joy for archaeologists because it is almost imperishable; once a culture starts to make pottery, it leaves behind a trail of broken shards, often distinctively decorated and therefore datable.) They wove baskets from reeds and textiles

from wool and flax and began to work metals like gold, silver, and copper. Finally, they discovered the wheel and made wagons and pottery wheels, and they invented the plow, which superseded digging sticks and hoes. Food surpluses freed some members of the community, generally males, to become at least part-time specialists: smiths, potters, weavers, artists, and perhaps priests.

Gender roles in Neolithic communities were affected by the production of food surpluses. Plow agriculture required the physical strength of males, rather than of females, whose energies were taken up by pregnancy and the nursing and rearing of children. Animal husbandry, too, was likely a male occupation. The males' control of surpluses of livestock, meat, pelts, and grain gave them an economic advantage that translated into the leisure to develop and engage in specializations. In short, males managed production, while to women fell the time-consuming and labor-intensive tasks of reproduction.

Once the Agricultural Revolution had occurred in the Fertile Crescent, it quickly spread to other regions in Asia, North Africa, and Europe. By contrast, farming emerged independently in North and South America. In all these areas, the revolution in food production enabled humans to take the next major step toward civilization—from village to city. Before turning to that major change, we will consider Neolithic culture elsewhere in the world.

Neolithic Times in Europe

The earliest agricultural villages in Europe appeared about 6500 B.C.E. in Greece, probably as a result of colonization by Anatolians across the Aegean. The farmers lived in square mudbrick buildings, sometimes with one larger building as a meeting place. Their economy centered on the raising of sheep and the cultivation of wheat and legumes. By 4000 B.C.E., Neolithic settlements had spread throughout Europe along two major routes: the Vardar-Danube-Rhine corridor, and the coastal areas of the Mediterranean Sea. Wooden longhouses were more common than mudbrick huts outside the Balkans. Initially, the pattern of farming settlements was dictated by the location of fertile soil that had resulted from the weathering of loess (layers of windblown dust that had formed like silt along the rims of glaciers in earlier times). Eventually, however, as incoming farmers carved land from the European forests, the hunters who had lived there since the early postglacial period (c. 10,000 B.C.E.) left their former mode of life to swell the ranks of the agriculturalists.

The earliest progress toward civilization on the European continent took place along the Mediterranean

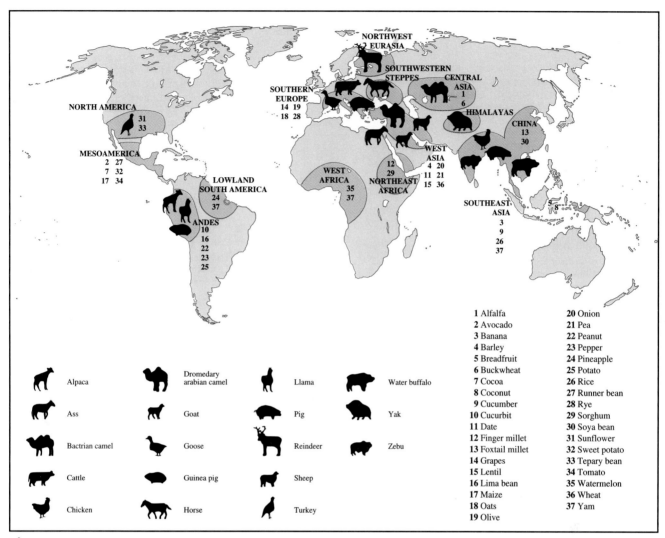

MAP 1.1 The Origins of Agricultural Crops and of Domestic Animals. This map shows the areas where particular plant and animal species were first cultivated or domesticated. Some species (e.g., the pig) seem to have developed independently in different areas. In most cases, however, the contact between neighboring cultures facilitated the rapid spread of plant and animal cultivation around the globe.

coasts, especially in the Balkan and Italian Peninsulas. Northern and western Europe was another matter; this area made few contributions (mainly in the form of natural resources) to the general advance of civilization before 500 C.E. It was largely unreceptive to external cultural influences (metalworking was an exception). Literacy, for example, came very late, imposed by conquerors. However, one ancient European art form does remain noteworthy: the megalithic (literally "large stone") constructions scattered from Scandinavia in the north to Corsica, Sardinia, and Malta in the south. Some of these are older than the Great Pyramids of Giza in Egypt, though they are by comparison very crude in both form and arrangement. Many of the megaliths are tombs; others are laid out in symmetrical patterns selected for reli-

gious or astronomical reasons. The most famous megalithic structure is Stonehenge in southern England. Here, in the late Neolithic and early Bronze Ages, (c. 2800–1800 B.C.E.), the prehistoric builders collected about 136 massive stones, some as large as thirty feet long and weighing fifty tons. The megaliths, transported over some eighteen miles, were assembled in a circle a hundred feet in diameter with an inner horseshoe consisting of five massive post-and-lintel gateways. The structure as a whole is aligned to the movements of sun, moon, and stars at specific points in the year and thus constitutes a kind of gigantic observatory. All this argues a remarkably precise awareness of astronomical movements, unassisted by the mathematical theorems later developed by the Babylonians and Egyptians. Stonehenge also bespeaks both an elaborate cooperation of labor and a careful organization of religious and social observances.

Neolithic Times in Africa

The Neolithic Revolution spread to the Nile Valley between 5000 and 4000 B.C.E. Wheat and barley and goats, sheep, and pigs were very likely introduced from the Fertile Crescent, especially Palestine and Mesopotamia. Irrigation by control of the Nile flood started at this time. Such developments laid the agricultural foundations for the first historical dynasties of ancient Egypt, beginning about 3000 B.C.E. (discussed in Chapter 1). Elsewhere, African peoples in the Saharan region, which did not become uninhabitably arid until after 3000 B.C.E., adopted the domestication of animals and, more slowly, the practice of agriculture from the neighboring Nile Valley. With the desiccation of the Sahara, these peoples carried their Neolithic skills with them in migrations to central and western Africa, though hunting-gathering cultures persisted in many areas. The barrier that the Sahara imposed by 2500 B.C.E. prevented the spread of the urban civilization that flowered with such magnificence in Old Kingdom Egypt. It was not until the first millennium B.C.E. that settled agricultural life and the practice of metallurgy became more widespread in sub-Saharan Africa. In all cases, however, the scarcity of water has meant that African peoples engaged in long-term agriculture have lived within the limits of a precariously balanced ecological system.

A very few African peoples remained at the hunter-gatherer stage till quite recently. Thus anthropologists could observe directly the cultural implications of the change to an agricultural mode of life, for example, among the !Kung San people (formerly called "bushmen") of southern Africa (the ! symbolizes an explosive sound or "click" common to the language). Here the transition to settled farming meant a shift from the mentality of sharing to that of saving. Among hunter-gatherers, survival of the group depends on the sharing of food collected into a common supply by all members, and all who contribute in any way to the general store of food are valued equally, regardless of sex. Among farmers, by contrast, a desire to conserve for oneself what one has produced is predominant. Farmers are also intensely possessive of the land that they have labored long and hard to make productive and are even willing to fight for it. Socially, hunter-gatherer !Kung exhibited little differentiation in status or rigidity in the definition of sex roles. Among agriculturalist !Kung, however, women are confined to work in the fields, while men tend to animals. Because there is often a surplus of animals but not of crops, the men gain power by controlling cattle as a medium of exchange for other goods or for money; thus the work of the women is undervalued. The division of gender roles begins even in childhood: in hunter-gatherer societies, children play together in the same manner. By contrast, the children of !Kung farmers split by sex: girls' play is modeled on the behavior of women, boys' play on that of men.

Neolithic Times in Asia

The Neolithic Age in India dates from about 5000 B.C.E. It was centered in modern-day Baluchistan and Sind in northwestern India, then a well-watered and wooded area, but today almost a waterless desert. Several distinct cultures evolved, distinguished from each other by different types of painted pottery and burial practices. Pottery figurines made by these Neolithic peoples show that they practiced fertility rites (mother goddess, phallic symbols) and that the bull was important to them. The Neolithic Age came to an end around 2500 B.C.E. with the beginning of the Indus civilization, a subject for Chapter 2.

The Neolithic Age began in China about 6000 B.C.E. with three separate Neolithic cultures. The first, called the Yangshao culture, was located in North China; its people lived in semisubterranean round and rectangular houses and cultivated millet. Another was located in the Hwai (a river in east-central China) and lower Yangtze Valleys, where rice was grown. A third, which extended along the South China coast and possibly included coastal Southeast Asia and Taiwan, cultivated edible tubers (taro and yam) and fruit. Each culture had its distinct and characteristic pottery. In time each outgrew its immediate surroundings and interactions resulted. Around 3000 B.C.E., silkworms were domesticated and the weaving of silk cloth began. At about the same time, the ability to work nephrite jade, an extremely hard stone, was developed. The Chinese have been making jade tools, ornaments, and ritual items ever since.

Around 2500 B.C.E., an advanced late Neolithic culture, the Lungshan, developed in northeastern China. Its people made a thin, high-fired, almost porcelain-quality pottery on the wheel, began to work metals, had specialized crafts, and began to live in small urban settlements. Differentiated graves indicate the development of a ranked society. According to traditional accounts, great rulers of this period created the first dynasty, called the Hsia. To date, though, we have no documentary evidence of the Hsia dynasty. Undoubtedly, however, the Lungshan culture provided a basis for later development of the first documented dynasty, the Shang, which began around 1700 B.C.E. The Shang dynasty and its immediate successors will be examined in Chapter 2.

Although the earliest Japanese written records date from about 500 C.E., archaeology and Chinese records enable us to reconstruct information for earlier periods. The archaeological record shows that the first Japanese culture, called the Jomon (rope pattern), appeared during the third millennium B.C.E. It is named after pots made and decorated by coiling clay. Jomon people did not practice agriculture, but were hunters and gatherers. To judge from the huge shell mounds they left behind, shellfish was important to their diet.

About the third century B.C.E. in western Japan emerged a Neolithic culture that made pottery on wheels, knew both bronze and iron, and used irrigation to grow rice. It is called the Yayoi culture after one of its sites. Strong Chinese influence is suggested in the introduction of irrigation and in the Han bronze mirrors, weapons, and coins found at Yayoi sites. Technology transfer is evident in the local imitation of metal prototypes introduced from China.

The earliest Chinese historical records containing definite references to Japan were compiled in the third century C.E. They provide interesting information about the political and social organization of an island people whom the Chinese called Wa. According to the records, the Wa were divided into many tribes, ruled over by hereditary kings and queens. The most powerful tribe, called the Yamatai (possibly a rendition of Yamato, the old capital district of the later Japanese imperial line), was ruled by a queen who was also a high priestess. The Chinese also commented on the marked social differences between members of Wa society.

Neolithic Times in the Western Hemisphere

In the Western Hemisphere, undisputed evidence of farming before 7000 B.C.E. exists in the semiarid Mexican highlands, but the climate, at least in the areas where the first civilizations arose, is less favorable to preserving the evidence archaeologists need than are the deserts of Mesopotamia and Egypt. Nevertheless, the early Middle Americans had domesticated gourds by 6500 B.C.E., and they selectively bred maize (commonly called "corn") into a cultivated staple between 7000 and 3500 B.C.E. In comparison, cereals were first grown in the area of present-day Europe about 3000 B.C.E.

Maize would be the agricultural basis for the development of later civilization in Middle America, filling the role that rice did in Asia and cereals did in the Middle East. Weighed against those staples, maize produces more nourishment with less effort than rice or wheat and can grow in drier conditions. The Middle American peoples recognized their debt to their crop: maize gods figure in every Middle American culture the equals, at least, of rain and other environmental deities.

From 3500 to 2500 B.C.E., roughly contemporaneously with the civilization of Sumer in Mesopotamia and the founding of Egypt's dynasties, permanent Neolithic settlements appeared in Middle America. The oldest pottery found dates to about 2500 B.C.E. By 1500 B.C.E., full-time agriculturists had appeared in the central highlands and the Gulf Coast regions of Middle America. The earliest known civilization in the Western Hemisphere, the Olmec, appeared here south of Vera Cruz; it will be taken up in Chapter 1.

Turning to South America, in Peru some farming of both gourds and cotton took place before 2500 B.C.E. In this early phase, many cultural centers existed in different river valleys, but the intervening highlands limited contact between them. We know from the archaeological record that sedentary cultures evolved between 2500 and 1800 B.C.E. in most of the river valleys, where the people built temples and altars, as did some of the highland groups. On the seacoast, the basis of the economy was not agriculture, although farming was done in the fertile soil that seasonal flooding left on the rivers' banks. The main source of food was the sea, which provided not only fish, shellfish, and birds but also seaweed. By the end of this period, some highlanders grew maize, the cultivation of which had spread from Middle America, although most still depended largely on hunting and gathering. Unlike the Middle Americans, the Peruvians domesticated animals: they had the dog, guinea pig, and fowl for food and the American cousins of the camel family—the llama, alpaca, guanaco, and vicuña—for carrying burdens and also for wool. Along the central coast, pottery appeared about 1800 B.C.E. and may represent a diffusion of the technology from Colombia, where it was being made by about 3100 B.C.E. The potato, whose later export to Europe profoundly affected the Old World, was cultivated wherever the climate was suitable. During the period when pottery was just beginning, some of the Peruvian coastal cities also began to raise peanuts and manioc. Because those plants originated east of the Andes, their presence on the Peruvian coast argues for the existence of long-range trade.

Selected Sources

Annaud, Jean-Jacques, director. *Quest for Fire.* 1982. This film depicts a variety of Stone Age discoveries, including fire starting and spoken language.

Barber, Elizabeth W. *Women's Work: The First 20,000 Years: Women, Cloth, and Society in Early Times.* 1994. An informative book that draws on archaeological and other evidence for the development of weaving and many other aspects of women's lives; covers the era from later Paleolithic times through classical Greece.

*Bronowski, Jacob. *The Ascent of Man.* 1973. Chapters 1 and 2 of this best-seller, based on the BBC television series, offer a lively account of Stone Age developments.

*Chang Kwang-chih. *The Archaeology of Ancient China.* 3d ed. 1977. The most authoritative book on the subject. Many illustrations, maps, and charts make it interesting and informative.

*Ehrenberg, Margaret. *Women in Prehistory.* 1989. An interesting study of deductions that can be made about the important role of women in Stone Age cultures.

Fagan, Brian M. *The Journey from Eden: The Peopling of Our World.* 1990. A useful treatment of human evolution and migration patterns in Paleolithic times.

Fiedel, Stuart J. *Prehistory of the Americas.* 1988. A recent and splendid attempt to integrate the new knowledge about pre-Columbian America that has appeared in many fields.

Gimbutas, Marija A. *The Civilization of the Goddess: The World of Old Europe.* 1991. A good examination of prehistoric religions and the place of mother goddesses in early human culture.

*Hawkes, Jacquetta. *The Atlas of Early Man: The Rise of Man across the Globe from 35,000 B.C. to A.D. 500.* 1976; rev. ed. 1993. An extremely well-written book, enhanced by more than 1,000 superb illustrations and maps.

*Leakey, Richard E., and Roger Lewin. *Origins Reconsidered: In Search of What Makes Us Human.* 1992. A readable and well-illustrated update of the popular first edition of Leakey's discussion of human origins.

Mohen, J. P. *The World of Megaliths.* 1990. A current discussion of the megalithic monuments and their builders in the Neolithic era.

Piggott, S. *Prehistoric India.* 1950. Still the classic work on this subject.

Wilson, Peter J. *The Domestication of the Human Species.* 1988. Particularly strong on prehistoric social evolution, land settlement patterns, and dwellings.

*Available in paperback.

Internet Links

Atlas: Stone Age in the Kalahari?
http://www.turknet.com/atlas/97september/bushmen/hunter.html
An online look at the lives of the !Kung people of the Kalahari Desert in northeast Namibia. Excellent text and graphics.

Human Prehistory: An Exhibition
http://users.hol.gr/~dilos/prehis.html
A series of "Exhibition Rooms" featuring helpful graphics and text discussing the progress of our understanding and study of human prehistory.

Paleolithic Art
http://www.mc.maricopa.edu/anthro/exploratorium/art/paleoart.html
An excellent selection of paleolithic rock art such as the Lascaux paintings, with helpful text, including a *Time* magazine article, "Behold the Stone Age," by Robert Hughes.

Stone Pages
http://joshua.micronet.it/utenti/dmeozzi/HomEng.html
"Stone circles, dolmens, standing stones, cairns, barrows and hillforts: welcome to the most comprehensive online guide to European megaliths and other archaeological sites."

The Defining Characteristics of Civilization

*Appetite for food and sex is nature.**

*The range of variations is infinitely wider in food than in sex. . . . People who have the same culture share the same food habits, that is, they share the same assemblage of food variables. People of different cultures share different assemblages of food variables. We might say that different cultures have different food choices.***
 *Kao Tzu, fourth-century B.C.E. philosopher.
 **K. C. Chang, *Food in Chinese Culture: Anthropological and Historical Perspectives* (New Haven: Yale University Press, 1977), p. 3.

The first cities appeared in the Fertile Crescent and Egypt about 3000 B.C.E. as a result of the Agricultural Revoluton, which began in those regions after about 10,000 B.C.E. This momentous achievement enabled humans to acquire food with much greater efficiency and regularity and in greater quantities than had been possible during the earlier hunting-gathering stage. Thus larger groups of people could live from the produce of less land. As food production increased, so did population and consequently population density. More efficient food production led to a surplus that allowed some people to engage in specialized occupations. Trade developed as a result. These advances changed the human condition so significantly that they are collectively termed the Agricultural Revolution.

Some historians speculate that agriculture spread from the Fertile Crescent and Egypt to other parts of the globe. This thesis is difficult to prove, however, and it is possible that agriculture was independently invented in several areas of the world and under different geographical conditions. For example, most early centers of the Agricultural Revolution in Asia and North Africa were located in the temperate zones, and most early civilizations began in large river valleys: the Tigris-Euphrates in Mesopotamia, the Nile in Egypt, the Indus in India, and the Huang Ho in China. However, the Amerindians of Mesoamerica and South America developed advanced civilizations in tropical jungles, in hot arid highlands and coastal areas, and on cool plateaus and uplands, but not along major river valleys. These cultures differed in their food assemblages (for example, cereal grains in West Asia, rice in East Asia, maize in Mesoamerica), which helped them in the evolution of their different cultures.

Many people use the word *civilized* to mean "urbane" or "sophisticated." The term is often applied to one's own group; other groups are deemed to be less civilized or uncivilized "barbarians." For example, the Greeks considered the Persians "barbarians" because they did not speak Greek and embrace Greek cultural values; in the same way, the Persians called the Arabs barbarians, and the Chinese referred to most of their neighbors by the same epithet. In North America, the Inuit and Sioux spoke of themselves as "human beings" or "the people," as if those outside their group were somehow less than human. The origin myths of many peoples support such claims.

Scholars who deal with the past use the word *civilized* in a neutral, descriptive way. Increasingly, historians tend to define civilization in terms of urbanization. Whatever the particular circumstances of their origin, early civilizations manifested similar urban characteristics: new and specialized vocations, advances in the arts and technology, and complex political and cultural institutions. Physically, a city is functionally distinct from the surrounding countryside, often with defensive walls demarcating the entire city or at least its religious and administrative center. It also includes palaces, temples, private residences, and markets. Socially, most early cities included people of distinct social classes and occupational groups, ranging from the ruling elite and religious leaders to artisans, merchants, and slaves.

The city-centered government also ruled surrounding territories, often by military force. It also organized labor for public works. Depending on the resources at their disposal, governments devoted great technological and artistic skills to building canals and dikes, roads, temples, palaces, rulers' tombs, and monuments.

Another approach to defining civilization is to link it with writing. In the opinion of some, no matter how urbanized and how technologically, culturally, and artistically advanced a culture is, it must also have a system of writing to be termed civilized. Applying this criticism to Amerindian cultures, the Maya and the Aztecs were civilized but the Olmec and the Inka were not.

Another issue related to the concept of civilization is the meaning of the term *prehistoric*. Most of us use the term to mean "primitive," as in the sense of Neolithic "cave dwellers." Some professionals, however, use *prehistoric* in a special technical sense to denote a culture that had no writing or whose writing has not been deciphered. According to this point of view, an era is designated *historic* if written materials provide us with a deeper understanding of its culture than can be gained from archaeological artifacts alone. Thus, although the people of the Indus civilization used writing, their civilization is prehistoric, because the few surviving samples of their writing remain undeciphered.

(continued)

This essay has defined civilization and its preconditions largely in material terms. In closing our discussion, we must also remember that every civilization represents a triumph of the human spirit. In the words of Arnold J. Toynbee, a renowned historian of world civilizations:

> How are we to describe . . . any . . . of the ten or twenty civilizations which we can count up on our fingers? In human terms . . . , each of these civilizations is . . . a distinctive attempt at a single great common human enterprise . . . , an effort to perform an act of creation. (A. J. Toynbee, *Civilization on Trial* [New York: Oxford University Press, 1948], p. 55)

The next two chapters will focus on the distinguishing features and achievements of the world's oldest known civilizations in West Asia and Africa, along the Mediterranean, in Central and South America, and in South and East Asia.

Chapter
1

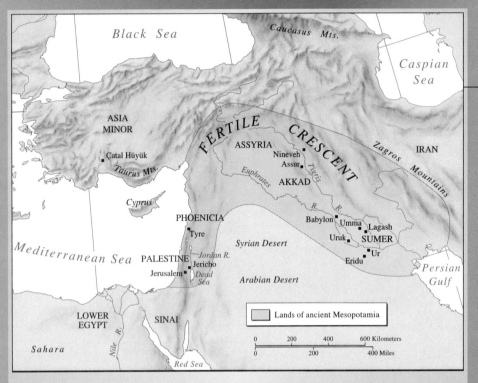

Ancient Mesopotamia

Greece and the Aegean Basin

Early Mesoamerican Civilization

Early Civilization in West Asia, Africa, the Aegean, and the Western Hemisphere

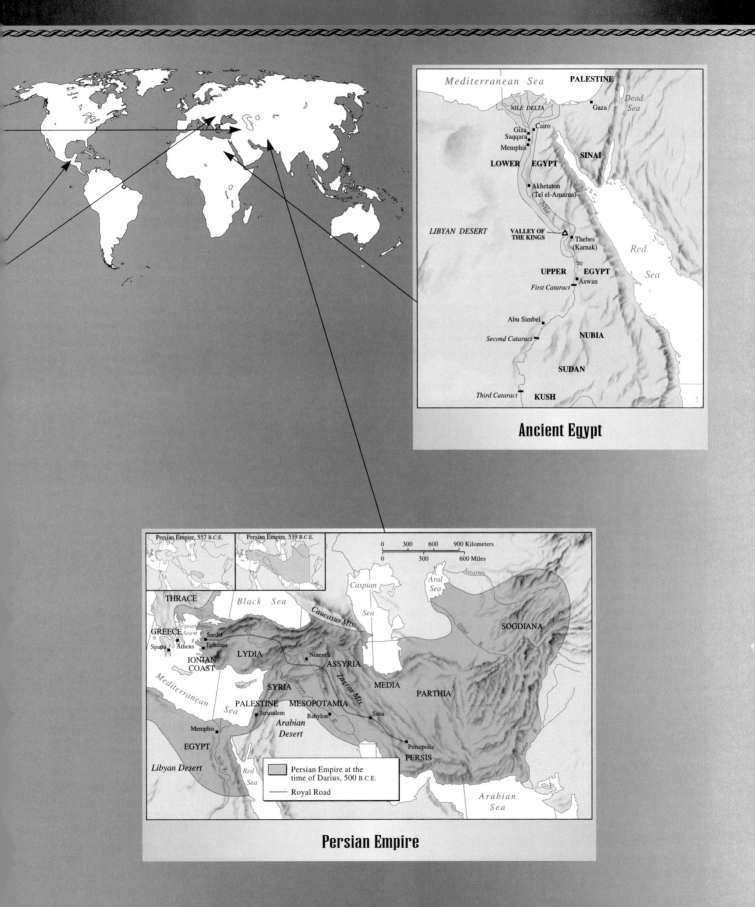

Ancient Egypt

Persian Empire

T̲he study of ancient civilizations is rewarding for several reasons. There is the allure of origins, of people in remote times and distant places who were first in so many crucial endeavors. The early inhabitants of West Asia, Egypt, the Aegean area, and, in the Western Hemisphere, Mesoamerica and the Andean region confronted the problems of survival and succeeded in developing the earliest examples of civilized life. The cities of Mesopotamia, Babylon, and Ur of the Chaldees, the ever-fascinating great pyramids at Giza, the massive sculpted heads at the Olmec city of La Venta, the Lion Gate in the imposing walls at Mycenae, and the spectacular royal palace at Persepolis in Iran—all are the visible signs of energetic people who had marvelous creative talents and ambition to match. Because of their remoteness in time, these civilizations have an air of the exotic and mysterious. We cannot help but be curious about the conditions of life and the personal motivations of the people who fashioned these ancient worlds: in short, what made them tick? To pursue this question is to explore the early, prototypical accomplishments of the human race. Such study is its own reward.

For the student of history, there are additional reasons for studying ancient civilizations. This chapter and the next examine the cultural traits of a number of peoples who built some of the earliest societies based on an urban mode of existence. The preconditions for those societies and their political, social, economic, and cultural common denominators were sketched in the preceding comparative essay. Though the early civilizations we will examine died out in the course of history, they hold special interest precisely because they were the first in the world. They demand attention because of the lasting contributions they made to subsequent societies: the devel-

opment of writing, city living, metalworking, hydraulic engineering, complex governments, rational codes of law, and quasi-monotheistic religions. In all these endeavors, the ancient civilizations, even though they themselves vanished, provided the building blocks for many later advances.

For students living in Western societies, the study of ancient civilizations, as indeed of world history itself, is a good antidote to Eurocentrism (overemphasis on European historical achievements). Not only were West Asia and Africa the cradles of the very earliest civilizations, but it is also becoming increasingly clear that the first European civilization, ancient Greece, owed a large debt to its non-European predecessors. Furthermore, great civilizations were emerging in the rain forests and highlands of Mesoamerica and on the Peruvian coast and the adjacent slopes of the Andes long before the heyday of the classical Greeks.

M̲esopotamian Civilization

The fenlands are in bloom, the fields are green,
The uplands are drenched, the dykes are watered;
Ravine and slope carry down the mountain-torrents
That rush into the dykes, watering the fields.
The soil . . . becomes a plantation,
The grass grows in wood and in meadow,
The bountiful womb of the earth is opened,
Giving plenteous food for cattle and abundance for the
    homes of men.
An ox and a horse struck up a friendship.

3000 B.C.E.

King Menes unifies Egypt
Bronze metallurgy in West Asia
Great Pyramids at Giza
Olmec agricultural villages in
  Mesoamerica

2000

Indo-Europeans arrive in Balkan
  Peninsula
Hammurabi's Code
Hyksos domination in Egypt
Height of Minoan civilization on
  Crete
Eruption of Thera
Akhenaton and Nefertiti rule in
  Egypt
Rise of Olmec civilization in
  Mesoamerica
Introduction of chariot warfare by
  the Hittites
The Trojan War
Collapse of Mycenaean civilization

1000

Spread of iron metallurgy
Kushite kingdom in Africa
Amerindian Chavin culture begins
  to flourish in Peru
Greeks adopt Phoenician alphabet
Homer composes *Iliad* and *Odyssey*
Zoraster in Persia
Nebuchadnezzar builds the
  Hanging Gardens in Babylon
Persian royal road network
Conquests of King Cyrus

500

The rich pasture had sated their bellies,
And glad of heart they lay resting.
The ox opened his mouth to speak, and said to the horse,
    glorious in battle:
"I seem to have been born under a lucky star:
From beginning to end of the year I find food;
I have fodder in abundance and spring water in profusion. . . .
Change thy way of life and come away with me!"
[Said the horse:] "Strong brass to cover my body
Have they put upon me, and I wear it as a garment.
Without me, the fiery steed,
Nor king nor prince nor lord nor noble fares upon his way. . . .
The horse is like a god, stately of step,
Whilst thou and the calves wear the cap of servitude."*

*Sabatino Moscati, *The Face of the Ancient Orient* (Garden City, N.Y.: Doubleday, 1962), pp. 85–86.

This Assyrian beast fable offers a parable of the contrasting aspects of civilized life. The ox praises the settled and orderly life of peace, an idyllic life in a land made lush and fertile by the efforts of men and women who build dikes, divert water, sow seeds, reap the harvest, and tend the animals. The horse, by contrast, praises war, scorning the slavish life of its bovine friend and glorying in the armor and magnificence of the great warriors, lords, and kings who depend on it for success in battle. This section examines both peace and war in several ancient Mesopotamian civilizations.

The Sumerian Exemplar of Civilized Life

The constituents of civilization appeared first in Mesopotamia (Greek for "the land between the rivers") in the Tigris and Euphrates River valleys of West Asia. Climatically, Mesopotamia, a region larger than Texas, was sometimes a hot, arid dust bowl, but at other times it suffered from unpredictable floods and unhealthy swamps. To surmount these problems, a succession of peoples over the centuries—Sumerians, Babylonians, Assyrians, and Chaldeans—mobilized large, well-organized labor forces that gained control over the water supply by constructing and maintaining a system of canals, dikes, drainage ditches, and reservoirs. Properly irrigated and cultivated, Mesopotamian crops yielded as much as a hundredfold return on seed planted and thus supported a much larger population than regions outside Mesopotamia still practicing Neolithic agriculture.

Soon after 3500 B.C.E. the Sumerians began to exploit the potential of the lower Tigris-Euphrates Valley. They built several city-states of 10,000 to 50,000 inhabitants, notably Ur, Uruk, and Lagash, and sustained themselves both by the agricultural produce of the land they controlled and by trade, which provided various imported

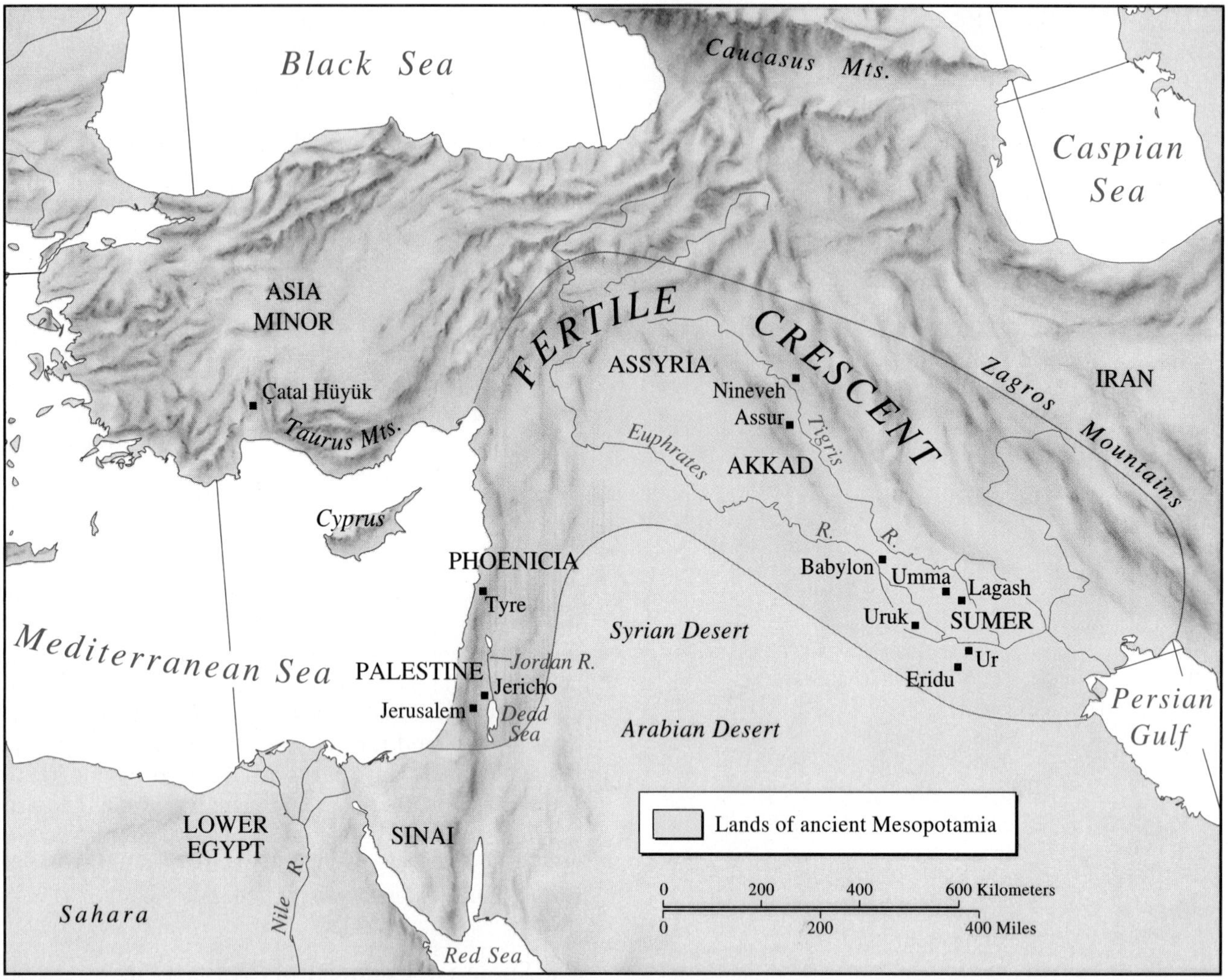

MAP 1.1 Ancient Mesopotamia. The two great rivers of ancient Mesopotamia flow out of Anatolia (present-day Turkey): in Mesopotamia the Euphrates runs some 800 miles and the Tigris about 440, from northwest to southeast, before they join as the present-day Shatt al-Arab, whose 100-mile course ends in the Persian Gulf.

goods and materials in exchange for surplus crops of cereals and vegetables. Over the next 1,500 years, on this agricultural base the Sumerians erected a civilization of great sophistication and durability essentially centered on a cluster of independent city-states that occasionally made war on each other. Because the Sumerians established enduring patterns for Mesopotamian civilization, they receive the greatest attention here.

The Sumerian city-states showed a striking advance in agriculture, architecture, engineering, and technology over the farming villages of the Neolithic era. The Sumerians parceled out the land in tracts of almost geometrical regularity and efficiently watered them through an elaborate irrigation system of dams and canals, with smaller channels supplying individual plots. They built a network of roads and waterways and used donkeys, wagons, boats, and barges to carry goods to the urban centers.

Sumerian social, economic, and political life was as elaborately organized and controlled as its natural surroundings. Around 85 percent of the inhabitants of a city were little more than human farm machines. Most were slaves or tenant farmers who went out from the city to their plots or to the water-control works and, by ceaseless toil, produced the abundant crops that sustained their society. They exchanged part of their produce for the wares of the city's artisans—metalworkers, weavers, potters, and others. They also bartered for the foods available from fisherfolk, bakers, and brewers and for the merchandise brought from outside Mesopotamia by a host of traders.

This intense economic activity made Sumerian cities very impressive indeed. Fortifications were common. The city wall at Uruk, for example, was nearly six miles in circumference; it enclosed about 1,000 acres and contained some 900 defense towers. Within the walls were thousands of humble farmers' hovels and the more elaborate homes of civic and priestly officials and other members of the upper class. Though some avenues were broad and straight, the city as a whole gave the impression of a densely packed hive. Most conspicuous were the temples, set apart in walled-off enclosures and often raised on distinctive, stepped artificial mounds called *ziggurats* (the probable inspiration of the biblical tower of Babel).

Much of the peasants' produce went to support the many religious and civic activities controlled by the temples. Increasingly, in the Sumerian period the secular leaders of the state became identical with the religious hierarchy. The *ensi* (city ruler) was considered the agent of the city god and acted on his behalf. The ruler coordinated the various temple communities within the city and assigned work on public buildings and on the water-control installations. He imposed taxes and made legal decisions of various kinds. The city ruler also dictated the foreign policy of the state, including its defense policy and trade relations. The soldiers were under his direct command. Recognized by his subjects as the supreme earthly authority, the *ensi* was given gifts and shown other signs of deference.

Writing is one of the most notable achievements of the Sumerians. Archaeologists have found thousands of clay tablets inscribed in cuneiform ("wedge-shaped"; see the illustration) dating from nearly all periods of Mesopotamian civilization. These tablets mainly record business transactions, inventories of supplies, production and taxation figures, and wage payments. They show, too, that the Mesopotamians employed such mathematical functions as multiplication and division and had devised both a base 12 system of numerical computation and a calendar correlated with the phases of the moon.

Cuneiform records give us invaluable insights into the Sumerians' view of the world. Anthropomorphic (having human forms and/or personalities) deities, all-powerful and often fickle, populated their religion. The gods were chiefly personifications of natural forces: Inanna, goddess of fertility; Enlil, storm god of earth, wind, and air; Ereshkigal, queen of the underworld; and Dumuzi, god of vegetation, who underwent an annual cycle of death and rebirth. Humans were subject to these and a whole host of lesser but still awe-inspiring divine forces.

Sumerian religion offered no comforting theology of love and salvation and no clearly defined ethical code by which men and women might order their individual lives. Humans might only hope to ensure the security of their society by the proper observance of rituals, involving the sacrifice of animals, demanded by imperious gods. The following hymn to the god Ninurta gives some sense of the intensity of the "fear of the lord" in ancient Sumer:

> Lord Ninurta who vanquishes the houses of the rebellious
>   lands, great lord of Enlil,
>   You, with power you are endowed. . . .
> Lord Ninurta, when your heart was seized by anger,
>   You spat venom like a snake. . . .
> Lord Ninurta, of the house of the contentious and
>   disobedient, you are its adversary,
>   Of their city, you are its enemy. (trans. S. N. Kramer)

Furthermore, after death one could expect to experience only a shadowy, limbolike existence in the underworld. The outlook here is in striking contrast to the more optimistic expectations of Egyptian religion. Still, there was a time for laughter and dancing as well as for weeping and

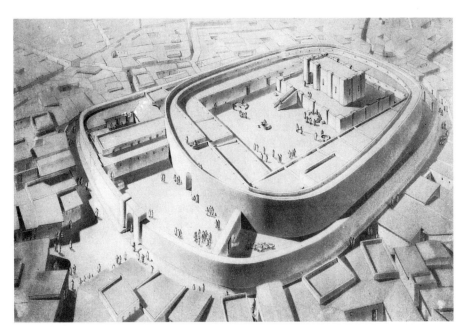

✻ Sumerian Temple. A reconstruction of an early temple at Khafajah in present-day Iraq. Such elevated buildings dominated the vista of the city as the gods dominated the Sumerian worldview. Because the Sumerians worked chiefly with sun-baked mud-bricks, the resulting architecture was and is less impressive than that of the Egyptians and Greeks, who used limestone, granite, and marble in more elaborate and durable structures.

Courtesy of the Oriental Institute/University of Chicago

❧ Evolution of Sumerian Writing. After earlier experimentation with pictographic writing, the Sumerians devised a script called cuneiform (wedge-shaped). Since this system of signs transcribed sounds rather than pictures or ideas, it was adaptable to other languages as well; thus cuneiform writing was later used by the Babylonians and Assyrians.

Original pictograph	Pictograph in position of later cuneiform	Early Babylonian	Assyrian	Original or derived meaning
				Bird
				Fish
				Donkey
				Ox
				Sun Day
				Grain
				Orchard
				To plow To till
				Boomerang To throw To throw down
				To stand To go

mourning, as may be seen in such literary remains as the great *Epic of Gilgamesh*.

Political and Cultural Developments of the Babylonians, Assyrians, and Chaldeans

After 2400 B.C.E. the land of Mesopotamia witnessed political upheavals and shifts in centers of power. New peoples rose to prominence by gradual infiltration or by conquest. The rulers of Akkad (2350–2150 B.C.E.), known as Sargonids after King Sargon I, subjugated the city-states of Sumer and forced them into a federation under Akkadian direction. However, this early instance of empire building was terminated by the violent incursion of outside groups. A later reassertion of Sumerian control (2150–1950 B.C.E.) was cut short by an invasion of the Amorites, who organized the city-states of Sumer and Akkad into an empire centered at Babylon.

This Old Babylonian Empire lasted four centuries. The Babylonians assimilated and refined many of the elements of Sumerian civilization, just as Rome later built on Greek cultural foundations. To cite one example, the

law code of Hammurabi (reigned 1792–1750 B.C.E.), Babylon's most famous dynast, set out in an orderly way, in some 280 articles, the body of law as it had evolved over 1,500 years of Mesopotamian history. Designed to replace capricious blood feuds as the basis for justice, Hammurabi's laws dealt in a ponderous, rational manner with a wide variety of actionable offenses. Most of the code was concerned with indebtedness and breach of business contracts (reflecting the Mesopotamians' commercial orientation), but it also dealt with marriage, adultery, divorce, legitimacy and inheritance, incest, treatment of slaves, personal injury and property damage, and even medical malpractice. Clearly evident in the code is a stratification of society into upper, lower, and slave classes. The penal aspects are dominated by the law of retaliation, "an eye for an eye." Like many other early codifications of law, Hammurabi's code imposed harsh penalties, including capital punishment for many crimes; the severity of the penalty usually depended on the status of the aggrieved party. For example, the code stipulated that "if a physician performed a major operation on a free man with a bronze lancet and has caused the free man's death,

"Fill Your Belly with Good Things"

Gilgamesh, where are you hurrying to? You will never find that life for which you are looking. When the gods created man they allotted him death, but life they retained in their own keeping. As for you, Gilgamesh, fill your belly with good things; day and night, night and day, dance and be merry, feast and rejoice. Let your clothes be fresh, bathe yourself in water, cherish the little child that holds your hand, and make your wife happy in your embrace; for this too is the lot of man.*

The attractive and nubile Siduri, barmaid and vintner to the gods, gives this consoling advice to the hero Gilgamesh during his unsuccessful quest for eternal life. The *Epic of Gilgamesh* was composed in the third millennium B.C.E., some 1,500 years before the earliest European literature (Homer). It was known to the Babylonians, Hittites, Assyrians, and perhaps to the Greeks. A seventh-century B.C.E. copy inscribed in cuneiform on clay tablets was found by excavators at Nineveh in 1853.

*N. K. Sandars, trans., *The Epic of Gilgamesh*, rev. ed. (Baltimore: Penguin, 1972), p. 102.

King Sargon I. Sargon I, ruler of Akkad, founded a dynasty that dominated the cities of Sumer for two centuries. This impressive sculptural head was found at Nineveh and dates to around 2350 B.C.E. Iraq Museum, Baghdad. Photograph: AKG London.

or he opened up the eye-socket of a free man and has destroyed his eye, they shall cut off his hand" (trans. Theophile J. Meek), while the same offense against a slave entailed only replacement of the damaged "property." The general severity of the law code was necessitated in part by the absence of a highly developed ethical doctrine in Mesopotamian religion.

The Babylonians also improved on Sumerian innovations in mathematics and science, especially astronomy. In religion, their deity Marduk presided over a pantheon of Sumerian gods with Babylonian names: for example, Babylonian Ishtar was equivalent to Sumerian Inanna. These deities would survive in various guises through the periods of Assyrian and Chaldean predominance.

Around 1550 B.C.E., the sudden arrival of the Kassites from the neighboring Iranian highlands to the east brought another transition in the sequence of Mesopotamian civilizations. The Kassites in their turn melded with existing Babylonian civilization and remained dominant in Sumer and Akkad for some 400 years.

During the Kassite period, the focus of Mesopotamian development shifted northward. Between about 1300 and 900 B.C.E., the Assyrians rose to prominence in northern Mesopotamia. Although the Kassites for a time prevented consolidation of the entire Tigris-Euphrates Valley, ruthless Assyrian militarism won out after 900 and reached its peak in the careers of a succession of victorious warrior-kings. By the seventh century nearly all of Asia Minor (present-day Turkey), Mesopotamia, Syria, Palestine, and Egypt were at one time or another under Assyrian domination.

In 612 B.C.E., however, another Iranian people, the Medes, allied with resurgent Babylon, succeeded in destroying Assyrian power at its center, the capital of Nineveh. The Neo-Babylonian or Chaldean era that followed was a time of conquests of foreign lands, though not on the Assyrian scale. The most famous Neo-Babylonian king, Nebuchadnezzar (reigned 604–562 B.C.E.), beautified Babylon with such adornments as the Hanging Gardens (an elaborate terraced garden area) and the magnificently decorated Ishtar Gate; he also sought to revive Babylonian religious devotion.

"I Cut Their Throats Like Lambs"—Memoirs of an Assyrian Warrior-King

With the weapons of [the god] Assur, my lord, and the terrible onset of my attack, I stopped their advance, I succeeded in surrounding them [or turning them back], I decimated the enemy host with arrow and spear. All of their bodies I bored through like a sieve. . . . Speedily I cut them down and established their defeat. I cut their throats like lambs. I cut off their precious lives [as one cuts] a string. Like the many waters of a storm, I made [the contents of] their gullets and entrails run down upon the wide earth. My prancing steeds, harnessed for my riding, plunged into the streams of their blood as [into] a river. The wheels of my war chariot, which brings low the wicked and the evil, were bespattered with blood and filth. With the bodies of their warriors I filled the plain, like grass. [Their] testicles I cut off, and tore out their privates like the seeds of cucumbers. . . . Their hands I cut off. The heavy rings of brightest gold [and] silver which [they had] on their wrists I took away. With sharp swords I pierced their belts and seized the girdle daggers of gold and silver which [they carried] on their persons. . . . The chariots and their horses, whose riders had been slain at the beginning of the terrible onslaught, and who had been left to themselves, kept running back and forth. . . . I put an end to their [the riders'] fighting. [The enemy] abandoned their tents and to save their lives they trampled the bodies of their [fallen] soldiers, they fled like young pigeons that are pursued. They were beside themselves . . . they held back their urine, but let their dung go in their chariots. In pursuit of them I dispatched my chariots and horses after them. Those among them who had escaped, who had fled for their lives, wherever they [my charioteers] met them, they cut them down with the sword.*

The ruler who records one of his military successes with such relish in this inscription was Sennacherib (reigned 704–681 B.C.E.). This typically brutal Assyrian warrior-king established an imperial capital at Nineveh on the Tigris River, using thousands of slave-laborers to construct the royal palaces and monuments of the new city.

*Daniel D. Luckenbill, *Ancient Records of Assyria and Babylonia*, vol. 2 (Chicago: University of Chicago Press, 1927), pp. 126–128.

Assyrian Relief Sculpture. This sculpture, done in low relief, shows the Assyrian king Assurbanipal (reigned 668–630 B.C.E.) participating in a hunt. The elaborate dress of both horse and rider signify the high status of the king. Hirmer Verlag

During the Chaldean period, the gods came to be identified with planets: for example, Ishtar (later, Venus) was equated with the planet we call Venus, and Marduk (later, Jupiter) with Jupiter. The Chaldeans were the best astronomers of the ancient world; they developed a detailed method of time reckoning, employing a seven-day week and a day of twelve 120-minute hours. Astronomy also had a religious or astrological function. The Chaldeans believed that charting the positions and movements of the planets and the stars provided a key that would reveal the intentions of the gods, thus enabling humans to foresee future events.

The long story of Mesopotamian civilization closed in 539 B.C.E., when the Persian ruler Cyrus conquered Babylon and incorporated Mesopotamia into his huge empire.

African Civilization

One generation of men passes to another, and God, who knows characters, has hidden Himself, . . . so worship God upon his way. . . . The soul goes to the place it knows. . . . Beautify your mansion in the West, embellish your place in the necropolis with straightforwardness and just dealing; . . . more acceptable is the character of the straightforward man than the ox of the wrongdoer. Serve God, that He may do the like for you, with offerings for replenishing the altars and with carving; . . . God is aware of whoever serves Him. Provide for men, the cattle of God, for He made heaven and earth at their desire. He suppressed the greed of the waters, He gave the breath of life to their noses, for they are likenesses of Him which issued from His flesh. He shines in the sky for the benefit of their hearts; He has made herbs, cattle, and fish to nourish them. He has killed His enemies and destroyed His own children, because they had planned to make rebellion; He makes daylight for the benefit of their hearts, and He sails around in order to see them, . . . and when they weep, He hears.*

*Leonard H. Lesko, trans., "Egyptian Religion: An Overview," in *The Encyclopedia of Religion*, vol. 5, ed. M. Eliade (New York: Macmillan, 1987), p. 41.

This passage comes from an ancient Egyptian "coffin text" (so called because it was painted inside a coffin) of about 2040 B.C.E. It provides a concise summary of the theology and philosophy of the religion of Re, the sun god, whose cult was preeminent through most of Egyptian history. Re is a hidden, all-knowing, and just god. His gifts of life and of the good things of the world must be matched by humans' worship of his godhead and fair treatment of their fellow human beings. The pyramids of Giza are the most lasting testi-

mony of the Egyptians' enduring belief in the power and justice of their gods and of the kings thought to be descended from them. The pyramids also bespeak a thriving society where the labor of thousands—skilled and unskilled—was mustered and directed by a highly sophisticated organization. Ancient Egyptian civilization, the earliest to develop on the continent of Africa, has fascinated later ages both because of its great antiquity and because of the marvelous works of art and architecture that have outlived it.

The Land of the Nile and the Emergence of Egyptian Civilization

Because of the topographical uniformity of its location, Egyptian civilization (see Map 1.2) was more homogeneous, both geographically and politically, than was the case in Mesopotamia, with its numerous, densely populated city-states. Compared with Mesopotamia, Egypt had few cities; administrative activity was highly centralized and concentrated in a few major capitals, such as Memphis and Thebes. The mass of people in Egypt lived in thousands of villages more or less evenly distributed in the 12,000 square miles of arable land in the valley and delta of the mighty Nile, where the dependable pulse of the river's yearly cycle of flood and subsidence regulated Egyptian life. The arid land was fertile only where the waters reached or could be made to reach.

Besides bringing water during its annual flood stage from June to October, the Nile deposited some 200 million tons of rich, fertile soil and minerals on Egyptian farmlands each year. By diverting the floodwaters and draining swamplands in the Nile Valley, Egypt became the most productive agricultural land of the ancient world. The reliable rhythm of the Nile also affected the people of Egypt in subtler ways: in particular, it fostered a more optimistic outlook on life, a confidence in the natural order of things that is not evident in, for example, Mesopotamia.

Menes, the first king of Egypt's First Dynasty (royal family line), is credited with unifying Upper and Lower Egypt around 3000 B.C.E. The next 2,000 years of Egyptian history are customarily divided into three periods of strong political unity, the Old, Middle, and New Kingdoms, separated by periods of weak central government, social unrest, and foreign invasions.

The preeminent central authority in the Old Kingdom was the pharaoh, a god-king, seen variously as the son or the manifestation of certain deities. He exercised his supreme will through a simple but rigid hierarchy ranging from royal agents and elite nobles to local officials who ruled some forty administrative districts. This political superstructure and the many building projects and other activities it supervised were supported by the tremendous agricultural surplus produced by the mass of peasants. This god-governed state engaged in exploration of and trade with neighboring lands, including Nubia, Ethiopia, the Sinai Peninsula, and Phoenicia. To build monuments or flood-control installations, the pharaohs dictated the enlistment and provisioning of a large, skilled labor force: masons and stonecutters, sculptors, carpenters, and painters, as well as construction managers, surveyors, draftsmen, scribes, and others. These worked chiefly during the inundation phase of the Nile's cycle, when transport by water was easiest and farm workers were free to quarry, haul, and position stone building materials.

The pharaoh wielded such extensive powers because service to him on any state project was a religious as well as a civic duty. Egyptian religion, like that of Sumer, was a thoroughgoing polytheism (belief in many gods), in which most major and minor divinities were associated with the agrarian rhythms of fertility and germination, death and regeneration. The gods were mainly anthropomorphic but could also have the form of a beast, such as a beetle, bull, or snake, or a half-beast, such as a human torso with the head of a jackal, crocodile, or cow.

Egyptian religion had a slight ethical emphasis and concern for justice that we do not see in Mesopotamia. The gods ruled a cosmos based on the Egyptian notion of moral right. The pharaoh was expected to treat his subjects equitably, and those subjects in turn were required to be fair in their dealings with one another. Those with the means to do so were to assist the less well off, such as widows and orphans.

Perhaps the most universal Egyptian myths concerned the god Osiris, slain by the evil Set but reborn through

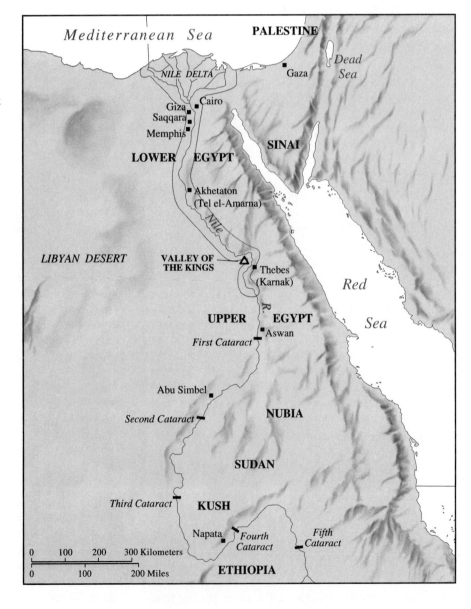

✳ MAP 1.2 Ancient Egypt. The Nile—the longest river in the world—literally defines the country of Egypt. Its sources are in the lakes of Ethiopia and Uganda, which give rise to the Blue and White Niles. These two join at Khartoum in Sudan. The river is about one-half mile wide, and its valley is about five miles wide down to a point just north of present-day Cairo, where the river divides to form the great Nile delta on the Mediterranean. Throughout Egyptian history, 95 percent of the population has lived in the Nile valley and delta.

Diverse Burial Customs

Death, birth, and marriage are the cardinal events in all societies throughout history. Humans have evolved a wide range of rituals of celebration and mourning. Burial practices vary depending on the climate and topography in which societies have emerged. In tropical, hot regions where bodies decompose quickly, or in densely populated areas like India, corpses are often cremated and the ashed returned to the land, air, or sea. In hot desert regions like the Middle East, simple burials are usually held within twenty-four hours of death.

As civilizations became more complex, so too did burial practices. Powerful and wealthy rulers and elites were often buried in huge, ornate tombs and adorned with costly jewels and clothing. In Han China, rulers were buried with full regalia and replicas of their armies, horses, and trappings of power. Similarly, in the Western Hemisphere, Chaco and Aztec warriors were buried with their armor, gold jewelry, and armaments.

The burial customs of the ancient Egyptians were among the most complex in human history. The pyramids in Giza and tombs in the Valley of the Kings and Queens are 3,000-year-old monuments to the Egyptian preoccupation with death and the afterlife. The burial chamber of the pharaoh Tutankhamon, uncovered by Howard Carter in 1922, contained a veritable treasure trove of artifacts. Upon seeing the chamber for the first time, Carter exclaimed that he saw "wonderful things, strange animals, statues and gold, everywhere the glint of gold." One elaborately painted chest took Careter three weeks to unpack. The items found in "Tut's" tomb—including gold jewelry, alabaster vases, and a jewel-inlaid, golden funerary mask—continue to amaze and delight present-day viewers.

---

the efforts of his sister/wife Isis. Osiris was the father of Horus, who, in most periods of Egyptian history, was embodied in the person of the king. After death, the pharaoh became one with Osiris, the king of the dead who influenced the life cycles governing the natural world. In a continuing cycle, the new pharaoh, the son of the dead ruler, was the dutiful Horus, who led the state in the worship of his father Osiris. Thus the security not only of the state but also of the whole universe was directly linked to the well-being of the king, both during and after his life on earth. He had to be accorded all due honors and signs of deference in this life as well as in the next. This belief accounts for the practice of mummification, which was an attempt to ensure the continued comfort and goodwill of the deceased king in the afterworld. Hence, too, the fantastic expenditure of time and resources on funeral monuments, temples, and tombs, of which the pyramids are the most notable.

Early in their history, the ancient Egyptians evolved and perfected the pyramid, the architectural form that has ever after been the distinguishing mark of their civilization. Of the Great Pyramids built at Giza, the largest is that of Khufu (or Cheops), which dates from about 2600 B.C.E. It was 460 feet high and 755 feet on each side and was made from some 2.3 million stone blocks averaging 2.5 tons each. The whole was sheathed with limestone casing blocks (stripped in later centuries to supply building stone for new cities like Cairo) that gave the pyramid the appearance of one massive unit. The complex at Giza—the three Great Pyramids and the famous Sphinx—was only one of many Old Kingdom burial places in the region of Memphis; some eighty tombs are marked by pyramids. Although the pyramids provided an eternal home only for royalty, the existence of nobles' tombs indicates that the possibility of life after death was open to others besides the pharaoh.

The pyramids at Giza are among the best examples of Egyptian architecture, not only in scale but also in the precision of their construction. They are particularly remarkable considering the Egyptians' lack of sophisticated hoisting equipment. It is likely that earthen ramps were used to haul the stones up and into position. Moreover, the tombs and temples, here and elsewhere in Egypt, were adorned with magnificent sculptures (full-figure and relief), paintings, and hieroglyphic inscriptions. The last were perhaps inspired by a knowledge of cuneiform, but they differ from that script by combining pictographs with syllable signs and letter signs. Thus the Egyptians did not develop true alphabetic writing.

Discontinuities and the Rise and Decline of an Imperial Culture

Just as Sumerian archetypes gave an enduring pattern to Mesopotamian civilization, the Old Kingdom originated many aspects of the political, religious, and artistic worldview of the Egyptians. In Mesopotamia, change often came as a result of intrusions from the Iranian uplands to the east and north or from Arabia to the west and south. Egypt, by contrast, was better protected from invasion by vast tracts of uninhabitable desert wasteland.

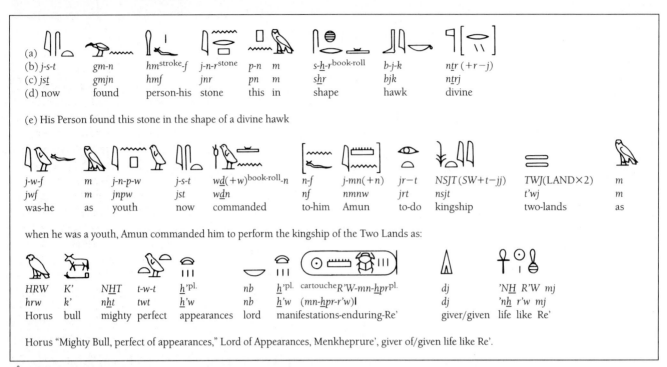

(a)
(b) *j-s-t*   *gm-n*   *hm*stroke-*f*   *j-n-r*stone   *p-n*   *m*   *s-ḥ-r*book-roll   *b-j-k*   *nṯr* (+*r*−*j*)
(c) *jst*   *gmjn*   *hmf*   *jnr*   *pn*   *m*   *sḥr*   *bjk*   *nṯrj*
(d) now   found   person-his   stone   this   in   shape   hawk   divine

(e) His Person found this stone in the shape of a divine hawk

j-w-f   *m*   *j-n-p-w*   *j-s-t*   *wd*(+*w*)book-roll-*n*   *n-f*   *j-mn*(+*n*)   *jr−t*   *NSJT* (*SW*+*t*−*jj*)   *TWJ*(LAND×2)   *m*
jwf   *m*   *jnpw*   *jst*   *wdn*   *nf*   *nmnw*   *jrt*   *nsjt*   *t'wj*   *m*
was-he   as   youth   now   commanded   to-him   Amun   to-do   kingship   two-lands   as

when he was a youth, Amun commanded him to perform the kingship of the Two Lands as:

HRW   *K'*   *NḤT*   *t-w-t*   *ḥ'*pl.   *nb*   *ḥ'*pl.   cartouche*R'W-mn-ḫpr*pl.   *dj*   *'NḤ R'W mj*
hrw   *k'*   *nḥt*   *twt*   *ḥ'w*   *nb*   *ḥ'w*   (*mn-ḫpr-r'w*)| *dj*   *'nḥ r'w mj*
Horus   bull   mighty   perfect   appearances   lord   manifestations-enduring-Re'   giver/given   life like Re'

Horus "Mighty Bull, perfect of appearances," Lord of Appearances, Menkheprure', giver of/given life like Re'.

❋ Egyptian Hieroglyphic Writing. This example of Egyptian hieroglyphic writing is from a temple of Thutmose IV (reigned 1406–1398 B.C.E.). Line *a* shows original hieroglyphics, *b* and *c* show two kinds of transliteration, *d* gives a word-by-word translation, and *e* gives a smooth English version. Hieroglyphic writing passed out of use around 400 C.E. It remained undeciphered until the discovery of the Rosetta stone (now in the British Museum) by the French during their occupation of Egypt in 1799. The stone bears an inscription from the reign of Ptolemy V (196 B.C.E.) in three versions—hieroglypic Egyptian, demotic Egyptian, and Greek. Using this as a key, the French scholar Jean François Champollion was able to decipher hieroglyphic writing in 1822.

Internal social and political upheavals, however, occasionally led to weakness and disunity.

During the first intermediate period (2150–2050 B.C.E.), the central administration was replaced by a fragmented system of hereditary local leadership. The succeeding Middle Kingdom (2050–1750 B.C.E.) had its capital at Thebes, some 400 miles up the Nile from Memphis. Once again Upper and Lower Egypt were reunited. About 1750, however, either a succession of weak kings or stiffer competition from local nobles with royal aspirations apparently once again eroded central authority. Vulnerable because of its domestic disarray, Egypt suffered the "Great Humiliation," a successful invasion, probably from Palestine, by a people whom the Egyptians called the Hyksos. Unlike the Amorites or the Kassites, who were ultimately absorbed by the civilizations they attacked in Mesopotamia, the Hyksos remained an alien force. They maintained themselves in Lower Egypt by superior military ability and technology: the horse-drawn chariot and improved weapons. After about 200 years, they were ejected by Theban rulers, who were in turn followed by the ambitious and imperialistic kings of the New Kingdom era.

The Egyptian Empire, as the New Kingdom (1550–1150 B.C.E.) is sometimes labeled, restored much of the prestige lost during the Hyksos occupation. Egyptian control again reached across the Sinai into Palestine and Syria and to the Euphrates. At home, foreign conquest meant peace and prosperity; tribute and valuable materials poured into Egypt. Strong trade contacts were developed, for example, with the land of "Punt," in the region of modern Somalia, and with Arabia; these contacts brought incense, ivory, myrrh, and slaves to Egypt in exchange for jewelry, weapons, and tools. The Egyptians' pride in these achievements can be seen in the art and architecture sponsored by the conquering pharaohs of the New Kingdom, who launched massive building programs to honor the gods and to publicize and magnify their own accomplishments. The colossal temple complex of Amon at Karnak near Thebes is an especially noteworthy example, as are the huge, lavishly furnished temples and tombs in the Valley of the Kings across the Nile from Thebes and at Abu Simbel above Aswan. The tomb of an unimportant king, Tutankhamon (reigned 1352–1344 B.C.E.), which escaped grave robbers, gives us a tantalizing glimpse of the wealth of the kings and nobles of imperial Egypt. The discovery of the tomb of Tutankhamon (or "King Tut") by the British archaeologist Howard Carter in 1922 caused a worldwide sensation and a frenzy of interest in ancient Egypt, seen in new styles of architecture and interior decoration, as well as in such popular entertainments as the horror film *The Mummy*. As Carter himself said in recalling the discovery:

> A feeling of intrusion had descended heavily upon us with the opening of the doors, heightened, probably, by the almost painful impressiveness of a linen pall, decorated with golden rosettes, which dropped above the inner shrine. We felt that we were in the presence of the dead King and must do him reverence, and in imagination could see the doors of the successive shrines open one after the other till the innermost disclosed the King himself.

Amenhotep IV (reigned 1369–1353 B.C.E.), unlike most of the militaristic pharaohs who preceded him, was most notable for his innovations in religion. A rebel in his attitudes toward art and theology, he recognized as gods only himself and the solar disk, Aton. He changed his name to Akhenaton ("it pleases Aton") and founded a new capital called Akhetaton ("place of the Glory of Aton") at present-day Tel el-Amarna (see Map 1.2). In contrast to the polytheism prevalent in the ancient world, his religion closely approached monotheism. Akhenaton and his queen, Nefertiti, are familiar from artistic depictions. The pharaoh's reform efforts, however, were short-lived. His successor, Tutankhamon, reinstated the previous polytheism with Amon as chief deity, pleasing the numerous priests who derived wealth and prestige at the restored capital of Thebes and elsewhere. Indeed, the ever-rising power of the various priesthoods, which Akhenaton had tried to curb, was a principal symptom of yet another decline of the central authority.

After 1100 B.C.E., Egypt was only intermittently a unified state. Despite sporadic reassertions of independence, Egypt proper never regained the political autonomy and confident imperialism of its glorious past. Ancient Egyptian history became an adjunct of Kushitic, Assyrian, Persian, Macedonian, and Roman history.

The Kushite Kingdom in Upper Egypt and the Sudan

Once an extension of the ancient Egyptian Empire, the Kushite kingdom emerged as an independent power by 700 B.C.E. Located around the border of present-day Egypt and Sudan, with their capital at Napata, the Kushites had long served as intermediaries for the transport of goods traded between the Egyptian kingdom and East Africa. In the course of their contacts with, and eventual subjugation by, Egypt, the Kushites assimilated many of the cultural, religious, and social values of ancient Egypt.

Career Counseling in Ancient Egypt

The washerman's day is going up, going down. All his limbs are weak, [from] whitening his neighbor's clothes every day, from washing linen.

The maker of pots is smeared with soil, like one whose relations have died. His hands, his feet are all full of clay; he is like one who lives in the bog.

The cobbler mingles with vats. His odor is penetrating. His hands are red with madder [dye], like one who is smeared with blood. He looks behind him for the kite, like one whose flesh is exposed.

The watchman prepares garlands and polishes vasestands. He spends a night of toil just as one on whom the sun shines.

The merchants travel downstream and upstream. They are as busy as can be, carrying goods from one town to another. . . . But the tax collectors carry off the gold, that most precious of metals.

The ships' crews from every house [of commerce], they receive their loads. They depart from Egypt for Syria, and each man's god is with him. [But] not one of them says: "We shall see Egypt again!"

The carpenter who is in the shipyard carries the timber and stacks it. If he gives today the output of yesterday, woe to his limbs! The shipwright stands behind him to tell him evil things. . . .

The scribe, he alone, records the output of all of them. Take note of it! . . . Set your sight on being a scribe. . . . You will not be like a hired ox.*

T his passage is from an ancient Egyptian document (the *Papyrus Lansing* in the British Museum) dating to about 1150 B.C.E. It is part of a letter of advice written to a young man about to decide on a profession. The document provides some interesting reflections on the conditions of work in a variety of jobs.

*Miriam Lichtheim, comp., *Ancient Egyptian Literature: A Book of Readings*, vol. 2, *The New Kingdom* (Berkeley: University of California Press, 1976), pp. 168–173.

As Egypt declined in military strength and cultural dynamism, the Kushite kingdom evolved into a distinctive Sudanic empire. By 750 B.C.E., Kushite kings began attacking the weakened Egyptian forces and, under King Shabako (reigned 707–696 B.C.E.), conquered Egypt. After almost one hundred years of rule over Egypt, the Kushite Empire was attacked by the stronger military might of the Assyrians. Following the Assyrian conquest of Egypt, the Kushites hastily withdrew to the Sudan. By 591 the Egyptians renewed their attacks on the Kushites, who then moved their capital further south to Meroë. Meroë, located approximately one hundred miles north

✳ Temple at Abu Simbel. Pictured is the façade of the great temple at Abu Simbel with its colossal figures of Ramses II (reigned 1290–1224 B.C.E.), more than sixty feet in height. At a cost of $40 million, a UNESCO team of German, Italian, French, and Swedish engineers dismantled and moved the temple to higher ground to prevent its being submerged by the rising waters of Lake Nasser after the completion of the Aswan High Dam; the move took four years (1964–1968). Telegraph Colour Library/FPG

of contemporary Khartoum, had substantial deposits of iron ore and wood, good grazing land for cattle, and a navigable harbor; it also had control of the rich gold mines of the Sudan (known in Rome as Nubia).

In Meroë, the Kushites prospered from trade with Egypt and East Africa. Documents and relics indicate that the Kushites also had indirect contacts with China, India, and Arabia. Following the Macedonian conquest of Egypt in 332 B.C.E., they also established close relations with the Greeks. Much of Meroë's prosperity was based on the production of high-grade iron used to manufacture weapons. Meroë was known throughout the Hellenistic world as an iron-producing center, and remnants of slag heaps from smelting factories are still visible around the ancient monuments of the city. As Meroë declined in wealth and power, some Kushites may have migrated to West Africa, carrying with them their skills in iron production and knowledge of the lost-wax process for bronze casting. At present it is not known whether these skills were transmitted from East Africa or whether West African societies developed the techniques independently.

Once literate in the Egyptian language, the Kushites gradually developed a written language of their own based on hieroglyphics, but the signs have yet to be interpreted. As a result, much of what is known about Kushite society comes from accounts by foreign travelers, traders, or historians who had contact with the Kushite Empire.

It is known that the Kushites had an extremely hierarchical society similar to that of ancient Egypt. The ruling families lived lavishly, owned slaves, and were probably revered as divine. Most Kushites earned their livelihoods from herds of cattle, sheep, and goats. The many depictions of royal women in sculptures and reliefs on temples suggest that the society may have been matrilineal. Documentary evidence reveals that the Kushite kingdom was ruled by a queen in 45 B.C.E. The extensive ruins of temples, palaces, and pyramids around Meroë attest to the wealth, building skills, and complexity of the society. Pottery, sculpture, and other objects show influences of pharaonic, Hellenistic, and sub-Saharan African societies. As in Egypt, Kushite royalty and nobility, along

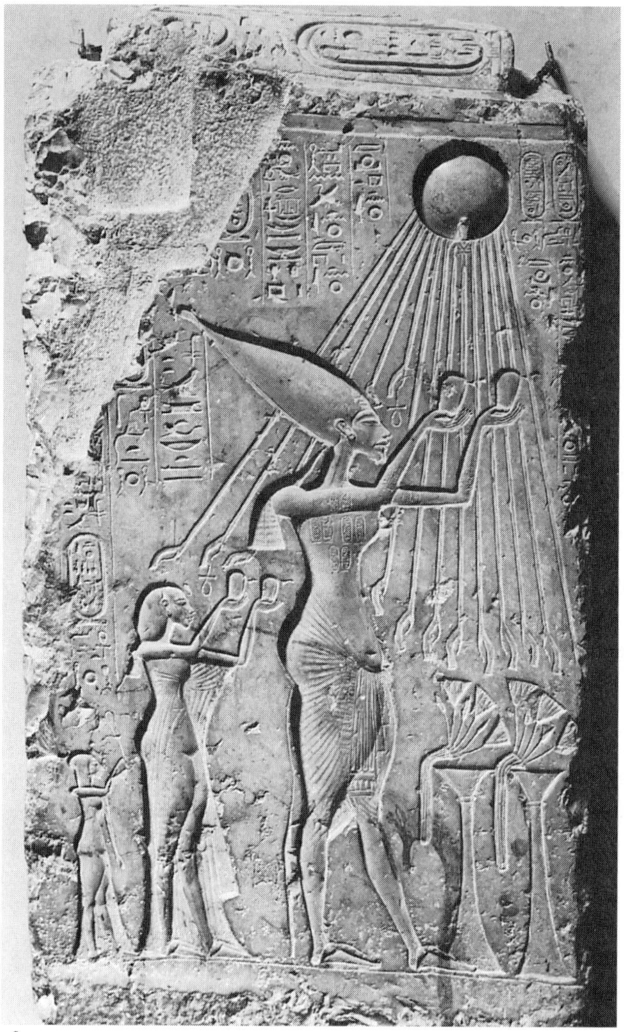

Akhenaton Worshiping Aton. This limestone sculptural relief shows Akhenaton with his queen, Nefertiti, and one of their children presenting gifts to Aton, the solar disk. Note that some of the hands at the ends of the solar rays hold the Egyptian emblem of life known as the *ankh*. Metropolitan Museum of Art

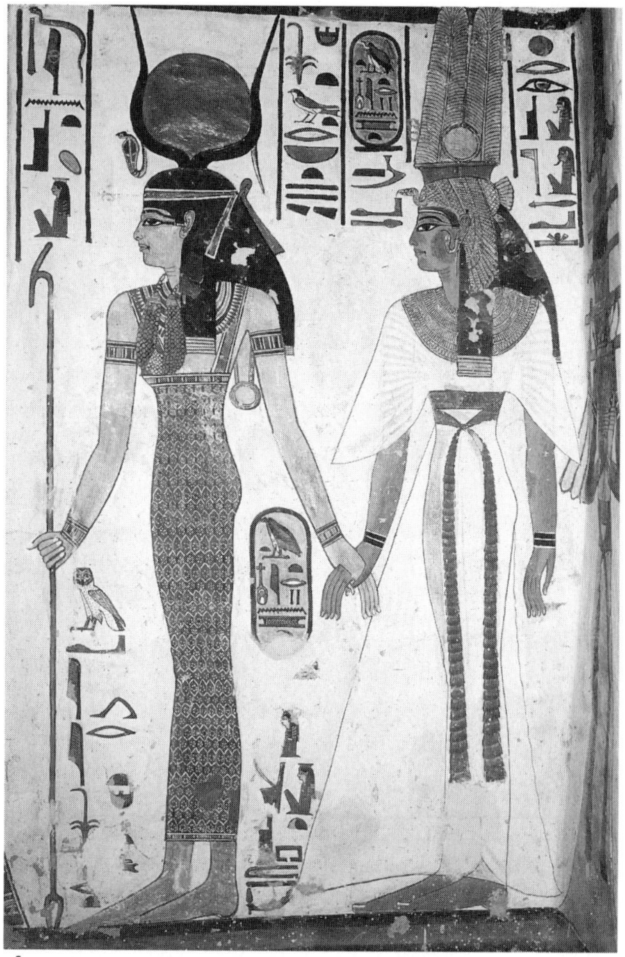

Tomb of an Egyptian Queen. Shown here is a painting of Nefertari, the favorite wife of Ramses II. This scene from the queen's tomb, which is among the most beautifully decorated Egyptian tombs, shows Nefertari accompanied by the goddess Isis. Giraudon/Art Resource

with their personal possessions, were buried in lavish tombs. Some of these tombs have provided archaeologists with a rich source of information about the Kushites; however, many of these tombs and other Kushite monuments have not yet been excavated, and much remains to be learned.

Amerindian Civilization

*I [came] face to face with Colossal Head Number 1, buried up to its eyes near the base of the great mound at La Venta. Now, retrieved and revered anew, it stares sightlessly with a certain air that seems to me to verge on smugness, perhaps because it has survived a span of time that began long before the Parthenon rose on the heights above Athens.**

*George E. Stuart, "New Light on the Olmec," *National Geographic* 184 (November 1993): 104.

These intimidating sculptures portraying the rulers of the city-states of the early Olmec culture of Mesoamerica stand up to eleven feet tall. They are among the most impressive archaeological finds from the early Amerindian civilizations that arose in the Western Hemisphere beginning in 1800 B.C.E., some 1,200 years after humans had established civilizations in Mesopotamia and Egypt. One cultural center, Andean civilization, emerged on the Pacific coast of present-day Peru and quickly extended into the Andean highlands from

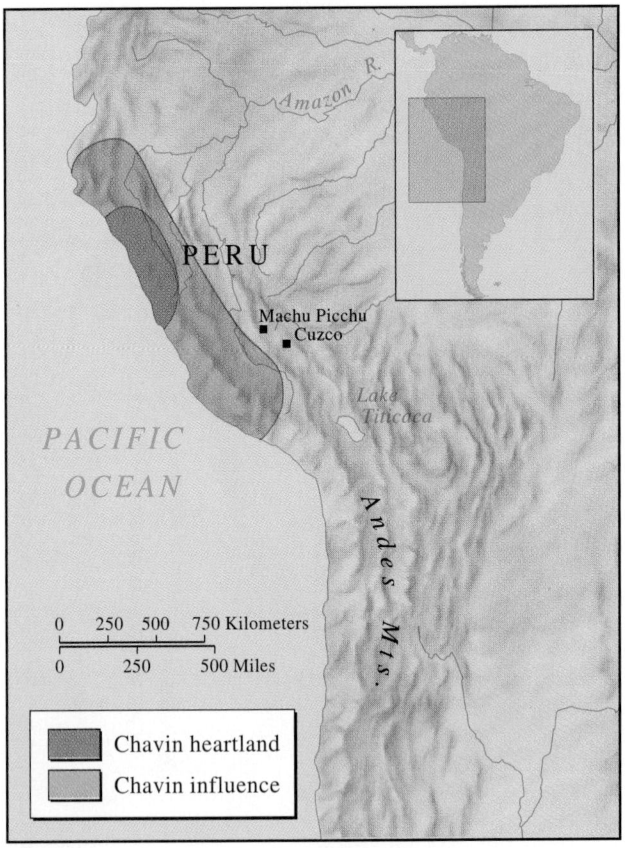

MAP 1.3A. Early Peruvian-Andean Civilization. The Chavin culture (900–300 B.C.E.) was the first stage of a series of increasingly sophisticated Amerindian cultures that first flourished on the coast of present-day Peru and spread up into the high plateaus of the Andes. The Chavin built monumental religious structures and were experts in making fine pottery and exquisite gold jewelry.

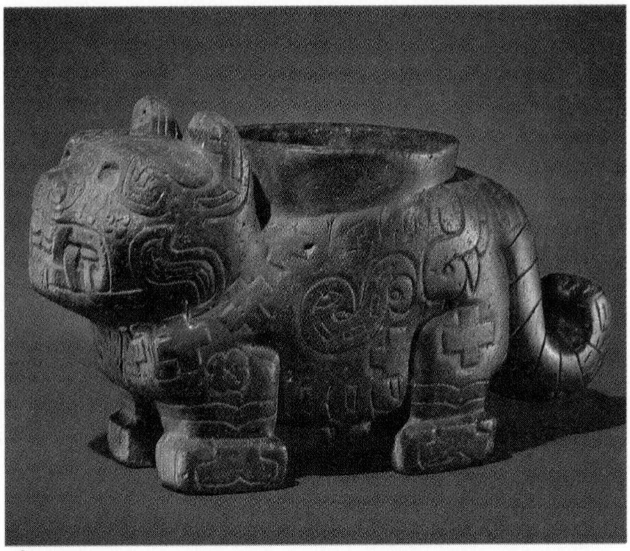

A Chavin Jaguar. This stone mortar was carved in the shape of a puma, or jaguar. Stone carving was a specialty of the Chavin, and the jaguar was an important figure in Peruvian and Andean culture as well as in Mesoamerica. The University Art Museum, University of Pennsylvania, neg. #T4-132c3

Ecuador to Chile. The other center of civilization arose in Mesoamerica (present-day eastern Mexico, Guatemala, Belize, El Salvador, and western Honduras) about 400 years later.

Archaeologists are currently undertaking extensive projects in both Mesoamerica and Peru, and their investigations have greatly enlarged our understanding of the antiquity, complexity, and geographic extent of these Amerindian civilizations. In this section, we focus on the two earliest Amerindian cultures: Chavin society along the arid coast of Peru and Olmec society in the humid rain forests along the Gulf of Mexico southeast of Vera Cruz.

The Opening of Andean Civilization: The Chavin Culture

The Andean cultural area is a region of great environmental diversity that is best conceived of on a vertical rather than a horizontal scale. The high mountain valleys of the Andes lie only seventy to ninety miles east of the Pacific coast. Off the coast, a cold current supports a rich marine life that usually supplies a major element of the diet of the dwellers on the narrow, arid coastal plain. On occasion, however, the waters run warm, producing the effect called El Niño, which destroys marine life and disrupts the interior climate. The narrow coastal plain is cut by some forty rivers that carry the fertile soil down from the highlands. Amerindian farmers grew maize, vegetables, avocados, potatoes, and peanuts on the soil deposits in these short, narrow valleys. Rainfall increases as one moves into the Andean foothills and mountains, and the puna, a high plateau of varying elevations interspersed among the Andean mountain ranges, is well watered. The Amerindians living in these uplands grew maize at the lower levels and potatoes farther up and herded llamas and alpacas on the high grasslands. Some Andean villagers attended to all three areas by walking a few miles up or down the slopes. The warm eastern face of the Andes drops down into the Amazon basin; here the inhabitants grew cotton and coca and gathered tropical fruit.

All that remains of Peru's history before the Spanish conquest is the archaeological record of nonliterate peoples, which can reveal much about the way that people lived, but less about why they did so. Such studies indicate that by 3000 B.C.E. the Amerindians had established permanent agricultural settlements on the coast; shortly thereafter they expanded into the Andean highlands, and by 2700 they were making pottery. By 1800 B.C.E. Amerindians were establishing religious centers marked by large stone buildings throughout Ecuador and Peru, both on the coast and in the highlands.

The first widespread civilization in Peru was the Chavin culture, which flourished from 900 to 200 B.C.E. Archaeologists have uncovered some aspects of this culture, and it is known that the Chavin religion promoted two deities archaeologists call the Smiling God and the Staff God. The Chavin religion was so powerful that in less than a century it spread throughout Peru; yet to date scholars have little understanding of its ideas or rituals. Chavin artwork was as influential as the religion. Chavin artisans worked in ceramics, textiles, and jade; jaguars were a key motif. Metals began to be smelted for the first time during these years, but were used almost solely for decoration. Chavin artisans worked first with gold and copper and later with silver, platinum, and tin. They also began to cast bronze, but it too was usually used for decoration, not for tools or weapons.

About 350 B.C.E. major changes occurred. Coastal populations began to build major irrigation works, a hint that population growth may have been exerting pressure on natural resources. Many Peruvian cities began to erect strong fortifications, and their art began to feature warriors, an indication that cities were warring with each other over control of neighboring farmlands. Urban centers constructed fortifications, undertook prolonged wars, built irrigation systems, and allocated water, suggesting that strong central authority and stratified social systems had developed by this stage. By 200 B.C.E. the Chavin culture had faded away.

The Advent of Mesoamerican Civilization: The Olmec

Mesoamerica is a geographic area of great variety in altitude and rainfall, and the Amerindian cultures there developed in many different environments. The great mountain spine that extends from Alaska to the tip of South America dominates the physical terrain of Mesoamerica, where it runs close to the Pacific coast. There are also extensive lowlands along the Gulf of Mexico and the Caribbean Sea, especially in the Yucatán Peninsula. Rainfall varies over the different lowland and highland areas.

Olmec society appeared about 1400 B.C.E. and dominated Mesoamerican civilization until about 500 B.C.E. Most archaeological excavations have centered on the area southeast of Vera Cruz, but work at new sites in the highlands south of Mexico City and in southern Guatemala has revealed additional centers of Olmec culture.

As early as 2200 B.C.E., the Olmec were living in agricultural villages in the lush, steamy environment along the gulf coast, where they cultivated large maize crops and supplemented their diet with abundant seafood and shellfish, game, and dogs. The plentiful food supply supported an increasingly populous and sophisticated village and town life.

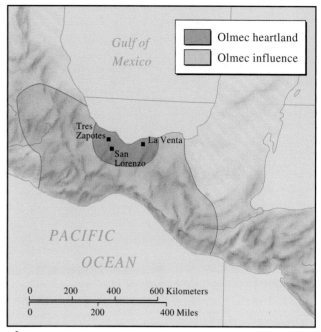

MAP 1.3B. Early Mesoamerican Civilization. The Olmec culture (1200–500 B.C.E.) was the first stage of a series of increasingly sophisticated Amerindian cultures centered in Mesoamerica (present-day eastern Mexico, Guatemala, Belize, and western Honduras) for almost 3,000 years. The Olmec built large earthen temple mounds, imported huge boulders that they carved into likenesses of their rulers, and set up an extensive trading network throughout the area.

The Olmec were traders as well as farmers and fisherfolk. They prospered by selling and trading throughout Mesoamerica. They trafficked in tar, rubber, salt, fine clay for pottery, metal ores for coloring, basalt for monuments, shells, skins, exotic bird feathers, cacao, jadite, incense, medicines, textiles, obsidian (volcanic glass), and jadeite (a special variety of jade). The Olmec especially prized obsidian and jadeite. In cultures without smelted metals, obsidian is particularly valuable because, properly worked, it can be made into razor-sharp, though somewhat brittle, tools and weapons. Access to obsidian sources in the highlands near present-day Mexico City was an important element in the rise and fall of Mesoamerican civilizations. As for jadeite, the Olmec desired it for religious purposes.

Where traders went, cultural influence was not far behind. Artifacts found over a wide area of Mesoamerica indicate that the Olmec traders spread their culture to less advanced maize-growing villages in the central highlands of Mexico and founded a major city, Copan, in southern Guatemala 400 miles from the Olmec heartland.

Like the Chavin before them and the Maya after them, the Olmec lived in a world of ministates. In the Olmec heartland there were three major centers based on temple

❊ The Head of an Olmec Ruler. The most striking artistic expressions of the Olmec culture are the heads carved from basalt boulders, apparently advertising the authority of specific rulers. This particular six-foot representation was carved about 700 B.C.E.   Foto Film/Art Resource

complexes: San Lorenzo (1400–900 B.C.E.), Tres Zapotes (900–350 B.C.E.), and La Venta (900–350 B.C.E.). San Lorenzo was the first religious center in the Western Hemisphere, and the sacred ball game may have originated there. As with the Chavin culture, our knowledge of the Olmec comes from archaeological assessments. At this stage in Olmec culture, there is no sign of writing.

La Venta, the largest Olmec city, best illustrates the basic aspects of Olmec culture. The city proper, which contained a population of about 18,000, was situated on an island; another 350,000 people lived in adjacent areas. La Venta was symmetrically laid out on an axis eight degrees west of true north and was dominated by a pyramid of packed earth more than one hundred feet high, probably flattened on top to serve as a center for religious ceremonies. A number of lower mounds were probably the sites of other public buildings or homes for the nobility. In the hot climate, both private homes and public buildings were apparently constructed with thatched roofs and open walls to catch any cooling drafts. The city was guarded by huge, stern-visaged heads that proclaimed to all outsiders, human and nonhuman, the temporal and spiritual power of La Venta's rulers.

The Olmec, and the Amerindian cultures that succeeded them in Mesoamerica, constructed their temples and other major buildings without the wheel, metal tools, or draft animals. Olmec farmers, probably working in the dry season as forced labor, hauled burdens such as the ten-ton monumental heads to the religious centers. They used rafts on waterways where possible and sleds and rolling poles on land where necessary. Historians of ecology see the absence of draft animals as the Olmec's greatest handicap, because these animals not only perform labor but also provide a ready source of high-protein food.

La Venta was a center for artisans, traders, and farmers who lived in a highly stratified society dominated by a class of nobles and absolute rulers. Unlike the Chavin, Olmec artisans did little metalworking, but rather concentrated their efforts on sculpting, whether huge stone heads or tiny jadeite jewelry. Overall, the artistic and spiritual power of the Olmec artisans was immense. Most of the numerous Mesoamerican cultures that followed the Olmec—including the Maya and the Aztec— show distinct Olmec influence. Recent studies now indicate that both writing and the famous Mesoamerican calendar (see the discussion of the Maya in Chapter 7), first known to be employed at Monte Alban in the highlands about 450 B.C.E., may have originated in Olmec civilization.

La Venta was above all a religious complex. What precisely the Olmec asked of their gods is not clear, because they had plenty of rain, an unfailing agriculture, and no strong enemies. Perhaps, as in many religions, they sought the continuation of the natural order, praying that their state would not fall to social anarchy or natural catastrophes.

The Olmec and later Mesoamericans depicted most of their gods as part human and part animal, a practice also common in ancient Egyptian and Indian religions. At different times, the eagle, the serpent, the alligator, and the jaguar rose to special distinction. The jaguar, a fearsome predator in nature, was even more terrible and powerful when deified; jadeite was the medium chosen to represent the jaguar god.

Like all humans, the Olmec had death rituals. They evidently believed in an underworld. The seated figures they commonly carved may have been their rulers sitting in the passageway to that underworld. The rulers, in animal-shaman form, could perhaps pass in and out of the underworld as mediators and determine who went there and under what conditions.

The Olmec developed the "divine" or "sacred" ball game that later spread into almost every Mesoamerican culture, although the Olmec did not construct the walled enclosures for it that became typical later. The ball game was an athletic contest in which the object was to put a heavy rubber ball through a tight-fitting ring set vertically in a wall at both ends of the court. The players could not use their hands, but powered the ball by bouncing it off heavy plates on their forearms, chests, and hips. There may have been professional teams that played for money and glory; apparently there was considerable betting.

A Were-Jaguar. The jaguar, depicted here on a ceremonial axe carved before 600 B.C.E., was an important motif in Olmec-influenced areas of Mesoamerica. The ferocious eyes and extended fangs show how the Olmec had created a fearsome supernatural world. Courtesy of Library Services, American Museum of Natural History, neg. 1298

In later Mesoamerican civilizations and probably in the later Olmec, the players in the sacred ball game often fought for the highest stakes—their lives. In these instances, the ball game served as a ritual for the perpetuation of the state. A captured ruler and his men, suitably weakened, were forced to play in a hopeless contest against the local ruler and his well-rested men. The captives eventually lost the game and were sacrificed to the gods.

Early Aegean Civilization

At a depth of twenty-five feet from the surface of the [Mycenaean] Acropolis, [Heinrich] Schliemann cried out, "Sophia! Sophia!"

When she joined him . . . she exclaimed, "My God!"

He had found three bodies "smothered"—Schliemann's word—in gold. Each body was draped with five gold diadems; two of the bodies were each adorned with gold laurel leaves. The sepulcher, cut out of rock, also contained "many curious objects," including cow-shaped idols, fragments of colored glass, small knives of obsidian, the fragments of a gold-plated silver vase, a bronze knife. The bones and skulls had been preserved, but they had suffered so much from moisture that when he reached out and touched them, they dissolved as if in a dream. . . .

*Returning to the surface in a frenzy, he ordered the work gangs to dig up the whole area beneath the other grave markers. Schliemann behaved like a man possessed.**

*Arnold C. Brackman, *The Dream of Troy* (New York: Mason & Lipscomb, 1974), pp. 180–181.

This passage captures the thrill of discovery that makes archaeology so appealing. Of course, when Heinrich Schliemann was excavating at Mycenae in 1876, the science was in its infancy and many mistakes were made; as one scholar put it, Schliemann excavated as if he were digging for potatoes, and the atmosphere was more that of a treasure hunt than of a scientific investigation. Today, as a mature field of study, archaeology involves careful examination of sites and painstaking methods of handling, labeling, and recording materials brought to light. Nevertheless, the romantic allure of revealing the lives of men and women who lived thousands of years ago still remains. The romance of archaeology provided much of the inspiration for Schliemann, who later claimed to be seeking to verify the Homeric poems, with their glorious and bloodthirsty kings and warriors, magnificent palaces, and heroic quests and warfare. However rudimentary his efforts at Troy and "golden Mycenae," Schliemann proved that Homer's world of heroes was not merely a figment of poetic imagination. This section explores that world by focusing on the earliest civilizations of the Aegean region.

The Flowering of Minoan Civilization

The Aegean world encompassed the southern end of the Balkan Peninsula (see Map 1.4), the west coast of Asia Minor, the islands that dot the Aegean and Ionian Seas, and the large islands of Crete and Cyprus. This region (in area about the size of Alabama) was not as blessed as Mesopotamia or Egypt with fertile soil or other natural resources. Its physical geography consisted of many mountains, small and scattered coastal plains and river valleys, and the ever-present sea.

The mountainous topography contributed to both the political fragmentation of the Aegean world and the

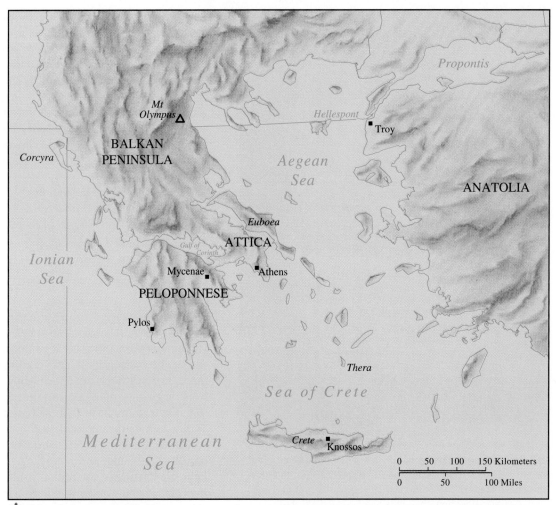

✻ MAP 1.4. Greece and the Aegean Basin. Shown in this map are the mainland regions and islands that were the home of Aegean civilization. Some of the more important Bronze Age sites are indicated.

scarcity of arable land; less than 20 percent of the land was fit for cultivation, and even in antiquity the region suffered from deforestation and generally poor soil management. The area was hot and arid in summer but cool and moderately watered by rainfall in winter. Though wheat and barley were grown on virtually every acre of suitable land, the soil and weather of the region were actually better suited to the grapevine and the olive tree. There was sufficient grazing land for sheep and goats, but usually not for cattle and horses. The Aegean region was and is a beautiful country, a land of stunning contrasts, of crystalline skies and "wine-dark" seas, of brilliant, sun-drenched vistas of steep river valleys and mountain peaks.

Human beings had lived in the Aegean area in the Neolithic era (7000–3000 B.C.E.) and, in a few places, even earlier. Around 3000, a change occurred, marked by new types of pottery and the introduction of metallurgy (specifically in bronze, hence the term *Bronze Age*). This

transition from the Stone Age to the Bronze Age likely reflects the arrival of a new people. In the next 1,500 years, the most rapid cultural advances in the region took place on the large island of Crete (approximately 150 miles long by 35 miles wide), on the southern edge of the Aegean Sea, where the Minoan civilization flourished.

The culture of the Minoans was unknown until modern times when Sir Arthur Evans excavated Knossos (see Map 1.4). Beginning in 1899, he uncovered a vast, multistory palace complex and eventually found that the astonishingly rich and distinctive Minoan civilization had pervaded the whole island. The palace walls and floors were brightly decorated with fresco paintings showing plants and animals, aquatic and marine life. People were pictured in a wide variety of activities, including ritual sports such as the famous bull-jumping events. The style of this art was vivid and distinctively impressionistic.

Less is known about the people who built and adorned the palaces. The architectural grandeur implies

LIVES AND TIMES ACROSS CULTURES

Risking Death to Gain the Favor of the Gods

Many early cultures around the world sought to pay homage to supernatural powers by means of perilous athletic contests. Among the Olmec, for example, such competitions centered on ball games in which the losing participants often forfeited their lives. Spectators at these events no doubt also felt the presence of supernatural forces. The general intent was probably to placate the gods and ensure their good will toward the community.

Similarly, the Minoan people of Bronze Age Crete appear to have enjoyed life-threatening feats of acrobatic skill. A number of famous wall paintings and sculptures depict young athletes performing death-defying vaults over charging bulls. As archaeological evidence from Crete features bulls in contexts of religious sacrifice, it seems likely that the bull-jumping events, like the Mesoamerican athletic competitions, were designed to honor or influence the gods. So, too, in classical Greece and Rome, athletic games were held at Olympia, Delphi, and hundreds of other sites to honor gods such as Zeus and Apollo, although these games were generally not life endangering.

The Roman gladiatorial contests are perhaps the best-known examples of the association of physical competition with the awe-inspiring force of death. Though they became thoroughly secularized, the bloody Roman games likely originated with an earlier, Etruscan practice of a specialized type of human sacrifice, in which pairs of warriors fought to the death as part of the funeral rites in honor of a deceased nobleman.

a strongly centralized administration, as does the evidence of two nonalphabetic forms of writing, called Linear A (used to transcribe the language of Crete) and Linear B (used to transcribe Greek). Inscribed clay tablets record inventories of raw materials, manufactured goods, agricultural production, and stored goods. These tablets suggest that Crete was heavily populated and that the various palace centers controlled surrounding farmsteads, pastures, and villages.

A king called "Minos," perhaps an honorific title, controlled the palace complex and was assisted by a corps of specially trained bureaucrats and scribes who supervised and recorded the activities of farmers, artisans, and slaves. Priests may have been in charge of religious observances, in which the bull figured prominently; whether the animal was a sacrificial offering or a god image is unclear, but it may have provided the kernel of the myth of the Minotaur, a monster usually depicted as a man with the head of a

Knossos. An artist's rendering of the great Minoan palace complex discovered by Sir Arthur Evans at Knossos on Crete. The palace's mazelike complexity may have inspired the myth of the labyrinth, in which the Greek hero Theseus slew the Minotaur.

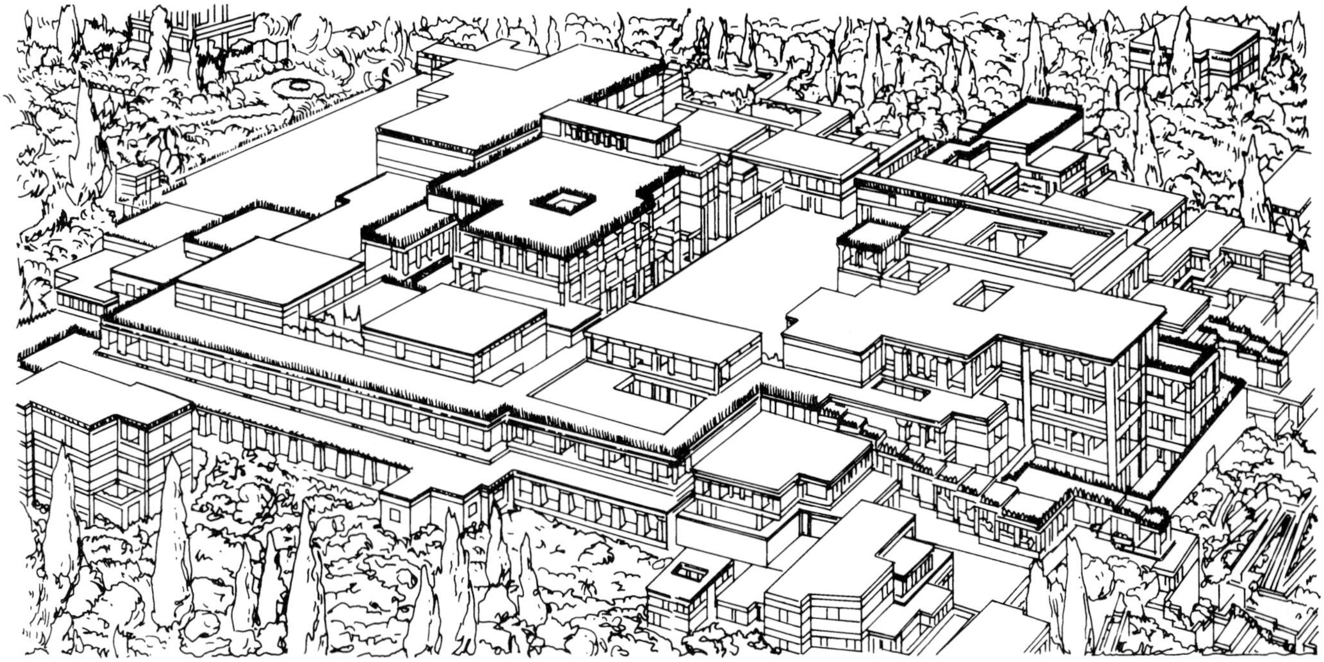

bull, who was slain by the Athenian hero Theseus. Snake-handling mother goddesses, sacred trees, and caves also figured in Minoan religion. As in Egypt and Mesopotamia, fertility, death, and regeneration were major concerns.

The people of Crete had learned from Egypt how to construct ships that could sail the Mediterranean. Though we have stories of Cretan naval vessels dominating neighboring islands and even mainland sites, the influence of the Minoans appears to have been commercial and cultural rather than imperialistic. Unlike the Mycenaeans later, they neither protected their palaces by fortifications nor included military scenes and weapons in their art.

The Minoan civilization was dealt crippling blows by a devastating earthquake around 1700 B.C.E. and a huge volcanic eruption on the neighboring island of Thera around 1625. The Minoans seem not to have recovered fully from these disasters when their palaces were again destroyed sometime after 1380, this time by Indo-European invaders, the Mycenaeans. Minoan traditions, however, continued to live in the culture of the conquerors.

The Coming of the Indo-Europeans

Beginning in the third millennium B.C.E. and continuing into the first millennium C.E., a new linguistic class of people, the Indo-Europeans, radiated out from the steppe region north of the Black Sea into Greece, Anatolia (Asia Minor), Iran, and India. Written records for the earliest periods of Indo-European migration are very scarce and appear only after the migrating peoples settled in their new homes. The languages recorded are distinct (including Greek, Hittite, Persian, and Sanskrit) and reflect a mingling of immigrant and indigenous populations. There are no written specimens whatever of the parent Indo-European language, which antedated the advent of writing. Although there is controversy regarding particular word roots, it is possible to re-create some of the basic vocabulary by arguing backward from later, "descendant" languages. Thus many dictionaries list reconstructed Indo-European roots (usually preceded by an asterisk [*]) for words in modern languages. For example, **bhrater* lies behind Sanskrit *bhratar,* Greek *phrater,* Latin *frater,* German *Bruder,* French *frère,* Italian *fratello,* and English *brother, friar,* and *fraternal.*

Since so many modern tongues, including English and most other languages of Europe as well as those of Iran and, to a lesser extent, India, are Indo-European (see the illustration), linguists and historians have given special attention to the history of its speakers. By re-creating the vocabulary of this protolanguage, specialists may reconstruct details of the lives of its speakers and their community. Deductions from vocabulary provide a different perspective on a society than do assessments based on archaeology. The lack of a general word for sea argues that the original Indo-Europeans were an inland people,

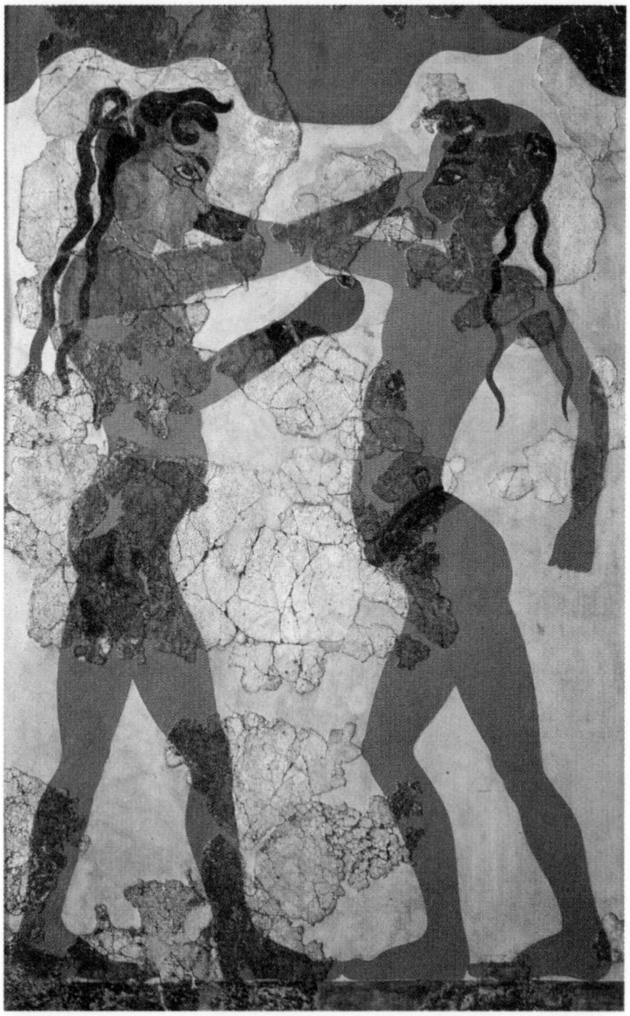

Boxing Children. This charming fresco painting comes from the island of Thera and dates to the time of the volcanic eruption around 1625 B.C.E. The fresco is in the typical, naturalistic style of the Minoan civilization of Crete and surrounding islands. AKG London/John Hios

unfamiliar with seafaring. Indo-Europeans had words for time and the seasons that reflect life in an agricultural society. Words for plowing, sowing, plucking, and grinding, as well as for furrow, wheat, and rye, point to the cultivation of grains. The vocabulary also attests to the domestication of animals (cows, sheep, pigs, horses) and, in the technical sphere, to weaving, pottery manufacture, metalworking (copper and possibly bronze), and the use of carts with solid (not spoked) wheels. That the Indo-Europeans had a word for apple trees, but not for citrus fruits, indicates a northern rather than a Mediterranean locale. Words for fish were rare and there were none for camel, lion, or tiger.

As regards socioeconomic matters, the Indo-Europeans had many terms for familial relations within a strongly patriarchal (father-ruled) society and for the household or tribal groups of households as basic units. There were

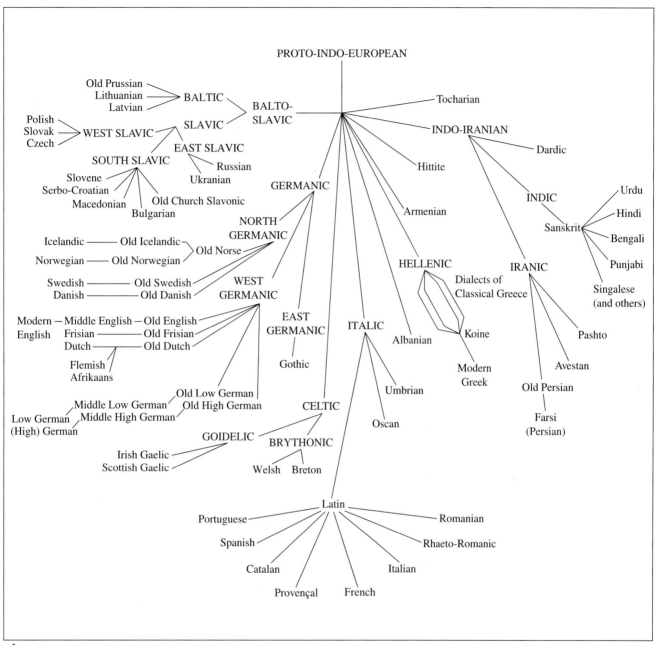

❄ The Indo-European Family of Languages. This chart shows the principal languages of the family in an arrangement indicating genetic relationships and geographic distribution.

also words for fortified high places. Kingship or warlordship and priesthood appear to have been complementary aspects of political sovereignty. The principles of gift exchange and mutual obligation binding hosts and guests, familiar from later Greek customs, existed in Indo-European society. The invaders infused various indigenous Neolithic peoples with an active, mobile, patriarchal, and aggressive culture. When they conquered and joined or merged with civilized societies, they often adopted or assimilated many elements of those cultures.

The impact of an early Indo-European culture may be gauged from the accomplishments of the Hittites in the second millennium. Although Mesopotamia and Egypt

enjoyed for two millennia the best natural resources and strongest political organizations in West Asia, archaeologists have shown that another very significant power was located in Asia Minor. Sometime before 2000 B.C.E., the Hittites came to this region as part of the general movement of Indo-European peoples. Between 1600 and 1200, the Hittites played a major role in the power politics of West Asia. This was in part due to a technology they monopolized for a time: ironworking. The use of iron weapons, together with another innovation, the chariot, gave the Hittites a decided advantage in warfare. They also used iron to manufacture improved farming implements. The Hittites successfully invaded Babylonia and fought a great battle against New Kingdom Egypt at Kadesh in Syria. The Egyptian pharaoh, Ramses II, later decorated many temple walls with carved depictions of his exploits at this battle, though in fact the battle was a draw. The Hittites themselves subsequently fell to a new wave of Indo-European invaders after 1200.

In western Asia Minor, the chief successor state of the Hittites was the kingdom of Lydia, which rose to prominence beginning in the eighth century. The Lydians enjoyed the economic advantages of excellent farmland and rich natural resources. The Greek cities that had sprung up in western Asia Minor became tribute-paying subject states of Lydia. In Greek accounts of his life, the last and most famous of Lydian kings, Croesus, became an archetype of the fabulously wealthy eastern potentate. It is thus fitting that the Lydians' principal gift to posterity should have been the invention of coined money.

The Rise and Fall of Mycenaean Warrior-Kings

The Greeks, another Indo-European people active at the same time as the Hittites, played a more influential role in world history. Around 2000 B.C.E., the first Greek speakers arrived on the tip of the Balkan Peninsula and founded powerful states centering on citadels at Athens, Pylos, Mycenae (from which the culture gets its name), and other sites. These were the heroes that the Greek poets spoke of, people called Achaeans in Homer's epic poems. The uncovering of Troy and Mycenae by Heinrich Schliemann in the 1870s sent shock waves through the scholarly world.

Each Mycenaean site was a heavily fortified center from which a king governed the surrounding territory. Administrative organization was quite intricate and, as on Crete, was overseen by a corps of bureaucrats and scribes who classified, counted, and recorded millions of bits of information in Linear B.

Bronze Age Bureaucrats

Astonishing and significant is the omniscience, the insatiable thirst for intimate detail [of Mycenaean officials]. Sheep may be counted up to a glittering total of twenty-five thousand: but there is still a purpose to be served by recording the fact that one animal was contributed by Komawens and another by Etewano. Restless officialdom notes the presence in Pesero's house of one woman and two children; the employment of two nurses, one girl, and one boy, in a Cretan village; the fattening of an insignificant number of hogs . . . ; the existence somewhere of a single pair of brass-bound chariot wheels labelled "useless"—these things and hundreds more of the same type were duly recorded in the palaces of Pylos and Knossos.*

The records described in this passage come from thousands of clay tablets inscribed with the nonalphabetic script called Linear B. For a half century after the tablets were first discovered by archaeologists in 1900, it was thought that their language was not Greek. Then, in 1952, a young British architect named Michael Ventris deciphered Linear B and showed it to be a primitive form of Greek. This amazing discovery forced researchers to rewrite the history of Greek civilization.

*Denys L. Page, *History and the Homeric Iliad* (Berkeley: University of California Press, 1959), p. 181.

This civilization was wealthy and, at least in its art, cosmopolitan. The Mycenaeans imported amber from the Baltic Sea coast, ivory from Syria, alabaster from Crete, lapis lazuli from Mesopotamia, and even ostrich eggs from Nubia in Africa. Excavations at Mycenae revealed royal graves exceedingly rich in grave goods, including

❧ Mycenaean Gold Death Mask. This is the most impressive and best known of a number of gold masks found in the shaft graves in the citadel of Mycenae. Heinrich Schliemann erred by three centuries when he identified the portrait as that of Agamemnon. The mask was actually made around 1525 B.C.E. by the repoussé process, in which a thin plate of metal is hammered into a mold from the back.
René Burri/Magnum

The Creation of Homer's Epic Poems

The Homeric poems belong to the period of transition from an oral to a literary technique.... Homer ... was an oral poet living in an age of writing. Oral songs can be collected either by phonograph apparatus, which is obviously out of the question here; or by dictation to a scribe; or by a literate oral poet who has been asked to write down his song for someone else who, for some reason, wants it in writing. The last of these possibilities is highly unlikely, because the oral poet, if he is at all literate, can have only a smattering of writing, if he is to remain an oral poet. Had he enough facility in writing to record 27,000 lines of text [of the *Iliad* and the *Odyssey*], his style could not be that of an oral technique, which Homer's demonstrably is. In my own mind there remains no doubt that Homer dictated the *Iliad* to someone else who wrote it down, because the Homeric poems have all the earmarks of dictated texts of oral epic songs.*

A lbert Lord reached these conclusions about the origins of our texts of the Homeric poems on the basis of knowledge gained while he did field research with his teacher and mentor, Milman Parry. This research was conducted among illiterate singer-poets in Yugoslavia during the 1930s. Lord's theory of the oral dictated text has won wide acceptance among students of Homer and other early oral traditions of epic poetry.

*Albert B. Lord, "Homer's Originality: Oral Dictated Texts," *Transactions of the American Philological Association* 84 (1953): 131.

❊ The Lion Gate at Mycenae. Shown here is the massive structure of the main entrance to the citadel at Mycenae. The lions stand symmetrically in a heraldic pose on either side of a central, Minoan-style column resting on two altars. This earliest piece of monumental sculpture in Europe (c. 1250 B.C.E.) symbolizes the religious and political power of the Mycenaean king.
Walter S. Clark/Photo Researchers, Inc.

crowns, sword scabbards, pommels of ivory and gold, bronze daggers inlaid with scenes of lion hunts, vases of gold, silver, bronze, and alabaster, numerous articles of jewelry, arrowheads, boars' tusks like those of a helmet in Homer's *Iliad,* axes, tridents, and many other valuables. The workmanship is very fine and points to influence from Asia Minor, Egypt, and especially Crete. Schliemann thought one of the gold masks he found was the death mask of Homer's King Agamemnon, and indeed the stern and angular features do give an impression of majesty and a will to power.

How did Mycenaean royalty acquire such wealth and power? A far-flung network of trade contacts and a firm agricultural base are part of the answer, but warfare played an important role too. The weapons buried with the warrior-kings show this, and so do the massive walls built later to protect Mycenaean fortresses. The walls at Mycenae were adorned by the Lion Gate, the first large-scale sculpture in Europe. Indeed, the Mycenaeans engaged in one of the most famous military conflicts in ancient history. Around 1200 B.C.E. they attacked and destroyed Troy, located at the northwest corner of Asia Minor near the Dardanelles. The Trojan War was celebrated in heroic song orally transmitted by epic poets down to the eighth century, when the *Iliad* and the *Odyssey* of Homer were recorded in a written form made possible by the adaptation of the Phoenician alphabet to the transcription of the Greek language (see Chapter 3).

Homer's great poems are the earliest landmarks of European literature. Greek myth told of the abduction of Helen, the most beautiful woman on earth, from her husband Menelaus by the Trojan prince Paris. In the legend the Greeks mounted an expedition to Troy to recover Helen and became bogged down in a war that lasted ten years. In fact, the real goal of the mission was the wealth of Troy, which was a great center of textile manufacturing and likely also extracted toll payments from ships passing through the nearby Dardanelles Strait. Whatever the actual goal and the true scale of the Trojan War of legend, it was for the Greeks the earliest major event in their history.

Around 1200 B.C.E., most Mycenaean centers were devastated by roving warriors known as the "Sea Peoples" who raided the eastern Mediterranean region. There followed a large-scale influx from the north of Dorians, a culturally backward Greek subgroup. Internal strife may also have hastened the Mycenaean world's demise. By 1050 a whole civilization had disappeared, with its royal ruling elite, administrative apparatus, writing system, monumental art and architecture, transport and trade networks, armed forces, fortifications and citadels, and elaborate burial practices. In the period that followed, the Greek dark age, which lasted until 800 B.C.E., the population of Greater Greece fell by about 80 percent. Many people had died in the times of trouble just before and during the Dorian invasion; others fled to new settlements on the western coast of Asia Minor. Although Lefkandi on the island of Euboea and a very few other sites continued to trade with cities in the eastern Mediterranean, commercial contacts with lands outside the Aegean basin virtually ceased, and in most cases loosely organized tribal groups replaced the former strongly centralized governments.

The Dorians completed the ethnic picture of the Greek people and created a great divide in Greek history. Greece in the dark age underwent a transition to another, quite distinct civilization, which will be discussed in Chapter 3.

Ancient Persian Civilization

When I entered Babylon as a friend and . . . established the seat of the government in the palace of the ruler under jubilation and rejoicing, Marduk, the great lord, induced the magnanimous inhabitants of Babylon to love me, and I was daily endeavoring to worship him. My numerous troops walked around in Babylon in peace; I did not allow anyone to terrorize any place of the country of Sumer and Akkad. . . . As to the inhabitants . . . , I abolished the yoke which was against their standing. I brought relief to their dilapidated housing, putting an end to their main complaints. Marduk, the great lord, was well pleased with my deeds and sent friendly blessings to myself, Cyrus, the king who worships him, to Cambyses, my son . . . as well as to all my troops, and we all praised his godhead joyously, standing before him in peace.

All the kings of the entire world from the Upper to the Lower Sea, those who are seated in throne rooms . . . , as well as all the kings of the West lands living in tents, brought their tributes and kissed my feet in Babylon.*

*James B. Pritchard, ed., The Ancient Near East: An Anthology of Texts and Pictures (Princeton: Princeton University Press, 1958), pp. 207–208.

Leaders of new regimes often sing their own praises while damning their predecessors. In this passage, Cyrus the Great, founder of the mighty Persian Empire, describes the allegedly happy acceptance of his rule by the conquered people and gods of Babylon. Although civil discord during the reign of the last Chaldean king, Nabonidus, had in fact made life miserable for many, we may doubt that Cyrus's contemporaries fully realized the significance of the changes the "king of kings" had made in the political map of ancient West Asia.

The Rise of the Persian Empire

The Persians lived in a number of tribes dispersed throughout southwestern Iran. They were ethnically related to their overlords, the Medes, a warrior people who temporarily controlled Upper Mesopotamia, Syria, and Iran. During the reign of Cyrus (559–530 B.C.E.), the Indo-European–speaking Persians achieved a spectacularly swift rise to power that radically changed the political map of West Asia. In 550 they not only freed themselves from Median authority but conquered their former masters and annexed their territory. The Lydian king, Croesus, now made the mistake of attacking the Persians; in 547 he lost both his life and his kingdom. The realm of the Chaldeans, which was suffering from political disorder internally, fell to Persian arms in 539.

Cyrus next turned his attention to the northeastern quadrant of his far-flung dominions. In 530 B.C.E. he died in Bactria (modern Turkestan) defending the Persian Empire's frontier on the Jaxartes River against nomadic invaders. Cyrus's son and successor, Cambyses (reigned 530–522 B.C.E.), added Egypt to the empire. Faced with a major revolt within his empire and perhaps afflicted with mental illness, Cambyses committed suicide in 522. After a period of bloody civil strife, a rather distant relative of the royal Achaemenid family, Darius I (reigned 522–486 B.C.E.), became king.

During his long reign, Darius proved as energetic and effective as his forerunners. He eventually enlarged the empire to the Indus River in the east, the Caucasus Mountains in the north, and Upper Egypt in the south, while in the west he seized a foothold in Europe.

Darius's most significant contribution was his creation of a model for the organization and administration of large empires composed of ethnically, religiously, and linguistically diverse groups. Royal inscriptions, for example, were written in three official languages: Persian, Elamitic, and Babylonian. In the ancient world, only the Roman Empire would surpass the Persian in the degree of unity achieved despite cultural differences among subject peoples. Imperial China attained a similar degree of administrative unity, but its population was much more culturally and ethnically homogeneous. The empire Darius and his predecessors had fashioned embraced vari-

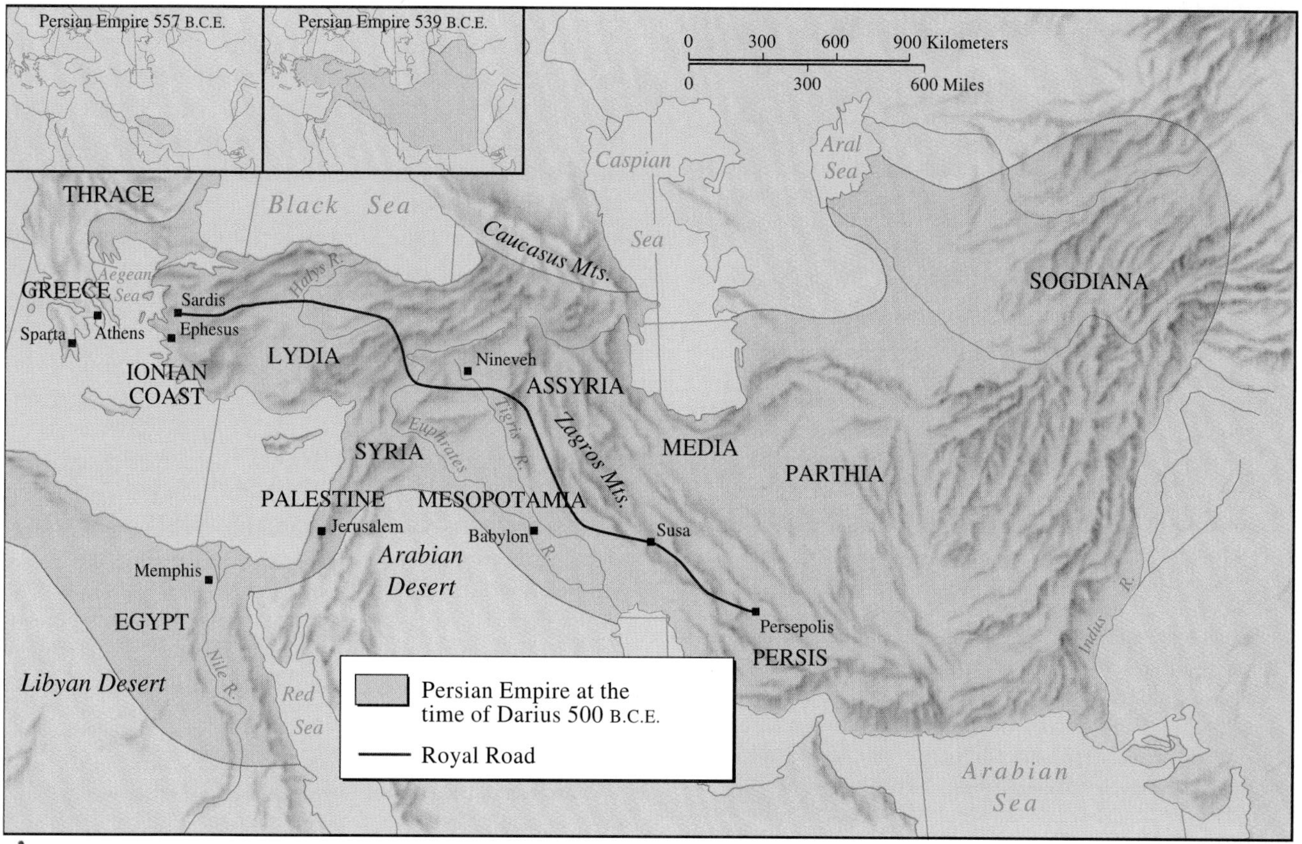

MAP 1.5. Persian Empire. Shown here is the Persian Empire at its greatest extent. It was by far the largest of the ancient West Asian empires.

ous tributary kingdoms and twenty provinces. Although strategically stationed garrisons ensured military control, the Persians allowed the local governments considerable autonomy and respected their subjects' religious preferences. The relative leniency of Persian rule as compared with the earlier Assyrian hegemony enabled Darius to recruit willing mercenary forces both for maintaining internal security and for defending the borders.

Military and civil officials were drawn primarily from the elite of the Iranian nobility. Darius appointed provincial governors called satraps, who enjoyed considerable individual autonomy, to collect tribute, taxes, soldiers, and military provisions for delivery to the king, whose personal supervisors, called "Eyes and Ears," made regular rounds of the provinces. The revenue generated by this method not only paid administrative expenses but also ensured brimming royal treasuries. Although internal uprisings did occur, especially at times of transition in leadership, the administrative apparatus Darius set in place endured until Alexander's conquest in 330 B.C.E.

To ease the task of governing their huge empire, the Persian monarchs created the most elaborate public works system yet seen in West Asia. Communication (including a postal system) and transport were facilitated by an extensive network of good roads, including the Royal Road from Ephesus on the Aegean to Susa, some 1,600 miles away in Iran. These were traveled by armies, ambassadors, distinguished visitors, prisoners of war, caravans, and merchants. Only Han China and the Roman Empire equaled or surpassed the Persian Empire in their elaborate public works systems. Darius also provided for a uniform standard of weights and measures and, borrowing an idea from Lydia, introduced gold and silver coinage.

Master of all this was the supreme autocrat, Darius, the earthly viceroy of Ahura Mazda, the Zoroastrian god of light. To quote one inscription, he was "the great king, king of Kings, king of the countries possessing many kinds of people, king of this great earth far and wide." The earlier Mycenaean kings in the Greek world had been mere local warlords by comparison; the powers of the Persian kings were to be rivaled by a Greek only briefly in the reign of Alexander the Great, who saw himself as their supplanter and successor. Roman emperors provide the closest analogy to the Persian model of absolute monarchy, although the earlier (and wiser) emperors tried to avoid the appearance of such unlimited monopoly of power.

Persian Culture and Religion

Persia's artistic and intellectual accomplishments did not match its military and governmental performance. Little literature was produced, except for the Avesta, the col-

The Great King Darius Crushes a Rebellion

I am Darius, the great king, the king of kings, the king of Persia, the king of the provinces, the son of Hystaspes, the grandson of Arsames, the Achaemenian. . . .

Says Darius the king—There are eight of my race who have been kings before me; I am the ninth; nine of us have been kings in succession . . . .

Says Darius the king—Then I went to Babylon against that Nidintabelus, who was called Nabochodrossor. The people of Nidintabelus held the Tigris; there they were posted, and they had boats. There I approached with a detachment in rafts. I brought the enemy into difficulty. I carried the enemy's position. Ahura Mazda brought help to me. By the grace of Ahura Mazda I crossed the Tigris. There I slew many of the troops of Nidintabelus. On the 26th day of the month Atriyata, then it was we so fought.

Says Darius the king—Then I went to Babylon. When I arrived near Babylon, at the city named Zazana, on the Euphrates, there that Nidintabelus, who was called Nabochodrossor, came with his forces against me, to do battle. Then we fought a battle. Ahura Mazda brought help to me. By the grace of Ahura Mazda I slew many of the troops of that Nidintabelus—the enemy was driven into the water—the water destroyed them. On the 2nd day of the month Anamaka, then it was we so fought.

Says Darius the king—Then Nidintabelus with the horsemen that were faithful to him fled to Babylon. Then I went to Babylon. By the grace of Ahura Mazda I both took Babylon, and seized that Nidintabelus. Then I slew that Nidintabelus at Babylon.

Says Darius the king—While I was at Babylon, these are the countries which revolted against me: Persia, Susiana, Media, Assyria, Armenia, Parthia, Margiana, Sattagydia, Sacia. . . .

Says Darius the king—[After his lieutenants had quelled many of the revolts] then I went out from Babylon. I proceeded to Media. When I reached . . . a city . . . named Kudrusia, there that Phraortes, who was called king of Media, came with an army against me, to do battle. Then we fought a battle. Ahura Mazda brought help to me; by the grace of Ahura Mazda, I entirely defeated the army of Phraortes. On the 26th day of the month Adukanish, then it was we thus fought the battle.*

This passage is from an inscription carved around 520 B.C.E. on the face of a cliff near the site of one of Darius's famous battles. The Persian king records a successful mission to quell a rebellion mounted against him after the death of his predecessor, Cambyses.

*Henry Rawlinson, trans., "The Behistun Inscription of Darius" [1847], in *The Greek Historians,* vol. 2, ed. Francis R. B. Godolphin (New York: Random House, 1942), pp. 623–628.

lected sacred scriptures of Zoroastrianism. Science and mathematics did not advance beyond the substantial inheritance from Babylonia and Egypt. In art and architecture, Assyria, Babylonia, Greece, and Egypt often provided the models and sometimes the expertise: Greek stonecutters and sculptors, for example, worked on the mammoth palace complexes at Susa and Persepolis. In at least one respect, the Persian structures were novel, for they were erected to celebrate not the gods but an earthly ruler of a mighty empire, the all-powerful "king of kings."

The Persians did show great originality in religion. The traditional Iranian religion was a typical Indo-European polytheism, whose chief officials were magi (priest-astrologers). In the early sixth century, however, a reformer named Zoroaster (Zarathustra in Persian) removed the magical elements from the religion. According to the new faith, Zoroastrianism, the world was ruled not by a horde of supernatural beings but by one only. Representing goodness, light, and truth, Ahura Mazda was the supreme being, but he was opposed by another supernatural power, Ahriman, who represented darkness and evil. The two were locked in a universal struggle,

Archers of the Persian Royal Guard. This relief sculpture, done in colored brick, depicts two members of the imperial guard. It adorned the palace of King Darius I at Susa.
Giraudon/Art Resource

With a history of some three thousand years, Zoroastrianism is one of the most ancient living religions. It is the most important and best-known religion of ancient, or pre-Islamic, Iran. . . . It was . . . the religion of Iran under the rule of the Iranian-speaking Aryan populations, members of the Aryan or Indo-Iranian group of the more extended Indo-European family. Another name for Zoroastrianian, Mazdaism, is derived from the name of the religion's supreme god, Mazda ("wise"), or Ahura Mazda ("wise lord"). . . . The primary innovation of Zoroastrianism, which sets it apart from the religions of other Indo-European peoples, . . . is its emphasis on monotheism. . . . The concept of Ahura Mazda as the creator of heaven and earth, day and night, and light and darkness, . . . as well as the ethical context in which Zarathustra conceived his answer to the problem of evil, demonstrates that the prophet was an original thinker, a powerful religious figure who introduced radical changes to the spiritual and cultural world in which he was reared.*

In assessing the achievement of the Persians, it is important to avoid the bias of ancient Greek historians like Herodotus. In writing of political and military affairs, they often labeled the Persians "barbarians" and saw their civilization as culturally decadent and, because it was monarchical, politically despotic. The truth is that Persian religious beliefs at any rate were in crucial ways very much in advance of contemporary Greek polytheism.

*Gherardo Gnoli, "Zoroastrianism," in *Religions of Antiquity*, ed. R. M. Seltzer (New York: Macmillan, 1989), pp. 128, 131.

which Ahura Mazda was destined to win. On a future judgment day, all human beings, living and dead, would be consigned to heaven or hell. This notion of a last judgment later figured significantly in Christianity and Islam. Zoroastrianism was a strongly ethical religion; it taught that men and women possessed free will and were expected to avoid sin and abide by divine laws. Each person's choices mattered in the struggle. The king of kings himself was a devotee and example to his people. Later, Mithras, Ahura Mazda's lieutenant, played a prominent part in the religious ferment of the Roman Empire. Zoroastrianism, though modified by a resurgence of old Iranian ritual and magic and by contact with other religious traditions, survived the fall of the Persian Empire to Macedon and the subsequent period of Hellenistic overlordship. After the Arab conquest, it was handed on from generation to generation during the Mongol hegemony and the reign of Muslim rulers in Persia. Today there are small Zoroastrian communities in Iran and more influential ones among the Parsee of India (for example, in Bombay) and Pakistan.

In warfare, politics, religion, and material culture, the Persian Empire equaled or surpassed its West Asian predecessors. It brought lasting stability to a vast region of diverse peoples and cultures. In the ancient world, only the Roman Empire and Han China would match that achievement.

Summary and Comparisons

The story of civilization begins in West Asia, where Mesopotamia, a fertile land claimed from swamp and desert by dint of hard work, became the locus for the development of cities. Abundant cereal crops in the lower Tigris-Euphrates Valley had created a relatively dense, even overcrowded, agricultural population, a key precondition for the appearance of urbanization. Around 3500 B.C.E. the Sumerians, who lived in that region, began an urban mode of life. A sophisticated social structure, with elaborate diversification of labor, typified life in Sumerian cities. The world's first fully developed writing system made possible not only more efficient transaction of public and private business but also the recording of the creations of a rich literary tradition. The Babylonians added further refinements in the areas of mathematics, astronomy and the calendar, and law, with the famous code of Hammurabi. Assyrian achievement was in imperialism and military conquest. The final phase of the distinctively Mesopotamian civilization, known as Chaldean or Neo-Babylonian, was also one of military conquest, though not on the Assyrian scale. It was an era of revitalization under Nebuchadnezzar.

In Egypt, too, regular crop production, ensured by careful and laborious management of the annual Nile flood, supported a vibrant and long-lived civilization. In the Old Kingdom, the god-king pharaoh presided over a strongly centralized government that deployed massive labor forces to build utilitarian projects such as dikes and canals and religious structures like the Great Pyramids. As in Mesopotamia, an assemblage of priests and temple personnel supervised the rituals of an elaborate polytheism. After a period of disruptions and comparative weakness in government, the New Kingdom pharaohs built an Egyptian Empire that extended into West Asia. They immortalized the empire and the gods who had sanctioned it by an extensive building program at

Karnak, Abu Simbel, the capital city of Thebes, the Valley of the Kings, and other places in the Nile Valley. The New Kingdom also witnessed a brief flirtation with a form of monotheism during the reign of Akhenaton and Nefertiti.

In the Western Hemisphere, civilization appeared in the Mesoamerican rain forests and highlands and also in the coastal and Andean region centered in present-day Peru. These Amerindian cultures, like those of early West Asia and Egypt, were sustained by a thriving agriculture. Conversely, the Amerindian cultures were marked by cities built around religious complexes. There was extensive internal trade within the cultures, but apparently little or none between them. The Chavin culture in Peru, like that of the Mesopotamians, demonstrated advanced engineering skills in constructing an extensive irrigation system.

The systems of religious belief in these societies flourished and spread widely; typical of the Amerindians were painstakingly constructed and decorated temples and also arenas for playing the sacred ball game. The early Amerindian civilizations also featured impressive artwork, including the monumental sculpted heads of the Olmec and the advanced metalwork of the Chavin culture. In these matters the earliest civilizations of the Western Hemisphere were as advanced as those of West Asia, the Aegean, and Africa.

The Aegean region, Crete, and the lower Balkan Peninsula were the center of the Minoan-Mycenaean civilization, which flourished in the second millennium B.C.E. The fully developed Mycenaean culture resulted from the absorption of indigenous elements and borrowings from Minoan Crete by a Greek-speaking Indo-European people who moved into the Balkans around 2000 B.C.E. The Minoan-Mycenaean culture brought forth remarkable achievements in painting, sculpture, jewelry, and architecture. The Linear A and Linear B writing systems show that there was a degree of literacy in both Crete and Greece, though it was restricted to a class of scribes and clerks. A combination of disruptive forces, including foreign invasions, brought an end to the Mycenaean world.

The Persians, also an Indo-European people, reshaped West Asia beginning in the reign of Cyrus. They fashioned an imperial system more extensive and better organized than any up to the Roman Empire. An overarching central administration with the great king himself at its top supervised racially, linguistically, and religiously diverse populations through a carefully devised system of semiautonomous local governments. The public works infrastructure, especially the imperial road network, far surpassed those of earlier periods in West Asia. Culturally, Persian Zoroastrianism brought a new stage in religious beliefs about the nature of the divine; it superseded an older, more traditional Iranian polytheism and was destined to have a lasting influence.

The magnitude of the material and intellectual developments of the early civilizations described in this chapter is impossible to overestimate. Certainly, the differences stand out. Geographically, some cultures, like Egypt and Mesopotamia, developed in great river valleys, others on the edge of the sea or in steaming jungles. For some of these cultures, urbanization meant large cities that reorganized a prosperous agricultural society for commerce, as in Mesopotamia. For other societies, like Egypt and the Olmec, it meant having a religious center for the most effective communication with the powers of the next world. Some, such as Persia, were conquering civilizations that could sustain military operations in far away lands; some, like the Chavin, stayed home. Some civilizations, like Mesopotamia, Persia, and the Olmec, added to the sum of human knowledge in mathematics, astronomy, highway engineering, hydraulics, and the calendar; others specialized in body adornments. Though some of these early cultures remained completely illiterate, in others literacy could mean prayers for priests only, commercial and stockyard receipts, or even transcriptions of poetry.

If one were to seek a common denominator, perhaps the most pervasive underlying factor in the human experience was the striving for order. The impulse to exploit the order of nature had earlier led to agriculture. The need to impose order on the relationships of men and women to the environment and to one another now led to civilized communities. The attempt to detect order in the dispositions of the invisible powers also stimulated more complex intellectual speculation. Egyptians, Mesopotamians, Amerindians, and Indo-European peoples like the Hittites, Persians, and Greeks all attempted to grasp and somehow control the workings of their world and have influence on the other world. They did this by developing mathematics and astronomy, some by creating writing systems, and all by applying their religious insights. In all these arenas, later participants in the various civilizations of the world were heavily indebted to their ancient forebears. Chapter 2 will round out the picture of early civilizations by examining those of South and East Asia.

Selected Sources

Archaeology. This reasonably priced magazine (six issues annually) provides information on recent discoveries and interpretations of archaeological sites around the world. Excellent photographs.

Brosius, Maria. *Women in Ancient Persia (559–331 B.C.)*. 1996. An excellent, very current examination of a neglected subject.

*Burstein, Stanley, ed. and trans. *Ancient African Civilizations: Kush and Axum*. 1997. Based on Greek and Roman sources,

this collection describes the cultures and governments of two major African kingdoms.

*Castleden, Rodney. *Minoans: Life in Bronze Age Crete*. 1990. A very attractive presentation of the evidence about Minoan Crete.

*Chadwick, John. *The Mycenaean World*. 1976. A well-written general account with helpful illustrations.

*Crawford, Harriet. *Sumer and the Sumerians*. 1991. A good, concise treatment of the Sumerian people and their achievements.

*Ferry, David, trans. *Gilgamesh: A New Rendering in English Verse.* 1992. A recent, lively translation of the world's first heroic epic.

Ghirshman, Roman. *Persia: From the Origins to Alexander the Great.* Trans. S. Gilbert and J. Emmons. 1964. An excellent, highly readable survey.

*Gurney, O. R. *The Hittites.* Rev. ed. 1990. A good, concise work on the subject.

*Harris, James E., and Kent R. Weeks. *X-Raying the Pharaohs.* 1973. This description of a radiological examination of mummies in the Egyptian Museum in Cairo includes an astounding "Portfolio of Pictures."

Hawkes, Jacquetta. *King of the Two Lands.* 1966. A historical novel set in the time of Akhenaton and Nefertiti, by an eminent British archaeologist.

*Hobson, Christine. *The World of the Pharaohs: A Complete Guide to Ancient Egypt.* 1987; reprinted 1993. A clearly organized treatment with marvelous color illustrations.

*Knapp, A. Bernard. *The History and Culture of Ancient West Asia and Egypt.* 1988. A succinct, current survey.

Lamberg-Karlovsky, C. C., and Jeremy A. Sabloff, eds. *The Rise and Fall of Civilizations: Modern Archaeological Approaches to Ancient Cultures.* 1974. A valuable anthology of thirty-three selected readings: includes material on both Western and Eastern Hemisphere archaeology.

Lanning, Edward P. *Peru before the Incas.* 1967. Looks at the Chavin Cult and other pre-Inka civilizations.

Latacz, Joachim. *Homer: His Art and His World.* Trans. James P. Holoka. 1996. This recent study places the great Greek epic poet in his historical and literary contexts. Contains helpful discussions of the *Iliad* and the *Odyssey.*

*Mallory, J. P. *In Search of the Indo-Europeans: Language, Archaeology, and Myth.* 1989. A recent work with many illustrations; includes a judicious assessment of rival theories.

Markman, Roberta H., and Peter T. Markman. *The Flayed God: The Mythology of Mesoamerica.* 1992. A combination of original text and contemporary commentary that leads the reader into the mythology of the Mesoamerican cultures.

*Phillipson, David W. *African Archaeology.* 2nd ed. 1993. A revised version of the author's broad survey of the archaeology of Africa, beginning with the origins of humankind. Well illustrated.

*Pritchard, James B. *The Ancient Near East: An Anthology of Texts and Pictures.* 1958. A convenient, widely available collection containing interesting and important materials.

*Romer, John. *Ancient Lives: Daily Life in the Egypt of the Pharaohs.* 1984. A fascinating study of daily lives of the people—on all social strata—in a village near ancient Thebes.

Soustelle, Jacques. *The Olmecs: The Oldest Civilization in Mexico.* Trans. Helen R. Lane. 1985. The distinguished French anthropologist shows his affection for the Olmec in this work.

Stuart, George E. "New Light on the Olmec." *National Geographic* 184, no. 5 (1993): 88.

Wilber, Donald N. *Persepolis: The Archaeology of Parsa, Seat of the Persian Kings.* 1969. A well-written and well-illustrated presentation of the ancient Persian capital.

*Wood, Michael. *In Search of the Trojan War.* 1985. A well-illustrated and clearly written account of the archaeological adventures of the search for ancient Troy; a companion to the six-part BBC television series.

*Available in paperback.

Internet Links

La Cultura Chavín
http://nazcanet.com/cultura/culturas_preincas/chavin.html
This Spanish-language website offers a succinct account of Chavin culture: its origins, social structure, architecture, art, and technology.

Greek Art and Architecture: Mycenaean Civilization
http://harpy.uccs.edu/greek/mycenae.html
A collection of excellent photographs of the site and environs of Mycenae and of the major architectural remains.

History of Ancient Egypt
http://www.library.nwu.edu/class/history/B94/
This website, developed as part of a course on the history of ancient Egypt at Northwestern University, contains extensive text, visual aids (maps, photos, diagrams), bibliography, and internet links to other resources pertinent to both Egypt and Nubia.

Minoan Civilization
http://dilos.com/region/crete/evans.html
This site, drawing in part on the holdings of the Iraklion Museum on Crete, offers succinct text material and a superb Image Gallery relevant to most of the major sites of Minoan civilization.

Olmecs
http://udgftp.cencar.udg.mx/ingles/Precolombina/Olmecas/docs/olmin.html
A concise description of Olmec culture, especially strong on the themes and forms of Olmec art. Good illustrations.

Oriental Institute Virtual Museum
http://www-oi.uchicago.edu/OI/MUS/QTVR96/QTVR96.html
Maintained by the University of Chicago's Oriental Institute, this is an excellent source of information about the ancient Near East, based on the holdings of the Institute.

Sumerian Mythology FAQ [Frequently Asked Questions]
http://pubpages.unh.edu/~cbsiren/sumer-faq.html
This site contains helpful identifications of the major gods and goddesses, a discussion of Sumerian religion, and a good bibliography.

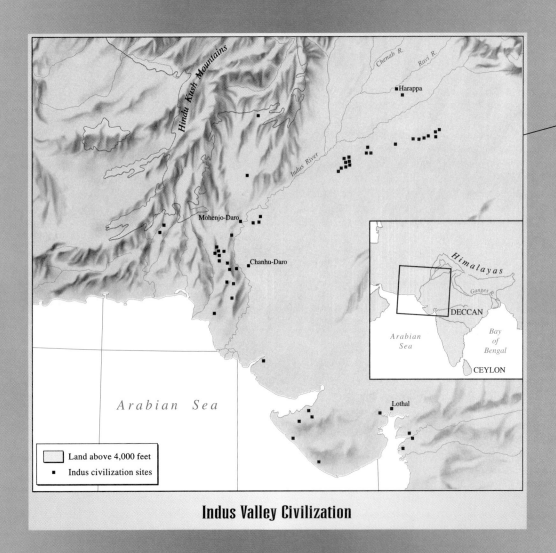

Indus Valley Civilization

The Early Civilizations of South and East Asia

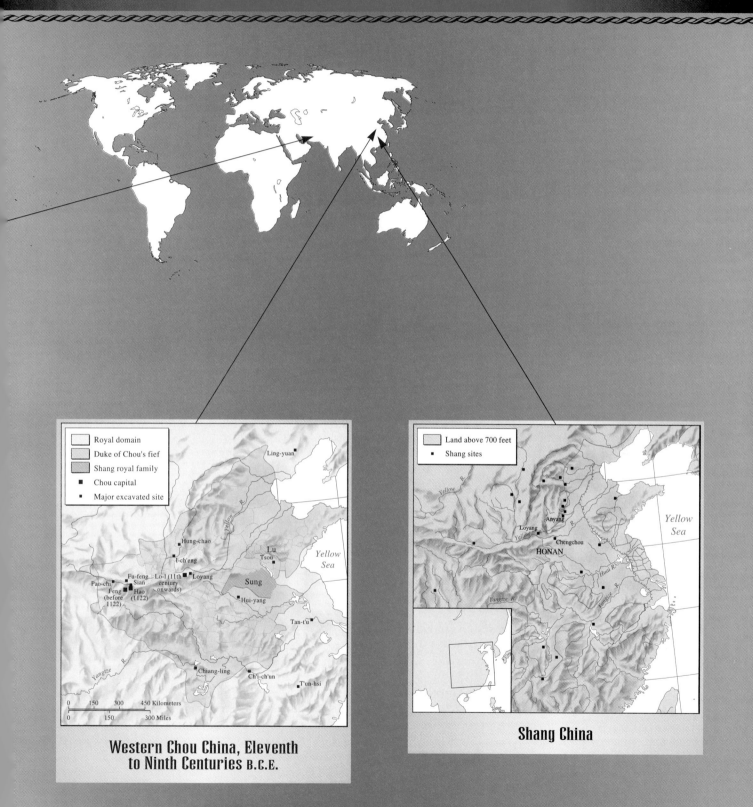

Royal domain
Duke of Chou's fief
Shang royal family
■ Chou capital
▪ Major excavated site

Ling-yuan

Hung-chao

I-ch'eng

Lu
Tsou

Yellow
Sea

Pao-chi   Fu-feng
Feng   Sian   Lo-I (11th
(before   Hao   century   Loyang
1122)   (1122)   onwards)

Sung

Hui-yang

Tan-t'u

Chiang-ling   Ch'i-ch'un   T'un-hsi

0   150   300   450 Kilometers
0   150   300 Miles

Western Chou China, Eleventh to Ninth Centuries B.C.E.

Land above 700 feet
■ Shang sites

Yellow R.

Anyang

Loyang   Yellow
Chengchou
HONAN

Yellow
Sea

Huai R.

Yangtze R.

Yangtze R.

Shang China

The Indian subcontinent is also called South Asia. It is bounded by the Hindu Kush in the northwest and the Himalayas in the northeast, the Arabian Sea in the southwest and the Bay of Bengal in the southeast. It includes modern India, Pakistan, Bangladesh, and Sri Lanka, and culturally it is heir to the civilizations of ancient India. East Asia lies east of the great mountain ranges (the Tien Shan and Altai) and the Gobi Desert, which bisect Asia. Comprising China, Japan, and Korea, East Asia finds its cultural antecedent in the ancient civilization of China. The influence of early South and East Asia on the development of later civilizations of Southeast Asia cannot be overestimated. Over half of the world's total population currently lives in these combined regions.

While the earliest civilizations in West Asia, India, and China exhibit certain similarities, significant differences are also apparent. As in Mesopotamia and Egypt, civilizations first emerged in India and China along major river valleys in temperate climatic zones. The rivers provided water for irrigation and transportation, and their periodic floods renewed the soil's fertility. Although the Indus River valley in northwestern India is most accessible by land from West Asia, and the Yellow River valley in North China is least accessible via land from India and West Asia, clear evidence of early contact among these regions has not been found. Archaeology has not yet been able to pinpoint definitively the source of South and East Asian civilizations. Indeed, pottery, tools, plants, and animals suggest independent, indigenous development in both regions.

The major difference between early India and China is that invaders of a different race and culture partly superseded the earliest Indian civilization, but China experienced no early invasions or migrations. Modern Chinese are the direct descendants of the early hominids of that region. The people who overthrew China's first historic dynasty belonged to the same culture and did not disrupt its development. Thus, unlike the civilizations of ancient Egypt and West Asia, and to a certain extent the civilization of India, Chinese civilization, once begun, has continued in the same tradition to the present. This chapter will investigate the beginnings of civilization on the Indian subcontinent and in China and will provide an overview of the first 2,000 formative years of both civilizations, to approximately the middle of the first millennium B.C.E.

The Indus River Civilization

Hitherto it has commonly been supposed that the pre-Aryan peoples of India were on an altogether lower plane of civilization than their Aryan [Caucasian, Indo-European] conquerors; that to the latter they were much what the Helots were to the Spartans . . . a race so servile and degraded, that they were commonly known as Dasas or slaves. . . . Never for a moment was it imagined that five thousand years ago,

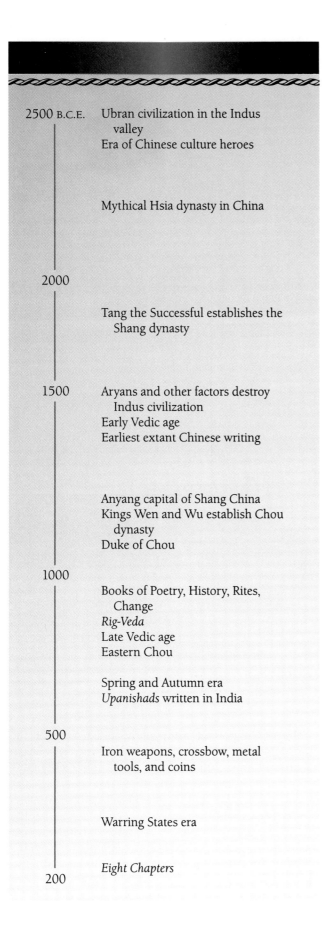

2500 B.C.E.	Ubran civilization in the Indus valley
	Era of Chinese culture heroes
	Mythical Hsia dynasty in China
2000	
	Tang the Successful establishes the Shang dynasty
1500	Aryans and other factors destroy Indus civilization
	Early Vedic age
	Earliest extant Chinese writing
	Anyang capital of Shang China
	Kings Wen and Wu establish Chou dynasty
	Duke of Chou
1000	
	Books of Poetry, History, Rites, Change
	Rig-Veda
	Late Vedic age
	Eastern Chou
	Spring and Autumn era
	Upanishads written in India
500	
	Iron weapons, crossbow, metal tools, and coins
	Warring States era
200	*Eight Chapters*

before ever the Aryans were heard of, the Punjab and Sind, if not other parts of India as well, were enjoying an advanced and singularly uniform civilization of their own, closely akin but in some respects even superior to that of contemporary Mesopotamia and Egypt. . . . They exhibit the Indus people of the fourth and third millennia B.C. in possession of a highly developed culture.*

*John Marshall, ed., *Mohenjo-Daro and the Indus Civilization* (Delhi: Indological Book House, 1973), pp. v, vii.

These were the words of Sir John Marshall, who headed the first systematic excavation of Indus sites between 1922 and 1927 and brought to light the earliest civilization on the Indian subcontinent, a discovery as exciting and important as Heinrich Schliemann's excavations at Troy in Asia Minor and Mycenae in Greece. In the pages that follow, we will examine the important characteristics and achievements of the Indus civilization and the reasons for its decline and fall.

The Land of India

The Indian subcontinent is a little less than half the size of the United States. It is bordered on the north by the Hindu Kush and the Himalayas, the latter the world's tallest mountain range; with their extensions to the east and west, these mountains separate India from the rest of Asia and make it a distinct subcontinent. Formidable though the mountains are, they did not prevent settlers, traders, and warriors from negotiating the passes to and from India from the northwest. The mountains are also the source of two great river systems. To the west is the Indus, which gave its name to India and empties into the Arabian Sea. To the east flows the Ganges, which joins the Brahmaputra to form the largest delta in the world, as the channels of the two mighty rivers empty into the Bay of Bengal. The Thar, or Desert of Rajastan, divides the Indus valley from the plain of the Ganges River. In more recent times the Gangetic Plain, together with that of the Brahmaputra, has been the heartland of India.

South of the great river plains is peninsular India, whose core is the Deccan Plateau, bordered by the Eastern and Western Ghats, or hills, and beyond them, the coastal plains. The Tamil Plain lies at the southeastern tip of the peninsula and is the home of a distinct ethnic and cultural group. Geographically, the island of Sri Lanka (formerly Ceylon) is a continuation of southern India. From north to south, the subcontinent spans approximately 2,000 miles.

India has a wide variety of climates, from cold winters in the Himalayan foothills to searing summer heat in the northern plains, to year-round hot temperatures in the

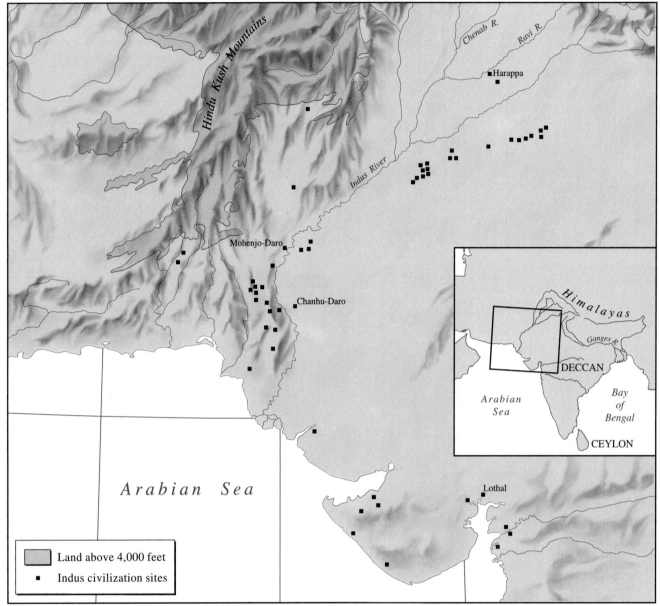

✵ MAP 2.1 Indus Valley Civilization. The earliest civilization on the Indian subcontinent flourished between 2500 and 1500 B.C.E. in an 800-mile stretch along the banks of the Indus River and its tributaries, to the coast of the Arabian Sea. Indus cities were planned and prosperous, and the peoples traded with other parts of India and Mesopotamia.

south. Climate and natural conditions have also undergone significant changes since the dawn of civilization. From Neolithic times down through the third and second millennia B.C.E., when the first civilization developed and thrived along the banks of the Indus and its tributaries, the region was well watered and was covered in part by marshes and jungles. Over time the climate of the lower Indus became drier. These climatic and ecological changes contributed to the decline of the Indus civilization. By the time Alexander the Great and his army reached this area in 326 B.C.E., much of it was already the barren desert that it remains today.

The most important feature of the Indian climate is the monsoon ("the rain"), which comes pelting down starting around June until September. Not only do the rains bring relief from the suffocating heat and turn the parched land green, but they make agriculture possible. To this day, much of the harvest depends on whether the monsoon brings too much or too little rain and whether it comes on time. Because of this dependence, Indians look on rain-laden dark clouds and thunder and lightning as beneficent signs from heaven. Between October and May, hardly a drop of rain falls in most of India, so irrigation is indispensable for farming.

✴ Indus Seals. Many seals of engraved stone have been found throughout the Indus valley and in Mesopotamia. A variety of animals and occasionally humanlike figures are found on the seals, as well as characters of a pictographic writing that is unrelated to any other known writing system and has not been deciphered. Robert Harding Picture Library

The Beginning of the Indus Civilization

In the third millennium B.C.E., Neolithic peoples who lived in the Indus valley evolved the first civilizations in India, in much the same manner as civilizations had emerged in the Nile and Tigris-Euphrates valleys. Unlike Egypt and Mesopotamia, however, where much of our knowledge comes from the written records of those civilizations, the Indus civilization must be reconstructed from other evidence. Although a system of writing developed in the Indus valley, to date archaeologists have not found any long inscriptions left by the Indus people. In fact, all we have of Indus writing are short pictographic inscriptions, carved on little seals about one inch square or in diameter. Most seals also have carved animals or deitylike figures. The carvings suggest that the seals were used to stamp ownership marks on merchandise and therefore represented personal or company names or perhaps short prayers. Thousands of these seals have been found throughout the Indus valley and also in Mesopotamia, but no Indian equivalent of a Rosetta stone has been discovered to unlock the secrets of this unique language. In any case, the messages on the seals are too short to allow meaningful glimpses into the Indus culture. Because so little written evidence has survived and because what has survived is as yet undeciphered, the Indus civilization continues to be classified as prehistoric.

Because we do not know the language, we must rely chiefly on archaeological evidence for our knowledge of this civilization. Over 1,500 Indus sites have been identified, covering an area of approximately 300,000 square miles, larger than the state of Texas and twice as large as the area occupied by ancient Egypt or Sumer. The geographic boundaries of the civilization stretch beyond the Indus valley to include all northwestern India from Kash-

mir in the north to Delhi in the east and the entire northern shore of the Arabian Sea. The three largest cities that have been excavated are Harappa in Punjab; Mohenjo-Daro in Sind, 400 miles to the southwest beside the Indus; and Lothal on the coast. Many features, such as the size of the bricks and the urban plans, including an elevated mound in each city center, were uniform throughout the area. Hence, archaeologists refer to the civilization as the Harappan culture or the Indus Empire.

An Urban Culture: Mohenjo-Daro

Since Mohenjo-Daro is the best preserved and one of the most systematically excavated cities of the Indus culture, it stands as the prototype for other cities in the region. Mohenjo-Daro was centered around an artificial mound, about fifty feet high, which was fortified by a brick wall with towers. Stores of ammunition stones indicate that this was a citadel. The citadel also has a great bath or tank, thirty-nine feet by twenty-three feet, flanked by a large pillared hall and small cell-like rooms. Archaeologists guess that the pool and hall served a religious or ritual purpose. Since no palace that might have housed royal rulers has been found, archaeologists further deduce that a high priest or a college of priests may have ruled the city. Scholars also surmise that the ritual tanks found alongside Hindu temples in later India may have had their origin in the great bath of the Indus cities. A magnificent granary of brick and timber, with loading platform and ventilation holes, completes the structures on the citadel.

Below the citadel spreads a well-laid-out city, perhaps the earliest example of urban planning. The main avenues were broad and oriented north-south; they were intersected by lesser east-west lanes in a grid system. Certain parts of the town were designated for shops; other areas were used by other occupational groups. All buildings were made of baked bricks of uniform size, suggesting a powerful, centralized authority.

Merchants' houses in the prosperous residential districts were substantial; the ground floor was about thirty feet square on average, and many had second and third stories. No windows faced the street; instead, the rooms opened onto a central courtyard. This style of house is still found in India today and throughout tropical and temperate areas from China to North Africa. On both the ground and second floors were bathrooms with drains flowing to underground sewers that ended in soak pits (like our septic tanks). Some houses had private wells, but public wells at street intersections provided water for those without them. These features, the state granary, and the sentry boxes scattered throughout the city could only have been maintained by a highly sophisticated government.

The workers' living quarters also indicate a prosperous economy. They lived in comfortable (by the standards of the era, and even by present-day living standards of Indian workers) two-room cottages, each unit being about twelve feet by twenty feet in Mohenjo-Daro and even bigger in Harappa.

Society and Economy

Anthropologists who have studied the skeletal remains of the Indus people conclude that several racial groups were represented among them. Adults ranged between five feet five inches and five feet nine inches in height. The average life span was around thirty years (the norm for Indians until the early twentieth century). Then as now, most of the noncity dwellers farmed. The main food crops were wheat, barley, peas, sesame, melons, and dates. We cannot be certain whether the Indus people irrigated their crops, but we do know that they were the first people in the world to grow and weave cotton. Their domestic animals included humped cattle, goats, sheep, pigs, and fowl. Elephants figure in the seals, but we do not know whether they had been tamed; in any case, their ivory was widely used.

Trade flourished. Boats carried goods along the Indus River and the seacoast to West Asia. Lothal, a major sea-

Granary at Mohenjo-Daro. This drawing of the granary at the citadel of Mohenjo-Daro is based on archaeological remains. The brick and timber structure had a recessed loading dock. Presumably bullock-drawn carts, similar to toy carts found at Mohenjo-Daro, delivered the grains for storage here. Such bullock carts are still a common sight in India. Robert Harding Picture Library

Layout of Mohenjo-Daro. The streets of Mohenjo-Daro followed a grid pattern. Houses had enclosed central courtyards. Many street intersections had public wells and sentry boxes for watchmen. A wall with watch towers enclosed part of the city. The excavations reveal a high degree of organization and a prosperous urban life. Robert Harding Picture Library

port, had the world's oldest scientifically designed docks in an artificial basin that took into consideration the water level of high and low tides. Land routes connected the Indus valley with other parts of India. A bead factory found at Lothal has ten rooms and measures 5,380 square feet. Indus artists made jewelry from lapis lazuli (a semiprecious stone possibly from Afghanistan), gold, turquoise from Iran, and locally mined carnelian. Perishable items such as textiles and woods may also have been exchanged. Numerous Indus seals and pottery items found in Mesopotamia testify to trade between the two civilizations. Sumerian and Akkadian cuneiform documents from around 2400 to 2000 B.C.E. mention a land called Dilmun or Telmun in the east with which there was organized trade; they may have been referring to the Indus civilization.

Indus artisans displayed talent in a wide number of basic crafts. They used the wheel to make pottery vessels of many shapes and sizes for food, drink, cooking, and storage. They also created utensils of stone, ivory, copper, bronze, and silver. They used the lost-wax method, as did the ancient Greeks, to cast metal ornaments and tools, in contrast to the piece mold method of the ancient Chinese. Some ivory combs, copper mirrors, and gold and silver jewelry show very fine workmanship and artistry. The many toys and games, such as miniature terra cotta animals, whistles, rattles, and bird cages, show the loving care that adults must have lavished on their children.

Indus Religion

It is difficult to write definitively about the religion of the Indus people in the absence of written documents. As we observed, archaeologists speculate that they used the great bath and the adjoining assembly hall in Mohenjo-Daro for religious and ritual purposes, and that a college of priests lived in the rows of small rooms nearby. Excavations have revealed neither temples nor monumental sculptures and large statues such as those in Egypt that are clearly religious in purpose. Large numbers of terra cotta figurines similar to those found in sites from Egypt to Iran have been discovered, however. The generally accepted view is that the pregnant-looking female figurines, which are often molded together with children, represent the great mother or nature goddess. Parallel instances of female nature deities are found throughout the eastern Mediterranean. There are also nude male figurines, the best example being that of a three-faced horned male figure, nude except for his jewelry. He is seated with crossed legs in the yoga position and is surrounded by four animals: an elephant, a tiger, a rhinoceros, and a buffalo. This god has been called proto- (early, primitive) Shiva.

🎋 Bearded Man Found at Mohenjo-Daro. Very little statuary from the Indus civilization has been discovered. We do not know whether this figure was a deity or a man. Government of Pakistan, Department of Archeology and Museums

Shiva is the later three-faced Hindu god of death, destruction, and fertility and the lord of beasts.

Indus people may also have worshiped certain trees and animals, including the bull, the animal most commonly found in the seals. In later Hinduism the bull is associated with Shiva. The cow, almost a universal symbol of later Hinduism, is, however, nowhere represented on Indus artifacts. The dead were carefully buried in cemeteries, laid out with their heads to the north and their feet pointing south. Grave goods, though not elaborate, include painted pottery jars, some weapons in graves of males, and sometimes a sacrificed sheep or goat. No royal graves have been found. Since we do not have contemporary written documents, we do not know the significance of the burial practices.

The End of Indus Civilization

Civilizations rise and fall as a result of complex factors. When a civilization is as widely distributed as the Indus, no uniform date or single reason can be given for its end. One cause was extensive and serious flooding, probably caused by deforestation and overgrazing. Even more im-

portant were the major geological changes in the beginning of the second millennium B.C.E. that caused coastal uplifts along the northern shore of the Arabian Sea and moved several Indus era ports as much as thirty-five miles inland. These geological changes had a ruinous effect on the lives and economies of the people in the lower Indus region, but do not seem to have disrupted the life of Harappa farther upriver. That they interrupted long-distance trade we may deduce from the almost complete disappearance of seals in the late levels of Mohenjo-Daro and Lothal. The uplift prevented the river's water from reaching the sea and created huge shallow lakes upstream. We do not know how long these periods of flooding lasted; some of them probably persisted for decades. The floods would also explain the layers of silt as much as seventy feet deep found around Mohenjo-Daro and the huge embankments, some twenty-five feet high, and other community projects built to keep out the floodwaters. Since public works such as embankments to control floods are major undertakings, it is safe to assume that small towns and settlements were simply abandoned to the floodwaters. In time the floodwaters spilled over the barrier, and the river resumed its course to the sea. The people of Mohenjo-Daro were then left with the task of reinforcing the flood-damaged buildings or rebuilding them.

This process was repeated at least five times at Mohenjo-Daro. The people must have been worn out and impoverished by their repeated efforts to fight the floods. The decline in their living standard toward the end is evident in the shoddier construction of later houses, which were built on the ruins of their predecessors or on artificial platforms that had been raised to keep above the flood crests. Economic decline and population pressures are visible everywhere as shantytowns superseded spacious residences and rabbit warrens spread onto once neatly laid-out streets. Around 1900 B.C.E. the Indus River changed course and a parallel river dried up, further contributing to the economic ruin.

Then invading barbarian settlers from the west descended on the Indus plains through the passes of the Hindu Kush, contributing to the decline of the Indus civilization. Defensive measures are evident in the last centuries of the Indus cities. Mohenjo-Daro's great citadel was fortified by a brick wall with towers, and Harappa built massive turreted walls forty feet wide at the base and thirty-five feet tall; its western gate was wholly blocked in to defend against invaders from the west. In the centuries after 2000 B.C.E., newcomers settled in villages in outlying areas. Their pottery was coarser and cruder than the vessels made by the Indus peoples. Fleeing refugees must have streamed into the walled cities for protection, causing further economic and social strains. A potter's kiln built in the middle of a street indicates collapsing municipal standards. Caches of hoarded jewelry speak eloquently of the breakdown of law and order.

Before the end came, most of the inhabitants of Mohenjo-Daro had fled. Several groups of skeletons have been found in dead-end streets, strewn helter-skelter with axe and knife wounds in the skulls or huddled by wells, then covered by debris. These remains vividly suggest how the last stragglers met their doom. Fires probably destroyed the sacked city. Most corpses must have been burnt in the fires or disposed of in other ways. The once flourishing urban life represented by Mohenjo-Daro came to an end.

Harappa and other nearby settlements, which had not suffered previous decline, were abruptly abandoned and not reoccupied. We do not know whether the inhabitants fled at the threat of invasion or were expelled. At Chanhu Daro farther downriver, Indus inhabitants were replaced by squatters, whose huts had fireplaces, a feature unknown to Indus architecture, suggesting that the owners had come from colder climates. Among the scattered remains of the newcomers are copper axes and swords with strengthening midribs superior to anything the Indus people possessed. The invaders also had horses, which were unknown to the Indus people.

By about 1500 B.C.E., the Indus civilization had perished. Although scholars still argue about the precise reasons for its fall, it is safe to conclude that it fell as a result of a combination of factors. Deforestation and degradation of the environment and natural catastrophes first weakened the morale as well as the economy of the Indus peoples. Then came waves of more dynamic and warlike invaders and settlers, from the north and west, called Aryans, wielding superior weapons and riding in swift and terrifying horse-drawn chariots.

The Aryan Invasion and Early Vedic Age

To Indra

I will declare the manly deeds of Indra, the first
that he achieved, the thunder-wielder.
He slew the dragon, then disclosed the waters, and
cleft the channels of the mountain torrents.

He slew the dragon lying on the mountain; his
heavenly bolt of thunder Tvashtar fashioned.
Like lowing kine in rapid flow descending the
waters glided downward to the ocean.

Impetuous as a bull, he chose the Soma, and in
three beakers drank the juices.
The Bounteous One grasped the thunder for his
weapon, and smote to death this first born of the
dragons.

When Indra, thou hadst slain the dragon's first
born, and overcome the charms of the enchanters,
Then, giving life to sun and dawn and heaven, thou
foundest not one foe to stand against thee.

Indra with his own great and deadly thunder smote
into pieces Vritra, worst of Vritras,
As trunk of trees, what time the axe hath felled
them, low on the earth so lies the prostrate
dragon.

He, like a mad weak warrior, challenged Indra, the
great impetuous many-slaying hero.
He, brooking not the clashing of the weapons,
crushed—Indra's foe—the shattered forts in
falling.*

*Robert O. Ballou, ed., The Bible of the World (New York: Viking, 1939), pp. 5–6.

These six verses of a hymn to Indra are from the Rig-Veda, the holiest book of the Aryan invaders and also of Hinduism, a religion that developed out of the beliefs of the Aryans and the indigenous Indian peoples. For generations the Aryan priests memorized the songs of praise in an Indo-European language that was closely related to Greek and Latin. About 1000 B.C.E., these songs were written down in Sanskrit, an alphabetical script of the Indo-European family. Indra was an important god in the Rig-Veda. This hymn portrays him as a hard-drinking warrior who killed dragons and demolished forts. He was also the god of thunder and the bringer of rain.

The word Aryan is the Anglicized form for Aryas in Sanskrit. It means "noble of birth and race," which is how the fair-complexioned invaders described themselves in contrast to the natives whom they called dasas, meaning dark skinned, or of "dasa color." Dasa in Sanskrit came to mean "slave." Sometime after 2000 B.C.E., the Aryans pushed through the mountain passes that separate Afghanistan from northwestern India. The movement spanned several centuries and included many tribes that sometimes fought each other. Tools and weapons of bronze and copper discovered in northwestern India in association with the early Aryans are very similar in type and date to those found in southern Russia, the Caucasus, and Iran. They suggest that the Aryan invaders of India were closely related to the Indo-Europeans who spilled over Europe and Iran in equally dynamic migrations in about the same period.

In material development, the Aryans were less advanced than the people of the Indus civilization. They were not city dwellers, and after conquering the Indus cities, they abandoned them to ruin. There were no significant cities in India for the next 1,000 years, and the remains of the villages with houses of wood and other perishable materials have long since vanished. Thus India from 1500 to 500 B.C.E. is almost an archaeological blank; our knowledge about it comes mainly from literary sources.

Early Vedic Society and Economy

The earliest literary sources for the history of India are the hymns and prayers of the *Rig-Veda,* the literature of the Aryan invaders. These hymns are primarily addressed to male deities. They were memorized by the priests for recital at religious ceremonies, as they are to the present day. After circa 1000 B.C.E. and the appearance of writing, the hymns were compiled and written down. Although primarily religious and metaphysical in character, the *Vedas* and other early writings do contain some historic reference points that supply information about the

life of the community during the 1,000-year period of the Vedic Age.

The Aryans were organized according to tribes, each ruled by a hereditary chief, called a *raja* (related to the Latin word *rex,* or "king"). The main function of the raja was to lead in war. He was not absolute and had to consult a tribal assembly before making decisions. He had no religious function except to order sacrifices and provide support for the priests. The priests played an important role in Aryan society because they composed, memorized, and passed down to succeeding generations of priests the hymns of the *Rig-Veda* and other sacred works. They also presided at ceremonies and conducted sacrifices to maintain cosmic order and ensure tribal prosperity in peace and victory in war.

Aryan society was already divided into social classes before the invasion. As the Aryans settled in India among

❊ Indra. An important Vedic god, Indra is depicted here as the king of heaven, trailing clouds and accompanied by celestial nymphs. This figure is part of a Buddhist cave wall painting that dates to between the fifth and the seventh century C.E. By then Indra had been supplanted in worship by other deities, but he remained a celestial god to both Hindus and Buddhists.
UNESCO World Art Series

From that all-embracing sacrifice
were born the hymns and chants,
from that the metres were born,
from that the sacrificial spells were born.

Thence were born horses,
and all beings with two rows of teeth.
Thence were born cattle,
and thence goats and sheep.

When they divided the Man,
into how many parts did they divide him?
What was his mouth, what were his arms,
what were his thighs and his feet called?

The Brahman was his mouth,
of his arms was made the warrior,
his thighs became the vaisya,
of his feet the sudra was born.

The moon arose from his mind,
from his eyes was born the sun,
from his mouth Indra and Agni,
from his breath the wind was born.

From his navel came the air,
from his head there came the sky,
from his feet the earth, the four quarters from his ear,
thus they fashioned the worlds.*

The preceding verses from a hymn in the *Rig Veda* describe the creation of the universe and all within it and justify the existence of a social order in which humans were divided into four major categories, each with its function. These four divisions are called "castes" in En-glish (*varna*, meaning "color," in Sanskrit). Each caste was subdivided into occupational or geographic groups called *jati*, which remain the foundation of Hindu society.*

*A. L. Basham, *The Wonder That Was India* (New York: Grove Press, 1954), pp. 240–241.

dark-skinned indigenous people, they put more stress on purity of bloodline and class divisions. By the end of the early Vedic period, society had been divided into four great classes; children were born into their father's class and could not change it. This division was given religious sanction. The groupings were based on function and on skin color, called *varna* in Sanskrit. Thus the old tribal class structure was expanded to include people of different skin complexion. In English the word *caste* or *class* is commonly used to refer to these groups. They were, in descending order, the priests (*brahmans*), the warriors (*kshatriyas*), the landholders and artisans (*vaisyas*), and the serfs and servants (*sudras*). The first three castes included the fair-skinned Aryans, while the fourth consisted of the dark-skinned natives. In later centuries the original racial distinctions became blurred as the religion of the Aryans outpaced their physical penetration of India. Thus in South India where there were few Aryans, members of all castes tended to be non-Aryans. These basic divisions, with many subdivisions, survived to the present.

The Aryan social unit was the patrilineal and patriarchal family. Marriages were usually monogamous and apparently indissoluble. Although the wife and mother enjoyed respect, a woman was definitely subordinate to her husband. Daughters were less desired than sons. The *Rig-Veda* describes unmarried young men and women mixing freely and does not indicate that married women were secluded, as became normal in later times.

The Aryans practiced a mixed pastoral and farming economy. They prized cattle for status and wealth; they valued horses as well, though mainly for military reasons.

Domestic animals included sheep (for wool), goats, and dogs. Cows did not have the sacred status of later times, nor were there strictures against eating meat. Most people were farmers and lived in villages. Arable land appears to have been privately owned, but grazing land was probably held in common and manuring and irrigation were practiced. Artisans such as carpenters, metalworkers, and tanners formed subcastes, plied their specialties, and lived in both towns and villages. Most trade was by barter, but cattle were also used as currency in important exchanges. There is no information about international trade in the Vedic Age as there was in the Indus era, and no Vedic Age artifacts have been discovered outside India.

Religion

Our knowledge of early Aryan religion comes from the *Rig-Veda*. By the time these hymns were written down hundreds of years after they had been composed, many of the words had become archaic and their meanings unclear. They represent an amalgamation of the beliefs of several different Aryan tribes and are not systematic. Nevertheless, hymns from the *Rig-Veda* are still recited at weddings and funerals and in the daily devotions of brahmans, and they remain part of the living Hindu tradition.

The objects of Aryan worship were the *devas*, a Sanskrit word related to *deus*, which means "god" in Latin. Foremost among the gods was Indra, who in some respects resembled the Greek god Zeus, a successful warrior who killed the dasas and demolished their forts. Agni was the fire god (compare Latin *ignis*, which means "fire"), also god of the hearth and home. He accepted the sacrifices offered by humans and carried them to the other gods and as such was an intermediary between gods and humans. Soma was both a god and a hallucinogenic drink made from a hemp-type plant and drunk at religious ceremonies. Yama was the lord of the dead. Rudra was the archer god, who was feared and avoided because his arrows brought disease; but he was also the healer god and gave good health to those he liked. Varuna, the emperor of heaven, was possibly related to the Greek heaven-god Uranus. Varuna was an ethical god and guardian of the moral order, who abhorred sin and punished sinners by inflicting them with disease, especially dropsy, and by condemning them to a gloomy House of Clay after death. Aryans who had performed the proper rites, however, were believed to feast forever in happiness after they died. The *Vedas* tell of many other gods, demigods, divine musicians, gnomes, goddesses, and *apsarases,* who were similar to the nymphs of the Greeks. Unfortunately, ancient India never had the equivalent of a Homer or Hesiod of ancient Greece, so we do not have a clear genealogy of the Aryans' deities, and their relationships are often unclear.

Aryan religion centered on many kinds of sacrifices, including the daily domestic hearth sacrifices performed by the head of the family as well as the great sacrifices ordered by rulers and chiefs, presided over by many brahmans, and requiring the slaughter of many animals. The goal in each case was to gain the favor of gods, who were believed to descend to earth, partake of the offerings, and then bless the participants by granting their requests for success in war, health, long life, children, good crops, or other forms of good fortune. The participants drank soma, felt bigger than life, and were rewarded with a sense of well-being. The main difference between the Aryans and the dasas was religion. Many passages in the *Rig-Veda* denounce the dasas for impiety and for their religious rites.

Aryan religious ceremonies became more complex with the passage of time. Their correct performance came to be regarded as essential not only to individual and community well-being but also for the maintenance of the cosmic order.

The Appearance of Writing

Sanskrit and all other Indo-European languages are related because they all trace back to the spoken tongue of common ancestors who lived in the steppes of the Eurasian plains around 4,000 years ago. Many key Sanskrit, Greek, and Latin words obviously share the same origin, and many grammatical rules of the three ancient languages are similar. The language of the *Rig-Veda,* which is written in the earliest surviving form of Sanskrit, bears the same relationship to later classical Sanskrit as Homeric Greek does to classical Greek.

By the time the *Rig-Veda* was written, its language was already archaic. Classical Sanskrit, which developed in the first centuries of the first millennium B.C.E., had a less complex grammar and included new words, many of them borrowed from non-Aryan languages. Even then it was probably never used by ordinary Aryan peoples, who spoke dialects with simpler grammar. The spoken or vernacular tongues were called Prakrits, which literally means "unrefined" or popular languages, as opposed to the "perfected" or "refined" or "Sanskrit" of the scholars. Because Sanskrit was used by the priests (and probably by other members of the upper class) and by government officials, it became a universal language for the subcontinent. Even now, brahmans from different parts of India can communicate with one another through Sanskrit.

Although writing began around 1000 B.C.E., no document from earlier than the third century B.C.E. has survived. By the time the *Vedas* were written down, classical Sanskrit had evolved so much from Vedic Sanskrit that scholars and priests concerned with preserving the purity of the religious texts developed the sciences of linguistics and grammar. The oldest extant Indian linguistic text dates to the fifth century B.C.E. and explains obsolete Vedic words. Toward the end of the fourth century B.C.E., a great grammar book, entitled *Eight Chapters,* was written. Sanskrit became standardized, and also perhaps fossilized, after the completion of the *Eight Chapters.* It ceased to develop, whereas the Prakrits evolved into modern vernaculars.

The languages of southern India belong to the Dravidian group. They are unrelated to Indo-European languages, although in time they incorporated many Sanskrit words into their vocabularies. The oldest Dravidian written language is Tamil. The earliest literature in the Tamil language dates to the first centuries C.E.

The Late Vedic Age

Satyakama son of Jabala said to his mother: "Mother, I want to be a student. What is my family?"

"I don't know your family, my dear," she said. "I had you in my youth, when I travelled about a lot as a servant—and I just don't know! My name is Jabala, and yours is Satyakama Jabala."

He went to Gautama Haridrumata, and said: "I want to be your student, sir. May I come?"

"What is your family, my friend?" he asked.

"I don't know my family, sir," he answered. "I asked my mother, and she said that she had me in her youth, when she used to travel about a lot as a servant. . . . She said that she was Jabala and I was Satyakama. I was to give my name as Satyakama Jabala."

"Nobody but a true brahman would be so honest!" he said. . . . "Go and fetch me fuel, my friend, and I will initiate you, for you have not swerved from the truth."

*Robert O. Ballou, ed., *The Bible of the World* (New York: Viking, 1939), p. 254.

This passage from an *Upanishad* extols the virtue of honesty. Ethical behavior was one of the qualities given high emphasis in the quest for truth and salvation that characterized the Late Vedic Age (about 1000–500 B.C.E.), the five centuries between the composition of the *Rig-Veda* and the age of the Buddha. Old rituals and sacrifices to the Aryan tribal gods had lost their appeal, and the goal of thinking people was to seek truth and understand the nature of the brahman, or the essential divine reality of the universe. In so doing, scholars brought about new philosophical developments within the existing religious pattern and founded new, breakaway religions.

Our sources for the period are still predominantly sacred literature and the *Upanishads,* essays that deal with religious and philosophical questions. In addition, we have epic tales about the period, though they were written later. The greatest of those epics is the *Mahabharata,* which survives in two versions; both tell the story of a gigantic war over the dynastic succession in the Kuru tribe that eventually involved all of India. Corroborative evidence shows that between the tenth and ninth centuries a great war did take place, probably centered in modern-day Delhi. The names of many of the heroes in the epic may indeed be those of contemporary chieftains. However, it is not possible to reconstruct accurate political history from the epic. Since the archaeological work on this era of Indian history is far less comprehensive than that done in Greece, the *Mahabharata* is of less use to the historian of India than the *Iliad* is to historians of ancient Greece. Both epics served the purpose of providing models of heroic behavior to their societies.

Despite the scarcity of sources, it is known that during the Late Vedic period Aryan society expanded across northern India along the Himalayan foothills and the Jumna and Ganges Plains to the Bay of Bengal. The center of culture and political power in India shifted from the Indus to the Ganges Valley. The earlier conquered lands of Sind and the Punjab (which means "five rivers" because of its location at the upper Indus, where five tributaries converge on the main river) were almost forgotten, and when mentioned, they were described as inhabited by the impure, that is non-Aryan, people. Tribal groups had formed into territorial states with permanent capital cities and rudimentary administrative systems. The kings, almost exclusively kshatriyas, now wielded judicial as well as military power. The formerly powerful tribal assemblies were discarded, replaced by courtiers who served the kings.

Late Vedic Society and Economy

The Late Vedic Age was more advanced economically and materially than the previous era. As the tribes settled down and cleared forests, agriculture became more important than animal herding. Most people lived in villages, but the texts mention cities; Ujjian, for example, retains its seventh-century name unchanged. Situated in the present state of Vindhya Pradesh, it was then the capital city of a kingdom and a holy city; it is still sacred to Hinduism.

The texts also mention many subcastes of craftsmen and new grain crops. While many continued to eat meat, others begin to regard meat eating with disfavor due to the development of new ideals of respect for animal life. There is some, but not conclusive, evidence that India once more traded with Mesopotamia in this period. Caste distinctions became more pronounced and rigid; the members of all four classes found their lives more strictly regulated. Brahmans and kshatriyas, however, increasingly enjoyed privileges denied to vaisyas and sudras, and the gap between the top and bottom of society grew wider. At the top, brahmans enjoyed immense power and prestige, for they were indispensable to the conduct of sacrifices and the maintenance of a correct relationship between this world and the cosmic order. At the lower end, the sudras were regarded as impure. The size of the sudra caste grew constantly, as conquered or assimilated tribal people were added to the Aryan-dominated society.

Unlike some other ancient civilizations, Vedic society did not have large numbers of slaves, and no caste of slaves as such existed. Nevertheless, slavery did exist. War captives became slaves to the victors until ransomed. Undesirable work that some societies relegated to slaves was given to people later known as outcastes or untouchables, a group lower than sudras. Outcastes were considered ritually impure; they were assigned menial and unpleasant tasks, served the rest of society, and were excluded from the Aryan social order. Some outcastes were descended from conquered aborigines. Others were descended from men and women who had been "outcasted" because of severe infractions of caste rules. Still others may have been members of professions that came to be considered impure in the new moral scheme.

Indirect evidence warrants the conclusion that in this period the position of women declined from its earlier relatively high level. Child marriages, in which young girls were sent to live under the authority of their husbands' parents, were common and had the effect of keeping young women subordinated. Another new practice allowed upper-caste men to take concubines or secondary wives from the sudra caste.

Religion

During the Late Vedic period, two religious trends emerged. First, brahman religious leaders challenged the kings' pretensions to political absolutism. Second, men not traditionally associated with religious leadership, as well as some brahmans who were dissatisfied with traditional ways, began to offer new religious ideas that challenged the established religious rituals and prescribed sacrifices. One of these ideas was the doctrine of *karma* (literally "deed"), which held that one's position in this life is the result of deeds and actions in past lives and that one's present deeds will affect future lives as the soul passes from life to life into infinity. This doctrine of transmigration of souls—that the soul moves from one body to another from life to life—gave an ethical content to one's actions, and it explained and justified the inequalities in Aryan society. It also linked all forms of life into one comprehensive system that included humans, animals, insects, and, according to some, even inanimate matter. The belief in karma, that one's conduct determined one's status in future existences, became fundamental to all religions originating in India.

The political changes discussed earlier and the development of new ethical and religious ideals combined to create a pessimistic outlook on the world that is characteristic of the Late Vedic period. This mood led to several developments; one was a trend toward asceticism. Ascetics were men, and occasionally women, of any caste, whose quest for wisdom led them to abandon the material world in favor of a life of wandering and meditation. They also performed mystical exercises requiring great discipline of both mind and body, with the goal of developing their psychic faculties and insights beyond ordinary understanding. Similarly, in classical Greece, Socrates, in the *Phaedo,* said that the true philosopher is in training for death (that is, the final separation of the soul from the body and its distractions). The ascetic way of life had ancient roots in India. Some hymns of the *Rig-Veda* even mention a class of holy men who, as a result of meditation and the practice of austerities, acquired great wisdom and powers of perception beyond ordinary people's understanding.

By about 600 B.C.E. toward the end of the Late Vedic Age, asceticism had become very widespread, and it was through the ascetics rather than the orthodox brahman priests that new religious teachings developed. Some ascetics, in groups or alone, wandered the country, teaching and debating with one another. Others lived rather permanently on the outskirts of towns and villages. Some groups were led by a senior teacher. The movement toward asceticism was certainly in part a protest against the pretensions of the brahmans and their sacrificial cult, though some brahmans who believed the traditional cult to be inadequate also became ascetics.

A Holy Man. Holy men have been revered in India since Vedic times because they have given up all material and emotional attachments. They wander singly or in small groups, visit holy sites, and spend long hours meditating. Robert Harding Picture Library

The *Upanishads*

The greatest creation of the Late Vedic era was the *Upanishads,* a collection of 108 essays dealing with ethical questions that was written between 800 and 300 B.C.E. Literally, *upanishad* means "sitting near" and refers to students sitting near a teacher to learn esoteric doctrines from him. Not all the essays are important, nor do they teach a consistent point of view. We know the names of some of the authors, but most of the essays were anonymous group efforts. Just as the Greek philosopher Plato and the Chinese philosopher Confucius explained their ideas in dialogue form, so many of the *Upanishads* contain dialogues, questions and answers between students and teachers.

The general tendency of the *Upanishads* was toward monism, a metaphysical system in which reality is conceived as a unified whole. Ritual and magic were discouraged as futile when applied without enlightenment, and faith and good works were considered inadequate. The goal of the *Upanishads* was to seek the knowledge and wis-

"Fetch me a fruit of the banyan tree."

"Here is one, sir."

"Break it."

"I have broken it sir."

"What do you see?"

"Very tiny seeds, sir."

"Break one."

"I have broken it, sir."

"Now what do you see?"

"Nothing, sir."

"My son," the father said, "what you do not perceive is the essence, and in that essence the mighty banyan tree exists. Believe me, my son, in that essence is the Self of all that is. That is the True, that is the Self. And you are that Self, Svetaketu!"

"Put this salt in water, and come to me in the morning."

The son did as he was told. The father said: "Fetch the salt." The son looked for it, but could not find it, because it had dissolved.

"Taste the water from the top," said the father. "How does it taste?"

"Of salt," the son replied.

"Taste from the bottom. How does it taste?"

"Of salt," the son replied.

Then the father said, "You don't perceive that the one Reality exists in your own body, my son, but it is truly there. Everything which is has its being in that subtle essence. That is Reality! That is the Soul! And you are that, Svetaketu!"*

The dominant theme of the *Upanishads* is the search for knowledge or understanding of the mystery of this unintelligible world and one's place in it. These two passages from an *Upanishad* assert that salvation is found through knowledge of or realization of the individual self (the *atman*) and the absolute self (*brahman*). The wise person realizes that the two are the same, and his highest quest is then to seek a synthesis of the two. When he realizes that, he is freed from transmigration.

*Robert O. Ballou, ed., *The Bible of the World* (New York: Viking, 1939), pp. 250–251.

dom that the *Vedas* did not give. Eventually, the ideas explored in the *Upanishads* found their way into the new orthodoxy of the Hindu religion that emerged from the synthesis of old and new ideas. In this way, the *Upanishads* became accepted as an orthodox part of the Vedic literature that for over 2,000 years has formed the basis of the thought and spirituality of Hinduism, the religion that emerged from early Aryan religion and later additions. The strength of the *Upanishads'* teaching is its all-embracing approach, which overrides all barriers of caste and every external and internal difference between believers.

The ideas expressed in the *Upanishads*, however, were so esoteric and complex that they influenced only the small number capable of understanding them. They were entirely too difficult for the vast masses of the people and hence did not permeate downward. The most immediate effect of the movement was to widen the gap between the intellectuals and ordinary people.

Meanwhile, the common people began to put their faith in hitherto unimportant deities who now seemed to answer their needs. Most important among them were Shiva and Vishnu, who replaced Indra and Varuna, who had been important earlier. Also known as Rudra, Shiva may have become popular because of his identification with a deity often depicted on Indus seals. Shiva was associated with death and destruction, but also with fertility, something everyone desired. Worshipers appealed to Vishnu for deliverance from distress; he was also identi-

fied with Krishna, who taught morality and virtue. These two gods continued from Late Vedic to modern times as the most popular deities in Hinduism.

Another result of the religious mood of the Late Vedic period was the development of two new religions that sought to change and reform some of the prevailing religious ideas and practices. These new religions were Buddhism and Jainism, which will be discussed in Chapter 4.

China from the Neolithic Age to the Shang Dynasty

Examining into antiquity we find that the Emperor Yao was called Fang-hsun. He was reverent, intelligent, accomplished, sincere and mild. He was sincerely respectful and capable of modesty, His light covered the four extremities of the empire and extended to Heaven above and the earth below. He was able to make bright his great virtue, and bring affection to the nine branches of the family. When the nine branches of the family had become harmonious, he distinguished and honored the hundred clans. When the hundred clans had become illustrious, he harmonized the myriad states. The numerous people were amply nourished and prosperous and became harmonious. . . .

[As he grew older Yao searched for a successor from among all his subjects, and found Shun the best qualified.]

The emperor said: "Come you, Shun, in the affairs on which you have been consulted, I have examined your words; your words have been accomplished and capable of yielding fine results for three years; do you ascend to the imperial throne." Shun considered himself inferior in virtue and was not pleased. But in the first month, the first day, he accepted the abdication of Yao in the Temple of the Accomplished Ancestor.*

*William T. de Bary, ed., *Sources of Chinese Tradition*, vol. 1 (New York: Columbia University Press, 1960), pp. 8–9.

Until the twentieth century, Chinese were taught that Kings Yao and Shun were historic figures who reigned around 2200 B.C.E. They were revered for their sincerity, reverence, and unselfishness and for the golden age that their reigns brought. Later rulers were exhorted to emulate them. Since there is no proof that these kings existed, we can only regard them as culture heroes. In this section we will find out how civilization began in China, how traditional Chinese looked at their past, and how modern archaeology has added to our knowledge of ancient China.

The Land of China

China, a country of continental dimensions, today extends some 2,500 miles from the Pamir Mountains in the west to the Pacific Ocean in the east and over 2,000 miles from the Amur River in the north to the Indochinese border in the south. At 3.7 million square miles, it is slightly larger than the 3.6 million square miles of the United States. This area varies greatly in topography, climate, and vegetation, ranging from subarctic taiga (evergreen forests) in the northeast to tropical jungles in the southwest, from the steppes and deserts of Chinese Turkestan in the northwest to the high plateau of Tibet in the west and the temperate river valleys of the east. Although it is possible to cross the broad deserts and scale the high mountains that separate China from the other civilizations of Asia, the length of the journey and the difficulties and dangers associated with such travel have tended to isolate China from other lands. Conversely, the great river valleys and coastal plains make internal communications relatively easy and thus have helped to unify the Chinese.

China can be divided into two broad parts, north and south. The Yellow River dominates North China. It brings the water and deposits the layers of silt on which agriculture depends; it has also since the earliest times brought the cruel floods that have given it the name

MAP 2.2 Shang China. Most archaeological sites of the Shang dynasty are found along the lower reaches of the Yellow River, the heartland of early Chinese civilization, although some are located along the Yangtze and its tributaries. The last Shang captial, Anyang, is located in modern Honan province.

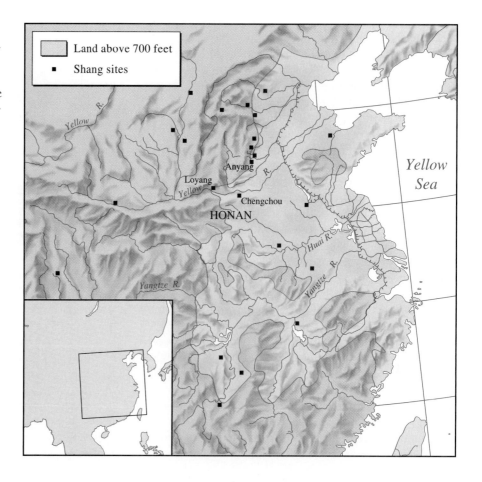

"China's sorrow." Hot in summer and cold in winter, the North China plains receive little rainfall. Here barley and millet are the main crops, and donkeys and oxen are the chief draft animals.

The Tsingling Mountains separate the drainage basins of the Yellow and the Yangtze Rivers. The Yangtze valley and the Hsi (West, also called Pearl) valley farther south constitute South China. A coastal plain of varying width extends along the entire coastline. Southern China receives abundant rainfall and has mild winters and hot summers. It is a land of double and triple crops each year, paddy rice and water buffalo, canals and lakes. Contrasts abound between the harsh north and the verdant south.

The Study of Ancient China

The Chinese have a tradition and history that have continued unbroken from the beginning to the present. Unlike the earliest Indian oral traditions and written documents, which dealt with religion and philosophy, ancient Chinese writings were from the beginning concerned with historiography, or the recording of historic events, with an emphasis on socially applicable morals and virtues.

Early records told of ancient culture heroes who ruled in succession starting from 2850 B.C.E. The greatest was Huang-ti (Yellow Emperor), considered the founding father of the Chinese state because he defeated the neighboring barbarians and united the Chinese people throughout the Yellow River plain. To this day, the Chinese call themselves descendants of the Yellow Emperor. He was followed by others such as Yao and Shun, whom posterity regarded as sage kings. Later writers point to their reigns as a golden age, and subsequent generations have been exhorted to emulate their virtues and achievements.

Another of these culture heroes was Yu, known as the Great, because he dredged the channels of the Yellow River, allowing the floodwaters to flow to the sea and solving the problem of recurring floods. He was so devoted to his work that he never returned home in over ten years, even when he passed by his gate and heard his wife and children weeping in loneliness. Yu was made ruler because of his successful flood-control work and was so loved that when he died, the people set aside the man he had chosen to succeed him and put his son on the throne. Thus began the first dynasty, the Hsia (c. 2205–1766 B.C.E.). Little is known about the Hsia kings until the last, who was a tyrant. He was overthrown by a subordinate named Tang the Successful, who founded the Shang dynasty (c. 1766–1122 B.C.E.). The last Shang king was a debauched tyrant, who in turn was deposed by his subordinate, who founded the Chou dynasty (1122–256 B.C.E.). This, in very brief outline, is how early history was taught to Chinese children until the beginning of the twentieth century.

❀ Neolithic Pots. Both pieces, a large earthenware jar and a bowl, were made by Neolithic farmers in northwestern China between 4000 and 3000 B.C.E. Found in graves, they originally contained food and were buried in the belief that people in the afterlife needed the same things they had in this life. These vessels were handmade by the coiling method and painted with abstract designs in red, black, and white. Collection of Jiu-Hwa L. Upshur; photograph by John Nystuen

The Rise of the Shang Dynasty, 1766–1122 B.C.E

In this year [1899], Liu Tieh-yun . . . was visiting in the capital [Peking] as a house guest of Wang I-yung. The host of Liu Tieh-yun was attacked by malarial fever. The doctor's prescriptions included an ingredient of decayed tortoise shell purchased at the drugstore. . . . On the tortoise shells Liu Tieh-yun saw seal characters, which he picked out and showed to his host; both of them were somewhat astonished at this discovery. Wang, a student of bronze inscriptions, immediately realized that these tortoise shells must be ancient. He went to the drugstore, to inquire about the source of supply of these ingredients. The manager told him that they came from T'ang-yin and Anyang of Honan province. They were sold at a very low price. . . . Liu Tieh-yun went to the drugstore in the city and purchased them all.

This account from the journal of an early modern scholar of ancient Chinese writing tells how a fortunate event led to the discovery of the earliest examples of Chinese writing on tortoise shells and animal bones and to the excavation of the capital of the Shang dynasty. Scientific excavations began at Anyang and other Shang sites in the 1920s, at about the same time that modern archaeology began in India, and have continued ever since.

The Agricultural Revolution, evident in the domestication of plants and animals and the appearance of pottery, began in China around 7000 B.C.E. Communities existed in isolation until about 4000, when they began to interact with one another, though they remained independent from the other emerging civilizations. Although archaeologists have found many remains that corroborate traditional accounts of the Hsia, no written

At the time when men still followed the Great Way, all under Heaven was owned in common. Men were chosen for their ability and talent. Their teaching was reliable and they cultivated harmony. People of ancient times treated not only their nearest relatives as relatives and not only their own children as children. . . . There was employment for the strong and the young were given the opportunity to grow up. Widows, orphans, those left on their own, and invalids were all provided for. Men had their work and women their shelter. They accumulated provisions because they did not wish anything to be thrown away, but they were not supposed to amass goods for themselves. They toiled because they did not wish goods to be anything but the result of their own efforts. But they were not supposed to do this for the sake of personal advantage. Therefore selfish schemes did not arise and robbers, thieves, and rebels were not in evidence. They went out without shutting the door. This was called the Great Harmony.*

Centuries later, Confucius and Confucians viewed the earliest antiquity as a golden age when virtue reigned and selfishness did not exist. They were undoubtedly exhorting the people of their own times to live up to high ideals and maintained that such ideals were realizable, because they had once been reality.

*Attributed to Confucius, from the *Li Chi*, vol. 1, trans. James Legge (1885; reprint, New Hyde Park, N.Y.: University Books, 1967), pp. 364–366.

construction of the Great Pyramids in Egypt, a huge labor force was mobilized to build such major Chinese public works. Experts calculate that it took 10,000 men working 330 days a year for 18 years to build the wall around Ao. The Shang government clearly had the organizational skill to supervise monumental projects.

Within the city walls were large palaces, residences for aristocrats, and ceremonial quarters. Pits with the remains of human sacrificial victims have also been unearthed. Artisans and workers lived close to their work in tamped-earth houses. Remains of these houses are found near kilns, bronze foundries, and workshop areas, located outside the walls. Scattered farmhouses dot the countryside. Artifacts made of bronze, jade, and other materials abound throughout, but no writing has been found, either here or at the other presumed pre-Anyang capitals. We can therefore only deduce from nonwritten information that Chengchow (Ao) was an important political and ceremonial center. Pottery and other artifacts of the last Shang phase at Chengchow are of poorer quality, which suggests that by then the center of power had moved elsewhere.

The last twelve kings of Shang ruled from Yin, near present-day Anyang, for 273 years until the fall of the dynasty; hence the last phase of the Shang is also called the Yin dynasty. When the curious purchasers of the "dragon bones" began to inquire as to their place of origin, the trail led to Anyang; in 1928 China's first major archaeological dig began there.

The excavations near Anyang reveal an impressive civilization. Eleven large tombs that belonged to the kings have been found. Twelve kings ruled from Anyang, but the twelfth and last died in his burning palace as his capital fell and was not given a kingly burial. Smaller tombs in the royal cemetery apparently belonged to other members of the royal family. Unlike the Egyptians, whose rulers were buried in pyramids and tombs carved into cliffs, the Shang kings were buried in underground chambers not unlike those found in the royal cemetery at Mycenae. Each tomb was about thirty feet deep, oblong in shape, with a central burial chamber containing a coffin surrounded by objects of jade, bronze, shell, pottery, and other materials. Remains of human sacrificial victims were found interred in the main chamber and scattered in other parts of the grave, as were dogs and horses harnessed to chariots. Chariot drivers were buried beside their vehicles. Similarities between Shang chariots and those discovered in burial mounds in the Caucasus region in western Asia led to speculation that Shang China might have had contact with cultures to the west.

All the royal graves excavated up to 1975 had been robbed in ages past, but in 1975 a hitherto undisturbed grave was found. It belonged to Lady Hao, one of the sixty-four wives of a powerful Shang monarch. That she was an important wife of the king is proved by the fre-

documents of that era have survived. Thus the Hsia dynasty remains prehistoric.

The Shang dynasty was centered in modern-day Honan province (an area south of the Yellow River in northeastern China). We are not sure of the extent of its political power or its relationship with the peoples of central and eastern China. Since the systematic excavation of its last capital at Anyang began in 1928, scores of other Shang sites have been found and investigated. Some major sites may have been earlier capitals of the dynasty. For example, Chengchow in northern Honan was probably the second Shang capital, called Ao in the ancient records. Excavations have been in progress at Chengchow since the 1950s, and study of the findings reveals that the area was continuously occupied since Neolithic times. The city was rectangular in shape, surrounded by a wall of rammed earth estimated to have been more than thirty feet in height, more than sixty feet at the base, and almost two and a half miles in circumference. As with the

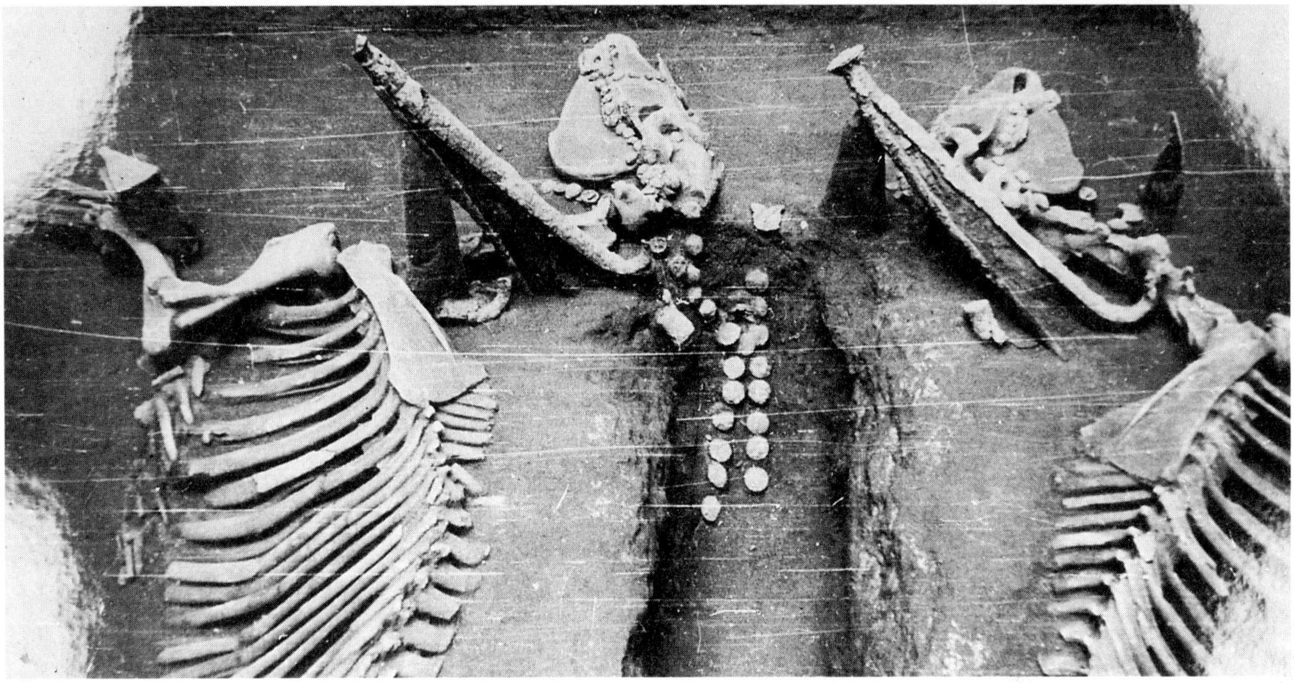

Royal Tombs at Anyang. Twelve kings were buried in huge underground tombs at the royal cemetery at Anyang, the last Shang capital. They were interred with thousands of precious items such as bronze ritual vessels and weapons, jades, and ivory ornaments. Dogs, horses, and slaves were sacrificed and buried in the tombs to serve their masters in the next world. This picture shows the remains of two horses lying in front of the chariot they once pulled. Robert Harding Picture Library

quency in which her name appeared in oracle bone inscriptions and by the lavishness of her grave. She led troops in war, owned her own estates, and was the mother of some of the king's children. Thus she merited an elaborate send-off to the next life. Her grave contains the remains of sixteen sacrificed humans and six dogs. It also held more than 1,600 objects, including many bronzes, jades, ivories, pottery, stone carvings, and 7,000 cowrie shells (used as currency). Originally, a building stood over the grave; it was used for ceremonies and sacrifices conducted in her honor.

The key "documents" that give us an understanding of the Shang dynasty are 20,000 inscribed oracle bones buried in Shang government archives. Questions to the gods were written on these bones, and answers from the gods were recorded there as well. Modern Chinese writing evolved from the script incised into these bones, usually the scapula bones of oxen or the inner shells of tortoises. Most of the words have been deciphered. We know that Shang scribes kept government records that they wrote down with brush and ink on slips of bamboo or wood that were bound together and rolled up in the fashion of modern slat screens, but these have long since perished. Some Shang bronze ritual vessels also had inscriptions cast into their lids or bases, but they contained only a few characters identifying the vessel and the clan names of the owners.

Shang Government

The oracle bones were used for divination, the art of telling future events by consulting the supernatural, a practice found worldwide that was also used by Neolithic peoples in China. Not until the Anyang period of the Shang dynasty did the bones contain writing. The Shang king's diviner would inscribe a question on the prepared bone or shell, dig a small pit part way through the piece, and then apply a heated metal rod to the pit, which would cause the shell or bone to crack. The nature of the crack indicated the answer. A typical bone or shell contains a date, followed by "The diviner X asks on behalf of the king . . ."; then comes the question, for example: "Is the drought caused by ancestor X?" or "If we raise an army of 3,000 men to drive X away from Y, will we succeed?" The diviner then recorded the answer. A final statement sometimes gave the outcome, which sometimes differed from the first answer. Many oracles were in the nature of reports to ancestors. Since it was believed that the spirits of royal ancestors could influence events, Shang monarchs regularly offered elaborate sacrifices to propitiate those spirits.

The Shang is a historic dynasty because in addition to archaeological evidence, we now possess copious contemporary documentation about it deciphered from the oracle bone inscriptions. The king's relationship to the

Royal Tombs in Bronze Age Greece and China

Many ancient cultures buried artifacts with the dead for use in the next world. Believing that the dead would need many of the same objects they had used in this world, ancient peoples included luxuries and items of daily use in the tombs. Discovery of these ancient tombs helps posterity reconstruct life in bygone times. Excavated tombs of Bronze Age rulers of Mycenaean Greece corroborate descriptions of objects in Homer's *Iliad,* just as the royal graves of Shang dynasty rulers at Anyang authenticate passages of the *Book of History* and the *Book of Poetry.* Conversely, the Aryans who settled in northern India after 1500 B.C.E. cremated their dead, so there are no grave sites to substantiate accounts in the *Vedas* and other literary works about that era in Indian history.

The following passage describes burial objects found by Heinrich Schliemann during his excavation of one of six shaft graves inside the city wall at Mycenae in Greece:

> The five bodies in Grave IV had been literally smothered in costly burial offerings. . . . Among the finds were . . . a silver vase in the form of a bull's head . . . with golden horns . . . ; three remarkable and awe-inspiring gold face masks . . . , apparently modeled on the actual features of the deceased; two large gold signet rings showing chariot scenes of battle and hunting; a massive gold bracelet; gold breastplates, diadems and a "shoulder-belt"; nine golden goblets and vases, including the famous "cup of Nestor"; . . . more than 400 beads of amber; . . . thirty-two copper cauldrons; . . . various adornments for armor and

weapons; obsidian arrowheads; perforated boar's tusks; forty-six bronze swords and daggers; four lances; three knives; numerous terra-cotta vases.*

The next passage is from an archaeological report listing items found in the tomb of a Chinese queen from the Shang dynasty in the fourteenth centure B.C.E. The tomb included human sacrificial victims, slaves killed to serve their masters in the next world.

> At lease sixteen human [sacrificial victims] were buried in the tomb. . . . There were also six dogs . . . more than 1,600 objects in addition to almost 7,000 pieces of cowrie shells [used as large-denomination money]. Of the 1,600 plus buried objects, there were more than 440 bronze pieces, over 590 jade items, over 560 bone objects; in addition there were over 70 stone objects, several ivory carvings, pottery objects, two made from sea shells and one from a large sea shell. After preliminary study of the burial items, and the deciphering of the inscriptions on the bronze vessels, it would seem that most of them had been the accumulated possessions of the owner of the grave; and that a minority of the pieces had been made expressly as sacrificial items of the person buried.**

*William A. McDonald, *Progress into the Past: The Rediscovery of Mycenaean Civilization* (Bloomington: Indiana University Press, 1967), pp. 61–62.
**Kaogu Xuebao, Peking Institute of Archaeology, Chinese Academy of Social Sciences (1977), pp. 59–60, trans. Jiu-Hwa L. Upshur.

---

ancestor who was the object of a sacrifice was important and was always clearly stated, allowing reconstruction of clear genealogies of the royal family. Oracle bone inscriptions also provide information about Shang government, state, society, and economy, as well as insights into the kings' private lives and relationships with their ancestors. The inscriptions have also corroborated much of the information about the Shang recorded in later histories.

The king was the central focus of both the Shang and the succeeding Chou dynasties. A poem written during the early Chou proclaimed:

> Everywhere under Heaven
> Is no land that is not the king's.
> To the borders of all those lands
> None is but the king's slave.

Historians are not sure whether the Shang state and society were based on tribal alliances or a form of feudalism, in which the king delegated power to noblemen who owed him allegiance and responsibilities such as taxes and contribution of troops in war. We do know that from

his capital city, the king ruled through a complex and highly stratified governmental network. Numerous offices and titles are mentioned in the oracle bone inscriptions, but we are not sure of the functions of many of them. Only the king could consult and offer sacrifices to his ancestors and other spirits. Although this was an important source of the king's power and its results affected the whole nation, the king himself, unlike the Egyptian pharaoh, was not considered divine. Ancestors and their living descendants had reciprocal obligations; therefore, for the health and safety of the state, the king had to offer the correct sacrifices to the particular ancestor at the appropriate times. A proper offering should secure the desired response from the ancestral spirit. The king should then make another offering to the ancestor in thanksgiving. This concept of reciprocal responsibility is the essence of ancestor worship as practiced by the Chinese.

The king was responsible for correct relations not only with ancestral spirits but with the wider spirit world as well. The most important spirit was the impersonal high god called Ti, who appointed kings to rule on his behalf and demanded moral uprightness and integrity from all kings, a concept called the mandate of heaven. Heaven appointed a worthy man to rule and allowed him to pass the kingship to his descendants so long as they ruled with justice and compassion and carried out their religious duties. If they failed to do so, heaven would cut its mandate and appoint another ruler.

Shang kings also led their troops in war. Sometimes calling up 5,000 or more men at a time, they conducted campaigns against neighboring groups, some of which belonged to non-Chinese cultures and were referred to as "barbarians." At first the Shang kings made war mostly in North China, but later they expanded southward along the coast and probably into the Yangtze region. The king and the nobles rode to battle in horse-drawn chariots. They and the common soldiers used a variety of bronze weapons, including axes, spears, daggers, and metal-tipped arrows. Prisoners of war were enslaved and might be sacrificed at royal burials or buried in building foundations. When not warring, the kings and their nobles held large hunts for sport and for food.

Society and Economy during the Shang Era

A great gap existed between the rulers and the ruled in Shang society. At the top of society were the royal and aristocratic families, who were organized according to patrilineal clans and kept careful genealogies. Since the royal family and the nobles practiced polygyny (one man with more than one wife), and since the economy could not have supported an ever-increasing leisure class, it is reasonable to assume that some offspring of the nobility must have been regularly demoted to commoner status. Nobles were rewarded with strings of cowrie shells acquired from South China and Southeast Asia, which were probably used for major transactions. There was also an artisan class such as jade carvers and bronzesmiths, who lived in or around the towns. We do not know their social status, but since they performed services that required skills, it is reasonable to assume that they were well treated. Most of the trade must have been in barter form since there was no coinage beside the cowrie shells.

At the bottom of society were the slaves. Some slaves were acquired deliberately in wars against the Shang's non-Chinese neighbors, while others were convicted criminals who were enslaved as punishment. Slaves were often sacrificed in royal burials and in other rituals. The vast majority of the people, however, were not slaves. They were farmers, who probably had the status of serfs, meaning that they were tied to the land and had to give part of their crops to their lord.

By Shang times the hunting-herding-farming economy of the Neolithic Age had given way to a predominantly farming one. Where the land was arable, the landscape was dotted with villages of semisubterranean houses of adobe and thatch. Fieldwork was primarily for men; the common word meaning "male" is a pictograph that combines a symbol representing a field and another meaning work. Since bronze was a luxury metal, farming implements were made of wood, bone, or stone. The major crops were millet, barley, wheat, and vegetables. Women tended silkworms, spun, and wove cloth. Domesticated animals include horses (used for chariot pulling only, not for riding or fieldwork), oxen, pigs, sheep, dogs, and fowl. Pork was the staple meat. Animal bones and tusks were used for arrowheads, small tools, and ornaments. Animals were sacrificed in ancestral and other rites; their

Shang Oracle Bones. Thousands of inscribed tortoise shells and scapula bones have been unearthed in Anyang, the last Shang capital. Used for divination, they are the earliest surviving examples of Chinese writing and are a rich storehouse of information on the Shang dynasty. Courtesy of the C. V. Starr East Asian Library, Columbia University

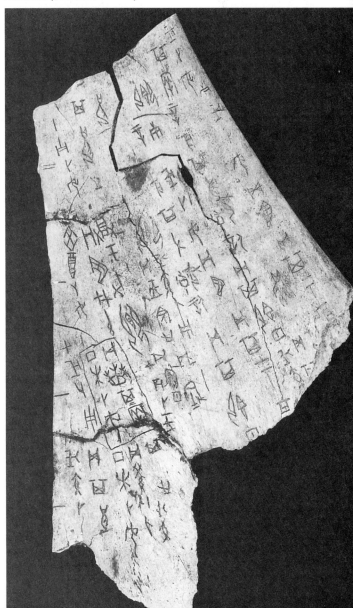

Feasting in Bronze Age Greece and China

We have considerable evidence of foods consumed by Bronze Age people. Although little documentary evidence about the diet of ordinary people is available, great literary writings from ancient Europe and Asia depict the feasts of rulers, nobles, and heroes.

The following excerpt is from Homer's *Odyssey*. The hero Odysseus has been washed ashore in the land of the peace-loving and somewhat decadent Phaiakians, who show him much hospitality and assist him on his journey home. In the passage quoted here, the Phaiakian king, Alkinoös, has ordered a great feast for his distinguished visitor, complete with musical entertainment by the blind minstrel Demodokos, who may be a self-portrait by Homer.

> [They] made their way to the great house of Alkinoös,
>   and the porticoes and enclosures and rooms were
>   filled with people
> assembling, there were many men there, both old and
>   young ones,
> and for them Alkinoös made a sacrifice, twelve sheep,
>   eight
> pigs with shining tusks, and two drag-footed oxen.
> These they skinned and prepared and made the lovely
>   feast ready.
> The herald came near, bringing with him the excellent
>   singer . . . .
> Pontonoös set a silver-studded chair out for him
> in the middle of the feasters . . .
> and set beside him a table and a fine basket,
> and beside him a cup to drink whenever his spirit desired
>   it.*

The second quotation, from the Chou dynasty, vividly describes the delicacies and sumptuous dishes that fam-

ily members have prepared in hopes of enticing the soul of a departed loved one to share the meal. The Chinese have always prepared elaborate dishes to commemorate special occasions involving beloved deceased family members. After ceremonially entreating the souls to enjoy their offerings, family members sit down to the lavish meal.

The Summons of the Soul

> Oh soul, come back! Why should you go far away?
> All your household have come to do you honour; all
>   kinds of good food are ready;
> Rice, broom-corn, early wheat, mixed all with yellow
>   millet;
> Bitter, salt, sour, hot and sweet; there are dishes of
>   all flavours.
> Ribs of fatted ox cooked tender and succulent;
> Sour and bitter blended in the soup of Wu;
> Stewed turtle and roast kid, served up on yam sauce;
> Geese cooked in sour sauce, cassaroled duck, fried
>   flesh of the great crane;
> Braised chicken, seethed tortoise, high-seasoned, but not
>   to spoil the taste;
> Fried honey-cakes of rice flour and malt-sugar
>   sweetmeats;
> Jadelike wine, honey-flavored, fills the winged cups;
> Ice-cooled liquor, strained of impurities, clear wine,
>   cool and refreshing;
> Here are laid out the patterned ladles, and here is
>   sparkling wine.**

*Richmond Lattimore, trans., *The Odyssey of Homer* (New York: Harper, 1965), pp. 122–123.
**K. C. Chang, ed., *Food in Chinese Culture: Anthropological and Historical Perspectives* (New Haven: Yale University Press, 1977), p. 32.

meat was probably eaten later. Animals were also buried with their owners.

There is no indication in Shang times or in later ages that the Chinese used milk or milk products from any of their milk-producing animals. Yet they were in constant contact with nomadic herders living on the northern rim of their world whose diet was heavy on milk products. In fact, one can observe a contrast in dietary patterns among the peoples of Europe and Asia based on their use or avoidance of dairy products. In East Asia the people of China, Korea, Japan, Indochina, and Malaya do not use milk products, while all Indo-Europeans (including the Aryans of India), the Semites, Scythians, Turks, and Mongols have used them since early times. The reason for this difference is not clear.

Science, Arts, and Crafts

Chinese tradition says that the Yellow Emperor first established the sixty-year cycle as the basis of calculating time and that the Hsia dynasty fixed the lunar calendar of 366 days a year. Even today the Chinese call the lunar calendar on which their traditional festivals are based the Hsia calendar. Many oracle bones of the Shang recorded solar and lunar eclipses and noted predictions of their occurrences. From this it would seem that the men who cast oracles were also astronomers and mathematicians. Records show that the decimal system originated during the Shang and was in use at least by the fourteenth century B.C.E. The ability to chart the movement of heavenly bodies, predict eclipses, regulate the calendar, and define

Shang Bronzes. Bronze ritual vessels made by Shang craftsmen are unsurpassed in artistry and technical virtuosity. Most are richly ornamented with stylized animal masks whose meanings are lost. Many have survived because they were buried with the dead. The Nelson-Atkins Museum of Art, Kansas City, MO (Purchase: Nelson Trust) 41–43

the agricultural season became recognized as the prerequisites for rulership. The Shang oracle specialists were probably the predecessors of the board of astronomers of the Chinese government of later eras.

The most remarkable products of the Shang dynasty are bronze ritual vessels that art historians consider unequaled in technical excellence and beauty. The art of bronze casting developed around 2000 B.C.E., in the Late Neolithic Age. In early West Asia, India, and Europe, bronze was made by the lost-wax method: a wax model of the object is encased in a clay mold; as molten metal is poured in, the wax melts (is lost) and is replaced by the metal. In contrast, the Chinese cast their vessels in ceramic piece molds. This way very large vessels could be made with complex decorations (the largest Shang vessels found weigh about 1,500 pounds). This method of bronze casting came naturally to the Chinese, who were already skilled in pottery making. Indeed, Shang potters made a high-fired, glazed pottery close to stoneware. Shang pottery and bronze pieces often shared the same shapes and forms of decoration. Pottery making was widespread, but bronze foundries were found only near major urban centers where they constituted large-scale operations with divisions of labor. Bronzesmiths must have been respected artisans.

Art historians have classified over two dozen distinct forms of bronze ritual vessels, which fall into three categories according to use: for storage, for food, and for liquids, mainly alcoholic beverages. Most pieces were decorated, some elaborately, with stylized masks of real or mythological birds and animals arranged symmetrically. Styles of decoration varied with time and region from abstract to realistic. Many pieces survived because they were buried with the dead, as the practice of ancestor worship dictated. For over 1,000 years, Chinese connoisseurs have collected Shang ritual bronze pieces; early collectors attributed magical qualities to these unearthed treasures, a belief that led to the looting of early tombs. Shang bronzesmiths also made weapons, chariot fittings, horse harnesses, and mirrors.

Shang artisans also worked extensively in jade and other materials. Like bronze, jade was a luxury item used in rituals and buried with the dead. The Shang jade carvers improved upon the skills of their Neolithic forebears. Their raw material came from the northwest, an area now called Chinese Turkestan, a considerable distance from the

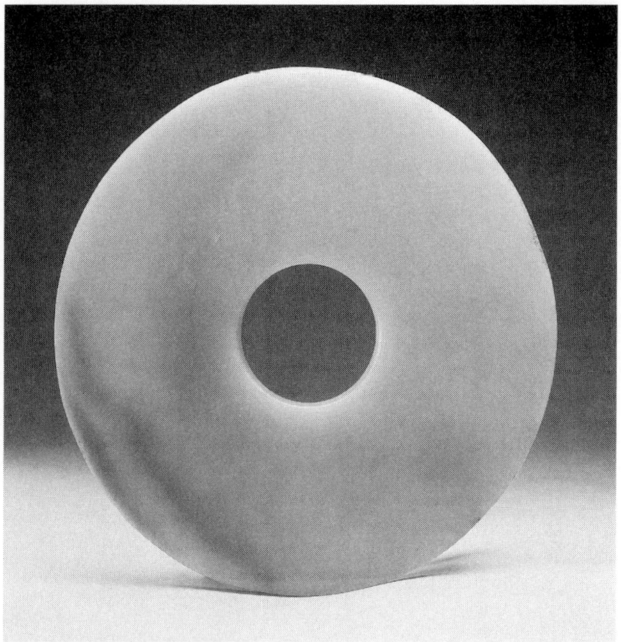

Jade Disk. From time immemorial, a circular disk with a perforated center was used in rituals to symbolize heaven. This jade disk dates to the period between the Late Neolithic Age and the Shang dynasty in the late second millennium B.C.E. The yellow nephrite jade came from central Asia, and its presence in China is evidence of long-distance trade. National Palace Museum, Taipei, Taiwan, Republic of China

Shang urban centers. The abundance of jade and cowrie shells in Shang culture, both of which came from lands beyond Shang political control, indicates international trade. Shang artisans also fashioned utilitarian and decorative objects from stone, ivory, and bone. They invented lacquer by extracting sap from a lacquer tree and applying the liquid to a surface such as wood to form a glossy, waterproof coating. They also worked in gold and silver. Gold was not abundant in ancient China, however, and gold objects did not have the significance there that they did in most other early cultures.

A Pictographic Script

Although signs and symbols are found on pottery as early as 5000 B.C.E., they are isolated and cannot be considered written language. The earliest extant written records date to the fourteenth century B.C.E., by which time the script exhibited a maturity of stylization that presupposes a centuries-long evolution.

Chinese writing is unrelated to other writings. It is a nonalphabetic script, consisting of symbols or graphs. A good modern dictionary will list more than 40,000 graphs, most of which have evolved since Shang times. There are three basic kinds of graphs: (1) Pictographs are conventionalized picture symbols of an object such as the sun or moon. (2) Ideographs frequently are formed by combining two or more pictographs; for example, pictographs of the sun and moon, placed side by side, mean "bright" or "brilliant." (3) Logographs are formed by combining either a pictograph or an ideograph to indicate meaning with a symbol to provide a key to the pronunciation. For example, the pictograph of a horse is pronounced "ma"; when it is combined with the pictograph for woman, the new word is still pronounced "ma" but means mother. The great majority of words in the Chinese vocabulary are logographs. All three kinds of graphs were evident in late Shang writing.

The Chou Dynasty

*Now that the king has received the mandate, unbounded is the grace, but also unbounded is the solicitude. Oh, how can he be but careful! Heaven has removed and made an end to the great state Yin's mandate. There are many former wise kings of Yin in Heaven, and the later kings and people here managed their mandate. But in the end [under the last king] wise and good men lived in misery so that, leading their wives and carrying their children, wailing and calling to Heaven, they went to where no one could come and seize them. Oh, Heaven had pity on the people of the four quarters, and looking with affection and giving its mandate, it employed the zealous ones [the leaders of the Chou]. May the king now urgently pay careful attention to his virtue . . . may he not neglect the aged elders. Then he will comprehend our ancient men's virtue, nay, still more it will occur that he is able to comprehend and endeavor to follow Heaven.**

*William T. de Bary, ed., *Sources of Chinese Tradition*, vol. 1 (New York: Columbia University Press, 1960), p. 11.

Thus the people of China heard their new Chou rulers justify their conquest of the Shang (Yin) dynasty as the will or mandate of heaven. Around 1120 B.C.E. the leaders of the Chou from northwestern China overthrew the Shang dynasty and set up their own rule. They then issued a series of proclamations to explain to the people why they had overthrown the Shang and why the people should submit to their rule. Appealing to the mandate of heaven, they told their new subjects that the last Shang king had forfeited his right to rule by his personal immorality and tyrannical government. Ti had then cut off the Shang's mandate to rule and transferred it to the deserving house of Chou. The concept of the mandate of heaven has remained the cornerstone of Chinese political thinking down to the twentieth century.

After the overthrow of the Shang in 1122 B.C.E., the Chou established the longest-lasting dynasty in Chinese history, ending in 256 B.C.E. This long period is subdivided into the Western Chou (1122–771 B.C.E.) and the Eastern Chou (770–256 B.C.E.).

The Chou Conquest

Toughened by years of fighting non-Chinese tribes, the Chou people emerged out of the plain of Chou, situated on the northwestern frontier of the agricultural basin of North China. Shang oracle bone inscriptions described them at different times as enemies and as allies. Although the Shang had looked on the Chou as semibarbarous country cousins, around the beginning of the twelfth century B.C.E. a Shang king made an alliance with the house of Chou by giving a kinswoman to the Chou leader in marriage and then conferring on him the title Chief of the West.

Parts of the earliest texts that have survived, the *Shu Ching* (Book of History) and *Shih Ching* (Book of Poetry) were written during the early Chou and described and justified their destruction of the Shang. The first undoubtedly historic leader of the Chou was King Wen (the Cultivated or Accomplished), who laid plans to take on the Shang. The *Shu Ching* justified his actions as being in obedience to heaven's wishes.

King Wen's son, King Wu (the Martial), defeated and destroyed the Shang. In accounts that clearly show a Chou bias, King Shou, the last Shang ruler, is described as dying a well-deserved death in his burning palace at Yin as the dynasty fell to Chou troops. Wu died soon after his victory and left the throne to his young son. Because the new king was only a boy, his uncle, the Duke of Chou, became regent. The duke completed the conquest of Shang lands and laid down the institutional basis for what became a long-lived dynasty. He lectured his nephew about the duties of the ruler and the people about bowing to the will of heaven. When his nephew came of age, the duke handed over the reins of government and retired. Chinese have ever since celebrated King Wen, King Wu, and the Duke of Chou as three of their greatest rulers and the early Chou as a golden age.

Several documentary sources contribute to our knowledge of the early Chou. Although Chou rulers also used divination to find out the will of heaven and of their ancestors, their oracle bones did not contain lengthy inscriptions. Instead, the Chou cast lengthy inscriptions on the surfaces of their bronze ceremonial vessels to document and report to their ancestors major events such as victories and the granting of fiefdoms to royal relatives or allies.

In addition to the information provided by the inscribed vessels, some documents in the *Shu Ching,* and some of the poems in the *Shih Ching,* we also have the *Li Chi* (Book of Rituals), which describes the organization of the Chou government and the rituals, ceremonies, and etiquette of the Chou court. Tradition says that the *Li Chi* was written by the Duke of Chou. Since the duke, his brother, and his father were considered exemplary rulers, later generations regarded the *Li Chi* as describing a golden age worthy of study and emulation.

Ruling a land approximately the size of modern France, Chou kings were unable to govern the entire kingdom effectively. Accordingly, they devised a political and economic system called feudalism. The king ruled a royal domain directly; he also supervised a central government assisted by six ministers, each responsible for an aspect of administration. The king assigned the remaining land as fiefdoms to his relatives and created marriage ties with meritorious nonrelatives, who also received fiefdoms. Assisted by royal inspectors, these lords administered the king's laws in their domains; they were expected to visit the royal court at prescribed intervals as demonstrations of their loyalty, to contribute substantive revenues to the king's treasury as well as symbolic tribute, and to provide military contingents when needed. The lords received their titles at investiture ceremonies at the Chou ancestral temple, and their heirs had to be confirmed by the king. Each fiefdom was called a *kuo,* represented by a pictograph of a walled and guarded territory. The Chou royal domain, the heartland of the nation, was called *chung-kuo,* meaning "central state." Later *chung-kuo* came to mean the Middle Kingdom or China.

Society and Economy in the Chou Era

The early Chou kings were city builders. Likewise the nobles built smaller towns from which they ruled their domains. The proliferation of archaeological sites throughout this long dynasty shows population growth and a trend toward urbanization. This trend was especially pronounced during the Eastern Chou; records show that at least seventy-eight cities were built between 722 and 480 B.C.E.

Hao, capital of the Western Chou (situated in the Chou homeland), and Loyang, built by the Duke of Chou as a second capital to administer the eastern conquests (and later the capital of the Eastern Chou), would under various names be the sites of China's capital for the next 2,000 years. So many Chou sites have been identified and excavated that a picture of the urban life of that time can be reconstructed. Most early Chou towns were administrative and ceremonial centers and were walled and fortified.

As under the Shang, rank and position were inherited, so people can be classified according to their hereditary social classes. At the top of the social ladder were the aristocrats, starting with members of the royal family; they were followed by a graded nobility down to the knights. The aristocrats were polygynous, organized into

Heaven then greatly ordered Wen Wang [King Wen] to destroy the great Yin [Shang] and greatly received its mandate; its state and people as a result became orderly. In contrast: "He [King Shou, last ruler of the Shang] was greatly excessive in wine. He did not think of ceasing his licentiousness. His heart was malign and he was unable to fear death. Crimes existed in the city of Shang and in the state of Yin, but for the extinction he had no anxiety. . . . Therefore heaven sent down destruction on Yin and had no mercy for Yin, it was due to his excesses. Heaven is not tyrannical, people themselves draw guilt upon themselves.*

* * *

King Wen is on high;
Oh, he shines in heaven!
Chou is an old people,
But the charge is new.
The leaders of Chou became illustrious;
Was not God's charge timely given?

King Wen ascends and descends
On the left and right of God.

August was King Wen,
Continuously bright and reverent.
Great, indeed, was the appointment of Heaven.
There were Shang's grandsons and sons,
Shang's grandsons and sons;
Was their number not a hundred thousand?
But the Lord-on-High gave his command
And they bowed down to Chou.

The charge is not easy to keep;
May it not end in your person.
Display and make bright your good fame,
And consider what Yin received from Heaven.
The doings of high Heaven
Have no sound, no smell.
Make King Wen your pattern
And all the states will trust you.**

Early Chou rulers frequently lectured their newly conquered subject peoples. They insisted that it was heaven's will that the people obey their new masters. In applying a moral dimension to rulership, however, the early Chou kings were introducing a double-edged weapon. In other words, heaven could just as easily turn against them if they failed to live up to high standards, as shown in the poem from the *Book of Poetry,* written soon after the Chou conquest. It sums up the Chou propaganda asserting that heaven has given them the right to rule because of their moral leadership. Conversely, it condemns the immorality of the last Shang king and explains how he forfeited the right to rule for himself and his descendants.

*The Chinese Classics, vol. 3, part 2, The Book of History, trans. James Legge (London: Trubner, 1865), pp. 284–288.
**William T. de Bary, ed., Sources of Chinese Tradition, vol. 1 (New York: Columbia University Press, 1960), pp. 12–13.

patrilineal clans, and concerned with keeping careful genealogies of their families. Unlike India, China had no priestly class after the Shang, because the kings and nobles officiated at their own ancestral sacrifices and ceremonies and appealed directly to their ancestors' spirits.

Farmers were serfs, bound to the land they tilled, and transferred with the land whenever it was invested in a new lord. Late Chou writers described an idealized land tenure system that they attributed to the Duke of Chou and called the well-field system. The name comes from the pictograph for a well (for drawing water), which resembles a tick-tack-toe design with nine components. Supposedly, early Chou villages were divided into units of eight families, each farming a plot. Villagers lived in the central plot (the ninth one), where presumably the well was located, and farmed it in common for the lord. Such a detailed land distribution was probably impossible for an ancient government. Yet the concept is so simple and just that it has inspired every reformer in China down to the twentieth century. It is another reason that later Chinese recall the early Chou as a golden age.

Artisans congregated in towns to serve the needs of the governing nobles and lived in their separate quarters. They probably enjoyed a higher status than the serfs. As the population grew, so did trade and a merchant class. Merchants and artisans in Chou China, as in medieval Europe, had no defined place in the feudal hierarchy, as they had in the Indian caste system. Slavery declined under the Chou, and slaves did not play an important role economically. Few excavated Chou tombs contain remains of human sacrificial victims.

As in Shang times, cowrie shells, strung in decimal units, were the big-denomination currency. Records tell of kings awarding lords ten to twenty strings of cowrie shells for meritorious service, and the notable event would be inscribed in a specially cast bronze vessel. Standard lengths of silk rolled in bolts, jade, pearls, dogs, horses, and measures of grain were also used as media of exchange. Metal coins did not come into widespread use until the fifth century B.C.E.

By the sixth century B.C.E., a number of major improvements in agriculture had taken place and become widespread: irrigation, animal-drawn plows, crop rotation, and fertilization. During the fifth century, iron farming implements were introduced. These improvements revolutionized agriculture, increased food production,

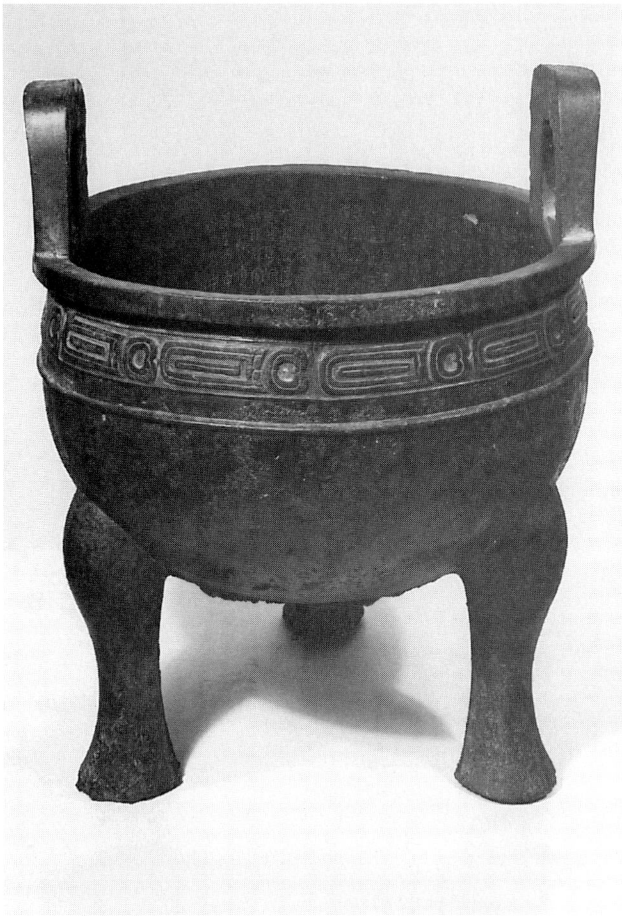

Inscribed Bronze Cauldron. Much of our knowledge of the early Chou dynasty comes from long inscriptions on bronze vessels that were cast to commemorate important events. This monumental three-legged cauldron, commissioned by the Duke of Mao, has a 500-word inscription cast into the interior (a rubbing of the inscription is shown below). National Palace Museum, Taipei, Taiwan, Republic of China

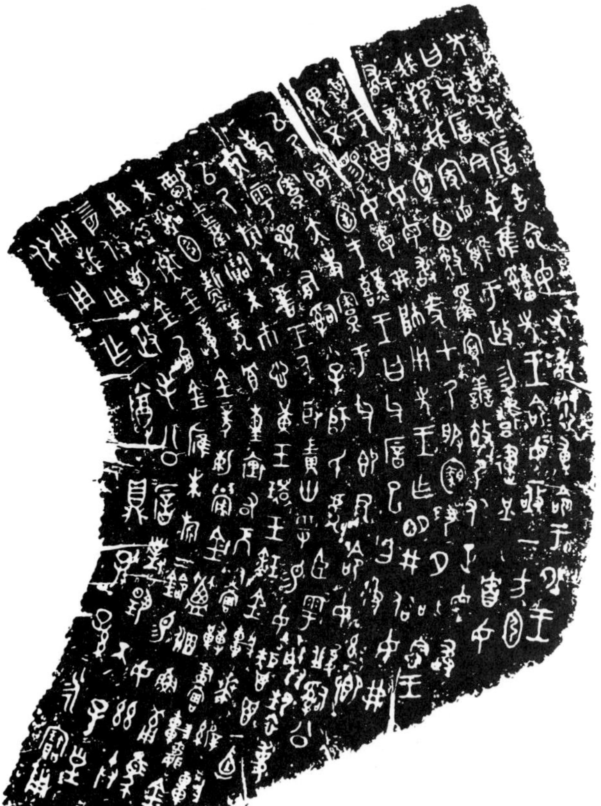

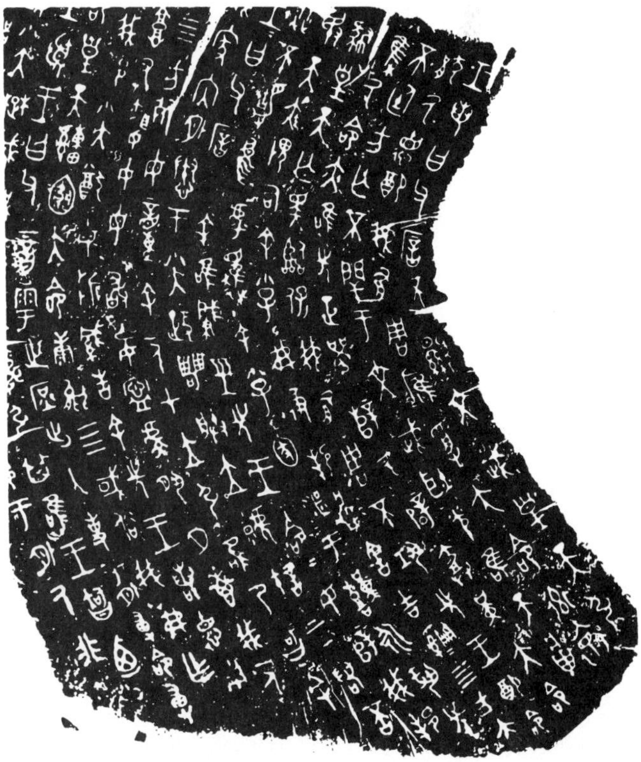

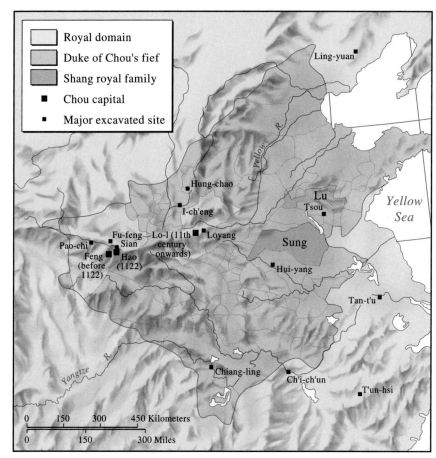

❊ MAP 2.3 Western Chou China, Eleventh to Ninth Centuries B.C.E. The victorious house of Chou divided its territories into fiefs and granted them to relatives, allies, and even surviving relatives of the previous Shang dynasty, while retaining only a core territory that it ruled directly as *chung-kuo* or royal (central) domain. During its initial centuries, the Chou royal house was powerful and exercised control over the feudal vassals.

and led to rapid population growth. Chinese began to move into lands hitherto occupied by aboriginal tribes. As land became scarce, all available land was used more intensively, and hunting and herding as a way of life were gradually abandoned in favor of agriculture.

Chou Religion

The religious practices of the Shang continued and evolved during the Chou period. The specialists or priests who had cast and inscribed oracle bones for Shang kings seem to have disappeared, and owing to the dominance of ancestor worship in religious life, they were not replaced by other priests or magicians. From king to commoner, each person invoked his own ancestors for blessing and assistance, and every family's life centered on its ancestral temple or shrine. All believed that in the life following death one would need essentially the same things one had needed on earth. Hence people buried food, drink, and other material goods, according to what they could afford, with the dead. The practice of sacrificing humans and animals to serve the powerful in death declined and died out, however, and came to be denounced in later Chou writings. Concern for the family extended to the future as well as the past. Most of the

commemorative bronze vessels cast and inscribed by Chou lords contained the following sentence, which expressed the hope that their descendants would be filial and remember them as they remembered their ancestors: "May my sons and grandsons forever treasure and use this vessel."

The king's ancestral temple was the center of affairs for the kingdom. All important state affairs took place there, and all events of consequence were reported to the king's ancestral spirits. Several separate altars were constructed, each for a specific purpose; for example, one was for worshiping heaven, another was for worshiping earth and the soil, and still others were in honor of various spirits. It was the king's responsibility to officiate at ceremonies in honor of heaven, the soil, and the various spirits at appropriate times.

In time, Ti, the high god of the Shang, came to be identified with Tien or heaven, the chief Chou deity. Tien may have begun as the "great man," as its pictograph, clearly that of a man, would suggest. In time, Tien became a "Great Spirit," a vast, impersonal, supreme deity. The Chou ruler bore the title of *wang*, or king, as had the Shang sovereign. However, in accordance with the doctrine that the Chou rulers had inherited the mandate of heaven, the Chou monarch was also called Son of

Heaven. This mandate theoretically could only be maintained by their descendants if they, too, carried out heaven's wishes. Otherwise, as had happened to the Shang, the mandate could be revoked and transferred to a more worthy recipient.

The Eastern Chou

During the dynasty's first three centuries, the Chou rulers expanded their realm and united all of North China under their rule. With the passing of time, however, early kinship ties loosened, the kings' authority declined, and the feudal lords began to identify more with their hereditary territories than with the royal court. By the ninth century, kings were experiencing difficulties in dealing with warlike barbarians in both the north and the south, and regional lords were beginning to ignore the king's orders and to fight among themselves. In 771 B.C.E., the king was killed in a campaign against a northern tribe, and the capital at Hao was overrun. The remnant government fled eastward to Loyang, which had been made the second capital of the dynasty by the Duke of Chou.

This flight marked the end of the exercise of real power by the Chou kings, who reigned but no longer ruled; in time, they were consulted only on such issues as genealogy and ritual. The period between 770 and 256 B.C.E. is called the Eastern Chou. The royal domain of the house of Chou was now tiny compared with the larger feudal states.

The Eastern Chou was an unstable and violent age, marked by many wars. Diplomacy was important, as evidenced by the many interstate alliances, often cemented by marriages. After 680 B.C.E., one ruler, but never the Chou king, was always recognized as the hegemon (*pa*), or predominant lord, who maintained some order. So many wars characterized the last 150 years of the Chou dynasty that it was called the Era of Warring States; during that time 132 states were finally reduced to one.

Since chariot warfare was unsuitable in the hilly northwest or in the wet Yangtze Valley, chariots were replaced by massed infantry and cavalry formations. If contemporary records can be believed, some states fielded infantry numbering in the hundreds of thousands. Military leaders who needed to counter the northern horse-riding nomads created cavalry units, which became the standard auxiliary of Chinese armies. By the fifth century more lethal iron weapons had replaced bronze ones. The crossbow, a Chinese invention that had a more powerful and longer draw than the composite bow and was worked by a precisely cast metal trigger mechanism, came into widespread use. Warfare became more destructive as a result.

In 256 B.C.E., King Cheng of the northwestern state of Ch'in eliminated the house of Chou; by 221 he had crushed the other warring states. In unifying all the land

❖ Bronze Bell. Most early Chou bronzes continued the Shang tradition, but new shapes were also introduced. This bell was part of a set; different-sized bells produced different notes when struck. Bells provided music during religious and court rituals. National Palace Museum, Taipei, Taiwan, Republic of China

that had once been in the Chou domain, he renamed the national dynasty Ch'in, which became China. That story will be covered in the next chapter.

Eastern Chou Society and Economy

The system of family government that had characterized the early Chou no longer sufficed for an increasingly complex society. Hereditary posts declined, replaced by a system in which promotions were determined by merit. For the first time in Chinese history, men of commoner status rose to important political positions. Most of the new bureaucrats, however, were not commoners, but belonged to the lower aristocracy of knights, called *shih*.

Others of the shih class who were disappointed in their quest for public office or who felt disaffected by the chaotic conditions became teachers and developed philosophies to correct the evils and problems of the age. Their ideas, too, will be explored in the next chapter.

The large number of cities built during the last centuries of the Chou indicates a growing population and the rise of a merchant class. Early Chou cities had been mostly administrative and religious centers created and inhabited by the feudal lords, their retainers, and the artisans who served their needs, but the new cities built during the Eastern Chou were industrial and commercial centers. Whereas the old cities had a wall that enclosed the lords' residences and government buildings, now a second enclosed area sometimes appeared for ordinary residential and commercial quarters. We have one population estimate for a city in the Warring States period: Lin-tzu, capital city of the state of Ch'i in northeastern China, had 70,000 households, or roughly a third of a million people. There are also accounts of Lin-tzu's bustling traffic, amusement quarters, street markets, and wholesale brokers' businesses.

Rulers eager to increase their revenues encouraged commerce. From the fifth century on, metal coinage became widespread. Inscriptions identified the states that issued the coins, and different sizes and weights distinguished the denominations. Early coins were shaped like miniature spades and knives. A round coin with a square hole in the center suitable for stringing was first issued by the state of Ch'in. After 221 B.C.E., that style became standard throughout China. Such coins strung in units of 1,000 remained the basic Chinese currency until the early twentieth century.

Three significant improvements in agriculture occurred during the Eastern Chou. First was water control, vital for bringing land in the upper Yellow River valley under cultivation, controlling floods, and allowing irrigated rice cultivation in the upper Yangtze plains. Engineers improved diking techniques, and systematic irrigation became widespread. Second was the introduction of fertilization and crop rotation. Third, and perhaps most important, was the introduction of iron farming implements, which significantly increased the amount of land an individual farmer could cultivate. Iron tools also facilitated the clearing of virgin lands. As the Chinese people expanded the area of land under cultivation and more intensely colonized the land they already occupied, the population rose to 60 million by the end of the era. As the population grew, the feudal land tenure system of the early Chou was gradually replaced with a system of freehold farmers. Rulers discovered that free farmers worked harder and produced more than land-bound serfs and also fought better to protect their interests. The northwestern frontier state of Ch'in took the lead in ending feudal land tenure and in building irrigation works. Both policies were key to the Ch'in's ultimate success in unifying China. By the end of the Chou dynasty, all the essential technological features of traditional Chinese farming had been introduced.

Summary and Comparisons

This chapter has examined the roots and early developments of two great Asian civilizations. In both India and China, the first civilizations grew directly from indigenous Neolithic cultures along or near major river valleys. Like the civilizations that arose farther west, these civilizations developed urban centers, commerce, art, and writing. Major archaeological work, begun in both India and China in the 1920s, has confirmed the information from some ancient texts and added enormous quantities of new knowledge.

The Indus civilization, a very advanced urban and trading culture, began in northwestern India about 2500 B.C.E. Also called the Harappan culture after one of the largest cities of the area and era, the civilization flourished for approximately one thousand years. Although the Indus people had a pictographic script, few characters have survived and they remain undeciphered. The huge cities along the Indus and beyond exhibited much uniformity and a high degree of urban organization and civic pride. They traded extensively among themselves and with the peoples of Mesopotamia.

After a period of gradual decline caused by extensive flooding and deforestation, the weakened Indus civilization fell by 1500 B.C.E. It was subsumed by the Aryans, Indo-European nomads from the steppes of Eurasia. The Aryans sacked and then abandoned some Indus cities, gradually settling along the Indus valley and later migrating eastward to the Gangetic Plain. They subjugated the darker-skinned indigenous people and developed a hierarchy of conquering and conquered peoples, which we call the caste system. The *Rig-Veda,* the most sacred text of the Aryans and of later Hinduism, contains hymns alluding to the Aryan conquest. It and other *Vedas* were composed and later written down in Sanskrit between 1500 and 500 B.C.E.

The millennium between approximately 1500 and 500 B.C.E. is divided into the Early and Late Vedic Ages because of significant differences between the two periods. By the Late Vedic Age, Aryan society had changed from predominantly pastoral to mainly agricultural, Aryan states had become territorial rather than tribal, and the economy had developed from predominantly subsistence to specialized and commercial.

These important social, political, and economic developments contributed to changing religious attitudes as well. Late Vedic Indians were no longer satisfied with the heroic gods of the *Rig-Veda* and the sacrificial cult of the brahmans. New religious ideas such as karma and reincarnation resulted in a widespread pessimistic outlook and soul searching for new answers. One outcome of this religious quest was the emergence into prominence of new gods and goddesses; another was the compiling of the *Upanishads,* a collection of essays that provided answers on human destiny. In time, the new deities and the *Upanishads* were incorporated into Hinduism.

China's Shang dynasty (1766–1122 B.C.E.) was centered in the Yellow River valley. Shang civilization was urban and literate and skilled in metallurgy. Twentieth-century archaeology in China has corroborated many of the early written records about the Shang dynasty as a historic era.

The oldest extant Chinese writing was incised on tortoise shells and scapula bones of large animals that were used for divination by Shang kings. These oracle bones tell us much about many aspects of Shang government, society, and beliefs. The modern Chinese language is directly descended from the script found on Shang remains.

The most beautiful objects from the Shang are bronze ritual vessels that were used in rites of ancestor worship and buried in royal and aristocratic tombs. They were made by the piece mold method, which is unique to China. Bronzesmiths and other craftsmen evidently enjoyed higher status than serfs, who farmed the land.

After ruling for approximately 600 years, the Shang dynasty was overthrown by the Chou in 1122 B.C.E. The Chou rulers in general continued beliefs and institutions as they found them, leaving Chinese civilization essentially unchanged. The Chou conquest, however, expanded the Chinese heartland geographically to include all of the Yellow River valley and the approaches to the Yangtze River valley. The gradual decline of the house of Chou after 771 B.C.E. resulted in political turmoil as powerful feudal lords competed for supremacy and for the right to impose a national dynasty on a reunified land.

There are striking similarities and notable differences between the two first great civilizations of South and East Asia. Both were rooted in indigenous Neolithic cultures; both were riverine, urban, literate, and metalworking. Both invented pictographic written scripts, which were unrelated. However, because the extensive written remains of the Shang have been deciphered, we know much more about this civilization than about that of the Indus valley, where the fewer extant writings engraved on seals are not yet understood. Our ability to decode Shang documents makes it a historic civilization, whereas the Indus remains prehistoric.

Contemporary documents give us information that cannot be gathered without them. For example, we know the names of all the kings of the Shang monarchy and their relations to one another. In contrast, we know nothing for certain about the Indus government or religion.

Because their buildings were constructed with bricks, there are extensive physical remains of Indus cities, whereas little survives of the wood and tamped-earth structures of the Shang. The Indus people buried their dead carefully in cemeteries; the Aryans, however, cremated their dead, a practice that continued in India, leaving archaeologists with few material remains. In China, on the other hand, the Shang and Chou peoples left tombs that are treasure troves because of the Chinese custom of burying the dead sumptuously with everything they might need in the next world.

The peoples of both India and China traded far afield. The Indus people traded with the older Mesopotamian civilization, where documents mention people we infer to be from the Indus region. There is no evidence as yet that the Vedic peoples carried on international trade, however. Both the Shang and the Chou traded with southeastern and central Asia, but these trading partners, being preliterate, left no written records.

Social organization is an area of sharp contrast. As the Vedic Age progressed, social delineations in India became sharper, apparently stemming from racial distinctions between the conquering Aryans and the indigenous dasas. In contrast, the Chinese were quite homogeneous racially, a factor that contributed to the gradual erasing of hereditary distinctions by the late Chou dynasty.

Both the Indus Empire and the Shang dynasty ended violently. While the Indo-Aryan conquerors had a different culture from the Indus people, on whom they imposed a new language, religion, and social organization, the Chou who overthrew the Shang shared the same traditions, beliefs, and written language, which continued to evolve uninterrupted by political change. For example, the Chou buried their dead with artifacts just as the Shang did, though they ended the human and animal sacrifices. Likewise Chou bronzewares were decorated like those of the Shang, showing shared artistic traditions and rituals. Thus the transition from one dynasty to another was much less disruptive in China than in India.

By the end of the Vedic Age in India and the Chou dynasty in China, each civilization had achieved a certain homogeneity. Homogeneity among Indians was based on shared religious beliefs, social organization, and, among northern Indians, languages derived from Sanskrit. Among Chinese, a common historical and political tradition, writing, and ancestor worship created cohesiveness. India had no tradition of political unity, but in China the ideal of political unity was indelibly rooted in the earliest folk memory.

Selected Sources

*Basham, A. L. *The Wonder That Was India.* 1954. Many maps and photos and a well-organized text make this book a pleasure to read.

———, ed. *Cultural History of India.* 1969. Numerous experts contributed to this informative book.

*Chang, Kwang-chih, ed. *Food in Chinese Culture: Anthropological and Historical Perspectives.* 1977. A storehouse of interesting information.

———. *Shang Civilization.* 1980. Professor Chang has pieced together a fascinating jigsaw puzzle from archaeological and textual evidence of China's first historic dynasty.

*———. *The Archaeology of Ancient China.* 4th ed. 1986. The most authoritative book on the subject. Many photos, illustrations, maps, and charts make it interesting and informative.

Cheng, Te-k'un. *Archaeology in China.* Vol. 1: *Prehistoric China.* 1986. A concise and clear account, with photos, charts, and maps.

———. *Archaeology in China.* Vol. 2: *Shang China.* 1960. Profusely illustrated with drawings and photos, this comprehensive book examines what archaeologists have learned about the Shang.

———. *Archaeology in China.* Vol. 3. *Chou China.* 1963. This book is as authoritative as Professor Cheng's other books in the series.

*de Bary, William T., ed. *Sources of Chinese Tradition.* Vol. 1. 1960. A source book of readings.

*———, ed. *Sources of Indian Tradition.* Vol. 1. 1958. A source book of readings with helpful introductions.

Fairservice, Walter A., Jr. *The Roots of Ancient India.* 1971. A comprehensive survey of India from the earliest humans to the Aryan invasion.

Feuerstein, Georg, Subash Kak, and David Frawley. *In Search of the Cradle of Civilization.* 1995. Provocative new studies and interpretations regarding ancient India.

*Hsu, Cho-yun. *Ancient China in Transition: An Analysis of Social Mobility, 722–222 B.C.* 1965. A brief, interesting account.

Ke, Yuan. *Dragons and Dynasties: An Introduction to Chinese Mythology.* 1993. Good stories, well explained.

Li, Chi. *Anyang.* 1977. Li supervised the first excavation of Anyang, the last Shang capital, during the 1920s and 1930s.

Majumdar, R. C. *Ancient India.* 1968. A clearly written history of India up to c. 1200 C.E.

———. *Concise History of Ancient India.* 3 vols. 1977. An authoritative work.

Piggott, S. *Prehistoric India.* 1950. Still the classic work on this subject.

Rawson, Jessica, ed. *Mysteries of Ancient China: New Discoveries of the Early Dynasties.* 1996. The first account in English of more than 200 new archaeological discoveries in China. Richly illustrated.

Smith, Brian K. *Classifying the Universe: The Ancient Indian Varna System and the Origins of Caste.* 1994. A scholarly book on the role of caste in ancient Indian religion and culture.

Spear, Percival, ed. *The Oxford History of India.* 4th ed. 1981. An authoritative book written by many experts and updated with new information.

*Temple, Robert. *The Genius of China: 3,000 Years of Science, Discovery and Invention.* 1986. Concise, well written, and beautifully illustrated, this book summarizes China's scientific contributions.

*Thapar, Romila. *A History of India.* Vol 1. 1968. A good, concise history from the beginning of Indian civilization to the sixteenth century.

Wagner, Donald B. *Iron and Steel in Ancient China.* 1993. Recent archaeological finds have been incorporated into this study of the development of an important technology.

Watson, William. *Early Civilization in China.* 1966. Lavishly illustrated and clearly written, this book traces the evolution of humans in China from Paleolithic times to the end of the Chou.

Wheeler, Mortimer. *The Indus Civilization: Supplementary Volume to the Cambridge History of India.* 3d ed. 1968. Written by the man who supervised the excavation of Harappa and other sites, with many photos and illustrations.

*Available in paperback.

Internet Links

Chronology: Ancient India
http://www.itihaas.com/ancient/index.html
> A helpful chronological outline with links to informative texts on the various eras and events of Indian history.

Harappa
http://www.harappa.com/welcome.html
> This very extensive site features detailed information about the Indus valley civilization; plentiful graphics with photographs, site plans, and maps; and a "walkabout" of the archaeological venue at Harappa.

Indus Valley Civilization Daily Life: 3000–1500 B.C.
http://members.aol.com/Donnclass/Indialife.html#INDUS
> This site provides information about daily life in ancient India, including food, clothing, housing, entertainment, transportation, and art. Links to other sites relevant to ancient Indian life and religion.

Timeline of the History of China
http://www.china5k.com/
> This is "the first interactive timeline representation of Chinese History, including culture, art, education, science, and government reference of China. The goal . . . is to enrich people's understanding about China and its culture through the electronic media."

The Upanishads
http://www.west.net/~beck/EC7-Upanishads.html
> This succinct summary of the *Upanishads,* their subject matter, ethical concepts, metaphysics, and key vocabulary includes well-selected quotations.

Great Faiths and Philosophies

1. And the angel of the Lord called unto Abraham . . . and said, "By myself have I sworn, says the Lord, for because you have done this thing, and have not withheld your son, your only son [Isaac]: That in blessing I will bless you, and in multiplying I will multiply your seed as the stars of the heaven, and as the sand which is upon the sea shore; and your seed shall possess the gate of his enemies; And in your seed shall all the nations of the earth be blessed; because you have obeyed my voice." (King James Version of the Holy Bible, Genesis, chapter 22, with slight changes)

2. Homer and Hesiod have ascribed to the gods everything shameful and reprehensible among mankind: theft, adultery, and mutual deceptions. (Xenophanes)

3. Regarding the gods, I can't tell if they exist or not, nor what they look like, for many things preclude such knowledge: the obscurity of the subject, and the brevity of our lives. (Protagoras)

4. We don't know yet how to serve men, how can we know about serving spirits? . . .

Devote yourself to the proper demands of the people, respect the ghosts and spirits but keep them at a distance—this may be called wisdom. (Confucius)

Although all peoples across the globe have believed in some supernatural power over the universe, their conceptions of that power have varied. The passages quoted here show some of these differing attitudes. Thus, in Judaism an all-powerful, monotheistic deity makes a promise to Abraham as the representative of the Hebrew people. In Greek religion, by contrast, polytheistic deities were often depicted as exhibiting the same vices and virtues as mere humans. This led certain Greek philosophers to be skeptical about the existence, or at any rate our conception, of such humanlike gods. On the other hand, though the Chinese philosopher Confucius did not question the existence of the gods, he recommended keeping a safe distance from them.

By the fifth century B.C.E., and even earlier in Palestine, a number of great religious and philosophical systems had evolved. Jews, Greeks, Indians, and Chinese learned from such remarkable thinkers as the Hebrew prophets, Socrates, Gautama Buddha, and Confucius.

What made these beliefs so appealing and durable? The primary fuction of religions and philosophies is to explain the meaning of human life and death and to find order in the universe. Religion and philosophy follow different paths and answer somewhat different needs. Religions demand faith and offer supernatural explanations for the human condition in this life and beyond. Philosophies, on the other hand, are concerned with existing life and society and seek explanations through rational inquiry. In some of the cultures discussed in Chapter 3,

many religions and philosophies competed for allegiance, and in the crucible of time only the most useful and appealing survived. For example, in China the era between 600 and 300 B.C.E. is called the "Hundred Schools"; out of this competition Confucianism eventually emerged triumphant.

Most early humans were awed by inexplicable occurrences in life and nature. They could not account for such rhythms of nature as the rising and setting of the sun and the cycle of the seasons, for meteorological events, or for the mystery of birth, aging, and death. Unable to explain these events, people attributed them to supernatural powers.

The belief that there was a power or powers beyond human control caused fear and anxiety and aroused the desire to ensure right relations with that power. The belief systems described here tried to assuage or lessen the anxieties that earlier faiths had failed to dispel. The great religions provided a sense of harmony and spiritual well-being by spelling out the terms for a right relationship with the divine. They taught their adherents to visualize the divine power as a person—for example, Buddha, Vishnu, and Yahweh—amenable to the supplications of human beings. The faithful believed they could communicate with the deity by prayer and ritual to ensure harmony and good fortune. The Jews, for example, codified their relationship with Yahweh through a covenant or pact. In return for obedience to him, Yahweh promised his worshipers prosperity and protection.

Greek philosophy and Confucian teaching, on the other hand, stressed universal patterns that could be grasped by human reason and understanding. Early Greek philosopher-scientists sought to explain the mystery of the universe and its workings by observation and rational analysis rather than through supernatural explanations. A knowledge of these patterns would allow people to order their lives in accord with them.

The major religions and philosophies survived because they offered codes of conduct and provided workable ethical bases for society. Their teachings were eventually codified in authoritative scriptures or canons. The Hebrew scriptures, the Buddhist canons, the Confucian Classics, the Taoist *Tao-te Ching,* and the Hindu *Upanishads* are among such guidebooks for right living. Although no Greek philosophical text attained the status of a sacred book, Greek philosphers were also concerned with questions of ethical conduct, in part because they found that traditional Greek religion lacked moral consistency. The lasting Greek contribution was thus not a code of religious beliefs, but rather a conviction that human reason, exercised in careful observation

and logical argumentation, might discover the laws that both govern the order of nature (physics) and provide the key for right living (ethics).

In summary, these religious and philosophical systems gave the men and women who embraced them a strong sense of security and purpose, and they provided effective guidance for a meaningful existence. Further, each system contained a distinctive mixture of precepts and ethical principles that exerted an especially powerful psychological attraction on its adherents.

We may ask why so many great belief systems arose across two continents in the same general time span. There is no definitive answer to this question. During this period, however, India, China, Greece, and Palestine all experienced profound social, economic, and political changes. These changes and the insecurities they generated stimulated philosophers and religious leaders to revise old, no-longer-sufficient philosophical and religious systems or to develop new ones. The resulting combinations of beliefs, practices, and perspectives obviously met very basic psychological and spiritual needs. Along with two later religions, Christianity and Islam, which shared many of the same characteristics as those discussed here, the belief systems discussed in Chapter 3 continue to be profoundly influential down to the present day.

Chapter 3

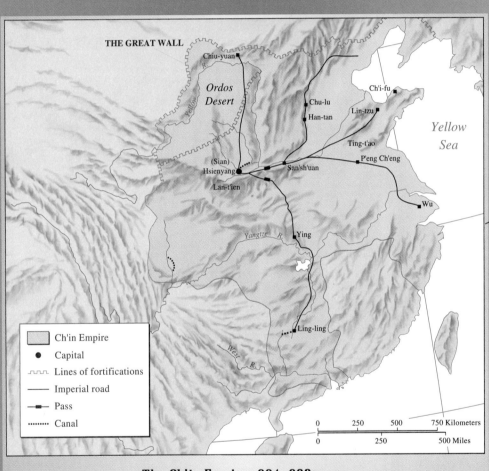

THE GREAT WALL

Chiu-yuan

Ordos Desert

Chu-lu

Han-tan

Ch'i-fu

Lin-tzu

Ting-t'ao

Yellow Sea

(Sian) Hsienyang

San'sh'uan

P'eng Ch'eng

Lan-t'ien

Wu

Yangtze R.

Ying

Ling-ling

Wei R.

	Ch'in Empire
●	Capital
	Lines of fortifications
	Imperial road
	Pass
	Canal

0   250   500   750 Kilometers

0   250   500 Miles

The Ch'in Empire, 221–206 B.C.E.

The Flowering of Great Faiths and Philosophies

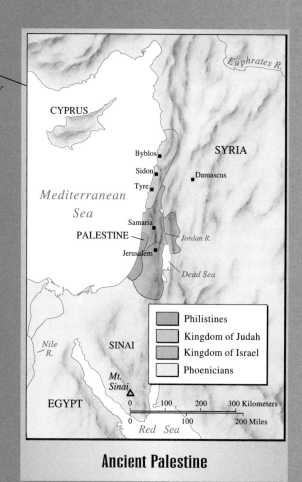

Ancient Palestine

On the Ancient Palestine map:

- CYPRUS
- Euphrates R.
- Byblos
- Sidon
- Tyre
- SYRIA
- Damascus
- *Mediterranean Sea*
- Samaria
- PALESTINE
- *Jordan R.*
- Jerusalem
- *Dead Sea*
- *Nile R.*
- SINAI
- *Mt. Sinai*
- EGYPT
- *Red Sea*

Legend:
- Philistines
- Kingdom of Judah
- Kingdom of Israel
- Phoenicians

0 100 200 300 Kilometers
0 100 200 Miles

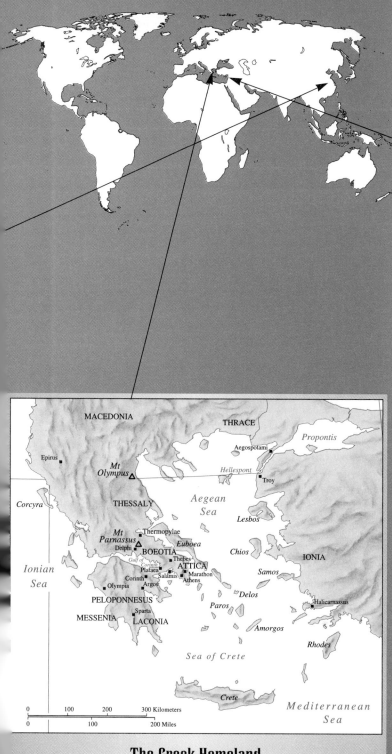

The Greek Homeland

On the Greek Homeland map:

- MACEDONIA
- THRACE
- *Propontis*
- Epirus
- *Mt Olympus*
- *Hellespont*
- Aegospotami
- Troy
- *Corcyra*
- THESSALY
- *Aegean Sea*
- *Lesbos*
- *Mt Parnassus*
- Thermopylae
- *Euboea*
- *Chios*
- Delphi
- BOEOTIA
- *Gulf of Corinth*
- Thebes
- ATTICA
- IONIA
- *Ionian Sea*
- Plataea
- Salamis
- Marathon
- *Samos*
- Corinth
- Argos
- Athens
- Olympia
- *Delos*
- Halicarnassus
- PELOPONNESUS
- *Paros*
- MESSENIA
- Sparta
- LACONIA
- *Amorgos*
- *Rhodes*
- *Sea of Crete*
- *Crete*
- *Mediterranean Sea*

0 100 200 300 Kilometers
0 100 200 Miles

Outline

The eminent historian Arnold Toynbee, Jr., described civilizations in terms of the characteristics of the spiritual life that permeated their society and culture. By this standard the cultures discussed in the present chapter would place at or near the apex. Across the Eurasian continent during the first millennium B.C.E., the Hebrews of Palestine, the Greeks of many city-states, the Indians of the Late Vedic Age, and the Chinese of the Eastern Chou dynasty all reached great heights of spiritual insight. The religions and philosophies they developed during these centuries would influence future generations well beyond their original homelands. As the Athenian statesman Pericles once confidently predicted, "future ages will wonder at us."

As we observed in the essay "Great Faiths and Philosophies," religions and philosophies based on the archaic past already permeated and gave structure to ancient civilizations. During the middle of the first millennium B.C.E., however, religious and philosophical innovators challenged, and sometimes discarded, old values and beliefs at critical junctures when they proved inadequate or outdated. In the process new religions, philosophies, and systems of government emerged.

This chapter begins with an examination of the evolution of the world's first great monotheistic faith: Judaism. The Hebrews' ethical religion was based on a covenant or pact with God that would sustain them through great adversities. Judaism, because of its influence on Christianity and Islam, represents how a people small in numbers can have more long-term influence in history than many huge empires.

Greek culture flourished with astonishing inventiveness in philosophy, government, the sciences, and the arts among the city-states of mainland and island Greece. The world is indebted to Greece for participatory government among other contributions. Like the Hebrews, the Greeks were not numerous and established no great empires. Again like the Hebrews, their contribution to the human spirit far outpaced their political sway and would guide and inspire much of humanity to the present.

In India, the middle centuries of the first millennium B.C.E. produced not only new philosophies that altered the direction of the Vedic religion (discussed in the last chapter), but also two new religions: Buddhism and Jainism. Buddhism became a universal religion and gave ethical meaning and guidance to countless millions across South, East, and Southeast Asia. It challenged Vedism/Hinduism in India, brought higher civilization to Southeast Asia, and was so influential in even a highly civilized land such as China that Chinese civilization can be divided by this encounter into the pre- and post-Buddhist eras.

The centuries that produced Buddhism and Jainism in India produced new philosophies in China. Of the many, or Hundred Schools of philosophies that developed in China during this era, two have dominated Chinese thought to the present: Confucianism and Taoism. Confucianism sought to instill in people the values of virtue, love, humanity, and duty to bring about a golden age. Taoism taught escape from a chaotic and immoral world. These two philosophies complemented each other. During the closing centuries of the first millennium B.C.E., the amoral philosophy called Legalism provided the discipline and force that restored unity to divided China.

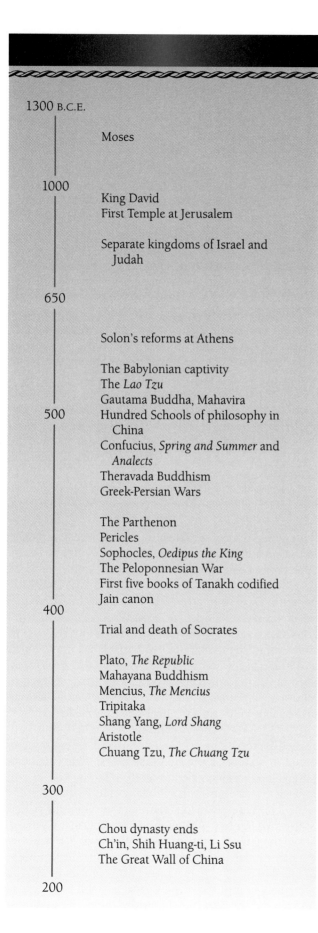

1300 B.C.E.

Moses

1000

King David
First Temple at Jerusalem

Separate kingdoms of Israel and
Judah

650

Solon's reforms at Athens

The Babylonian captivity
The *Lao Tzu*
Gautama Buddha, Mahavira
500   Hundred Schools of philosophy in
China
Confucius, *Spring and Summer* and
Analects
Theravada Buddhism
Greek-Persian Wars

The Parthenon
Pericles
Sophocles, *Oedipus the King*
The Peloponnesian War
First five books of Tanakh codified
Jain canon
400

Trial and death of Socrates

Plato, *The Republic*
Mahayana Buddhism
Mencius, *The Mencius*
Tripitaka
Shang Yang, *Lord Shang*
Aristotle
Chuang Tzu, *The Chuang Tzu*

300

Chou dynasty ends
Ch'in, Shih Huang-ti, Li Ssu
The Great Wall of China

200

Civilization in Palestine and Phoenicia

*The Lord said to Abram, "Go forth from your native land
and from your father's house to the land that I will show
you.*

> *I will make of you a great nation,*
> *And I will bless you;*
> *I will make your name great,*
> *And you shall be a blessing.*
> *I will bless those who bless you*
> *And curse him that curses you;*
> *And all the families of the earth*
> *Shall bless themselves by you."*

*Abram went forth as the Lord had commanded him.**

**Genesis 12:1–4, from *Tanakh: A New Translation of the Holy Scriptures
according to the Traditional Hebrew Text* (Philadelphia: Jewish
Publication Society, 1985), p. 18.*

Belief in a covenant, or special arrangement with
God, pervades the Hebrew scriptures and marks a
crucial ethical departure from the polytheistic systems of
Mesopotamia, Egypt, and Greece. In the developed Hebrew view, one and only one God existed; and this God
looked with special love upon the men and women who
worshiped him and duly obeyed his laws. Monotheism
(belief in only one God) made possible a self-consistent
code of ethics. This religion, not politics or military
conquest, was the Hebrew people's chief contribution to
civilization.

The part of West Asia known as Syria-Palestine and as
Canaan was not the center of any major kingdom or
empire; it was, however, the midpoint on the route that
conquerors from the powerful states of Egypt and Mesopotamia followed to attack each other. Its land was less
productive agriculturally than the fertile river valleys that
were home to powerful nations elsewhere in West Asia.
Nevertheless, two very important cultural groups, the Israelites and the Phoenicians, appeared in this region. The
Israelites conceived a religious faith that has exercised a
lasting influence on humankind. The Phoenicians created the alphabet and spread it with their trade throughout the Mediterranean world and beyond.

Israelite Political History

In the big picture of history, the Hebrews were neither numerous nor politically dominant. In fact, they were often
victimized by powerful neighbors. Their monotheism and
their recurrent covenants with God, however, made them
uniquely important in the history of civilization.

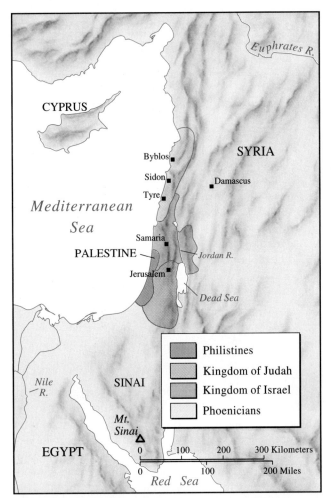

�֍ MAP 3.1 Ancient Palestine. This map shows the northern and southern kingdoms of the ancient Hebrews and the adjacent areas inhabited by the Phoenicians and the Philistines.

From about 2000 B.C.E. onward, the Semitic-speaking Hebrews moved from the deserts of Syria and Arabia, where they had subsisted as nomads, into less desolate regions of West Asia. According to their records, one contingent, led by Abraham, migrated from Ur in Babylonia to Canaan (Palestine). Later, sometime before 1600, certain Israelites (so called from Israel, another name for Jacob, Abraham's grandson) went to Egypt to avoid famine in Palestine; there they suffered oppression and fled in a mass exodus around 1300, under the leadership of Moses, who united his followers in the worship of God. Once again in Palestine, the Israelites exchanged their nomadic life for an agricultural mode of existence and engaged in military actions to acquire and defend territory. In time, they intermingled with the original population and adopted various aspects of Canaanite culture, including the institution of private ownership of property. The Israelites succeeded in gaining a hold on territory in Palestine, an area not then controlled by any powerful

state. After about 1200, however, another invading people, the Philistines, also entered the region; at first they settled along the coast, but then by force of arms, they began to push farther inland. The Philistines were militarily more advanced than their new Canaanite and Israelite neighbors, with better organization and superior (iron) weaponry.

As often happens in history, the Israelites responded to the threat of a strong external opponent by moving toward greater internal unity. During the period 1025–928 B.C.E., the twelve tribes of Israel were joined in a united monarchy under three successive king-generals. The first king of Israel, Saul (reigned 1025–1004 B.C.E.), did not attain the needed full cooperation of the various tribes and achieved little before meeting his death in battle at Gilboa against the Philistines. His successor, David (reigned 1004–965 B.C.E.), gained both victory on the battlefield and political harmony within the united kingdom. He ended the threat posed by the Philistines, ultimately restricting them to five towns in the coastal area near Gaza. David then annexed the remaining Canaanite areas and established a royal capital at Jerusalem, which became the political, military, and religious center of his realm. He forged strong ties with Phoenicia, thereby giving Israel access to the important ports of Tyre and Sidon, through which Israelite olive oil and grain could be traded for cedar, copper, and various luxury goods such as ivory and gold.

The economic and political prosperity continued in the reign of David's son, Solomon (reigned 965–928 B.C.E.), who spent lavishly on public construction projects. He built a magnificent temple and royal palace complex at Jerusalem and enlarged the fortifications begun by David. Such projects necessitated unpopular measures, however, specifically, heavy taxation and forced labor (already begun in David's reign). After Solomon's death, the Israelites could no longer endure a West Asian–style royal autocracy, and the kingdom (an area about the size of New Jersey) soon split into two parts: Israel in the north and Judah in the south. This division of resources weakened both kingdoms, however, and the Israelites eventually lost territories outside Palestine and became increasingly vulnerable to attacks by external foes.

In 722 B.C.E., the expanding Assyrian Empire absorbed Israel; its people were scattered, being remembered in history as the "ten lost tribes." The Chaldean king Nebuchadnezzar conquered Judah in 597. In 586 Jerusalem was destroyed, and many of its leading citizens were deported to Babylon, marking the end of the period of the First Temple. Although the Persian ruler Cyrus allowed the Jews (another name for Hebrews, derived from the name Judah) to return to Jerusalem after his conquest of Babylon in 539, many chose to stay in Babylonia. The returnees completed a new temple—with Persian approval—in 516. This was the beginning of the period of

✣ Relief Sculpture from the Palace of Sennacherib. This sculpture from the royal palace at Nineveh shows captive Israelites being presented to the Assyrian king Sennacherib (seated on throne) in 701 B.C.E. The British Museum

the Second Temple. Palestine remained under Persian control until the conquest of Alexander the Great in 332. It was thereafter absorbed by various Hellenistic kingdoms. Finally, after a last period of independence, it succumbed to the Roman Empire in 63 B.C.E.

Judaism

The religious history of ancient Israel is important out of all proportion to its political history. The various conquerors of Israel and Judah inflicted massacres, destroyed cities and sanctuaries, and sent many into the misery of exile. Whatever their condition, however, the Jews gradually managed to formulate and cling to a monotheistic religious tradition that differed notably from the polytheisms of Mesopotamia, Egypt, India, and China.

For this monotheism we have the evidence of a truly remarkable body of literature, the Tanakh (the Holy Scriptures, the first five books of which are called the Torah), known to Christians as the Old Testament. These writings comprise two-thirds of "the Book" or Bible (Greek *biblos*) that has codified Judaeo-Christian tradition throughout Western civilization. Tanakh is both a religious text and a rich work of literature. It is unique among West Asian documents in giving such a thorough

description of its composers' early history and in relating that history to a particular system of religious beliefs.

The most distinctive aspect of those beliefs is monotheism. Hebrew monotheism was characterized by an elaborate code of moral behavior. Unlike the gods of the West Asian and later Greco-Roman polytheisms, the Hebrew God presented men and women with a consistent code of morality and dictated a covenant under which humans would be rewarded for abiding by that code. The Ten Commandments of the Book of Exodus (20:1–17) are only its essence: Orthodox Judaism contains 613 commandments in the Law.

By contrast, the gods of Egypt and Mesopotamia set out no coherently formulated standards of behavior. Whatever ethical imperatives these deities stood for were vague and subject to suspension or cancellation. Thus mortals, even a hero like Gilgamesh, suffered from a deep-seated insecurity, often finding themselves in the double bind of being punished by one god for obeying another. Sometimes, like the polytheistic deities, the Lord God could be vengeful and jealous as well as paternally nurturing. His ways could be hard to fathom, as in the story of the wealthy and virtuous hero of Tanakh's Book of Job, who is overwhelmed by terrible misfortunes that he seems not to deserve. Nevertheless, Judaism normally

The Israelites . . . celebrated the dedication of the House of God with joy. And they sacrificed for the dedication of this House of God one hundred bulls, two hundred rams, four hundred lambs, and twelve goats as a purification offering for all of Israel. . . . They appointed the priests in their courses and the Levites in their divisions for the service of God in Jerusalem, according to the prescription in the Book of Moses.

The returned exiles celebrated the Passover on the fourteenth day of the first month, for the priests and Levites had purified themselves to a man; they were all pure. They slaughtered the Passover offering for all the returned exiles, and for their brother priests and for themselves. The children of Israel who had returned from exile, together with all who had joined them . . . to worship the Lord God of Israel, ate of it. They joyfully celebrated the Feast of Unleavened Bread for seven days, for the Lord had given them cause for joy by inclining the heart of the Assyrian king [Darius] toward them so as to give them support in the work of the House of God, the God of Israel.*

This passage from the Book of Ezra recounts the joy of the former inhabitants of Judah who had returned from the Babylonian Captivity and restored the destroyed temple at Jerusalem. The theme of exile and return is one of special pathos and power in the history and religion of the Jews. The Passover feast (celebrating the "passing over" of the homes of the Israelites when the firstborn of the Egyptians were slain) was itself a commemoration of another time of exodus or release from foreign captivity (in Egypt). Other exiles, however, like the ten lost tribes, were not so fortunate. And there would be further occasions of dispersal from the promised land, in particular, the great Diaspora ("scattering") after the Roman destruction of Jerusalem in 70 C.E. Still, somehow the God of the Israelites seemed to restore his chosen ones, particularly if they had obeyed his prophets (the word means chiefly "teacher") by repenting their transgressions of his laws. In the passage quoted here, the Lord is credited with controlling the mind of King Darius.

*Ezra 6:16–22, from *Tanakh: A New Translation of the Holy Scriptures according to the Traditional Hebrew Text* (Philadelphia: Jewish Publication Society, 1985), pp. 1500–1501.

---

furnished its followers with a comprehensive code of ethics by which to live their lives. It offered the assurance that the supreme creator looked on human beings as intrinsically valuable, not as mere playthings of the deities. Neither the Greeks nor the Romans, despite their emphasis on the potentials and achievements of humankind, were to formulate a theology that so emphasized the worth of every individual in the eyes of God.

Despite their code, the Jews, both individually and as a nation, broke the Law and disobeyed their God over and over in scriptural accounts. Moreover, in evolving their monotheistic religion, the Israelites were not insulated from the religious influences of their West Asian neighbors. Elijah, for example, had to prove to his people the superiority of their God to the Canaanite god Baal. Other prophets, like Amos, chastised the Jews for their shortcomings and, like Jeremiah, foresaw the coming of divine punishment in the guise of Babylonian conquest. During the exile in Babylon (586–539 B.C.E.), the "second Isaiah" and Ezekiel sang the praises of the one God and of his chosen people, urging repentance and holding out hope for a return to the promised land and a restoration of the temple at Jerusalem.

Judaic scriptures reflect the attitudes of a rigidly patriarchal society. Women's roles were restricted and their moral worth was often suspect. In part, this attitude stemmed from the struggle of monotheistic Judaism against the polytheistic worship of Canaanite deities, especially the popular fertility goddess Asherah. Judaism mandated the exclusive worship of a male Father-God, a worship eventually organized and administered by a strictly male priestly caste. Women could, of course, pray and study the scriptures, but one of the principal religious responsibilities of parents was to teach the Torah only to sons. When formal education was instituted in ancient Israel, it was limited to males.

The Book of Genesis describes the first woman, Eve, as created from the rib of the first man, Adam. She is thus a secondary creation, somehow inferior to the original male. So, too, Eve's role as the first to sin by eating of the forbidden fruit has often been interpreted as owing to the inherent weakness of the female sex. Though the scriptures do contain stories of virtuous and heroic women, such as Deborah, the prophetess and judge who helped deliver Israel from Canaanite oppression in the Book of Judges, the overall tone of Hebrew tradition and scripture is patriarchal.

The canonical (official) books of Tanakh were assembled between 400 and about 150 B.C.E. and constitute one of the most influential legacies of ancient West Asia. In religious thought, the Hebrews far outstripped their materially more fortunate neighbors. Judaism was to survive as a tremendously influential world religion, both in and of itself and as a major element in the evolution of Christianity and Islam.

The Phoenicians: Catalysts of Culture

By the early first millennium B.C.E., the Phoenicians had emerged in a coastal strip about the size of Connecticut west of the Lebanon Mountains and north of Palestine (see Map 3.1). Neither innovators nor originators of culture, the Phoenicians did facilitate its spread, especially between about 1000 and 700 B.C.E. They were the best mariners and traders of the ancient world, with major home ports at Tyre, Sidon, Berytus (modern Beirut), and Byblos. From these ports, Phoenician sailors and merchants fanned out to all the centers of commerce in the eastern Mediterranean and eventually even as far away as modern Spain and Great Britain (called the Tin Islands after the rich sources of that rare metal mined in Cornwall). Trade enabled them to maintain their civilized way of life despite the scarcity of fertile soil in their sector of West Asia. Imports included foodstuffs and raw materials such as grain and metals (for example, copper from Cyprus); exports were timber (cedar in particular) and various manufactured goods, including textiles, bronze and ivory artifacts, and a famous purple dye extracted from the shellfish of the region. On the north coast of Africa, in modern Tunisia, they founded Carthage, a prosperous city that later challenged Rome for control of the western Mediterranean.

The most enduring Phoenician gift to civilization, however, was the alphabet. This script, consisting of a small number of easily learned consonant signs, enormously facilitated the spread of literacy and cultural development. The actual characters seem to have descended from a script used at the town of Byblos. They were simpler to learn and to use than, for example, the more cumbersome and difficult Egyptian hieroglyphics. After 1500 B.C.E., the Phoenicians spread alphabetic writing principally through trade contacts. By the eighth century the Greeks had borrowed it, adding signs to represent vowels. They in turn passed it on to the Romans via the Etruscans. The Greek and Roman alphabets were subsequently adopted by virtually all modern European languages.

Classical Greek Civilization

I declare that our city is an education to Greece, and I declare that in my opinion each single one of our citizens, in all the manifold aspects of life, is able to show himself the rightful lord and owner of his own person, and do this, moreover, with exceptional grace and exceptional versatility. . . . Athens, alone of the states we know, comes to her testing time in a greatness that surpasses what was imagined of her. . . . Mighty indeed are the marks and monuments of our empire which we have left. Future ages will wonder at us, as the

present age wonders at us now. . . . For our adventurous spirit has forced an entry into every sea and into every land; and everywhere we have left behind us everlasting memorials of good done to our friends or suffering inflicted on our enemies.*

*Thucydides, History of the Peloponnesian War, trans. R. Warner (Harmondsworth: Penguin, 1954; rev. ed. 1972), pp. 147–148.

In this speech in honor of war dead in 430 B.C.E., the great Athenian statesman and general Pericles patriotically celebrated the civil and military accomplishments of his beloved Athens, assessing with prophetic insight their impression on posterity. The stage for these accomplishments was set in the Archaic Age, when the Greeks enjoyed freedom from outside interference. Beginning about 500, however, the Greek city-states faced a dire threat from the Persian Empire, which forced the Greek states for once to stand united. Greek victory in that conflict inaugurated a period of brilliant cultural and political achievement, particularly at Athens. Politically, the Persian Wars also resulted in the rise and triumph of the Athenian Empire in the era of Periclean Athens. The fifth century closed with the long, debilitating struggle known as the Peloponnesian War, which ended with the triumph of Athens' major rival, Sparta.

The Archaic Revival: New Patterns of Government

In the archaic period (c. 800–c. 500 B.C.E.), renewed contact with West Asia revived Greek architecture, metallurgy, pottery and textile production, and trade. Sea routes linked Greece with many points on the Mediterranean and Black Seas. The Phoenician alphabet was adapted for use in transcribing Greek, and the practice of coining money was adopted from Lydia (a kingdom in Asia Minor); both greatly expedited commercial activities.

In the Greek homelands, however, increasing population and relatively unproductive soil led to starvation, foreclosure, and enslavement for debt. One remedy was to acquire new land. Between 750 and 550 B.C.E., thousands of Greek colonists emigrated to Sicily, southern Italy, southern France, and North Africa, carrying Greek culture to the western Mediterranean in the process. Other Greeks emigrated northward to Thrace, Macedon, and the coasts of the Black Sea. The new settlements were independent states, not units within a unified empire such as the Romans later fashioned.

The Greek city-state or *polis* (compare English "political"), a city and its immediate rural environs, usually encompassing no more than a few hundred square miles, was the setting for momentous experiments in government. Citizen input into domestic and foreign policy set

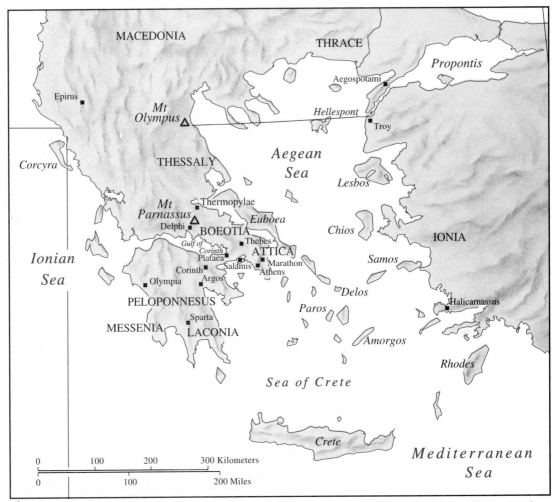

MACEDONIA

THRACE

Propontis

Epirus

Aegospotami

Mt Olympus △

Hellespont

Troy

THESSALY

Aegean Sea

Corcyra

Lesbos

Thermopylae

Mt Parnassus △

Euboea

Chios

Delphi

BOEOTIA

Gulf of Corinth

Thebes

ATTICA

IONIA

Plataea

Marathon

Ionian Sea

Corinth

Salamis

Athens

Samos

Olympia

Argos

Delos

PELOPONNESUS

Paros

Halicarnassus

Sparta

MESSENIA

LACONIA

Amorgos

Rhodes

Sea of Crete

| 0 | 100 | 200 | 300 Kilometers |

| 0 | 100 | 200 Miles |

Crete

Mediterranean Sea

✳ MAP 3.2 The Greek Homeland. This map shows major fifth-century Greek city-states, battle sites, and cultural centers in the Balkan Peninsula and on the islands and shores of the Aegean Sea.

the polis off sharply from its West Asian predecessors, where strong monarchies ceded few rights to the common individual. In the early archaic period, most Greek city-states were governed by an aristocratic oligarchy (a small ruling elite). After 675 B.C.E., however, innovations in military affairs brought changes in government. Greek soldiers now used new advanced, standardized equipment and were carefully drilled and deployed in a phalanx or mass formation of *hoplites* (heavy-armed foot soldiers). So efficient was this new infantry that all city-states quickly realized that a force of hoplites—the larger the better—was indispensable for "national security." Ordinary citizens, mainly farmers, serving in the hoplite army displaced aristocratic cavalry as the backbone of the military.

Social and political changes rapidly ensued, as the hoplites sought economic advantages and a voice in government befitting their military importance. They often acquired these by backing a tyrant, that is, a usurper-reformer, generally a disgruntled noble. Typically, the

tyrant overpowered his aristocratic opponents with a privately conscripted army of hoplite commoners. He rewarded the commoners by canceling debts and redistributing land. Paradoxically, at Athens tyranny led to democracy, when the tyrant abused his powers, became "tyrannical" in the familiar sense, and was overthrown and replaced by an elected leadership.

Full citizenship in a Greek polis was normally confined to adult male landowners. Women could not vote or hold office, nor could they be recognized in law courts without representation by some male, usually a father, husband, uncle, or brother. Women were, however, highly valued as a means of producing citizen children. In most city-states respectable women were carefully supervised and customarily confined to special quarters within the home to ensure that they had no contact with strange males and thus that the children they bore were legitimate. Women were given in marriage by their fathers or other male relatives who verified their citizenship. A substantial dowry accompanied the new wife;

although it reverted with her to her family of origin in the event of divorce. While she was married, the dowry money was managed by her husband. Respectable women all followed the same profession: bearing children, keeping house, and making clothing for family members.

Women who were not tied to a single male through a legal marriage were not considered respectable; such women, generally noncitizens or freedwomen, enjoyed greater freedom of movement outside the home and more diversity in occupations, including small-scale selling of clothing, perfumes, and foodstuffs, wet-nursing, and flute playing. Many, however, turned to prostitution, as *hetairai*, sophisticated call girls or "escorts" for males attending drinking parties, or as *pallakai* (concubines), who, though they lived with one male for a length of time, lacked citizenship status and could not bear legitimate children. Pericles himself fell afoul of this legal restriction when he had a child by his long-time companion, the captivating ex-hetaira (and noncitizen) Aspasia. He had to secure a special exemption to have his son, also called Pericles, recognized as a citizen.

Much of the labor force in the Greek city-states consisted of slaves, acquired through warfare or trade, who had no legal standing even as human beings. The Greeks and the Romans, though more liberal than, for example,

U.S. slave owners in freeing individual slaves, never abolished slavery; slaves could no more be given up than tools. Finally, there were intermediate statuses, like that of the *perioikoi* ("non-full-blooded" or "dwellers around") in Sparta and the *metoikoi* or metics (resident non-Athenians, but normally Greeks) in Athens. Both groups had legal protections, served as soldiers, and played a key role economically, but lacked the right to vote or hold office or sometimes even to own land. Political participation in ancient Greece was thus not as inclusive as in modern times.

Athenian and Spartan Social and Political Patterns

Throughout most of Greek history, the most important states were Athens and Sparta. Athens controlled the 1,000-square-mile peninsula of Attica (about the size of Rhode Island) and had the largest population of any Greek city-state (in the mid-fifth century B.C.E., around 300,000, at least one-third of whom were slaves or noncitizens). The lower classes profited when Draco supervised the first written codification of law at Athens (c. 621 B.C.E.). Like Hammurabi's code at Babylon, Draco's laws laid down harsh penalties; they were said to have been written in blood (thus the meaning of *draconian*). Still,

❊ The Chigi Vase. This archaic-era Corinthian vase (c. 650 B.C.E.) bears a very early representation of hoplite warriors. The phalanx is marching into battle in time to the playing of a piper. The standard hoplite weapons and arms are clearly depicted. Scala/Art Resource

Faking Citizenship: The Case against Neaera

Stephanus gave [Phano, the daughter of Neaera] in marriage, as being his own daughter, to an Athenian citizen, Phrastor, together with a dowry of 30 minas [the equivalent of about ten years' wages]. When she went to live with Phrastor . . . she was unable to accommodate herself to his ways, but hankered after her mother's habits and the dissolute ways of that household. . . . Phrastor observed that she was not well-behaved nor willing to be guided by him, and . . . he found out for certain that she was not the daughter of Stephanus, but only of Neaera [allegedly a concubine]. . . . Phrastor was most indignant at all this, and . . . turned the young woman out of his house after having lived with her for a year and when she was pregnant; and he refused to return the dowry.

Stephanus began a suit against him for alimony . . . according to the law enacting that if a man divorce his wife, he shall pay back the dowry. . . . Phrastor also brought an indictment against Stephanus . . . that Stephanus had betrothed to him, an Athenian citizen, the daughter of an alien woman, pretending that the girl was his own daughter, contrary to the following law . . . : "If any person give in marriage an alien woman to an Athenian citizen, pretending that she is related to him, he shall be deprived of his citizen status, and his property shall be confiscated."*

This passage is from a speech delivered in a court case at Athens around 340 B.C.E. At issue is whether Stephanus has given in marriage the daughter of a woman named Neaera, whom the prosecution has described as a prostitute/slave, formerly owned by various individuals in Elis, Corinth, and Athens, and now living as the mistress of Stephanus. To recognize the offspring of such a disreputable woman as citizens would threaten the structure of Athenian society and civil law. The harshness of the penalties imposed on offenders shows that this threat was taken very seriously.

*Kathleen Freeman, *The Murder of Herodes and Other Trials from the Athenian Law Courts* (New York: Norton, 1963), p. 205.

---

they did at least distinguish murder from manslaughter and in general shielded the lower classes from arbitrary judgments by aristocratic magistrates. At this time, the indispensable hoplite infantry had little control over their personal destinies. Because their land was not very productive, many were deeply in debt to aristocratic creditors. They often forfeited their farms or, worse yet, were sold into slavery. The situation grew potentially explosive.

To forestall violent revolution, aristocrats and commoners granted special powers to the chief *archon* (nine archons served as the chief executive officers) in 594 B.C.E. This archon, Solon (c. 640–c. 560 B.C.E.), spared the wealthy the radical measure of land redistribution, but canceled debts, forbade debt bondage, and recalled citizens sold into slavery outside Attica. By redefining social status and eligibility for office by wealth rather than birth, and by widening the jurisdiction and composition of juries of citizens, Solon broke the aristocratic monopoly of governmental authority. He also promoted economic development by extending citizenship to immigrant craftsmen, merchants, and traders.

In 508 B.C.E., another reformer, Cleisthenes, ensured more equitable representation of citizens by creating ten large political divisions (tribes), each composed of wards, with residence the chief requirement for citizenship. Each tribe annually elected one archon and chose fifty councillors by lot to serve in a Council of Five Hundred, which managed state finances and foreign policy and determined the agenda for the full assembly of citizens. The latter made the final decisions regarding all weighty matters of domestic and foreign policy and has remained the model of early democratic self-determination. There was also a panel of ten annually elected generals; because, unlike archons, they could be elected repeatedly, the generals came to possess exceptional authority in the Athenian state. Through another innovation, ostracism, the citizenry could vote, using pottery fragments called *ostraca*, to send a dangerously powerful person into a ten-year exile.

Sparta's government differed in many respects from that of Athens. For example, it retained the archaic institution of kingship; in fact, Sparta had two kings and two royal families. Though these kings were supreme military commanders, civil authority came to be vested in five elected *ephors*, similar to Athenian archons in responsibilities. There was, in addition, a council of thirty elders. An assembly restricted to full-blooded Spartans possessed powers of ratification.

Even more than Athens, Sparta contained a strong class structure. Members of the Spartan ruling elite were called *homoioi* (equals). The non-Spartan inhabitants or *perioikoi* were free citizens of their own communities but were obliged to serve in Sparta's army and to abide by its foreign policy. The largest population group was the helots or state-owned slaves. The Spartans defeated neighboring Messenia in the seventh century B.C.E. and enslaved its population, forcing them to work on Spartan-controlled land. Freed thus from farmwork, full-blooded Spartans made a lifelong, absolute commitment to the most rigorous discipline in education and military training (hence the term *spartan* for living under austere conditions), partly to maintain internal security in the face of a vastly larger subject population. The relationship between Spartans and helots was similar in some respects to that between Aryans and dasas in India. Sparta was the greatest military power in Greece until the fourth century, but it paid a high price for this supremacy. The Spartans aborted promising earlier developments in art and poetry to devote their energies exclusively to the code of the soldier. History shows a similar stunting of cultural growth among other excessively militaristic societies (for example, the Assyrians or, in modern times, fascist states).

The Persian and Peloponnesian Wars

In 499 B.C.E., some Ionian Greek cities revolted (unsuccessfully) against Persia. Because Athens had assisted the rebels, the Persians sent a punitive expedition against it in 490. At the plain of Marathon, 10,000 hoplites soundly defeated a Persian force more than twice as large. Although King Darius's death in 486 postponed a new assault, his son, Xerxes (reigned 486–465 B.C.E.), planned a much larger invasion with both land and sea forces. He ordered a mile-long bridge to be constructed out of ships cabled together across the Hellespont, which divided Europe from Asia, and a canal to be built through the peninsula at Mount Athos to avoid the risk of storms off its cape.

Fortunately for Greece, the Athenian statesman Themistocles (c. 528–462 B.C.E.) realized that seapower was critical. In 483 B.C.E., when a large new vein of silver was discovered in the state-owned mines at Laurium, Themistocles persuaded the assembly of Athenian citizens to use the bonanza to increase their fleet to 200 triremes and to improve the harbor installations. This democratically adopted decision determined the outcome of the Persian Wars.

In 481 B.C.E., Athens, Sparta, and some thirty other states formed a league to defend themselves against the Persians. In 480 Xerxes led about 150,000 troops on the 500-mile march to central Greece. The Persians annihilated King Leonidas's Spartan force at the mountain pass of Thermopylae and pushed on to seize Athens, burning the temples on the Acropolis.

Although the Greeks still possessed powerful forces, victory required coordination of the military and naval strengths of Sparta and Athens, respectively. Themistocles engaged the Persian fleet in the narrow strait between the island of Salamis and Attica. There, the Greeks used boarding parties of marines, superior oarsmanship, and effective ramming tactics to win a decisive battle. Xerxes withdrew to Asia Minor, leaving behind a large force, which Greek forces crushed at Plataea in 479 B.C.E. The victory ensured the independent development of the Greek city-states for another century and a half.

The Spartans' Last Stand at Thermopylae

Many of the invaders fell; behind them the company commanders plied their whips, driving the men remorselessly on. Many fell into the sea and were drowned, and still more were trampled to death by their friends. No one could count the number of the dead. The Greeks . . . fought with reckless desperation. . . . They resisted to the last, with their swords if they still had them, and, if not, with their hands and teeth, until the Persians, coming on from the front over the ruins of the wall and closing in from behind, finally overwhelmed them [with arrows and spears].*

For two days, 300 Spartans held the pass at Thermopylae against a much larger Persian force. On the third day, however, the Persians, assisted by a Greek collaborator, brought some of their troops around through the mountains and down to the coast behind Thermopylae. Leonidas and his men, specially chosen from those who had living sons, were thus caught in a slaughterous pincer movement.

*Herodotus, *The Histories*, trans. A. de Sélincourt (Harmondsworth: Penguin, 1954), pp. 492–493.

In 478 B.C.E., some 150 Greek cities of Asia Minor and neighboring islands turned to the strongest naval power, Athens, to form and lead a league called The Athenians and Their Allies (known in modern times as the Delian League because its treasury was on Apollo's sacred island of Delos). The league was created to defend the Aegean region and harass the Persians wherever possible. Members contributed either men and ships or money to maintain an allied fleet under Athenian direction. Sparta, which refused an earlier offer to head the league, did not join, but remained the *hegemon* (leader) of the land-based Peloponnesian League. These alliances of Greek city-states resembled those of the Chinese states during the late Chou, though on a smaller scale. In both cases, a common culture superficially united member states. The hegemonic states of the Eastern Chou tried, like Athens and Sparta, to control their allies.

At first, the Delian League benefited Greece by rooting out remaining Persian bases in the Aegean and Asia Minor, suppressing piracy, and fostering seaborne mercantile activity, but Athens transformed the Delian League into an Athenian Empire. The treasury at Delos was removed to Athens, which squelched attempts to leave the alliance and interfered highhandedly in the internal affairs of member states. Under Pericles' guidance, Athens became the richest and most powerful Greek

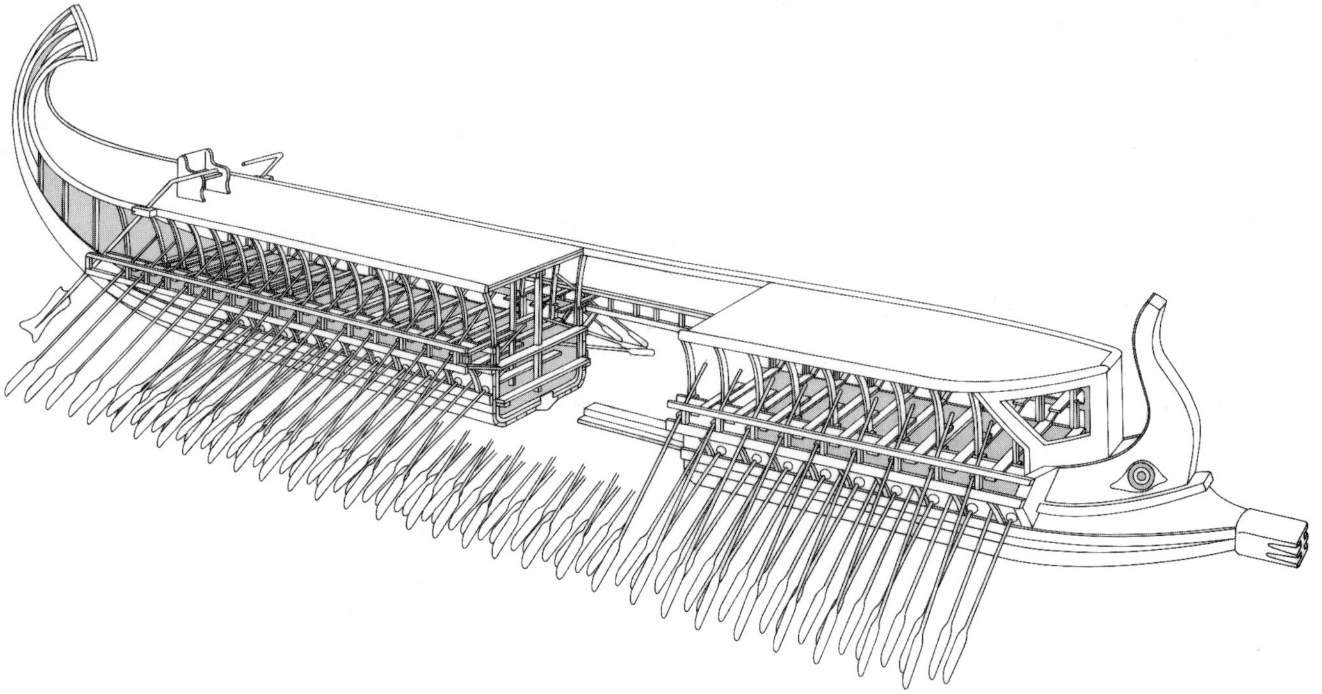

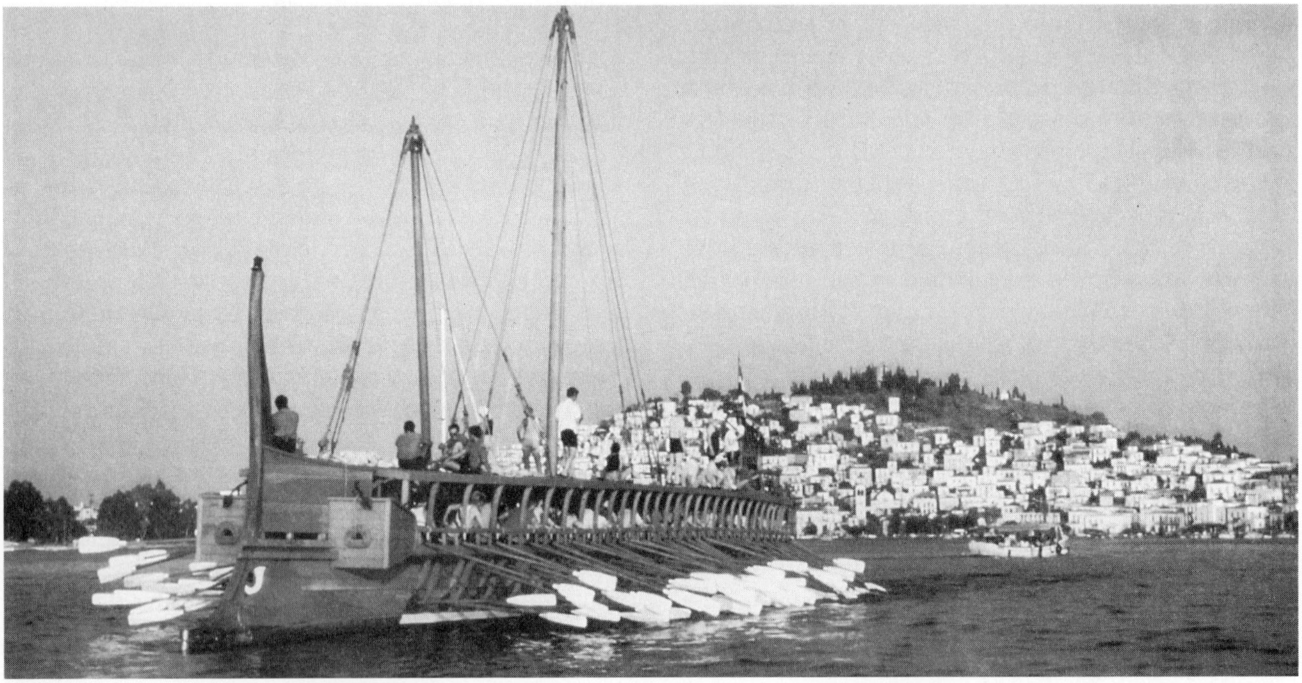

The Greek Trireme. *Above:* A cutaway view of a trireme, the standard Greek warship of the classical period. Such vessels were about 120 feet long by 12 feet wide, with crews of 150–175 rowers seated on benches in three tiers. The ram at the bow was the ship's main offensive weapon; note also the special steering oars at the stern.
Below: In 1987 Greek shipbuilders, working from plans made by a British classical scholar and former chief naval architect of the British Ministry of Defense, completed "the first trireme to be launched in 1,500 years." The *Olympias* was the result of two years' work and the expenditure of $700,000 by the Greek government. With a crew of 130 men and 40 women, mostly young Britons, the modern replica achieved a speed of 21.7 knots at thirty oarstrokes per minute. Susan Mulhauser/*Time*

city-state and the capital of intellectual and artistic activity. Pericles' mistress, the former Milesian prostitute Aspasia, made his home a social gathering place for the intellectual lights of the era. Pericles' imperialistic foreign policy went hand in hand with the increased prosperity of the lower socioeconomic classes at home. In particular, reliance on the fleet gave a new prominence to the thousands of rowers who were paid for manning the ships. This enabled Pericles to win election to the *strategia* (generalship) so routinely that the historian Thucydides wrote of Athens that "though the system was democratic in name, power was actually vested in the leading citizen."

Sparta and many other Greek states feared the growing power of Athens. When Athens attempted to control supplies of grain, timber, and precious metals at their source, the Spartans declared war and prepared to march on Attica. The Peloponnesian War began in 431 B.C.E. and lasted twenty-seven years. Although the Spartans used severely repressive tactics in maintaining the enslavement of the helots in their own country, they painted themselves as champions of Greek liberty in the struggle against Athenian imperialism. Pericles' chief task was maintaining morale, as may be seen from the speech he delivered at the funeral for the war dead in 430. A far greater crisis, however, arose when Athens lost perhaps one-fourth of its population, including Pericles, to a virulent plague. A peace was negotiated in 421.

In 415 B.C.E., the volatile, high-living Alcibiades (c. 450–404 B.C.E.) persuaded the Athenians to send the finest Greek naval force ever assembled to attack the powerful Greek city of Syracuse on Sicily and add the island, with its rich grain production, to the empire—just the sort of endeavor Pericles had advised against. In 413 the campaign ended in complete victory for Syracuse. Although Athens recovered partially from the Sicilian debacle, Sparta built a formidable fleet of its own, thanks in large measure to Persian subsidies, and shifted the theater of the war to Attica and the Aegean. In 405 a Peloponnesian naval victory severed Athens' grain supply route from the Black Sea. The starving Athenians surrendered unconditionally in 404. Their fortifications were dismantled, and they relinquished the empire and their navy.

Greek Intellectual History: From Myth to Philosophy

Despite their political fragmentation, all Greeks shared a religious heritage with roots in the Bronze Age. The images of the Olympian gods, named from their home on Mount Olympus, were already fully formed at the very beginning of the archaic period. Among the most important were Zeus, the supreme deity, a sky god and wielder of the thunderbolt; Athena, the warrior-goddess and patroness of intellectual endeavor; Aphrodite, the goddess

of erotic love; and Apollo, the god of music, prophecy, and medicine. The gods figured in the tales of poet-singers and in the art of vase painters, sculptors, and coin designers. The mythic stories often answered questions as yet unanswerable by science: What causes thunder? Where did a particularly strange black rock come from? They could convey a moral—treat a guest as you would like to be treated—or simply entertain, as good stories have always done.

Certain religious centers gained exceptional prestige among all Greeks. As was the case among the Chaldeans in West Asia and the Shang dynasty in China, the practice of divination was very prominent in Greece, for example, at Delphi, where the city-states vied with one another in erecting sacred monuments at Apollo's oracular shrine. The Greeks also held athletic contests to honor the gods at various sites, especially Olympia in the western Peloponnesus.

The principal occasions for the private citizen to worship in Greece (and indeed throughout the ancient world) were the numerous festivals throughout the religious calendar. Unlike most modern religious "services," the festivals of the Greek city-states were public, often state-sponsored, events embracing a broad range of activities and spectacles. The farmer and his family left their homestead and spent part or all of a day traveling, generally on foot, to the city, where for a day or perhaps a few days they attended religious events. During the festivals, they watched an impressive, Fourth of July-like parade of religious officials and worshipers wending its way to the shrine of a particular god or goddess. They might also attend athletic competitions, choral performances, poetic recitations, or tragedies and comedies staged to honor the deity. The farmers' visits to the city to pay homage to their gods were thus also civic activities and occasions for popular entertainment. Athenians enjoyed the annual Panathenaic (All-Athenian) festival when games, musical performances, and recitations of Homeric poetry from "authorized" versions were staged in honor of the birth of the goddess Athena.

As in most ancient religions, including early Judaism, the sacrificial festivals provided the chance for fellow citizens to socialize and, since the core of the actual rites in honor of the many Greek gods was the offering of sacrificial animal s and participation in special meals, to consume foods, especially meats, not normally available to them. The central ceremony took place in the open air; the notion of a church where one sat in quiet, pious, personal devotion to the god was quite alien to the ancient Greeks. The priests and other officials, wearing ornaments and wreaths, led a procession with the sacrificial animal, often a bull, which was also decorated with ribbons or gilded horns, to an altar near a temple or shrine of the god or goddess. A fire blazed on top of the altar; incense often wafted through the air, and typically there

Creation Myths and the Construction of Gender and Social Orders

Like other myths, creation stories often explain or justify "the way things are" by investing the current state of affairs with an aura of venerability and divine causation. The creation stories of the ancient Greeks, for example, are best known from the works of the poet Hesiod, a younger contemporary of Homer. Hesiod's very early version of creation foreshadows the patriarchal social system of the Greeks. According to the myth, man was created first and woman only later, as a punishment inflicted by vengeful gods for the Titan Prometheus's theft of fire for men.

> The father of men and gods [Zeus] . . . bade famous Hephaestus make haste and mix earth with water and to put in it the voice and strength of human kind, and fashion a sweet, lovely maiden-shape, like to the immortal goddesses in face. . . . [And] the Guide, Slayer of Argus [Hermes] contrived within her lies and crafty words and a deceitful nature at the will of loud-thundering Zeus, and the Herald of the gods put speech in her. And he called this woman Pandora, because all they who dwelt on Olympus gave each a gift, a plague to men who eat bread.*

Some three centuries later, the philosopher Plato wrote the *Symposium*, which recounts the after-dinner conversation of a group of Athenian writers and other intellectuals. One of the diners, the comic poet Aristophanes, tells a myth to explain the origins of human sexual preference. In his witty tale, humans were in the beginning double beings, with two heads, four arms and four legs, two sets of genitalia, and dual sets of all other organs. There were three sexes: male-male, male-female, and female-female. They were much stronger than later humans; they could, for instance, run much faster by cartwheeling along on their eight limbs. Soon they challenged the very gods for supremacy in the universe. Zeus in anger cut them into halves. Thus they (like us, their descendants) spent their lives seeking to find their true partners and to undo the division imposed by Zeus.

The early Aryan texts in India do not present a clearly defined creator god. This hymn from the *Rig-Veda* describes the sacrifice of the primeval man by the gods and tells how his body produced the universe and all within. Members of the four Hindu castes were created from different parts of his body, which sanctified the social ordering of Hinduism.

> When the gods made a sacrifice
>   with the Man as their victim,
> Spring was the melted butter, Summer the fuel,
>   and Autumn the oblation.
>
> * * *
>
> Then were born horses,
>   and all beings with two rows of teeth.
> Thence were born cattle,
>   and thence goats and sheep. . . .
> When they divided the Man,
>   into how many parts did they divide him?
> What were his mouth, what were his arms,
>   what were his thighs and his feet called? . . .
> The brahman was his mouth,
>   of his arms was made the warrior,
> his thighs became the vaisya,
>   of his feet the sudra was born.
>
> * * *
>
> With Sacrifice the gods sacrificed to Sacrifice—
>   these were the first of the sacred laws.
> These mighty beings reached the sky,
>   where are the eternal spirits, the gods.**

The earliest transmitted Chinese texts say nothing about creation. The later commonly accepted myth dates to the fourth century C.E.; it attributed creation to P'an Ku, as follows:

> Variously described as the chiseler of the universe out of chaos, he himself being the offspring of the *yin* and the *yang*, the dual powers of Nature, and as the actual creator of the universe. Pictured as a dwarf clothed in bearskin or merely in leaves or with an apron of leaves. He has two horns on his head. In his right hand he holds a hammer and in his left a chisel. He is also shown as attended in his labours by the four supernatural creatures—the unicorn, phoenix, tortoise, and dragon; others again draw him with the sun in one hand and the moon in the other, some of the first fruits of his stupendous labours. His task occupied eighteen thousand years, and having finished it he dissolved into the various concrete parts of the visible universe, from constellations to human beings, etc.***

*Hugh G. Evelyn-White, trans., *Hesiod, the Homeric Hymns, and Homerica*, rev. ed. (Cambridge: Harvard University Press, 1936), pp. 7, 9.
**A. L. Basham, *The Wonder That Was India* (New York: Grove Press, 1959), pp. 240–241.
***E. T. C. Werner, *Dictionary of Chinese Mythology* (Shanghai: Kelly and Walsh, 1932), p. 355.

was musical accompaniment. The priests or priestesses ritually washed their hands and sprinkled water on the victim. Grains of unground barley (the most ancient agricultural product) were scattered on the ground, the altar, and the victim, as prayers were uttered. The officiating priest took a knife and trimmed a few hairs from the animal's head and tossed them in the fire. The victim's throat was then cut, to the accompanying ritual screams of women; care was taken so that the blood fell on the altar, with a bowl sometimes being used to catch and pour the blood.

The sacrificial victim was next disemboweled and carved up. The bones and much of the fat were burned, the savory smoke ascending to the god while the meat itself provided the sacrificial meal for those attending the rite. This was the typical blood sacrifice of the ancient religions. It was the most common form of religious practice in ancient times and is still practiced in some religions today. Thus, for the average man or woman religion consisted of participating in or witnessing various ritual actions. Unlike the Jews, the Greeks had no sophisticated theology or body of dogma and no sacred book to give moral guidance; they relied on "the customs of our ancestors."

Despite the frequent, elaborate public rituals, the Olympian gods failed to provide answers to moral and ethical questions or to explain how the physical world worked. Early Greek philosopher-scientists, dissatisfied with simple mythic resolutions of scientific problems, sought to explain the universe by rational inquiry. Some believed that a controlling law (in Greek, a *logos*) underlay the arrangement of basic elements—earth, air, water, and fire. Others argued about being and becoming and the precise nature of appearances and motion. Pythagoras and his followers explored mathematical patterns in the structure of the cosmos and dabbled in theories of the transmigration and reincarnation of souls. In the atomic theory of Democritus, indivisible bits of matter were the basis of all reality. As we have seen, in India at approximately the same period, similar questions were being asked by philosophers who wrote their reflections in the *Upanishads*.

By about 450 B.C.E., however, the inconclusiveness of the natural philosophers led to the emergence of the Sophists (wise ones), traveling professors who provided instruction, for a fee, in everything from arts and crafts to medicine, philosophy, and oratory. The chief traits of the Sophists were skepticism and relativism. In their opinion, humans would never ascertain absolute right and wrong or good and evil. What was "good" for one might be bad for another. For the Sophists, the only subjects worth pursuing were those that gave individuals the means to acquire their own ends. In Athens, this meant rhetoric—the theory and practice of persuasive oratory. Skill in speaking could make even the worse case appear

✳ View of Delphi. This shows the temple of Apollo at the great pan-Hellenic oracular shrine at Delphi. The elaborate complex of religious buildings centered on the temple is spectacularly situated on the steep slopes of Mount Parnassus in central Greece. © Wolfgang Kaehler/Gamma-Liaison

to be the better; indeed, *worse* and *better* became meaningless terms. As the Sophist Gorgias put it, "The power of speech over the . . . soul can be compared with the effect of drugs on the bodily state: just as drugs by driving out different humors from the body . . . different words can induce grief, pleasure or fear; or again, by means of a harmful kind of persuasion, words can drug and bewitch the soul" (trans. K. Freeman). For the Sophists, using the appropriate words in the proper situation was all that mattered; ethical questions of absolute right and wrong were both unanswerable and irrelevant.

Socrates (469–399 B.C.E.) extended this questioning of old values. As a young man, he dabbled in natural philosophy, but later he shifted his focus to the right conduct of life: What is justice and can it be taught? What is love? Is the soul immortal? Unlike the Sophists, Socrates believed that absolute values did in fact exist and that one could strive to know them through dialectic. He solicited definitions from others and tested them by cross-questioning, a procedure that came to be known as the Socratic method of inquiry. Since the definitions nearly always crumbled, he sometimes made enemies, but he never lapsed into the relativistic skepticism of the Sophists.

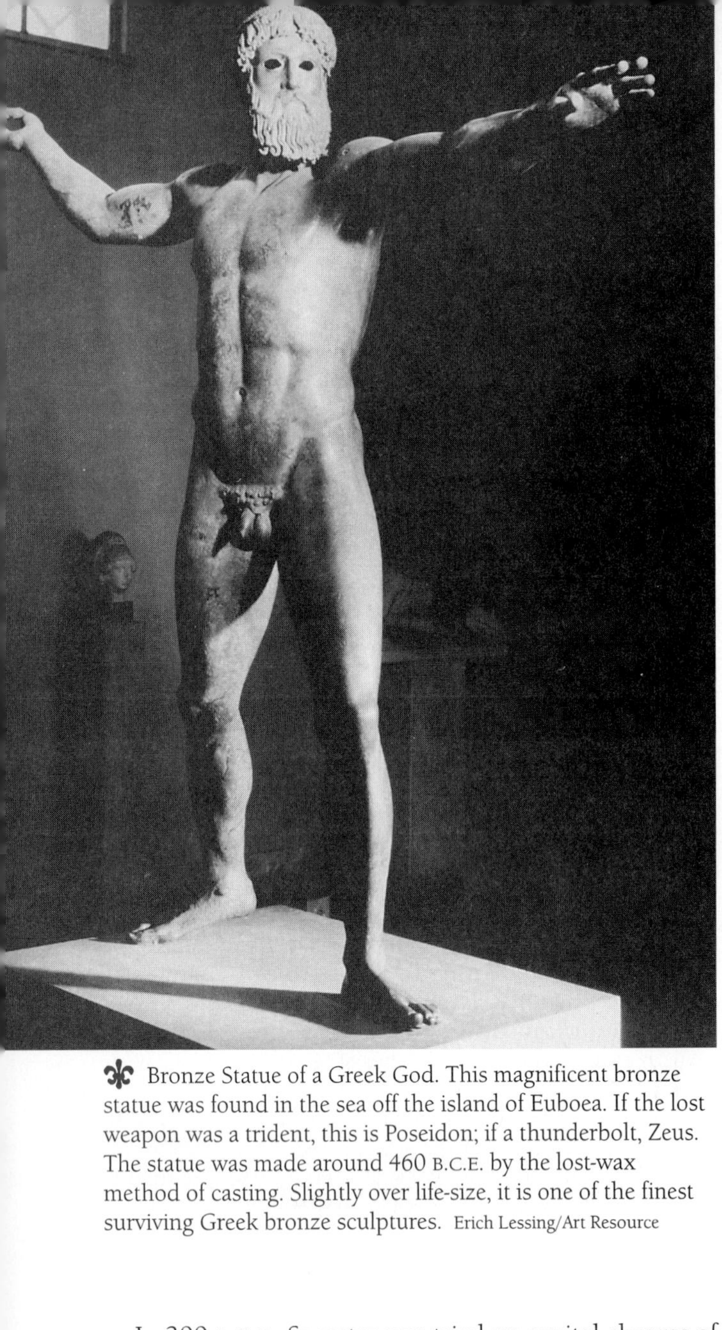

Bronze Statue of a Greek God. This magnificent bronze statue was found in the sea off the island of Euboea. If the lost weapon was a trident, this is Poseidon; if a thunderbolt, Zeus. The statue was made around 460 B.C.E. by the lost-wax method of casting. Slightly over life-size, it is one of the finest surviving Greek bronze sculptures. Erich Lessing/Art Resource

In 399 B.C.E., Socrates was tried on capital charges of atheism and corruption of the young (he made questioners of them). In defending himself against these charges, as recorded in Plato's *Apology* (defense), he portrayed himself as a victim of old prejudices, who had been wrongly lumped together with the amoral Sophists. He stoutly refused to stop his irksome inquiries, maintaining that the unexamined life was not worth living. Found guilty and sentenced to death, Socrates drank the lethal hemlock to show his respect for the laws of Athens, by which he had always abided. He argued on his last day that death—the separation of body and soul—was something to be desired, not feared, by the true philosopher, since philosophy was a "training for death." The wise man practices an ascetic way of life, as Socrates had famously done throughout his own life, to reduce the bodily distractions that prevent intellectual endeavors from reaching their goal. Death eliminates such distractions altogether. Socrates lived and died by these principles and bequeathed to humanity a method of inquiry and a style of living and seeking the truth, rather than a body of hard and fast doctrine.

Among the pupils of Socrates was Plato (c. 429–347 B.C.E.), whose philosophy profoundly shaped Western intellectual history. Plato's dialogues present brilliant, dramatic conversations between Socrates and his pupil-friends. Plato sharply distinguishes the reality of the five senses from the world of ideas, which is true and unchanging always and everywhere and thus is the only proper source of knowledge. The philosopher (lover of wisdom) must cultivate the soul, the seat of reason, and suppress the body's misleading sensory experiences. Plato applied this theory of knowledge to such concepts as beauty, virtue, and justice. In his *Republic*, for example, the participants seek to define the "just man" by constructing a detailed model of a perfectly just state, governed by philosopher-kings, whose education is described in detail. The result is an extraordinary mix of philosophy, political science, educational theory, sociology, psychology, and literary criticism. Some modern critics have called the political theory of the *Republic* oppressive and totalitarian, but it must be remembered that Plato aimed to define the just man and not to draw plans for an actual state.

Plato founded a school called the Academy. His best pupil was Aristotle (384–322 B.C.E.), known to his fellow students as "the brain." For a time the tutor of Alexander the Great, Aristotle later founded his own school, the Lyceum. He rejected Plato's emphasis on a separately existing, unchanging reality and based his own general concepts on logical argumentation and observation of natural phenomena. He systematized logic, ethics, political science, metaphysics, the natural sciences, and literary theory. In the Middle Ages, the Scholastics, including Thomas Aquinas, revered Aristotle, and his biological works remained definitive until the eighteenth century. Dante rightly called him "the master of those who know."

In their long tradition of philosophical inquiry, the Greeks succeeded in two major accomplishments. First, they provided an option to "blind faith." Although the old religious views persisted, thinking persons increasingly turned to a more rational, even scientific, way of explaining the world and seeking guidance to right living. While it brought no final answers to the mysteries of life, philosophy did give to human beings a confidence about their capacity to fathom issues of cause and effect, moral right and wrong, and the origins of things. Second, Greek rationalism established a very durable mind-set, or habit of thinking, for subsequent civilizations.

The Greek Origins of European Literature and Art

The impact of the Greeks on literature was as profound as their contributions to philosophical and scientific thought. The Greeks enriched older literary forms such as the epic and lyric, and the Athenians developed drama and history. Written Greek literature began with Homer's *Iliad* and *Odyssey* in the eighth century B.C.E. Behind them lay a long oral tradition of epic poetry dating back to Mycenaean times and furnishing a common Greek heritage of heroic myth. Children learned their alphabet with the Homeric epics before their eyes and in their ears. Homer's answers to the great questions of human potential faced by Achilles on the battlefield at Troy and by Odysseus during his journey home influenced the mental outlook of every educated Greek. The aristocratic ideal of *arete* (moral and physical excellence) set a standard of heroic behavior for the whole society.

The Indians and Chinese also had venerable oral traditions and heroic tales that served an educational purpose of transmitting ethical values as did the Greek heroic poems. The oral poetry of the early Aryans in India culminated in the composition of the *Mahabharata* and the *Ramayana*, which celebrated the deeds of gods and heroes. Homer's poetry was the closest thing to a holy book that the Greeks possessed. Though they were not taken as dogma or as a formal creed, his epics, together with the poet Hesiod's *Theogony*, which recounts the origins and genealogy of the gods, provided an authoritative, early record of the Greek polytheistic system of belief. By contrast, as we have seen, the *Rig Veda* of ancient India did not present a clear genealogy of relationships among the gods.

A more down-to-earth, practical strain also emerged in Greek literature in the archaic period. The *Fables* of Aesop normally relate anecdotes from the life of simple folk or animals that carry some moral, often illustrating shrewdness (or lack of it). The tale of "Vengeance at Any Price" is typical: "A wasp settled on a snake's head and tormented it by continually stinging. The snake, maddened with the pain and not knowing how else to be revenged on its tormentor, put its head under the wheel of a wagon, so that they both perished together." The moral is that "some men elect to die with their enemies rather than let them live" (trans. S. A. Handford).

The archaic Greeks also developed the lyric, a short poem usually sung to the accompaniment of a lyre. The most distinctive aspect of Greek poetry, as compared with that of ancient West Asia, was the prominence of the self-aware individual. The inner life of the poet was appropriate subject matter for serious and not-so-serious writing. Lyric poems were personal, immediate, and flexible in form and content, suitable for recording nearly any experience. The poetess Sappho described the emotional and physiological responses ignited by love:

> . . . my lips are stricken to silence, under-
> neath my skin the tenuous flame suffuses;
> nothing shows in front of my eyes, my ears are
> muted in thunder.
> And the sweat breaks running upon me, fever
> shakes my body. . . . (trans. R. Lattimore).

The Code of the Hero in Homer

And now [Sarpedon] spoke in address to Glaukos,
    son of Hippolochos:
"Glaukos, why is it you and I are honored before
    others
with pride of place, the choice meats and the filled
    wine cups
in Lykia, and all men look on us as if we were
    immortals,
and we are appointed a great piece of land by the
    banks of Xanthos,
good land, orchard and vineyard, and ploughland for
    the planting of wheat?
Therefore it is our duty in the forefront of the Lykians
to take our stand, and bear our part of the blazing of
    battle. . . .
Seeing that the spirits of death stand close about us
in their thousands, no man can turn aside nor escape
    them,
let us go on and win glory for ourselves, or yield it to
    others."*

Sarpedon, a son of Zeus and ally of the Trojans during their war against the Greeks, here summarizes the heroic code. As the price of nobility and the material advantages it confers, one must risk one's life on the battlefield. Humans are inescapably mortal. Death comes for us all, sooner or later. In Homer, the hero seeks to cheat death by winning glory, which will ensure both prestige in this life and continued life in the memories of men and women.

*Richmond Lattimore, trans., *The Iliad of Homer* (Chicago: University of Chicago Press, 1951), pp. 266–267.

The invention of drama in late sixth-century Athens was one of the most important Greek contributions to civilization. Tragedy evolved from choral lyrics sung at Athenian religious festivals, where singers impersonated gods or heroes and interacted with the chorus in dramatic dialogue. In the fifth century, at the Athenian City Dionysia (festival in honor of Dionysus), three poets each presented three tragedies in competition for prizes. The actors and the chorus of twelve or fifteen singers wore costumes and masks, but otherwise few props and little scenery were used. The theater itself was at first a hillside (the south slope of the Acropolis) with a stage and a circular orchestra in which the chorus danced and sang. Attendance was perhaps as large as 20,000. Admission was inexpensive, and in the time of Pericles the treasury paid for the seats of citizens. Large stone theaters came later, in Hellenistic and Roman times.

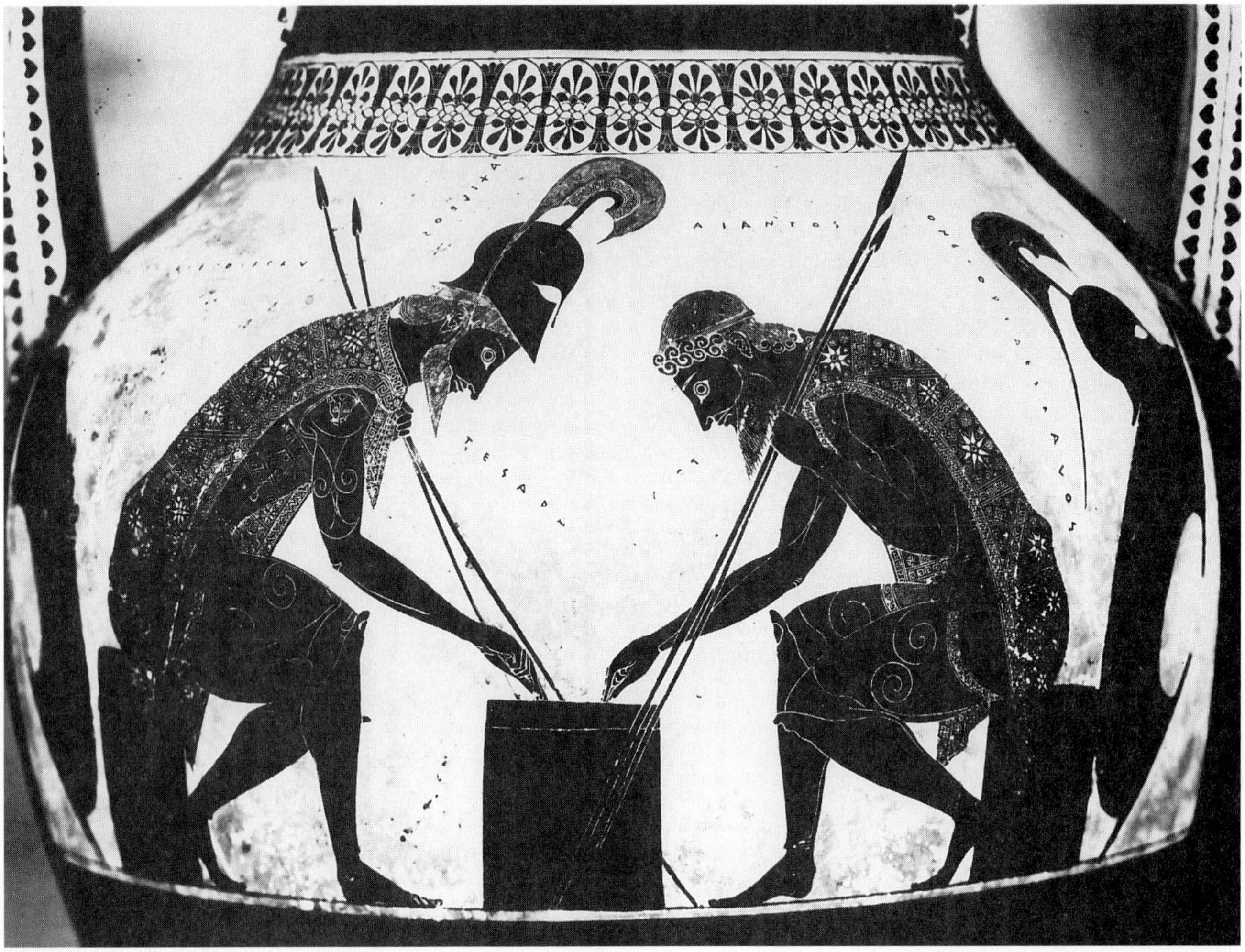

Black-Figure Vase. This splendid black-figure amphora was painted by Exekias c. 530 B.C.E. It shows the epic heroes Achilles (left) and Ajax (right) enjoying "R and R" between battles by playing dice; Achilles calls "four" and Ajax "three." Vatican Museum

For their subjects, playwrights selected and freely modified mythic tales of murder, incest, cannibalism, rape, insanity, parricide, fratricide, infanticide, and suicide. In his *Poetics*, Aristotle said that the crisis of the best plots involved a spectacular coincidence of fall from grace and shocking recognition for the central character, arousing fear and pity in the audience.

Aeschylus (525–456 B.C.E.) wrote plays concerned with major moral and theological issues. In the Oresteian trilogy (*Agamemnon*, *Libation Bearers*, and *Eumenides*), he wrestled with a thorny question of crime and punishment. Clytemnestra murders her husband Agamemnon, who had sacrificed their daughter Iphigenia to secure safe passage for the Greek expedition to Troy. (Similarly, in Hebrew scriptures, Abraham was willing to sacrifice his son Isaac at the command of God.) Clytemnestra's son Orestes then retaliates by killing her, thereby escaping the Furies (avenging spirits who attack those who kill their kin) of his father but attracting the wrath of his mother's Furies. Orestes escapes the appalling cycle of vengeance only after Athena authorizes a law court to hand down a binding decision. Orestes goes free and vendetta is eliminated, just as it had been historically under such lawgivers as Hammurabi and Draco. Though the human predicament is often painful in the works of Aeschylus, wisdom resulting from suffering ennobles the individual. The Olympian gods ensure ultimate triumph over the forces of darkness and madness.

In the tragedies of Sophocles (c. 496–406 B.C.E.), action arises from personalities subjected to wrenching changes in outlook and fortune. Characters learn not to exceed their limitations or challenge the gods. Inborn character traits, whether despicable or admirable, may lead to disastrous decisions. In *Oedipus the King*, a man has unwittingly killed his father and married his mother. Oedipus is a conscientious ruler, eager to rid Thebes of a terrible plague by apprehending the murderer of the previous king. Even after he suspects he is the guilty party, Oedipus doggedly pursues the truth. His discovery of that truth destroys his wife/mother and drives him to blind himself. Ironically, the man who at first saw with his eyes but not with his mind later gains inner sight but loses his eyes.

Euripides (c. 485–c. 406 B.C.E.) was attuned to the teachings of the Sophists. His plays are often psychological "thrillers" that question traditional morality. His most powerful works, however, deal with psychological abnormality, with the explosive emotions of men and especially women under stress. The traditional anthropomorphic gods symbolize psychic compulsions. Thus, in the *Hippolytus*, Aphrodite and Artemis represent extremes of sexuality and chastity in Phaedra and her stepson Hippolytus, respectively. Phaedra's supercharged sexual appetite draws her to Hippolytus, who adheres to a cult of virginity, redirecting his sexual urges into sadistically obsessive hunting of wild animals. When Hippolytus learns of Phaedra's illicit infatuation and denounces all women with maniacal bitterness, she hangs herself but leaves a note for her husband, Theseus, claiming Hippolytus has raped her. Theseus curses his son, who is trampled to death by his own horses before his father learns the truth.

The Athenians also invented comedy, which, in the Classical period, was strongly satirical. The eleven surviving comedies of Aristophanes (c. 450–c. 385 B.C.E.) are a fantastic mix of serious exposé and uproarious farce, with the humor often based on bodily functions. In the *Clouds*, for example, Aristophanes parodied the Sophists and natural scientists with an outrageous caricature of Socrates, whose eccentric looks and behavior invited such attacks. In the *Knights*, he portrayed the politician and general Cleon, then at the height of his success, as a contemptible demagogue and a blustering, vulgar, stupid upstart. Aristophanes' antiwar sentiments were given free rein in *Lysistrata*; in that play, Athenian women attempt to end the war by a sex strike against their soldier-husbands, who appear in humorously obvious states of agonizing sexual arousal. That Aristophanes could heap blistering abuse on prominent persons and attack their policies without reprisals attests to the remarkable freedom of speech in classical Athens.

Another major innovation of Greek writing was thoughtful narrative and analytical history, as compared to the rote chronicles of ancient West Asia. Herodotus (c. 484–c. 425 B.C.E.), called the Father of History, was born in Asia Minor but lived at Athens and later at an Athenian colony in Italy. His *History* (from Greek *historia*, "inquiry"), though concentrating on the Persian Wars,

Parthenon. The Parthenon was built by the architects Ictinus and Callicrates between 447 and 432 B.C.E. to replace an incomplete temple destroyed by the Persians in 480 and to symbolize Athenian imperial might and cultural superiority. The temple was nearly leveled in 1687 C.E. when a Venetian bombardment set off gunpowder stored in it by the Turks. Though it was restored in the late nineteenth and early twentieth centuries, deterioration caused by atmospheric pollutants and rusting iron clamps has necessitated a complete dismantling and re-restoration, currently in progress. FPG International

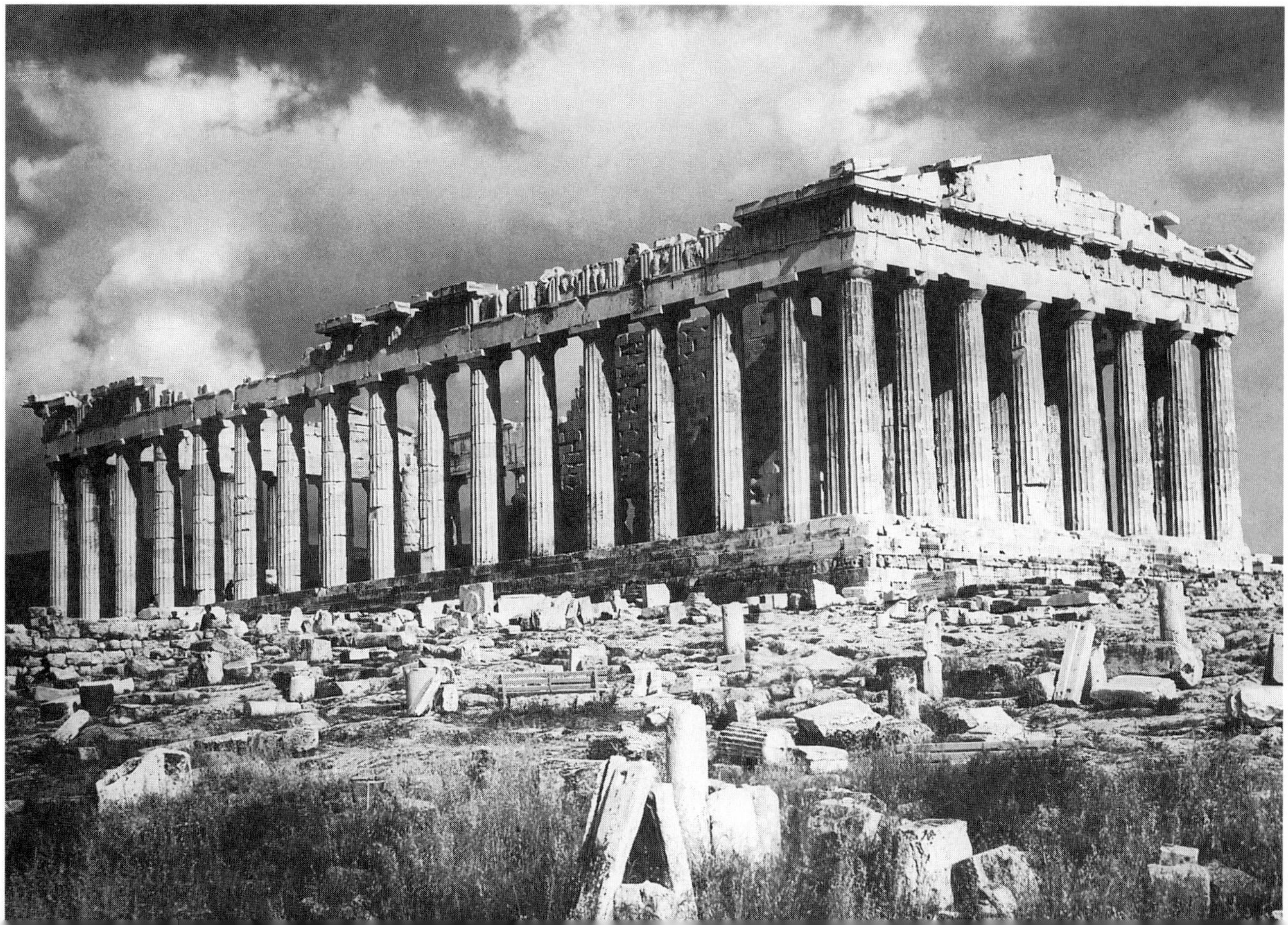

also compares the cultures of Persia and Egypt with that of Greece; enlivening the narrative are the author's accounts of his own eyewitness experiences and oral reports collected on his wide travels. The *History* is full of believe-it-or-not tales of amazing happenings, told in a leisurely and enjoyable style. It is also our best source of information about the Persian Wars. Herodotus combined the roles of cultural anthropologist, geographer, and naturalist with that of the historian. Yet for all its advance in trustworthiness over Greek mythology, Herodotus's *History* is still often unreliable. He naively accepted stories of oracular pronouncements, inspired dreams, and other divine interferences in human affairs. His chronology and statistics also are often faulty; for example, his number for the army of Xerxes—5,283,220—is ludicrous.

Thucydides (c. 460–c. 400 B.C.E.) came closer to the critical standards of modern historiography. An Athenian by birth, he began his *History of the Peloponnesian War* just after its outbreak, "expecting it to be a great war and more worthy of recording than previous ones." He served as a general, but in 424 he was stripped of his command for failing to relieve the besieged city of Amphipolis. His exile for the remainder of the war freed him to work exclusively on his *History*. Thucydides differed from Herodotus by concentrating on political and military events and by evaluating historical evidence more care-

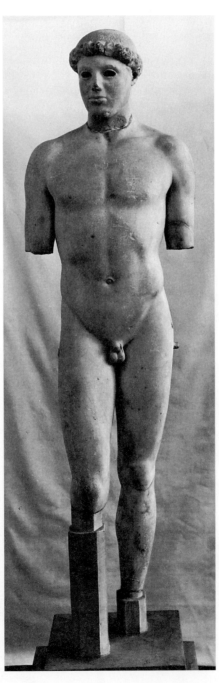

❇ *Left:* Archaic Youth Statue. Note the stiffly impassive frontal pose, left foot forward, arms at sides, hands clenched. These features, together with the broad shoulders, narrow waist, and small flanks, point to Egyptian or Mesopotamian inspiration; c. 600 B.C.E. *Right:* The Kritios Boy. This statue, done around 480 B.C.E., embodies the Greek ideal of physical perfection. The art historian Kenneth Clark called it "the first beautiful nude in art." The imbalance between the tensed, weight-bearing left leg and the free right leg and the sensual elasticity of the sculptor's rendering of flesh and skin mark a complete break from the four-square rigidity of the archaic youth figures.
Hirmer Verlag

fully. He believed the main purpose of history was to provide an accurate record and analysis of past events as a basis for intelligent decisions in later times. Thucydides adopted a sophistic skepticism by giving no place to the supernatural in human affairs. He believed individuals and states acted out of self-interest, not decency or morality; using a literary device sometimes criticized by modern historians, he composed set speeches to crystallize such motivations. He admired Pericles and the Athenian Empire, but realized that growth in the power of any one state inevitably upset the balance between states. Further, he believed that because states with power either used it or ceased to be powerful, war with its unforeseeable turns and brutalizing effects on people was inevitable.

Greek achievements in literature, philosophy, and science were matched by progress in architecture and sculpture. A marvelous sensitivity to balance and beauty in form marked the Greek visual arts as "classic" in their perfection.

The worship of the Olympian gods led to the Greek temple, with its encircling colonnade and carefully worked out proportions, probably inspired by Egyptian models. The Parthenon was among the finest architectural expressions of the Greek love of symmetrical proportion and an impressive monument to Athenian imperial strength and religious devotion. Unlike Roman temples or Gothic cathedrals, which were designed to be approached from one direction, Greek temples dominated their surroundings in all directions. The Parthenon was built of fine marble, hauled, at state expense, from quarries a few miles from the city. Forty-six columns surrounded a two-room inner chamber; the smaller room housed the treasury of the Delian League, the larger a magnificent ivory and gold statue of Athena. On the exterior were sculptures of the goddess's birth and scenes of warfare. The unique continuous frieze running along the top of the chamber illustrated a Panathenaic procession. A remarkable natural serenity pervades the building.

In free-standing, life-size sculpture, the Greeks' restrained realism produced a beautiful nobility in diverse renderings of the human figure. A handful of surviving fifth-century originals, like the Artemisium Zeus and the Kritios Boy, exhibit a stunning sense of proportion and dynamism.

The Rise of Buddhism and Jainism in India

The monk Gautama has given up injury to life, he has lost all inclination to it; he has laid aside the cudgel and the sword, and he lives modestly, full of mercy, desiring in compassion the welfare of all things living.

He has given up taking what is not given. . . . He accepts what is given to him and waits for it to be given; and he lives in honesty and purity of heart. . . .

He has given up unchastity. . . . He is celibate and aloof. . . .

He has given up false speech. . . He speaks the truth, he keeps faith, he is faithful and trustworthy, he does not break his word to the world. . . .

He has given up slander. . . . He unites those who are divided by strife, and encourages those who are friends. . . .

He has given up harsh speech. . . .

He has given up frivolous talk. . . .

He does no harm to seeds or plants. He takes only one meal a day. . . . He will not watch shows, or attend fairs with song, dance, and music. He will not wear ornaments. . . . He will not use a high or large bed. He will not accept gold or silver, raw grain or raw meat. He will not accept women or girls . . . fields or houses. . . . He will not buy or sell, . . . will never bribe, cheat, or defraud. He will not injure, kill or put in bonds, or steal, or do acts of violence.

*William T. de Bary, ed., Sources of Indian Tradition, vol. 1 (New York: Columbia University Press, 1958), pp. 114–115.

This passage is part of a long essay praising Gautama Buddha's moral virtues. These attributes, codified as the ten precepts or commandments, became the guiding principles for monks and, in modified form, for laypeople, too. Gautama founded a world religion called Buddhism. Although it later died out in its original land, India, it remains powerful in East and Southeast Asia.

There was much intellectual ferment in India in the middle of the first millennium B.C.E. It was a transitional period from Aryan tribal states to settled territorial kingdoms, from simple village culture to flourishing towns where artisans and merchants plied their trades and prospered, from old rituals and sacrifices to Vedic gods to new religious ideas and ideals. The previous chapter discussed how asceticism grew during this period and intellectual speculations preoccupied the learned. This section will examine the development of the two new religions that contested the domination of the brahmans—Buddhism and Jainism.

The Life of Buddha

Judged by his posthumous effects on the world, Gautama Buddha, founder of Buddhism, was certainly the greatest man ever born on the Indian subcontinent. Like many great men of ancient times, he was the subject of legends and stories that have become intertwined with the facts of his life. Nevertheless, scholars are reasonably sure about some events. He was born around 566 B.C.E., the son of the chief of the Sakyas, a small tribal kingdom in the foothills of the Himalayas near present-day Nepal, and his consort, Maya, who died after childbirth. His name was

Siddhartha, and his clan name was Gautama; in Buddhist literature he is called either Gautama or Sakyamuni, which means "sage of the Sakyas." He was brought up amidst luxury by his father and his aunt (who was also his stepmother), was married at sixteen to his beautiful cousin, whom he won in manly contest (as in Greek mythology, several noblemen competed in archery or other contests for the hand of a noble woman in marriage), and by whom he had a son. Visions of old age, sickness, and death troubled him deeply, however, and made him aware of the hollowness of human pleasures. Then one day he saw a holy man in a yellow robe, was attracted by his serenity, and decided to follow his path.

Now thirty years of age, one night Gautama left his father's household and, in an act called the Great Renunciation, stripped off his fine clothes and jewels, cut off his hair, and donned a yellow robe. For six years he wandered and meditated with five other ascetics, torturing himself to find enlightenment, but in vain. Then he decided to follow the middle path or the way of moderation. Accusing him of backsliding, his companions left him in disgust. One day he seated himself beneath a pipal or bo tree and vowed that he would not leave until he had found the solution to suffering.

For forty-nine days and nights, he remained beneath the tree meditating, while demons tempted him with pleasure and power and tormented him with pain, but he was unmoved. On the forty-ninth day, he knew the truth, the secret of sorrows and what he must do to overcome them. With this knowledge he was fully enlightened and became a Buddha, the Enlightened or Awakened One. He stayed by the tree, now called the *bodhi* tree (tree of wisdom, the holy tree to Buddhists), for another seven weeks, meditating. Then he journeyed to the Deer Park near Banares (or Varanasi, at a place called Sarnath, where later a great monument to Buddhism was erected) and preached his first sermon to his five former companions, thus "setting in motion the Wheel of the Law." They became his disciples.

Buddha spent the remainder of his life teaching. He and his disciples spent approximately eight months each year traveling throughout the Ganges valley, preaching and organizing Buddhist communities. According to one story, a distraught woman clutching her dead infant approached the Buddha and asked if he could restore its life. Buddha told her to go to the nearest town and obtain a handful of mustard seeds (a common spice), but stipulated that the seeds must come from a family that had not suffered death. She returned at the end of the day empty-handed, but though disappointed, she had learned that all suffer the pain of death. She too became a disciple. During the four monsoon months when travel was impossible, Buddha and his disciples rested and studied in places donated by the pious. As his fame grew, his converts came to include his father and other family members, kings, and humble people. At his stepmother's request, he allowed her to form a community of nuns. Unlike some other holy men who also appeared to challenge established traditions, he suffered no persecution.

Before his death at the age of eighty, Buddha admonished his disciples in these words:

> You must be your own lamps, be your own refuge. Take refuge in nothing outside yourselves. . . . A monk becomes his own lamp and refuge by continually looking on his body, feelings, perception, moods, and ideas in such a manner that he conquers the cravings and depressions of ordinary men and is always strenuous, self-possessed, and collected in mind. Whoever among my monks does this, either now or when I am dead, if he is anxious to learn, will reach the summit.

His sorrowing disciples gathered to cremate his remains and then divided his ashes among the various Buddhist communities. In accordance with local custom, *stupas* (mounds) were built over the places where the ashes were deposited, and bo trees were planted at these sites; they became pilgrimage sites because they commemorated his death and enlightenment, respectively.

Soon after his death, Buddha's disciples gathered together in council to compile his teachings. A second great council held during the fourth century and a third council called by Emperor Asoka around 240 B.C.E. further defined and completed the Buddhist scriptures or canons, called the *Tripitaka* (the Three Baskets, because the palm leaves on which the canons were written were rolled up and deposited in three basket containers according to classification), after the three sections into which they were divided. These sections were: (1) Conduct—rules of behavior for the *sangha* or orders of monks and nuns; (2) Discourses—a collection of sermons on doctrine and ethics, later enlarged by the birth stories (*Jataka*) that dealt with the previous incarnations of the Buddha; and (3) Supplementary Doctrine—metaphysical elucidations of ideas presented in the Discourses. The canons were written in Pali, a vernacular language of northern India. The canons and commentaries were completed in the second century C.E. Later additions by Buddhist scholars were not considered canonical works.

All Buddhists derive their views from the words of Gautama Buddha. In time, however, different schools of thought arose, based on different interpretations of the canons. Centuries after the master's death it was impossible to be certain what he had meant by certain words, and different people interpreted them according to their own emotional needs and the needs of the time. Eventually, each branch, and different sects within each branch, developed its own version of the canons.

The Orthodox: Theravada Buddhism

By the time of the Second Council, differing interpretations of the canons had led to a schism within Buddhism

❊ Temptation of the Buddha. This frieze from present-day Afghanistan depicts Gautama's temptation by Mara, the deity of sin incarnate, before his enlightenment. It is a fine example of Roman-Buddhist sculpture from third-century Gandhara. Courtesy of Richard Edwards

over monastic discipline. Those who claimed that they correctly followed the original teachings called their way the *Theravada*, or Teaching of the Elders, as opposed to the minority dissident camp, who called their way the *Mahayana*, which means the Great Vehicle. At the Third Council, the Theravada school was proclaimed orthodox and members of the Mahayana were expelled.

Gautama did not question the fundamental premises of Indian thought. He believed that *samsara*, or the transmigration of souls, and *karma*, which determines what we are and what we will be, were basic laws that governed the universe. All Indian philosophies agreed that there were endless rounds of rebirths, but they differed on what *dharma,* or doctrine, to follow in order to escape samsara.

In simple terms Buddha explained that life is transient and painful and that the pain is caused by desires, especially selfish and sexual desires, for they lead to reproduction, which stretches out the chain of life into new suffering. However, the pain can be ended by cultivating a sense of detachment from material things; this indifference toward material things can be achieved by following the Eightfold Path. The goal was *nirvana,* an indescribable state, which Gautama and Theravada Buddhists equated with "the blowing out" or extinction of craving and consequently of suffering; it was a tranquil state realized by those who are freed from desires. In an ever-changing universe, nirvana is the only constant, for it is not part of the universe. A living person can attain nirvana, and once he does, he will never lose it. When he dies, he passes into this state forever in the "final blowing out" that releases him from the cycle of reincarnation.

Gautama did not deny that there is happiness in life, but he argued that on balance sorrows always outweigh joy: "As the ocean has one flavor, the flavor of salt," he reputedly said in explanation. Although he did not deny the existence of gods, he insisted that they too are part of the universe and cannot help us. Gautama also taught that the universe is soulless and that the world soul or *brahman* of the Upanishads is an illusion. As he explained, nothing passes from one life to another in transmigration. Only a new life arises from a chain of events that includes the old. Thus Theravada Buddhism is a religion without gods, without souls.

The leaders of Buddhism were members of the order of monks and nuns called the *sangha*. Membership was by avocation, and it was not restricted by caste. Gautama did not attack the caste system directly, but he did not recognize it in his own order. Buddhism (and Jainism) were in part a kshatriya protest against the pretensions and domination of the brahman caste and a rejection of caste restrictions. Undoubtedly, Gautama's attitudes and activities weakened the caste system, and when Buddhism declined in India, the caste system reestablished its rigid order.

A person could join the sangha as a novice from age eighteen on, but could not gain full admission as a member until at least age twenty and only after a period of satisfactory study. A novice underwent a simple ceremony that involved head shaving, donning a yellow robe, and pronouncing the Three Jewels: "I go for refuge to the Buddha; I go for refuge to the Doctrine (dharma); I go for refuge to the Order (sangha)." The novice also promised to obey the Ten Precepts or commandments. Some of the

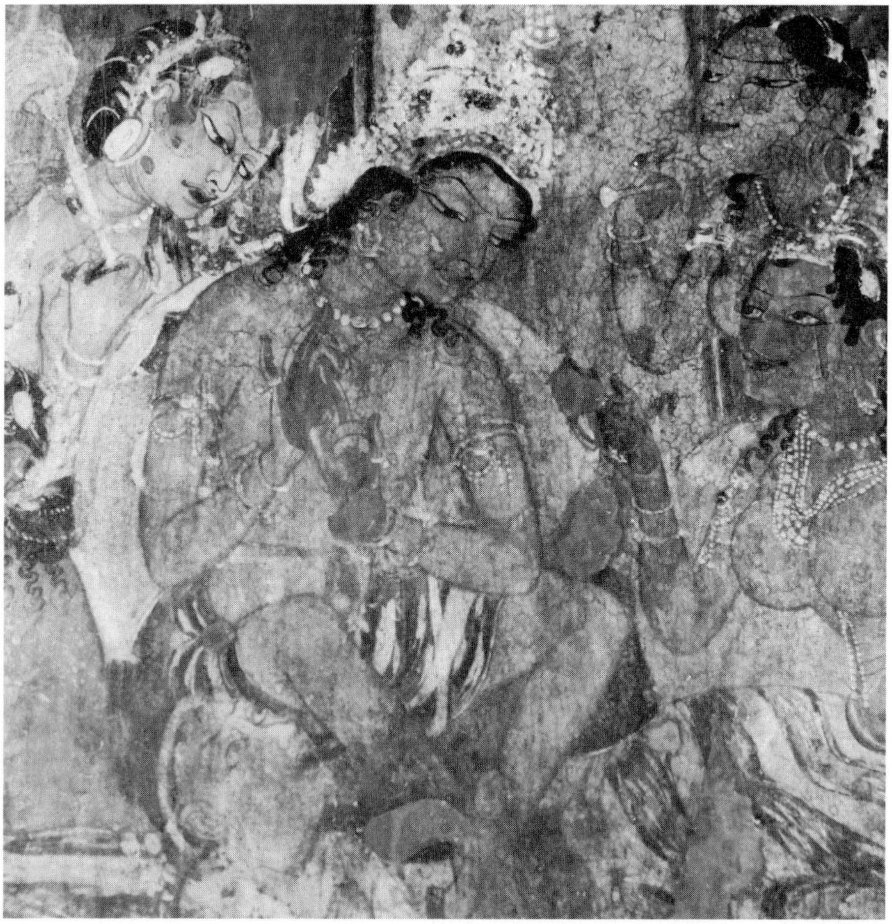

The Buddha in a Previous Life. *Jataka* stories tell about the Buddha's previous incarnations or about moral acts by humans and animals. They were popular among Buddhists as tools for teaching religious ideals. This fourth-century fresco from the Ajanta cave in India tells about the virtuous life of the Buddha in a former incarnation. V. Panijab/Superstock

commandments had equivalents in the later Christian monk's vows of chastity and poverty, but the Buddhist monk, unlike his Christian counterpart, swore no vow of obedience, for the sangha was essentially a community of free men or women with no central authority or chain of command. The monastic vow was not a lifelong bond (even now all young men in such Theravada Buddhist countries as Thailand and Burma are expected to take vows for a specified short period and then return to lay life). A monk might leave or even reenter the order freely, although backsliding was frowned upon.

Monks spent their time chiefly in study and religious exercises; of the latter, the most important were called the Four Sublime Moods, which required the monk to sit cross-legged, fill his mind with the four cardinal virtues—love, pity, joy, and serenity—and think of all living things in light of these virtues. Monks who reached higher levels meditated on more advanced themes with the ultimate goal of realizing nirvana. To remind them of their vow of poverty, monks went from door to door every morning to beg for food, which they shared with members of the community. As monasteries became wealthy (poverty was enjoined on the individual, not the community), the requirement to beg was either reduced to a formality or dropped entirely.

In a sermon titled "Address to Sigala," Gautama instructed a young man on familial and other relationships, duties, and responsibilities. It said in part:

> Husbands should respect their wives, and comply as far as possible with their requests. They should not commit adultery. They should give their wives full charge of the house, and supply them with fine clothes and jewelry as far as their means permit. Wives should be thorough in their duties, gentle and kind to the whole household, chaste, and careful in housekeeping, and should carry out their work with skill and enthusiasm.
>
> A man should be generous to his friends, speak kindly of them, act in their interest in every way possible, treat them as his equals, and keep his word to them. . . .
>
> Employers should treat their servants and workpeople decently. They should not be given tasks beyond their strength. They should receive adequate food and wages, be cared for in time of sickness and infirmity, and be given regular holidays and bonuses in times of prosperity. They (servants) should rise early and go to bed late in the service of their masters, be content with their just wages, work thoroughly, and maintain their master's reputation.

Unlike the sermon to Sigala, some other sermons and philosophical discourses were difficult for ordinary people to understand, but Jataka stories were not. They therefore became important vehicles for teaching. Like Aesop's *Fables* in ancient Greece, Jataka stories taught the value of caution and shrewdness in daily life, as well as generosity and self-sacrifice. In the Sibi Jataka, for example, the king of the Sibis (a previous incarnation of Gautama) ransomed a pigeon from a hungry hawk with flesh cut from his own body. Everyone could grasp the moral in these stories, which became popular favorites. Through sermons, stories, and examples, Theravada Buddhism taught that all could accumulate merit through individual effort and that all can attain nirvana.

Evolution of the Great Vehicle: Mahayana Buddhism

According to the Pali scriptures, Gautama was not a deity; he had gained enlightenment by his own efforts after many births, and when he finally entered nirvana, he ceased to affect the universe in any way. The scriptures also taught that there had been other buddhas before Gautama and that there would be others in the future; furthermore, buddhahood was something that everyone could attain, just as the holy monks who practiced Gautama's teachings had done. In so doing a holy monk became *arahant* (worthy) and an exemplar for others.

Though inspirational, these teachings also made most people feel inadequate before the challenge of achieving buddhahood. A new interpretation, called *Mahayana* (the Great Vehicle), developed to meet the needs of these believers. In this reinterpreted Buddhism, a great vehicle was found whereby more believers could be carried to nirvana with the help of compassionate beings, called *bodhisattvas*. Mahayana Buddhists called the orthodox school *Hinayana* (Lesser Vehicle), because the self-reliance it demanded of its followers allowed a lesser number to attain nirvana. The nature of nirvana also changed from extinction of the individual soul to a paradise of the blessed. Soon after Gautama's death his followers began to proclaim the phrase, "I go for refuge in the Buddha," as one of the Three Jewels of Buddhism (the other two being dharma and sangha). Mahayana Buddhists interpreted this statement to mean that the master, as distinct from his teaching, was still in some way present and able to help his followers. This point of view led to the deification of Gautama Buddha.

Early Buddhists worshiped outdoors and did not have statues or images. By the first century B.C.E., however, surviving Buddhist monuments show adoring worshipers honoring symbols of the Buddha, such as his footprint. A little later actual images of the Buddha began to appear as the focus of worship. Although Mahayana Buddhists led the way in this trend, eventually Theravadins followed suit, and Gautama came to be honored in all Buddhist shrines with statues, flowers, incense, and lamps. Bodhisattvas were a hallmark of Mahayana Buddhism. Gautama is portrayed as a bodhisattva in previous incarnations in some Jataka stories. Animals are the heroes in others. One heroic monkey saved his friends from death by making himself a living bridge over the Ganges River so they could escape from hunters by walking over him. Other stories told of wonderfully appealing and compassionate figures who had voluntarily postponed their own buddhahood in order to help other living things achieve the same goal.

Some bodhisattvas had specialized functions, but all answered prayers. Just calling the name of a bodhisattva in sincerity would give merit to the supplicant. In addition to answering prayers and extending their compassion, bodhisattvas also became spirits of suffering, taking on the pains and sorrows of the world. In comparison with the bodhisattvas, the arahants or holy monks admired by Theravada Buddhists seem cold and selfish. By the first century C.E., the idea of a suffering savior, who resembled the Christian idea of God who gave his life to

❧ Worshiping the Buddha. This second-century B.C.E. stone relief shows people bowing before an empty throne beneath a tree. Early Buddhist art does not present an image of the Buddha. Instead, he is symbolized by an empty throne or a footprint. Royal Smeets Offset

❧ Dancer and Musicians Perform for the Buddha. This late-seventh-century panel in the Buddhist cave shrine at Aurangabad in India shows a changed vision of nirvana in Mahayana Buddhism. Instead of obliteration of the self, nirvana is now a paradise of incredible, everlasting bliss. © John Listopad

redeem humanity, became important in Mahayana belief. Scholars agree that the Zoroastrian idea of a savior who will lead the forces of good against those of evil and darkness at the end of the world did influence the Mahayana Buddhist cult of *Maitreya*, or Buddha of the Future, a gentle figure who is worshiped as a bodhisattva.

Mahayana Buddhism also developed the notion that Gautama had been not a mere man, but rather the earthly expression of a great spiritual being. This being had three bodies, and of these only one, the Created Body, had been on earth. Another, the Body of Essence, eternally permeated the universe; the third, the Body of Bliss (called *Amitabha*, or Immeasurable Light), is the presiding deity of the Happy Land, the most important heaven where the blessed are reborn on lotus buds and live in bliss. Though presiding in heaven, Amitabha continues to take a compassionate interest in the world. Some Mahayana sects believe that calling his name in faith will ensure the faithful's rebirth in this Happy Land.

Thus the Great Vehicle not only created a pantheon of noble and compassionate bodhisattvas but also transformed nirvana into a land of joy for the blessed. The faithful no longer sought extinction but participation in a land of bliss. Many Mahayana believers preferred the idea of a suffering savior and compassionate saints who answer prayers to the Theravada notion that all humans must find their own way to salvation. Therefore, while both schools agreed that the world is full of suffering, Mahayana is more socially oriented and optimistic. In both forms, Buddhist teachings were less abstract than the nonviolence and abstinence of the *Upanishads,* and more attainable than the severe self-mortification demanded by Jainism. For these reasons Buddhism is called the religion of the middle way.

Jainism

Mahavira means "great hero." It is the title given to Vardhamana, founder of Jainism, the "religion of the conquerors," which also took shape during the Late Vedic Age. It too challenged Vedism and competed with Buddhism. Much of Mahavira's early life resembled that of Gautama Buddha. Like Gautama, Mahavira belonged to the kshatriya caste. Born about 540 B.C.E., the second son of a minor ruler of northern India, he married and had a daughter, but felt spiritually unfulfilled. After his parents' death, he left home at the age of thirty, with his elder brother's permission, to pursue a life of asceticism. When Mahavira started his wandering life, he wore a suit of clothes, but soon he discarded it as an encumbrance and, for the rest of his life, went about in complete nudity. For twelve years he meditated and subjected his body to the severest punishments. In the thirteenth year, Mahavira found full enlightenment and became a *jina,* or conqueror.

Like Gautama, Mahavira spent the remaining thirty years of his life traveling the Ganges valley with a band of disciples, teaching his new religion. His followers were called Jains, a derivative of the word *jina.* When he died in 468 B.C.E. at the age of seventy-two, reputedly of self-inflicted starvation, he left a disciplined band of naked monks and many lay followers to continue his work. Jain religious canons were first codified about 200 years after Mahavira's death, but they did not take final form until the fifth century C.E.

According to Mahavira, the universe is eternal, divided into an infinite number of cycles, each with an up and a down phase. There had already been twenty-three cycles, the era that spanned his life being the twenty-fourth. Universal emperors and other great men lived during each cycle. When a cycle is at its apex, giant people get all they want from wishing trees and have no need for laws and property. During Mahavira's lifetime the world was in decline and would so continue until the cycle reached its nadir, when the tide would turn and conditions would improve again.

Jainism holds that there are an infinite number of souls in the universe, all fundamentally equal, but differing in the extent to which the accretion of karmic matter from life to life has dulled the originally bright soul. Salvation is to be found by freeing the soul from matter so that it can regain its original pristine purity. Only then can it enjoy eternal bliss in nirvana, atop the universe, above the highest heaven.

Mahavira taught that life pervades the whole world and that all living things belong to one of five classes of life, locked in the process of birth and rebirth. The highest class includes gods, humans, and certain intelligent animals: lower classes include the lower animals, insects, and plants on down to inanimate objects such as rocks, fire, and water. Only monks (and nuns according to one Jain sect) have a chance of escaping the process of reincarnation because of their renunciation of the material life and their strict vows and practice of self-denial. Although laypeople cannot obtain release from rebirth in this life, they are nevertheless encouraged to lead strictly moral lives, to undertake frequent retreats into monasteries, and to fast often.

Because the five classes are locked together in the eternal cycle of reincarnation, any action that harms life brings adverse consequences. The following verses from the Jain Book of Sermons explain this belief:

> Earth and water, fire and wind,
>   Grass, trees, and plants, and all creatures that move,
> Born of egg, born of the womb,
>   Born of dung, born of liquids—
>
> These are the classes of living beings.
>   Know that they all seek happiness.
> In hurting them men hurt themselves,
>   And will be born again among them. . . .
>
> The man who lights a fire kills living things
>   While he who puts it out kills the fire;
> Thus a wise man who understands the Law
>   Should never light a fire.
>
> There are lives in earth and lives in water,
>   Hopping insects leap into the fire,
> And worms dwell in rotten wood.
>   All are burned when a fire is lighted.
>
> Even plants are beings, capable of growth,
>   Their bodies need food, they are individuals.
> The reckless cut them for their own pleasure
>   And slay many living things in doing so.

Hence, Jains are sternly enjoined to practice *ahimsa,* which means behaving in a nonviolent or noninjurious way toward living things. Jains are strict vegetarians, are not allowed to wear silk clothing (because silkworm larvae must be killed before the thread can be unwound), or engage in professions that entail killing living things. This includes farming, which involves accidental killing of living organisms and intentional killing of plant life. Hence, monks must eat only food obtained from begging, because they are forbidden to participate in the killing of life that food preparation entails or to light fires. Since Jains could not follow professions that harmed life, they became merchants, bankers, lawyers, and doctors. They are known for their honesty, hard work, and frugality and

dus, and brahmans are often called in to officiate on those occasions in Jain households. Hence, some Hindus consider Jainism a sect of Hinduism and Jains a separate group within the four great orders or castes in Hindu society. Such an attitude is typical of the tolerance Indians have traditionally felt toward people of different religious beliefs and practices. A Jain layman could call on a Hindu priest to perform a ceremony at his house and also donate to a Jain temple and go there for periodic retreats.

Indian culture owes a debt to Jainism. Many Jain monks were scholars of both religious and secular learning; some were noted mathematicians and astronomers. Great libraries associated with Jain temples have preserved many ancient manuscripts. In addition, Jains' fervent support of nonviolence has undoubtedly helped to spread the ideal among non-Jains as well. In modern times, Jainism had a significant influence on Mahatma Gandhi, who was born and raised in a part of India where Jainism was widespread. Gandhi wrote about the deep impression the saintly Jain ascetics made on him in his youth.

China: Confucianism, Taoism, and Legalism

Confucius said: "If a ruler himself is upright, all will go well without orders. But if he himself is not upright, even though he gives orders they will not be obeyed. . . . Lead the people by laws and regulate them by penalties, and the people will try to keep out of jail, but will have no sense of shame. Lead the people by virtue and restrain them by the rules of decorum, and the people will have a sense of shame, and moreover will become good."*

* * * * *

Mencius had an interview with King Hui of Liang. The king said:

"Venerable sir, since you have considered it worth while to journey so far to come here, I assume that you must have brought with you counsels to profit my kingdom—is it not so?"

Mencius replied, "Why must your majesty speak of profit? I have nothing to offer but benevolence and righteousness. If your majesty asks, 'What will profit my kingdom?' then the great officers will ask, 'What will profit our families?' and the lower officers and people will ask, 'What will profit our persons?' Superiors and inferiors will contend with one another for profit and the state will be endangered. But there has never been a benevolent man who neglected his parents, nor a righteous man who regarded his ruler lightly. Let your majesty then speak only of benevolence and righteousness."**

*William T. de Bary, ed., *Sources of Chinese Tradition,* vol. 1 (New York: Columbia University Press, 1960), p. 32.
**The Mencius I (1), in H. G. Creel, *Chinese Thought from Confucius to Mao Tse-tung* (New York: Mentor Books, 1953), p. 75.

✣ Adoration of a Jina. This page from a seventeenth-century illustrated manuscript shows various beings adoring a jina, one who has conquered desire. Los Angeles County Museum of Art, from the Nasli and Alice Heeramaneck Collection, Museum Associates Purchase

are a successful people. Splendid Jain temples, built more than a thousand years ago and still well maintained, attest to the wealth and piety of the community. Down to the present the Jain community maintains many charitable institutions for humans and animals. Their contributions to Indian society have been much more important than their present population of 7 million people would lead one to expect.

For two centuries after Mahavira's death, the Jains were a small community of monks and lay followers, and in keeping with traditional Indian tolerance, they were not persecuted. A schism or split occurred at the beginning of the Mauryan dynasty (third century B.C.E.) over the severity of monastic discipline. Two sects of Jain monks, the Space Clad or Sky Clad (naked) and the White Clad (robed in white cloth), emerged, and the schism has never healed.

Although Jains deny the authority of the *Vedas* and have their own canons, in time they accepted many Hindu gods, though in subordinate positions to the Jain universal emperors. Their domestic rites at birth, marriage, and death do not differ much from those of Hin-

After their deaths, Confucius and Mencius were honored as China's first and second sages. They were concerned with morals and good government and thought that rulers and educated men had an obligation to set good examples and rule by persuasion rather than threats of punishment. Like the Greek philosopher Plato, they had no success in installing a philosopher-king who would be amenable to their advice. Confucius devoted his later years to teaching and to the development of the philosophy that would be called Confucianism. Mencius, who lived two centuries later, became the greatest Confucian after the master. Around 100 B.C.E. Confucianism became China's state doctrine.

Philosophy flourished in China between approximately 600 and 300 B.C.E.; indeed, all the classic philosophies that molded Chinese civilization to the present were rooted in this period. The chaotic conditions of the Eastern Chou dynasty (771–221 B.C.E.) inspired many philosophers to offer their ideas, each claiming that he had the solution to reunite the Chinese world. The philosophies ranged from the very abstract to the very concrete, from idealistic to hedonistic. The great variety of views prompted later Chinese to dub this the era of a Hundred Schools, which happened at about the same time that Hebrew prophets were interpreting God's will in Israel, Greek scientists and philosophers were speculating on moral and cosmic issues, and great religious thinkers were teaching in India.

Some of the Chinese teachers were not philosophers in the strict sense. For example, Sun Wu, who wrote *The Art of War,* was a tactician who analyzed the factors involved in total war, including psychological warfare, intelligence gathering, strategy, and mobilization; the work remains useful and even now is often studied in military academies. The three schools that had the most influence on China, however, were Confucianism, Taoism, and Legalism.

The Idealist: Confucius and His Teachings

Like Buddha in India, Confucius is the best-known son of China. Few men have so profoundly influenced human lives and history. Confucius (551–479 B.C.E.) was a member of the *shih* (knight) class, the lowest among aristocrats. His family name was K'ung and his given name was Ch'iu, but the Chinese call him K'ung Fu-tzu or Master K'ung, which was Latinized to Confucius by Jesuit missionaries in the seventeenth century. His father died when Confucius was three years old, and he was brought up by his mother in rather humble circumstances. Still, his hobbies were archery and music, which indicate an aristocratic heritage, just as horse riding, music, and the sports of the gymnasium were part of the Greek aristocrat's daily life.

Confucius was ambitious. Because he did not inherit a government position, he had to earn one by his own efforts, for in his day the path to fame and effectiveness was through public office. Yet he was temperamentally unsuited for a successful career as a politician. His failure to attain responsible public office left him time to study and contemplate, and he finally resigned himself to teaching. He was probably the most learned man of his age. He had a dynamic and revolutionary view of education, which he saw as a means to make government serve the people, not as a vehicle for securing government positions. Unsurpassed as a teacher, he reputedly imparted his views on life and government to 3,000 students. Soon after his death, some of them compiled his sayings into a book called the *Lun-yu* or *Analects.*

From the *Analects* we know much not only about Confucius's views but also about the man; for example:

> In his leisure hours, Confucius was easy in his manner and cheerful in his expression. . . . Confucius fished but not with a net; he shot but not at a roosting bird. . . . When Confucius was pleased with the singing of someone he was with, he would always ask to have the song repeated and would join in himself.

He expressed his love of learning thus:

> At fifteen, I set my heart on learning. At thirty, I was firmly established. At forty, I had no more doubts. At fifty, I knew the will of Heaven. At sixty, I was ready to listen to it. At seventy, I could follow my heart's desire without transgressing what was right.

Confucius believed that human nature was innately good and that it was moral education that made some people superior: "By nature men are pretty much alike; it is learning and practice that set them apart." He also observed that "in education there are no class distinctions."

Confucius wrote a book called the *Chun Chiu* (Spring and Autumn), a chronicle of his native state of Lu from 722 to 479 B.C.E. The *Chun Chiu, Shu Ching* (Book of History), *Shih Ching* (Book of Poetry), *Li Chi* (Book of Rituals, see Chapter 2), and the *I Ching* (Book of Change), which dealt with divination and metaphysical concepts, are called the Five Classics. They are the most important canons of Confucianism and are accepted by all Chinese as the distillation of their heritage from ancient times. Some scholars credit Confucius and his disciples with compiling and editing the earlier classics. In any case they were conservators who prided themselves on preserving and handing down the heritage of the past.

Confucius taught that people must return to virtue and live the ideal of *jen,* which means "humanity, benevolence, and love." When jen is practiced together with *li* (moral and social propriety), society will return to a state of *tao,* or the moral way ordained by heaven and carried out by past sage rulers during the golden age of mythology and the early Chou dynasty.

All individuals exist within society. Moral worth, not birth, makes a person superior. Superior men devote

✻ Portrait of Confucius. This traditional portrait of Confucius is by an unknown artist. It shows a serene old teacher.
National Palace Museum, Taipei, Taiwan, Republic of China

themselves to public service to bring about general betterment. Leaders should be virtuous and rule by example rather than through coercion and fear. When a ruler asked Confucius about government, he replied: "If a ruler himself is upright, all will go well without orders. But if he himself is not upright, even though he gives orders they will not be obeyed." To this, he added: "Let the prince be prince, the minister be minister, the father father and the son son." Confucius called this concept the rectification of names, meaning that every name carries certain implications. Thus, when a man is called ruler, he should know what is expected of a moral ruler. If he acts according to those ideals, then he is truly a ruler in name as well as in fact. The same holds true for every name in social relationships.

Confucius taught that there are five basic relationships: ruler and minister, father and son, husband and wife, elder and younger sibling, and friend and friend. Each relationship is reciprocal; each person has obligations toward the other. For example, younger siblings should love and respect their older brothers and sisters, who should love and guide the younger ones. The impor-

tance of the family is shown by the fact that three of the five relationships are between its members. According to Confucius, the family is the state in microcosm. Older family members give the young ones their first lessons in morality. If the father is kind and just and sets a good example, the family will live in harmony. Likewise, if the ruler treats his subjects as a good father does his children, the state will be in good order. Confucius constantly urged filial piety, or love and reverence of the young toward the old, as a social duty. What if there is conflict between a son's duty to his father and a higher social duty? Confucius said: "In serving his parents a son may gently remonstrate with them. If he sees that they are not inclined to follow his suggestion, he should resume his reverential attitude but not abandon his purpose. If he is belabored, he will not complain."

Confucius founded a school of moral philosophy, not a religion. He believed in ancestor worship, as did all Chinese, but he shied away from speculating about the next world. When asked by a student about the worship of ghosts and spirits, he replied: "We don't know yet how to serve men; how can we know about serving the spirits?" In this he shows a kinship of spirit with Socrates, who similarly was skeptical of conventional notions about life after death.

The Reformer: Mencius and the Confucian Consensus

Confucius had many disciples, who continued his teachings, but the most famous early Confucian was Meng K'o (c. 372–c. 289 B.C.E.), whose Latinized name was Mencius, for Meng Tzu, or Master Meng. Like Confucius, he was born into a *shih* family and lost his father when he was very young. Mencius was raised by his mother, who struggled to give him a good education, moving several times until she found a place near a school. Regretting that he was born too late to know the master, Mencius studied under Confucius's grandson. For a while he traveled from state to state, vainly trying to convince rulers to adopt his ideas, but eventually he settled down to teach. His ideas are set out in a book called *The Mencius,* which became a major Confucian classic.

A brilliant debater, Mencius took on advocates of other schools of philosophy. He also expanded on some ideas not fully developed by Confucius and brought them to their logical conclusion. For example, Confucius said that men should practice jen in dealing with others, but did not fully explain why. Mencius explained that they should do so because human nature is originally good, so every man has the potential of sagehood, but goodness needs to be cultivated and cannot be achieved through a flash of enlightenment.

Mencius was even more insistent than Confucius that the state should be a moral institution and that the head of state should be a moral leader. He declared that such an ideal state had existed when sage men ruled in the golden age. What if the ruler failed to live up to the ideals? Developing Confucius's theory of the rectification of names to its logical conclusion, Mencius said that such a ruler is no king but a "mere fellow" and that the people have the moral right of revolution. He added that rulers should trust the administration to qualified officials and not interfere with their duties, for to do so would be as foolish as trying to tell a skilled jade carver how to carve jade. It is not enough, he continued, for a ruler merely to set good examples. He should also create an environment that will encourage the people to cultivate high standards of morality. He could do this by providing for the economic well-being of his subjects. This had been done, said Mencius, by the Duke of Chou when he created the well-field system. This land distribution system, so simple in concept, has fascinated reformers from Mencius's time to the present; many see it as the ultimate foundation of social justice in an agrarian society.

Mencius's idealism had a practical base. He argued that it is in the enlightened interest of a ruler to treat his people well, for he cannot expect his subjects to practice morality on empty stomachs. Conversely, Mencius warned that if a ruler abuses his people, they have the right to rise up and overthrow him. These teachings earned Mencius the title of the Second Sage (after Confucius), inspired the love of the people, and established his reputation as a scourge of tyrants.

Confucianism was a practical philosophy that emphasized proper conduct, virtuous life, and humanity, which can be learned through the study of history and the classics. It is also an optimistic philosophy that teaches that human nature is good, that both the individual and society are perfectible, and that life can be harmonious and fulfilling for all. Confucianism faced competition, however, from other schools of thought.

The Mystic: Lao Tzu and Taoism

The word *tao* means "the way." If most Chinese philosophers agreed upon one thing, it was that the turmoil of the era was the result of the loss of tao, however interpreted. While Confucians, the earnest "do-gooders" of the day, attempted to restore the perceived tao of the sage kings of antiquity by moral reforms, others reacted to the chaotic times by seeking to rise above the mundane. The *Analects* mentions hermits ridiculing Confucius for vainly attempting to save a world that they regarded as beyond saving. The philosophy these recluses developed to justify and give meaning to their nonaction is called Taoism. Next to Confucianism, Taoism is the most important traditional philosophy in Chinese history. In many ways it is precisely the opposite of Confucianism; paradoxically, though, the two doctrines have acted as necessary counterparts of each other, appealing to different sides of the Chinese character.

Tradition credits Lao Tzu (Old Master) with founding Taoism, but there is no proof that such a man existed. After Taoism had established a following, some Taoists claimed that the Old Master had been a senior contemporary of Confucius, that he came from the state of Ch'u located along the Yangtze valley, and that he had worked as an archivist in the royal Chou court. According to the same tradition, as an old man he had decided to leave China and head west but had been stopped by border guards who had asked him to write down his teachings. After doing so, some stories say, he went on to India where he converted the Buddha to Taoism.

The *Lao Tzu* or *Tao Te Ching* (The Canon of the Way and Virtue) is attributed to Lao Tzu. Considered the most important canon of Taoism, the *Lao Tzu* is mostly in poetic form and only 5,000 words long. It is a difficult book—terse, deliberately obscure, and thus open to many interpretations. These characteristics have contributed to its appeal through the generations. It begins thus:

> The Tao [way] that can be told of
> Is not the eternal Tao;
> The name that can be named
> Is not the eternal name.
> Nameless, it is the origin of Heaven and earth,
> Nameable, it is the mother of all things.

In another passage the *Lao Tzu* says: "Those who understand don't talk, and those who talk don't understand." Confucians have delighted in throwing this epigram back at the Taoists, saying that in writing this book, Lao Tzu may have proved that point conclusively!

While many passages of the *Lao Tzu* are puzzling, some are not; for example:

> Therefore a sage rules his people thus:
> He empties their minds,
> And fills their bellies;
> He weakens their ambition,
> And strengthens their bones.
> He strives always to keep the people innocent of
> knowledge and desires, and to keep the knowing ones
> from meddling. By doing nothing that interferes with
> anything, nothing is left unregulated.

This passage sums up the Taoist theory of government. Both Confucians and Taoists agree that a sage should rule, but whereas the Confucian sage-ruler should do many things for the people, the Taoist sage-ruler should do nothing at all. Taoists say the troubles of the world are caused not by governments failing to do enough but by governments doing too much. Before civilization corrupted people, there had been a golden age:

> It was when the Great Tao declined,
> That there appeared humanity and righteousness.
> It was when knowledge and intelligence arose,
> That there appeared hypocrisy.
> It was when the six relations lost their harmony,

That there was talk of filial piety and paternal
    affection.
It was when the country fell into chaos and confusion
That there was talk of loyalty and trustworthiness.
Banish sageliness, discard wisdom,
And the people will be benefitted a hundredfold.
Banish humanity, discard righteousness,
And the people will return to filial piety and
    parental affection.
Banish skill, discard profit,
And thieves and robbers will disappear.

By virtue (*te* in the canon *Tao-te Ching*), Taoists do not
mean the virtue achieved through a moral education, but
rather the natural, instinctive qualities of virtue, a concept similar to Plato's idea of the primitive man in the
Laws. Taoists therefore strive to return to primitive simplicity, to a time before people were corrupted by the fol-
lies of civilization. The *Lao Tzu* thus represents an
alternative solution to the political chaos and intellectual
turmoil of the late Chou. Like Confucianism, Taoism pro-
poses a way of life and philosophy of government for the
elite, the only people who could read and had the leisure
to withdraw to contemplate nature.

Chuang Tzu (Master Chuang, c. 369–286 B.C.E.) was
the second great figure, and a historical one, of the Taoist
school. He reputedly served as a minor official in one of
the states; little is known about him, however, for he
seems to have spent much time as a hermit. A book of essays called the *Chuang Tzu* is attributed to him. Like the
Lao Tzu, it does not depend on methodical argument to
convince. It is full of whimsy; animals and insects con-
verse philosophically while men speak nonsense. Moralists, especially Confucians, are lampooned with cutting
wit. The *Chuan Tzu* is sprinkled throughout with anecdotes, of which the following is an example:

> Once Chuang Tzu was fishing in the P'u River when the king
> of Ch'u sent two of his ministers to announce that he wished
> to entrust to Chuang Tzu the care of his entire domains.
>
> Chuang Tzu held his fishing pole and, without turning
> his head, said: "I have heard that Ch'u possesses a sacred
> tortoise which has been dead for three thousand years and
> which the king keeps wrapped up in a box and stored in his
> ancestral temple. Is this tortoise better off dead and with its
> bones venerated, or would it be better off alive with its tail
> dragging in the mud?"
>
> "It would be better off alive and dragging its tail in the
> mud," the two ministers replied.
>
> "Then go away!" said Chuang Tzu, "and I will drag my tail
> in the mud!"

Chuang Tzu agreed with the *Lao Tzu*'s thesis that the
tao is the underlying principle governing all existence. He
denied the Confucian concept that man is the measure of
all things. To Chuang Tzu, the human mind was clouded
by partial understanding, and only the tao was enduring
and eternal. He believed that people must free themselves
from their own prejudices and their tendency to judge
others in terms of themselves. A person who understood

and lived in unity with the tao would be happy and beyond change and death. Chuang Tzu regarded death as a
natural step that followed life in an eternal process of cosmic change; therefore it was not to be feared.

Such was the vision of the early Taoist sages. They extolled nature and urged people to attune themselves to it in
order to be happy. They offered no governmental programs
except that less is better, until people could return to the
state of childlike innocence of ancient times. A true Taoist
should not even urge others to follow the Tao because in
so doing he would be imposing his own value judgment.
However, being human, the Taoists joined in the competition with other schools of philosophy for acceptance.

The Totalitarians: Legalism

Legalism, the other main challenge to Confucianism, was
chronologically the last philosophy to emerge from the
Hundred Schools period. It had the greatest impact on
the political life of the time. Unlike exponents of the other
schools who did not hold high public office, Legalist leaders were high government officials with great power; their
primary concern was to find solutions to immediate problems, not to devise theoretical approaches. Like many
busy politicians, they were impatient with the debates of
philosophers, which they condemned as "vain talk." Legalism here does not mean jurisprudence; it refers to the
theory and method of political organization and leadership. It developed because the state needed a rational social and political organization that would enable it to
prosper and unite China by defeating its rivals in war.

The first book expounding Legalist ideas was *The Lord
Shang,* written by Shang Yang (d. 338 B.C.E.). Shang Yang
(later rewarded with the title of lord) was the chief minister of the northwestern state of Ch'in and was responsible for organizing a system of government that enabled
Ch'in to become powerful, overcome its rivals, and unify
China a century later. In his book Lord Shang described
the policies that he had successfully implemented, such
as the abolition of serfdom and the institution of a centralized, bureaucratic form of administration. He organized all families into mutual surveillance units, imposed
harsh punishments, and rewarded informers. Lord Shang
also emphasized the importance of rule by law from
which the school derived its name.

Han Fei (d. 233 B.C.E.) was another minister of Ch'in.
He too left a book named after himself that added to Lord
Shang's theories on Legalism. Han Fei later lost a power
struggle, was disgraced, and died in prison at the hands
of his fellow Legalist and rival, Li Ssu. Li served as chief
minister of Ch'in both during its final drive for unification and afterward. Li, who would also be murdered in
prison, synthesized the teachings of Lord Shang and Han
Fei and brought them to their highest development. The
deaths of Li and Han reflect the ruthless and violent
power struggles typical of the Legalists.

Legalists had no patience with the Confucians and Taoists who looked back in time for a golden age. They maintained that people in the present were neither better nor worse than people in the past; it was only that conditions were different. Rather than long for a restoration of the past, people should solve new problems with new measures. Han Fei's book cited a story to prove this point:

> There was a plow man of Sung in whose field was a tree stump. When a rabbit scampered headlong into the stump, broke its neck, and died, he abandoned his plow and kept watch over the stump, hoping it would get him more rabbits. But he got no more rabbits and became the laughingstock of the whole state of Sung. Now, wanting to apply policies of the former kings in governing people in these times belongs in the very same category as watching over the stump!

The idea that the human condition was a changing process was revolutionary at that time.

Whereas Confucians and Taoists were concerned with improving the plight of the people, Legalists believed that human nature was evil, that people were naturally selfish, lazy, disobedient, and reluctant to engage in war. Accordingly, the Legalists argued that the ruler should defend his absolute authority against the demands of the people through the stringent enforcement of strict laws. Those who contribute to the state should be rewarded lavishly, while wrongdoers should be punished with exemplary harshness. For example, when the crown prince criticized some laws as too harsh, Lord Shang held the prince's teacher responsible and had him branded. When some people then praised the laws, he ordered them banished for daring to voice their opinions. All learned to keep quiet and obey. Officials should receive job assignments on the basis of talent and not birth, and they should be held strictly responsible for their deeds. No one is above the law, and when the laws are complete, the system is foolproof. The ruler need only retain the authority to reward and to punish, and all else will run automatically.

The ultimate Legalist goal was to establish and perpetuate an all-powerful state, protected by all-embracing laws, impersonally administered. Legalists maintained that there were only two types of useful citizens: farmers and soldiers. The farmers' work created wealth, and good soldiers won wars that made the state powerful. Furthermore, the state should be able to mobilize its able-bodied farmers and use them as soldiers when needed. How does the state convince its citizens that they must fight? Lord Shang answered: "If there is no hope of fame except through service in warfare, the people will be ready to lay down their lives. . . . I would have the people told . . . if they fear harm, it will be only by fighting that they can escape it." He concluded: "A country that directed itself to these two ends [agriculture and war] would not have to wait long before it established hegemony or even complete mastery over all other states." He also observed that

❀ The Three Faiths. This sixteenth-century painting shows Confucius in the center and dominant; he is flanked by Gautama Buddha on his left, who is withdrawn in meditation, and Lao Tzu, founder of Taoism, on the right, looking contented. Legalism was rejected by the Chinese after the brief Ch'in dynasty and does not figure here. Nelson-Atkins Museum of Art, Kansas City, MO (Gift of Bronson Trevor in memory of his father, John Trevor) 76–10/12

"a ruler who can make the people delight in war will become king of kings."

Legalists disdained the classics and moral values such as filial piety, sincerity, and humanity. They feared that these books and values would dissuade the people from the single-minded pursuit of agriculture and warfare. They also wished to eliminate many classes of people:

Military Innovations

Late Chou China shared with classical Greece a high frequency of wars (468 wars were fought in China between 463 and 222 B.C.E.). The continual struggles for survival eliminated the lesser states until one, a frontier state called Ch'in, triumphed and unified China. The constant warfare produced armies of up to a million soldiers, new military tactics, and increased social mobility as success was rewarded by upward mobility and failure punished by a drastic drop in status, even by enslavement.

Wars were at first chivalrous affairs between aristocrats fighting individual combats from four-horse chariots; witness the question by one ruler to another in 632 B.C.E. before the opening of combat: "Will Your Excellency permit our knights and yours to play a game?" Later, large infantry forces using stronger weapons—forged from iron rather than bronze—and supported by cavalry largely replaced the war chariots. The change was dictated by the expense of maintaining chariots and the expansion of contested areas to regions unsuitable for the less maneuverable chariots. Chinese states near nomadic lands had adopted cavalry when fighting the horse-riding nomads; once in use, cavalry forces became common in all wars. Innovative military tactics also became important, leading to the rise of career tacticians. The most famous was Sun Wu (also known as Sun the Cripple or Sun Tzu—Master Sun) whose *The Art of War* is still studied in military academies throughout the world.

In ancient Greece, too, the style of warfare changed dramatically in the archaic era (c. 800–500 B.C.E.). At the beginning of the period, cavalry was the backbone of the military. Since only very wealthy, aristocratic families could afford to allocate precious land for raising horses, the nobles were as predominant in military as in civic affairs. In Homer's epic poems, too, we see great kings and heroes conveyed into battle by chariots; the battle itself consisted mostly of single combats between champions like the duel between Achilles and Hector at the climax of the *Iliad*.

Then, in the seventh century B.C.E., there was a shift toward reliance on infantry. State security came to rest on large numbers of specially trained citizen foot soldiers (much more numerous than the aristocrats), uniformly equipped with bronze and iron defensive armor and weaponry. Small-farmer militiamen and later professional infantrymen were the decisive factor in all the major land battles fought during the remainder of ancient Greek and Roman history. Commanders like the Spartan Pausanias, the Athenian Pericles, the Macedonian Alexander the Great, and the Roman Julius Caesar were gifted strategists with the remarkable ability to solve the logistical and tactical problems of mobilizing, moving, and deploying tens of thousands of men in large infantry forces. Not surprisingly, Caesar's *Commentaries* on his wars in Gaul were the favorite reading of a later military genius—Napoleon Bonaparte.

aristocrats because they were born to their privileges; artisans because they produced luxury items that catered to the aristocrats; innkeepers because they served travelers who were apt to be troublesome and to plot against the state; merchants because of their avarice; moralists (the Confucians) because they preached filial piety and loyalty to friends, which might create conflicts of interest and mitigate against total loyalty and obedience to the state; philanthropists because they helped the poor, whose condition was due to their own laziness and extravagance; recluses (Taoists) because they were unproductive and might teach the people falsehoods; sorcerers (diviners) because they taught the people to rely on divine guidance; and last, swashbucklers because they roamed in bands and used their "private swords" to carry out justice on behalf of the oppressed little folks. Legalists opposed formal education except in practical fields such as medicine and agriculture. They regarded history and philosophy books as especially dangerous because they taught people to think and question; such activities made people discontented.

Some modern scholars call this school Realism instead of Legalism. They argue that its adherents, who rejected tradition, supernatural guidance, and morality and insisted that government be based on the actual facts of the world as they existed, were realists. Moreover, they maintain, only such unsentimental and hardnosed policies could have succeeded in ending the chaos of the Era of Warring States and unifying China.

The Three Ideologies Compared

Although many schools of philosophy competed for acceptance during the late Chou, we can now say, with the benefit of hindsight, that Confucianism, Taoism, and Legalism were the most important.

Confucians were the idealists. They taught that the goal of life should be the pursuit of goodness and that people should be governed by morality and example, not by harsh laws and punishment. Although they looked back in history for the golden age, they did not extol the past for its own sake, but rather praised certain periods and persons in the past for their virtues and accomplishments. In the process, they also reinterpreted old ideas. For example, the ancient texts talked about li as rituals and rites of the aristocratic class. Confucius and Mencius

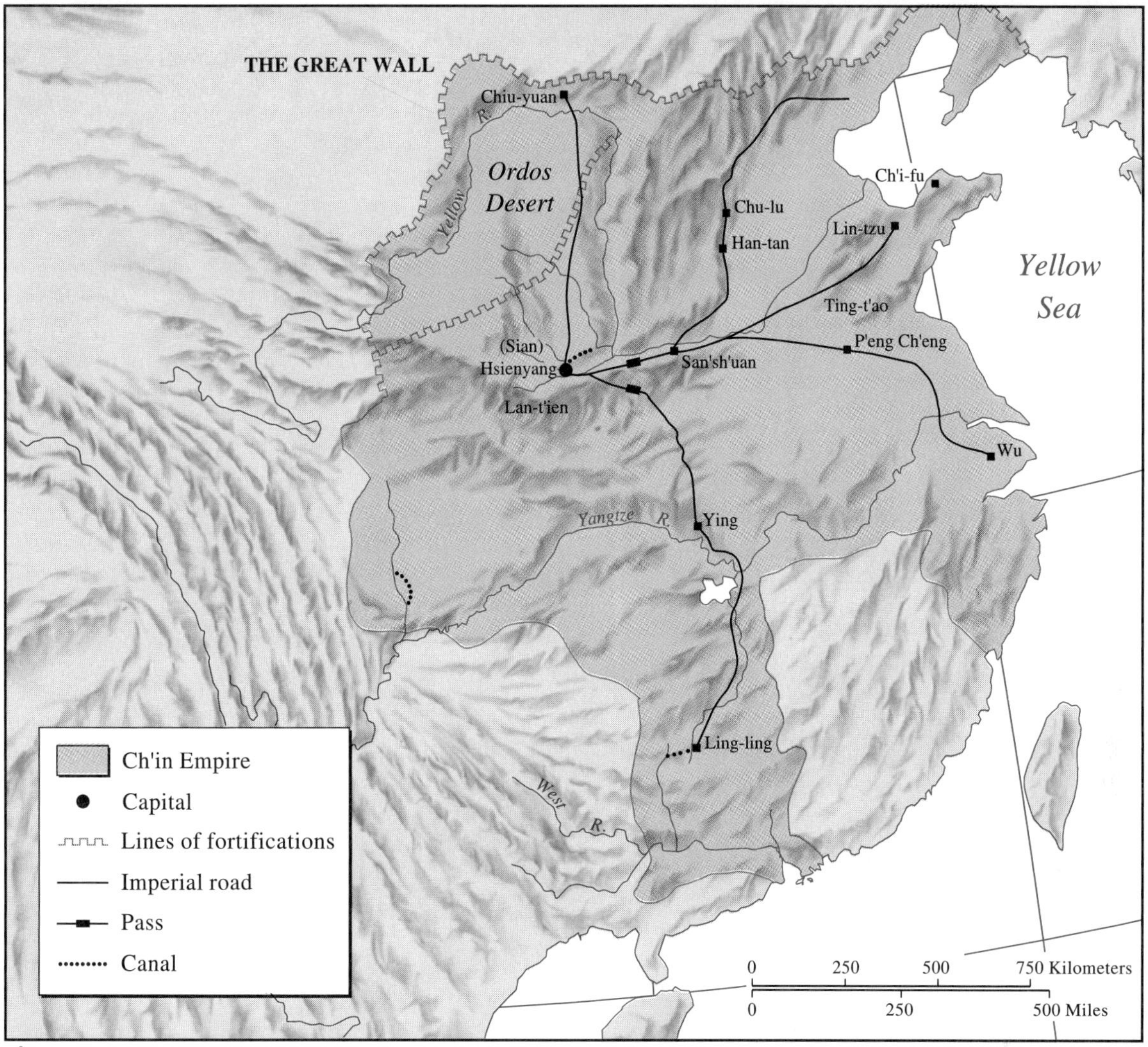

MAP 3.3. The Ch'in Empire, 221–206 B.C.E. China was unified in 221 B.C.E., when the Ch'in crushed its rival states. An ambitious program of roads and canals linked the outlying provinces to the capital, Hsienyang, while the Great Wall protected the northern frontiers against nomadic tribes.

gave li a moral dimension and insisted that it be applied to all people. They also insisted that the aristocracy should be based on merit and not on the accident of birth. Many centuries later, the founding fathers of the United States, John Adams and Thomas Jefferson, advocated a similar concept of the "natural" aristocracy of talent. These reinterpretations of traditional values made Confucians revolutionaries.

Taoists taught that humans were originally innocent, but were corrupted by civilization. They believed in a return to nature and innocence and that less is better, especially in government. They valued passivity and individual freedom and shunned worldly power and position. Although Taoism resembles a recent idea of government called laissez-faire, no government has tried to put Taoism into action as a political philosophy.

Legalists were cynical realists. To them individuals had worth only if they could serve the state, whose primary functions were war and expansion. Morality was irrelevant. Like Confucians, they believed there should be no privilege by birth; but instead of raising the common people to a higher standard of conduct by teaching them moral values, the Legalists demoted the aristocrats to ordinary people, discarded li, and subjected all to harsh impersonal laws. They were amoral technocrats and efficiency experts.

The Brief Rise and Fall of the Ch'in

Although the Era of Warring States was extremely fruitful in producing great philosophy, it was a difficult period for most Chinese. Many yearned for the reestablishment of a strong dynasty that would restore peace and order. In the rise of Ch'in, their hopes were both realized and turned into a nightmare. As a national dynasty, the Ch'in was short-lived, but its importance cannot be measured by its duration, for it left its imprint on the next 2,000 years of Chinese history.

Ch'in was located in northwestern China, in what had been the Chou homeland. Its rise in some ways was a repeat of the rise of the Chou almost 1,000 years earlier. Because they were tough frontier people, the people of Ch'in

Slavery and Volatile Social Status

During the late Chou (772–256 B.C.E.), the breakdown of the feudal order led to social mobility. For example, out of 713 persons mentioned in important historical works describing this period, over one-third or 34 percent came from obscure social origins, indicating that there were many opportunities for upward mobility. Meanwhile others lost status. Prisoners of war, especially captured "barbarians," often became slaves and were presented as rewards to victorious generals. In 594, for example, as a reward for adding territory to the state, a Ch'in general was awarded 1,000 families from the defeated barbarians. Nobles and officials from defeated states could also be enslaved; for example, a former official of a state named Kuo was sold as a slave for five pieces of sheepskin. According to a source from 655, the ruler of a defeated state and his minister were enslaved and given as part of the dowry of a princess of the victor state. An inscription mentions slaves being used, along with horses and silk, in lieu of money in commercial transactions. Other sources mention the freeing of slaves who had fought well in battle. Men convicted of certain crimes and their family members were enslaved as punishment, and people could also be enslaved for indebtedness. All of these examples indicate the volatility of social status in the wars that culminated in the Ch'in unification of China.

In both Greece and Rome, slavery was also an enduring institution throughout antiquity. In Greece, warfare was the most common source of slaves. Defeated enemies, if not put to the sword or ransomed, were enslaved. This practice is well attested in the Bronze Age Linear B tablets and in the epic poems of Homer (c. 725 B.C.E.). Later, the Spartans were able to concentrate on being soldiers because they conquered a neighboring territory—Messenia—and made its inhabitants state-owned serfs. In archaic Greece, citizens could be stripped of their citizenship rights and sold into slavery for failing to pay their debts. The Athenian statesman Solon (594 B.C.E.) enacted legislation to prevent Athenian citizens from being enslaved for debt, but he did not abolish the institution of slavery itself. After taking the island of Melos by siege during the Peloponnesian War, the Athenians put all the males to death and sold all the women and children into slavery. Indeed, slavery was so commonplace that the philosopher Aristotle speaks as if a natural law consigned some people to slavery, others to freedom.

The Romans, too, capitalized on the manpower made available by slavery. Roman success in warfare resulted in a flourishing trade in slaves and bustling slave markets throughout the empire. So many slaves were employed in farmwork by the second century B.C.E. that Rome suffered a series of "servile" revolts in which huge armies of runaway slaves defeated Roman legions in battle (see Chapter 4).

In the following letter, the Stoic philosopher Seneca (c. 4 B.C.E.–65 C.E.) reflects on the vicissitudes of fortune that made one person a master and another a slave:

> "These people are slaves." No: they are human beings.
> "These people are slaves." No: they are those with whom you share your roof.
> "These people are slaves." No: when you consider how much power Chance can exert over you both, they are fellow slaves.
> That's why I find it ludicrous that there should be people who think it shameful to have dinner with their slave. . . .
> Each time you remember how much you are entitled to do to your slave, you must remember also just how much your own master is entitled to do to you. "But I don't have any master," you object. The world is still young: perhaps there will come a time when you do have one.*

---

*Translated by R. Campbell, in Thomas Wiedemann, *Greek and Roman Slavery* (Baltimore: Johns Hopkins University Press, 1981), pp. 233–235.

were looked upon as semibarbarous country cousins by the more advanced Chinese of the heartland. Though their location had exempted the Ch'in from most of the wars with other Chinese states, they were nevertheless experienced in war through frequent fighting with nomadic tribesmen from the steppes.

To their original homeland in modern Shensi, the Ch'in had early added Szechuan in the southwest along the upper Yangtze valley. Both lands were rich in agricultural potential if irrigated. Ch'in engineers constructed large-scale irrigation and flood-control works (the systems they created in Szechuan are still in use). Despite harsh laws, Ch'in's abolition of serfdom attracted immigrants to settle and farm. Its location on the edge of the Chinese world also saved it from the ravages of the almost continuous warfare that disrupted the economies of the more centrally located states. As a result of the economic prosperity, the Ch'in built up huge grain reserves, which allowed them to divert workers from farming into the army for their final push for unification. Its strategic location made Ch'in territory easy to defend from invaders from the east (where most of the Warring States were), while the same mountain passes that protected it were easy staging points to invade the states to the east.

❇ A Terra Cotta Army. Ranks of life-size infantrymen, horses, and chariots made of pottery are drawn up in battle formation in underground pits that flank the tomb of the First Emperor of the Ch'in. They were intended to protect him in death. Robert Harding Picture Library

Quick to adopt advances in knowledge and technology, Ch'in soldiers even anticipated the mustard gas used in the trenches in World War I. They used bellows to pump toxic gas generated by burning mustard seeds and other materials into the tunnels dug by their enemies when besieging Ch'in cities. Ch'in mapmakers drew relief maps that showed the contours of the land, which Ch'in generals used in warfare. A relief map of the entire realm was reported to have been buried in the tomb of the first Ch'in emperor who later unified China.

Ch'in rulers welcomed talented men from other states. In 356 B.C.E., Lord Shang entered into the service of Ch'in from another state and held the office of chief minister until his death in 338. His Legalist policies made Ch'in the most efficiently run state of its time. Officials were chosen on merit and promoted or demoted on their performance, and free men and women worked as tax-paying and landowning peasants; men also fought as conscript soldiers. Lord Shang was followed by other

technocrats; like him, many were born in other states but attracted to Ch'in by the opportunities it offered.

In 247 B.C.E., King Ch'eng, a vigorous and ambitious young man, succeeded to the Ch'in throne with Li Ssu as his chief minister. They completed the conquest and unification of China in 221. Ch'eng decided that he needed a title greater than mere king to match his prestige. With supreme confidence, he called himself *Shih Huang-ti; shih* means "first" and *huang-ti* means "emperor," a title until then used only for high gods. He further decreed that since his house would rule China for all time, his successors would be designated only by numerals, as second emperor, third emperor, and so on. Although his family did not rule beyond the second emperor, the title *huang-ti* was retained by rulers down to the end of the imperial age in 1911.

Shih Huang-ti and chief minister Li Ssu formally abolished feudalism in the entire empire and instituted a centralized government. The country was divided into

Your Majesty possesses a unified empire . . . and has firmly established for yourself a position of sole supremacy. And yet the independent schools, joining with each other, criticize the codes of laws and instructions. . . . If such license is not prohibited, the sovereign power will decline above and partisan factions will form below. It would be well to prohibit this.

Your servant suggests that all books in the imperial archives, save the memoirs of Ch'in, be burned. All persons in the empire, except members of the Academy of Learned Scholars, in possession of the *Book of Odes*, the *Book of History*, and discourses of the hundred philosophers should take them to the local governors and have them indiscrim-

inately burned. Those who dare to talk to each other about the *Book of Odes* and the *Book of History* should be executed and their bodies exposed in the market-place. Anyone referring to the past to criticize the present should, together with all members of his family, be put to death. Officials who fail to report cases that have come under their attention are equally guilty. After thirty days from the time of issuing the decree, those who have not destroyed their books are to be branded and sent to build the Great Wall. Books not to be destroyed will be those on medicine and pharmacy, divination by the tortoise and milfoil, and agriculture and arboriculture. People wishing to pursue learning should take the officials as their teachers.*

Chief minister Li Ssu submitted this memorial (a memorial is a document submitted by an official to the ruler) to the First Emperor, who ordered its suggestions carried out. A nationwide book burning followed; anyone caught hiding books was executed.

These harsh acts had several purposes. The destruction of history books would end any comparisons between Ch'in and earlier dynasties that might put Ch'in in an unfavorable light. Philosophies that might promote another way of life would be prohibited. Anyone who dared to criticize the government would be punished with such harshness and cruelty that the people would be terrorized into obedience. Guilt by association and

holding groups of people mutually responsible would prompt people to spy on one another and to report wrongdoing, lest all be implicated.

In the short run, the policies seemed to work. But when the terror-inspiring First Emperor died, the system collapsed under pent-up popular resentment. Later governments would make use of some Legalist ideas and methods of ruling, but none dared espouse the hated doctrine. The discredited First Emperor and his ministers became the symbols of oppression and evil in Chinese history.

*William T. de Bary, ed., *Sources of Chinese Tradition*, vol. 1 (New York: Columbia University Press, 1960), p. 141.

---

commanderies (provinces), which were subdivided into counties. All offices were nonhereditary, and officials were ultimately responsible to the emperor. Uniform laws, weights, measures, coinage, and written script applied to the whole land. Shih Huang-ti ordered roads built to link parts of the country and to facilitate administration and military movements, in much the same way that the Persian emperors Darius and Xerxes had done and that the Roman government would do later. Carts using the roads were required to have axles of a standard length, so that the ruts they made would be uniform. His engineers dug a canal linking a tributary of the Yangtze River with the Pearl River in the extreme south to make it easier to supply an army campaigning in the area. The army conquered and annexed lands that today make up southern China and northern Vietnam. In the north, existing walls built by the feudal states against the nomads (and sometimes against one another) were linked together to form a single defense system called the Great Wall. This monumental engineering project was built with conscript and convict labor; although its construction caused enormous hardships, it provided security along a long and vulnerable frontier.

Shih Huang-ti also built a magnificent capital near the first Chou capital, Hao. Because of the fertile agricultural

lands and strategic location, China's capital would continue to be in this general area for the next thousand years. Very little remains of the Ch'in capital, although the huge (forty-eight meters high) artificial hill enclosing the tomb that Shih Huang-ti started to build for himself soon after he unified the country is still a major landmark. Records tell us that tens of thousands of men spent years building the tomb and that it was furnished with fabulous treasures. Nearby, archaeologists have recently excavated three huge underground pits containing over 7,000 life-size terra cotta horses and men, an army to guard the emperor in death.

Despite his real achievements, the First Emperor has been universally reviled in Chinese memory. Popular folktales denounce his cruelty and tyranny. Millions were conscripted and many died to build his walls, canals, palaces, and tomb. Many more paid crushing taxes to support the projects. Scholars abhorred his attempts at thought control. With the Ch'in unification, the Hundred Schools came to an end. Legalism prevailed; all other schools were outlawed. The government prohibited all intellectual discussion; to question the government's policies became treason. In 213 B.C.E., a law ordered all books other than histories of the House of Ch'in and works on agriculture, medicine, and divination confiscated and burned; the penalty for disobeying was death. Scholars were appalled; many, especially the Confucians, spoke out in protest. The emperor had 460 of them arrested and executed. Even the crown prince was not exempt; when he protested the harshness of the punishment, he was banished to duties along the Great Wall. The book burning destroyed forever many ancient texts, creating gaps in our knowledge of the pre-Ch'in eras. Such techniques of totalitarianism and thought control have been used by other tyrants in other eras throughout the world, attesting to the power of the written word. After the fall of the dynasty, when it was again legal to engage in intellectual activities and to write books, accounts were written of the Ch'in rule; most of them had little good to say about the First Emperor and his policies.

Since all decisions came from the all-powerful emperor, he toiled long hours to do his work. In 210 B.C.E., while on an inspection tour that had as its second goal a search for the elixirs of long life, the First Emperor suddenly died at age fifty, probably from overwork and other excesses. A power struggle followed. Li Ssu and the chief eunuch (eunuchs were castrated males who served in the households of monarchs) destroyed the emperor's will and forged an order commanding the crown prince to commit suicide, which he did. Li and the eunuch put a weakling younger son of the emperor on the throne as Second Emperor so they could rule in his name. Soon the conspirators fell out and Li was murdered. The eunuch then murdered the Second Emperor and put a son of the late crown prince on the throne. The new ruler had the eunuch executed. By then revolts had broken out everywhere. Loyal generals rushed hither and yon trying to put them down, and many defected when they could not, for failure was a crime punishable by death. In 206 B.C.E. the third Ch'in ruler surrendered to the rebels, thus ending the dynasty.

Summary and Comparisons

This chapter has examined several major cultures that flowered in the first millennium B.C.E. and shared a concern with religion and morals. Soon, new developments in religion and philosophy created revolutions in thought that led to the abandonment or modification of previous traditions in favor of new systems of belief.

There had been experiments in the direction of monotheism in Egypt under Akhenaton and Persia in the time of Zoroaster, but these movements had failed to prevail against the established polytheistic religions of the time. In Greece, India, and China, intellectual speculation did not evolve in the direction of monotheism. The Hebrews, therefore, were the originators of the first true monotheistic faith, which proved to be one of the most durable and influential in history. The Hebrew scriptures are a treasured legacy, whether they are regarded as literature, history, or religious revelation. They assert a covenant with God that both comforts human beings and imposes moral responsibilities. Although the political and military triumphs of the ancient Hebrew state were short-lived and had little impact outside Palestine, the Hebrew people nevertheless made a momentous contribution to the future of the human spirit through their religion. Judaism furnished its followers with an elaborately formulated and self-consistent ethical code.

The achievements of the Phoenicians were pragmatic. Their sophisticated ports and expert sailors linked West Asia with distant parts of the Mediterranean. Their sailors and merchants also carried an artifact on which no price could be put—the alphabet. The simplicity of the alphabet compared to the writing systems devised by earlier cultures from Babylon to China made literacy potentially available to more than a tiny minority of scribes and priests.

In the archaic period, the Greek world rebounded materially and culturally from the Dark Age. Male citizens increasingly participated in the affairs of their city-states. At the beginning of the fifth century, Greeks repelled the threat of absorption into the Persian Empire by standing together in common defense of their city-states. Athens emerged as the preeminent naval power and the leader of a large confederacy of Greek city-states. Pericles broadened the bases of democracy and made Athens a focus of economic and artistic activity. The growth of Athenian power, however, led to the Peloponnesian War and ultimately to the dismantling of the Athenian Empire and the hegemony of Sparta and its allies.

Greece was the center of philosophical investigation into the nature of the universe. Greek commitment to the highest intellectual ideals laid the groundwork for subsequent philosophical inquiry. This inclination to rationalistic inquiry also extended to the investigation and recording of past deeds, in short, to the writing of the first histories.

Greek literature and art explored the physical and intellectual potential of human beings. Within a century of their invention, both tragedy and comedy reached the highest levels of artistry, thanks to the city-states' commitment of time, energy, and money to cultural activities. In architecture and the figural arts, also, the Greeks delighted in balance and symmetry of structure and put human beings and society at the center of focus.

In India during the Late Vedic Age (c. 1000–500 B.C.E.), Aryan culture spread eastward to the Ganges valley and southward to the Deccan Plateau and peninsular India, adapting to contacts with native peoples and experiencing economic transformations. The changes of the Late Vedic Age led many to feel pessimistic about human destiny and to reject the ancient gods, brahman dominance, and Vedic rituals. One result of these changes was the philosophical writings called the *Upanishads,* which explained the human experience and the relationship with the ultimate; the changes also led to the formulation of two breakaway religions, Buddhism and Jainism. Each played an important role in the future of India, and Buddhism spread to become a key religion in many parts of Asia.

As every new system arises to some degree out of its predecessor, both Buddhism and Jainism were outgrowths of ancient Vedism. Despite some differences, the basic views of Jainism, Buddhism, and orthodox Vedism (and Hinduism, a later outgrowth of Vedism) did not disagree: life was governed by universal law or dharma, and karma or deeds determined reincarnation with its painful results; as their final goal, all aimed at release, resulting in nirvana. Both of the new faiths, however, denied the validity of the *Vedas,* the authority of the brahmans, and the caste system. Similarly, in Greece, Pythagorean teaching about transmigration of souls abandoned traditional religious thinking and offered new, alternative beliefs about the next life

Gautama Buddha taught the middle way in his Four Noble Truths and Eightfold Path. Many Indians were ready to receive his new teachings. The greater gains of Buddhism compared with Jainism were due to Buddhism's moderation and more attainable lifestyles and especially to the popular doctrine of Mahayana Buddhism.

Mahavira, founder of the extremely demanding Jainism, taught a rigorous ethical system that put special emphasis on the ascetic way of life and self-denial. So too, in classical Greece, Socrates sought true knowledge in part by reducing or overriding the physical demands of his body.

Just as political and social ferment in India and Greece around 500 B.C.E. had led to important intellectual and religious developments, similarly, in China, the increasing political chaos of the Eastern Chou (771–256) initiated a period of intellectual turmoil known as the Hundred Schools of philosophy. Most Chinese philosophers dealt with human relationships in this world, as had the Greek Sophists. The only exception was the school known as Taoism, which advocated passivism, renunciation of civilization, and return to an innocent primitive past. In its advocacy of simplicity and asceticism, Taoism may be likened to Buddhism. This similarity later contributed to the ready acceptance of Buddhism by many Chinese.

Like the itinerant Greek Sophists, who sought pupils in different city-states, many Chinese philosophers traveled from state to state and attempted to persuade rulers to accept their point of view. Confucius and his disciples were foremost among these dedicated men; they believed that the practice of morality, family responsibility, and virtuous government would bring about a return to the golden age. Confucians were ridiculed by Taoists who maintained that activism was counterproductive and that the way to achieve peace with oneself was by rising above worldly concerns.

Although Confucianism and Taoism later became the twin mainstreams of Chinese thought, Legalism had an immediate impact on the time. Legalism was devoid of morality and ethical content; in fact, the men who devised it had contempt for such values. Legalists were cynics about human nature and the nature of power and were interested only in efficiency and result. Their final goal was an all-powerful state ruled by harsh and impersonal laws. So too was the perfectly just state in Plato's *Republic* marked by an authoritarianism that rigidly determined all the social, political, military, and educational aspects of life. With Legalism as its guiding ideology, the Ch'in triumphed over the other Warring States and unified China in 221 B.C.E. Between 221 and 206, the Ch'in ruled China ruthlessly and by terror, obliterating many old institutions. As a system of ruling, however, Legalism was intolerable, as the speedy collapse of the Ch'in empire proved. Legalism was never attempted as a state ideology again.

All of the major Eurasian civilizations examined in this chapter took great strides in developing important new religious and philosophical systems. All fostered remarkable innovations in religious and ethical thought that had a profound influence on many aspects of life both at the time and in later centuries.

Selected Sources

*Baldry, H. C. *The Greek Tragic Theater.* 1971. Especially valuable on the social context of the dramatic festivals and on the mechanics of mounting productions.

*Basham, A. L. *The Wonder That Was India.* 1954. A long chapter deals with religions; includes quotations.

Ben-Sasson, H. H., ed. *A History of the Jewish People.* 1969; trans. 1976. A very thorough, recent account from earliest times to the mid-twentieth century by several eminent historians.

*Boardman, John. *Greek Art.* 4th ed. 1996. A good basic introduction to ancient Greek art and architecture from the archaic period to the Hellenistic. Many fine illustrations.

Cook, J. M. *The Persian Empire.* 1983. A good, readable, up-to-date introduction to the political and cultural history of ancient Persia. Nicely illustrated.

Cotterell, Arthur. *The First Emperor of China.* 1981. The author makes full use of recent excavations of the terra cotta army to bring to life the life and times of the First Emperor.

Creel, H. G. *Confucius the Man and the Myth.* 1949. Creel first gives a biographical account, then explains the development of the myth, the triumph of Confucianism, and its worldwide relevance.

———. *Chinese Thought from Confucius to Mao Tse-tung.* 1953. Concise, well written, and easy to read.

*de Bary, W. T., ed. *Sources of Indian Tradition.* Vol 1. 1958. Good, short introductory passages explain readings in Buddhist and Jain canons.

*Doody, Margaret. *Aristotle Detective.* 1978. A highly entertaining detective story in which the great philosopher solves the mystery of the violent murder of a prominent Athenian citizen. Realistic background detail.

Edward, J. Thomas. *The Life of Buddha as Legend and History.* 1931. An account of the man and his teachings, the growth of Buddhism, and the myths that surround it.

*Fantham, Elaine, et al. *Women in the Classical World: Image and Text.* 1994. This very current collection of essays by a number of experts includes material on the representation of women in literature, the arts, science, and philosophy throughout Greek and Roman history.

*Guthrie, W. K. C. *The Greeks and Their Gods.* 1950. A lively account of the ways in which the gods, both major and minor, permeated all aspects of ancient Greek life and culture.

*Hesse, Hermann. *Siddhartha.* 1922; Eng. trans. 1951. A novel about one man's search for enlightenment.

Hirakawa, Akira. *A History of Indian Buddhism: From Sakyamuni to Early Mahayana.* Ed. and trans. Paul Groner. 1990. Good, comprehensive book.

Hornblower, Simon, and Anthony Spawforth, eds. *The Oxford Classical Dictionary.* 3d ed. 1996. The most comprehensive, one-volume resource for all aspects of the world of ancient Greece and Rome. Includes contributions from hundreds of leading specialists.

Jaini, P. S. *The Jain Path of Purification.* 1979. Good summary of Jain teachings.

Lange, Nicholas de. *Judaism.* 1986. A recent account of the characteristics and importance of this world religion.

Levi, Jean. *The Chinese Emperor.* 1987. A novel on the life and times of the First Emperor; describes the murderous intrigues and horror of life in a Legalist state.

*Mazar, Amihai. *Archaeology of the Land of the Bible: 10,000–586 B.C.E.* 1990; rev. ed. 1992. The best available work on the topic; thorough and attractively presented.

Moscati, Sabatino. *The World of the Phoenicians.* 1968. A good, readable history by the director of Semitic studies at the University of Rome.

Potok, Chaim. *Wanderings: Chaim Potok's History of the Jews.* 1978. A riveting account of 4,000 years of history by the noted American Jewish novelist, scholar, and rabbi.

*Renault, Mary. *The Last of the Wine.* 1956; reprinted 1975. One of Renault's excellent historical novels; set during the Peloponnesian War.

Robinson, Richard H., and William L. Johnson. *The Buddhist Religion: A Historical Introduction.* 1982. Covers the development of Buddhism in India and elsewhere.

*Starr, Chester G. *Individual and Community: The Rise of the Polis, 800–500 B.C.* 1986. A good, recent presentation of the cultural, economic, and political achievements of the citizens of the Greek polis.

Twitchett, Dennis, and Michael Loewe, eds. *The Cambridge History of China.* Vol. 1: *The Ch'in and Han Empires, 221 B.C.–A.D. 220.* 1986. Definitive treatment by many experts; Chapter 1 deals with the Ch'in Empire.

Vaux, R. de. *The Bible and the Ancient Near East.* 1972. A useful assessment of biblical narratives within the context of the history of the Near East.

*Waley, Arthur. *Three Ways of Thought in Ancient China.* 1939. A short, lucid study of Confucianism, Taoism, and Legalism, with many quotations from original writings of the three schools.

*Available in paperback.

Internet Links

Atlas of the Greek and Roman World
http://www.unc.edu/depts/cl_atlas/
This site features nearly 100 detailed topographical maps.

A Bequest Unearthed: Phoenicia
http://www.concentric.net/%7eshaal/toc.html
A well-conceived and informative website, covering virtually every aspect of ancient Phoenician civilization: history, law, literature, art and archaeology, language, religion, trade, and military history.

Diotima: Materials for the Study of Women and Gender in the Ancient World
http://www.uky.edu/ArtsSciences/Classics/gender.html
A good source of guidance for the study of women's lives in ancient Greece, Rome, Egypt, and West Asia, including extensive course materials, bibliography, links to databases of images and texts in translation.

Introduction to Biblical Judaism
http://www.acs.ucalgary.ca/~elsegal/J_Transp/J01_JudaismIntro.html
Offers a very clear chronological outline of ancient Judaism and the early history of the Jews. Several illustrations and maps.

Mahavira and Jainism
http://www.west.net/~beck/EC8-Mahavira.html
This site provides a helpful outline of Jainism, with biographical information, lucid explanations of terms and concepts, and well-chosen quotations from ancient documents.

Perseus Project
http://www.perseus.tufts.edu/
This "evolving digital library" provides access to virtually all classical Greek texts (in translation as well as in the original) commonly read in colleges. Maps, archaeological site plans, and a large collection of photographs and other illustrations make this an invaluable research tool. Includes search facilities.

Resources for the Study of East Asian Language and Thought
http://www.acmuller.gol.com/index.html
This site offers links to several "virtual libraries" relevant to Buddhism, Confucianism, and Taoism, among other subjects, as well as helpful glossaries of technical terminology.

Su Tzu's Chinese Philosophy Page
http://mars.superlink.net/user/fsu/philo.html
"This page has been designed for the purpose of organizing the resources on Chinese philosophy that can be found in 'cyberspace.'" Contains links to bibliographies, large text repositories, and other relevant websites.

The Defining Characteristics of Great Empires

Most noteworthy by far and most marvelous of all is the grandeur of your concept of citizenship. There is nothing on earth like it. For you have divided all the people of the Empire . . . into two classes: the more cultured, better born, and more influential everywhere you have declared Roman citizens . . . the rest vassals and subjects. . . . Everything lies open to everybody; and no one fit for office or a position of trust is an alien. There exists a universal democracy under one man, the best *princeps* [emperor] and administrator.

(Aelius Aristides, in N. Lewis and M. Reinhold, eds., *Roman Civilization, Sourcebook II: Roman Empire* [New York: Harper, 1966], pp. 135–136)

Several great empires—the Hellenistic kingdoms, the Roman Empire, and the Mauryan and Han Empires—flourished between c. 300 B.C.E. and 200 C.E. Each unified under one government diverse and often previously antagonistic peoples and states. Each was maintained by huge resources of manpower and materials. The quotation above praises the Roman imperial achievement and the many benefits the empire brought to its citizens.

Empires were secured by powerful military forces, effective bureaucracies, and diplomatic alliances that often included the exchange of hostages and arranged marriages between ruling families. A poem by a homesick Han princess attests to the high individual human cost of dynastic marital alliances:

My family sent me off to be married on the other side of heaven;
They sent me a long way to a strange land, to the king of Wu-sun.
A domed lodging is my dwelling place, with walls made of felt;
Meat is my food, with fermented milk as the sauce.
I live with constant thoughts of my home, my heart is full of sorrow;
I wish I were a golden swan, returning to my home country.
(Hsu-chun, in James P. Holoka and Jiu-Hwa L. Upsher, eds., *Lives and Times: A World History Reader,* vol. 1 [St. Paul: West Publishing, 1995], p. 173)

Although they varied considerably in size and longevity, each empire controlled much more territory and larger populations than a single city or group of settlements. Each of the empires discussed in Chapter 4 controlled lands at least the size of the United States east of the Mississippi. Each had a population numbering in the tens of millions and endured for at least two centuries. Other empires had appeared earlier in history (e.g., the Egyptian, Assyrian, and Persian), while others would form later (e.g., the Aztec, Inka, Ottoman, and Mongol). Although each was distinct, most great empires shared numerous common characteristics.

Successful empires were stable and durable for the following reasons: each had centralized leadership and an efficiently run government. Empires were often headed by a more or less stable hereditary dynasty, bolstered by a social and political elite like the Roman patricians or the great families in Han China. Most successful imperial administrations also recruited at least some officials on the basis of merit, not birth. This was true of the Hellenistic states, Rome under the emperors, and Han China. In fact, many empires relied on their schools to fill administrative positions; the successful ones also gave efficiency ratings and on-the-job training to promising officials and based promotions on performance. In Han China, administrators were chosen from a pool of formally educated men on the basis of recommendations, examinations, and efficiency ratings. An imperial university for training bureaucrats had over 30,000 students at its peak. In the Hellenistic states, literacy in Greek was essential for successful advancement in both the public and the private sector.

Great empires had uniform currencies and standards of weights and measures that simplified tax collection, government finance, and trade. Rulers issued coins that publicized themselves and their political programs. Reasonable fiscal and tax systems generated sufficient revenues to run the government without overburdening the population. When greed or overwhelming needs caused extortionate taxation, disaffection or rebellion often resulted, presaging eventual decline and fall. The maintenance of an adequate military force always took up the largest share of tax revenues and much manpower.

All empires also required service from their citizens, either as soldiers or as laborers. For example, in Rome all male citizens were obligated to serve in the army, initially without pay. Likewise, the Han government demanded military and corvée service (compulsory, unpaid labor) from its adult males. In time, in both China and Rome, full-time, professional forces superseded inadequate part-time citizen soldiers.

Successful empires possessed weapons and military technology superior to those of their enemies; they also supplemented this technological superiority with defensive installations such as the Great Wall in China and Hadrian's Wall in Roman Britain. Vital empires were almost invariably aggressive, often attacking and absorbing their weak or hostile neighbors. Military strength and wealth from booty brought safety and provided the preconditions for further economic expansion and technological innovation. The resulting prosperity contributed to social harmony and political stability. However, the great expense of garrisoning vast territories with professional soldiers also imposed huge financial burdens that drained treasuries.

Empires had uniform legal codes, which the governments enforced. Examples are Rome's Twelve Tables (and later Justinian's code) and the Mauryan code engraved on stone pillars. The Roman legal system became the foundation for many later European codes. Similarly, later Chinese and other East Asian legal systems were based on the Han legal code. Muslim empires often based their legal systems on the Qur'an.

All great empires built elaborate public works. Although often constructed by forced labor, the roads, aqueducts, granaries, and irrigation works generally provided long-term benefits for all inhabitants, often outlasting the states that built them. The Persians, Romans, and Inka were especially good civil engineers. Their roadways expedited troop movements, domestic commerce, and international trade. Even today, many Roman highways are still in use. An international overland route, called the Silk Road, linked the Roman and Han Empires. Safe trade and travel along this 6,000-mile route were possible because of the Pax Romana and Pax Sinica. Such domestic and international peace maintained over long periods promoted well-being for millions of people. The mapping and policing of sea-lanes and the building of harbors and lighthouses also promoted both domestic and international trade. All empires built lavish public monuments, especially in their capital cities. Temples, tombs, and palaces, which had no tangible benefits for ordinary people, nevertheless provided spiritual consolation and inspired pride. Even in ruin, the Roman Colosseum, Asoka's pillars, and the Mayan pyramids at places like Copán in Central America still inspire awe and admiration.

Great imperial governments also patronized learning, expressed in literature, art, and philosophy. In Han China, the government-sponsored writing of history set the example for succeeding generations. In Ptolemaic Egypt, the government supported research in the sciences and a great library at Alexandria. The emperor Augustus's encouragement of writers resulted in masterpieces of Latin literature such as Vergil's *Aeneid*. The political integration of vast imperial territories also brought about linguistic integration. Latin became the universal language of western Europe, Greek of the eastern Mediterranean, and Chinese of East Asia.

Successful empires instilled a sense of strong allegiance and a spirit of public service in their people. Even after the empires fell, memories of their grandeur continued to capture the imaginations of later generations. For centuries, western Europeans longed to resurrect the glories of the Roman Empire. The very name of Rome, the eternal city, led Constantinople to be called the "Second Rome," and after Constantinople's fall to the Muslim Ottoman Empire, Russian rulers designated Moscow the "Third Rome." So, too, the Chinese have continued to call themselves the Han people. Asoka's lion serves as the national symbol for modern India.

In Chapter 4 we shall examine several of the world's earliest great empires: the Hellenistic, Roman, Indian, and Chinese. Each had many of the characteristics outlined in this essay.

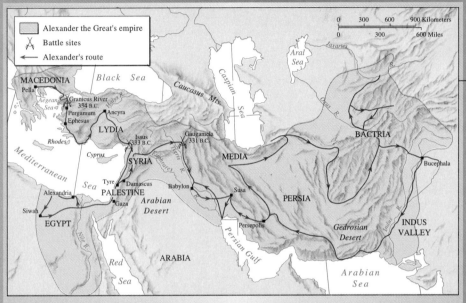

Conquests of Alexander the Great and the Hellenistic Kingdoms

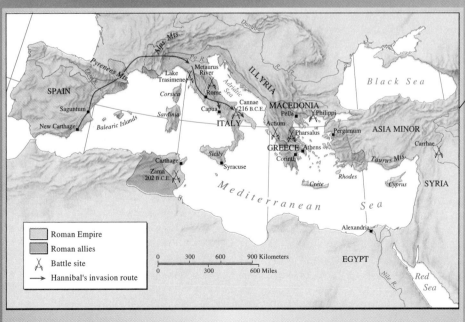

The Roman World at the Time of the Late Republic

The Age of Great Empires

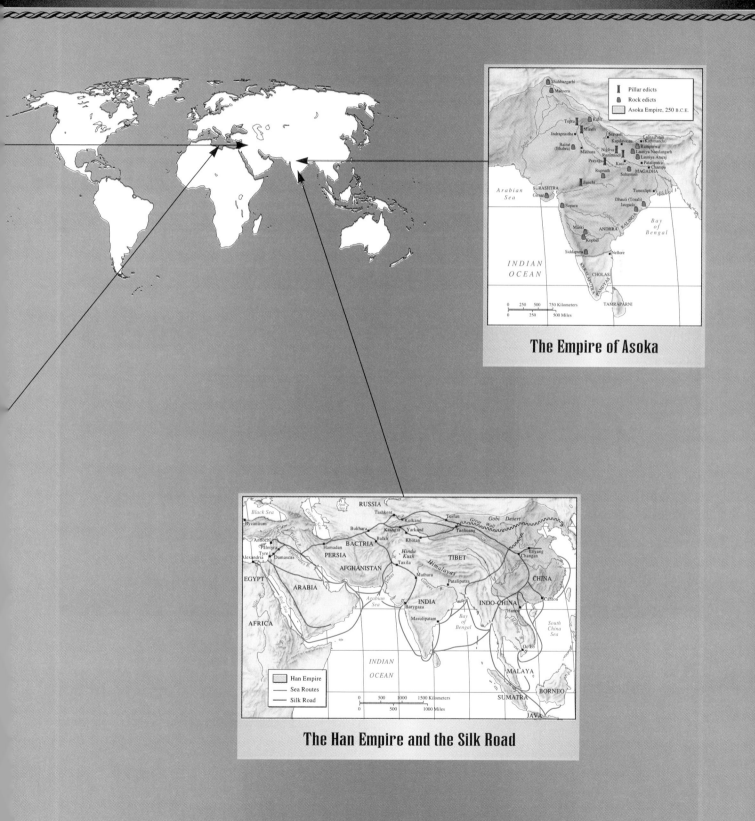

The Empire of Asoka

The Han Empire and the Silk Road

Outline

This chapter highlights the principal achievements of four of the greatest empires of the ancient world. The Hellenistic kingdoms succeeded in bringing Greek culture to large, politically unified territories in a way that the old classical city-states had never been able to do. The Roman Empire brought political unity to the entire Mediterranean basin and spread Greco-Roman culture throughout Europe and much of West Asia. India of the Mauryan Empire, particularly under Emperor Asoka, witnessed both political and religious unification to an unprecedented extent. In China under the Han dynasty, a remarkable flowering of culture accompanied military and governmental successes.

A Greek citizen of the Roman Empire, Aelius Aristides, once praised Rome in the following terms:

> You have surveyed the whole world, built bridges of all sorts across rivers, cut down mountains to make paths for chariots, filled the deserts with hostels, and civilized it all with system and order. . . . Before your rule, things were all mixed up topsy-turvy, drifting at random. But with you in charge, turmoil and strife ceased, universal order and the bright light of life and government came in, laws were proclaimed, and the gods' altars acquired sanctity.

Though there is some exaggeration in this hymn of adulation, its essence is true, and similar words could rightly be addressed not only to Rome but to any of the empires examined in this chapter.

Macedonian Conquest and Hellenistic Empires

*You [Philip] are called to action . . . by your ancestors, by Persian effeminacy, by the famous men, true heroes, who fought against Persia, and most of all by the fitting hour which finds you in possession of greater strength than any previous European, and your adversary in deeper hatred and wider contempt than any monarch in history. . . . What will be the praises sung of you, when it is realized that in the political field you have been the benefactor of all Greek states, and in the military the conqueror of Persia? No achievement can ever be greater than to bring us all out of such warfare to unity of spirit.**

*Isocrates, "Philip," in *Greek Political Oratory*, trans. A. N. W. Saunders (Harmondsworth: Penguin, 1970), pp. 164–165.

The Greek city-states of the fifth century B.C.E. had achieved remarkable triumphs in their economic, cultural, and intellectual life, but they failed to overcome interstate rivalries and to unite their world in a lasting political organization. In the wake of the debilitating Peloponnesian War, no Greek state was powerful enough to

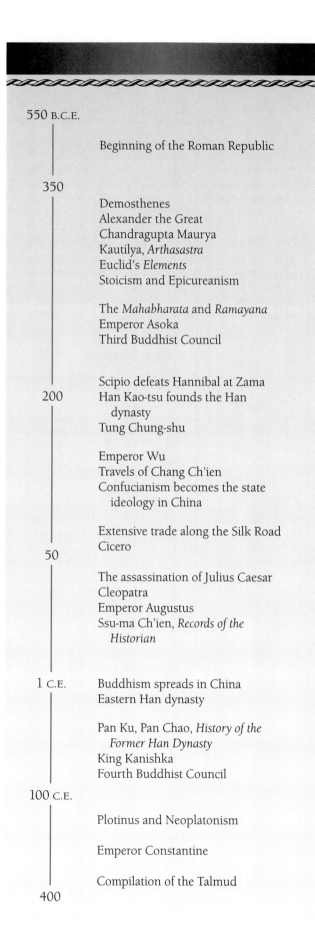

550 B.C.E.

Beginning of the Roman Republic

350

Demosthenes
Alexander the Great
Chandragupta Maurya
Kautilya, *Arthasastra*
Euclid's *Elements*
Stoicism and Epicureanism

The *Mahabharata* and *Ramayana*
Emperor Asoka
Third Buddhist Council

Scipio defeats Hannibal at Zama
Han Kao-tsu founds the Han
dynasty
Tung Chung-shu

200

Emperor Wu
Travels of Chang Ch'ien
Confucianism becomes the state
ideology in China

Extensive trade along the Silk Road
Cicero

50

The assassination of Julius Caesar
Cleopatra
Emperor Augustus
Ssu-ma Ch'ien, *Records of the
Historian*

1 C.E.

Buddhism spreads in China
Eastern Han dynasty

Pan Ku, Pan Chao, *History of the
Former Han Dynasty*
King Kanishka
Fourth Buddhist Council

100 C.E.

Plotinus and Neoplatonism

Emperor Constantine

Compilation of the Talmud

400

control or rally the rest for any great length of time. This situation changed forever with the careers of Philip II (reigned 359–336 B.C.E.) and Alexander the Great (reigned 336–323 B.C.E.). The two Macedonian leaders enlarged the Greek world and dramatically changed it both politically and culturally.

In the quotation above from an open letter to Philip II, the Athenian orator Isocrates urges the Macedonian king to lead Greece in a crusade against the Persians. He appeals to long-standing Greek prejudices: freedom-loving, rational, masculine Greeks are contrasted with enslaved, barbarian, effeminate Persians. As usual, however, the Greek states were fatally incapable of united action, and Philip was more interested in gaining supremacy for Macedon than in saving Greece from its chronic internal strife.

By 338 B.C.E. Philip had taken advantage of the weaknesses of the old city-state system to establish Macedon as the dominant political and military force in the Greek world. After Philip's death, his son Alexander capitalized on this military superiority to conquer vast territories in Asia and Africa. On his death they were divided into several very large kingdoms, which we designate Hellenistic (the word indicates postclassical Greek civilization from the death of Alexander in 323 into the first century B.C.E.).

The Father: Philip

After the Peloponnesian War, the Spartans for a time maintained a shaky predominance among the Greek city-states, but they lacked the diplomatic and financial savvy of the Athenians. By the mid-fourth century B.C.E., Greece was still a disunified collection of independent city-states. The common folk, disenchanted with endless warfare, lost their patriotic enthusiasm for the polis. Greek soldiers often served as mercenaries for the highest bidder, whether Greek or not.

Before the reign of King Philip II, Macedon was an underdeveloped region in northernmost Greece. Many Greeks thought of Macedonians as hard drinking, backward, and uncivilized. In fact, Macedon was a sleeping giant, with valuable natural resources and huge manpower reserves. Similarly, in China during the Warring States era, the frontier Ch'in people were regarded as uncouth country cousins by the more advanced Chinese of the heartland. Nevertheless, the Ch'in were able forcibly to unify China as Philip and Alexander subjugated Greece.

Philip first reformed the army, making it fully professional, with the highest standards of discipline and elite units called companions. He increased its size to more than 25,000 men divided among infantry, light-armed skirmishers, archers, slingers, and cavalry. He also introduced a new, fifteen-foot thrusting spear, better siege machinery, and more effective infantry tactics. Philip funded this crack army by seizing the gold and silver mines of Mount Pangaeus. He then defeated the Balkan neighbors who had long plagued Macedon. Philip next unified and modernized his country by redistributing the population into new urban centers and by making better use of arable land. He ushered Macedon into mainstream Greek culture by promoting education and encouraging artists and intellectuals to come to the new royal capital at Pella, where Alexander was born. Philip also dared to aim at political domination of Greece.

The Greek city-states feared this growth of Macedonian power and influence. In a series of speeches known as *Philippics,* the Athenian statesman Demosthenes portrayed Philip as addicted to power. Deciding the time had come for a showdown, the Athenians and Thebans confronted the Macedonians at the battle of Chaeronea in 338 B.C.E. and were crushed by Philip and eighteen-year-old Alexander. Chaeronea ended the tempestuous history of the city-state as the primary Greek political unit. Henceforth, large empires absorbed the Greek states into new political structures. Greece was only the first of many territories that fell to the expanding power of Macedon.

After Chaeronea, Philip announced his intention to avenge Persian offenses, especially Xerxes' burning of Greek temples 150 years earlier, and envisaged a campaign of glorious conquest in Persia. In 336 B.C.E., however, with preparations for this expedition well under way, he was murdered by a disgruntled member of the royal bodyguard. After Philip's assassination, the troops proclaimed Alexander king; the chance for glory in the Persian campaign went to the son, not the father.

The Son: Alexander

The nineteen-year-old Alexander possessed tremendous determination and an unquenchable thirst for power. As a youth, he underwent thorough training in athletics and the use of weapons; he was a fast runner and rode a horse almost before he walked. Nor was his intellectual development neglected: Philip hired the philosopher Aristotle to be Alexander's tutor. His education gave him a scientific curiosity about the natural world and a deep love for literature, especially the epics of Homer and the odes of the great Boeotian lyric poet, Pindar. Alexander's military training culminated at Chaeronea where he commanded the attacking wing of the Macedonian forces. By the time his father was assassinated, he was a great favorite among the troops.

In 336 B.C.E., when Alexander was occupied with putting down invasions by Macedon's semibarbaric neighbors, the Greek city-states thought they saw a chance to regain their freedom. When Thebes revolted (with Athenian encouragement), Alexander marched swiftly into Greece and destroyed the city (except for the house Pindar had lived in) as a horrifying example to other would-be rebels. He treated Athens much more leniently out of respect for its cultural history and espe-

The Boy Alexander and the Black Stallion

Philonicus the Thessalian brought the horse Bucephalas to Philip, offering to sell him for thirteen talents; but when they went into the field to try him, they found him so very vicious and unmanageable that he reared up when they endeavored to mount him, and would not so much as endure the voice of any of Philip's attendants. Upon which, as they were leading him away as wholly useless and intractable, Alexander [about ten years old at the time], who stood by, said, "What an excellent horse they are losing for lack of courage and know-how!" Philip . . . said, "Do you reproach your elders, as if you knew more and could better control him yourself?" "I could manage this horse," replied Alexander, "better than others do." "And if you do not," said Philip, "what will you forfeit for your rashness?" "I will pay," answered Alexander, "the whole price of the horse." Everyone laughed at this; and as soon as the wager was settled between them, Alexander immediately ran to the horse, and taking hold of the bridle, turned him directly toward the sun, having noticed that he was disturbed by the movement of his own shadow. Then letting him go forward a little, still keeping the reins in his hands and stroking him gently, when he began to grow eager and fiery, he shed his upper garment and with one bound mounted him firmly. When he was astride him, he gradually drew in the bridle and controlled him without blows or spurs. Then, when he was quite relaxed and ready to run, he let him go full speed, urging him with his voice and his heels. Philip and the others gazed in silence and some anxiety, but seeing him return rejoicing in what he had done, they burst into applause. Philip shed tears of joy and kissed the boy as he dismounted, saying "O my son, look for a kingdom worthy of you, for Macedon is too little for you."*

Philip's words were, of course, prophetic. Alexander kept the mighty Thessalian stallion and rode him in most of the major battles of his career. When the great warhorse died, some twenty years later, in the Indus region after the battle of the Hydaspes River, Alexander named a settlement Bucephala in his honor.

*John Dryden, trans., "Life of Alexander," sect. 6, in vol. 2 of *Plutarch's Lives,* ed. A. H. Clough (New York: Dutton, 1910), p. 467 (with slight modifications).

cially its naval power. Alexander now began his campaign against Persia, crossing the Hellespont in 334 precisely where Xerxes had crossed to attack Greece in 480—the symbolism was obvious. Besides his army of 65,000, Alexander brought with him technicians, road builders,

132   CHAPTER 4

surveyors, administrators, financial officers, and secretary-journalists. In addition, geographers, botanists, zoologists, astronomers, and mathematicians collected information that formed the basis of European knowledge of West Asia and India for many centuries afterward.

In the next decade, Alexander conquered the whole Persian Empire (see Map 4.1). While he was in Asia Minor and Syria-Palestine, Alexander ran the risk that the Persian navy might attack Greece or cut his supply lines at the Hellespont, forcing him to withdraw from Asia. The Persians, however, unwisely decided to give battle on land, first at the Granicus River in 334 B.C.E. and then, under King Darius III himself, at Issus in 333. Alexander won both battles and added the Mediterranean portion of the Persian Empire to his conquests. He marched into Syria and Palestine, where he took Tyre, a key Persian naval base. In Egypt, where he was proclaimed pharaoh, Alexander founded the city of Alexandria in 331. Alexandria later became the principal center of Hellenistic cultural development, the most important port in the eastern Mediterranean, and the second most populous city (after Rome) in the history of the ancient world. Alexander also underwent a decisively important religious experience when he consulted the oracle of

Ammon, whom the Greeks equated with Zeus, at the oasis of Siwah. Though he never revealed the oracle's message, Alexander henceforth believed himself marked out by the gods for even greater achievements than merely punishing the Persians.

Alexander next set out to conquer the heartland of the Persian Empire—modern Iraq and Iran. He beat Darius decisively at Gaugamela near the Tigris in 331 B.C.E. The beaten king escaped and was shortly thereafter assassinated by dissatisfied allies. Alexander then marched triumphantly into Babylon, Susa, and Persepolis, seizing massive booty in gold and silver. At Persepolis, he burned the great royal palaces and temples, avenging the Persian destruction of Greek temples. Turning his war machine eastward to the Indus valley, Alexander and his troops ran into winter weather in mountainous terrain and torrential monsoon rains. In the main pitched battle of this part of the expedition, Alexander defeated the Indian potentate Porus at the Hydaspes River in 326. Reluctantly yielding to the wishes of his weary troops, Alexander abandoned his plan to march even farther east. The journey back to Persia proved perilous, as the army encountered heavy fighting and suffered tremendous loss of life during a disastrous trek through the Gedrosian Desert.

❈ MAP 4.1 Conquests of Alexander the Great and the Hellenistic Kingdoms. After the death of Alexander, his far-flung empire, which had never really been stabilized administratively, was carved up during a long series of struggles among his successors. Three major kingdoms emerged by the mid-third century B.C.E.—the Macedonian, the Seleucid, and the Ptolemaic.

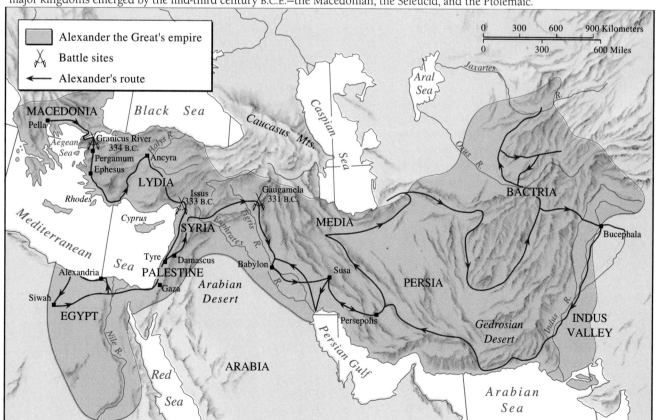

✣ Silver Tetradrachm. This four-drachma piece shows a divinized Alexander wearing the royal diadem and the ram's horns symbolic of Zeus Ammon, whose oracle he consulted at the oasis of Siwah. For the first time in Western civilization, coins bore the image of human rulers, as well as of gods. The coin, minted after Alexander's death, demonstrates the artistry of Greek coin designers and die cutters.   The Granger Collection

During his long campaign of conquest, Alexander assumed many of the trappings of Persian royalty, since he saw himself as the successor of the Great King and had come to admire Persian customs. He married the Sogdian princess Roxane and encouraged his officers to marry into Iranian nobility. He also promoted a plan of race fusion of his Macedonians and Persians but without much success. He treated Persians and other Iranians as his subjects rather than enemies and recruited a special corps of Iranian troops into the Macedonian army. He even demanded typically Persian signs of obeisance, specifically, prostration before the king. Since the Greeks associated such actions only with the worship of the gods, many of Alexander's veterans resented the apparent arrogance and inaccessibility of their leader.

Alexander was not one to rest on his laurels or devote his life to the administrative tasks of achieving political and social stability in conquered lands. Instead he planned new expeditions to the Arabian Peninsula, Africa, and perhaps the western Mediterranean. In 323 B.C.E., however, he died at Babylon of a fever of unknown origin, possibly malaria. The long journey, wounds suffered in battle, and probably advanced alcoholism had finally exhausted Alexander's marvelous stamina. Although Roxane bore a son, Alexander IV, after Alexander's death, both were murdered.

When Alexander was asked on his deathbed to whom he wished to leave his empire, he answered, "To the strongest." The result was ultimately a division of the empire into three Hellenistic kingdoms: Macedon and Greece; the Seleucid Empire, extending from Asia Minor to India; and the Ptolemaic kingdom, embracing Egypt and, at times, parts of Palestine. These kingdoms differed markedly from the classical city-states. Much larger in territory and ethnically more diverse, they were administered by an elaborate hierarchy headed by a remote,

godlike king of Macedonian descent who made the laws, owned much of the land, and was deified after death. Private citizens counted for much less politically than had their fifth-century ancestors and consequently felt little patriotic fervor.

The Hellenistic kingdoms endured for about two or three centuries. Macedon and Egypt fell entirely under Roman domination. The overextended Seleucid Empire lost territory too, as the culturally Hellenized kingdoms of Bactria and Parthia split off in its central and eastern sectors; its western portions succumbed to Roman armies. Ultimately, the Parthians would rule from the Euphrates to the Indus and, with superb cavalry, pose an insoluble military problem for the Romans; they also exploited their profitable position as brokers in the trade between East and West.

A Sophisticated, Cosmopolitan Society and Economy

Although wars occurred, an unprecedented level of cooperation among cities and among the Hellenistic kingdoms brought stability and prosperity. Greek educators, artisans, merchants, and soldiers moved into recently conquered regions. Trade relations were more secure and extensive, and Greek language and culture pervaded the newly formed kingdoms, at least among the upper classes.

Although most Hellenistic families were farmers, a remarkable growth in manufacturing and international commerce took place. Each region produced special commodities, which were exchanged around the Mediterranean and southwestern Asia: grain from Egypt, the Black Sea, and Sicily; olive oil from Attica; wines from Ionia and Syria; salt fish from Byzantium; cheese from Bithynia; prunes from Damascus; glass from Sidon; parchment from Pergamum (in present-day western

A Prenuptial Agreement from Hellenistic Egypt

Apollonia agrees to live with Philiscus in obedience to him, as is appropriate for a wife to her husband, possessing with him the property that they have in common. Philiscus . . . is to provide her with every necessity and a cloak and other possessions . . . at a level appropriate to their means, and Philiscus [may not] . . . bring into the house another wife in addition to Apollonia or a concubine or a catamite nor is he permitted to beget children with another woman so long as Apollonia is alive, nor to set up another household unless Apollonia is in charge of it, and he promises not to throw her out or insult or mistreat her and not to alienate any of their joint property in a way that would be injurious to Apollonia. If Philiscus is shown to have done any of these things or if he has not provided her with the necessities or the cloak or the other possessions as specified, Philiscus must immediately return the dowry of two talents and four thousand drachmas of copper money.

Similarly, Apollonia is not to stay away for a night or a day from Philiscus' household without Philiscus' knowledge, nor is she to live with another man or to cause ruin to the common household or to bring disgrace on Philiscus in whatever brings disgrace to a husband. If Apollonia voluntarily wants a separation from Philiscus, Philiscus is to return her dowry intact within ten days.*

This passage is from a papyrus found at Tebtunis in Ptolemaic Egypt and dates to 92 B.C.E. By ancient standards, this is an equitable marriage agreement. The basic responsibilities of both husband and wife are stipulated, and the disposition of the dowry and other communal property is carefully defined. The woman Apollonia has been well served by the male relatives who negotiated this marriage contract on her behalf.

*Mary R. Lefkowitz and Maureen B. Fant, *Women's Life in Greece and Rome: A Source Book in Translation*, 2d ed. (Baltimore: Johns Hopkins University Press, 1992), p. 90.

Turkey); bitumen (used in Egypt for embalming) from the Dead Sea; marble from Paros and Attica; timber from Macedon and Lebanon; precious purple dye from Tyre; ivory from India and Egypt; gemstones from India and Arabia; frankincense (used as a burnt offering in many religions) from Arabia; balsam from Jericho; and slaves from Thrace, Syria, and Asia Minor. Enhancing our knowledge of the Hellenistic world are many finds of papyrus in the arid soil of Egypt. The papyri record all sorts of official administrative dealings, as well as private communications and documents including wills, receipts, accounts, letters, lists, and memoranda. Others record agreements regarding marriage, divorce, adoption, apprenticeship and employment, and loans and sales of property and goods.

Hellenistic governments promoted and safeguarded these trade relations. Existing road networks, including those of the Persians, were maintained and expanded; the water supply along caravan routes was ensured; efforts were made to suppress piracy; and standard monetary systems were adopted. Certain cities—Rhodes, Delos, Corinth, and Ephesus, in particular—grew wealthy as transit depots. With the rise of Rome in the third century and after, new Italian markets further stimulated commerce.

An Age of Scientific Advances

The Hellenistic kingdoms supplied funding for various cultural enterprises. The Ptolemies of Egypt, for example, built and supported two important facilities, the first of their kind in history: the great Library of Alexandria and the affiliated "think tank" known as the Museum. Eminent librarians presided over the collection of some half-million volumes (papyrus rolls), and the world's first textual critics carefully edited the great works of Greek literature.

The scientific contributions of Hellenistic scholars were especially significant. By 300 B.C.E., Euclid had clearly explained the principles of geometry in his *Elements,* the basic textbook for the next 2,000 years. The brilliant inventor and mathematician Archimedes of Syracuse (c. 287–212 B.C.E.) worked on the geometry of spheres and cones and established the value of pi. Astronomers made surprisingly accurate calculations: a sun-centered theory of the universe was proposed, but the older earth-centered theory won out, and its formulation by Claudius Ptolemy was not superseded until the work of Copernicus, Galileo, and Newton in the sixteenth and seventeenth centuries. Eratosthenes accurately calculated the circumference of the earth by comparing the angles of shadow at noon during the summer solstice at two widely separated locations on the same meridian. In biology and medicine, dissection of cadavers and even of living convicts (supplied by King Ptolemy) advanced understanding of anatomy, including the function of the brain and central nervous system and the distinction between veins and arteries.

Hellenistic thinkers showed little interest in applied science and engineering. Under pressure from their rulers and patrons, however, they did produce some new military hardware. Archimedes was as famous for his machines and weaponry as for his mathematical genius; for

Take me and cast me where you will, for there I shall keep my divine part tranquil . . . if it can feel and act according to its proper constitution. Is this change of place sufficient reason why my soul should be unhappy and worse than it was, depressed, expanded, shrinking, frightened? . . .

If you are pained by any external thing, it is not this thing that disturbs you, but your own judgement about it. And it is in your power to wipe out this judgement now.

But if anything in your own disposition gives you pain, who hinders you from correcting your opinion? . . .

Remember that the ruling faculty is invincible, when self-collected it is satisfied with itself, if it does nothing which it does not choose to do, even if it resist from mere obstinacy. . . . Therefore the mind which is free from passions is a citadel, for humans have nothing more secure to which they can fly for refuge and for the future be inexpugnable.*

In this passage, Marcus Aurelius preaches the Stoic doctrine of self-control. The right-thinking person understood that human suffering was a result of an inner response to an outer occurrence. If the mind was correctly trained and attuned to the true nature of the universe, no accident could harm it. Indeed, "accidents" were entirely neutral—simply things that occurred. The

Stoic individual possessed a refuge in reason that offered absolute protection from the seemingly harmful events in the surrounding world.

*Marcus Aurelius, *Meditations*, book 8, sects. 45–48, trans. George Long, in *The Stoic and Epicurean Philosophers*, ed. Whitney J. Oates (New York: Random House, 1940), p. 550.

---

example, he invented a giant catapult that could hurl 200-pound missiles up to 200 yards.

Escapism and Individualism in Hellenistic Culture

Religion in Hellenistic times was directed more to the spiritual and escapist needs of the individual than to the promotion of civic responsibility. Since the individual was no longer an integral part of a civic group watched over by guardian deities, the old state religion lost its meaning. Needing more immediate emotional satisfaction and assurance of self-worth, people turned to the impressive secret ceremonies of popular new sects known as mystery religions. Cults like those of Dionysus from Greece, Isis from Egypt, and Mithras from Persia offered an escape to a joyful hallucinatory experience of union with a god or goddess—an experience induced by alcohol or drugs, delirious dancing, and sexual frenzy. The promise of immortality was a further attraction. Mystery religions remained popular in the Roman Empire and helped pave the way for Christianity.

For many educated persons, two new philosophical systems—Stoicism and Epicureanism—filled the vacuum left by the waning of the old religion. Zeno of Citium (335–263 B.C.E.) taught in Athens at the Stoa Poikile (painted hall), and his doctrine is thus called "Stoic." Its principal tenets were as follows: First, goodness is based on knowledge. Only the wise person is really virtuous. Second, the truly wise person lives in harmony with nature by means of reason, which is part of the divine, universal reason (equivalent to God) governing the natural world. Third, it follows that the only good is harmony with nature. External "accidents" like sickness, pain, and

death cannot harm the truly good person. Stoicism's emphasis on outwardly directed concepts like duty and civic responsibility later ensured its popularity in the Roman Empire. Indeed, the Roman emperor Marcus Aurelius was a practicing Stoic, whose book of *Meditations* is a masterpiece of Stoic philosophy.

Epicurus (341–270 B.C.E.), who taught at Athens about the same time as Zeno, preached the following principles: First, nothing exists but atoms and void. The soul, like all else, is material and disintegrates like the body; thus it cannot suffer after death. Second, the only good in this life is pleasure, a perfect equilibrium or inner tranquillity, defined as the absence of pain or stress. Third, all our actions should be directed toward the minimizing of pain, that is, toward pleasure. Epicureanism was an inwardly directed system, recommending withdrawal from society and public life. Its emphasis on pleasure invited charges of vulgar hedonism: Eat, drink, and make merry, for tomorrow you die and will not be held accountable. These perceptions are reminiscent of the charges that some Chinese leveled against the Taoists. Despite such accusations and misconceptions, the Epicureans exerted great influence and found their most eloquent proponent in the Roman poet Lucretius.

Stoicism and Epicureanism both offered ethical systems suited to the conditions of life in the Hellenistic world. Rather than focusing exclusively on the search for knowledge about the nature of the universe, they stressed the ability of properly educated individuals to ensure their own happiness. In different ways, each promised release from the psychological and spiritual pain of life in a cosmopolitan world where traditional values were dying.

After the masterpieces of the classical era, literature in the Hellenistic period is disappointing. Menander

✣ Statue of a Boxer. One of the favorite subjects of Hellenistic art was the human figure in the throes of intense physical exertion or pain. In this statue of a boxer, probably resting between bouts (there were no rounds), we see a veteran of many fights, which have left him with battle scars, including a broken nose and a cauliflower ear. The leather straps and pads he wears on his forearms and fists, known as "sharp gloves," were designed as much to inflict damage on an opponent as to protect the wearer.   Terme Museum, Rome. Photo © Archivi Alinari/Art Resource

(c. 342–c. 290 B.C.E.) perfected the New Comedy, whose emphasis, typical of the era, was on private family squabbles rather than the sharp-witted satirical depictions of current events and public policy found in Aristophanic Old Comedy. Recent papyrus finds give a clearer impression of this comedy of manners, which features young lovers, upstart slaves, crotchety old men, and the like. Mistaken identity, contrived or accidental, often motivated the plot. An immensely popular form, New Comedy's influence extended to the Roman stage, in the work of Plautus and Terence, and later to Shakespeare's comedies. The situation comedies of television are modern analogues.

Hellenistic art, best represented in sculpture, is both more ornate and more individualistic than classical art,

particularly in its representation of extreme emotion. Artists could still capture classical Greek nobility of form, as in the superb winged Nike of Samothrace, but the supple sensuality of the Venus de Milo is more typical. Humbler subjects were chosen too; for instance, a gnarled old boxer waiting his turn to compete and a little boy-jockey, frozen in mid-gallop. The famous Laocoön group, showing the Trojan priest Laocoön and his two sons being attacked by two sea serpents, symbolically captures the essence of war's hellish human price. Its style differs markedly from the sublimity of most classical sculpture. The discovery of the Laocoön at Rome during the Renaissance created a sensation and profoundly influenced Michelangelo (who viewed it within hours of its discovery), Titian, and, later, Gotthold Lessing.

Hellenistic artists practiced their art at the behest of the royal families or wealthy private citizens. Unlike their classical predecessors, they did not create adornments for the greater glory of the beloved city-state or the gods who watched over it. In this regard, they followed the same trend toward individualism and escapism that can be seen in Hellenistic philosophy and literature.

The Rise and Decline of Roman Power in the Mediterranean World

The study of history usefully provides a record of all manner of experiences inscribed as it were on a glorious monument. From that record, the reader may choose examples worthy of imitation by himself and by his nation and examples of behavior that are thoroughly disgraceful and to be avoided. If I am not deceived by my love of the work I have set myself in writing history, no republic was ever greater, more virtuous, or more abundant in good examples. Into no state did greed and self-indulgence come so late. In no state was there such respect for so long a time for frugality and an austere way of living.*

*Livy, *Ab Urbe Condita*, book 1, praefatio (translated by James P. Holoka).

These words of praise come from the historian Livy's preface to his magisterial history of Rome. Writing in the late first century B.C.E., he had witnessed the violent upheavals that attended the political transition from republic to empire. It was a time of disillusionment for many Roman intellectuals, but Livy found solace in writing the history of his state from its very beginnings, for he found there the record of great achievements and remarkable moral probity. While we may apply a more critical standard in our assessment of Rome's rise to power, the value of studying its history is

✳ Bronze She-Wolf. This bronze statue (fifth century B.C.E.) represents the most famous city-symbol ever devised. The wolf was a kind of totem animal from earliest times: When Romulus and Remus were exposed on the banks of the Tiber by their evil great-uncle, a she-wolf rescued and suckled them. The statue is a fitting symbol of the Roman virtues of warrior prowess and unflinching dedication to family (the twins are a Renaissance addition). Scala/Art Resource

assured by the influence Roman examples have exerted in the story of civilizations.

Rome had humble beginnings, however, and Romans were not always masters of the world. To explain Rome's rise, we must consider its origins, the social and political practices that gave it internal strength, and the military exploits by which it overcame external threats and conquered great reaches of land. We will examine the resulting Greco-Roman civilization that so shaped the culture and thought of later ages. Finally, we will consider the factors that led to the collapse of Roman power.

The Early Roman Republic

Centrally located in the Mediterranean, Italy has hot and dry summers and mild winters with moderate rainfall. As in Greece, the mountainous terrain separated the population into numerous city-states in valleys or coastal plains, but with abundant timberland and more cultivable land, Italy could support large populations.

The history of Rome begins in the eighth century B.C.E., when three major ethnic groups inhabited the Ital-

ian Peninsula. Greek colonists of the archaic period built towns throughout southern Italy and on Sicily. The Etruscans, who had immigrated in the same period, possibly from Asia Minor, occupied the territory between the Tiber and the Arno Rivers and exerted a crucial influence in culture and religion. Constituting an older ethnic strain than the Greeks and Etruscans were the Italic peoples—Latins, Sabines, and others—in whom were combined a Mediterranean people, perhaps from North Africa, and Indo-Europeans from across the Alps. They were a hardy stock, primarily farmers and herders.

The archaeological record shows that Rome in the eighth century was inhabited by shepherd folk: Latins and Sabines. Etruscan influence in the next three centuries brought progressive urbanization. The Tarquins of Roman myth likely reflect a historical period of Etruscan political and cultural domination. Rome's expulsion of its overlords marked the start of a period of government by elected officials under a republic.

In the early republic, the population of Rome was sharply divided into patricians and plebeians. The patricians were a hereditary aristocracy that accepted high

When a debt has been acknowledged . . . thirty days must be the legitimate time of grace. After that, the debtor may be arrested by laying on of hands. . . . The creditor may . . . bind [the defaulter] either in stocks or in fetters . . . with a weight no more than fifteen pounds, or with less if he shall so desire. . . . Unless they make a settlement, debtors shall be held in bonds for sixty days. During that time they shall be brought before the praetor's court in the meeting place on three successive market days, and the amount for which they are judged liable shall be announced; on the third market day they shall suffer capital punishment or be delivered up for sale abroad, across the Tiber.

Quickly kill . . . a dreadfully deformed child.

A child born ten months after the father's death will not be admitted into legal inheritance.

Females shall remain in guardianship even when they have attained their majority . . . except Vestal Virgins.

Persons shall mend roadways. If they do not keep them laid with stone, a person may drive his beasts where he wishes.

It is permitted to gather up fruit falling down on another man's farm.

If any person has sung or composed against another person a song such as was causing slander or insult to another, he shall be clubbed to death.

If a theft has been done by night, if the owner kill the thief, the thief shall be held lawfully killed.*

The Twelve Tables, Rome's earliest written code of law, represented a victory for the plebeian order. Though the code seems to mete out a rough justice, the very fact that it existed in written form shielded, for example, the poor (plebeian) debtor from completely arbitrary punishment by a patrician magistrate. Also, once the law was written down, it could subsequently be amended and refined to create a more rational and humane system of justice. The Twelve Tables also furnish invaluable evidence for the human condition in early republican Rome: it was an agrarian world, much concerned with questions of property, debt, law and order, and the various rights of family members.

*Naphtali Lewis and Meyer Reinhold, eds., *Roman Civilization, Sourcebook I: The Republic* (1951; reprint, New York: Harper, 1966), pp. 103–104, 106–107.

civic responsibility, not just for the sake of power but also because of the dignity conferred by public recognition of services rendered. The plebeians, who comprised the great mass of the free population—farmers, shepherds, small merchants, and artisans—suffered from poverty and oppression by aristocrats. By going on strike or threatening secession, however, the plebeians eventually secured certain essential individual rights and freedoms for all citizens, not just patricians. These included the right to vote for magistrates, the right to have marriages between citizens legally recognized, the right to secure legally binding commercial contracts, and the right to due process in any criminal proceedings.

Although the plebeians respected the political competence of the patricians, they successfully agitated for the right to intermarry with patricians and for a written code of law. The Twelve Tables (449 B.C.E.) marked the beginning of a distinguished history of Roman law, which extended down to Justinian's code in the sixth century C.E. Though excluded from patrician status, plebeians could rise to the rank of *equites* (knights), if they possessed the financial resources to keep horses and serve as cavalry in the army. They also eventually won the right to serve in the highest public offices. By the early third century, such guarantees of fair play and opportunities for advancement, won by hard struggle, were the inalienable right of every Roman citizen.

Rome, like Greece, was a slave-owning society. Perhaps one-fourth of the population throughout antiquity consisted of slaves acquired through warfare, piracy, and trade. Slaves provided the bulk of the labor force, performing household tasks and the heavy work of farming and mining. Slavery in ancient Rome was also a mechanism for the assimilation of new peoples. The common practice of freeing slaves as a reward for loyal service gave rise to a class of second-class citizens called freedpersons; so many non-Romans were given their freedom that by the late republic perhaps one-half of the citizenry of Rome had slave ancestors.

Although republican Rome never allowed common citizens to participate as much in key governmental decisions as classical Athens had, it did allow for representation of various elements of its society and adjusted to changing needs. The various magistracies were normally annual in tenure and divided among colleagues. Two consuls, elected annually for a one-year term, were the chief civil authorities within the city and commanders of the armed forces. They were empowered to appoint a dictator for a six-month term in times of dire emergency. Other elected officials had responsibility for administering justice, supervising public works, putting on games, races, and contests, maintaining official financial accounts, and conducting the census. In addition to the civic magistracies, the Romans elected for life the *pontifex maximus* (chief priest), who presided over the entire apparatus of the state religion. Finally, the Roman Senate was a key advisory body of ex-magistrates who held membership for life. *Senatus Populusque Romanus* (the Senate and Roman People; abbreviated SPQR) was the logo of Roman jurisdiction.

Roman society was based on "piety," a value system that emphasized devotion to the gods and to members of one's family, both living and dead. Romans honored the memory of their forefathers and held to a morality of hard work and self-discipline in service to gods, family, and state. As in the teachings of Confucius, the family was a microcosmic state: the father was effectively king and chief priest of the miniature nation of his family. Like their Greek sisters, Roman women were educationally and legally disadvantaged, but they could aspire to be *matronae* (mothers of families). In return for her fidelity, fertility, and domesticity, the Roman woman could expect to be revered within her family and Roman society.

Roman religion, like that of the Greeks, was polytheistic and involved civic as well as personal duty. Roman beliefs were shaped by foreign influences. The old Italic agricultural gods were modified to parallel Etruscan and/or Greek gods. Venus was equated with Greek Aphrodite, Jupiter with Etruscan Tinia and Greek Zeus, and so on. The goal of Roman religion was *pax deorum* (peace with the gods). Prayers, vows, sacrifices, and acts of purification or atonement were all designed to appease gods who were easily angered and liable to inflict punishment on an entire group, guilty and innocent alike. Divination of various kinds was practiced in an effort to ascertain the will of the gods: soothsayers read the stars and the flight patterns of birds, and professional "gut watchers" discerned the future in the entrails of sacrificial animals. In return for observance of religious rituals, Romans hoped for favorable answers to their requests for divine assistance.

The Roman Conquest of Italy and the Mediterranean

After 509 B.C.E., Rome joined, and later dominated, a league of Latin cities that defended its fertile plains against the frequent incursions of neighboring hill peoples like the Sabines. Success against these enemies led ultimately to their political absorption and the replacement of Oscan language dialects by Latin. After the setback in 387 of a shattering defeat at the hands of Gauls, fearsome Celtic invaders from across the Alps, the Romans embarked on campaigns of conquest against Gauls and Etruscans to the north and against Samnites and Latins to the south. By 290, Rome controlled more than half of the Italian Peninsula.

Roman predominance in the Italian Peninsula at the beginning of the third century B.C.E. rested on a shrewdly conceived system of annexations and alliances. Rome also established colonies of citizens or, more often, of allies, thus increasing its territory, available manpower, and military strength. Rome's conquests were achieved by an army of unpaid militia conscripted for each campaigning season. Discipline, obedience to authority, and ability to endure adversity combined with first-rate training and drill to make the Roman soldier the best the world had yet seen. The efficiency and preparedness of its military machine were to stand Rome in good stead during its coming struggles against major powers outside the Italian Peninsula.

In the third century, Carthage was the major power in the western Mediterranean. Originally founded as a Phoenician colony (called *Poeni* in Latin, giving the adjective "Punic"), its central position in the Mediterranean, near modern Tunis, and its excellent harbor made Carthage a preeminent trading city. It controlled the exchange of gold, silver, and tin from Spain and Africa for wine, textiles, and manufactured goods of its own or from the Hellenistic east. The rise of Rome to a rival first-class power imperiled that advantage.

When Carthage began to expand in Sicily (see Map 4.2), Rome decided in 264 B.C.E. to send troops to the island, thus starting the First Punic War. After Rome built a fleet to match that of the Carthaginians, final victory came in 241 at the high price of 200,000 men and 500 ships lost. Rome's Italian allies and colonists had supplied the needed reserves of manpower and matériel. The fruits of the hard-earned triumph were sweet. Carthage paid an indemnity of 3,200 talents (200,000 pounds in weight) of silver over the next ten years and ceded its territory in Sicily and, eventually, in Corsica and Sardinia. Rome had acquired its first overseas possessions, and the long process of adapting its government to the requirements of a far-flung empire began in earnest.

Initial hostilities in the Second Punic War were ignited by friction in Spain, where members of the Barca family—Hamilcar and later his son Hannibal (247–183 B.C.E.)—had been directing the creation of Carthaginian colonies. In 219 B.C.E., Hannibal took by siege the Spanish town of Saguntum, which had contracted an alliance with Rome. War broke out the following year.

Hannibal surprised the Romans by leading men, horses, and combat elephants across the Alps into the Po Valley. By his tactical brilliance and his superior cavalry, he defeated Roman troops sent to stop him, but could not take Rome itself, for the allied cities of central Italy held firm. Instead, he established himself in southern Italy, where he devastated the territory of cities that resisted and accepted the cooperation of others.

The tide turned in Rome's favor with the appointment of a brilliant general, Publius Cornelius Scipio (236–183 B.C.E.). He succeeded in taking New Carthage, the nerve center of Punic power in Spain, in 209 B.C.E. Later, Scipio carried the war to North Africa and, after Hannibal was recalled by Carthage, defeated the great general at Zama

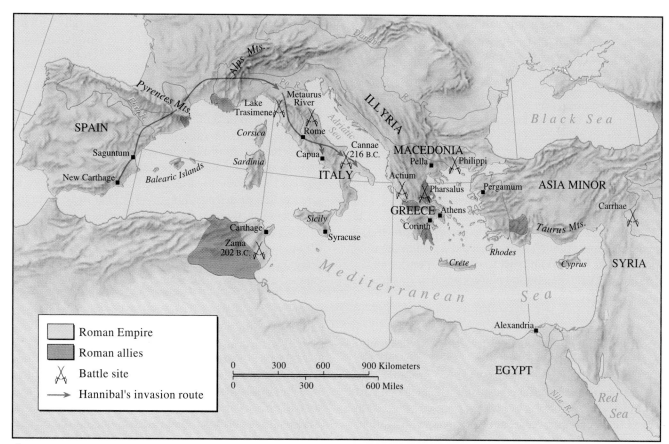

✳ MAP 4.2 The Roman World at the Time of the Late Republic. Shown here is the territory under Roman control by about 30 B.C.E. Some of the larger provinces and a few important battle sites are indicated.

in 202. In 201 Carthage capitulated, surrendering Spain and agreeing to pay an indemnity of 10,000 talents. The once-mighty city survived, only to be razed in 146, after the Third Punic War. Rome, now the foremost power in the western Mediterranean, was ready to turn to the Hellenistic east.

As Cicero later said in his *Republic,* "Our people, by defending allies, have become masters of the entire world." When Rhodes and Pergamum appealed to Rome, its armies defeated the Macedonian king in 197 BC.E. Rome later went to war with the Seleucid kings, again with Macedonia, and with a confederation of Greek states called the Achaean League. The result in each case was Roman victory and the creation of new provinces or puppet states from formerly independent Greek territories. Attalus III (138–133 BC.E.), the last king of Pergamum, bequeathed his kingdom to Rome, and Rome possessed its first province in Asia.

Between 264 and 133 BC.E., Rome had won important victories because of the bravery and discipline of its loyal legionary soldiers and the competence, and sometimes brilliance, of its generals. Rome's military success cost its opponents dearly, as Roman soldiers hunted down and butchered or enslaved Spaniards, Gauls, and Sardinians. Nor were civilized adversaries spared plunder, enslavement, rape, and extortion. As the historian Tacitus cyni-

cally said, "Plunder, murder, theft, these they misname empire; and where they make a desert, they call it peace."

By 133 B.C.E., empire building had become Rome's chief industry, a source of glory for the Roman nobility and of profits both for the state and for entrepreneurs, businessmen, publicans (tax collectors), and provisioners of the army. New trade routes and markets proliferated in the Mediterranean region. Many others, however, shared little in these profits of empire. The small farmer who had been the mainstay of the early republican state began to disappear. Devastation by Hannibal's army and neglect for long periods in the second century when their owners were in military service ruined many farms. Wealthy senatorial aristocrats bought up the holdings of failed farmers and combined them into vast estates worked by the plentiful slaves obtained through foreign conquests. Dispossessed free men drifted to Rome in search of work or handouts, swelling the ranks of a restless urban population.

For the citizens of Rome, the downside of the greatly enlarged slave labor force was the threat of revolt. Although many literate and skilled slaves from the Greek east found a comfortable life in the homes of wealthy Romans, the great majority of slaves were consigned to hard labor in the fields and mines. Runaways turned to banditry in the Italian countryside and posed a problem of national security: for example, 100,000 rebellious slaves led by the gladiator Spartacus were crushed in 71 B.C.E., but only after two years at large, during which they inflicted several defeats on Roman legions.

Provincials, too, often suffered from the predations of Roman governors, who were frequently less interested in fair administration than in enriching themselves through excessive taxation. Inclusion in the empire was thus a mixed blessing.

The Breakdown of the Republic and the Rise of Augustus

By 133 B.C.E., Rome had long since outgrown the makeshift constitution that had served it well in the early phases of its history. The vast territorial expansion of the empire and the tremendous powers wielded by generals and politicians finally strained the whole framework to the breaking point. Roman history became a tale of seizures of power, assassinations, mob violence, political collusion, and, in general, an utter disregard for republican habits of government.

After 133 the political atmosphere in Rome was charged by tension between *populares,* who included both patricians and plebeians but whose policies generally favored the common people, and *optimates,* who again included both patricians and plebeians but whose policies generally favored the entrenched senatorial elite. Gaius Marius (157–86 B.C.E.) solved Rome's recruitment problem and acquired a private army by transforming farmer-militia into paid professional soldiers. Land grants to discharged veterans accelerated Romanization of outlying parts of the empire and shifted soldiers' allegiance from the civil authorities to the military commander.

Marius's former subordinate, Sulla, now set the precedent of using military force to achieve his own political ends. Beginning in 83 B.C.E., he fought a bloody civil war against his *populares* opponents and had himself appointed dictator. Because Sulla needed land and money to reward his troops, he set forth proscriptions, lists of public enemies who could be murdered for a reward, including many whose only offense was their political opinion or their wealth.

In the next thirty years, three new strongmen accumulated fantastic military and political power. Gnaeus Pompeius (106–48 B.C.E.), called Pompey the Great, Marcus Licinius Crassus (c. 112–53 B.C.E.), and Gaius Julius Caesar (100–44 B.C.E.) cooperated for a time to subvert the republican system in favor of their own personal goals, but the uneasy balance of mighty egos finally collapsed.

Julius Caesar had family connections to important *populares* and had served in various high offices. His phenomenal success in the Gallic wars of 58–50 B.C.E. upset the tripartite balance of power. He gained for Rome the territory from the Alps to the Atlantic and the North Sea.

He also won tremendous booty, shared liberally with his devoted army, which grew from two to thirteen legions. Meanwhile Crassus's dream of military glory died with him and most of his seven legions on the plains of Mesopotamia, near Carrhae, in 53. The Parthians proudly displayed the captured legionary eagle standards (and Crassus's head on a pike) as trophies. Events now swiftly brought Caesar to supreme power. When the Senate voted that he should lay down his command before returning to Italy, Caesar chose rebellion. He forced Pompey and an army loyal to the Senate to withdraw to Greece. Caesar defeated him in 48 at Pharsalus. Escaping to Alexandria, Pompey was stabbed to death.

Caesar soon settled matters from one end of the Mediterranean to the other. He established Cleopatra (reigned 51–30 B.C.E.) as queen of Egypt, where he remained almost a year. At Rome, Caesar reduced the number of grain dole recipients, carried out public works programs, and revised the calendar, making it solar rather than lunar. Caesar spared Roman citizens who had fought against him in the civil war and even secured offices for former aristocratic opponents, but he continued to monopolize power. His assumption of the prerogatives of *dictator perpetuus* (dictator for life) in 45 angered jealous aristocrats and alarmed true republicans, including Marcus Junius Brutus (85–42 B.C.E.), who murdered Caesar at a meeting of the Senate on the Ides (fifteenth) of March 44 B.C.E.

In the first years after Caesar's assassination, no one individual leader was able to consolidate all his powers. Caesar's grandnephew, Gaius Julius Caesar Octavianus, or Octavian (63 B.C.E.–14 C.E.), used his vast inherited riches to raise armies and buy influence. After the group responsible for assassinating Caesar was eliminated, Octavian turned his attention to Marc Antony, a colleague of Julius Caesar's, who was in control of the eastern provinces of the empire. Octavian persuaded the western provinces, Italy, and most of the surviving Roman aristocracy that Antony meant to make Cleopatra joint ruler and shift the center of empire to Alexandria. In 31 Octavian crossed to Greece and defeated Antony and Cleopatra at the naval battle of Actium. At Alexandria the following year, Antony committed suicide to avoid capture, as did Cleopatra, the last Hellenistic ruler in the Ptolemaic line from Alexander's day.

Octavian, now left as the single all-powerful ruler, inaugurated the imperial period of Roman history, an epoch that witnessed a fusing of West Asian, Greek, and Roman cultural traditions. He accepted the name Imperator Caesar Augustus (*augustus* means "venerable" or "majestic") and announced his intention to restore republican institutions. However, the next forty-one years brought instead a steady, calculated implementation of a new monarchy, as Augustus's shrewd outward show of respect for republican institutions disguised his monopoly of power. Actually, Augustus genuinely respected

When [Cleopatra] first met Antony she sailed on a golden barge, dressed like Aphrodite. She was not so beautiful as some earlier Macedonian queens, but she possessed a magical charm and a beautiful voice. She was well educated and spoke many languages including Egyptian (unlike many male Ptolemies). . . . Since Antony did not have intellectual aspirations, Cleopatra entertained him as he desired. The two of them enjoyed Oriental luxury, Cleopatra playing the exotic companion to Antony's pleasure, though the debauchery and drunkenness ascribed to her are not in keeping with the traditions of Hellenistic queens, and, as far as we know, she had sexual liaisons with only Caesar and Antony. Legends built up by her enemies are doubtless the source of unflattering accounts, since Cleopatra's competence as a ruler was never questioned, and Egypt remained loyal to her. . . .

She resembled Alexander the Great in her ability and quest for world empire. She posed a major threat to Octavian and Rome. . . . When Octavian finally declared war after Antony had formally divorced Octavia [Octavian's sister], he declared war on Cleopatra alone. . . .

After being defeated by Octavian, Antony committed suicide and died in Cleopatra's arms. Rather than grace Octavian's triumph, Cleopatra killed herself by allowing an asp to bite her breast. . . . She dominated Antony, and, if she loved him, she certainly never let emotion divert her from her schemes. The Romans feared her as they had feared only Hannibal, and they created a legend that survives to this day.*

More than any other woman of the ancient world, Cleopatra has captured the imagination of biographers, historians, and creative writers. Shakespeare, in particular, in his tragedy *Antony and Cleopatra,* made famous the story of this Hellenistic queen. Whatever the romantic embroidery on her life, as the lover of Julius Caesar and the wife of Marc Antony, she played a major role in the turbulent last years of the Roman republic.

*Sarah B. Pomeroy, *Goddesses, Whores, Wives, and Slaves: Women in Classical Antiquity* (New York: Schocken, 1975), pp. 187–188.

most Roman traditions and tried to revive a society demoralized by civil strife.

The emperor's powers were virtually unlimited. He kept exclusive control of the military, which meant ultimate civil authority as well. Augustus's stupendous personal wealth allowed him to win and maintain the people's favor. He built new forum areas, renovated temples, improved roads, and, to keep the urban poor from growing restive, financed public games and kept grain prices artificially low, thereby setting the precedent for later emperors.

Unlike Alexander the Great, Augustus engaged in conquest not for its own sake but to secure borders and to promote the arts of government within them. He succeeded both by his own administrative skills and by those of the men he selected for positions of power. This stable government had economic consequences as well: commercial and manufacturing activity flourished during the *Pax Romana* (Roman peace). Augustus also reopened and made secure trade routes both inside the Mediterranean and outside it, for example, with Arabia, India, and China via the Red Sea and Indian Ocean.

Roman Cultural Developments

Roman military conquest of the Greek east was paralleled by Greek cultural conquest of Rome in the third and second centuries B.C.E. Greek ways of living and thinking so penetrated Roman society that, as the poet Horace put it, "Captive Greece captured its crude conqueror and brought the arts to hayseed Latium."

Service in campaigns in the Hellenistic kingdoms gave Roman soldiers a taste for things Greek. The Romans admired the magnificent temples and elaborate festivals, enjoyed dramatic performances in the splendid theaters, and engaged in athletic exercises in the palestras. They indulged in the creature comforts of public baths, luxurious mansions adorned with works of art, and of sumptuous meals skillfully prepared by master chefs. In imitation of what they had seen in the Hellenistic kingdoms, Roman aristocrats beautified their homes with sculptures and vases and their bodies with jewelry and fabrics from the Greek east. Slaves trained as barbers, doctors, painters, personal secretaries, and tutors brought high prices. Bakeries and taverns began to dot the streets and served imported wines as well as domestic varieties. Dates, peaches, apricots, lemons, plums, cherries, and spices were introduced to Italy from the east.

Also in the second century B.C.E., Epicurean and Stoic philosophers brought their teachings to Rome. Mystery cults, too, like that of Bacchus (in Greek, Dionysus) and of the great mother-goddess Cybele, imported from Asia Minor, first began to make inroads in the traditional beliefs. These alarmed Roman authorities because of their particularly strong appeal to the downtrodden members of society. Bacchus's worshipers were often women seeking to satisfy religious feelings and perhaps to register a disguised protest against male social dominance.

A Sound Mind in a Sound Body

Since earliest times people have been interested in, sometimes obsessed with, physical fitness. To encourage the birth of strong, healthy babies, Spartan women engaged in vigorous physical training. Roman mosaics show women working out and throwing the discus. The Greeks held hundreds of annual games, and the most famous, the Olympic games, were held quadrennially, as today. The Maya in Latin America were perhaps the most avid game players. Their elaborate ball game had no time limit, and the winners played until the losers died.

As civilizations evolved and men and women moved away from active lifestyles to more sedentary habits, maintaining one's physical well-being became a problem. As Hippocrates noted, "Eating alone will not keep a man well; he must also take exercise." Early Greeks and Romans stressed a wide variety of physical performance, including formal competitive events—running, jumping, throwing—and informal leisure-time activities such as hunting and fishing and various ball games.

Many societies, including those of Rome and Islam, believed in the therapeutic effects of hot baths and mineral waters. References to herbalists and health foods are found in regions as diverse as the Western Hemisphere, Africa, and Asia. The Greeks in particular stressed the importance of balance and moderation, especially in dietary and drinking habits. Many believed that "you are what you eat."

Under the influence of Greek culture, Roman literature made its debut in the late third and early second centuries B.C.E. Plautus (c. 254–184 B.C.E.) and Terence (c. 190–159 B.C.E.) adapted the Greek comic drama of social mores to produce the first Latin masterpieces. The treasure house of Greek literature entered the school curriculum, and soon nearly every educated Roman was bilingual and well versed in Greek classics.

Roman literature came of age in the late republic and reached its zenith in the early empire. The first truly great master of Latin language and style was Cicero (106–43 B.C.E.). Among his best-known speeches are the verbal cannon blasts of the *Philippics,* directed against Mark Antony. In a lighter vein are the treatises *On Friendship* and *On Old Age,* delightful reflections on ethical living by a man wise in experience. So great was Cicero's authority as a Latin stylist that, centuries later, one Christian prelate found himself unable to refer to the Holy Spirit in a Latin sermon because there was no word for it in Cicero.

The greatest Roman poet of the republic, Lucretius (c. 94–c. 55 B.C.E.), wrote the *De rerum natura* (On the Nature of Things), presenting the central axioms of Epicurean philosophy with consummate artistry and fervent commitment. Lucretius especially admired Epicurus for dispelling the terrors of conventional Greco-Roman religious belief.

Another interesting poet, Catullus (c. 84–c. 54 B.C.E.), was a member of a chic group of avant-garde writers called New Poets. Many of his poems were inspired by his love (and later hatred) for the woman he called Lesbia:

> Let's do some living, my Lesbia, and loving,
> and not give a damn for the gossip
> of all those stern old moralists;
> suns can set and then rise up again,
> but our brief sunburst goes out just once,

and then it's curtains and the big sleep.
Gimme a thousand kisses, then a hundred,
another thousand, another hundred,
then still another thousand and hundred,
then let's make so many thousands
that we lose track, no counting 'em at all,
so those envious fools can't jinx us
by toting up our kisses.
(Poem 5, trans. Lawrence Smith and James P. Holoka)

According to various sources, this intriguing woman was beautiful, aristocratic, witty, ultrafashionable, nymphomaniacal, adulterous, and perhaps murderous. Other poems relate practical jokes, a visit to the distant grave of a beloved brother, a mock funeral lament for a pet sparrow, and the delight of homecoming after a long absence.

An important aspect of literary production in this period was the influence of the emperor himself. Augustus possessed an exceptional ability to induce the best literary talents to restore Roman morale by writing poetry and history that advocated nationalistic ideals of patriotism and morality. Maecenas, the great literary patron of Vergil and Horace, was an indispensable aide to Augustus in this area.

Between 30 and 19 B.C.E., the greatest Roman poet, Vergil (70–19 B.C.E.), created the *Aeneid,* a masterpiece of world literature. The epic describes the exploits of the hero Aeneas after the fall of Troy. The gods choose Aeneas to lead a band of Trojan refugees on a perilous journey to Italy, where his descendants are to mingle with native Italians and found Rome. Since the gods in the epic gradually disclose the manifest destiny of the Roman Empire, the poem was both foundation myth and mission statement for the Roman people. Without being jingoistic, it gave the Roman world its national epic. The self-effacing Aeneas differs from Homer's more egocen-

When human life lay prostrate on the earth oppressed by the heavy burden of religion which seemed to show its head in the heavens, threatening human beings with a terrifying face, it was a Greek who first dared to lift his head and resist its power. He feared neither the tales of gods nor their lightning bolts nor their thunder in the heavens. All these things only spurred his brave spirit to break through the constricting boundaries of nature's gates. The vital force of his intellect carried him past the flaming walls of the universe as he traversed that immense realm in his mind and soul. In triumph he returned to us with knowledge of all that can or cannot come to be, of how each thing has its potentials defined and regulated. In this way, religion was cast down in subjection and we human beings raised to the heavens by his victory.*

Lucretius believed that humankind had lived in a benighted and unreasonable state of religious fear before Epicurus developed his philosophy. In particular, men and women lived their lives badly, committing such crimes as human sacrifice and unjust war, because they feared reprisals by gods who made contradictory and often irrational demands on them. The typical polytheistic belief in vengeful, fickle, and immoral gods had too long kept people in ethical and intellectual darkness. Epicurus freed humankind from such fears by daring to shed light on the universe with the power of his intellect, which revealed that the gods, if they existed, in fact played no part in our lives and thus posed no threats of punishment.

*Lucretius, *De rerum natura*, book 1, lines 62–79; translated by James P. Holoka.

Others will cast more tenderly in bronze
Their breathing figures, I can well believe,
And bring more lifelike portraits out of marble;
Argue more eloquently, use the pointer
To trace the paths of heaven accurately
And accurately foretell the rising stars.
Roman, remember by your strength to rule
Earth's peoples—for your arts are to be these:
To pacify, to impose the rule of law,
To spare the conquered, battle down the proud.*

In these lines, Vergil identifies the distinctive Roman achievement in history as the art of government: the manifest destiny of the Romans was to unify the earth's peoples into a peaceable order. In Vergil's eyes, this was something to be proud of, surpassing even the artistic and scientific achievements of those "others," the Greeks.

*Virgil, *The Aeneid*, trans. R. Fitzgerald (New York: Random House, 1983), book 6, lines 847–853.

---

tric heroes. He follows the commands of the gods, even when it means that he must leave the homeland he loves or a woman who loves him. Willingness to place duty above personal interest was precisely the ideal Augustus wished to hold up as a model of patriotic devotion in troubled times.

Another first-magnitude poet of the Augustan period was Horace (65–8 B.C.E.). His *Odes* are compact poems on such universal subjects as love, pleasure, the brevity of life, and art and nature. They are filled with memorable gemlike phrases like *carpe diem* (seize the day) and with patriotic sentiments ("sweet and fitting it is to die for one's country"). Horace also extolled the blessed security and social regeneration of the Augustan Age.

Livy (59 B.C.E.–17 C.E.) wrote a massive history of Rome from the founding of the city down to his own day.

The *History,* like the *Aeneid,* furnished models of patriotic heroism and morality. Although Livy was less critical in his judgments and handling of sources than, for example, Thucydides, the *History* was both an immediate popular success and influential in later ages.

The greatest Roman historian, however, was Tacitus (c. 56 C.E.–c. 120), whose *Histories* and *Annals* are our best and most extensive narrative of the period from 14 to 96 C.E. Tacitus wrote from the perspective of a man disgusted with both the emperors' abuses of power and the subservience of the aristocratic classes. In his pages, we meet the mistrustful emperor Tiberius listening to the charges of informers and indulging in sexual perversions at his villa on Capri; the genial but naive emperor Claudius, manipulated by scheming wives and freedmen; and, of course, Nero with his uncontrolled passions and delusions of artistic grandeur.

While Tacitus attacked the political impotence of the aristocratic class, the satirist Juvenal (c. 60 C.E.–c. 135) trained the powerful weapon of his biting criticism on its social and moral degeneration. He mercilessly denounced those he felt were corrupting Roman society, especially the immigrant "Greeklings" who excelled in unsavory jobs while seducing the wives and children of native Romans. The satires attack, among others, upper-class married women, Egyptians, homosexuals, soldiers, hypocritical philosophers, and the evil emperor Domitian. Juvenal's transformation of painful moral indignation into literary art has made him the archetypal satirist.

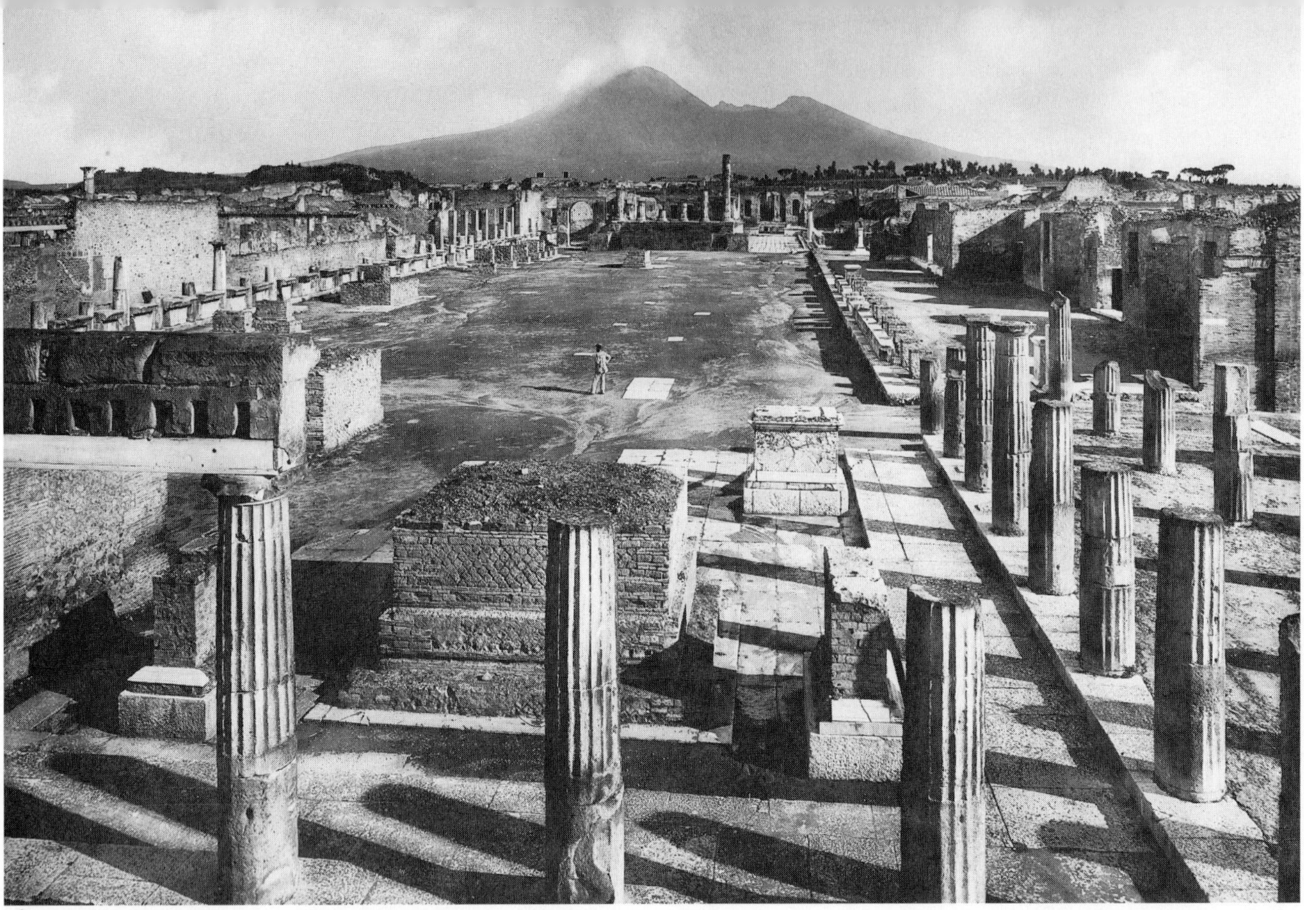

View of a Roman Town. This photograph shows the "downtown" area of the typical Roman town of Pompeii, which was buried by the volcanic eruption of Mount Vesuvius in 79 B.C.E. The large open space is the forum, surrounded by various commercial, civic, and religious buildings. Editorial Photocolor Archives/Art Resource

Roman sculpture and painting derived almost entirely from Greek models. Indeed, the thousands of exact Roman reproductions are often our best source for the lost Greek originals. Roman artistic innovation was confined to the ultrarealistic depiction of actual persons, warts and all, particularly in the busts of worthy Romans that adorned homes and tombs. In architecture, however, the Romans did advance beyond Greek models. In particular, they used concrete to alter traditional building types in momentous ways. Roman architects were able to create curvilinear forms—the arch, the vault, the dome—while respecting Greek aesthetic norms of balance and symmetry. These distinctively Roman designs strongly influenced the architecture of later times, particularly the Romanesque.

Huge public baths, sports arenas, and temples were the most typical structures of the new imperial architecture. The amphitheater—essentially a 360-degree version of the Greek theater—first appeared in southern Italy, but the most famous was the Colosseum. It accommodated some 50,000 spectators and was the site of gladiatorial contests, wild animal "hunts," executions of Christians, and even mock sea battles.

The most durable and impressive example of the new imperial architecture was the Pantheon (Temple of All Gods). Unlike Greek temples, which impress by stunning exterior views, the Pantheon depends on its huge enclosed space for its effect. Its dome was the world's largest until the building of St. Peter's in Vatican City. The Pantheon strongly influenced Renaissance architects and, through them, Thomas Jefferson, in his design for the library rotunda at the University of Virginia.

The Roman spirit emphasized stability, order, and smooth practical function. Although much earlier the Indus people (see Chapter 2) and, of course, the Greeks (see Chapter 3) had practiced urban planning, Roman civil engineers operated on a much larger scale throughout the vast empire. Every significant town and city in the Roman Empire possessed walls, paved streets, efficient water supply and waste disposal systems, facilities for the preparation, storage, and distribution of food, centers for political, administrative, and judicial functions, temples and associated structures, commercial shops, and recreational and cultural complexes.

Roman engineers built the most durable roads in the world, providing vital transportation and communication arteries throughout the empire. The huge Roman imperial highway system was some 50,000 miles in extent. Construction was done by soldiers or forced labor (slaves and prisoners of war), always with careful attention to good foundation, choice of material, smooth paving, and proper drainage. The Romans were also excellent hydraulic engineers. Large reservoirs situated on high ground fed fountains, baths, and private residences. A constant flow of water through public latrines carried waste out to the sea through the sewer system. When sources were lacking nearby, water was diverted, sometimes over long distances, by aqueducts. At Rome, more than a dozen aqueducts kept 1 million people plentifully supplied, and an extensive underground drainage system emptied into the Tiber.

Politics, Society, and Economy in the Early Empire

Although the immediate successors of Augustus, like him members of the Julio-Claudian family, could not match his managerial skills, they nevertheless maintained stability in domestic and foreign policy. The empire survived despite the eccentricities and even mental aberrations of some of the emperors themselves. Caligula (reigned 37–41) and Nero (reigned 54–68) were psychopaths who committed incest and murdered close family members; Nero even murdered his own mother. Despite such problems at the top, the system Augustus installed was remarkably resilient and durable.

By the second century C.E., succession based on the support of the army and the accident of birth into the imperial family was replaced by a system in which each emperor selected and legally adopted his own successor, usually a capable and experienced administrator and/or general. Trajan (reigned 98–117) pleased the masses in Rome by his major building programs and gifts of money. He also enlarged the empire by the addition of Dacia (modern Romania). Hadrian (reigned 117–138) tirelessly traveled throughout the provinces of the empire, personally attending to military security along the borders. He everywhere indulged his strong interest in the arts and architecture by constructing and renovating magnificent temples (including the Pantheon), markets, and other facilities. The general prosperity in the empire continued until 165, when an epidemic (possibly smallpox) caused great loss of life. This severely compromised Rome's military strength, as decreasing Roman manpower and increasing Germanic pressure along the Rhine-Danube frontier overtaxed a defensive system designed to repel only one border incursion at a time.

During the early empire, the Roman world was a vast cosmopolitan collection of more than 5,000 towns (see Map 4.3) and their surrounding hinterlands inhabited by

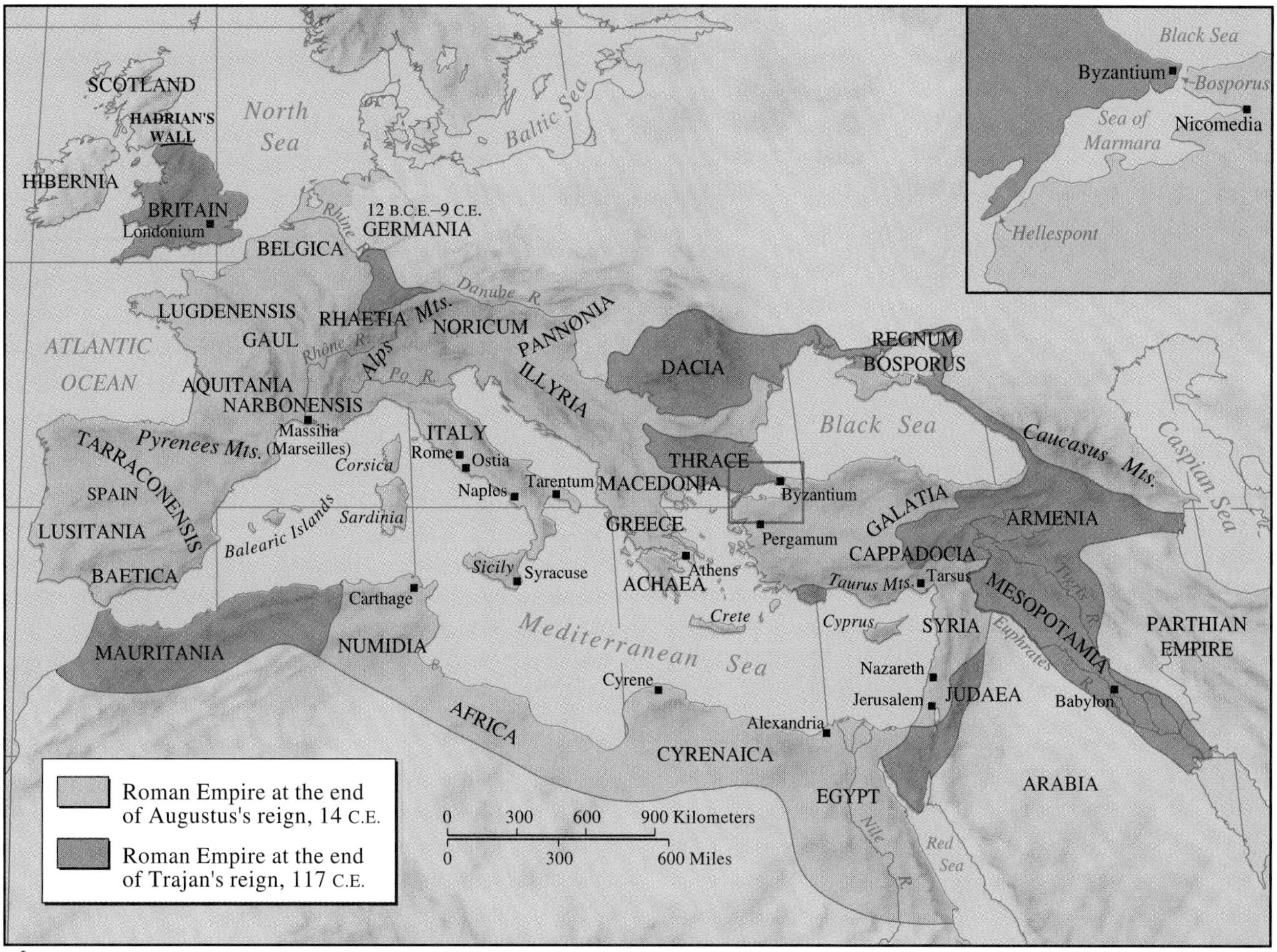

MAP 4.3 The Roman Empire from 14 to 117. Shown here is the Roman Empire in the reign of the emperor Augustus and, a century later, in the reign of the emperor Trajan, when it had reached its greatest extent.

"The Going Rate": Wages and Prices in the Roman Empire

In 301 C.E., the emperor Diocletian attempted to control the rampant inflation plaguing the late Roman Empire by issuing the Edict on Maximum Prices, which set limits on wages and prices. Although the edict failed to have the desired effect, it provides modern students with valuable insights into personal income and the cost of goods and services. We can, for example, get an idea of the relative earnings of people in various professions by comparing their wages. Sewer cleaners, camel and mule drivers, shepherds, and farmhands made 25 denarii per day. Scribes made the same amount for 100 lines of fair copy. Wall painters made 75 denarii per day, a sum that arithmetic teachers made per month for each pupil they instructed. Teachers of rhetoric or public speaking made 250 denarii per pupil each month. Barbers made 2 denarii per head. Tailors made 60 denarii for cutting and finishing a hooded cloak of first quality.

Although it is impossible to convert ancient Roman monetary units into present-day dollar equivalents, we can get some sense of the real cost of specific items by restating prices in terms of a day's wage. According to Diocletian's edict, for example, a carpenter or a baker earned up to 50 denarii per day; on that basis, the following prices obtained:

Item	Cost (in days' wages)
20 lb. wheat	2
20 oz. best-quality wine	.6
20 oz. cheap wine	.2
20 oz. beer	.1
20 lb. salt	2
20 oz. best-quality honey	.8
1 lb. pork	.25
2 chickens	1.2
1 lb. best-quality fish	.5
100 oysters	2
1 pair soldier's boots	2
1 pair women's boots	2
1 lb. best-quality wool	3.5
1 lb. second-quality wool	1
1 lb. white silk	240
1 lb. silk, dyed purple	3,000
1 lb. gold	1,000

a population of 50 to 60 million. Commercial activity flourished because of the uniform currency system, the suppression of piracy, the highway network, and the maintenance of harbors and dockyards. Roman ports saw a constant flow of textiles, grain and other foodstuffs, metals (gold, silver, copper, tin, lead, iron), manufactured goods (glass, pottery, jewelry, paper), and luxury items (silk, ivory, precious gems, spices) from all over the Mediterranean world as well as from Arabia, India, and China.

In addition to these material advantages, Roman intellectual culture also became widespread in the empire. Citizens in the western part of the empire learned the Latin language. The modern Romance languages (French, Italian, Spanish, Portuguese, Romanian) are its direct descendants. In the east, Greek persisted in preference to Latin, while in the west educated people were generally bilingual, as the literature and philosophy of both Greece and Rome were transmitted to succeeding generations. Rome showed special originality by creating law schools and recognizing medicine as an important specialization.

Decay and Temporary Recovery in the Later Roman Empire

After 180, however, the Roman Empire experienced a time of troubles. The era of Roman imperial peace and tranquillity was over. Armed conflict among would-be successors effectively militarized the civil authority of the emperor. Between 235 and 284, more than twenty emperors assumed power, as mutinous legions or imperial guards deposed or murdered the same claimants they had earlier conspired to put on the throne.

Rome also faced increasing defense problems. In the east, the Persians, under the Sassanid dynasty, pushed back Roman legions in the area. The capture of an emperor, Valerian (reigned 253–260), by Persian forces was a conspicuous blow to Roman self-esteem. Elsewhere, Germanic tribes made incursions along the Rhine-Danube border and in Britain, and the Dacians frequently broke into the Balkans.

The chaos of the third century was temporarily checked by the reforms of the emperor Diocletian (reigned 284–305). Diocletian staffed the imperial bureaucracy with the best available talent, reorganizing provinces into smaller districts supervised by more officials. In light of the frequency of barbarian invasions, Diocletian believed that the empire had become too large for one man to rule and split it into four administrative sectors. In each, a tetrarch (one-fourth ruler) held supreme authority. Rome was not one of the four imperial capitals and thus faded further into the background. To meet the defense needs of the empire, Diocletian enlarged the army from 300,000 to 500,000, in part by enlisting barbarians. After Diocletian's resignation in 305, the tetrarchy soon disintegrated in a complicated series of civil

wealth from the more prosperous eastern half of the empire to sustain the overburdened west. Increases in spending on defense and the ever-growing imperial bureaucracy led to dire economic difficulties, as imperial tax collectors tightened the screws on a shrinking population of taxpayers. Debasement of the coinage caused rampant inflation. Attempts to impose wage and price controls were no help. Individuals had to be forced to remain in certain essential, but now much less profitable, occupations; these included soldiering, farming, and grain shipping, among others. The nobility retained only honorific titles; true power was in the hands of thousands of petty bureaucrats. Well-to-do landowners, who had in the past voluntarily put their skills and funds at the disposal of government, were now taxed to their limit and burdened with legal obligations of public service. The ultimate collapse was near.

✾ Constantine. This titanic marble head, eight and a half feet in height, remains along with a right hand and sundry other outsized limb fragments of a colossal seated statue of the emperor. The distant gaze of the eyes bespeaks concentration on realms far beyond the ken of puny mortals. The statue (c. 313) graced the basilica of Constantine in Rome. Brian Blake/Photo Researchers

wars fueled by personal ambition and the reversion to dynastic inheritance.

By 324 Constantine (reigned 306–337) had emerged as the sole ruler of the Roman Empire. In general, Constantine followed the governmental policies of Diocletian, ruling autocratically and consulting only a few trusted appointees. Constantine prepared the way for the empire's split into eastern and western halves by founding a new imperial capital, Constantinople, on the site of Byzantium. Constantinople (modern Istanbul) commanded a peninsula on the European shore of the Straits of Bosporus, convenient for the direction of military operations along the Danube to the north and against Persia to the east. For over a thousand years, this "second Rome" preserved a residue of Greco-Roman civilization (see Chapter 5) until its fall to the Ottoman Turks in 1453.

The troubles of the third and fourth centuries exerted a powerful disintegrative force on Roman society, economics, and culture. The emperors were forced to siphon

The Mauryan Empire in India

But this last combat with Porus [king of northwestern India] took off the edge of the Macedonians' courage, and stayed their further progress into India. For having found it hard enough to defeat an enemy who brought but twenty thousand foot and two thousand horses into the field, [the Greeks] thought they had reason to oppose Alexander's design of leading them on to pass the Ganges too, which they were told was thirty-two furlongs broad and a hundred fathoms deep, and the banks on the further side covered with multitudes of enemies. For they were told the kings of the Gandaritans and Praesians expected them there with eighty thousand horses, two hundred thousand foot, eight thousand armed chariots, and six thousand fighting elephants.*

*Aubrey Stewart and George Long, trans., *Plutarch's Lives*, vol. 3 (London: Bell, 1925), p. 73.

Alexander's incursion into India in 326 B.C.E. was an epoch-making event for both sides. His soldiers were shocked by the war elephants the Indians used in battle, the very size of India, which seemed to stretch on endlessly, and the prospect of determined Indian resistance. Eventually, they refused to march any further, and Alexander was forced to turn back, even though he had won every engagement he fought in India. The Indians in the northwestern part of the subcontinent who faced Alexander were stunned by the successes scored by the Macedonians. After Alexander's retreat and later death, northwestern India was thrown into chaos, which propelled an ambitious young Indian to found the first great Indian empire.

Although Alexander briefly held only a small part of India, his invasion had important and lasting consequences. It opened up direct lines of communication, by land and sea, between India and lands to the west. The Hellenistic kingdoms that Alexander's generals founded in western Asia continued the contacts. Hellenistic artistic traditions influenced Indian art, especially Buddhist art in later centuries. Some scholars believe that contact with Greek mythology modified some Indian Buddhist teachings. Indian astronomy was indebted to Hellenistic astronomy and borrowed many terms from Greek.

This section will begin with Alexander's conquest of northwestern India and go on to look at the Mauryan Empire, the first great Indian empire. It will also explore some of the cultural interactions between India and lands to the west. Since, unlike the Greeks, Romans, and Chinese, the ancient Indians left few historical works, we must rely extensively on archaeological remains, coins, inscriptions, and the accounts of foreign (mainly Greek and Chinese) observers. Thus the historical information for ancient India is rather scanty.

Persian and Greek Precursors

Throughout history great upheavals have often preceded the formation of empires. This was also true in India, where several upheavals culminated in the founding of the Mauryan Empire around 313 B.C.E. As we have seen, an economic and social revolution had produced Buddhism and Jainism in the sixth century. These religions offered their followers new ethical and social standards that emphasized the individual rather than tribes or castes.

Persian and then Macedonian invasions of northwestern India also added to the trauma of the period. In 518 B.C.E., King Darius of Persia had conquered a part of northwestern India and made it the twentieth satrapy (province) of the Persian Empire. It was ruled by Persian appointees, and as one of the wealthiest satrapies in the empire, it paid substantial taxes and supplied numerous soldiers, some of whom participated in the Persian invasion of Greece. The Persians introduced new ideas of government and military organization to India, but Persian power gradually weakened, and the empire fell to Alexander.

In 326 B.C.E., Alexander's conquering army reached northwestern India and found many warring states in what had once been the Persian satrapy. Some states submitted to him, others he subdued. He then confronted King Porus (also called Puru), the most powerful ruler in the upper Indus valley. After a hard-fought battle, Porus was brought captive before Alexander, who was so impressed that he confirmed him as a vassal king, restored his lands, and even added to them.

Alexander was preparing to advance eastward, but India was spared further conquest when his weary sol-diers mutinied and he was forced to return to Babylon. After Alexander died in 323 B.C.E., his successors, fighting one another to partition his empire, withdrew from newly conquered northwestern India. Local revolts broke out; by 317, the last Greek general had left India.

The Rise of Chandragupta Maurya

Taking advantage of Alexander's death, Chandragupta Maurya, an Indian who may have known the Macedonian conqueror, drove out the remaining Greek forces. He then subdued the tribes in the northwest, marched east, and overthrew a kingdom located along the Ganges. Taking over its capital city, Pataliputra, he proclaimed himself ruler around 313 B.C.E.

Alexander's empire in Asia went to Seleucus Nicator set off to reconquer India in 305 B.C.E. He was defeated by Chandragupta in battle. The two sides then agreed to a settlement in which Seleucus gave up his claim to India and ceded the Kabul valley in present Afghanistan to Chandragupta in return for 500 elephants. The agreement was cemented by a marriage and resulted in lasting peace. Seleucus sent an ambassador, Megasthenes, to reside at Pataliputra. Chandragupta also exchanged ambassadors with the Ptolemies in Egypt and with other Hellenistic rulers.

Megasthenes wrote a detailed account of India and of life at Chandragupta's court that became the standard source for later classical accounts of Indian history. Although Megasthenes' record is not always accurate, it is nevertheless valuable because it was the first authentic and lengthy account of India by a foreign observer. Another source on this period is the *Arthasastra (Treatise on Polity)*, a book reputedly written by Kautilya, a minister to Chandragupta, who some think was the real architect of the Mauryan Empire. The *Arthasastra* is a detailed book that dealt with the theory and practice of government and the laws and administration of the Mauryan Empire.

The imperial administrative system described in the *Arthasastra* was a highly organized and thoroughly efficient autocracy. The ruler was assisted by a council of ministers and an elaborate bureaucracy. He was supreme in military and civil affairs and the final arbiter of justice. As in Persia a network of spies reported directly to the ruler. If accounts can be believed, Chandragupta's army included 600,000 men, 9,000 elephants, chariots, and a naval auxiliary. All were paid directly by the royal treasury.

The capital city, Pataliputra (modern Patna), situated at the confluence of the Ganges and Son Rivers, was a grand place. Megasthenes described it as enclosed by a wooden wall approximately nine miles long by two miles wide with 570 towers and sixty-four gates, all protected by a moat. The palaces and other buildings were also made of wood, a good precaution against earthquakes, but highly perishable. Archaeological excavations have confirmed the Greek ambassador's claim that the opulence of the palaces rivaled that of the Seleucid palaces at Susa.

We learn from the *Arthasastra* that a council of thirty men governed the capital city, administering its finances, sanitation, water supply, public buildings, and gardens. The council was divided into six committees, each with a clear-cut function, such as supervising industries or taking care of foreigners and pilgrims.

Chandragupta ruled for twenty-four years. Megasthenes wrote admiringly of his energetic administration of justice. Kautilya's account of the emperor's busy schedule tells us that his days were divided into ninety-minute segments, which he devoted to meditation, meeting with ministers, or receiving reports. His rare public appearances were occasions of pageantry and grandeur as he rode in a golden litter or an elephant-drawn chariot, dressed in embroidered robes of gold and purple and surrounded by a bodyguard of women. His favorite diversion was hunting in the royal game preserve, where he shot arrows at game driven before him by beaters. Elaborate precautions were taken to protect him from assassins; he reputedly slept in a different bedroom every night. We know little about his family life or of his end. Jain tradition of doubtful authenticity says he abdicated the throne, became a Jain monk, and fasted to death in the manner of Jain saints.

Bindusara, a son of Chandragupta, succeeded him in 300–299 and ruled until around 272. He was known as the Slayer of Foes, which suggests that he was a successful warrior. Stories say that he had sixteen wives and 101 sons; the latter may be an exaggeration, since the names of only four sons are known.

The Rule of the Emperor Asoka

Asoka was not Bindusara's eldest son, but while he was still young, he was given major responsibilities as governor of two strategically located provinces in the northwest, at crossroads of international trade. His first wife was a devout Buddhist woman; they had a son and a daughter. Buddhist sources tell of a war of succession in which Asoka defeated his inept elder brother and then had all his other brothers and possible rivals killed. That Asoka was not crowned until four years after his father's death strongly suggests a disputed succession.

By 269–268 B.C.E., Asoka was firmly in control of the largest empire to that date in Indian history, a realm that included most of modern Afghanistan and all of India except the extreme south. Little is known of the first eight years of his reign. Presumably, he spent his time on governing, family life, and the accepted pastimes for royalty, including lavish entertaining. As he later said, "Formerly

Asoka Transformed by the Horrors of War

Eight years after his coronation King Devanampiya Piyadasi [of Gracious Mien, and Beloved of the Gods— a title by which Asoka was addressed] conquered the Kalingas. In that [conquest] one hundred and fifty thousand were deported [as prisoners], one hundred thousand were killed [or maimed] and many times that number died. Thereafter, with the conquest of Kalinga King D. P. [adopted] the practice of morality, love of morality and inculcation of morality. For there arose in King D. P. remorse for the conquest of Kalinga. For this purpose this rescript on morality has been written that my sons and great grandsons should cease to think of new conquests and in all the victories they may gain they should be content with forbearance and slight punishment. For them the true conquest should be that of morality; all their delight should be delight in morality for benefit in this world and the next.*

Deep remorse over the suffering his conquest of Kalinga in southeastern India had brought about Emperor Asoka to renounce war as an instrument of policy for himself and his successors. He had this statement carved on a rock pillar as a public confession and manifesto. He also converted to Buddhism and devoted much of his remaining years to the propagation of morality and righteousness according to Buddhist teachings. This fascinating man is revered by Indians as the greatest ruler in their history. Indeed, he ranks as a great ruler in the pageant of humanity.

*Edict 13, in B. G. Gokhale, trans., *Asoka Maurya* (New York: Twayne Publishers, 1966), appendix.

in the kitchen of King [Asoka], many thousands of [animal] lives were daily slaughtered for [making] curries."

Asoka's conquest of Kalinga in southeastern India later filled him with such remorse that he changed the direction of his government and his personal life. He gave up eating meat and commanded his kitchen to prepare only vegetarian dishes for everyone. He replaced hunting with pilgrimages to places associated with the life of the Buddha. He also labored hard as king, declaring: "At all times and in all places, whether I am dining or in the ladies' apartments, . . . official reporters should keep me informed of the people's business. . . . At any hour and at any place, work I must for the commonweal." He devoted the rest of his reign to realizing Buddhist teachings in laws and deeds. His enthusiastic espousal of Buddhism contributed to its spread in India and beyond. He was to Buddhism what the Roman emperor Constantine would be to Christianity.

❊ An Asokan Pillar. Many of the pillars that Asoka ordered erected still stand. The lower part of this pillar is inscribed with the emperor's edict. © MacQuitty International Collection

Asoka also enjoined his people to cultivate such virtues as obedience to parents, kindness to servants, generosity to friends, and respect to holy men. He told them to be honest, speak the truth, and give to charity.

Asoka was even ready to hand down unpopular orders if he believed certain popular pastimes contravened Buddhist ideas. For example, he banned certain festivals where people had a good time eating, dancing, drinking, and watching performances, because he thought they were immoral. He created a new category of officials called morality officers to ensure that his officials conformed to his ideals and lived up to his code of behavior. The morality officers were allowed to pry into people's private lives, even those of the emperor's brothers and sisters. Similarly, Augustus saw moral exhortation and legislation as part of his duties as ruler of Rome.

Asoka also worked in practical ways to improve people's daily lives. He set up botanical gardens to cultivate medicinal plants and erected hospitals for both people and animals. He constructed highways and built and maintained rest houses and wells along the routes. He also had fruit and shade trees planted along the roads for the benefit of all users.

Asoka also built grand religious edifices and founded new cities. According to Buddhist literature, he had the Buddha's remains further divided and enshrined in great mounds (*stupas*) throughout his empire; these became pilgrimage destinations. A Chinese Buddhist pilgrim who visited India in the seventh century C.E. recorded more than eighty stupas and other structures associated by tradition with Asoka. That so many had survived or were still remembered a thousand years after Asoka's time certainly testifies to his munificent patronage of Buddhism.

Asoka also supported Buddhist missionary activities outside India. Two of his children entered the Buddhist order and are credited with bringing Buddhism to Ceylon (modern Sri Lanka). They took with them cuttings of the pipal tree under which Gautama had meditated and achieved enlightenment. Some ancient pipal trees on the island reputedly are descended from those cuttings. At a great rock fortress at Sirigaya in Ceylon, one can see frescoes of Buddhist heavenly nymphs from the sixth century C.E. that resemble the wall paintings of Ajanta (see Chapter 6), an indication of the close cultural (and sometimes political) ties between southern India and Ceylon. Most Ceylonese religious buildings and art are closely linked with the Theravada Buddhist traditions in India, although with local variations. Recent archaeological studies show that Indians dominated maritime trade in South and Southeast Asia between 200 B.C.E. and 300 C.E.; Buddhist missionaries from India and Ceylon were instrumental in spreading religion as well as Indian commerce and culture throughout the region. They were the forerunners of Indian settlements that would flourish in many parts of Asia in later centuries. Asoka also ordered

We know much about Asoka's rule because he had his laws and pronouncements carved on stone pillars and on rock surfaces throughout the empire, many of which have survived. He ordered his officials to read these edicts at public gatherings so that ordinary citizens would learn of his commands.

"All men are my children," said Asoka, and although he tolerated all religions, he nevertheless attempted to reform his "children" according to the teachings of Buddha. In application, this meant replacing some traditional practices with the ethics of Buddhism. He relaxed somewhat the stern laws that applied to criminals, although he did not abolish the death penalty. Those condemned to death were given three days' grace to settle their affairs before their sentences were carried out. He prohibited animal slaughter in religious ceremonies, declared many species protected, and encouraged people to become vegetarians, or at least to abstain from eating meat on certain days.

✻ Wall Painting from Ceylon. This fine wall painting of a divine maiden is but one example from a fortress at Sirigaya, in Sri Lanka (Ceylon). The paintings date from the sixth century and are very close stylistically to the wall paintings of Ajanta in India. Since Indian missionaries converted the people of Sri Lanka to Buddhism, that island has remained closely tied culturally to India. © Roger-Voillet

his ambassadors at the courts of Egypt, Macedonia, the Seleucid Empire, and other states in the west to spread Buddha's message, but with no apparent results.

Around 240 B.C.E., Asoka convened the Third Buddhist Council at Pataliputra. It dealt with differences within the monastic order and completed compiling the canons. He then appointed special officers to enforce monastic discipline and had disobedient monks expelled from their orders. The Roman emperor Constantine later did much the same thing in dealing with disputes among Christians.

Although an enthusiastic Buddhist, Asoka was tolerant of other faiths. As one of his edicts instructed: "All sects deserve reverence for one reason or another. By thus acting a man exalts his own sect and at the same time does service to the sects of other people." In another edict he advised all to honor brahmans and ascetics. A story about his father Bindusara illustrates the Mauryans' cosmopolitan outlook on religions and philosophies. Bindusara sent an ambassador to the court of Antiochus Soter, king of Syria, to request figs, grapes, and a good

Greek philosopher, for whom he said he would pay a high price. Antiochus sent him the exotic edibles, but said that he could not find a philosopher for sale.

Perhaps later generations have become too intrigued with Asoka the moralist at the expense of Asoka the ruler of a mighty empire. We should remember that although he renounced war, he did not disband his army. He warned primitive tribal people on the borders of his empire that if they failed to be persuaded by his *dharma* (moral duty) and infringed on his empire, he had the force to punish them. In other words, like any astute ruler, he continued to maintain a large military for its deterrent effect. His renunciation of war as an instrument of state policy was in itself a great innovation, unique among successful rulers. Some scholars, however, attribute the rapid decline and fall of the Mauryan Empire after Asoka's death in part to his pacifist policy, which they suggest weakened the military.

Although Asoka's edicts are couched in Buddhist terms, they show no interest in theology. Thus it is possible that Asoka used Buddhism as an instrument to unify the heterogeneous empire that he had inherited. Nevertheless, he imbued statecraft with high moral aims. That he was also tolerant of other faiths is proof of his realism as well as his magnanimity.

Little is known of Asoka's last years. Some sources say that he became reclusive toward the end and was succeeded by his son, while others say that he was deposed by a grandson. In any event, soon after Asoka's death around 232 B.C.E. his sons and grandsons divided the empire. The last king of the main branch of the line was killed in 185, but several minor families that claimed Mauryan descent ruled parts of India for centuries. From the rapid disintegration of his empire after his death, one might conclude that Asoka's pacific policy had failed. In another sense, however, he had laid the foundations for one of the greatest conquests in history—the peaceful conquest by Buddhism of India, central Asia, Ceylon, Southeast Asia, China, and Japan. The success of Buddhism would not have been possible without Asoka. For this reason Asoka is better known to history than his grandfather Chandragupta, whose political and military achievements were more remarkable than those of his grandson.

Culture of the Asokan Age

Asoka's long reign, the wide extent of his empire, and contacts with Persia and the Hellenistic world brought about an unprecedented flowering of culture in India. Buddhist art also began in this period.

The artistic achievements of the Asokan Age, however, can only be understood against the background of what had preceded it. The history of art in India between the Indus civilization and the third century B.C.E. is mostly a blank. Whereas the Indus people had built in enduring materials, mainly brick, their successors had built with wood, which quickly perished in the humid Indian climate. Likewise sculptures of wood and clay and paintings in perishable media have all vanished. While the Mauryan palaces and even the city wall of Pataliputra continued to be made of wood, India's first monumental stone sculptures date to Asoka's reign.

Thirty spectacular stone pillars, some engraved with inscriptions, were erected at various sites in the Mauryan Empire under Asoka. Ten have survived in almost perfect condition, others are damaged, and still others have disappeared. They are between thirty and forty feet high and weigh at least forty tons each. They are made from a hard gray sandstone polished to a lustrous shine. Each pillar is surmounted by a capital and topped by animal sculptures, either singly or in groups, carved in the round. The animals have symbolic importance to Buddhism. They are the lion, whose roar compares with the Buddha's preaching; the horse, which stands for Buddha's renunciation of the world; the elephant, which

symbolizes his conception by his mother; the bull, representing strength; and the goose because, according to legend, Buddha was the king of geese in an earlier incarnation. The wheel, which represents the sacred law or dharma, is also found on the pillars, placed below the animals. When India gained its independence from Great Britain in 1947, the four-lion Asokan capital was chosen as the nation's emblem, and the wheel of law became the centerpiece of the national flag. That leaders of secular and predominantly Hindu modern India would choose these Buddhist emblems as national symbols bespeaks the enduring memory of Asoka and his association with a great past.

Asoka's piety and his devotion to spreading Buddhism undoubtedly were behind his decision to erect the pillars. In a manner similar to all successful rulers, he also wanted to proclaim the grandeur and extent of his empire. The artistic inspiration for these monumental pieces is difficult to trace. A case can be made for indigenous roots for the bull, lotus, and elephant motifs, which were frequently found in the Indus civilization seals. The lion and horse motifs, on the other hand, have a long history in Persian and West Asian art and are probably imported.

The high quality of the sculptures can only have resulted from generations of technical and artistic experience with the medium. We do not know who the stone sculptors were. But since no Indian stone sculptures have been found prior to the Asokan period, and since this art form vanished at the end of his reign, the Asokan monuments were probably made by Hellenistic artists invited to the court of Asoka or by Indians influenced by them.

The earliest cave shrines and dwellings also date to Asoka's reign and continued under his successors. For centuries ascetics had taken shelter in caves during the monsoon season. But the sudden acquisition of skills in stone working, which led to the enlarging of natural caves and to polishing and decorating their surfaces, again suggests Persian and West Asian inspiration. These techniques already had a long history in Persia and West Asia.

Asoka continued the Vedic and early Buddhist custom of erecting mounds to enshrine the funeral remains of great people. Gautama's disciples had divided his ashes at the First Council and enshrined them under stupas. As Buddhism grew, it became a meritorious act for the pious to worship at such sites. Asoka is credited with a further division of the Buddha's remains so that more people could benefit from visiting them. We know little of the decoration of Asoka's stupas because they have been built over in later ages. They were probably hemispheric mounds set on platforms, with flights of steps from four directions that lead to the base. Later on, railings, gateways, and arches were added to enclose and decorate the sites, and these were profusely ornamented with scenes from the Buddha's life and from *Jataka* stories.

The earliest extant examples of writing since the Indus civilization also date from the reign of Asoka. They have survived because they were engraved on stone rather than written on perishable materials. They are Asoka's edicts—his proclamations, exhortations, and sermons engraved on pillars, rocks, and cave walls throughout the Mauryan Empire. Persia and Mesopotamia are again the likely sources of inspiration because Indians were first introduced to official proclamations and panegyrics engraved in stone by King Darius I. Even the format of Asoka's edicts, which begin, "The Beloved of the gods, King Priyadarsin spoke thus," may have been adapted from the Persian model, "Says Darius [or another name] the King." The language and lettering of the rock edicts varied, indicating that several vernaculars were current in different parts of the Mauryan Empire. The great majority, however, were written from left to right in the Old Brahmi script. The script is the parent of most of the scripts now current in India. As with ancient Egyptian hi-

eroglyphics, the characters' meanings were lost, and they were not deciphered until 1837, when modern scholarship on ancient India, called Indology, began.

Extant Buddhist and Jain canons and commentaries on them were substantially completed during Asoka's time. Nonreligious works, such as the early versions of the epics *Mahabharata* and *Ramayana* also date from approximately this period, although both were added to and reworked later.

In its final form, the *Mahabharata* is seven times as long as the *Iliad* and the *Odyssey* combined. Like the *Iliad*, it is a tale of an epic war fought by gods and men; stories of knightly chivalry, love, piety, duty, and devotion are interwoven with violence and gambling. Written in verse form and narrative style, the following passage tells how Princess Damayanti chose as her husband her true love Nala, even though four gods had taken on his appearance in the hope that she would pick one of them by mistake. The theme of competition for a beautiful, royal woman is

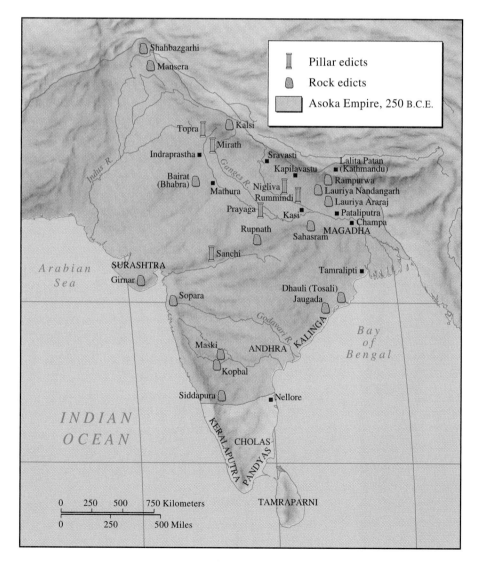

✹ MAP 4.4 The Empire of Asoka. Asoka expanded the empire he inherited so that all the Indian subcontinent except the southern tip plus part of modern Afghanistan were incorporated into one administration. India was prosperous, and the capital, Pataliputra, was a grand city.

familiar from the Greek stories of Helen's betrothal and, in the *Odyssey*, the contest for the hand of Penelope.

> Then, when the right time had come,
>   at the auspicious day and hour,
> King Bhama invited
>   the lords of earth to the bride-choice.
>
> When they heard, the lords of earth,
>   all sick at heart with love,
> in haste assembled,
>   desiring Damayanti.
>
> Like great lions the kings entered
>   the hall firmly founded,
> with its splendid porch
>   and shining golden columns.
>
> Then on their several thrones
>   the lords of earth sat down
> all decked in fragrant garlands,
>   with bright gems on their ears.
>
>   *   *   *

An Asokan Column Capital. This capital, which adorned one of Asoka's columns, shows powerful stylized lions standing atop the Buddhist wheel of the sacred law. This capital is the official symbol of the Republic of India. Robert Harding Picture Library

> Then fair-faced Damayanti
>   entered the hall,
> stealing with her splendor
>   the eyes and thoughts of the kings.
>
> When the glance of the noble
>   spectators fell on her limbs
> there it was fixed,
>   and never wavered.
>
> Then, while the names of the kings
>   were being proclaimed,
> the daughter of Bhama saw
>   five men of the same form.
>
> Whichever of them she looked at
>   she recognized as Nala.
> Wondering in her mind,
>   the fair one was filled with doubt.
>
>   *   *   *
>
> Thus thinking over and over,
>   and pondering again and again,
> she resolved that the time had come
>   to take refuge in the gods.
> "I heard from the mouth of the swans
>   that Nala had chosen me as his bride,
> and so, if that be true,
>   may the gods show him to me!
>
>   *   *   *
>
> May the great gods, the world-protectors
>   take on their own true form,
> that I may recognize
>   the king of men, of good fame!"
>
> When they heard Damayanti,
>   mournful and piteous
> they did as she had asked,
>   and put on their true forms.
>
> She saw the four gods
>   sweatless, not blinking their eyelids,
> their garlands fresh and free from dust,
>   not touching the ground with their feet.
>
> But the king of Nisadha had a shadow,
>   his garlands were withered,
> his body bore dust and sweat,
>   and he blinked his eyelids.
>
> The modest long-eyed girl
>   seized the hem of his garment,
> and on his shoulder she placed
>   the loveliest of garlands.
>
> She chose him for her lord,
>   she of the fair complexion,
> and suddenly all the kings
>   together shouted and cheered.
>
> And all the gods and sages
>   thereupon cried bravo,
> and shouted at the wonder,
>   praising Nala the king.

Krishna, an incarnation of Vishnu, and beloved of millions in later Hinduism, is a hero in this great poem.

Woven into it is the *Bhagavad-Gita,* a lofty philosophical poem from which Hindus have since learned lessons about morality and religious law. Here Krishna teaches the ideal of duty and action to fulfill one's function in society without personal desire or ambition.

The briefer *Ramayana* resembles the *Odyssey* in that it tells about the hardships and wanderings of the hero and his faithful wife who waits patiently for his return. The couple's cause triumphed, and they were reunited with the help of the monkey king and his monkey soldiers (hence Hindus revere the monkey and there are temples to Hanuman, the monkey god and Rama's helper). Hindus revere Rama and Sita, the hero and heroine of the *Ramayana,* as the ideal man and woman.

Life under the Mauryans

The large Mauryan empire was richly diverse. In addition to the capital city, Pataliputra, there were several other sizable cities surrounded by strong walls, punctuated by lofty watchtowers, and pierced by gates. Texts mention city streets lit by torches at night, pleasure parks, assembly halls, and gambling places as well as trading booths and artisans' quarters.

As in the Roman Empire, rulers often sponsored public entertainments for city people. The entertainments were usually associated with religious festivals and consisted of singing, dancing, dramatic presentations, chariot races, jousts of arms between men, and animal combats. Asoka was offended by the violence and immorality associated with the festivals and sought to restrict them. Girls and boys from upper classes amused themselves with music, singing, and dancing, and boys and men also gambled with dice, played a game like hockey, and a board game that later became chess.

Most people lived in the countryside. The texts mention three main groups by occupation: farmers, herders, and hunters. Most farmers lived in simple mud-and-thatch houses in villages, and most seemed to own their land. Large estates were rare and were worked by hired hands, not by slaves. Slaves existed, but not in large numbers; most slaves worked as domestic servants. Villages were largely autonomous but paid taxes and dues to the government, customarily one-sixth of the harvest. Agriculture was highly regarded, and farmland was supposed to be spared from ravages during wars. Farmers organized themselves for communal projects such as digging irrigation ditches, but were exempted from military and other government services. Then as later, farmers suffered from periodic famines brought on by natural disasters and by locusts. The *Arthasastra* enjoined rulers to store extra food for emergencies and to distribute seeds and food during hard times.

The herders and hunters often lived in tents beyond the pale of the villages. Cattle were always important as a food source to Indians but were rarely butchered for meat. Hunters and trappers were responsible for getting rid of pests, clearing virgin lands, and sometimes also for providing food; for their work, they were rewarded by the government.

Artisans were important in both cities and villages. Pataliputra's municipal government had a board that supervised artisans in that city. Some villages specialized in one craft, and specialties tended to be passed from father to son. The artisans included ivory and stone workers, painters of frescoes, metalsmiths, jewelers, textile weavers, embroiderers, oil millers (extractors of edible oils from seeds), bamboo workers, toolmakers, and potters. Each guild was headed by a foreman or elder who supervised the workers; guilds also performed some of the functions of modern banks. The textile industry employed many women; some worked in shops while others worked at home. New subcastes of artisans were recorded during this time, proof of the proliferation of manufacturing.

Transportation by water was highly developed. Seagoing ships sailed as far away as Burma, the Malay Peninsula, Ceylon, and the Persian Gulf. They navigated by the stars. Most water trade was along northern India's well-developed waterways, the Indus and Ganges Rivers and their tributaries. The Mauryan government even established a bureau that built ships and leased them to merchants.

The chief items of trade were silk and cotton textiles, ivory, jewelry, and gold. Some trade was by barter, but it was being replaced by silver and copper coinage. Pataliputra had a special board that supervised trade and commerce. It regulated weights and measures and placed a stamp on items it had inspected. Later as trade with the Roman Empire flourished, gold and silver coins from Rome became plentiful in India, supplementing locally minted coins. Romans from Pliny the Younger (61–c. 113 C.E.) on regretted their people's appetite for Indian luxuries, especially fine cotton textiles, bought with precious metals. From the west Indians imported sweet wines, exotic fruits, luxury handicrafts, entertainers, and beautiful girls for the harems of the rich.

Marriages were monogamous for most, polygynous for rulers and aristocrats. Polyandrous marriages (one wife with several concurrent husbands) existed in several isolated regions. Most men and women were expected to marry, but some of both sexes (fewer women) became ascetics and lived celibate lives and were honored for it. Although some upper-class women and female ascetics were well educated, most women were not literate, but neither were most men. *Sati,* or the custom of immolating a widow on her late husband's funeral pyre, was practiced. Both men and women wore adornments: upper-class women were especially noted for the richness of their clothing and jewelry.

The Kushan Empire: A Flourishing Buddhist State

The Maurya empire faded away and gave place to the Sunga dynasty, which ruled over a much smaller area. . . . In central Asia the Shakas or Scythians had established themselves in the Oxus Valley. The Yueh Chih, coming from farther east, drove them out and pushed them into north India. These Shakas became converts to Buddhism and Hinduism. Among the Yueh Chih, one of the clans, the Kushans, established their supremacy and then extended their sway over northern India. They defeated the Shakas and pushed them still farther south, the Shakas going to Kathiawar and the Deccan. The Kushans thereupon established an extensive and durable empire over the whole of north India and a great part of Central Asia. . . . This borderland state, called the Kushan empire, with its seat near modern Peshawar, and the old university of Taxila near by, became the meeting place of men from many nations. There the Indians met the Scythians, the Yueh Chih, the Iranians, the Bactrian Greeks, the Turks, and the Chinese, and the various cultures reacted on each other.*

*Jawaharlal Nehru, The Discovery of India, ed. Robert Crane (New York: Doubleday, 1960), pp. 89–90.

This is how Jawaharlal Nehru, first prime minister of independent India, described the confusing array of invaders that entered India after the Mauryan Empire, long in decline, ended in 185 B.C.E. The failure to restore unity to the subcontinent had two consequences similar to what happened in Europe after the collapse of Rome. First, a looser structure of government with less central control emerged. Second, civil wars became endemic as military adventurers ousted one another in quick succession. In this situation the borderlands became victim to invaders of varying backgrounds and levels of civilization. While there are some parallels between western Europe after the fall of the Roman Empire and India after the fall of the Mauryan Empire, there are many differences as well. For example, intellectual and artistic life were not devastated in India as they were in western Europe. On the contrary, the invaders introduced Roman, Hellenistic, Persian, and central Asian art, which enriched Indian artistic traditions to form a new synthesis.

The Kingdom of Kanishka

Because Indian scholars were primarily interested in religious and philosophical matters and seldom paid attention to recording mundane historical happenings, we must rely on sketchy and often unreliable documentary sources for historical information. Bactrian Greeks, Parthians (Iranians or Persians), and Scythians invaded northwestern India and set up local kingdoms. Mauryan power had never been strong in southern India, and that region remained unaffected by the invasions that disrupted the north during the succeeding centuries.

The Yueh-chih, strongest of all the invading groups, entered India toward the end of the second century B.C.E. They had earlier been driven westward from China's northern border by more powerful nomads, the Hsiung-nu, ancestors of the Huns that later invaded the Roman Empire and ravaged Europe. By 60 C.E. one of the Yueh-chih tribes, the Kushans, had established an empire that stretched from northern India westward to the Caspian Sea. They converted either to Hinduism (mostly to a sect that chiefly worshiped Shiva) or to Buddhism. Kanishka (reigned c. 78–111 C.E.), the greatest Kushan king, was a patron of Buddhist religion and art. After the death of Kanishka, decline set in, and the empire broke up during the third century, although remnants survived until the sixth century.

The precise reasons for the fall of the Kushan Empire remain shrouded in mystery. It may have been due in part to the loss of Afghanistan to Persian control and with it fresh sources of manpower for the army. Nehru postulates that an undercurrent of nationalism on the part of Indians who were not reconciled to Kushan rule also contributed to the empire's undoing. Thus it appears that the Kushans fell as a result of a combination of factors. Over a century later, Kushan was replaced by the empire of an Indian dynasty, the imperial Guptas (see Chapter 6).

Kushan Culture: Buddhism in a Cosmopolitan Setting

The chaos of the post-Mauryan era had no adverse effect on the spread of Buddhism within and beyond India. From northwestern India missionaries traveled the Silk Road west to Persia and central Asia and east to China (see the next section). The large number and quality of Buddhist temple remains in communities in the Kushan realm and along the Silk Road, rich even in ruin, show both the devotion of the believers and the prosperity brought by this international trade in luxuries.

King Kanishka was revered by some Buddhists almost as a second Asoka, and indeed there are many parallels. Like Asoka, Kanishka succeeded to a prosperous and powerful empire and waged victorious wars early in his reign, annexing additional lands. Although a Buddhist, he tolerated other religions, as is shown by coins from his reign with images of many gods from several faiths. They include the Hindu god Shiva, the Roman god Hercules, and Persian deities. Like Asoka, he patronized Buddhism by building and repairing shrines and encour-

Above: Panoramic View of Rock-Carved Temple at Bamiyan, Afghanistan. This broad valley was located at the junction of the Silk Road that linked China, India, central Asia, and the Roman Empire. It was a trade center and also became a pilgrimage site, after the completion of the rock-carved temple that housed several thousand monks. Two huge Buddha statues dominated; the smaller (120 feet), seated Buddha can be seen here.
Left: Colossal Buddha. This enormous Buddha statue stands 175 feet high in a niche shaped as a body halo. Located at a crossroad of international travel, it made an indelible impression on all who passed and was a prototype for similar monuments in China. Photos courtesy of Richard Edwards

aging missionary work. About the year 100 Kanishka called the Fourth Buddhist Council at his capital city, near modern Peshawar on the Pakistan-Afghan border. Five hundred monks attended the council to settle disputes in Buddhism and to collect and compile commentaries on the Tripitaka. Kanishka also lavishly patronized Buddhist art.

By the first century, many Buddhists favored community worship of the Buddha as a savior god, and some aspired to be saintly bodhisattvas who delayed their own entrance to nirvana to help suffering living beings achieve enlightenment. Many of the devout, however, wished there was an image of the Buddha to assist them in their prayers.

The first images of the Buddha date to Kanishka's time, although the origins of the Buddha images are in dispute. Some scholars argue that the likenesses of the Buddha evolved from images of *yakshas,* or earth spirits of Hinduism, and therefore are Indian in origin. Others point out that the Kushans were a non-Indian dynasty and that early Buddhist images show strong Greco-Roman influences. Evidence supports both sides. The two artistic sources depict the same subject matter: the image of the Buddha and the stories of his life and previous lives, along with bodhisattvas and other deities associated with Buddhism, including Vedic gods.

Large numbers of the Gandharan, or Greco-Roman–influenced, Buddhist sculptures have been found in the ruins of Taxila, a northern Indian center of international commerce and art, and at various sites in Afghanistan and Pakistan. Most are statues of the Buddha and bodhisattvas, or reliefs that depict the Buddha's life or scenes from Buddhist texts. They are characterized by realistic molding of the human body and accurate delineation of muscles. Many of the stone and stucco (painted plaster) statues and relief carvings of the Buddha and others in Gandhara are so beautifully robed and coifed in contemporary Roman styles that they would not have been out of place in imperial Rome. They are distinguishable from their secular counterparts only by their halos (a western import) and their religiously significant hand gestures.

Later Gandharan artists were especially fond of stucco as a medium. This was perhaps due to close sea contacts with Alexandria in Egypt, where at that time the art of working with stucco was well developed. Apparently, a continuing influx of artists and artisans from Roman provinces arrived in India throughout the Kushan period. The imported artists must also have trained local people in their media and styles. It is not surprising then that deities of Greece and Rome are sometimes found in Buddhist scenes.

In the prosperous Bamiyan valley in Afghanistan, at the crossroads of the Silk Road, monks in the fifth century honeycombed a towering cliff wall of the Hindu Kush with grottoes and cells and crowned the complex with three colossal Buddha statues carved from the cliffs. The tallest stands 175 feet high in its own niche. The statues were finished with lime plaster and decorated with paintings. The site welcomed pious Chinese pilgrims as they approached India after their long journey and inspired Chinese Buddhists to excavate similar rock grottoes in their homeland. After the eighth century, Bamiyan and other Buddhist sanctuaries in Afghanistan were desecrated by Muslim invaders. They have stood since then amid empty ruins, pockmarked by artillery shells of later Muslim cannons, for which they served as targets. Even in ruin, they testify to the energy and creativity that marked the Buddhist centuries in Afghanistan and northwestern India.

Mathura was already an art center when the Kushan Empire took over. The red sandstone religious statues that its artists produced would adorn Buddhist, Hindu, and Jain holy places for centuries to come. Whereas the Gandharan Buddhas had the face of the Greco-Roman god Apollo and wore togas, those from Mathura are dressed like Indians in thin *dhotis* (loin cloths); *yaksha* spirits became bodhisattvas, surrounded by *nagas* (anthropomorphic serpent figures of ancient Indian lore) and other symbols of Indian mythology. The Mathuran art style survived the fall of the Kushan Empire and reached its ultimate development in the following Gupta era. At both centers Kushan art mirrored social life. Scenes of drunken orgies abound; Gandharan ladies' dresses could have been worn by matrons in any city of the Roman world, while nudity or scanty dress in the Indian fashion is conspicuous in Mathuran figures. Later, when Buddhism spread to China, Korea, and Japan, Greek, Roman, and Persian art forms were introduced to the farthest shores of East Asia.

Coins provide much information and a great deal of the chronology of post-Mauryan dating, since there is very little reliable chronological record otherwise. The Greeks popularized coinage as the medium of exchange, and Indian rulers followed suit. Indian coins usually carried the image of the issuing ruler on one side and of a deity on the other, along with an inscription. The large quantity of Roman coins found in India supports the contention that India enjoyed a favorable balance of trade with Rome, a circumstance that Roman leaders bemoaned. Roman coins probably circulated as an international currency, which might explain why gold coins issued by Kanishka conformed to the Roman standard. An interesting gold coin bears the image of Buddha on one side and of Kanishka on the other. Kanishka wears the baggy trousers and tall boots of central Asia, suggesting his nomadic heritage. Although a Buddhist, he is pouring an offering on a fire altar, a Persian religious practice.

Gold Coin of Kanishka. This gold coin was issued by the Kushan king Kanishka in the late first to early second century.
American Numismatic Society

These coins suggest that initially the conquering rulers worshiped their Hellenistic and Persian deities. But since the invaders were numerically few, in time they were assimilated and became Indianized.

Several centuries of contacts with the west left other legacies. A number of words in Sanskrit and modern Indian languages are borrowed from Greek, especially in the sciences and in astrology, where Indian scholars were very alert to new information. A work titled *Questions of Melinda* (an Indianized name of a minor Hellenistic king, Menander, who converted to Buddhism), though Buddhist in content, shows the stylistic influence of the philosophical dialogues of Plato.

China's First Imperial Age: The Han Dynasty

*"Gentlemen, for a long time you have suffered beneath the harsh laws of Ch'in. . . . I hereby promise you a code of laws consisting of three articles only: (1) he who kills anyone shall suffer death; (2) he who wounds another or steals shall be punished according to the gravity of the offense; (3) for the rest I abolish all the laws of Ch'in. Let the officials and people remain undisturbed as before. I have come to save you from injury, not to exploit or oppress you. . . ." He sent men to go with the Ch'in officials and publish this proclamation. . . . The people of Ch'in were overjoyed and hastened with cattle, sheep, wine, and food to present to the soldiers, but Liu Chi declined all such gifts, saying: "There is plenty of grain in the granaries. I do not wish to be a burden to the people." With this the people were more joyful than ever and their only fear was that Liu Chi would not become King of Ch'in.**

*William T. de Bary, ed., *Sources of Chinese Tradition*, vol. 1 (New York: Columbia University Press, 1960), pp. 154–155.

In victory Liu Chi displayed the essential qualities of compassion and justice that were in such sharp contrast to the oppression and tyranny of the government that he had rebelled against. A poor commoner with little education, he was nevertheless a profound psychologist, identifying with the common people and soldiers. These qualities won him the support and respect of the people and explain his success against both the Ch'in and other contenders for power. Liu became the first commoner to found a dynasty. Known as the Han, it was one of the longest lived and most successful dynasties in Chinese history. It is the reason why 95 percent of Chinese up to now call themselves the Han people and their language the Han language. Because Chinese fame spread far and wide during this dynasty, Koreans and Japanese too call the written Chinese script Han writing. Thus the Han dynasty is to China and East Asia what the Mauryan dynasty is to India and Buddhists throughout Asia. The following pages will explore the history, achievements, and legacy of the Han dynasty.

The Western Han Dynasty, 202 B.C.E.–9 C.E.

Several contenders sought to fill the vacuum created by the fall of the Ch'in dynasty in 206 B.C.E. The winner was Liu Chi (also called Liu Pang), who was proclaimed emperor of the new Han dynasty in 202. History knows him as Han Kao-tsu or High Ancestor of the Han. He was the first commoner to ascend the throne, an event made possible because of the Ch'in abolition of feudalism and the opportunities created by the wars of the preceding centuries. Kao-tsu and his supporters had suffered through the harshness of Ch'in rule and were well aware of the feelings of the people. Though they retained the basic structure of the Ch'in government, they moved quickly to remove the abuses.

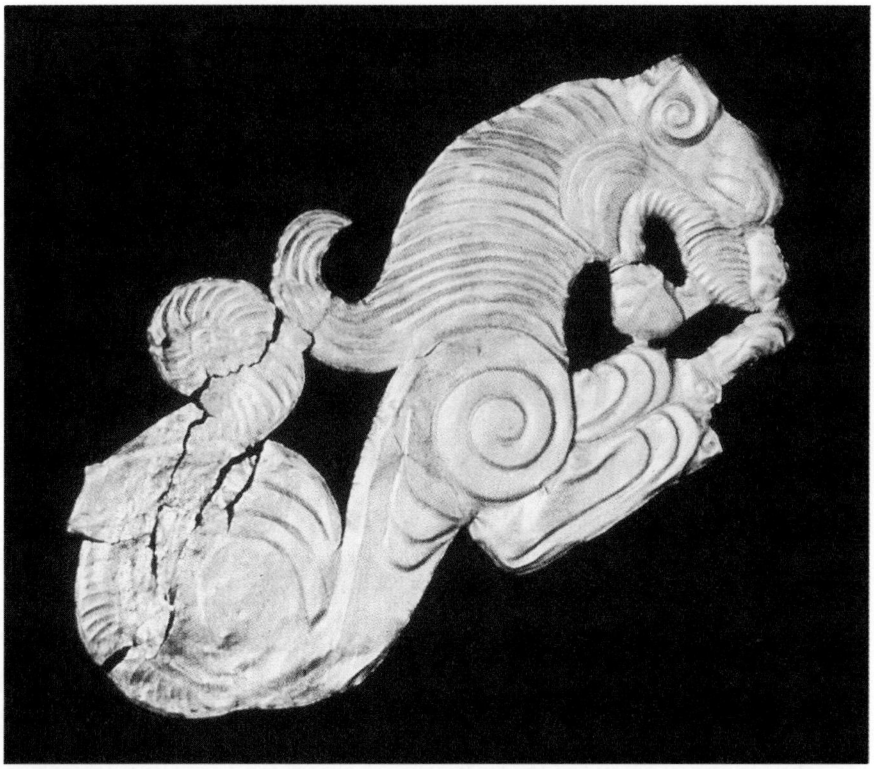

Bronze Figure of a Kneeling Warrior and Lion Ornament in Gold. Both of these items were excavated in northwestern China and date to circa 500 B.C.E. The warrior (left) is a nomad, probably a Hsiung-nu, with non-Mongolian features, prominent nose, and non-Chinese dress. The gold animal ornament (right) is typical of nomadic art. Photos courtesy of Dolkun Kamberi

Establishing his capital at Changan (near the Ch'in capital Hsienyang), Kao-tsu moderated the cruel Ch'in penal code, lifted the ban against intellectual activities, and lightened taxes from two-thirds of the farmer's crop as under the Ch'in to one-fifteenth. To give the people a chance to rest and recover from years of war, Kao-tsu pursued a domestic policy of peace and order and a foreign policy of conciliation and appeasement toward the powerful northern nomads called Hsiung-nu. In the third century, these nomads had formed a powerful confederacy that menaced China across the entire northern frontier. The Great Wall had not deterred these horse-riding raiders from the steppes. After a disastrous war against the Hsiung-nu, Kao-tsu was forced to bribe them with "gifts" of gold (1,000 pieces annually), grain, silks, and a princess as a bride. Kao-tsu died prematurely in 195 B.C.E. Soon afterward the king of the Hsiung-nu proposed marriage to his widow, Empress Lu, with the following letter:

> I am a lonely widowed ruler, born amidst the marshes and brought up on the wild steppes in the land of cattle and horses. . . . Your Majesty is also a widowed ruler living a life of solitude. Both of us are without pleasures and lack any way to amuse ourselves. It is my hope that we can exchange that which we have for that which we are lacking.

Although furious, she was forced to refuse him politely:

> My age is advanced and my vitality is weakening. Both my hair and teeth are falling out, and I cannot even walk steadily. The *shan-yu* [title of the Hsiung-nu king] must have heard exaggerated reports. I am not worthy of his lowering himself. But my country has done nothing wrong, and I hope he will spare it.

Empress Lu ruled for the next fifteen years and continued Kao-tsu's policies, as did her successors. With peace and frugal government, the economy expanded and production soared, so that despite a further tax cut to one-thirtieth of the crop, the state treasury was full and granaries bulged.

When Emperor Wu (the Martial, reigned 141–87 B.C.E.) ascended the throne, the Chinese people, now fully recovered and confident, were willing to support a vigorous and aggressive foreign policy. Wu campaigned in the south and regained control of the Pearl River valley and the Red River valley in modern Vietnam (which had seceded at the fall of the Ch'in). Another campaign brought southern Manchuria and Korea into the Han Empire. After his conquests Wu established a Chinese-style government in the newly annexed regions. He also sponsored Chinese immigration, which gradually resulted in the assimilation or Sinicization (from the Latin *Sinica,* meaning "China") of the local people.

These early wars were preparation for a showdown with the Hsiung-nu; however, Wu needed an ally. Much earlier, the Hsiung-nu had defeated the Yueh-chih, an Indo-European nomadic group north of China, and had driven them westward. As we have seen, the refugees finally settled in Bactria, in modern Afghanistan and northern Pakistan, where they established the Kushan state and many converted to Buddhism.

In 138 B.C.E., Emperor Wu sent a young courtier named Chang Ch'ien to find the Yueh-chih and offer them an alliance against the Hsiung-nu. Chang's journey was one of the most daring travel epics in antiquity. To reach the Yueh-chih, he had to cross Hsiung-nu territory; he was captured, given a Hsiung-nu wife, and lived among them for ten years, raising a family before escaping. Chang finally found the Yueh-chih, but they had no desire to cross swords with the Hsiung-nu again. En route home Chang was recaptured by the Hsiung-nu; again he escaped and finally returned to Changan in 126 with only two of his original staff of a hundred.

Even though he failed in his primary assignment, Chang Ch'ien's account of this trip and his later diplomatic mission to central Asia opened the Chinese to new horizons, peoples, cultures, and products. His informa-

tion led to further exploration and trade by land and sea between China, India, Persia, and other lands. His report of "blood-sweating" horses (the bleeding was actually caused by the bites of tiny mites) later sent Chinese armies campaigning across central Asia in search of them.

In 133 B.C.E., Wu launched an eighteen-year campaign that evicted the Hsiung-nu from an area bounded by a southward dip of the Yellow River. In 129 four generals cleared them from the entire Chinese northern border from Inner Mongolia across Turkestan. Some 700,000 Chinese colonists were sent out to settle the conquered lands, and the Great Wall was extended westward. Beyond it, a string of fortified outposts stretched into central Asia. Chinese protectors-general to the western regions supervised local vassal kings, who were required to pay homage and tribute at Changan and to leave their sons there to be educated and to serve as hostages in a pattern similar to Rome's arrangements with its client states. In return, vassal kings received Chinese titles, lavish gifts, and the right to trade. These conditions were so attractive that rulers in regions like Kashmir in India, which had not been conquered by the Han, voluntarily enrolled as vassals. No more Chinese princesses were sent as brides to nomadic chieftains. Wu's successors continued his policies against the Hsiung-nu, shattering their power. In 51 the southern branch of the Hsiung-nu

✳ The Flying Horse of Kansu. The Han government waged wars, used diplomacy, and traded to obtain the fast horses bred in central Asia. This bronze horse, found in the tomb of a Han general in Kansu in northwestern China, epitomized the qualities of strength and speed the Chinese prized in these "blood-sweating" horses. Robert Harding Picture Library

The High Cost of Empire

Lament of Hsi-chun

My people have married me
In a far corner of Earth;
Sent me away to a strange land,
To the king of the Wu-sun.
A tent is my house,
Of felt are my walls;
Raw flesh my food
With mare's milk to drink.
Always thinking of my own country
My heart is sad within.
Would I were a yellow stork
And could fly to my old home!

To His Wife, by General Su Wu, c. 100 B.C.E.

Since our hair was plaited and we became man and wife
The love between us was never broken by doubt.
So let us be merry this night together,
Feasting and playing together while the good time
  lasts
I suddenly remember the distance that I must travel;
I spring from bed and look out to see the time.
The stars and planets are all grown dim in the sky;

Long, long is the road; I cannot stay.
I am going away on service, away to the battle-ground,
And I do not know when I shall come back.
I hold your hand with only a deep sigh;
Afterwards, tears—in the days when we are parted.
With all your might enjoy the spring flowers,
But do not forget the time of our love and pride.
Know that if I live, I will come back again,
And if I die, we will go on thinking of each other.

Parting from Su Wu by Li Ling

I came ten thousand leagues
Across sandy deserts
In the service of my Prince,
To break the Hun tribes.
My way was blocked and barred,
My arrows and swords broken.
My armies had faded away,
My reputation is gone.
My old mother is long dead.
Although I want to requite my Prince
How can I return?*

Individual men and women paid a high price for the nation's military and diplomatic successes. These poems illustrate this point. The first is by Princess Hsi-chun. Around 100 B.C.E., she was given in marriage to a client king of Wu-sun, whose land supplied the Han with fine horses. Her husband was already an old man and the couple had no common language, so during their occasional meetings they only drank a cup of wine together. The second poem is by General Su Wu, who wrote it for his wife before he set out to campaign against the Hsiung-nu. He was captured during the war and held for nineteen years before being released. While Su Wu returned home, a fellow captive chose to stay. In the third poem he explains why.

*Arthur Waley, *Translations from the Chinese* (New York: Knopf, 1941), pp. 18, 52, 53.

---

submitted to Han rule, while another branch was defeated by the Han in Samarkand and fled westward. The flight of the Hsiung-nu set off a vast westward migration as numerous peoples were pushed west in a domino effect that continued until the fourth century C.E., when some of them reached the borders of the Roman Empire.

The Eastern Han Dynasty, 23–220 C.E.

Wu's successors were undistinguished. Between 9 and 23 C.E. an imperial in-law usurped the throne and attempted to establish his own dynasty. He failed, and a descendent of the house of Liu reestablished the Han dynasty in 23 C.E. The capital was moved to Loyang, located east of Changan; hence the era is known as the Eastern (or Later) Han. In retrospect, the period between 202 B.C.E. and 9 C.E. is called the Western Han. Loyang

is situated on the bank of the River Lo, a tributary of the Yellow River, and was strategically important. It had been the capital of the Eastern Chou dynasty.

Chinese power and prosperity were restored under the Eastern Han. Chinese arms again overawed much of central Asia, and trade and culture flourished. General Pan Ch'ao campaigned all the way to the Caspian Sea, and his vanguard reconnoitered the shores of either the Persian Gulf or the Black Sea. Chinese protectors-general continued to supervise kingdoms across central Asia in the furthest extension of power in Chinese history. Caravans carrying the international luxury trade traveled in safety. The Pax Sinica in the east matched the Pax Romana in the west; together the two empires dominated most of the ancient world.

By the second century, however, problems developed. Minors on the throne, power struggles between powerful consort families, and economic inequities led to rapid dynastic decline. The upper class became hedonistic, dabbling either in escapist Taoism or the new foreign religion, Buddhism. Downtrodden peasants revolted, and generals sent to quell them seized power, ending the dynasty in 220. Nevertheless, four centuries of Han rule had firmly established the foundations of traditions and institutions that would continue to the present century and had spread Sinitic civilization across eastern Asia. The Han became the yardstick against which all later dynasties would measure themselves.

Han Government

Han emperors presided over a centralized, bureaucratic government headed by a prime minister. The government included a number of ministries and bureaus, each with clearly defined functions such as fiscal and judicial affairs, imperial rituals, and the metropolitan police force. The basic local government unit was the county (there were between 1,000 and 1,400 counties); ten to twenty counties formed a commandery (later called a province), headed by a governor. The three-tier government system remains in effect in China to the present and is similar in organization to the three tiers of county, state, and national government in the United States. A governor had to submit detailed annual reports to the central government with statistics on economic conditions, finance, education, justice, and other matters in his commandery. Inspectors sent from the capital regularly investigated local affairs and checked on local officials in a manner similar to the special officials who acted as the "eyes and ears" to the Persian kings.

Kao-tsu had created a number of principalities and lesser fiefdoms for imperial relatives and in-laws and as rewards for meritorious officials. He did not revive full-blown feudalism, however, because the recipients received revenues rather than political power from their fiefs, and their domains were subject to the inspectors and other officials of the central government. Wu's reforms virtually wiped out the princely and noble domains. This separation of government positions from family prerogatives was a great advance in political institutions.

Although Kao-tsu and his successors pursued policies that precluded royal relatives from challenging the throne, they failed to control the ambition of their wives, mothers, and in-laws. An empress could be powerful because she assisted the emperor in performing rituals and was considered the "mother of the empire," but she was legally subordinate to her husband and could be demoted. Dowager empresses (mothers and grandmothers of reigning emperors) were infinitely more powerful, however, because filial piety required sons to obey their mothers. Empress Lu set the precedent by presiding over the government after Kao-tsu's death, even though her

❋ Model of a Watchtower. This second-century earthenware model of a watchtower standing in a moat has crossbowmen on guard on the parapet of the second-floor balcony. Walls, parapets, and watchtowers guarded China's northern frontier against nomadic raids and invasions. Courtesy of the Arthur M. Sackler Museum, Harvard University Art Museums. Gift of Earl Morse, Law School, 1930.

son was nominally ruler. He could not stop her domineering ways, and her extreme cruelty to her husband's concubines and their children caused him to suffer a nervous breakdown shortly after ascending the throne. He later abandoned himself to drinking, dying young after a seven-year reign. Dowager Empress Lu then appointed, dismissed, and killed several stepsons in succession; she also appointed members of her family to powerful posts and ruled for fifteen years until her death. During the Han, seven other dowager empresses ruled as regents while their sons were minors; some continued to rule in fact even after their sons became adults. As regents they appointed and dismissed officials, often appointing their relatives and eunuchs to powerful positions, and issued laws. Some even dismissed and appointed emperors. When there was more than one dowager empress (for example, when a mother and grandmother were both

Mathematical Problems in the Ancient World

Although the Han schoolboys' curriculum consisted mainly of the classics and history, they were also given some training in mathematics and exercises related to everyday affairs. Here are some examples:

1. A fast horse and a slow horse set out together on the 3000-li (900-kilometer; 558-mile) journey from Chan-gan to Ch'i. The first day the fast horse travels 193 li, thereafter increasing his speed by 13 li each day. The slow horse covers 97 li on the first day, thereafter reducing his speed by ½ li each day. After reaching Ch'i, the fast horse starts his return journey and meets the slow horse. When does the meeting take place and how far has each horse traveled? Answer: The horses meet after $15^{135}/_{191}$ days; the fast horse has traveled $4,534^{46}/_{191}$ li, and the slow horse $146^{145}/_{191}$ li.

2. A man is hired as a salt porter. If he is paid 40 cash for carrying two measures of salt for a distance of 100 li, how much will he be paid for carrying 1.73 measures for a distance of 80 li? Answer: $27^{11}/_{15}$ cash.

During his school days in the third century B.C.E., Eratosthenes of Cyrene (in North Africa) was known to his fellow pupils as "Beta" because he excelled in so many subjects as to be nearly (or "second") best in each. In his later life, he was an astronomer, mathematician, poet, and chief librarian at the great Library of Alexandria in Egypt. The most famous mathematical problem he solved had to do with the circumference of the earth. Eratosthenes had noticed that during the summer solstice, the sun's rays fell vertically at Syene (modern Aswan) some 500 miles up the Nile, but at an angle of 7° at Alexandria to the north near the mouth of the Nile. Applying basic Euclidean geometrical principles to this observation, Eratosthenes calculated the circumference of the earth. Although the precise equivalent in feet or meters of his unit of measure (the stade) is not known, it is nevertheless clear that his computation was amazingly accurate. He also measured the degree of obliquity, or tilt of the earth's axis.

---

alive), feuds between them and their families resulted in coups and battles. Although some dowager empresses were able rulers, others, together with their families and eunuchs, abused their power.

Han government was administered by a professional civil service rather than by hereditary nobles. Men were assigned to positions based on their education, merit, and ability to deal with people effectively. The first requirement for an aspiring official was an education. This requirement favored the rich because books, which were copied on silk, wood, or bamboo slips, were expensive and rare. Since public service was rewarded with honors and riches, a popular saying held that it was better to bequeath books than gold to one's sons. Local officials were annually required to recommend educated young men of good moral character, who were sent to the capital city and given written and oral exams. Those who passed then received posts. They served on probation during the first year, and received permanent appointments if they acquitted themselves satisfactorily. Every sixth day was a day of rest, and leaves were granted for illness and for mourning the death of parents. In 124 B.C.E., a national university was established at the capital with the task of preparing young men for the civil service. The curriculum was the Confucian classics. Enrollment was based on a geographical quota so that all areas of the empire would be represented; from an original fifty students, their numbers had grown to 30,000 by the second century. Along with the Ch'in edict that had unified the writ-

ten language, this massive national educational network for training officials proved invaluable in holding together a huge and diverse empire.

Every third year each official received an efficiency rating and report from his superior and was either promoted, demoted, transferred, or dismissed, based on his rating and the recommendation of his superior. Aged officials received pensions on retirement. A law of avoidance forbade a man to serve as governor or county magistrate in his home area to ensure that civil servants would be rotated throughout the country and that no one built a power base that might challenge the throne. This rule remained in force until the twentieth century. Subordinate officials in each unit of local government, however, were drawn from that area to ensure that local voices and interests were heard.

The military was an integral part of Han government. The Han ideal, as in Rome, was the citizen soldier. Adulthood began at twenty, and every male was liable for one year of military service at age twenty-three. The three-year delay was to allow the citizen time to accumulate savings so that he could serve without pay. Every year after the harvest, until they were fifty-six, men were liable for one month of reserve military duty. Actually, the citizen-soldier concept was not practical for a country as large as China with its need to defend distant frontiers. Therefore draft-eligible men who did not wish to serve could pay "substitute money" which was used to pay draftees and volunteers for longer-term service.

Ruins of hundreds of Han outposts, fortresses, watchtowers, walls, and ramparts across the entire northern frontier testify to the enormous burden of maintaining the Pax Sinica. Frontier garrisons protected the agricultural settlements and horse stud farms (for cavalry horses), delivered the mail, and secured the trade and diplomatic links between China and countries to the west. Because of northwestern China's dry climate, many reports, inventories, regulations, and personal accounts from the Han period have survived. They tell of a rigorous life of military duty, farming, discipline, and organization that kept the empire secure and its prestige high. One wooden slip said: "The order will be put up where it can be seen by the soldiers of the section of each post so that all may know it by heart and understand it; a close watch is to be kept and as soon as there is a fire signal the section of the post shall light one in turn." (As in the Roman army, a smoky fire would be lit by day and a bright fire at night for maximum visibility.) A fragment of silk from an officer's letter said plaintively: "The distance is long; contacts are rare; my rank is low and my person is humble; exchanges of letters are difficult." Most soldiers were infantrymen who carried 40-inch-long steel swords, twice as long and much stronger than the bronze swords of earlier times. Iron was also used for javelin tips and arrowheads, knives, and chain-link and fish-scale armor.

Cavalry units, essential for fighting the Hsiung-nu, supported the infantry in battle; in one campaign 130,000 horses participated—fewer than 30,000 returned. Thus the government gave top priority to obtaining good horses from friendly nomads and to controlling horse-breeding country. The powerful central Asian breeds, unlike the smaller ones native to China, could carry a fully armored soldier into battle. Horses also became a status symbol for rich citizens. The combination of superior iron weapons, leadership, organization, martial spirit, and cavalry enabled the Han to triumph over the nomads and preserve the peace. Around the end of the Han dynasty, the Chinese first cast stirrups from metal. This important invention gave the rider greater control over his horse, freed his hands, and made mounting and dismounting easier. Nomads spread this Chinese invention westward until it was universally used.

Soldiers' Orders. This wooden slip came from a Han military outpost in northwestern China along the Silk Road. It gives instructions for signaling between posts as follows: "The order will be put up where it can be seen by the soldiers of the section of each post so that all may know it by heart and understand it; a close watch is to be kept and as soon as there is a fire signal the section of the post shall light one in turn. . . ." The British Library

The Land and People

According to the census of 1 C.E. the Han population numbered just under 60 million; in 157, it was 56.5 million, perhaps more populous than the Roman Empire of the same period. Most Chinese were farmers. Land was privately owned and could be freely bought and sold. According to contemporary estimates, the typical farm family consisted of husband and wife and three children, working about seventeen acres. In the north, millet,

wheat, and barley were the grain crops; in the south, rice. Pigs and fowl were the common meat animals. Fish and tortoise raised in ponds also provided protein. Wind-powered bellows lowered the cost of making cast-iron tools, which were now used everywhere; plows were now made entirely of iron (as opposed to the iron-tipped wooden plow of the Warring States era). Other technical innovations included a three-legged seeder that could plant three rows of seeds simultaneously, an iron harrow, and a leveler. Paired or singly yoked oxen pulled the machinery; by using the nose ring, an innovation, one man could control a team of oxen. Archaeologists have found some giant plowshares thought to be ditchdiggers.

Iron tools enabled the government to construct large irrigation projects. Old reservoirs were enlarged and new ones built to hold water for irrigation. Han engineers built the world's first canals designed to follow the contour of the land as a way around or over hills. Also common were wells with winches to draw the water and brick-lined spill troughs to funnel water for irrigation.

The government encouraged planting mulberry trees and sericulture (raising silkworms and spinning and weaving silk cloth), which became widespread. Silks were China's most desired export commodity, and bolts of silk were used as currency and given as state gifts. To maintain China's monopoly in silk production, the government prohibited the export of silkworm eggs. Tending silkworms and carding and spinning silk were women's work, and each family in silk-producing areas was required to pay a tax in silk floss and fabric.

Everyone paid a poll tax, and cultivators paid a small land tax. During many years when the state treasury was full, taxes were remitted altogether, once for as long as eleven years. Male citizens also spent one month a year in corvée labor (corvée was compulsory labor for the state without pay; France, China, and several other countries required this service of males), mostly on public works projects after the harvest season.

Despite the general prosperity of the Han period, the small farmers, as in Rome at this time, found themselves in trouble. Without reserves to tide them over times of poor weather or other difficulties, farmers often went into debt, and if they could not pay their debt, they lost their land and had to work as sharecroppers, paying 50 percent of their yield to the landowner. Some left the land to become laborers, and the most unfortunate, like poor Athenian farmers before Solon's reforms, had to sell their children or themselves into slavery to pay off their debts. Government attempts at direct relief and schemes to resettle the dispossessed on virgin lands did not solve the fundamental problem of inequity in a free land-tenure system. Those with capital to invest, like wealthy contemporary Romans, accumulated great estates worked by tenants and slaves. Rich estate owners who also enjoyed

political connections could often evade taxes. That put a greater strain on the remaining small freeholders. Just as in Rome, the fall of the free peasantry had its corollary in the rise of great families. The Han elite was not an aristocracy by birth, but of wealth and political influence. Individual great families rose and fell, and the government tried to limit the size of estates, but as a class the landowning magnates continued to prosper.

Land ownership thus became an acute social issue. As the dynasty declined, the power of the great families increased unrestrained, until some fielded private armies that challenged the government. In the second century, the worsening economic crisis led to large-scale peasant revolts, which precipitated the dynasty's downfall.

Cities, Manufacturing, and Commerce

Large urban centers were a characteristic of Han China. Enclosed by a wall sixteen miles in circumference, the capital city of Changan was one of the largest cities in the world, and like Rome, it was cosmopolitan and luxurious. Changan was a planned city of palaces, temples, markets, and private residences; the widest avenues measured 150 feet across. Whereas the Greeks and Romans built in stone, the Chinese (and Indians) used mainly wood, a highly perishable material. Thus not much remains standing from Han times except the tomb mounds for rulers and aristocrats, portions of city walls, and foundations of buildings.

Loyang was smaller, but at its peak it had a total population of half a million, most of whom lived outside the city walls. In 131 the state university campus on its outskirts had 240 buildings, which housed classrooms and dormitories for 30,000 students. Then as now, citizens complained that many students spent their time boisterously having fun rather than studying. Many towns had specialized functions, such as manufacturing silk or iron, and others were noted for trade or served as garrison and administrative headquarters.

Both manufacturing and commerce flourished, and entrepreneurs grew rich. Merchants made fortunes dealing in grain, iron, and salt. The iron industry produced not only weapons and agricultural tools but common household items such as cooking pots, knives, scissors, and needles. One government-owned mine was allotted 100,000 corvée laborers each year to mine iron ore. Blast, reduction, and "steel puddling" furnaces were all in use.

Debates over proper government economic policy raged through much of the period. Confucians agreed with Legalists that merchants were social parasites; both groups scorned the profit motive as unworthy. Thus they put merchants and entrepreneurs at the bottom of the social order below scholars, farmers, and artisans. Emperor Wu promulgated sumptuary laws that forbade mer-

chants to flaunt their wealth and regulated their activities. He also nationalized the iron and salt industries and established a liquor licensing system, setting up a pattern that persisted to the twentieth century. He also set up state granaries to stabilize grain prices and to discourage speculation. State-owned factories and workshops were formed in many other fields. Despite these state actions, merchant princes continued to amass fortunes.

The crafts flourished along with commerce, as artisans created an extensive array of beautiful objects. Excavated tombs reveal that the metropolitan styles of Changan and Loyang were copied as far afield as central Asia and Lolang in modern Korea. Gorgeous Han silks were prized throughout the ancient world, and the beautiful articles of lacquer have not been surpassed since. Potters made a wide range of vessels for daily use, some glazed in rich green and amber colors. They also made scaled-down models of houses, animals, and tools that were buried in tombs for "use" by the dead in the spirit world. These grave goods enable us to reconstruct much of Han life.

Bronzesmiths made articles for ritual as well as for daily use and decoration. These goods were so reasonably priced that even the middle class could afford them. Bronze mirrors were especially prized; thousands have been excavated, some still with their prices marked on. Some mirror makers took to advertising their wares by casting words of praise on them; for example: "The substance of this mirror is pure and bright; the rays it radiates could be compared to those of the sun and moon," and "The mirrors made by the Ye family are handsome and great. They are as bright as the sun and the moon; indeed they are rare to find."

Jade was another ritual item as well as luxury item. The securing of the northwest, where nephrite jade was found, made for a steady supply. Popular superstition had it that jade could preserve the body from decay, so royalty had jade burial suits made for themselves. Archaeologists have recovered several jade suits from princely tombs. The bodies they enclosed, however, have long since turned to dust.

The Silk Road: Link between East and West

As the centuries passed, the great civilizations of Eurasia came into increasing contact with one another. Alexander's conquest of northwestern India in 326 B.C.E. failed, however, to open significant trade or contacts between China and western countries. Contacts had to wait until Emperor Wu defeated the Hsiung-nu, who blocked access; after that he exchanged ambassadors with King Mithridates II of Parthia (modern Iran). Wu gave presents of silk to Mithridates and received acrobats and ostrich eggs in return. Trade between China and Parthia followed. Roman descriptions of Crassus's defeat at Carrhae in 53 B.C.E. told of the gleaming silk banners that preceded the Parthian soldiers. Less than ten years later, when Julius Caesar entered Rome in triumph, his procession also had silk banners.

During the early Roman Empire, wealthy women developed an almost insatiable demand for silk fabrics—to the disgust of Roman moralists. The Roman political leader and philosopher Seneca complained: "I see garments in which there is nothing to cover either the wearer's body or her shame." Emperor Diocletian's Edict

Wages and Prices in Ancient India and China

Although neither India nor China had anything equivalent to Diocletian's price regulations during a similar period, we do have some information on wages and prices for Mauryan India and Han China.

For example, a table from Kautilya's *Arthasatra* specifies the following fees and wages (although it is not clear whether these are real or idealized figures or what time period is intended, such as weekly or monthly):

- 48,000 panas (each pana contained just under a half-ounce of silver) for the chief priest, prime minister, crown prince, queen mother, and chief queen.
- 24,000 panas for the chief police officer, guardian of the harem, head of the revenue department, and royal treasurer.
- 12,000 panas for princes and their mothers, the commander of the army, and the supervisor of manufacturers.
- 8,000 panas for the guild masters, regional commanding officers, and inspectors.
- 4,000 panas for chief supervisors.
- 2,000 panas for commanders of war chariots and physicians.
- 1,000 panas for fortunetellers and professors of repute.
- 500 to 1,000 panas for spies.

- 500 panas for trained infantry, scribes and accountants, a slave, and an elephant.
- 120 panas for wages for craftsmen.
- 60 panas for servants and medical assistants.
- 50 panas for a female slave, the average cost for maintaining one man for a year.
- 24 panas for a horse (as fine).
- 12 panas for an ox (as fine).
- 1 pana for 400 pounds of grain.

In Han dynasty China, the poll tax, which together with the land tax constituted the chief source of revenue, was levied at 120 coins per head for the adult population and 23 coins for each child between seven and fourteen years old. A Han inscription of 90 C.E. says that a ten-yard roll of undyed silk cloth weighing thirteen ounces had a value of 618 coins. We may compare this with the monthly stipend of between 360 and 3,000 coins paid to officers serving in the northwestern frontier guard. In one case an officer whose monthly stipend was 900 coins was paid two rolls of silk. Another document from northwestern China during the Han era stated that 20,000 coins could purchase two adult female slaves, twenty ox-carts, or ten draft horses.

---

on Maximum Prices in 301 rated raw white silk by weight at one quarter the value of gold; if dyed purple, raw silk was rated at triple the value of gold.

The Silk Road that connected the Chinese and Roman Empires and the lands in between began in the Han capital of Changan and proceeded westward to Tunhuang, the last Chinese settlement. After crossing mountains and deserts and stopping at oases, it ended at a port of the eastern Mediterranean, where the goods were shipped to Rome. No one merchant made the entire trip. The goods were transshipped many times before reaching their destination, making many trading stations en route prosperous. With the Han and Roman Empires in control of most of the route, roads were kept open and secure. Silk, both woven and raw, was China's major export, although skins, iron, lacquer, and spices were also exported. From the Roman Empire, China imported wool and linen fabrics, amber, coral, Syrian glass, Egyptian papyrus, wines, and acrobats and entertainers—the latter were status symbols in aristocratic Han households—but above all, gold coins and bullion.

In the first century C.E., the Romans developed a sea route to the east, which had a twofold advantage over the land route: ships carried more than draft animals, and

they bypassed territory controlled by the difficult and often hostile Parthians. During the reign of Augustus, as many as 120 Roman ships sailed from Red Sea ports for southern India every year. Some of them proceeded further to Southeast Asia and Canton in southern China, bringing to China Indian and Southeast Asian products such as ivory, tortoise shell, gems, pearls, precious woods, and spices. Some Roman leaders became alarmed by their unfavorable balance of trade, which caused a drain on the empire's precious metal reserves. As Emperor Tiberius complained, this outflow paid for "articles that flatter the vanity of women. . . . In exchange for trifles our money is sent to foreign lands and even to our enemies." In the second century, Pliny the Younger claimed that annually this trade drained the Roman treasury by 55 million sesterces paid to India and 45 million to China and Arabia. For comparison, a Roman soldier was paid about four sesterces per day.

Chinese records say that in 166 C.E. a Roman embassy from Marcus Aurelius arrived in Loyang with gifts. Since there is no mention of such an embassy in Roman sources, most likely this was a case of private merchants from the Roman Empire passing themselves off as ambassadors. The distances were so great that the Chinese

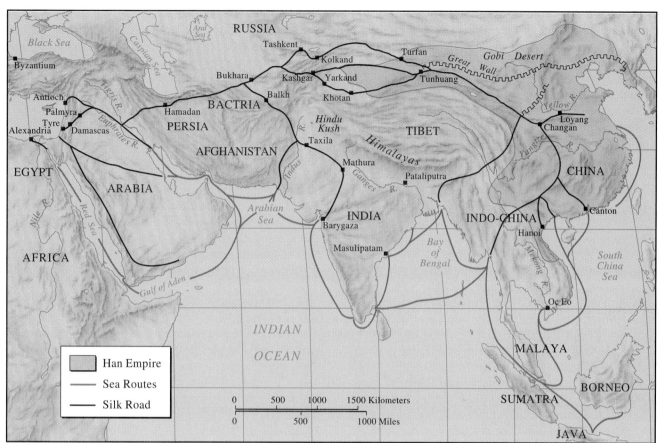

✳ MAP 4.5 The Han Empire and the Silk Road. In addition to controlling China, northern Korea, and Vietnam, Han outposts and garrisons dominated central Asia, allowing trade to cross the Silk Road to India, Persia, and the Roman Empire.

and Roman governments did not attempt direct communications. The contacts that developed involved an exchange of goods and not ideas. Trade dropped off after the third century, when political conditions deteriorated first in China and then in the west.

Religious and Intellectual Life

Emperor Kao-tsu and his immediate successors were practical men with no professed philosophical preferences. Nevertheless, they realized Legalism had become a liability because of its association with the hated Ch'in dynasty. What they needed was dedicated men to help run the government and to dignify it with proper rituals. Enter the Confucians, whose conviction that the place of a scholar was in government and that *li* or rituals were important in human relations made them natural allies of the imperial system. In 136 B.C.E., Emperor Wu declared Confucianism the official state philosophy and banned students of Legalism from government service, though in fact the autocratic Wu's policies were essentially Legalistic. In this respect he differed from Asoka of India, who favored Buddhism mainly out of moral conviction. However, Wu also established a state university

with a curriculum based on Confucian works and an embryonic examination system. These measures ensured the dominance of Confucians in the bureaucracy. Paradoxically, once in government the Confucians found that they needed to enact certain Legalist techniques and practices in order to govern effectively.

Tung Chung-shu (c. 179–c. 104 B.C.E.) was largely responsible for creating the examination system that became the institutional basis of Confucianism as the state ideology. He reinterpreted Confucian teachings and added current ideas to make Confucianism the theory of the unified empire. The universe, Tung explained, consisted of heaven, earth, and humans. The emperor was the highest representative of humanity. As such, it was up to him and the government to interpret the will of heaven and, by moral and beneficent government, to help people develop their potential for goodness and maintain harmony. It was also the emperor's duty to set a good moral example, take care of the economic needs of the people, make it profitable for them to become virtuous, and help them achieve moral fulfillment.

Should he fail or use his power improperly, the emperor risked disrupting cosmic harmony and forfeiting the mandate of heaven. To prevent such disasters, Confucians counseled rulers to seek their advice and to take warning from natural portents, which they reported and interpreted. Seasonable weather and abundant harvests meant that heaven was satisfied, while droughts, floods, and strange happenings portended heaven's displeasure. The ruler or son of heaven indeed had heavy responsibilities.

Thus a reinterpreted and eclectic Confucianism was proclaimed the state ideology. Other schools were not suppressed, however. Confucius was exalted as a sage, not a god or king. The spirit of his teachings influenced laws, but he was not a lawgiver. In this permissive climate, philosophical Taoism enjoyed a revival, and commentaries were written on the *Lao Tzu* and *Chuang Tzu*. Taoist ideas of cultivating self-contentment and seeking harmony with nature provided an outlet from Confucian strictures and allowed a degree of individualism to prevail.

Religious or popular Taoism came into its own at this time. Rooted in a hodgepodge of folk beliefs and superstitions, it was concerned with finding drugs and potions to prolong life and attain immortality and with using alchemy to produce gold from base materials. These interests led to experiments and new knowledge in chemistry, pharmacology, and other sciences and to the discovery of the compass, which greatly helped navigation, and later of gunpowder. Many persons may have achieved premature immortality from taking the drugs and potions, but that did not disillusion the true believers, who asserted that the immortals, men and women who had found the secret of everlasting life, had merely pretended to die in order to confound those of little faith. Others participated in group worship and believed in salvation. In the late Eastern Han, one religious Taoist group spread so fast that the government, which feared the political implications of the movement, acted to suppress it. Thereupon its adherents rebelled, donning a yellow head scarf for identification. The Yellow Turban uprising of 184 C.E., which capitalized on peasant discontent, precipitated the fall of the Han dynasty.

By the first century C.E., Buddhism had begun to take root in China. There were three centers of Buddhism: the capital city, Loyang, where Buddhism was brought overland via the Silk Road; Tonkin in the south (now Vietnam), where missionaries had come by sea; and the lower Yangtze valley. By the second century, a number of monks from Persia, central Asian kingdoms, and India were translating Buddhist canons into Chinese, assisted by Chinese monks.

Buddhism introduced new concepts such as karma and reincarnation and reinforced existing ideas about compassion. Buddhist meditation and yoga were akin to Taoist practices, leading some Chinese at first to think that Buddhism was a Taoist sect. Indeed, Buddhist translations freely borrowed Taoist vocabulary. Many Taoists seized on the idea that Buddhism was derived from Taoism because, they said, Lao Tzu had gone to India and converted Gautama to Taoism. Thus second-century Han emperors saw no contradiction when they placed deities of both faiths on the same palace altar and worshiped them together.

In retrospect, the introduction of Buddhism was one of the greatest events in Chinese civilization. After several centuries of assimilation and accommodations, Buddhism would be accepted as one of the three teachings of China, alongside Confucianism and Taoism. As a result, it has had a major influence on Chinese thought, art, and literature.

The greatest literary glory of the Han was the writing of history. We have already noted in previous chapters that historical writing is deeply rooted in Chinese civilization and traces to the earliest antiquity. Han historians contributed two great works. The first was the *Shih Chi* (Records of the Historian), a comprehensive history of the world then known to the Chinese, from the era of the culture heroes to the first century B.C.E. It was written by a father-and-son team, and its format and elegant prose were held up as models for succeeding historians. The work was divided into five sections: basic annals (narrative of important events), chronological tables, monographs (analytical essays on topics of special interest such as music, astronomy, and economic affairs), histories of great families of the past, and biographies (which included lives of statesmen, thinkers, rogues, and assassins).

This multifaceted approach to history set a standard for later dynastic histories that continued to the present century. Ssu-ma Ch'ien, the son and the more famous of the duo, believed that history had two purposes: to give information and to provide moral instruction. Like the Athenian historian Thucydides, he invented speeches and dialogues that he felt were suited to the historical characters and their situation and would bring the people and events to life.

The second great work was titled *The History of the Former [Western] Han Dynasty*. It was begun by Pan Ku (32–92 C.E.), brother and uncle of the great generals, father and son conquerors of central Asia, and finished by his equally famous sister Pan Chao, who also wrote a book of moral instructions for upper-class women.

Other literary works of the Han dealt with philosophy, poetry, and fiction. In the bibliographical section of the *History of the Former Han Dynasty*, Pan Ku listed 1,380 works of fiction, but none has survived.

Summary and Comparisons

This chapter has examined the development of several great empires. Each rose after a prolonged period of intellectual ferment and political turmoil in its cultural area and succeeded by imposing unity and order. All the empires shared important characteristics, yet they differed in other significant ways. In the Greek and Roman worlds, empires replaced republican governments with dynastic governments; in India and China where the dynastic system was already deeply rooted, powerful emperors replaced the earlier and less exalted regional kings. All dynasties were headed by men, but powerful women, mostly mothers and wives of rulers, sometimes governed through male figureheads. Murderous palace intrigues characterized politics during certain periods in each empire.

The fragmented and weak Greek city-states and their intellectual longings for the classical period allowed a backward and semi-Greek frontier state called Macedon to rise to ascendancy, first under Philip and then under his more famous son, Alexander. Alexander the Great conquered the Persian Empire and extended Macedonian dominance over a vast region from Egypt across the eastern Mediterranean to India.

Further west on the Italian Peninsula, Rome rose to dominance amidst numerous and diverse states of Greek, Etruscan, and Latin cultures. After ousting their Etruscan monarchs and forming a republic, the Romans first dominated the entire peninsula; between 264 and 30 B.C.E., they wrested control of the western Mediterranean from Carthage and of the eastern Mediterranean from the Hellenistic kingdoms, the successor states to Alexander's empire.

In India two important trends led to the formation of the first great territorial empire. One was the intellectual ferment that had produced the *Upanishads,* Buddhism, and Jainism (see Chapter 3). The second was the force of foreign influence, from both the Persian and Macedonian Empires, that culminated in Alexander's brief incursion into the Indus valley in the northwest. That event inspired an Indian prince, Chandragupta Maurya, to found a dynasty and conquer an empire in the fourth century B.C.E. that eventually controlled all but the southern tip of the subcontinent. After the fall of the Mauryan Empire, northwestern India suffered many invasions by Greeks and Persians, which reinforced earlier contacts between India and West Asia. The most successful invaders, however, were nomads who entered the region from their earlier homeland along China's northwestern frontier. Called the Yueh-chih by the Chinese, they established dominion from the Caspian Sea to Kashmir and called their state the Kushan Empire. Kushan power and culture reached its zenith under the great monarch Kanishka around 100 C.E., but even so, the Kushan Empire did not unify the whole Indian subcontinent.

Further east, the Han dynasty (202 B.C.E.–220 C.E.) succeeded in unifying all Chinese peoples after a long era of cultural flowering known as the Hundred Schools of philosophy and prolonged civil wars by rival states similar to those between the city-states of classical Greece. Founded by a commoner named Liu Chi, who was attentive to the needs of the people, the Han dynasty succeeded by relaxing the harsh laws of its Legalist predecessor, the Ch'in dynasty.

These major empires did not enjoy the same degrees of success, nor were they equally enduring. Alexander's short-lived empire broke up into three major Hellenistic states. Each was governed by an elite of Macedonian and native civil and military administrators under a supreme monarch. They were all finally absorbed by Rome.

The Roman Empire reached its zenith during the first two centuries C.E. Dramatic deterioration set in after the third century, however, largely because of civil strife. Strong-willed and able autocrats postponed the empire's collapse, but at the price of hastening its division into two portions, the east and west.

The Mauryan Empire reached its zenith under Emperor Asoka, the founder's grandson, but disintegration set in after his long reign. The lack of early historical documents has hampered scholars from reconstructing Mauryan and Kushan history with the same detail and precision they have achieved with the history of the Roman and Han Empires.

The Han Empire reached a high-water mark under Emperor Wu, who conquered a huge domain and, much like Rome, buffered it with client states along its critical frontiers. Han power paralleled Roman power, and the two empires nearly touched at their boundaries. Weak rulers in the later Han eventually lost control, as economic problems and revolts brought the dynasty to an end.

The formation of successful and enduring empires accelerated cultural growth, exchange of ideas, and assimilation between different peoples. Alexander's conquests and the division of his empire among his generals accelerated the spread of Greek culture throughout the eastern Mediterranean, into West Asia, and eastward to India. Cosmopolitanism reigned among the upper classes, commerce and manufacturing reached unprecedented levels, and the arts and sciences prospered. Alexandria became a hub of cultural and commercial exchange between the Mediterranean world and—via Arabia and the Red Sea—India and China.

Because Persia had ruled portions of the Indus valley prior to Alexander's conquest of that region, Persian culture became particularly influential in India: Chandragupta's centralized bureaucracy, his spy network, and the pomp and ceremonials of the Mauryan court were traceable to Persian models, as were the rock inscriptions of Asoka and the workmanship of his stone pillars and capitals. His conversion to Buddhism and his energetic patronage made the faith a world religion. Because the Kushan Empire straddled crucial trade and missionary routes across East, Central, and West Asia and because the Kushan people adopted Buddhism, the beautiful temples they built were adorned with art and statuary that combined Greco-Roman, Persian, and Indian traditions. Since missionaries and pilgrims between India and China traveled through Kushan territories, the Kushan Empire played a key role in the transmission of Buddhist art and culture to China.

Of the major empires discussed in this chapter, the Roman and Han Empires in particular played many similar and comparable roles and shared similar traits. Both emphasized historical writing and relied on divination to ascertain the wishes of the gods. Both established peace and order over large territories directly and indirectly through client states. The Pax Romana and Pax Sinica they imposed across most of the Eurasian continent made possible the most extensive international trade the world had seen—via the famous overland Silk Road and by sea.

Both empires endured many centuries due to their sound institutions—the election of officers in the Roman republic and a civil service system rooted in merit and learning in China. Each initially depended on citizen soldiers who regarded military service as a patriotic duty, but had to rely on a professional military and even foreign mercenaries in their later stages. Both were lawgivers and civilizers of numerous peoples and cultures they conquered and ruled.

The transmission of civilization was often a two-way process—at least for the Romans. During the Han era, the Chinese were primarily transmitters of civilization, not borrowers. By the end of the Han, however, Buddhism had made its way into China, and contacts with India had been established, thereby setting the stage for the significant debt that China ultimately would owe to Indian Buddhism.

During the period covered here, however, Rome played a dual role as recipient of classical and Hellenistic culture and as its transmitter to wide regions and the many less advanced subjects of the Roman Empire. Similarly, just as the rest of East Asia would later convert to Buddhism and learn about Greco-Roman–influenced Buddhist art through China, northern Europe would later learn about classical and Hellenistic Greece through Rome. In rather different manners, much of Europe and Asia adopted Hellenistic culture through trade and the widespread settlement of Greeks in lands Alexander and his successors opened up. At the other end of the spectrum, Indian Buddhism and Indian culture spread primarily through missionary activities and trade, with no military intervention.

The size and complexity of large empires often resulted in a sense of impersonality and alienation that caused many people to embrace new religious and philosophical systems. In the Hellenistic and Roman Empires, these included philosophies such as Stoicism and Epicureanism that appealed to the elite and mystery religions that comforted the masses. Han China saw the continued popularity of philosophical Taoism, the evolution of religious Taoism, and the introduction of Buddhism. These philosophies and religions challenged the traditional piety of Rome and the official Confucianism of Han China.

All five great cultures discussed in this chapter contributed to cultural growth and influenced posterity. The great achievements of the Roman, Mauryan, and Han Empires have left an enduring legacy to the peoples of Europe, India, and China beyond the empires' actual borders.

Selected Sources

Balsdon, J. P. V. D. *Life and Leisure in Ancient Rome.* 1969. The best book on Roman everyday life; based on a critical assessment of literary, inscriptional, and archaeological evidence.

Begley, Vimala, and Richard D. De Puma, eds. *Rome and India: The Ancient Sea Trade.* 1991. Essays by many experts on different topics.

*Boardman, John, et al., eds. *The Roman World.* 1988. This volume of the *Oxford History of the Classical World* contains essays by leading authorities on all aspects of Roman civilization; excellent illustrations.

*Bryher, Winifred. *The Coin of Carthage.* 1963. An entertaining historical novel about the fortunes of two Greek traders trying to make their way in a world convulsed by the Second Punic War.

*Christ, Karl. *The Romans: An Introduction to Their History and Civilization.* Trans. C. Holme, 1984. A well-informed, up-to-date, relatively brief history.

Ch'u, T'ung-tsu. *Han Social Structure.* Ed. Jack L. Dull. 1972. Comprehensive in scope and full of human interest and anecdotes.

*Demand, Nancy. *A History of Ancient Greece.* 1996. An up-to-date and clearly written survey of Greek history from Neolithic times through the career of Alexander the Great.

Erdosy, George. *Urbanism in Early Historic India.* 1988. Deals with the development of cities between 1000 B.C.E. and 300 C.E.

Frye, Richard N. *The Heritage of Central Asia: From Antiquity to the Turkish Expansion.* 1996. This book shows how central Asia connected all the ancient cultures of Europe and Asia.

Gokhale, B. G. *Asoka Maurya.* 1966. A good biography of the man and his age.

Green, Peter. *Alexander the Great.* 1970. This engaging and superbly illustrated biography of Alexander provides a well-balanced assessment of his accomplishments. Covers the career of Philip II also.

*Jones, A. H. M. *Augustus.* 1970. The best recent account of the life and times of the first Roman emperor and of the system of government he instituted.

Langguth, A. J. *A Noise of War: Caesar, Pompey, Octavian, and the Struggle for Rome.* 1994. A riveting account of a turbulent era by a popular biographer.

Loewe, Michael. *Everyday Life in Early Imperial China.* 1968. Many pictures and drawings help bring to life the China of 2,000 years ago.

*Long, A. A. *Hellenistic Philosophy.* 2d ed. 1986. This very helpful study covers Epicureanism, Skepticism, and Stoicism.

*McCullough, Colleen. *The First Man in Rome.* 1990. *The Grass Crown.* 1991. *Fortune's Favorites.* 1993. *Caesar's Women.* 1996. These four richly detailed historical novels trace the careers of Marius and Sulla and the rise of Pompey the Great and Julius Caesar.

Nilakanta Sastri, K. A., ed. *Age of the Nandas and Mauryas*. 2d ed. 1967. Many experts contributed to this book, which deals with the many facets of India before Alexander's campaign.

Pirzzoli-t'Seerstevens, Michele. *The Han Dynasty*. 1982. A beautifully illustrated volume with easy-to-read text.

*Plescia, Joseph. *The Bill of Rights and Roman Law: A Comparative Study*. 1995. A fascinating and concise comparison of the development of citizens' rights in ancient Rome and in the U.S. Bill of Rights.

*Pomeroy, Sarah. *Women in Hellenistic Egypt*. 1984. A fascinating account of the lives of women on all social levels during the period.

Power, Martin. *Art and Politics in Early China*. 1992. Examines interactions between the government and art in Han China.

*Renault, Mary. *Funeral Games*. 1981. A vivid fictionalized treatment of the bloody and chaotic struggle for power by Alexander's successors after 323 B.C.E.

*Scarre, Chris. *The Penguin Historical Atlas of Ancient Rome*. 1995. Contains, in addition to excellent full-color maps and illustrations, a quite detailed, topic-by-topic history of ancient Rome.

Soren, David, et. al. *Carthage: Uncovering the Mysteries and Splendors of Ancient Tunisia*. 1990. By far the best general account of ancient Carthage and its civilization from the ninth century B.C.E. to the sixth century C.E.

*Walbank, F. W. *The Hellenistic World*. 1982; rev. ed. 1993. A concise, accurate, up-to-date presentation of political and cultural developments of the era.

Yu Ying-shih. *Trade and Expansion in Han China: A Study in the Structure of Sino-Barbarian Economic Relations*. 1967. Deals with the interaction between politics and economics.

*Available in paperback.

Internet Links

The Ancient Greek World
http://www.museum.upenn.edu/Greek_world/Index.html
This well-designed site from the University of Pennsylvania Museum has sections on Land and Archaeological Time (including Hellenistic), Daily Life, Economy, and Religion and Death. Superb graphics throughout.

Augustus: Images of Power
http://www.lib.virginia.edu/etext/augimage.html
A detailed look, through informative text and good graphics, at several Augustan publicity masterpieces: the Mausoleum, the Altar of Peace, the Prima Porta statue, and the Gemma Augustea.

China: The Imperial Era
http://www-chaos.umd.edu/history/imperial.html#first
A succinct account of the unification of China in 221 B.C.E., the Han dynasty, the Great Wall, and the Silk Road.

Images from World History: The Kushan Empire
http://www.hartford-hwp.com/image_archive/kushan/index.html
A good selection of graphics depicting art objects and artifacts from the Kushan Empire.

In the Footsteps of Alexander the Great
http://www.pbs.org/mpt/alexander/
This site, based in part on Michael Wood's PBS series, offers concise outlines of Alexander's life and career, together with capsule biographies of important figures, a helpful timeline, and hyperlinks to other internet resources.

Mauryan Period (323–185 BCE)
http://jefferson.village.virginia.edu/pompeii/page-1.html
A collection of images—art works, site plans, etc.—relevant to Mauryan India.

Pompeii Forum Project
http://www.village.virginia.edu/pompeii/page-1.html
An online examination of the downtown area of a typical Roman town of 20,000. Excellent site plans and text.

Stoicism, the Philosophy of Rome
http://home.fia.net/~n4bz/gsr4/gsr403.html
This source provides well-chosen quotations from Epictetus and Marcus Aurelius, with valuable connecting narrative and explication by the website authors.

The Decline and Fall of Empires

Why do great empires crumble away or crash? Are their deaths inevitable? Over the centuries, historians have postulated numerous reasons for the demise of empires. For example, Chinese scholars accepted a cyclical theory of history, namely, that growth and prosperity are inevitably followed by decline and fall. Chinese writers also accepted the proposition that periods of unity are followed by disunity and chaos, which in turn give way once more to unity. These views were shared by the great fourteenth-century Arab historian Ibn Khaldun. Judeo-Christian historians, on the other hand, believed that historic progression served God's purpose and that history would end when God's kingdom was established on earth. In the nineteenth and twentieth centuries, modern theories range from the Marxist view that all history is the result of class struggle based on economic causes to Arnold Toynbee's hypothesis that empires rise when they meet the physical and spiritual challenges of the people and time and fall when they no longer do so.

The problem with broad theories such as these is that they may lead their exponents to bend, distort, or use facts selectively to prove their case, while ignoring or dismissing important factors that fail to serve their thesis. In fact, the rise and fall of great empires result from many complex reasons, some of which are shared, while in other instances they are specific and unique. Therefore it is difficult and unwise to force the explanation for the fall of all empires into a uniform framework. This essay identifies some of the important reasons for the decline and fall of empires. As we shall see in the chapter that follows, as well as in later chapters, empires have characteristically declined and collapsed as a result of a combination of factors.

1. *Dynastic succession.* To paraphrase the great twentieth-century British statesman and historian Winston Churchill, although democratic governments are imperfect, they are nevertheless superior to all other forms of government. In particular, constitutional democracies built on the rule of law have clear rules concerning acquiring, holding, and relinquishing power. No major ancient empire was democratically governed. All were hereditary dynasties, ruled most of the time by men, but sometimes by women. Succession to power was often based on primogeniture or some other form of selection within the ruling family. Inevitably, after some generations, ruling families produced weak heirs due to wine, song, sexual excess, mental deficiency, or other causes, or they left minor heirs who were incapable of governing. Ineffectual leaders and disputed successions generally led to revolts, usurpations, and civil wars that toppled the rul-

ing dynasty and contributed to the decline and fall of the empire. For example, the lack of an adult male heir spelled the breakup of Alexander's empire. A disputed succession broke up the Mongol Empire two generations after its founding by Genghis Khan. Inferior rulers and minor rulers manipulated by relatives and eunuchs brought about the end of the Mauryan and Han Empires. Disputed succession led to coups that severely undermined the strength of the Roman and Inka Empires and ended the unity of the Muslim Empire a generation after Muhammad's death.

2. *Bureaucratic corruption.* All effective empires relied on an honest bureaucracy and created checks and balances to ensure it. For example, the Romans emphasized the duty of the upper class to set moral examples and to devote their lives to public service. Han China created state universities and an examination system to educate and select men of integrity and ability for public service. In time, however, all bureaucracies succumbed to corruption, and corrupt governments provoked rebellions; for example, a peasant revolt called the Yellow Turban rebellion contributed to the fall of the Han Empire.

3. *Inequitable economic burdens.* Successful empires depended on sufficient revenues to support the military, bureaucracy, and other arms of government. Sufficient revenues depended on a prosperous population engaged in agriculture, trade, and industry. Those who could evade taxes, however, generally the powerful, often found ways to do so, thereby enhancing their incomes and becoming richer. The resulting shift of the tax burden to the poor and powerless inevitably led to decreased revenue for the government and aroused resentment among the taxpayers. A resentful population often revolted, and impoverished governments frequently lacked the resources to put down the revolts or to ameliorate the discontent that provoked them. Nor did the governments have the resources to mount defenses against external enemies. A vicious cycle of decline and fall resulted. For example, the rise of large plantations and the concomitant fall of a free farming citizenry greatly contributed to the fall of both Rome and the Han. The inability of the Gupta Empire in India to collect revenues to pay all its officials contributed to its collapse.

4. *Regional, racial, or ethnic tensions.* Great empires were usually composites of numerous racial, ethnic, and religious groups who resisted full integration. The Hellenistic empires never fully integrated the ruling class of Greeks and the subject Egyptians, Persians, and other ethnic groups. In India the reversion to regional

states divided by language and ethnicity demonstrates how difficult the Mauryan task of attempting to unite the subcontinent had been. A major weakness of the Aztec Empire was its tenuous control over restless subject peoples, who were often ready to join outsiders against their current masters. Widely disparate regional interests led Emperor Diocletian to divide the Roman Empire into four administrations with four capitals and four leaders. In time the division solidified into two separate empires, each with its official language, traditions, and culture.

5. *Decline of martial spirit.* The existence of a will to fight, or, put another way, the willingness of a populace to sacrifice property or life itself to defend the state, is an intangible but important factor in the rise and fall of many empires. The success of the Roman Empire was in part due to its male citizens' pride in military service. When that spirit declined, Rome was forced to recruit unreliable mercenaries. The need to pay mercenaries drained the treasury. This was also true of the Han and T'ang Empires in China. When the T'ang government needed to recruit barbarian units for the army, the result was a rebellion that almost toppled the dynasty. According to some, the Indian emperor Asoka's emphasis on pacifism and moral persuasion as state policies sapped the martial spirit of the Indians and contributed to the fall of the Mauryan Empire after his passing.

6. *Moral decline.* This is also an intangible factor. Nevertheless, from Augustus on, Roman leaders decried the decline of their citizens' moral fiber and their increasing self-indulgence and hedonism. Similarly, in Han China, the hedonism and extravagance of the upper classes were blamed for the decline of the dynasty. Emperor Asoka of India appointed morality officers to uphold high moral standards, with dubious results.

7. *Escapist or otherworldly religions.* The eighteenth-century historian Edward Gibbon blamed Christianity, which stressed heavenly rather than earthly rewards, for declining civic spirit and other ills of the Roman Empire. He also blamed religious strife among Christians for the increasing chaos of Rome. Likewise, many upper-class Han Chinese indulged in otherworldly Buddhism or escapist philosophical Taoism. Emperor Asoka's encouragement of pacific pursuits and the nonviolent teachings of Buddhism and Jainism may also have contributed to weakening the Mauryan Empire.

8. *External enemies.* All successful empires were forged through conquest and maintained through military strength. While defeated enemies schemed for revenge, the wealth generated by powerful empires inspired envy, especially among less affluent neighbors. Thus outsiders awaited opportunities to breach the defenses of the Han and Roman Empires and to loot, settle, and rule the lands they coveted.

9. *Costly technology.* All successful empires created engineering wonders that helped to sustain them. From China to India, West Asia, the Mediterranean world, and South America, imperial governments built and maintained roads, harbors and waterways, irrigation projects, defensive walls, and other installations. They maintained granaries to provision troops defending their borders, to relieve famine, and to enhance their economies. The Great Wall of China, the Roman roads and aqueducts, the enormous granary complex of the Inka, and the Ptolemaic irrigation works along the Nile River are major examples of the energies expended to maintain safety and enhance the economies of those empires. Whatever their intrinsic merit, however, the expense of initiating and maintaining projects of such magnitude often impoverished the governments that supported them, turning what was originally an advantage into a liability.

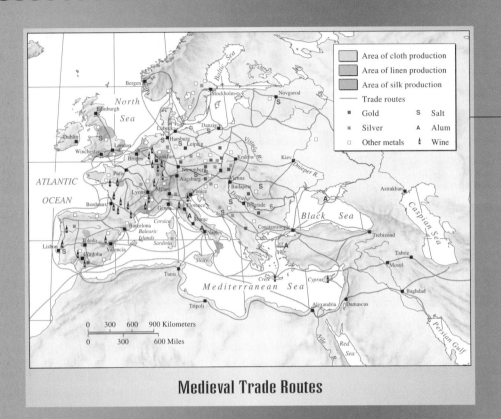

Medieval Trade Routes

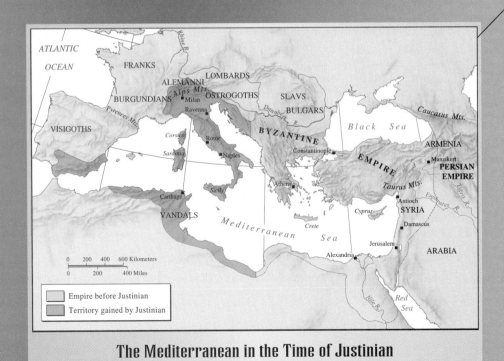

The Mediterranean in the Time of Justinian

Disruption and Renewal in West Asia and Europe

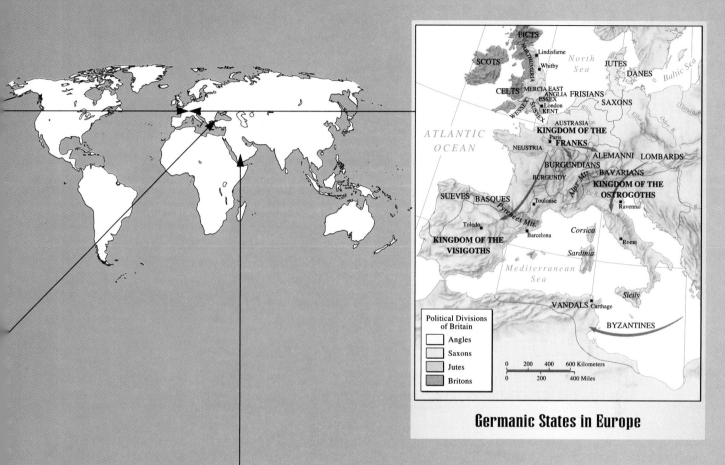

Germanic States in Europe

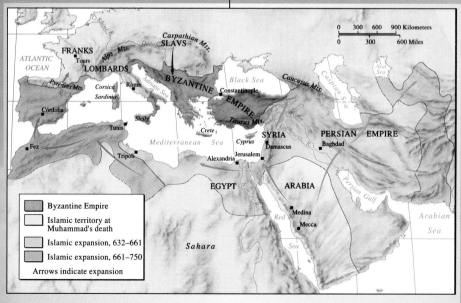

The Expansion of Islam

As noted in the preceding comparative essay, the reasons for the death of empires are many and varied. Although scholars disagree over the precise reasons for the fall of Rome or Constantinople, there is no doubt that the rising power of the Germanic tribes in Europe and the emergence of a dynamic new Muslim Empire in Arabia first threatened and then overtook the older Roman Empires. After first describing religious and social conditions in first-century Palestine and the spread of Christianity throughout the Roman Empire, this chapter will trace the long decline and destruction of the western Roman Empire and the gradual disintegration of the eastern Byzantine Empire.

As we shall see, Germanic peoples and Eurasian nomadic invaders made massive incursions into Europe and western Asia, destroying the western portion of the Roman Empire. This opened the way for a new civilization in western Europe during the Carolingian era and the Middle Ages. At the same time, in the eastern portion of the Roman Empire, the Byzantines fashioned a durable imperial government and a distinctive tradition in art and literature. Eventually, however, their empire also manifested symptoms of internal decay.

Beginning in Arabia in the seventh century, Islam rose to prominence among the major religions of the world. Unlike the Huns and other destructive invaders, the Mus-

lims were agents of constructive change. Like Christianity, Buddhism, and the other great faiths, Islam shaped not only the spiritual but also the temporal lives of its millions of adherents, from India to Spain. In the process Muslims spread their own culture and assimilated elements of Greco-Roman culture, which they later transmitted to western Europe.

Political, Religious, and Social Unrest in Palestine: 63 B.C.E. to 73 C.E.

What has become of that great city, the metropolis of the Jewish people, with its protective walls and forts and towers, bursting with war materials and thousands of defenders? The city we thought God had founded? It has been destroyed root and branch, and now the only sign of its existence is the camp of the enemy that destroyed it. A few hapless old men sit and weep by the ashes of the temple precinct; a few women kept alive to sate the lust of the enemy. Who among us in this situation could bear to look on the sun's light any longer, even if he could himself live in safety? Who among us is such an enemy of his fatherland, such a coward, such a

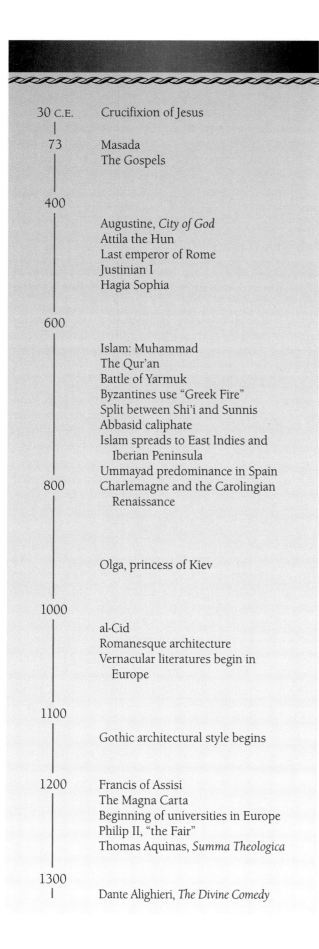

30 C.E.	Crucifixion of Jesus
73	Masada
	The Gospels
400	
	Augustine, *City of God*
	Attila the Hun
	Last emperor of Rome
	Justinian I
	Hagia Sophia
600	
	Islam: Muhammad
	The Qur'an
	Battle of Yarmuk
	Byzantines use "Greek Fire"
	Split between Shi'i and Sunnis
	Abbasid caliphate
	Islam spreads to East Indies and Iberian Peninsula
	Ummayad predominance in Spain
800	Charlemagne and the Carolingian Renaissance
	Olga, princess of Kiev
1000	
	al-Cid
	Romanesque architecture
	Vernacular literatures begin in Europe
1100	
	Gothic architectural style begins
1200	Francis of Assisi
	The Magna Carta
	Beginning of universities in Europe
	Philip II, "the Fair"
	Thomas Aquinas, *Summa Theologica*
1300	
	Dante Alighieri, *The Divine Comedy*

lover of life, that he does not regret being alive to see all this? We should all have died rather than see that holy city sacked by enemy hands, that sacred temple so ruined and profaned. We cherished the noble hope of avenging the city. Since that hope has now left us, let us hurry to die honorably. Let us show mercy to ourselves, our wives, and our children, while it is still in our power to do so. For we and our children were fated to die; even the fortunate cannot escape death. But nature does not impose on men the necessity of bearing disgrace, slavery, and the sight of our wives and children shamefully treated; such things come to those who refuse to avoid them by seeking death. . . . Let us die unenslaved; as free men with our children and wives, let us depart this life together.*

*B. Niese, ed., Flavii Iosephi opera, vol. 6: De bello Judaico libri vii (Berlin: Weidmann, 1895; reprinted, 1955), trans. James P. Holoka.

This passage is from a speech given to Jewish rebels by their leader, Eleazer, at the fortress of Masada in 73 C.E. Aware that the besieging Roman army is about to break through the fortress's defenses, Eleazer encourages his men to cheat the Romans of their victory. The next day some 960 rebels and their families committed suicide rather than be killed or enslaved by Roman soldiers. This stunning act of defiance marked the last gasp of a revolutionary movement intended to throw off Roman overlordship.

This section will examine the remarkable political, social, and religious conditions of life in Palestine during the century and a half leading up to the failed revolt. This was a crucially important era both for the subsequent history of the Jews and Judaism and for the new world religion—Christianity—that now entered the stage in Palestine.

Palestine under Roman Rule

The direct Roman control of Palestine that Pompey the Great had instituted in 63 B.C.E. was loosened during the reign of King Herod the Great. With Rome's backing, Herod seized power and held it throughout a long reign (37–4 B.C.E.) during which Palestine enjoyed peace and prosperity. His new port city of Caesarea Maritima and his lavish reconstruction of the Temple of Solomon are symbols of the affluence the small Jewish nation enjoyed under Herod. In the latter part of his reign, however, Herod was preoccupied with issues of dynastic succession that led him to monstrous acts such as the execution of members of his own family and the slaughter of the infants after the birth of Jesus (Matthew 2:16–18).

After Herod's death, the Roman authorities divided his kingdom among his sons. This arrangement did not last long, however, and beginning in 6 C.E., the various parts of the Jewish state again began to come under the

✴ Masada: This nearly impregnable fortress near the Dead Sea was one of several refuges originally built by Herod the Great in nearly inaccessible places. Held by rebel forces in 73 C.E., it fell to a Roman army after a six-month siege and the mass suicide of its defenders. The Romans finally took the site by constructing a massive earthen ramp.

© Baron Wolman/Woodfin Camp

direct authority of Rome as the province of Judaea. Roman prefects, including Pontius Pilate (26–36) familiar from the New Testament, and then imperial officials known as procurators ruled the province. These Roman administrators often behaved brutally toward the Jewish population and tolerated massacres of Jews by Greek-speaking inhabitants of the province. These abuses led to uprisings by various militant Jewish groups who used guerrilla tactics in hopes of regaining their freedom.

The subversive and terrorist activities of political resistance groups, especially the Zealots and the Sicarii or "dagger-men," as the Romans called them, eventually caused Rome to take decisive action. The Roman generals (and later emperors) Vespasian and his son Titus led a force of 60,000 troops into the province and crushed the rebellion in a bitterly fought war that resulted in the capture of Jerusalem and the destruction of its great temple in 70 C.E. Some few pockets of resistance, such as the fortress of Masada near the Dead Sea, were rooted out by 73.

The failure of their revolt and the loss of their temple as a central religious and political focus caused the Jews

to be scattered around the eastern Mediterranean and even farther afield in a dispersal known as a Diaspora. The character of Jewish life altered profoundly. In these new circumstances, Jewish leaders called rabbis began to place greater emphasis on observance of religious and social customs in Jewish communities. Essential to preserving and teaching these customs was the Talmud, a multivolume encyclopedia of Jewish religion. It had been orally accumulated over several centuries in Palestine and Babylonia, receiving final codification early in the sixth century C.E.

Religious Ferment

Reflecting in part these dramatic changes in political life in Palestine under Roman rule, various religious factions emerged within Judaism or became more sharply defined. These groups are familiar from the Christian Gospels and from the writings of the historian Flavius Josephus (born Joseph Ben Matthias), a Jew and Pharisee who became the protégé of the Flavian emperors, Vespasian and Titus.

The Pharisees were mainly laypeople of various social classes and occupations. They espoused adherence to the Torah (law) in every aspect of life, though they allowed for some flexibility in interpretation of the law. They also stressed prayer, fasting, and the paramount importance of ritual purity. They believed that a savior or Messiah would come to lead their nation against the forces of unbelievers and looked forward to an afterlife with God after the resurrection of the dead.

The Sadducees were a much more socially exclusive party; they belonged to aristocratic families whose members often served as priests. They did not, however, have the same degree of popular approval as the Pharisees, from whom they differed in several key doctrinal matters. For example, the Sadducees did not accept the comparatively new doctrines of resurrection of the dead and an afterlife. Along with the Pharisees, they had a prominent voice in the Sanhedrin (supreme religious and judicial council of the Jews). This theologically conservative party sought accommodation and peaceful coexistence with the Roman political authorities.

The Zealots advocated revolutionary overthrow of the Roman authorities so that they could establish a free nation based on their religious teachings. Like present-day fundamentalist Muslim revolutionaries, they espoused a very literal reading and strict application of the law. The Zealots and other radical groups, such as the Sicarii, escalated their acts of resistance to the point of open revolt in 66 C.E., with ultimately disastrous results for Judaea, as we have seen.

The preservation and transmission of the Jewish religious doctrines embodied in Mosaic law were the specific responsibility of a class of teachers and legal experts

Detail of the Arch of Titus. This relief sculpture from the triumphal arch erected in the Roman forum shows Roman soldiers carrying off spoils from the sacked city of Jerusalem, including the distinctive menorah, or candelabrum. Detail from Arch of Titus, Rome, © Alinari/Art Resource

known as scribes. This very honored (though unpaid) occupation drew its practitioners from all social classes and included Pharisees, Sadducees, and Zealots.

A Noble Social Experiment: The Essenes

While the Pharisees, Sadducees, and Zealots pursued their rivalries, other groups sought to opt out of the doctrinal strife and bitter political conflicts altogether. These groups withdrew to deserted corners of Judaea to form new communities where they might live according to their own utopian social and religious practices.

One of these separatist groups—the Essenes—is especially well known to us because of a sensational archaeological discovery. In 1947 an Arab shepherd came upon a cave in the hills at Qumran, a mile or so from the northwest coast of the Dead Sea. In it and several others excavated later were hundreds of scrolls written in Hebrew and Aramaic, a related dialect. The Dead Sea Scrolls and extensive archaeological remains at Qumran reveal a monastic community that had its own set of theological tenets and pursued a simple, self-sufficient existence.

The founder of the community, called the Teacher of Righteousness in the scrolls, probably lived in the mid or late second century B.C.E. Theologically, the Essenes were similar to the Pharisees in their emphasis on the law of Moses, ritual purity, and scrupulous observance of the Sabbath. Unlike the Pharisees, however, they did not believe in the resurrection of the dead. They also considered the Pharisees and other traditional Jewish groups to be corrupt and depraved and saw their own group as the one true Israel, called upon to fight under the leadership of a Messiah in an apocalyptic battle of Light against Darkness.

The scrolls indicate that initiation into the community was a three-year process, culminating in an oath that bound members to be just in their dealings with others, to be truthful, to show piety to God, and to discharge the other duties stipulated by the leaders of the sect. Baptism marked the repentance of initiates and entry into the fellowship of "God's elect."

By the time of Roman rule in the first century C.E., the Qumran community had built an aqueduct and large reservoirs to supply water, a pantry and large kitchen with five fireplaces, a pottery workshop, flour mills and ovens, living quarters, and cemeteries holding the remains of over a thousand people. Another room, where a bench, three tables, and two inkwells were found, appears to have been a writing room—a forerunner of the scriptorium of medieval monasteries. This is likely where the famous scrolls were transcribed.

New Testament scholars have studied the Essene community at Qumran in comparison with elements of Christian doctrine and the communal style of life of early Christian groups. We do not know whether the community had ties to the Zealot groups whose theological outlook was rather like their own. Though they do not seem to have shared the Zealots' enthusiasm for armed insurrection and terrorism, the Essenes suffered the same fate as other Jewish settlements, and the Qumran community was destroyed by Vespasian's legions in 68 C.E.

Palestine in the first century C.E. was a hotbed of religious ideas—reactionary, revolutionary, and conservative. In an atmosphere of political oppression, thinking Jews were wrestling with the question of whether their religious convictions could accommodate to life under Roman rule. Some thought cooperation was the best path; others, like Eleazer's rebel band on Masada, preferred death to despotism. And for many, the best hope for salvation—both political and spiritual—seemed to lie in the coming of a savior or Messiah. Christianity was born in these conditions.

These are the rules by which they shall judge at a Community Court of Inquiry . . . :

If one of them has lied deliberately in matters of property he shall be excluded from the pure Meal of the Congregation for one year and shall do penance with respect to one quarter of his food. . . .

If any man has uttered the Most Venerable Name even though frivolously, or as a result of shock or for any other reason whatever, while reading the Book or praying, he shall be dismissed and shall return to the Council of the Community no more. . . .

Whoever has deliberately lied shall do penance for six months. . . .

Whoever has borne malice against his companion unjustly shall do penance for . . . one year; and likewise, whoever has taken revenge in any matter whatever.

Whoever has spoken foolishly: three months.

Whoever has interrupted his companion while speaking: ten days.

Whoever has lain down to sleep during an Assembly of the Congregation: thirty days. . . .

Whoever has spat in an Assembly of the Congregation shall do penance for thirty days.

Whoever has been so poorly dressed that when drawing his hand from beneath his garment his nakedness has been seen, he shall do penance for thirty days.

Whoever has guffawed foolishly shall do penance for thirty days. . . .

Whoever has gone about slandering his companion shall be excluded from the pure Meal of the Congregation for one year and shall do penance. But whoever has slandered the Congregation shall be expelled from among them and shall return no more.*

This passage from the Dead Sea Scrolls illustrates the rigorous rule under which the Qumran community lived. Like Calvin's followers in sixteenth-century Geneva (see Chapter 9), members of the sect believed that those chosen to be among the elect by God had to live up to much higher standards than those of other, more conventional believers. The regulations laid down here would have satisfied the strictest monastic orders of medieval Christianity (see the discussion later in this chapter).

*Geza Vermes, *The Dead Sea Scrolls in English*, 2d ed. (Harmondsworth: Penguin, 1975), pp. 82–84.

Early Christianity

Two cities have been formed by two loves: the earthly by the love of self, even to the contempt of God; the heavenly by the love of God, even to the contempt of self. The former, in a word, glories in itself, the latter in the Lord. For the one seeks glory from men; but the greatest glory of the other is God, the witness of conscience. . . . In the one, the princes and the nations it subdues are ruled by the love of ruling; in the other the princes and the subjects serve one another in love. . . . The one delights in its own strength, represented in the persons of its rulers; the other says to its God, "I will love Thee, O Lord, my strength."

*Augustine, *The City of God*, trans. M. Dods (New York: Random House, 1950), p. 477.

Augustine wrote these words in the final days of the Roman Empire in the west. From the vantage point of an eminent Christian man of learning, he contrasts the earthly city of humanity—most fully realized in Rome itself—with the heavenly city of the Christian God. As the empire of Rome began to show signs of its mortality, many of Augustine's contemporaries also turned their eyes toward visions of more enduring, timeless realms of spiritual truth and divine love. This section describes the rise and ultimate victory of the Christian religion within the Roman Empire.

The Origins of Christianity

The old Greco-Roman polytheism continued as the official creed of the Roman state during the imperial period. Beginning with the deification of Julius Caesar, the ruler cult expanded the roster of deities, as the Roman Senate voted divine honors for successful and popular emperors after their deaths. In fact, however, a conglomeration of religions had begun to replace the traditional Roman religion during the late republic. As we have seen, mystery religions in honor of Bacchus and Cybele had won enthusiastic followings in Italy by the second century B.C.E. By 100 C.E. the cults of the Persian god Mithras and the Egyptian goddess Isis, among others, had attracted many believers and begun to replace the old religion in the hearts of Roman citizens. Though new to the Roman world, these mystery religions had roots in the distant past of ancient West Asia; their elaborate initiation rituals satisfied deep-seated desires for unity with the deity. The worn-out rituals of Greco-Roman polytheism could not match such powerful inducements to belief.

Amid the Jewish religious fragmentation of the first century C.E., an itinerant Jewish preacher, Jesus of Nazareth (c. 6 B.C.E.–c. 29 C.E.), inaugurated a new religion, Christianity. Many Jews who embraced this faith believed that Jesus was the Messiah (anointed one or savior) whose coming was frequently alluded to in the Old Testament. The Book of Ezekiel, for example, prophesied that a future prince of the house of David would bring salvation to the Jews at the time of the final destruction of the world. Under first Seleucid and then Roman rule, many Jews looked with great expectancy for the coming of an earthly savior who would destroy their oppressors and establish the preeminent power of Israel.

Jesus, however, directed his followers' hopes away from this world toward an otherworldly realm. His teaching emphasized the imminent "coming" of the kingdom of God, a new age of love and justice under God's reign. To prepare for God's kingly rule, men and women were enjoined to love God and their fellow human beings. Like Buddha, Jesus was an "enlightened one." As Buddha had spent forty-nine days and nights in meditation and temptation by demons (see Chapter 3), so Jesus spent forty days and nights in the wilderness, where he fasted and was tempted:

> Jesus was then led by the Spirit into the wilderness, to be tempted by the devil. For forty days and nights he fasted, and at the end of them he was famished. The tempter approached him and said, "If you are the Son of God, tell these stones to become bread." Jesus answered, "Scripture says, 'Man is not to live on bread alone, but on every word that comes from the mouth of God.'" . . .
>
> The devil took him next to a very high mountain, and showed him all the kingdoms of the world in their glory. "All these," he said, "I will give you, if you will only fall down and do me homage." But Jesus said, "Out of my sight, Satan! Scripture says, 'You shall do homage to the Lord your God and worship him alone.'" Then the devil left him; and angels came and attended to his needs. (Matthew 4:14, 8–11, Revised English Bible.)

Although Jesus respected the Jewish scriptures, he opposed the Pharisees on matters of Sabbath observance, food laws, and ritual purity. He also believed the priestly Sadducees had corrupted the temple at Jerusalem for personal gain. Jesus' popularity with the masses, who "heard him gladly," and his ties with some Zealots caused the recently established Roman authority in Judaea to perceive him as a threat. When Jesus arrived in Jerusalem, Roman and Jewish officials arrested, tried, convicted, and crucified him as an agitator.

After Jesus' death, his followers announced he had risen from the dead and was the long-awaited Messiah (in Greek, *Christos,* "anointed one"). Their dynamic preaching of Jesus' story added large numbers to their ranks. Converts underwent ritual baptism; this rite and the common meal of bread and wine (the Eucharist or Lord's Supper) became central ceremonies of Christian observance.

A Jewish convert to Christianity, Paul of Tarsus (c. 3–c. 67 C.E.) carried the new faith to Greek-speaking non-Jews in a series of extensive missionary journeys in Asia Minor, Greece, and Rome. He represented Jesus as a dying and resurrected savior-god who taught that sin so alienated humans from God that only God's grace could save them. According to Paul, God had offered that grace through the life, death, and resurrection of Jesus the Christ.

Paul, who has been aptly called "the apostle to the Gentiles [non-Jews]," was the only first-century partisan of the Christian faith to leave a substantial written legacy. His letters constitute one-fourth of the New Testament, and the Book of Acts is a detailed account of his career. Paul also established numerous Christian churches in Asia Minor and the eastern Mediterranean. He was executed by the authorities in Rome in the time of Nero.

As the new religion attracted large numbers of adherents, Roman authorities abandoned their usual policy of religious toleration. The first recorded persecution of Christians took place after a terribly destructive fire in the city of Rome in 64, when Nero tried to curb rumors blaming him for the disaster by pinning responsibility on the Christians in the city. He imposed horrible penalties, including burning people alive, a common punishment for arson. Before the third century, however, there was no consistent empirewide policy of persecution. Provincial governors only sporadically enforced the laws against Christianity. For instance, when Pliny the Younger wrote to ask Trajan what should be done about persons accused of being Christians in his province of Bithynia, the emperor answered, "No hard and fast rule may be set down. They are not to be hunted down; if they are brought before you and convicted, they should be punished. Nevertheless, anyone who denies he is Christian and verifies it by supplicating our gods should be pardoned accordingly, however suspicious his past life" (Pliny, *Epistulae,* book 10, no. 97, trans. James P. Holoka). With few exceptions, Trajan's rather enlightened policy was adhered to until the mid-third century. Whatever persecutions did occur tended to enhance Christianity's appeal.

Christianity competed effectively with the mystery religions in the Roman Empire in part because of its literature and its organization. Certain lives of Jesus (the Gospels or "good news"), letters by missionaries like Paul, and accounts of Christian teaching were eventually collected in the New Testament, which was joined to the body of Jewish scriptures, termed the Old Testament, to create the Christian Bible. Christian organization early showed a remarkable diversity of specializations, including prophets, teachers, healers, and administrators. Committees composed of elders—members distinguished for

After these [executions in the amphitheater], on the final day, they brought in Blandina and a boy named Ponticus about fifteen years old. These two had been made to watch the torments of the other martyrs on previous days. The authorities tried again to constrain them to swear allegiance to their idols, and the mob was enraged by their stubborn refusal to do any such thing. Thus, they ignored the tender years of the boy and did not balk at torturing a woman. They proceeded to put them through the whole course of brutal torments, but could not make them swear allegiance to their gods. Encouraging and assuring Ponticus was his sister, as the pagans [believers in traditional Greek and Roman deities] all witnessed; thus strengthened, he courageously bore the torture and surrendered his spirit in death. Blessed Blandina, kept to the last, counseled her children like a virtuous mother and sent them triumphant to meet the Lord their King. She then eagerly went forth to the same torments her children had suffered, actually glorying in her death as if she were attending a wedding feast and not herself being feasted on by wild animals. She was whipped, torn by beasts, burned by iron, and finally put in a basket and gored by a bull, which savaged her for some time, though she was now unconscious and quite impervious to the pain, thanks to her faith and adherence to her instruction and her communion with Christ. Thus when Blandina was sacrificed, the pagans all granted that no woman had ever endured so many and such awful torments.*

This passage from the church historian Eusebius describes a particularly savage persecution that took place at Lyons in Gaul in 175–176 C.E. The Roman Empire had been suffering from barbarian invasions and an outbreak of a virulent plague; consequently, a kind of mass hysteria, uncontrolled by an incompetent provincial governor, may explain the brutality of the attacks on Christians. The amazement and sometimes even sympathy of pagans who witnessed the uncanny poise and staunch faith of their Christian victims are common motifs in many biographical accounts of early martyrs. As the Christian writer Tertullian (c. 160–c. 240) put it, "the blood of the martyrs [those killed for their faith] is the seed of the church."

*Eusebius, *Ecclesiastical History,* vol. 1, ed. Kirsopp Lake (Cambridge: Harvard University Press, 1926), book 5, chap. 1 (trans. James P. Holoka).

their faith and maturity—regulated the activities of each local congregation, while its religious services were conducted by a presbyter (priest or minister). Where several congregations existed in the same city, they came to be supervised by a higher official, the bishop.

The Triumph of Christianity

By the late third century, Christianity had become an increasingly divisive factor in the Roman world. While many were attracted to Christianity for its apparent stability, order, and morality, others blamed it for sapping the empire of its strength by diverting the interest and loyalty of its citizens away from their civic responsibilities. Persecutions became more frequent and widespread. The most notable was begun by Diocletian in 303 and accelerated by his successor, Galerius (reigned 305–311). Churches were destroyed, and Christians, especially bishops and other leaders, were hunted down and executed. Sacred scriptures were burned, and church holdings seized.

The status of Christianity in the Roman Empire changed with startling suddenness during the fourth century. In 311, on his deathbed, Galerius recognized the failure of his religious policy and issued an Edict of Toleration, permitting Christians to practice their faith and rebuild their churches. Constantine, influenced by his mother's devout Christian faith and a prebattle vision of a Christian cross ("In this sign you will conquer") confirmed this toleration by his Edict of Milan in 313, which also restored confiscated Christian properties. He also granted the Christians special favors such as lands and buildings, tax exemptions for their clergy, and permission for their bishops to act as imperial judges. Constantine perhaps envisaged Christianity as a new imperial ideology that could provide unity to a sadly battered empire. Later emperors followed and extended his pro-Christian policies, until by the end of the fourth century Christianity and Judaism were the only legal religions in the empire.

Besides the crucial factors of sincere belief in the Christian God and imperial encouragement of that belief, we may note four reasons for Christianity's final victory over competing faiths and fearsome persecution. First, it was simple in its demand for absolute allegiance, brushing aside the welter of alternative religions and requiring a single, irreversible commitment to one creed. It offered permanent values at a time when political and spiritual absolutes were fast disappearing from the Roman horizon.

Second, it was equalitarian. Like the Hindu *Upanishads,* which ignored barriers of caste and other differences among believers (see Chapter 3), Christianity stressed the value of every individual soul. It was open to any and all, from the lowest slave (even female slaves) to the emperor. Every soul could be saved, regardless of ethnic origin or social status: "There is no question here of

✼ Mosaic from the Tomb of Galla Placidia. This fifth-century mosaic in Ravenna shows (left) bookshelves with texts of the four Gospels. Because Christianity emphasized the good word of Jesus' life and teachings, a new, more easily consulted and durable book form—the codex—replaced the older *volumen* (papyrus roll). The compact codex (about ten by seven inches) usually consisted of vellum (calfskin) or parchment (goatskin) sheets bound together as in a modern book. Constantine had fifty copies of the Christian scriptures written on vellum for the churches of Constantinople. Scala/Art Resource

Greek and Jew, circumcised and uncircumcised, barbarian, Scythian, slave and freeman; but Christ is all, and is in all" (Colossians 3:11, Revised English Bible).

Third, Christianity held out the hope of a better life in the world of the heavenly city. This was a compelling enticement when the foundations of the earthly world of the Roman Empire were shaking. Though various mystery cults similarly promised immortality, in the case of Christianity the courage and equanimity of the martyrs who endured torturous deaths lent credence to the notion that true believers would gain eternal bliss in the presence of their God. "I am the resurrection and the life. Whoever has faith in me shall live, even though he dies; and no one who lives and has faith in me shall ever die" (John 11:25–26).

Finally, Christianity satisfied the universal need to belong. Founded on the injunction to "Love thy neighbor," the Christian community shared a value system and manner of living as well as a body of ritual. Persecution only strengthened this bond, as the church assumed the responsibility of caring for its own in a hostile environment, ministering to the indigent and sick, supporting orphans and widows, and supplying a source of self-respect in the lives of thousands of urban poor. Such activities, which

were foreign to Greek and Roman religious expression, made the believer's earthly life more tolerable and meaningful, even in the face of adversity, quite apart from the prospect of a life after death.

As the Christians became preeminent in the empire, they devoted increasing attention to defining their beliefs. Ironically, efforts to make simple and clear formulations of the tenets of Christian belief often produced only complexity, confusion, and conflict. Special councils were held to resolve disagreements. From the Council of Nicaea in 325 emerged the distinctive Christian doctrine of the trinity and a definitive statement of essential beliefs of the Christian faith, the Nicene Creed.

The writings of the church fathers also helped to clarify Christian dogma. Jerome (c. 348–420) mastered Greek and Hebrew and produced a Latin translation of the whole Bible known as the Vulgate (common or ordinary), because it used an everyday style of language. His translation remained standard for a thousand years.

The greatest church father was Augustine (354–430). As a teacher of rhetoric, he had explored most Roman beliefs and enjoyed many of life's pleasures before embracing Christianity. His *Confessions* recounted the sinfulness—particularly sexual sins—of his earlier life and

✤ Christian Communal Meal. This third-century wall painting in the Catacombs of Saint Callixtus depicts the miracle of the loaves and fishes as a prefiguration of the Christian "love feast," or eucharistic meal. This shared Sunday meal commemorated the Last Supper and demonstrated one's membership in the community of the Christian faithful. Scala/Art Resource

the importance of God's grace to his rehabilitation. In his *City of God,* written shortly after the Visigothic sack of the city of Rome in 410 (see the next section), Augustine argues that the destruction of the Roman Empire may be part of God's plan and that humans ought to give their permanent allegiance not to the empire but to the city of God.

Some Christians practiced a rigorously disciplined religious life called monasticism and formed communities of monks and nuns, organized in much the same way as the Buddhist *sangha,* though with greater hierarchic stratification and centralized control than in Buddhist orders. Typically, they vowed themselves to poverty, sexual abstinence, and obedience to superiors. Their day was divided into periods for physical needs such as eating and sleeping, prayer and meditation, study, and, in the Latin west, work. Such communities speeded the Christianization of the countryside, contributed new models for spiritual leadership, and preserved much of classical civilization while transforming it to serve Christian purposes.

The papacy also developed during the period between 300 and 500. Archbishops in the empire's major cities became known as patriarchs. Although there were several patriarchs in the east, in the west there was only one, the patriarch of Rome, also called pope (from Latin *papa* or "father"). The Roman popes asserted that Jesus had granted jurisdiction over the whole church to the apostle Peter (Matthew 16:16–19), later the first bishop of Rome. The popes claimed that they, as successors of Peter, were the heirs of that authority. This claim caused bitter conflicts in the Roman Empire's Greek-speaking eastern portions. In the Latin-speaking west, however, where no other patriarch existed, papal claims to authority were enforced by a decree that required all bishops in the western Roman Empire to accept them. The following section will describe how the papacy became a symbol of Christian unity in the west as the Germanic migrations nullified the political power of the Roman emperor in that area.

Upheaval and Transition in Western Europe

WAITING FOR THE BARBARIANS

What are we waiting for, packed in the forum?

> *The barbarians are due here today.*

Why isn't anything going on in the senate?
Why have the senators given up legislating?

> *Because the barbarians are coming today.*
> *What's the point of senators and their laws now?*
> *When the barbarians get here, they'll do the legislating.*

Why did our emperor set out so early
to sit on his throne at the city's main gate?

> *Because the barbarians are coming today*
> *and the emperor's waiting to receive their leader. . . .*

Why have our two consuls and praetors shown up today
wearing their embroidered, their scarlet togas? . . .

> *Because the barbarians are coming today*
> *and things like that dazzle barbarians.*

And why don't our distinguished orators push forward
as usual to make their speeches . . . ?

> *Because the barbarians are coming today*
> *and they're bored by . . . public speaking.*

Why this sudden bewilderment . . .
(How serious everyone looks)?
Why are the streets . . . rapidly emptying,
everyone going home so lost in thought?

> *Because . . . the barbarians haven't come.*
> *And some people just in from the border say*
> *there are no barbarians any longer.*

Now what's going to happen to us without them?
The barbarians were a kind of solution.*

*C. P. Cavafy, *Selected Poems,* trans. E. Keeley and P. Sherrard (Princeton: Princeton University Press, 1972), pp. 6–7.

In this poem, the Greek author Constantine Cavafy (1863–1933) imagines the state of mind of Romans in the twilight of their empire, as ancient ways of living were giving way before the force of new peoples and new patterns of life. It was, of course, a frightful process, but the Roman Empire had, by the fifth century, lost its strength and its ability to guarantee a secure life for its inhabitants. In this sense, the "barbarians" were, as Cavafy's poem suggests, "a kind of solution" both politically and culturally in the history of western Europe. This section will describe the fall of Rome and the rise and triumph of the various states that replaced it in western Europe, in particular, the Carolingian Empire.

The Fall of the Roman Empire in the West

After the death of Constantine in 337, the Roman Empire struggled unsuccessfully to resist the submersion of its western half under waves of Asiatic and Germanic invaders and immigrants. The Huns, fast-moving horsemen from the steppes of Asia, provided one catalyst of change. Related to the Hsiung-nu who harassed Han China and the Huna or "White Huns" who invaded India, they pushed into central Europe to the north of the Roman Empire and later, under their king Attila, raided into the empire itself. In the process they displaced many of the German tribes living outside the empire; the Germans in

❋ Map 5.1 German Invasion Routes. This map shows the avenues of invasion and immigration followed by the various Germanic tribes that finally overwhelmed the Roman Empire's defenses beginning in the late fourth and early fifth centuries.

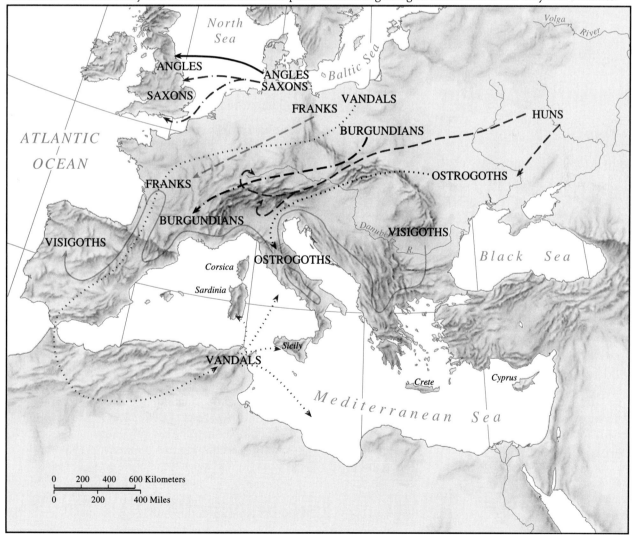

The Roman Tax Collector— "Like a Wild Beast"

What a terrifying individual [the tax collector] could be is nicely illustrated in . . . the *Life of St. John the Almsgiver*. . . . The Saint is represented as thinking about the dreadful monsters he may meet after death, and the only way he can adequately express the appalling ferocity of these wild beasts is to say that they will be "like tax-collectors." Certainly, tax collection from the poor in Roman times was not a matter of polite letters and, as a last resort, a legal action: beating-up defaulters was a matter of routine, if they were humble people. . . . In [Roman-controlled] Egypt . . . local officials would seize taxpayers whom they alleged (rightly or wrongly) to be in default, imprison and ill-treat them, and, with the aid of soldiers and local levies, burn down their houses. . . . According to [the historian] Ammianus [Marcellinus], an Egyptian in the late fourth century would blush for shame if he could not show on his back scars inflicted by the tax-collector's whip.*

O ne aspect of the economic crisis of an empire that had to support a bloated bureaucracy and a huge military machine was an unfair system of taxation. The rich were often able to evade taxes, while the poor were at the mercy of relentless government officials and tax collectors. In this respect at least, the replacement of Roman authority by Germanic states actually brought relief to many of the empire's inhabitants.

*G. E. M. de Ste. Croix, "The 'Decline and Fall': An Explanation," in Donald Kagan, ed., *The End of the Roman Empire: Decline or Transformation?* 3d ed. (Lexington, Mass.: Heath, 1992), p. 58.

their turn, desiring a more settled existence in the fertile cleared land to the south, poured into the Roman Empire. Emperors perished in battle, large tracts of land were successively ceded or stripped away, and finally Rome itself was sacked in 410. In 476, the last western emperor was deposed by the German leader Odoacer, who became the first barbarian king of Italy (reigned 476–493). The once brilliant light of Roman power in the west flickered out as Visigoths and Ostrogoths, Franks, Burgundians, Vandals, and others divided the territories of the old western empire.

Ancient and present-day scholars have offered various responses to the question of what caused the fall of Rome. Those who emphasize decay from within point to economic crises caused in part by the bloated imperial bureaucracy and the financial strain it placed on an empire whose inhabitants were overtaxed and decimated by

plagues, poverty, and declining birthrates. Some believe Christianity, with its emphasis on the heavenly kingdom of God, discouraged the patriotic virtues that had sustained Rome in earlier days; similarly, the later Han Chinese dabbled in escapist Taoism and otherworldly Buddhism. Others cite a loss of traditional Roman moral values as non-Italians and even barbarians gained prominence within society, the civil administration, and the ranks and officer class of the army. Soil exhaustion, protracted drought, the gradual poisoning of the aristocracy by lead water pipes and lead-containing food storage and cooking vessels, and slavery as an impediment to technological advance are still other causes of decline that scholars have suggested, some more plausibly than others. However, many of these weaknesses also affected the eastern half of the empire, which did not collapse.

The best explanation for the fall of the Roman Empire in the west is the intensified barbarian pressure directed against defense forces spread thin by the great length of the Rhine-Danube frontier. This pressure had been felt since the second century, but as Germanic migration steadily increased in the late fourth and throughout the fifth century, insupportable demands were placed on the military and financial resources of the western half of the empire, where the economic and social structure had long been crumbling.

The Germanic States of Western Europe

In contrast to the Byzantine and Islamic institutions of imperial government and urban life, Germanic society featured family and tribal structures in a rural setting. German families who owned or held land were subject to military service and tax assessment. They sometimes lived in isolated farmsteads, but more often clustered together in villages. The tribe or people was the aggregate of all persons who lived under the same law, fought in the same army, and recognized a common king. Germanic tribes were patriarchal, and women, on all levels of society, had subordinate roles.

Tribes contained free persons, slaves, and half-free persons later known as serfs. Slaves became less common as settled life replaced migration and raids to capture slaves became less frequent. Also, over time many individuals rose out of slavery to become half-free, while free persons fell to half-free status under the protection of noble lords. The half-free had to remain on the land they worked, but were not another's personal property. The merchants, clergy, and nobles became the only fully free persons. Nobles maintained their status by intermarrying and collected benefits and privileges from Germanic kings.

Most Germans depended on agriculture for their livelihood. In the great plains of northern Europe, where rainfall was generally plentiful and the seasons moderate, the heavy, wet soil produced two crops per year. However, poor, locally made tools and lack of fertilizer kept crop yields low, until a heavy plow came into wider use after the sixth century. Because their only method of restoring soil fertility was to let land lie idle, the Germans needed large areas to support relatively few people. They usually settled in small, densely populated communities widely separated from one another, in which all members cooperated in necessary agricultural activities.

The rulers of these scattered peoples retained and modified traditional features of Germanic kingship. Kings moved beyond the status of tribal chiefs by becoming successful war leaders who conquered and ruled territories, not merely people. They gave gifts to loyal followers, just as the war bands had formerly divided booty. The kings maintained the tribal laws and settled disputes between free persons, while lords judged disputes among their serfs and slaves. The kings now embodied the tribe's common origin and history, and their succession came to depend on dynastic (family) right rather than individual right.

Germanic rulers also incorporated Christian and Roman elements into their government structure. They used Latin in royal documents and law codes and adopted the biblical practice of anointing the king at accession. Under the church's guidance, kings regarded their subjects as Christians and defense of the faith as one of their royal tasks.

In contrast to the Byzantine and Islamic Empires described later in this chapter, the Germanic peoples of western Europe had difficulty controlling their own territories and were harassed by warlike neighbors. Large

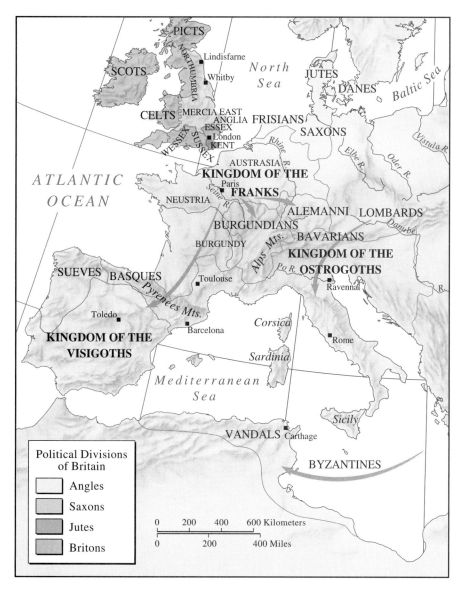

✤ MAP 5.2 Germanic States in Europe. Major German states about 500 are shown here; arrows indicate important German advances after that date.

landed estates dominated agricultural activity and sought economic self-sufficiency. While trade dwindled and towns decayed, the only significant international institution, the church, became the heir of much of the Roman cultural tradition.

The Triumph and Disintegration of the Carolingian Empire

Out of the preceding patterns of Germanic life, one people, the Franks, rose to prominence under the leadership of a dynamic ruler, King Clovis (reigned 481–511). Instead of separating Romans and Germans, Clovis chose to merge them by requiring both peoples to do military service and permitting intermarriage. Clovis's baptism as a Roman Catholic Christian shortly before 500 separated the Franks from the other Germans, who were Arian Christians. The Franks championed Roman Catholic orthodoxy against the Arians (heretics who denied that the Father and the Son "are of the same substance") and won the support of the Christianized Roman aristocracy of Gaul. The Roman Catholic clergy supplied Frankish kings with educated advisers and other benefits, such as the flattering legend that the Holy Spirit had descended directly from heaven for Clovis's baptism. The Byzantine emperor later designated Clovis an honorary consul.

The German custom of dividing property among all of a deceased father's sons meant that the sons of Frankish kings often fought among themselves to gain control of all the territories of their father. Successive generations of Clovis's descendants followed this process, weakening the monarchy and allowing the Frankish nobles to aug-

ment their political power and to assimilate royal lands and wealth.

In the eighth century, the Carolingian family (from the Latin *Carolus*, for Charles) took control of the Frankish monarchy. The leading Carolingian monarch was Charles the Great, better known as Charlemagne (reigned 768–814), who expanded the Frankish kingdom to include most of present-day France, Belgium, the Netherlands, and Luxembourg, and portions of Germany, Italy, Switzerland, and Spain. Most of this territory was wrested from the Franks' German neighbors and some of it from Muslims in Spain (see the Islamic section of this chapter) and Asiatic tribes from central Eurasia.

The Carolingians were able to amass their empire because they had created the most effective armed forces in western Europe. Usually enjoying a decisive numerical advantage over their opponents, Carolingian armies consisted primarily of well-armed and highly disciplined infantry, supported by smaller groups of cavalry; the soldiers wore helmets and coats of mail and were armed with swords and spears.

Under Charlemagne the Carolingian Empire was transformed into a restored Roman Empire. When Pope Leo III was hounded from the city of Rome by his enemies, Charlemagne marched to Rome and restored the pope to power. A few days later, on Christmas Day in the year 800, the pope crowned Charlemagne emperor of Rome, thus bestowing prestige beyond that of any other German ruler. Although the pope's actions were motivated mainly by gratitude for Charlemagne's aid, the coronation was clearly intended to cast a Roman aura on the Frankish monarch. The pope deliberately used the

✠ Baptism of Clovis. In this artistic re-creation of the historic event, bishops on the left and nobles on the right witness the ritual. Above the king, a dove, representing God's Holy Spirit, descends with oil for the ruler's anointing.
Bibliothèque Nationale de France, Paris

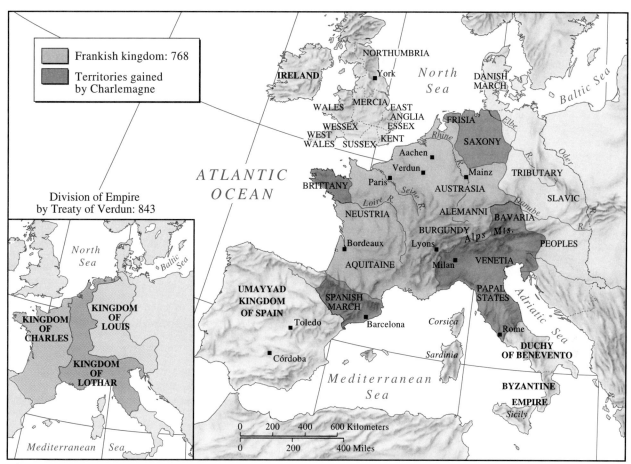

❋ MAP 5.3 The Carolingian Empire. Shown here are the boundaries of the Frankish kingdom before 768 together with surrounding territories acquired during the reign of Charlemagne. The inset shows the division of the Carolingian Empire among Charlemagne's grandsons.

Roman titles emperor and Augustus, together with the Byzantine procedures of patriarchal coronation and popular acclamation. Charlemagne, rising from prayer and crowned by God, probably reminded many of Constantine, the first Roman emperor to become a Christian, by whose authority the pope claimed to act. The idea of Rome as the model of a universal state would persist in the notion of a Holy Roman Empire down to 1806.

At the center of the Carolingian state was a reorganized royal household that included officials supported by the extensive lands held by the royal family. Lacking money, the kings paid their officials with land grants and exemptions from both taxation and visits by royal administrators. Such grants were also made in return for military service, especially service by mounted warriors who required land to maintain themselves and their horses. As deteriorating clan and tribal organizations ceased to provide customary protection and services, many warriors became personal and economic dependents of noble landowners.

Carolingian dukes had the responsibility for governing large frontier areas known as marches. Counts, who administered smaller areas (called counties) in accordance with local custom, were the essential personnel of Carolingian administration; each count served as the king's governor and military commander in one province, assisted by a viscount and one or more judges. To prevent the counts from building up their power at royal expense, they were required to make frequent public declarations of loyalty and were assigned to areas where they had no personal connections. The monarchs also sent inspectors to review and when necessary correct the counts' activities. In addition, the kings strictly prevented the counts from passing on their offices to their children. Hampering royal control, however, were an insufficient number of counts and supervisors and slow long-distance communications. Strong kings could crush rebellions of counts and dukes, but under weak kings, the nobles sometimes became independent. Nevertheless, Carolingian administration was fairly stable. Although there were differences, the

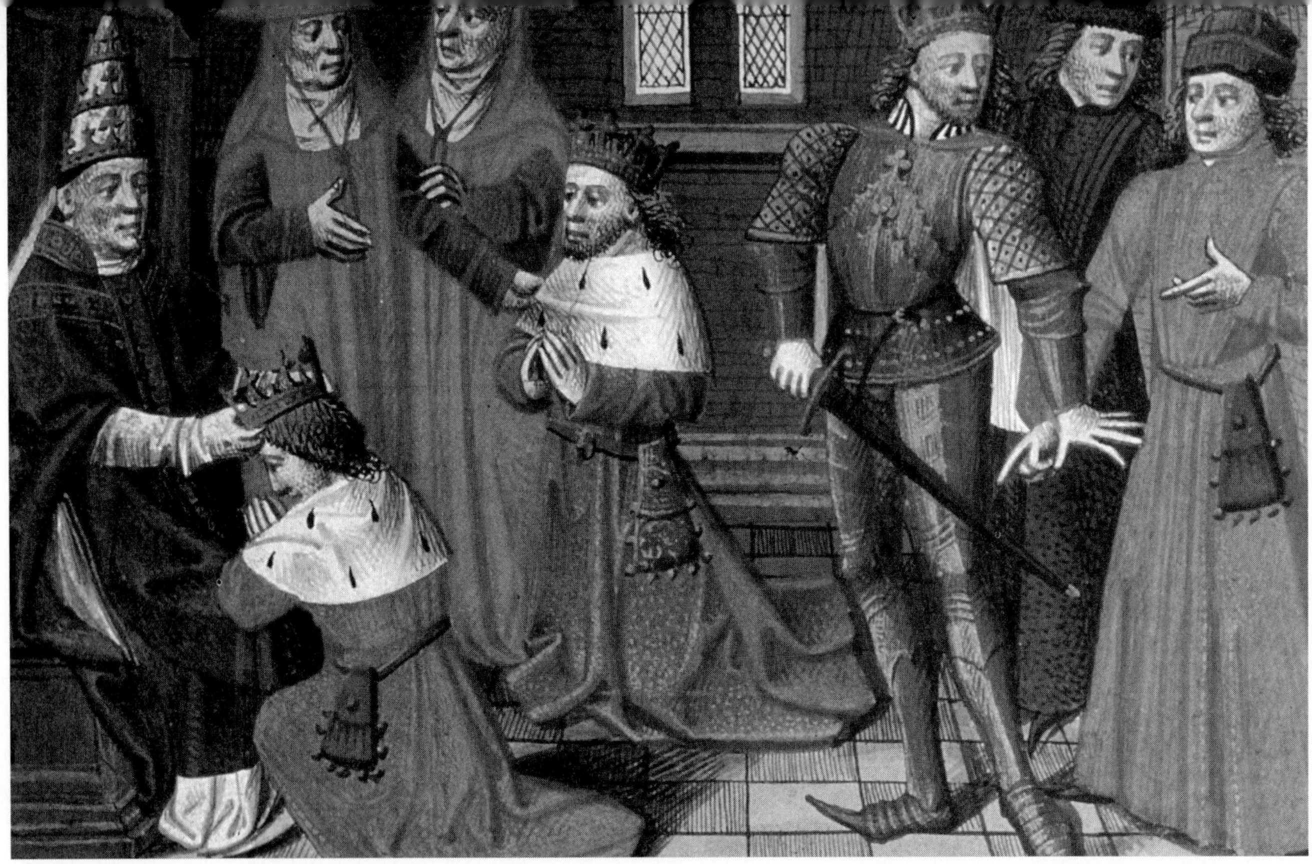

⚜ The Coronation of Charlemagne. According to some contemporary writers, the coronation was an unwelcome surprise to Charlemagne, although it clearly required advance preparation and apparently had the monarch's approval. Giraudon/Art Resource

political system established by the Carolingians in many ways resembled the feudal order reputedly established by early Chou kings of China.

Charlemagne owed his success to broad support from church leaders and laity, an effective army, and the weakness of his enemies. However, only a powerful ruler able to enforce loyalty and obedience could manage the weakly unified Carolingian state. Charlemagne's successors lacked that ability, and during the ninth century, the Carolingian Empire disintegrated. Charlemagne's son, Louis, divided his empire and the crown lands among his sons upon his death in 840, thus precipitating a series of civil wars that broke up the empire. Out of the collapse emerged what became a French monarchy and a German monarchy. The nobles, however, increasingly disregarded any central authority and enlarged their own power by in effect dividing the kingdoms into large territorial principalities, further eroding the remnants of Carolingian royal government. Such developments are reminiscent of what happened in China during the late Chou dynasty.

Religious and Cultural Developments in Early Western Europe

In an increasingly Germanized western Europe, the Christian church faced numerous problems as it assumed the moral, spiritual, and cultural leadership formerly exercised by the Roman Empire. Disappearance of Roman rule in the west deprived the church of imperial support, and the expansion of Islam reduced the territory of Christendom. Furthermore, the Greek and Latin churches developed different beliefs, practices, and forms of organization. Superstition, violence, and immorality characterized popular life; most people only vaguely understood or followed Christian teachings. Religious leadership frequently fell to uneducated and morally lax priests and to bishops better qualified to wield political power than to provide spiritual guidance.

The church responded to these problems on a number of fronts. It infused its ideas of justice and mercy into codes of law, maintained schools and hospitals, and assisted widows, orphans, and slaves. Monasticism, although introduced to the west before 500, was reformulated by Benedict of Nursia (reigned 480–547). He wrote a moderate and humane rule of life for monastic communities based on study, prayer, and physical labor.

To counter the luxury, sexual laxity, and disregard for authority that afflicted some of the clergy, Benedict required vows of poverty, chastity, and obedience, and submission to the absolute authority of an abbot. Pope Gregory I (reigned 590–604) wrote a *Life of Benedict* and promoted the spread of Benedictine monasticism in Europe. Monks and nuns following the Benedictine rule won converts to Christianity and instructed those converts in basic Christian belief and practice.

The other prominent Christian institution, the Roman papacy, gained increasing significance, primarily through the efforts of Gregory I. By adroit land management and

Food for Buddhist and Christian Monks

Buddhist monks and nuns were strictly forbidden to eat meat. In addition, on specified days they had to fast after the noonday meal. On special occasions such as the Buddha's birthday and other days of religious significance or secular celebrations, vegetarian banquets were held at temples for both clerics and laypeople.

Between 838 and 847, a Japanese monk named Ennin traveled and studied in China and kept a detailed diary of his stay. Ennin described a feast for about 750 participants, including monks, nuns, men, women, and children at a famous temple at Mount Wutai. All received equal portions, with seconds given on request. Although he did not describe the dishes, we gather from other sources that some of them were fashioned to resemble the forbidden meat dishes. Even today Buddhist restaurants in Chinese communities serve "chicken," "meat," and "fish" made from soybeans.

At about the same time, in the Europe of Charlemagne, monasteries complying with the Benedictine rule of life also featured a menu that seems rather ascetic by modern standards. Monks took only one daily meal in winter and two in summer. Although meat (especially pork, beef, mutton, venison, and poultry) was eaten in some monasteries on special feast days, for the most part the menu was vegetarian. The typical meal consisted of three dishes of dairy products such as cheese, vegetables, and bread or a kind of grain porridge that served as the principal staple of the diet. The members of more austere monasteries restricted themselves to barley bread (often mixed with ashes), gruel, and vegetables, with even poultry and fish forbidden. On Sundays the great treat consisted of a little cheese thinned with water.

---

shrewd negotiations with Byzantines and Lombards (a Germanic people who had settled in Italy), Gregory made the papacy financially and politically independent. His *Book of Pastoral Care* helped the clergy perform their duties effectively. He also worked to convert German kings from Arianism and in 597 sent missionaries to England, which in 664 agreed to follow the Roman observance. The Roman hierarchy was aggressive in converting the German and Slavic peoples of central Europe and the Irish, thereby providing western Europe with religious unity.

Ireland became an important center of early medieval cultural and religious activity. Its conversion to Christianity, traditionally attributed to Patrick (389–461), a Roman citizen educated in Gaul, opened the island to continental influences. Irish monasteries became centers of intellectual activity; each had its *scriptorium* (writing room) for the essential work of copying both Christian and classical manuscripts in excellent clear handwriting and elaborate decorative calligraphy. The Irish copyists also developed the art of illumination (painting brightly colored pictures on manuscripts).

England's conversion to Roman Catholic Christianity stimulated an outburst of literary productivity. The Old English epic of the eighth century, *Beowulf,* recounts the hero's slaying of monsters and a fire-breathing dragon. Although composed in the Germanic heroic tradition, the poem is altruistic in spirit, and it may have been intended as a Christian allegory.

As part of their responsibility for the Christians in their realm, the Carolingian rulers reorganized the administration of the Frankish church, restored old bishoprics and established new ones, and vigorously upheld Latin Christian theology against its challengers. Pepin (the founder of the dynasty) and Charlemagne enriched Frankish monasteries and restored them to compliance with the Benedictine rule. The monasteries in turn provided scribes and advisers for royal service. Charlemagne also devised a broadly conceived program for peacefully introducing Christianity among the pagan Saxons and Slavs.

Believing that the quality of the clergy determined the quality of spiritual life, Charlemagne promoted both classical and Christian education, mandating, for example, a teacher of grammar for each cathedral and a teacher of theology for each archbishop's cathedral. Monastic schools concentrated on the liberal arts, and a special palace school was established for educating the sons of Frankish nobles. Scholars whom Charlemagne recruited for this school built a collection of classical writings that preserved and made available earlier knowledge.

Charlemagne stimulated monasteries to become active centers for producing accurate, hand-copied manuscript books, including the Bible, manuals for the conduct of worship services, and the Benedictine rule for monks, which would form the basis of monastic reforms during the next several centuries. The monks also produced manuscripts of classical writers as well as of church fathers. More than 8,000 Carolingian manuscripts still exist, and over 90 percent of surviving Roman literature was passed on to later ages through Carolingian manuscripts. This outburst of intellectual and literary activity is sometimes termed the Carolingian Renaissance (rebirth).

Magical Practices in the Carolingian Era The Last Day of the Roman Empire

Maleficia [sorcery/witchcraft] appeared in many forms. It could impede the growth of another's grain by magic powers . . . or incantations. It rendered a neighbor's cattle sterile or brought harm on others through making knots in a dead person's girdle. Love potions to excite a husband's passion or attract a lover were made from sperm, menstrual blood, and aphrodisiac plants. . . . Bones of the dead, cinders and ashes, hair, pubic hair, different colored strings, various herbs, snails and snakes were used in *maleficia,* sterilizing potions, and abortifacients.

By far the most popular magical practices were those designed to protect and cure. Prisoners seeking to be free of their bondage, or peasants who feared that their horses would injure themselves, all recited the formulae preserved in Germanic texts. Sick children were carried to the peak of the roof while medicinal herbs were cooked to the recited incantations. Amulets and phylacteries [protective charms] endowed with particular characteristics were sold to anyone who wanted their protection. . . . Models of human limbs were hung from trees or placed at crossroads to procure the healing of an arm or leg. . . . Divination was practiced . . . by . . . paying heed to the direction of smoke, or examining the excrement or liver of animals, climbing to the rooftops, interpreting dreams or opening books at random. . . . Some of the manuscripts which the monks copied carry the magical squares which predicted the course of an illness by combining the letters of the victim's name and the number of the day on which he fell ill.*

The belief in the efficacy of magic or sorcery is both ancient and stubborn. Even in the face of official disapproval (and sometimes active persecution) by civil and religious authorities, many people have always tried to mobilize magical powers to their own benefit or to the detriment of others. The Carolingian Empire, despite its Christian allegiance, was no exception to this sort of activity.

*Pierre Riché, *Daily Life in the World of Charlemagne,* trans. Jo Ann McNamara (Philadelphia: University of Pennsylvania Press, 1978), pp. 184–185.

Crucifixion of Christ. Ornate animals and use of curving lines for decoration typified much Germanic art. Here, the Greek letters *alpha* and *omega* hang suspended from the cross's arms to recall Jesus' words, "I am the beginning and the end." A bird representing the Holy Spirit perches atop the cross. Bibliothèque Nationale de France, Paris

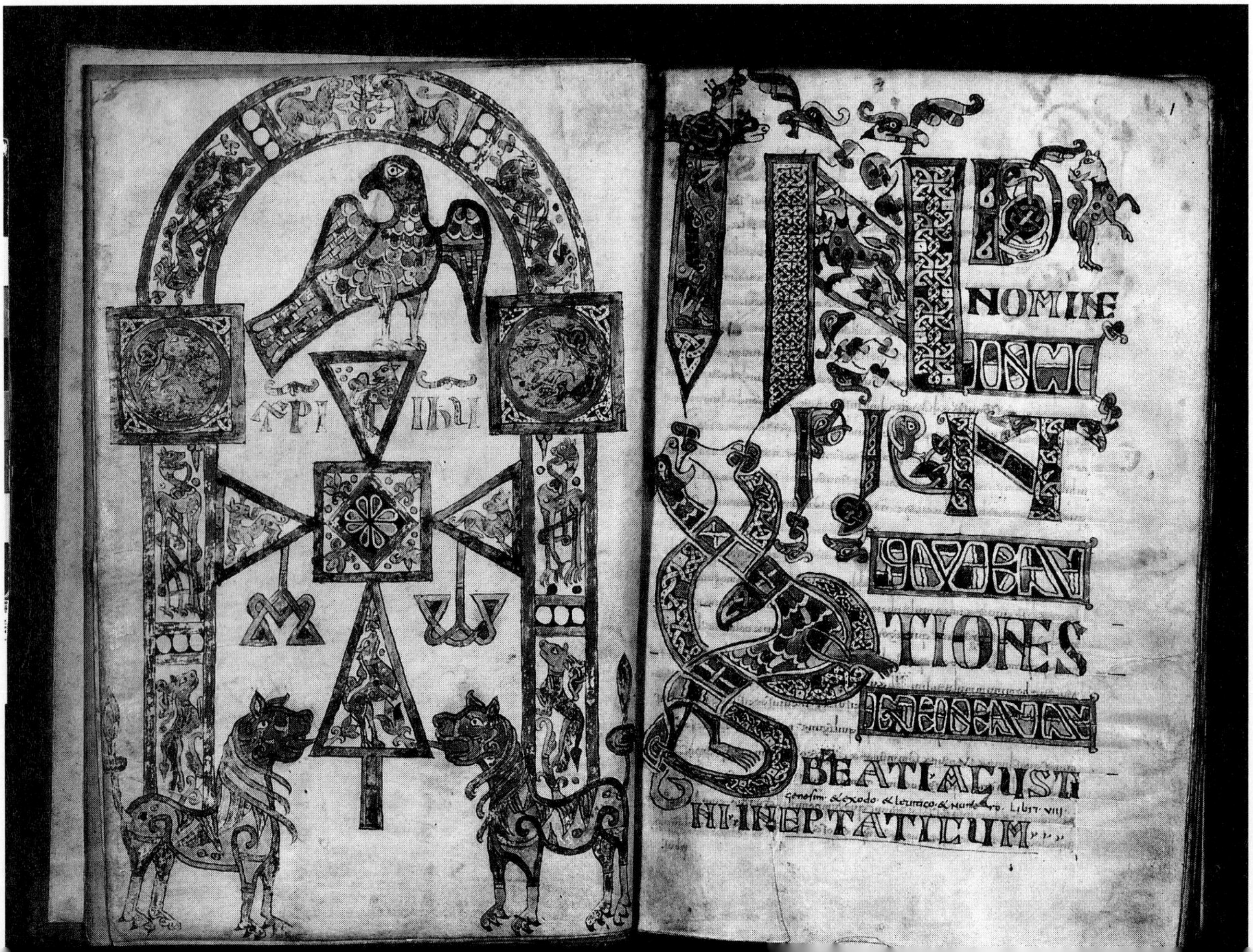

The grim demon was called Grendel, a notorious ranger of the borderlands, who inhabited the fastnesses of moors and fens. This unhappy being had long lived in the land of monsters, because God had damned him along with the children of Cain. . . . From Cain were hatched all evil progenies: ogres, hobgoblins, and monsters, not to mention the giants who fought so long against God. . . .

[Beowulf] stood upright and gripped Grendel so tightly that the talons cracked to bursting. The monster fought to escape but Beowulf closed with him. . . . The hall thundered with the hubbub. Every one of the Danes who lived in the stronghold, soldiers and chieftains alike, was seized with extreme panic. . . . A stupendous din went up. Pure terror laid hold of the Danes, and of everyone outside the hall who heard the howling; the dreadful scream of God's adversary wailing his defeat; the prisoner of hell bellowing over his wound. He was fast in the clutch of the strongest man alive.*

Beowulf, the subject of the only native English heroic epic of the Middle Ages, has many of the characteristics of the pagan heroes of Germanic tradition. As is clear in this passage, however, he is also cast as the champion of God in a struggle against the forces of evil; the heinous, half-human Grendel (and later his mother) are "adversaries of God" and not merely monstrous freaks of nature like, for example, some of the opponents that Herakles subdued.

*David Wright, trans., *Beowulf* (Baltimore: Penguin, 1957), pp. 29, 44–45.

Carolingian art, like literature and education, evolved from religious activity and employed late Roman and contemporary Byzantine models and techniques. For example, books priests used to conduct worship services were beautified by illuminations, consisting of separate pictures, elaborately decorated book or chapter titles, or large initial letters using traditional Germanic art forms of animals and interlaces. Builders of Carolingian churches usually followed the Roman basilica style, occasionally roofing the atrium to form a porch or adding an enclosed prayer room above the atrium. The architects of Charlemagne's chapel at his capital city of Aachen copied Byzantine imperial models to produce an octagonal building symbolizing the emperor joining together earth and heaven with divine aid; Justinian's church of Hagia Sophia at Constantinople served a similar symbolic purpose. Paintings on church walls generally made little use of scriptural themes and human forms in order to avoid the appearance of idolatry.

Europe under Siege: A New Wave of Invaders

As the Carolingian Empire disintegrated in the late ninth century, the face of Europe was transformed by new waves of invaders. The Magyars and Vikings produced widespread destruction and disrupted existing institutions and patterns of living. Amid the resulting disorder, successful resisters to those attackers began to establish new social, economic, and political patterns and to form new centers of European development.

Invited from western Asia by the Byzantines to aid in war against the Bulgars, the Magyars, nomadic ancestors of modern Hungarians, occupied the Hungarian basin of the Danube by 900 and soon were raiding Italy, Burgundy, and other Frankish and Germanic territories.

Another group of invaders, Vikings from Scandinavia, raided widely throughout Europe. Their motives included a desire for plunder, dislike of increasing royal authority in Denmark, Norway, and Sweden, overpopulation, climate change, and sheer love of adventure. The Norwegians raided and established settlements in western England and Ireland. Danish Vikings attacked lands on both sides of the English Channel. They conquered the eastern half of England and also seized land at the mouth of the Seine River in Francia, which became the nucleus of the duchy of Normandy. Well might western Europeans pray "From the fury of the Northmen, O Lord, deliver us." Swedish Vikings crossed the Baltic and worked their way southward across Russia on the extensive north-south river systems, reaching Persia and Constantinople via the Caspian and Black Seas, respectively. They became so numerous that the Latin name *Rus* (for ruddy) that distinguished them from the resident Slavs came to be applied to the entire land and all its people.

The Vikings also sailed westward across the North Atlantic and in 874 settled in Iceland, establishing the oldest continuously functioning democratic community. Erik the Red, an exile from Iceland, landed on the island of Greenland, and settlements of Europeans soon followed. In 1000, Erik's son Leif sailed farther west and briefly occupied Vinland, probably northern Newfoundland. As royal authority and Christianization increased in Scandinavian lands during the tenth century, the great age of Viking expansion ended.

The absence of effective imperial power in the disintegrating Carolingian Empire left local leaders to develop

✤ Viking Ship. This ninth-century vessel could carry approximately forty men. Although shallow of draft, these ships were quite seaworthy, carrying Viking raiders across the seas, along the coasts, and up the rivers of Europe. Culver Pictures

their own responses to the invaders of the ninth century. In England, Viking raids and English resistance combined to produce a united monarchy. The Danes destroyed all of the Anglo-Saxon kingdoms except Wessex, where King Alfred the Great (reigned 871–899) effectively combated the Vikings at sea and fortified and garrisoned towns as defensive strongholds. Gradually, Alfred gained authority over Anglo-Saxon lands in the west of England that had escaped Viking rule. By gathering scholars from various lands, he revived literature and learning in England, creating a solid basis for its future development.

In Italy, independent towns, grown prominent as Carolingian authority waned, led the resistance to Magyar and Muslim invaders. Within these towns, bishops became the principal leaders, building town fortifications and collecting tolls and other monies to pay for them. The bishops secured powers and privileges from kings and exercised control of urban defenses, revenues, and courts. Powerful bishops and strong, independent cities continued to play important roles in subsequent centuries of Italian history.

In the eastern regions of the empire, where Carolingian rule was recent, earlier German tribal divisions reemerged in five large duchies, areas dominated by dukes who seized royal lands and powers and controlled the churches in their districts. When the last Carolingian

ruler died in 911, the dukes chose one of their number as king to validate their rights and titles to land and to coordinate common defense measures. In the face of persistent Magyar invasions, an able, new dynasty of Saxon rulers (919–1024) emerged to reassert royal authority over the land, which became known as Germany.

In the Carolingian Empire's western areas, the invasions accelerated the decentralization of government, as counts and other nobles, who offered the only meaningful opposition to the invaders, acquired lands and goods and usurped royal authority. Although Carolingian kings continued to rule, by 987, when the last of the line died without heirs, his sexual impotence mirrored the political impotence of the monarchy. In their place, aggressive local lords exercised warfare and defense responsibilities and managed royal courts and revenues.

Feudal Relationships

As Carolingian government deteriorated, nobles seeking to provide protection and administer justice combined two well-established Carolingian practices—the personal relationship of vassalage and the landed relationship of benefice or fief—in a set of relationships, new in the West, called feudalism (from Latin *feudum,* "fief"). In vassalage a free man (the vassal) proclaimed his dependence on and faithfulness to another free man (the lord) and promised to serve him, usually militarily. The lord, in return, granted the vassal useful possession, but not ownership, of land called a benefice or fief. Similarly, in China under the Chou dynasty, lords contributed both revenues and homage to the kings and received in return confirmation of their social status and of their fiefdoms.

Counts and dukes held their lands as fiefs of the king, lesser nobles held their estates as vassals of counts or dukes, and they in turn granted smaller fiefs to their own vassals. Hence the same person might be the vassal of a greater lord and the lord of lesser vassals. Thorny complications arose when vassals held fiefs from different lords who became enemies. A woman had no property rights, and if, as sole survivor, she inherited lands or money from her father, the property became her husband's.

The personal pledges and obligations between lords and vassals theoretically ended when one of them died, but in practice sons normally assumed the loyalties and duties of their fathers. Typically, a vassal owed not only his own personal military service, but often also that of additional knights from his own estates. In addition, he was expected to serve in the lord's court of justice and to feed and house the lord and his traveling companions when required. Vassals also helped to raise a ransom if their lord was captured and gave the lord money on the occasion of the knighting of his eldest son, the marriage of his eldest daughter, and the succession of a son to his father's fief. In return, the lord provided the vassal with military protection and justice through his court.

At first nobles held large estates, whereas lesser vassals, often termed knights, held few if any lands; the nobles led armies into battle, whereas knights followed and obeyed. As time passed, the knights gradually gained extensive lands, privileges, and jurisdictional rights. As they married into old noble families, eventually a single aristocracy was formed.

In theory, lesser lords and vassals were armed and trained as warriors to preserve the privileges of communities and maintain the safety of the church, but in practice, most fought to acquire land and wealth or for the sheer joy of fighting. The armed and mounted knights dominated offensive warfare. Defensive warfare centered on castles, the nobles' fortified homes, which had evolved by the twelfth century into structures built of stone.

Europe in the Middle Ages

Society is divided into three orders. The ecclesiastical order forms one body. The nobles are the warriors and the protectors of churches; they defend all the people, great and small. The unfree is the other class. This unfortunate group possesses nothing without suffering. Supplies and clothing are provided for everyone by the unfree because no free man can live without them.

Therefore the city of God which is believed to be one is divided into three; some pray, others fight, and the others work. These three groups live together and could not endure separation. The services of one of them allows the work of the other two. Each, by turn, lends its support to all.*

*Adalberon, "Carmen ad Rotbertum regem," in Robert Boutruche, Seigneurie et féodalité (Paris: Aubier 1959), pp. 371–372, trans. in Norton Downs, ed., The Medieval Pageant (Princeton: Van Nostrand, 1964), p. 93.

This description, written about 1000, reflects the traditional medieval view of European society as an unchanging interrelationship of three orders or estates. (The terms medieval and Middle Ages refer to the conventional Western division of history into ancient, medieval, and modern.) Although it accurately described many aspects of medieval society, this view did not take into account a number of important changes that were underway, changes that would dramatically move Western society away from this three-class division. The present section examines developments in Europe in the period between 900 and 1350.

Economic and Social Changes in the Countryside

From 1000 to 1300, the economy of Europe developed and prospered. Available farmland tripled, and the food supply increased notably, enabling the population to increase as well. Europeans resettled lands that had been depopulated by the ninth- and tenth-century invasions and also opened new lands for farming, especially forested and marginal areas, those east of the Elbe River in central Europe, and lands conquered from the Muslims in the Iberian Peninsula. To ensure productivity, medieval farmers adopted the three-field system of cultivation in which only a third (rather than half) of the land lay fallow (to restore fertility) during the year. Technological improvements, including the heavy plow, the shoulder collar for horses, metal horseshoes, and more efficient water and windmills, contributed to the jump in the food supply. Between 500 and 1300, Europe's population grew from 25 million to more than 70 million.

During the fourteenth century, however, Europe's economic and demographic growth underwent a sharp reversal. The climate became colder and rainier, causing harvests to shrink and prices to soar. War seemed to be waged almost constantly during this period, and ravaging armies destroyed crops, barns, and mills. Famine became a fact of life. Adding to these troubles, bubonic plague

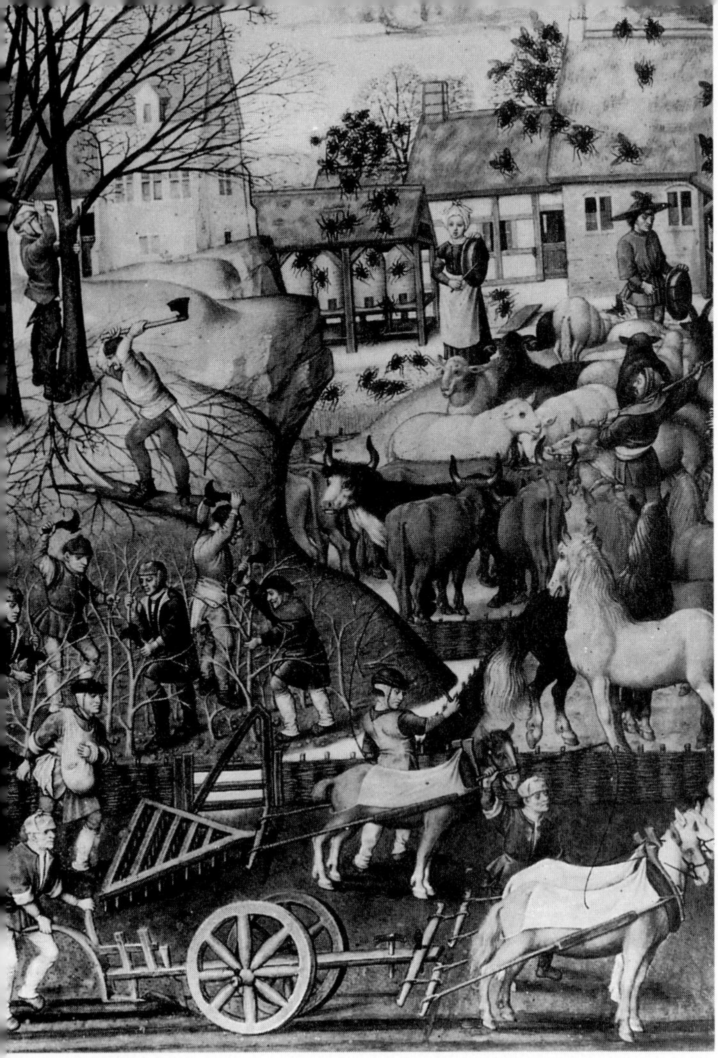

Village Scene. Animals and agricultural workers led a busy existence in a medieval village. At the upper left are wood gatherers. At the bottom, horses fitted with shoulder collars unwillingly draw a heavy-wheeled plow, mainstay of medieval farming, and a harrow is followed by a planter who spreads seeds from the bag slung over his shoulders. Fotomas Index

(the "Black Death") ravaged the population. Between 1348 and 1354, perhaps one-third of all Europeans died as the plague spread, in the words of one contemporary, "like fire when it comes in contact with large masses of combustibles." The population did not fully recover until about 1600.

Whether times were easy or hard, peasant farmers and their life pattern constituted the core of medieval society. Most of the farming people of Europe lived in villages ranging in size from ten to several hundred peasant families. The villages were located on manors, units of political governance and economic exploitation controlled by ecclesiastical establishments or by secular nobles. The manors were organized so that they would contain enough villages to produce nearly everything needed by their lords.

A manor's workforce consisted primarily of families of serfs, semifree persons linked to the lord and to the land who could not be sold away from their lands. Their village was a cluster of huts surrounded by fields. Each family was assigned several plots or strips, some on the more fertile and some on the less fertile land available to the village. On these plots each family produced food that it used for its own consumption, for barter, and for paying tithes to the church and dues to the lord. Also near the village would be pasture where plow animals, sheep, and cattle grazed and a wooded area where the peasants gathered fuel and building materials and pigs foraged. Usually, the village was located near a stream that supplied fish and powered the water mill. Typically, a village contained none of the schools, hospitals, or other amenities sometimes found in medieval towns. The parish church was the center of activity, where villagers celebrated religious holidays, baptisms, and marriages; in the churchyard they found their final resting place. Church bells provided the only timekeeping most people knew, and feast days marked the year's seasons.

Each farm family retained about half their own produce after paying the lord a percentage of the crop for the use of the pasture and woods and fees for the use of the lord's mill and oven. The lord also collected payments when a serf's son inherited his father's holdings or when a serf's daughter married outside the manor. Moreover, the church collected its tithe (10 percent). Serfs also performed labor services for the lord, working his land, repairing roads, or carrying firewood.

By 1300 some lords, seeking to attract workers to bring new lands under cultivation, offered milder terms of service to peasants and improved the working conditions of their serfs. Some freed them from labor obligations in return for cash payments and allowed them to pay rent in money rather than crops. On occasion, lords granted peasant communities charters that freed them from performing the obligations of serfs and permitted them to pay their dues collectively rather than individually. As wages and prices rose in the west during the fifteenth century, manorial lords sought to increase their cash incomes by raising cattle or sheep or growing commercial agricultural products such as dyestuffs, which required fewer laborers and gave high returns for low costs. Thus, by 1500, most western European peasants were no longer serfs owing labor and goods to their lords but renters who had traded the security of serfdom for the freedom to earn money or to lose it along with their livelihood. The gradual waning of feudalism in western Europe resembles what happened in China during the late Chou dynasty.

While western European peasants were enjoying greater freedom, eastern European peasants were losing what freedom they had. The lords in that area preferred to grow grain for export to western Europe and took advantage of fourteenth- and fifteenth-century wars and other upheavals to acquire large landholdings. They enforced manorial obligations and imposed serfdom even upon formerly free peasants.

In the west, meanwhile, freedom proved to be a mixed blessing, as lords sought to wring maximum rents from their tenants. Moreover, the ravages of war and the taxes of monarchs fell most heavily on peasants, since clergy and nobles were largely exempt from royal taxation. Peasant discontent with the status quo sometimes exploded into rebellions, which were easily defeated by regular armies. Still, the peasants' grievances persisted and reappeared to trouble later lords and rulers.

The Growth of Trade and the Development of Towns

European commercial activity expanded dramatically from the tenth through the fourteenth century. Whereas early medieval trade had largely been conducted by local merchants who exchanged perishable items and local commodities for salt, wine, and metals in village markets, by the eleventh century long-distance trade had begun to revive.

Descendants of Viking raiders now traded across the northern seas, bartering furs, timber, fish, and wax for textiles, grain, and wine. To the east, they established commercial relations with the Byzantine and Islamic Empires via the Baltic Sea and the river routes of Russia, trading for Islamic silver or Byzantine gold. By the thirteenth century, Germans had replaced Scandinavians as the primary merchants of northern Europe. The northern trade was primarily in staples: grain, butter, cheese, fish, timber, metals, and salt. German trading towns united in a Hansa (confederation) to preserve their dominant position in commerce.

In the ninth and tenth centuries, Italian port cities, particularly Venice, revived the Mediterranean trade. Byzantine merchant citizens in some Italian ports traded easily with both the Byzantine Empire and with the Muslims; religious differences between eastern and western Christians and between Christians and Muslims posed no obstacles when it came to commercial relations. During the eleventh century, Genoa and Pisa wrested control of the western Mediterranean from the Muslims, but by the late fourteenth century Venice had taken control of the lucrative trade with the east.

The eastern Mediterranean trade was based upon a sophisticated intercontinental commercial network. Venetian merchants exported slaves, timber, iron, and tools to the lands east of the Mediterranean and imported furs, silks, spices, and perfumes from the Byzantines and Muslims, who had brought them from India and China. For a brief time the Mongols permitted Europeans to bypass Islamic middlemen (see Chapter 8) and to trade directly with East Asia. The Venetians sold the Asian luxuries to the upper classes in western Europe and often invested the proceeds in new manufacturing establishments that were beginning to spring up in Italy.

From the northern and southern seas, trade quickly expanded inland. By the late twelfth century, merchants were moving continuously along Europe's rivers and roads, and commerce was fast displacing agriculture as the most dynamic force in European economic life. During the disastrous fourteenth century, European commercial activity faltered, as the population decline diminished markets and wars interfered with commerce.

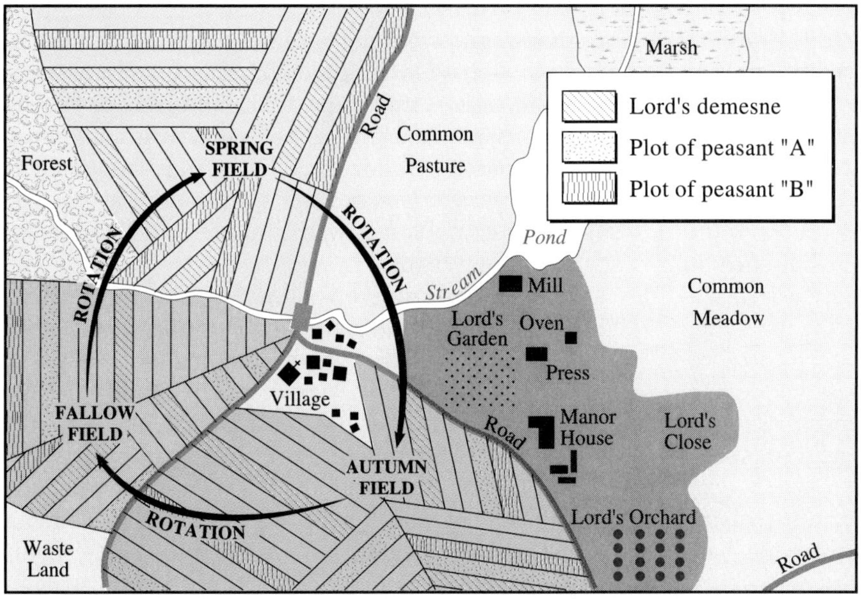

MAP 5.4 A Manor. The noble lord dominated the manor; he controlled the best land and the essential services of oven, mill, and press. The operation of the three-field system and the division of land into strips prompted villagers to work together at common tasks.

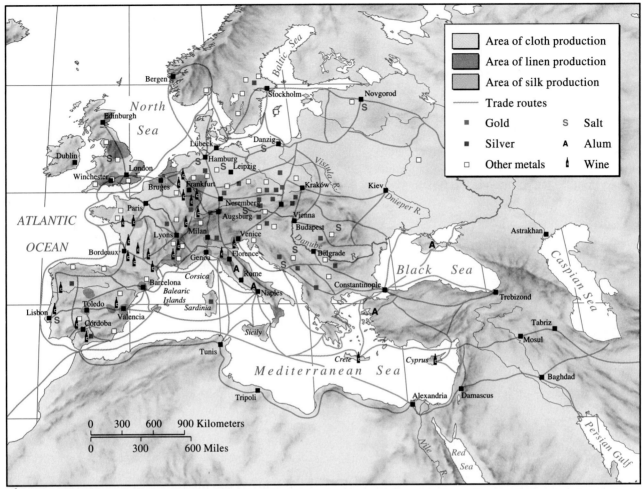

MAP 5.5 Medieval Trade Routes. By the end of the thirteenth century, trade routes covered most of western and central Europe. Vikings in early centuries and the German Hansa later controlled commerce in the northern seas. In the south, the Italian cities of Genoa and Venice dominated Mediterranean trade. Overland routes used rivers whenever possible to reduce transportation costs. In eastern Europe, however, trade routes were few, and the economy remained primarily agricultural.

Manufacturing developed later than trade in western Europe. Medieval "manufacturers" were typically artisans who produced goods in their own shops and sold them directly to the public. Both the construction industry and the textile industry, however, employed workers and developed complex systems of organization during the medieval period. Members of the building trades found employment erecting churches and public buildings in the growing towns and cities. As many were wage earners and owned neither the materials nor the tools they used, they resembled factory laborers. Some entrepreneurs, especially in the textile industry, used a "domestic" system in which they distributed raw materials to and collected finished products from workers who labored in their homes rather than in a factory.

Expanding agricultural productivity and increasing commercial activity sparked a growth of town life. Various forms of the German word *Burg* ("fortress")—burg, bourg, or borough—came to apply to the town, whose inhabitants were called burghers, later known as the bourgeoisie. Compared to the countryside, towns displayed a volatile juxtaposition of individuals and groups in close quarters. Besides merchants and artisans, there were free peasants, runaway serfs, and ambitious younger sons of lesser nobles, as well as masters and students at schools or universities.

Medieval cities and towns were small by present-day European standards. A substantial eleventh-century trading city, such as Bruges, might have had only 5,000 inhabitants. Towns grew with commerce, and by 1300 several Italian cities had 100,000 inhabitants each; Venice had 200,000. Elsewhere, Paris had a population of 80,000, London half that. The Black Death struck cities exceptionally hard, killing up to half of their inhabitants.

As the new elements in medieval society, town-dwelling merchants and manufacturers had to struggle to obtain acceptance for their activities, which did not fit the traditional concept of the three estates. To obtain freedom from servile and burdensome tax obligations, they sought charters from the local lord of the land. A lord might grant a charter for a money payment, but sometimes towns had to defeat lords in battle to obtain such documents. A charter usually provided the town's inhabitants freedom from servile obligations, typically permitting them to hold land and buildings for a money rent and forbidding the arbitrary seizure of their property. It also allowed burghers to maintain courts and make laws.

Burghers in northern Italy, whose towns were under the jurisdiction of the Holy Roman Emperor, went still further, seizing control of the cities' defenses, revenues, and courts and extending their authority over the surrounding countryside. City leaders began to develop important aspects of a new political order: corporate authority, delegated power, and representative government.

To regulate economic activity, merchants and artisans formed guilds. Merchants' guilds protected their members' interests against outsiders and secured each member a share in the trade available, generally by regulating prices and competition. Similarly, artisans set up craft guilds that supervised wages, prices, labor conditions, quality standards, and methods and amounts of production. Socially, guilds conducted banquets and sponsored religious festivals. They also saw to the proper burial of deceased members and cared for widows and orphans.

Women as well as men found economic opportunities in craft guilds. By 1300, at least 15 of 100 guilds in Paris were entirely female, including the guilds of the garment makers and workers in silk and embroidery. After 1300, however, economic activities for women were increasingly restricted or eliminated. The economic decline of German towns in the period between 1300 and 1500 was due in part to the suppression of flourishing female industries and the replacement of skilled women by unskilled men.

The Theory and Practice of Christianity

Like kings and princes who strove to create stable and effective governments, medieval religious leaders endeavored to centralize the organization and improve the quality of the medieval church. Although by 1000 the rulers of most European peoples had adopted Christianity for themselves and their subjects, the problems of ordering Christian society remained formidable. Viking and Magyar invasions had destroyed not only churches and monasteries but also ecclesiastical institutions, as monarchs converted bishops into vassals with fiefs and diverted the resources of the church to private, family, and "state" purposes.

Significant religious abuses arose from the feudalization of the church and the accompanying lay domination

The Growth of a Town

After this, because of the work or needs of those living in the chateau, there began to stream in merchants—that is, dealers in precious goods—who set themselves up in front of the gate, at the chateau's bridge; then there followed tavern-keepers, then innkeepers to provide the food and lodging for those who came to do business in the presence of the prince, who was often there. Houses began to be built and inns to be made ready, where those were to be lodged who could not be put up inside the chateau. . . . So many dwellings accumulated there that right away it became a large town.*

These words of a contemporary observer describe the beginnings of Bruges (meaning "the bridge"), one of northern Europe's foremost medieval towns. In central and eastern Europe, outside the territories of the old Roman Empire, new towns were usually founded by colonies of merchants who settled around a fortified stronghold, such as a castle or monastery, strategically located on a major trade route or at the intersection of two or more routes. Such settlers needed services that others came to provide, and settlements quickly grew into towns.

*Documents relatifs à l'histoire de l'industrie et du commerce en France: Collection de textes pour servir à l'étude et l'enseignement de l'histoire, vol. I, ed. Gustave Fagniez (Paris: Picard, 1898), pp. 54–55, trans. Carolly Erickson, The Records of Medieval Europe (Garden City: Doubleday, 1971), pp. 152–153.

of church offices. Christians frequently decried the ineptitude and immorality of the clergy, who were often ill-educated and appointed for political rather than spiritual reasons. Such appointees sought personal advancement and the control of ecclesiastical property, while taking a shallow, mechanical attitude toward religious life. Many ignored the church's rule of celibacy and either married or had sexual partners, creating further possibilities for the diversion of church lands.

By 1000, efforts to reform the church to eliminate such abuses were under way. As an alternative to local lords controlling the church, eleventh-century reformers created a centralized church bureaucracy under papal control, with its own officers, laws, and resources. By the early thirteenth century, the popes directed an extensive bureaucracy through the papal Curia; its specialized departments were staffed by well-trained clerics handling correspondence and records, finances, judicial cases, and the application of church law. Popes directly asserted their authority over lower levels of church administration either through correspondence or by special emissaries.

Execution of Heretics. Frequently, as in this thirteenth-century painting, heretics were executed by burning. At left, King Philip II of France sits on his horse. In the upper right, note the scaffold for mass hangings. Bibliothèque Nationale de France, Paris

A formidable tool for eradicating error in this period was the judicial process known as the Inquisition. Twelfth-century popes ordered bishops to conduct inquests concerning heretics within their dioceses and to punish the guilty by excommunication. Pope Innocent III added confiscation of goods and property to the punishment of heretics. The accused were denied legal counsel, interrogated by torture, and required to prove their repentance by identifying accomplices. Although some found guilty were sentenced to penance or a prison term, the Inquisition was less bloodthirsty than has been presumed; most convicted heretics were in fact put to death by the secular authorities, not by the church.

As in earlier centuries, the regimen of the stricter monastic orders such as the Cluniacs revitalized monastic discipline. Another monastic group, the Cistercian order, popularized the role of Mary, the mother of Jesus, who became the object of special devotion and veneration as the Blessed Virgin. Important religious feasts were established in her honor, and churches and cathedrals were dedicated to her. Jesus Christ's love and compassion could be secured through Mary, who would intercede on behalf of all sinners. The series of prayers known as the rosary deepened popular devotion to Mary.

Pressing religious needs in towns and cities and the threat of heresy prompted the development of mendicant (begging) orders during the early thirteenth century. Mendicant friars rejected life in monasteries and worked in the world while living under a spiritual rule. Relying on donations for the necessities of life, they made Christianity relevant to the lives of town dwellers by preaching and performing charitable deeds. Dominican friars were well educated and specialized in preaching and teaching; they subsequently joined university faculties. Dominicans energetically preached the Gospel to non-Christian Europeans and sought conversions in eastern Mediterranean lands and India.

The Franciscans, founded by Francis of Assisi (1182–1226), espoused a world-embracing joyousness; they spread rapidly throughout Europe, and some became missionaries in Syria and North Africa. They also engaged in scholarship and university teaching, forming notable centers of theological study in Paris and Oxford.

Many women, too, found religious withdrawal from the world attractive. In addition to the professed nuns, nunneries included lay sisters from peasant or artisan families who performed many menial tasks. Nunneries gave their residents both self-esteem and the respect of society. They also offered women good education and the chance to use organizational and management skills that might otherwise be wasted.

By the thirteenth century, Roman Catholicism was widely prevalent among Europeans, and the beliefs of medieval Christians formed a coherent and integrated system. They believed God was one, almighty, all-knowing, just, and merciful. The universe, created by God, was orderly, and in it human beings had a special place and destiny. By sinning, people had disobeyed God, thereby losing their original righteousness and God's supernatural grace and forfeiting their hope of heaven. Sin rendered men and women incapable of doing good by their own efforts. Therefore, God had sent Jesus Christ to redeem humans and qualify them for heaven.

As the custodian of God's grace, the church was an essential intermediary between God and the faithful. Through the seven sacraments, the church claimed to bring God's grace to all members at critical junctures of life. Baptism cleansed individuals of original sin and initiated them into the Christian fellowship. At puberty, confirmation reaffirmed young people's membership in the church and gave them additional grace for adult life. Two people might unite their lives in the sacrament of holy matrimony, or a person might "marry" the church in holy orders. Extreme unction (anointing with consecrated oil) prepared the dying for events after death. Christians could receive forgiveness from sin's consequences through the sacrament of penance. They could even receive Jesus Christ's body by partaking of the Eucharist, in which bread and wine were miraculously changed by means of the sacrificial mass into Christ's body and blood.

Saints, too, were believed to intercede with God on behalf of humans. Each town, each trade, and even each disease had its appropriate saint, and prayers and devotion to them were supposed to be especially efficacious. A lively traffic in holy relics (remains of saints and biblical figures) developed. A pilgrim to Venice about 1400 reported seeing there the arm of one saint, the staff of another, the ear of St. Paul, and a tooth of Goliath.

Pilgrimages (journeys to holy sites), although arduous and dangerous, also became increasingly popular acts of devotion and a means to secure grace. Geoffrey Chaucer's *Canterbury Tales,* written in the 1390s, vividly describes the members of such an expedition. A pilgrimage combined religious duty and holiday relaxation; hence pilgrimage routes came to be carefully arranged. Rome and Jerusalem attracted pilgrims from throughout Christendom.

The extent of popular piety, however, should not be exaggerated. The illiterate masses remained uninstructed about basic Christian beliefs and minimally involved in religious observances. Pre-Christian religious practices persisted in many places. Demons and mysterious powers were thought to fill the world and to require appeasement. Persons skilled in "white" magic, knowledgeable in healing through the judicious use of herbs and "home remedies," and able to "see" what the future had in store were in great demand.

Jews in Medieval European Life

After Rome had dispersed the Jews in the first and second centuries C.E., they settled throughout West Asia and around the Mediterranean. Life in Christian lands, certainly as compared to Islamic Spain, was difficult and often dangerous for Jews. They were excluded from most occupations, except trading and moneylending; the latter was forbidden to Christians by the church. For self-serving reasons, most Christians unreasonably believed that Jews were collectively responsible for Christ's death, were active servants of Satan, murdered Christian boys and used their blood for secret rituals, and poisoned wells and spread disease throughout the land. As a result, Christians executed, lynched, and banished large numbers of Jews. The warriors of the First Crusade massacred Jews in several Rhineland towns. The Third Lateran Council (1179) forbade Christians to live near Jews, thus spurring the growth of the ghetto, a walled section of a city in which Jews were compelled to live. European rulers in need of money exploited popular feeling by expelling Jews and seizing their abandoned property.

Beginning in the ninth and tenth centuries, the ongoing Christian reconquest of Spain forced many Jews to leave Spain in flight from both Muslim and Christian persecution. They joined meager groups of their coreligionists in southern and northeastern France and in the German Rhineland, where they established vigorous centers of Jewish life. Other Iberian Jews found refuge in North Africa and Turkey. As persecutions continued in western Europe, many Jews migrated into Poland and Lithuania, forming a major new Jewish population center there.

Feudal Monarchy in Western Europe

During the period from 900 to 1300, kings in some parts of Europe managed to replace the severely decentralized political order of the ninth and tenth centuries with more organized political structures known as feudal monarchies. The office of the king was endorsed by church and scripture, the person of the king was considered sacred, and kings continued to receive honor and prestige. Their primary functions were to provide justice and enforce the king's peace within their realms and to raise and lead national armies against external foes.

In addition, as previously discussed, feudal monarchs were overlords of the greater and lesser nobles within the system of feudal relationships, a system they exploited to extend their control. Feudal kings not only had the right to demand various services and dues in return for their grants but also to recover possession of fiefs forfeited by unfaithful vassals or lost by a vassal's failure to produce heirs.

Despite many rights and responsibilities, feudal monarchs did not have direct authority over the mass of their subjects. Under the feudal structure, monarchs had contact primarily with their chief vassals and the inhabitants of the royal family's own domains. Between the kings and the remainder of their subjects were various levels of lesser vassals, many of whom exercised the rights to wage war, coin money, and dispense justice. Feudal kings thus exercised overlordship while sharing power, rather than wielding unlimited direct authority.

Diffused government was another distinctive aspect of feudal monarchy. In the autocratic and centralized Roman and Byzantine Empires, the ruler used an extensive military and civilian bureaucracy to carry out government services. In contrast, medieval European feudal monarchs, like the Chinese feudal monarchs of the Chou era, governed through a series of relationships in which both they and their vassals personally performed essential public services, administered justice, and waged war.

Feudal monarchies lacked the resources to provide more than limited services. The king derived income primarily from the royal domains and estates he personally owned, feudal payments from vassals, fines, and monies paid by certain churches and monasteries. A council composed of the king's great vassals formally recognized a new king, furnished him with advice and counsel, and judged certain important cases in his name. Between meetings, a smaller body of officials carried on council functions. The great vassals administered local government theoretically in the name of the king, but in fact often quite independently.

The feudal monarchies had varied histories. The Holy Roman Empire, inheriting the eastern areas of the former Carolingian Empire, was an example of a feudal monarchy that failed. In the late Middle Ages, the empire was headed by a succession of German kings who engaged in a shifting power struggle with the popes. Although early German rulers succeeded in creating a strong feudal monarchy, their additional imperial responsibilities complicated the task of their successors. Emperors had duties in both Italy and Germany but usually lacked the resources to make their power truly effective in both places.

The Holy Roman Empire had little significance in European political and religious developments after the death of Frederick II (reigned 1212–1250). Although it eventually expanded to embrace an area as large as that ruled by Charlemagne, the empire itself was merely a loose union of principalities and states. The medieval ideal of an earthly empire peaceably cooperating with the church's dominions remained illusory.

In contrast, by combining features of Anglo-Saxon and Norman society, England initially became an extremely successful feudal monarchy. During long years of struggle against the Danes, Anglo-Saxon institutions gained strength and maturity, while the descendants of the Danes in Normandy developed efficient feudal governing arrangements there. After conquering England in 1066, William of Normandy fused the two sets of institutional relationships. England's small size, its lack of internal divisions, and the swiftness and thoroughness of William I's conquest made its experience unique.

During the twelfth century, royal administration became more elaborate and efficient as Henry II (reigned 1154–1189) made England Europe's best-governed state. He closely supervised royal officials and established some government departments at a permanent royal capital at Westminster, near London. Under Henry, royal law replaced a previous patchwork of local laws and customs with a common law governing all English subjects and made justice uniform as well as equitable throughout England.

During most of the thirteenth century, Henry's successors exhibited neither his ability nor his interest in government, and royal authority diminished. In 1215, the barons forced King John (reigned 1199–1216) to issue a Great Charter (*Magna Carta* in Latin). This committed kings to obtain baronial consent before levying new taxes, to administer justice according to established procedures rather than in an arbitrary and capricious manner, and to recognize and permit subjects to enjoy various rights and liberties. Later generations viewed the Magna Carta as a guarantee of fundamental human rights for all.

The reign of Edward I (1272–1307) saw the development of the English Parliament. Edward summoned barons, prelates, royal judges, administrators, knights from the shires (counties), and members of town governments to parliaments, or formal conferences, to provide advice on important issues and to support him in times of crisis. The knights and town representatives began to meet separately from the barons and thereby laid the basis for the division into a House of Commons and a House of Lords. Through the English common law and the operations of Parliament, English kings and their subjects defined their respective rights and responsibilities and forged elements of a national unity.

In France, feudal monarchy developed more slowly than in England, but eventually became a model for other European lands. The reign of Philip IV (1285–1314) brought the development of the medieval French monarchy to its apex. Philip brought additional territories under royal control and consolidated the royal system of justice by making the court of appeals (the Parlement of Paris) its center. His successful effort to tax the French clergy convincingly demonstrated how powerful and secure the French monarchy had become.

To obtain public support for his opposition to the pope, Philip created the Estates General, a parliament-like body composed of members of the three great social classes, or estates: the clergy, nobles, and townspeople. French monarchs used the body as a sounding board for royal policy and a means of stirring up support for royal decisions. However, the Estates General was never permitted to gain the authority that the English Parliament possessed. It had no power base from which to bargain with the king and never became an integral part of French government. In France, the crown remained the one great unifying concept, and nobles retained provincial or regional rather than national interests.

The failure of feudal monarchy in the Holy Roman Empire long postponed the development of national unity in Germany and Italy. By contrast, in England and France, the success of feudal monarchy, though in varying degrees, led to strong national states at a comparatively early date.

The Spiritual and Intellectual Life of the Later Middle Ages

During the eleventh and twelfth centuries, expanding royal bureaucracy, an increasingly complex ecclesiastical organization, and reviving commercial activity created a growing demand for educated persons to perform clerical and administrative tasks. Before 1000, most education in Europe had taken place in schools set up in cathedrals or monasteries. In response to the new demand, schools revised their curricula to stress study of the seven liberal arts derived from Greco-Roman civilization: grammar, logic or dialectic, rhetoric, arithmetic, geometry, astronomy, and music. By this time, a flood of new knowledge, primarily from the classical Greeks but transmitted and enlarged by Muslim and Jewish schol-

ars, had become available. As artisans and merchants had done previously, scholars organized themselves into guilds known as universities (from Latin *universitas,* meaning "guild" or "society").

The term *university* came to mean a group of scholars working in close proximity and providing a basic program of instruction in the seven liberal arts and in one or more of the higher disciplines of theology, law, or medicine. By completing the six- to eight-year program, a student obtained a master's degree and a license to teach. Bachelor's programs of four to five years' duration developed later, but they did not authorize their holders to teach. Universities were highly mobile, and relations between them and their hometowns were frequently strained and occasionally violent. Sometimes students and masters left town and established separate universities elsewhere. Gradually, wealthy patrons endowed colleges and universities with buildings and funds to pay for housing, feeding, and instructing students.

In northern Europe, the focus of study was theology, and scholars labored to improve their understanding of the Christian faith. During the eleventh century, some investigated the value of human reason in comprehending religious truth. Anselm of Bec (1033–1109), who later became archbishop of Canterbury, emphasized the use of logical reasoning in theology, even as a way to prove God's existence. Still, he ultimately subordinated reason to faith: "I do not seek to understand that I may believe, but I believe that I may understand; for this I also believe, that unless I believe I will not understand." By contrast, Peter Abelard (1079–1142) insisted that "by doubting we are led to question, and by questioning we arrive at the truth."

Scholars called "Scholastics" (because they worked in the medieval schools) responded to a challenge posed by the work of Aristotle. The most influential Scholastic thinker was Thomas Aquinas (1225–1274), who, in his massive *Summa Theologica* (Summary of Theology), recognized theology and philosophy as separate realms of knowledge and maintained that properly conducted rational inquiry would support the principles of revelation.

As works of Jewish, Islamic, and Greek philosophy were translated into Latin after their piecemeal recovery from Byzantium and formerly Islamic lands in the twelfth century, studies in logic expanded. Aristotle's *Organon,* with its emphasis on syllogism and deductive and inductive logic, provided Scholasticism with a much-needed tool. At the same time, Aristotle's rationalism challenged scholars to harmonize the findings of natural knowledge with the conclusions of religious faith.

Science became another prominent area of medieval intellectual activity, especially with the translation of Greek and Arabic scientific works during the eleventh and twelfth centuries. During the thirteenth century, Roger Bacon (1214–1294), among others, made Oxford

Nigher still, and still more nigh
Draws the day of Prophecy,
Doom'd to melt the earth and sky.

Oh, what trembling there shall be,
When the world its Judge shall see,
Coming in dread majesty!

Now the books are open spread;
Now the writing must be read,
Which condemns the quick and dead.

Now, before the Judge severe
Hidden things must all appear;
Nought can pass unpunish'd here.*

In the third place, I
    will speak
Of the tavern's
    pleasure;
Nor shall I find it
    till I greet
Angels without
    measure,
Singing requiems
    for the souls
In eternal leisure
In the public-house
    to die
Is my resolution;
Let wine to my lips
    be nigh
At life's dissolution:
That will make the
    angels cry,
With glad elocution,
"Grant this toper,
    God on high,
Grace and absolution!"**

Both poems treat the theme of life's end, but in markedly different manners. The first, part of the majestic *Dies Irae* (Day of Wrath), depicts the somberness of the Last Judgment through words, meter, and rhyme. The second presents a very different attitude toward life, which the poet's technique helps to emphasize. Both moods were part of medieval life.

*F. J. E. Raby, *A History of Christian-Latin Poetry from the Beginnings to the Close of the Middle Ages,* 2d ed. (Oxford: Clarendon Press, 1953), p. 443.

**John Addington Symonds, ed. and trans., *Wine, Women, and Song: Medieval Latin Students' Songs* (1884; reprint, New York: AMS Press, 1974), pp. 65–66.

a major center of scientific studies. Bacon promoted an inductive investigation method involving observation and experimentation with appropriate instruments and methods. He described the nerve system of the eye, made magnifying glasses, and proposed high-technology warfare employing gigantic mirrors to focus the sun's rays and incinerate opponents.

Medieval Literature, Art, and Architecture

In addition to numerous scholarly writings, medieval writers composed a great quantity and variety of imaginative literature. Several Latin hymns from this period, such as the *Dies Irae* (Day of Wrath), are still sung in churches today. Secular writers also used Latin to produce nonreligious poetry about all aspects of life.

In both quantity and artistic quality, poetry in vernacular languages such as French, German, and English be-

came more important than Latin poetry. During the eleventh century, northern French minstrels began to compose *chansons de geste* (songs of great deeds) and to sing them for audiences of nobles. These action-packed narratives vividly described battles, usually against non-Christian foes, and praised bravery in battle, loyalty to the lord, and generosity to all (including the minstrel!). The French *Song of Roland* related with much fictional elaboration a bloody battle between Saracens (Spanish Muslims) and a detachment of Charlemagne's army ambushed in the pass at Roncevaux in the Pyrenees Mountains. Its heroic characters became as well known as those of the *Iliad* and the *Aeneid.* Epics soon appeared in other languages: the Spanish *Song of the Cid,* for example, told of the noble deeds of the eleventh-century heroic "Lord Champion" in the golden age of medieval chivalry. Though often glorifying Christian victories against the Muslims, these poems and the music of the minstrels were frequently based on forms and images copied from Islamic societies, particularly in Spain.

Meanwhile, minstrels known as troubadours composed lyric poetry in the Provençal dialect of southern France. Troubadour lyrics elaborated an entire art of love that emphasized a lover's good manners and refinement rather than skills in battle and induced nobles to acquire some knowledge of music, poetry, and history. The idea of selecting a marriage partner on the basis of love and serving her faithfully for years made the marriages of some nobles more than business transactions.

A third literary form, the romance, emerged from the interaction of the troubadour and *chanson de geste* traditions. Romances generally started with a theme or a person of the remote past but completely disregarded historical accuracy in their treatments. A prominent figure in the romances was Arthur, a semilegendary sixth-century English king who, by the twelfth century, had become a literary archetype of the ideal monarch. Arthur's court at Camelot, full of charming ladies and chivalrous knights, became the imaginary setting for religious sentiment and romantic love.

In addition to epics, lyric poetry, and romances for noble audiences, medieval writers produced fables, fabliaux, and dramas for town dwellers. Fables were brief moralistic stories featuring animals that symbolized people and their characteristics. Many popular fables came from France and related the exploits of Reynard the Fox, a wily character who consistently outwitted his moral but stupid adversaries. Fabliaux were satirical poems depicting the lives of ordinary people with vigorous and coarse humor while ridiculing conventional morality. In these forerunners of the modern short story, all priests and monks are gluttons and lechers, all women are lustful and easily seduced, and praise goes to those who outwit others.

Medieval drama developed from short skits depicting events associated with Christmas and Easter that were performed in church during religious ceremonies. In time, new scenes and incidents were invented, stock characterizations and crude scenery developed, and guilds assumed responsibility for producing plays. By the thirteenth century, these morality plays emphasized three distinct subjects: saints' lives, biblical stories, and the personification of correct behavior.

Although French and German remained the leading vernacular literatures into the thirteenth century, an Italian, Dante Alighieri (1265–1321), produced the greatest medieval literary masterpiece, *The Divine Comedy*. It describes a journey through hell, purgatory, and paradise, concluding in the awesome presence of God. Dante's guides for that journey were, respectively, Vergil, a spokesman for classical rationalism, Beatrice, an object of romantic and unconsummated but now spiritualized love, and Bernard of Clairvaux, the epitome of Christian

sanctity. The result is a majestic vision of the entire medieval universe.

The artists and artisans of the medieval era created impressive works of architecture, sculpture, and painting that matched the accomplishments of the scholars and writers. So many churches were built (more than 1,500 in France alone during the eleventh century) that a writer shortly after 1000 remarked that the earth was being covered with a white robe of churches.

The architectural style of the eleventh and twelfth centuries is called Romanesque because it used Roman-type building materials and architectural features. Medieval builders employed the Roman basilica plan with certain alterations; it featured a large open rectangular area, called the nave, for accommodating worshipers, and a semicircular apse for the altar and the conduct of religious services. Intersecting aisles were arranged in a cross-shaped floor plan. A continuous barrel-vault roof was supported

✿ Love Scene. Troubadour poets sang of the loves of lords and ladies like the aristocratic couple in this illustration from a fifteenth-century German manuscript. The bird is a falcon, trained and used by nobles in hunting for sport.
Universitätsbibliothek Heidelberg

Façade of Rheims Cathedral. Elaborate decoration was a typical feature of Gothic architecture and sculpture; note especially the magnificent stained glass window above the central doorway.
Ulf Sjöstedt/FPG International

by massive piers and arches and thick walls with few windows and doors. The atmosphere was one of mysterious darkness but also of castlelike protection.

The twelfth century saw a major innovation in architecture, the Gothic style. Influenced by contemporary writers' emphasis on illumination through prayer and meditation, Gothic architects featured space, light, and height. They unified interior space by replacing the rounded Romanesque arch with the pointed arch, which raised roofs higher above the floor. External buttresses replaced the thick walls of Romanesque churches; the support provided by the buttresses permitted the walls to be pierced by large stained glass windows that flooded the building's interior with multicolored light. Sculptors decorated Gothic churches with secular and biblical subjects. The Gothic style remained the dominant European art style into the sixteenth century except in Italy, where interest in classical artistic forms led to the distinctive art style of the Renaissance.

The cathedral became the town's religious center. It was both physically and spiritually an ordered unity like that of Thomas Aquinas's *Summa Theologica* or Dante's *Divine Comedy*, combining several distinct but related elements into a structurally coherent whole.

The East Roman or Byzantine Empire

*As the inner part of the temple was seen, and the sun lit its glories, sorrow fled from the hearts of all. And when the first gleam of light, rosy-armed driving away the dark shadows, leaped from arch to arch, then all the princes and peoples with one voice hymned their songs of prayer and praise; and as they came to the sacred courts it seemed to them as if the mighty arches were set in heaven. Whenever anyone enters the church to pray, he realizes at once it is not by any human power or skill, but by the influence of God that it has been built. And so his mind is lifted up to God, and he feels that He cannot be far away, but must love to dwell in this place He has chosen.**

*Procopius, *Buildings*, trans. H. B. Dewing and G. Downey (London: Heinemann, 1940), pp. 11–17, 25–29.

So wrote a Byzantine in contemplation of the magnificent Church of Hagia Sophia (Holy Wisdom) in Constantinople. Like the Gothic cathedrals in western Europe, the Hagia Sophia was a symbol of the Byzantine

Empire's glorious cultural achievements. As we have seen, Germanic peoples had destroyed the Roman Empire's Mediterranean unity by 500 and ruled large portions of Rome's former domain in the west. Most of the eastern portion of the empire, however, remained under the emperor's control and became the Byzantine Empire, named after Byzantium, a Greek town incorporated in the imperial capital, Constantinople. Containing the richer and more populated half of the old Roman Empire, the Byzantine state retained Rome's political and social structures and preserved its cultural heritage for a thousand years (476–1453). Justinian I (527–565), perhaps the greatest Byzantine emperor, combined the cultural heritage and political order of classical Greece and Rome with the vitality of the Christianity religion. In so doing, he foreshadowed many Byzantine contributions to civilization that rivaled the work of the architects of Hagia Sophia. This section examines Byzantine accomplishments during the period from 500 to about 1400.

Life in the Byzantine Empire in 500

Freed of heavy expenses for the military defense and economic development of the west, the Byzantine Empire prospered economically, while remaining socially and ethnically diverse. A top layer of Greek aristocrats ruled a majority population of Slavs, Arabs, Armenians, Jews, and others. In rural areas, aristocratic nobles held large landed estates, worked by free tenant renters (sharecroppers) called *coloni*. Although the coloni were technically free, they were actually tied to the land by economic necessity.

During the eighth to eleventh centuries, the empire enjoyed relative economic prosperity and agricultural plenty. The government controlled the prices of the staples of the Byzantine diet, bread and olive oil, and manipulated the currency to maintain stability. As in earlier empires from Asia to Europe, the authorities in the Byzantine Empire supervised the upkeep of roads and ports to facilitate trade. Industries, especially the manufacture of brocaded textiles, flourished. In a manner similar to guilds in the west, guilds held monopolies over some manufacturing specialties like textiles, and foreign merchants were encouraged to establish businesses.

The capital, Constantinople, was one of the biggest cities of the age and at its zenith may have had a population of one million. The main street, a sweeping thoroughfare, was lined with shops and a terraced promenade decorated with statues of emperors and popular actresses. An enormous hippodrome or stadium, with seating for 60,000 spectators, was the site of spectacular and exceedingly popular chariot races. Betting on favorite teams such as the "blues" or "greens" was a popular pastime, and it was not uncommon for the supporters of rival teams to come to blows. These fights sometimes developed into full-scale riots that occasionally threatened the survival of the government.

The wealthy frequently owned slaves to work in their private homes. Many merchants, artisans, educators, and administrators lived lives of great luxury in large cities or

Hagia Sophia. With its towering dome, the Church of Hagia Sophia (Holy Wisdom) was a major architectural achievement of which Byzantine rulers were justifiably proud. It remains a major monument in present-day Istanbul; the needle-shaped minarets were added by the Ottomans. By placing the dome atop two half-domes, the Byzantine builders created a huge open space. The achievement astounded sixth-century contemporaries, who asserted that the dome had been let down from heaven. Erich Lessing/Art Resource

seaside villas located in the European and West Asian sections of the empire. Although members of the ruling elite lived well and reaped the benefits of empire, most people lived on the margin of starvation in one-story city tenements or village huts. As in earlier Greek traditions, society was dominated by men, and the lives of most women centered on their families and homes; few held any position of political, cultural, or economic importance.

Throughout its long history, the empire steadfastly maintained its identity as the living embodiment of the Roman Empire, but its culture, language, and lifestyle became increasingly Greek. The state paid the instructors at the university of Constantinople, and students often paid low or no tuition. Students studied classical Greek writings and followed classical educational traditions taught in classical Greek. The coloni and workers, however, spoke a different version, a common vernacular Greek.

Although Christianity was the official religion, the empire's Christians were divided by theological differences. The church leaders and elite were notoriously disputatious and constantly debated the smallest points of Christian theology, particularly questions involving the nature of Christ and the Trinity. The Orthodox upheld the conclusions of religious councils regarding the Trinity and the nature of Christ, but many non-Orthodox churches, branded as heretical by the Byzantine rulers, differed widely in their beliefs. For example, in eastern Europe (as well as in most of the German states of western Europe) most Christians believed that Jesus was not equal to God. Syria and Egypt, where the populations retained their own rich cultural traditions and local languages and scorned their Greek-speaking rulers, were also strongholds of nontrinitarian Christianity. From Egypt, the Coptic Christian church spread into Ethiopia in eastern Africa where it established a Christian society that has survived until the present day (see Chapter 7).

Centered around the eastern Mediterranean, the Nestorians believed that Christ had two separate natures, while the Monophysites argued that Christ's divine nature had absorbed his human nature. Some of these communities still live in present-day Syria, Iraq, and Lebanon. Nestorian missionaries also converted tens of thousands in southern India and China. Some authorities claim that by the ninth century, the Nestorians were the single largest Christian group in the world. Although many of the eastern Christians in West Asia ultimately converted to Islam, theological disputes about the nature of Christ have continued up to the present throughout the Christian world.

Within the Byzantine Empire, the emperor exercised absolute authority over both religious and political matters. He appointed and dismissed officials, issued edicts, sat as the final court of judicial appeal, commanded the military and naval forces, and conducted foreign policy, often seeking to avoid war with rulers and peoples outside the empire. Initially, emperors were chosen from the imperial family by the army and confirmed by the Senate in Constantinople; the mothers and wives of the emperors also often played a key role in the selection of successors. By the fifth century, the patriarch of Constantinople, representing both the people and the church, crowned and consecrated the emperor.

Justinian I

Justinian I (reigned 527–565), the greatest Byzantine emperor, was an able and active ruler. He was responsible for keeping harmony in what he regarded as a Christian Roman state. He saw his duties as both ecclesiastical, ministering to spiritual needs, and political, attending to earthly affairs. His able and courageous wife Theodora (c. 500–548) assisted in those tasks. She restrained his religious zeal and eased tensions between governmental authorities and heretics. Early in his reign, a riot between supporters of rival chariot racing teams spread throughout the city, prompting Justinian and his advisers to consider fleeing the capital, but Theodora urged them instead to stay and fight. They did as she advised, quelled the riot, and secured the throne.

Theodora. This spectacular mosaic depicts Theodora arrayed in a jewel-encrusted gown and robe. Dynamic and resourceful, Theodora was a trusted adviser to her husband, Emperor Justinian, and became a powerful political figure in her own right. Scala/Art Resource

Justinian also improved governmental administration and the collection of revenues. He beautified Constantinople with a large-scale building program that ensured employment for laborers and also for artists, who added mosaics, sculptures, and icons (pictures of religious figures) to many buildings. Byzantine art became nearly as important as the Greek language in defining Christian faith.

Justinian also systematized Roman law: he directed a committee to compile all Roman legislation and legal commentaries of jurists and to produce a standard textbook for students. The resulting *Corpus Juris Civilis* (Collection of Civil Law) became the basis for the civil law of many European and Latin American nations.

In addition, Justinian sought to complete the Christianization of the empire. In 529 he closed the ancient, pre-Christian philosophical schools in Athens. He also restricted the civil rights of so-called heretics; for example, Jews, other non-Christians, and non-Orthodox Christians were prohibited from living within the walls of Constantinople and were barred from many public offices and teaching positions.

Under Justinian, Byzantine literature and learning flourished. Christian teachers stressed the best elements of classical moral training, philosophical thought, and literary craftsmanship. They taught the classical tradition from the Christian viewpoint and wrote on both classical and Christian topics, producing epigrams in the classical Greek manner, poems in elegant Homeric verse, and histories in the style of Herodotus and Thucydides. The subject matter, as well as the style, tended to focus on the past; Byzantine writers and artists were not noted for innovation or experimentation.

The Empire's Neighbors

Although he devoted enormous energy to internal matters, Justinian spent most of his reign and much of the empire's wealth on the reconquest of the western Mediterranean, particularly the German-occupied territories in North Africa, the southern coast of Spain, and Italy. Following his death, the Visigoths reconquered southern Spain, and a new Germanic group, the Lombards, advanced from the Danube valley to seize much of northern and central Italy. As a result, the Byzantine presence in the west was reduced to North Africa, Sicily, and some regions on the Italian coast, with Ravenna serving as the imperial administrative center.

Justinian's warfare in the west weakened the empire's eastern and northern defenses and created serious problems for his successors. To the north, the Slavs, an Indo-European agricultural people, moved southward through the Danube valley, now vacated by the Lombards. They entered Macedonia and Greece by 600 and soon thereafter assaulted Constantinople. To counter the Lombards and Slavs, seventh-century Byzantine emperors placed

Theodora, Empress of Many Talents

Theodora, the belly-dancer whom Justinian defied convention to marry . . . was possessed of no ordinary beauty, charm and intelligence. She was a born actress and enjoyed being the centre of attraction as the great lady of the imperial court; and in contrast to her austere husband she revelled in the luxury, pomp and elegance of life in the Great Palace at Constantinople. She shared to the full his conception of the majesty of the Roman Empire. But whereas Justinian belonged to the Latin world and thought like a Roman, Theodora was a Greek or perhaps one may say a Byzantine. But as man and wife they complemented one another. Justinian was devoted to her, and her death in 548 marked a turning-point in his career.*

The wives or mistresses of eminent rulers have often exerted great influence on the course of history. The first Roman emperor, Augustus, found in his wife Livia a source of strength and dependably good advice. By contrast, Agrippina, the wife of the emperor Claudius, ruthlessly manipulated (and finally murdered) her husband in his doddering last years, even inducing him to prefer Nero, her son by a former marriage, over his own direct offspring. Justinian's Theodora, like Pericles' Aspasia, was one of those forceful personalities who overcame a dubious background to capture (and more than repay) the attentions of an important leader.

*Donald M. Nicol, "Justinian I and His Successors, A.D. 527–610," in *Byzantium: An Introduction*, ed. Philip Whitting (New York: Harper, 1973), p. 18.

civil and military authority in the hands of regional military commanders, and the region's civilian population became the defending army. This measure ensured the survival of the empire but changed it into a society mobilized for continual warfare. The Byzantines also long enjoyed naval supremacy, thanks in part to "Greek fire," a petroleum-based incendiary substance that could be discharged from tubes and was not extinguishable by water.

Farther east, Justinian's successors went to war with Persia soon after 600. The Persians, under the Sassanian dynasty that had replaced the Parthians, enjoyed early successes, quickly conquering Syria and Egypt and attacking Constantinople. However, the Byzantines countered by invading Persia and occupying its capital, Ctesiphon (in present-day Iraq). By 628, the Persians were forced to seek peace.

The war with Persia, which brought the Byzantines no territorial gains, exhausted the empire economically and made it vulnerable to attacks by vigorous foes. The Arabs,

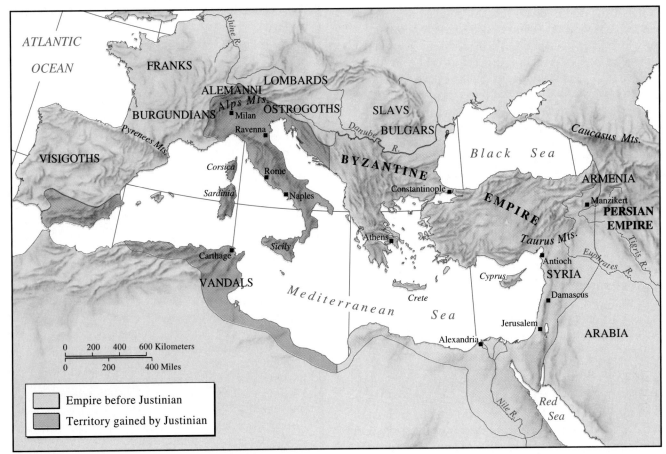

�֎ MAP 5.6A The Mediterranean in the Time of Justinian. Around 525, after the Germanic migrations into western Europe, the Byzantine Empire occupied only the limited area shown. Justinian I expanded the empire by recovering territories from Goths and Vandals, but some of these gains were lost soon after his death.

newly united under Islam, seized Syria and Egypt from the Byzantine Empire and Mesopotamia from the Persians shortly after 630. Two Arab sieges of Constantinople in 674–678 and 717–718 were unsuccessful; thereafter, the Taurus Mountains dividing Asia Minor from Syria became the Byzantine-Arab frontier. Another Asiatic people, the Bulgars, entered the Balkans from the north late in the seventh century, gaining control of the lower Danube valley. They integrated the local Slavic peoples into a Bulgar-dominated state. Thus the outer fringes of the empire were lost to increasingly powerful rivals.

Religious Issues

Byzantine wars had religious as well as political dimensions. Justinian fought the Germans as much because they were Arians as because they were occupiers of imperial territory. His successors similarly opposed the Slavs and Bulgars as non-Christian pagans. Following Zoroastrianism and Islam, respectively, the Persians and Arabs easily conquered Syria and Egypt in the seventh century, in part because non-Orthodox and Orthodox

Christians failed to mount any collective opposition to the invading forces.

The Arab and Persian conquests removed Jerusalem, Alexandria, and Antioch from the empire, leaving Constantinople and Rome as the major Christian centers. As time passed, leaders in those two centers often disagreed on religious issues. Believing it was their duty to maintain orthodoxy, Justinian and his successors tried to reestablish doctrinal unity. The bishops of Rome (popes), however, claimed primacy over the church and regarded the definition of Christian faith as their responsibility. Doctrines acceptable in the east and proclaimed by bishops in councils under the direction of the patriarch of Constantinople often encountered papal opposition, whereas doctrines the west could support were often rejected by eastern Catholics. Church councils in the sixth and seventh centuries failed to resolve such conflicts.

In the eighth century, Emperor Leo III (reigned 717–741) created a new rift between Christians. He believed that many of the empire's bright and able men were diverted from state service because they were interested in monastic practices that involved the worship of icons

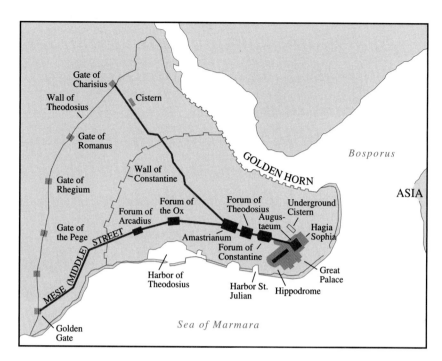

🎇 MAP 5.6B Constantinople. The capital of the Byzantine Empire, Constantinople was a large city with a lavish complex of imperial buildings and churches. Its location astride the Bosporus provided it with natural defenses that were further strengthened by a series of walls around the city. This map also shows the Hippodrome, where the famous games were held, the Hagia Sophia, and the long Mese, or middle street.

(images of sacred Christian figures). Leo accordingly tried to discredit monasticism by attacking the misuse of icons in eastern churches as idolatrous and by prohibiting their use. This sharply divided the empire's population into iconoclasts (image breakers) and iconodules (image users). Many of the latter fled to monasteries or to western imperial territories in southern Italy and Sicily. Because the popes opposed the iconoclasts, Leo retaliated by transferring many rich papal lands in Italy to the patriarch of Constantinople. Iconoclasm polarized Latin and Greek Christians and divided the Byzantine Empire even after the ecumenical Council of Nicaea in 787 restored relations between Rome and Constantinople. The dispute over icons was eventually resolved by the Empress Irene (reigned 780–802), who required priests to provide instruction to parishioners on the appropriate use of icons. Irene ruled by brute force and succeeded in imposing her son as successor. For her service to Christianity, the church subsequently declared her a saint.

Decline of Empire

During the ninth century, the Byzantine Empire gradually regained some of its former power; the emperors reestablished use of icons and restored the empire's financial and military resources. In 867 an ambitious son of Armenian peasants assassinated the reigning emperor and seized the throne as Basil I. Basil established the long-lived Macedonian dynasty (867–1054), which ably led the empire for nearly two centuries.

Byzantine cultural and religious life flourished under the early Macedonians. Literary output grew, while edu-

cational activity and interest in classical authors revived. Poems and hymns in praise of saints and prose accounts of their lives were published while histories and lexicons attested to the Byzantine fascination with the classical past. The emperor Constantine VII (reigned 912–959) patronized scholarly activity and authorized important works describing the administration of the empire and Byzantine court ceremonies. Out of the recurring border wars with the Muslims came the *Epic of Digenes Akritas* ("the border warrior born of parents from different ethnic groups"), which resembles western European works such as the *Song of Roland* and the *Song of the Cid.*

In art, the iconoclastic controversy triggered interest in the forms of Greek art popular during Alexander the Great's time, in the historical and secular rather than the ecclesiastical and spiritual, and in Islamic art and its use of ornament. This second golden age of Byzantine art was characterized by the pursuit of dignity, grace, restraint, balance, and refinement.

Under the Macedonian rulers, Byzantine artists and writers continued to copy classical Greek models in which secular taste often contrasted with religious sensitivity. In the decorations of aristocratic homes and in manuscript illuminations, classical themes and mythological or allegorical scenes were popular. The exploitation of their classical inheritance gave the Byzantines superiority over Latin Christianity in literary and artistic achievements in the ninth and tenth centuries.

Byzantine vitality also contributed to cultural and religious expansion. Byzantine emperors considered the late ninth-century conquests and subsequent conversion of the Serbians and Slavs to Orthodox Christianity to be one of their greatest accomplishments. The Bulgars negotiated with both Latin and Byzantine Christians, but the work of Byzantine missionaries and the diplomacy of the Byzantine emperors and patriarchs induced the Bulgar ruler to adopt Eastern Orthodox Christianity. By the tenth century, the Bulgar capital of Preslav had become a center for training Slavic clergy. They were taught in Old Church Slavonic, a literary language devised by Byzantine missionaries that became a means by which Byzantine culture infused into eastern and southeastern Europe.

During the tenth century, Kievan Russia began to enter the Byzantine cultural orbit. As trade with the Byzantines grew, Kievan rulers sought closer ties with Constantinople. Prince Vladimir (reigned alone 980–1015), a baptized Christian, married Anna, sister of the Byzantine emperor Basil II (reigned 976–1025). The Bible, saints' lives, and religious service books translated at Preslav from Greek into Old Church Slavonic formed the earliest Russian Christian religious literature.

In southeastern Europe, though, the Byzantine Empire declined rapidly. Although a series of vigorous emperors from 1081 to 1185 asserted imperial authority, increased commercial connections with Italian cities, and restored Constantinople as a leading cultural center, a subsequent succession of short-lived rulers weakened the empire. By 1200 rebellions in Serbia and Bulgaria had led to the establishment of independent states. In 1204 Latin crusaders sacked the capital of Constantinople and incorporated most of the Byzantine Empire into a Latin Empire that lasted until 1261. Although the Paleologi dynasty (1261–1453) was able to destroy the Latin Empire and recover Constantinople and much of northern Greece, from 1300 onward the Byzantine Empire, like central Europe, became increasingly politically fragmented. Like the Greek and Roman Empires before it, the Byzantine Empire, which had persisted for more than a millennium, disintegrated and finally disappeared. Byzantium was to be replaced during the fifteenth century by a new, non-Christian power, the Ottoman Turks, who, like the Byzantines, had a tradition of absolute rule (see Chapter 8).

Islam and Islamic Empires

The apostle of God became a young man. God protected him from the loose behavior of the pagans. He was the most generous of his people . . . kind to his neighbors, courteous, faithful. . . . He was the bravest of men.

[Muhammad's reactions when he had his first vision as he meditated in a desert cave:] "One came to me with a written scroll, while I was asleep, and said 'Read!' I said 'I cannot

read. . . .' He pressed me with it, until I thought death must be nigh. . . . And he said, 'Read in the name of thy Lord who created; He created man from a sensitive drop of blood' [Qur'an 96:1–2]. And he departed. . . .*

And I awoke. . . . And it was as if the scripture were written on my heart."*

*Emel Esin, *Mecca, the Blessed; Madinah, the Radiant* (New York: Crown, 1963), pp. 70, 76.

Thus did the prophet Muhammad's Arabian contemporaries describe the Prophet and his first revelation of what was to become one of the world's major religions. Just as Buddha and Jesus had gone to meditate in remote areas, so too did the prophet Muhammad. There he experienced a series of revelations that were transmitted first to converts in Arabia and then to growing numbers in Africa and eastern Asia.

Although the peoples of pre-Islamic Arabia were predominantly tribal nomads, Mecca and Medina had been major centers for religious pilgrimages and trade, particularly frankincense and myrrh from Yemen, for generations. A few Jewish and Christian communities were also scattered about the peninsula; these communities continued to maintain some commercial and cultural ties with the Byzantine Empire, which controlled most of the eastern Mediterranean. Merchants and city dwellers enjoyed a fair degree of prosperity, but most of the population of the Arabian Peninsula lived either in scattered desert oases, where they eked out a subsistence livelihood growing grains, vegetables, and date palms, or as nomads who traveled with herds of camels, goats, and sheep from one life-giving watering hole to the next. The majority of these *bedouin* (tribal people) were animists (believers that inanimate objects like stones, trees, and animals possess spirits or souls), living in what Islamic society would term ignorance.

Muhammad: A Religious and Political Leader

The prophet Muhammad, who came from the Hashim family or branch of the Qurash tribe, was born in Mecca around 570 or 571. He was raised by his grandfather and as an adult married an older widow, Khadijah. Muhammad rapidly gained a reputation as an honest and successful businessman. When he was around forty years old, Muhammad became increasingly religious and began to spend long periods of time in deep meditation. As early as 610, Muhammad began to have revelations from Allah (God), which were transmitted through the angel Gabriel. Muhammad began to preach the word of Allah and slowly gained adherents to the new religion, Islam (submission to God). The believers in Islam were known as Muslims, or those who submit to the will of God.

Muslims believe in one God and in the prophets of the Old and New Testaments; they include Christ as a prophet. They also believe in progressive revelation, the existence of angels, and the doctrine of the day of judgment. Islam, like Christianity, is a universal religion in which all people who accept the belief in one God and in Muhammad as his prophet are regarded as equal before Allah and within the community. For Muslims, Islam is the perfection of all previous religions, including Judaism and Christianity. As Islam spread and attracted converts around the world, its universal nature and equal treatment of all believers proved to be two of its major strengths.

The revelations from Allah received by Muhammad were set down in the *Qur'an (Koran),* which contained instructions governing all aspects of human life. As the Islamic community grew in numbers and expanded over vast territories, the Qur'an was supplemented by the *Hadith,* which is a collection of the sayings and traditions of the prophet Muhammad. Six authoritative collections of the Hadith are accepted by Muslims. In addition, a complex body of law, the *Shari'a,* gradually evolved. The Qur'an, Hadith, and Shari'a provide the guidelines for the conduct of Muslim societies. Over several centuries, differing interpretations of the Qur'an, the Hadith, and the Shari'a led to the formation of several different schools of Islamic law.

A large percentage of Islamic law deals with family matters. In Arabia, where women had previously enjoyed no legal status, Islamic injunctions were a major improvement. As the Prophet was known to have said, "Paradise is at the foot of the mother." Under Islamic law, a widow was guaranteed a portion of her husband's estate and could own and dispose of property; women also had the right of divorce in specific instances. These legal rights were granted in Islam centuries before most women in the Christian west obtained such rights. Muslim law permitted the practice of polygamy, which was common in Arabia and much of the rest of the world at the time. A Muslim male could have four wives at any one time if he treated them all equally. In actual practice only the wealthy could generally afford more than one wife.

In eras when religious tolerance was generally unknown, Islam enjoined believers to grant safe havens to people of the book (Jews and Christians) and usually to Zoroastrians and not to force conversions or to persecute

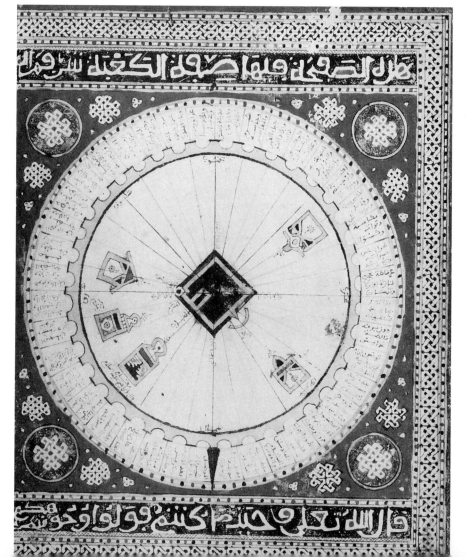

❊ Frontispiece of an Atlas. This Arabic atlas (1551) shows the Ka'bah surrounded by the names of the Islamic nations, connected by lines showing their location relative to the Ka'bah. Surrounded by a huge walled courtyard, the Ka'bah remains the holiest site in Islam.
Bibliothèque Nationale de France, Paris

these communities unless they waged war against Muslims. This tolerance, however, was not extended to animists or polytheists such as Hindus.

The Qur'an also provides regulations for marriage (including divorce), lending of money (interest is forbidden), diet, the treatment of women, orphans and slaves, and the behavior of government. Muslim theologians and legal experts who interpreted and explained Islamic canons were known collectively as the *ulema*. Importantly, Islam, in contrast to early Christianity, did not separate church from state.

Every true Muslim was instructed to follow the five basic pillars: belief in Allah and Muhammad as his prophet, prayer five times a day, the giving of alms, fasting from sunrise to sunset during the month of Ramadan, and the *hajj,* or pilgrimage to Mecca, once in a lifetime. The observance of these five pillars still serves as the principal means of salvation for Muslims, and nonobservance is believed to lead to eternal suffering in the afterlife.

The hajj commemorates the *hijrah* (flight) in 622 of Muhammad and his followers from the merchants of Mecca, who feared that this new religion would threaten both their preeminent political and social status and the

wealth they enjoyed from pilgrims coming to worship in the city. The hajj centers on the *Ka'bah,* a cube-shaped shrine in Mecca, which had long been a place of pilgrimage for tribal peoples in the Arabian Peninsula. In addition to its spiritual meaning, the hajj has also proved to be an excellent means through which the diverse and ultimately widely scattered Islamic peoples could exchange ideas and goods while maintaining a cohesive structure.

After the hijrah, the new Islamic community took refuge in Medina. The fledgling community soon became the dominant political and social force and began to attract more and more converts. Alarmed by the growing political and financial power of Muhammad and his followers, the leaders of Mecca launched several armed attacks against the new community. When the Muslims successfully repelled these attacks, they gained more converts. By 629 the Muslims led by Muhammad were strong enough to mount a force of more than a 1,000 believers to march on Mecca; by 632 Muhammad had successfully incorporated the city within the new and growing Muslim community. Just a few months after his return to Mecca, however, Muhammad died of a fever. Because the Prophet had left no specific instructions regarding a successor, the commu-

The Sacred Mosque and Ka'bah at Mecca. This contemporary photograph shows the holiest site in the Muslim world during the time of pilgrimage. Although the courtyard can hold half a million pilgrims, in recent years it has been too small to contain the crowds, which often exceed 2 million worshipers. © Robert Azzi/Woodfin Camp

❋ An Inscribed Bowl. Islamic/Arab societies, like the Chinese, held the art of pottery making in extremely high esteem. Ceramic centers flourished in the Islamic world, and pieces were frequently decorated with Arabic inscriptions from the Qur'an or with sayings from the Prophet. The inscription on the bowl shown here reads, "Excellence is a quality of the people of paradise." Courtesy of the Freer Gallery of Art, Smithsonian Institution, Washington, DC

nity of the faithful immediately gathered together and by consensus selected the first caliph, or leader.

The First Four Caliphs and Islamic Conquests

The first caliph, Abu Bakr, had been one of the original converts to Islam. As Muhammad's faithful friend, Abu Bakr was known for his devotion and was widely respected for his wisdom and good humor. Following Muhammad's death, a number of the Arabian tribes had broken with the Islamic community. Abu Bakr immediately appointed loyal chiefs to subdue these revolts. Subsequently, many of the tribal leaders participated in the military conquests of the entire Arabian Peninsula and in expeditions into Syria and Iraq.

After Abu Bakr's death in 634, the Islamic community selected the energetic Umar as the second caliph. Umar's administration was marked by a period of military conquest, as Muslims assimilated widely different areas and peoples into an Islamic Empire. In the east, the Iraqi territories of the old Sassanid Empire were conquered, and in 637 the capital at Ctesiphon fell to Arab/Islamic domination. These military victories brought vast wealth,

which was lavishly bestowed upon the soldiers. With promises of military victories and booty, the Islamic armies had little difficulty attracting recruits.

Over the next years, Muslim armies achieved similar military successes against the Byzantine Empire. Damascus fell to Khalid's forces in 635, and at the decisive battle of Yarmuk in 637, the forces of the Byzantine emperor were decisively defeated. Jerusalem was incorporated into the Arab/Islamic Empire in 638. The Muslims then turned their energies toward Egypt and Africa; in 639 they reached the banks of the Nile, taking Alexandria in 641. Two years later most of Persia had fallen.

Arab women and children accompanied the armies on military campaigns, and women frequently joined the fighting. The Byzantine soldiers, accustomed to women remaining secluded at home, were shocked to see Arab women on the battlefields. At Yarmuk, when the Arab army started to retreat, women seized swords and tent posts and urged the soldiers to rejoin the battle; the result was a complete rout of the Byzantine army.

The extremely rapid expansion of the Arab/Islamic Empire was attributable in part to the weakness of the Sassanid and Byzantine Empires. More important to the Muslims' success, however, were their fervent religious belief and the equalitarian nature of their religion, which treated converts as equals within the community. The Muslims' treatment of their their new subjects also contributed to their success. In contrast to leaders of earlier empires in Egypt and China, for example, Umar did not attempt to force the conquered peoples to assimilate or to adopt Arab customs. Umar's decision to interfere as little as possible with the conquered peoples was perhaps his most important contribution to the continued success and endurance of the Arab/Islamic Empire. During Umar's caliphate, provincial governors were appointed to administer the new territories; their major job was to collect taxes, which, in many cases, were far lower than those collected by the Byzantine and Sassanid Empires. Hence, many peoples actually welcomed the new rulers and were rapidly absorbed within Islamic society. Non-Muslims were not forced to convert and were allowed to maintain their own laws, as well as to practice their own religions. They were not permitted to bear arms, however; nor, for example, could their church towers be taller than the highest minaret in a town. In contrast to other societies of the age, which often forced conversions and persecuted or killed people of differing beliefs, the Arab/Islamic Empire became known for its relative tolerance of minorities and non-Muslims.

Similarly, Islamic law strictly regulated the treatment of slaves. Muslims could not enslave other Muslims, and the freeing of slaves was encouraged. In contrast to many other societies, particularly in the Western Hemisphere, slaves in the Islamic world were not generally used as

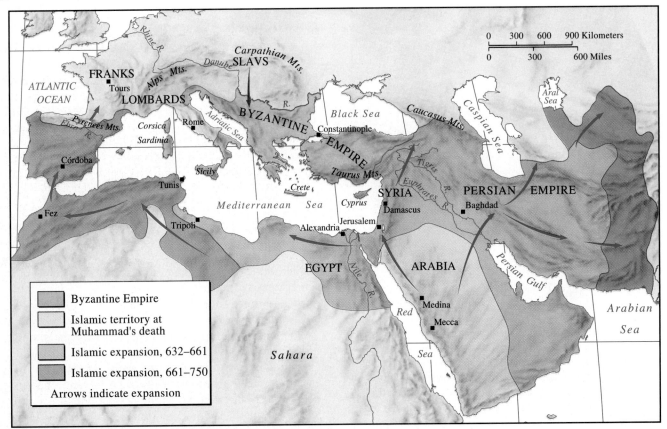

�֍ MAP 5.7 The Expansion of Islam. Most of Islam's early territorial gains were at the expense of the Persian and Byzantine Empires. The former was entirely absorbed, and the latter, already diminished by German gains, lost Syria, Egypt, and all of its North African possessions. Muslims then advanced into the Iberian Peninsula and France in the west and toward the banks of the Indus River in the east.

agricultural labor on huge plantations, but were kept only as workers and protectors for domestic households or as soldiers in the army.

As the "second founder of Islam," Umar also established a single authoritative version of the Qur'an; all other copies were destroyed, and the Qur'an has remained unchanged since that time. Unfortunately, while praying in Medina, at the very peak of his power, Umar was fatally wounded by a disgruntled slave. On his deathbed Umar appointed a committee of six prominent merchants to select the next caliph.

After some debate the committee chose Uthman, from the powerful Umayyad family, as the third caliph. An elderly man in his seventies, Uthman was not as forceful a leader as his predecessors, and he was widely criticized for favoring members of his own family over the rest of the *umma* (the Islamic community). For example, Uthman appointed his cousin Mu'awiyah governor of the flourishing province of Syria. Mu'awiyah proved an able ruler and military strategist, however, ordering the building of the first Islamic fleet, which immediately conquered the islands of Cyprus and Rhodes. With his army and fleet, which made him the dominant military force

in the eastern Mediterranean, Mu'awiyah emerged as a powerful leader in his own right.

The caliph Uthman's leadership was increasingly opposed by faithful Muslims in Medina and in provincial towns on the eastern frontier. An open revolt began in Kufah in Iraq in 655 and soon spread to Medina. In 656 the rebels broke into the caliph's home and assassinated him. Political assassination has often triggered unrest and accelerated changes in the course of history. For example, the assassinations of Uthman and Julius Caesar both sparked struggles for power that ended with the emergence of able administrators and founders of dynastic lines (Mu'awiyah and Augustus).

After Uthman's death, once again the Muslim leaders gathered to select a leader; after a week, the notables agreed to appoint Ali, Muhammad's son-in-law, as the fourth caliph. From the very beginning of his reign, however, Ali met with widespread opposition. So many in Medina were against him, including some who believed he had been implicated in Uthman's death, that Ali fled the city and established his capital in Kufah (in present-day Iraq). Nevertheless, the discontent continued. Aisha, Muhammad's favorite wife, disliked Ali, who had once accused her of infidelity. Astride a camel, Aisha led her supporters into a bloody battle against Ali in 656. Defeated at the so-called Battle of the Camel, in which many of the original followers of the Prophet were killed, Aisha was forced to retire to Medina where she died of natural causes several decades later.

Mu'awiyah proved much more dangerous to Ali's supremacy. He refused to resign as virtual ruler of Syria, and he had the support of the powerful Umayyad family. In 657 he challenged Ali's leadership at the battle of Siffin, in northern Syria. Although the battle was essentially a standoff, more and more provinces aligned with Mu'awiyah, who clearly held the preponderance of power. Some of Ali's original followers now turned against him. Known as *Kharijites* (seceders), they were against any sort of compromise and now opposed both Ali and Mu'awiyah. The Kharijites considered themselves to be the only true revolutionaries in the Muslim world. In 661 a Kharijite murdered Ali. His death ended the age of the "rightly guided" caliphs—the first four caliphs, all of whom had either been related to Muhammad or been his close compatriots.

The Umayyad Caliphate

After Ali's death, Mu'awiyah declared himself caliph in Jerusalem in 661 and established Damascus as the new capital of the Islamic Empire. He granted a substantial pension to Hasan, Ali's eldest son and a possible rival; Hasan retired from politics and spent the rest of his life in Medina. Mu'awiyah generally appointed able and vigorous governors to oversee the far-flung empire and engaged in lively discussions on government policies with the notables in Damascus. Many of the officials were Syrians or had been administrators in the Byzantine Empire. Thus many Byzantine traditions and cultural achievements were assimilated within the Umayyad caliphate. Commanding the strongest army within the empire, Mu'awiyah launched a series of attacks against the remaining territories of the Byzantine Empire in present-day Turkey and, as previously noted, tried but failed to take Constantinople, the Byzantine capital.

Simultaneously, Muslim forces in Egypt and North Africa continued to extend their influence. With Berbers from North Africa and other new African recruits from the sub-Saharan regions, they succeeded in crossing the Strait of Gibraltar in 710 and 711. From there, Tarik, the Berber commander, smashed the Visigoths and incorporated half of Spain under his command. The Muslims called the territory Al-Andalusia (Land of the Vandals), and proceeded to create in Spain a vibrant civilization that was to last for nearly eight centuries. The Muslim forces, known as Moors in western Europe, also made continual forays across the Pyrenees, advancing as far as Tours, only 234 miles south of Paris. Although they re-

mained a military threat for decades, they never succeeded in incorporating France into their empire.

During the Umayyad caliphate, similar expansions occurred in central Asia. Al-Hajjaj, viceroy in the eastern provinces, conquered Samarkand and surrounding territory in central Asia. Simultaneously, Muslim forces marched into northern and western India, conquering the lower Indus valley (Sind) in 712. The majority of the populations in these territories gradually converted to Islam, and the areas became part of the Islamic world.

The Split between Sunni and Shi'i

Before his death, Mu'awiyah had his son, Yazid, accepted as his heir, thereby instituting the practice of hereditary accession to the caliphate. Yazid was a better warrior than administrator, and during his reign a major schism of immense importance to the future Islamic world occurred. After the death of Ali's eldest son Hasan, his younger brother Husayn became the leader of those who had continued to support Ali's cause and to oppose Umayyad rule. Husayn refused to recognize the legitimacy of Yazid. With a small, poorly equipped force, he advanced against Yazid's army. The two rival forces clashed on the field of Kerbala, a city south of contemporary Baghdad, on the tenth of Muharram (10 October 680). Husayn and his badly outnumbered supporters were killed. Husayn's head was cut off and presented in a triumphal display to Yazid.

Husayn's martyrdom became the rallying point for opponents of the Umayyad caliphate throughout the empire. Their opposition was based on a political division over who should rule rather than on spiritual differences. The Shi'i, or party of Ali, maintained that the line of leadership should follow directly through the Prophet's family. The Sunni, or orthodox majority, contended that leadership could be bestowed on any able believer.

Kerbala, where Husayn was buried, became a major pilgrimage center for the Shi'i who marked his death in the month of Muharram with passion plays and ceremonies of self-flagellation. Ultimately, the Shi'i would become predominant in present-day Iran, which already differed from the Arabian Peninsula owing to its largely Farsi-speaking population and its unique cultural and historical identity. Shi'i also make up a sizable portion of the populations in present-day Iraq, Lebanon, the eastern Arabian Peninsula, and some other areas of the Islamic world.

The Shi'i ultimately split into a number of different sects, the most important of which were the Twelvers. They recognized the *Imams* (leaders) through Husayn's children and believed that the twelfth Imam, Muhammad al-Muntazar, disappeared into a cave in 878. According to Twelver Shi'i belief, Muhammad al-Muntazar did not die but went into occultation, a state in which other religious leaders could commune with him while he remained invisible. Twelvers believed that Muhammad al-Muntazar would return as the Mahdi (the rightly guided one) to save the world. As a result, the *mullahs* (clergy) assumed a special role within the Shi'i communities, which continued to look to the clergy for direction and leadership. The Shi'i clergy also established a hierarchy in which particularly knowledgeable and esteemed mullahs became known as *Ayatollahs*. In contrast, the orthodox, or majority, Sunni Muslims had neither an established clergy nor a hierarchy of religious notables.

In addition, a number of other splits developed among the Shi'i. Some argued that the fourth Imam, Zayid, was the last real Imam; they became known as Zayidis and in the contemporary era are found mostly in Yemen. Others held that Isma'il, the seventh in line, should have been recognized as the last infallible Imam. They ultimately established communities in Tunisia and India. From Tunisia their leaders, the Fatimids, established an independent Fatimid caliphate in Cairo in 969. Cairo subsequently became a rival for power and glory to the eastern capital in Baghdad.

The Establishment of the Abbasid Caliphate

The Ummayad caliphs in Damascus had increasing difficulties keeping the diverse and widely scattered peoples of the empire under their sole control. From the outset, the provinces in North Africa, Spain, and Egypt had been largely self-governing under their local provincial governors.

Meanwhile, the growing wealth and increasingly secular behavior of the Umayyad rulers aroused mounting opposition, even in Syria and Arabia. The rulers' lavish lifestyles had also corrupted many within the elite circles, and it became increasingly difficult to attract recruits to fight for the Umayyads. Rumors that the Umayyad caliphs drank wine, expressly forbidden to Muslims, and that one caliph even swam in a pool filled with wine were all used by the Umayyads' opponents to gain adherents from among the devout Muslim/Arab communities.

Rebellions became increasingly frequent. One group, the Abbasids, who were led by the great-grandson of the Prophet's uncle, gathered support from the Shi'i and from disgruntled groups in Iraq and Iran. In 747 the Abbasids called for an open revolt against the Umayyad caliphate and within three years had defeated the Umayyads at a decisive battle near the Tigris River. In 750 Damascus fell, and the Abbasids promptly attempted to eliminate all members of the Umayyad family. One, Abd al-Rahman I, fled to Spain where he established a new dynasty that lasted for nearly 300 years. The Abbasid leader, Abu al-Abbas, was proclaimed caliph at Kufah in 749 and proceeded to establish a new caliphate, which lasted for almost 500 years (see Chapter 8).

Summary and Comparisons

As the Roman Empire declined, the Christian church effectively replaced the collapsing political system as the temporal ruler. In Europe Christianity swept aside all other competitors and outlived the Roman Empire.

In the fourth and fifth centuries, barbarian invasions finally overwhelmed the defenses of the western Roman Empire. In contrast to China, where one dynasty led to another with a continuation of most cultural and political institutions, the collapse of Rome led to sharp changes in European institutions and society. Although internal deficiencies of the type discussed in the comparative essay preceding this chapter played a part in its collapse, Rome perished more from assault than from senility. From this point on, the distinctive Greco-Roman civilization was modified at the hands of the Germanic kingdoms of western Europe and the Byzantine Empire to the east, both of which were already on the scene by 500. Another heir, the Islamic Empire, was emerging just over the horizon.

In the Latin west, Germanic peoples practiced subsistence agriculture in tribal societies under weak kings; many African societies were organized along the same lines. In Europe one people, the Franks, became prominent. By adopting Roman Catholic Christianity and requiring Romans and Germans to work together, King Clovis provided a basis for new political and cultural development. Creative individuals preserved elements of the classical heritage, and innovative religious leaders gave new directions to western European life.

During the period 750–1000, Carolingian rulers unified the Frankish kingdoms and dominated western Europe. They created an adequate, if loosely organized, governmental administration and used an effective army to expand their territories. They also stimulated a modest outburst of mostly religious literary and artistic achievement, sometimes called the Carolingian Renaissance. Charlemagne, the greatest Carolingian ruler, was crowned Roman emperor by the pope in 800. During the ninth century, however, Carolingian rulers engaged in civil wars, and the empire disintegrated into small, weak states, just as similarly organized central powers in western and eastern Asia had disintegrated in earlier centuries.

During the ninth century, Muslim, Magyar, and Viking invaders completed the breakup of the Carolingian Empire, and local warlords rose to prominence. Different European regions responded by creating a variety of social and political relationships. Feudalism, a system of mutual obligations between lords and vassals, was the most notable of these new relationships. Kings struggled with popes and the nobility and in many cases increased their political control.

During the medieval period, western and central Europe underwent important economic and cultural changes. The population doubled, agriculture expanded, and town life, trade, and manufacturing grew. Christianity remained vigorous; in particular, monasteries met the religious needs of a generally pious population. Religious minorities generally were not well treated, however, and Jewish communities, especially in western Europe, suffered increasing discrimination.

A lively cultural life emerged in Europe during this era. The founding of the first European universities during the late Middle Ages encouraged philosophic and theological studies. The rudiments of the modern scientific method and outlook were also established, thanks in part to the translation of Greek and Arabic scientific works. In the late Middle Ages, literature, art, and architecture also reached great heights.

Despite the German conquest of the western portions of the Roman Empire by 500, the eastern Roman or Byzantine Empire continued to prosper. Its rulers retained Rome's political and social structures and fostered both Christianity and secular Greek culture. Justinian I, the greatest Byzantine ruler, streamlined the government, codified the law, and promoted intellectual and artistic activity.

Just as Rome, weakened by domestic problems, succumbed to outside conquerors, the Byzantine Empire ultimately did too. After Justinian's death, Slavs migrated into the Balkan Peninsula, Lombards seized parts of Italy, Persians conquered the empire's eastern provinces, and the growing Arab/Islamic Empire took large pieces of Byzantine territory. By 1200 rebellions in the Balkans had led to the creation of independent states in areas once under Byzantine control. In the thirteenth century, Latin crusaders propped up the Byzantine state for a short time, but the state never regained its former vitality. This left the way open for its final overthrow by the rising power of the Ottoman Turks.

Whereas the history of the Byzantines was one of gradual decline, that of the Muslims was one of explosive expansion. Islam proved to be not only a dynamic new religion but also a force for political and economic unity. From 622 to 632, under the leadership of the prophet Muhammad, Islam was accepted by most of the tribes in the Arabian Peninsula. The first three caliphs following Muhammad's death in 632 initiated a series of military conquests that had established Islamic societies from the Indus River in the east to Spain in the west by 750. Like earlier centrally organized empires in Asia and the Western Hemisphere, the Umayyad caliphs at Damascus fostered a vibrant new culture by encouraging the arts and education. Islamic universities flourished in Cairo and North Africa. Like universities in Christian Europe, Islamic institutions of higher education emphasized theology and philosophy, albeit from a differing religious and world viewpoint. All in all, Islamic expansion from West Asia to Africa and East Asia was one of the most rapid and far-reaching advances in human history.

Eventually, the Muslim community, like the earlier Byzantine, Mesopotamian, and Egyptian Empires and some Chinese dynasties, also fell prey to civil strife. This ultimately fragmented the Islamic world into a number of competing political centers. In addition, the community of Muslims split between the Sunnis, who thought the right to rule could be exercised by any believer, and the Shi'i, who maintained that rule should follow through Muhammad, Ali, and their suc-

cessors. This schism was the major cause of the collapse of the Umayyad caliphate in Damascus and the emergence of the rival Abbasid caliphate in Baghdad. Similar divisions in Christianity would later threaten the hegemony of the Catholic church and fragment political leadership in Europe.

Selected Sources

Abu-Lughod, Janet L. *Before European Hegemony: The World System A.D. 1250–1350.* 1990. An intriguing discussion of the patterns of cultural and commercial interaction across Eurasia in the period covered.

*Amt, Emilie, ed. *Women's Lives in Medieval Europe: A Sourcebook.* 1993. A valuable collection of primary documents.

*Angold, Michael. *The Byzantine Empire, 1025–1204.* 1997. This political history provides a fine overview of the empire during a key period of change.

Armstrong, Karen. *Muhammad: A Biography of the Prophet.* 1992. Concise, balanced account of Muhammad and Islam.

*Bayard, Tania, ed. and trans. *A Medieval Home Companion: Housekeeping in the Fourteenth Century.* 1991. A handbook of instructions written for his fifteen-year-old bride by an elderly citizen of Paris around 1393.

Benjamin of Tudela. *The Itinerary of Benjamin of Tudela: Travels in the Middle Ages.* Rev. ed. 1987. This twelfth-century travelogue by a Jewish native of Navarre contains fascinating descriptions of hundreds of cities, including Baghdad, Constantinople, Alexandria, and Jerusalem.

*Benko, Stephen. *Pagan Rome and the Early Christians.* 1984. A good account of the collision of paganism and Christianity in the Roman world.

*Brown, Peter. *The World of Late Antiquity: A.D. 150–750.* 1971. Especially valuable for its coverage of religious and cultural developments of the transition from antiquity to the Middle Ages.

"The Byzantine Empire." Insight Media. A two-part video (thirty minutes each) tracing the empire's glory and long decline.

Chuvin, Pierre. *A Chronicle of the Last Pagans.* Trans. B. A. Archer. 1990. A newer account of the momentous changes in religious life in the Roman Empire as seen from the pagan vantage point.

*Davis, R. H. C. *A History of Medieval Europe: From Constantine to Saint Louis.* 2d ed. 1988. A thorough, highly readable, and up-to-date history.

*Esposito, John. *Islam: The Straight Path.* Rev. ed. 1991. A readable survey of Islam, its major tenets, and historical development.

"The Five Pillars of Islam." Films for the Humanities. A video on the Islamic faith in historical context.

Fleischer, Richard, director. *The Vikings.* 1958. A film that treats Viking activities within the context of an adventure story; filmed on location in Norway and Brittany.

*Gardner, John. *Grendel.* 1971. An enthralling short novel that retells the Beowulf story, but from the point of view of the monster!

*Gottfried, Robert S. *The Black Death: Natural and Human Disaster in Medieval Europe.* 1983. An engrossing account of the causes, course, and consequences of the great plague.

*Gregory of Tours. *The History of the Franks.* Trans. Lewis Thorpe. 1976. In this work, a sixth-century bishop describes the history of his people and illuminates their life.

*Hinks, Roger. *Carolingian Art.* 1962. Provides a useful insight into the ideas and values of the period as expressed in painting and sculpture.

*Hourani, Albert. *A History of the Arab Peoples.* 1991. Includes splendid chapters on social development, demographic movements, and historical issues.

"Islam and Christianity." Films for the Humanities and Sciences. This thirty-minute video explores the long and often hostile relations between two major world religions.

*Kaegi, Walter. *Byzantium and the Early Islamic Conquests.* 1992. A military history of the early clashes between the Byzantine and Islamic Empires.

*Kagan, Donald, ed. *The End of the Roman Empire: Decline or Transformation?* 3d ed. 1992. A good anthology of essays constituting a helpful, brief survey of major theories.

*Kennedy, Hugh. *The Prophet and the Age of the Caliphates.* 1986. An excellent introduction to the rise and growth of Islam to the eleventh century.

*Loverance, Rowena. *Byzantium.* 1988. A good concise overview, with splendid illustrative materials.

*Mattingly, Harold. *Christianity in the Roman Empire.* 1967. An extremely concise and cogent account of the subject; originally a series of lectures.

Medieval Epics. Trans. William Alfred et al. 1963. Includes *Beowulf,* the *Song of Roland, The Nibelungenlied,* and the *Poem of the Cid.*

Momigliano, Arnaldo. *Essays on Ancient and Modern Judaism.* Ed. S. Berti, trans. M. Masella-Gayley. 1994. The essays on the Jews in ancient Greek and Roman society are especially valuable.

*Moriarty, Catherine. *The Voice of the Middle Ages in Personal Letters, 1100–1500.* 1989. This compendium of 200 letters includes selections from Petrarch, Dürer, da Vinci, and Eleanor of Aquitane.

Nicol, Donald MacGillivray. *The Byzantine Lady: Ten Portraits, 1250–1500.* 1994. A fascinating account of women within the empire.

*Pirenne, Henri. *Mohammed and Charlemagne.* 1939. Pirenne's emphasis on the importance of Islam in the making of Europe turned historical investigation in new and fruitful directions.

Reynolds, Susan. *Kingdoms and Communities in Western Europe, 900–1300.* 2d ed. 1997. An excellent, very current study that stresses both social and political history.

*Riché, Pierre. *Daily Life in the World of Charlemagne.* Trans. Jo Ann McNamara. 1978; reprinted 1988. A fascinating survey of the topic; gives an engrossing account of the activities, values, and preoccupations of people in all strata of society.

——. *The Carolingians: A Family Who Forged Europe.* 1983; trans. M. I. Allen, 1993. A thorough investigation of the Carolingian era in medieval history.

Todd, Malcolm. *The Early Germans.* 1992. An account of the changes brought about by the migration of Germanic tribes throughout Europe and North Africa between 400 and 600.

*Tuchman, Barbara W. *A Distant Mirror: The Calamitous 14th Century.* 1978. A riveting account that focuses on the life of a French knight.

Vermes, Geza. *The Complete Dead Sea Scrolls in English.* 1997. This is the best and most complete edition of the scrolls published to date.

Williams, Marty, and Anne Echols. *Between Pit and Pedestal: Women in the Middle Ages.* 1993. Features lively, accurate recreations of the everyday lives of women of many social classes and occupations.

*Wilson, David M. *The Vikings and Their Origins: Scandinavia in the First Millennium.* 1989. An excellent recent treatment of the subject; good illustrations.

*Winston, Richard. *Charlemagne: From the Hammer to the Cross.* 1954. A lively biography of the emperor by a modern popular writer.

Ziegler, Philip. *The Black Death.* 1969. A useful discussion of the social and economic consequences of the plague that swept through Europe in the fourteenth century.

*Available in paperback.

Internet Links

The Glory of Byzantium
http://www.metmuseum.org/htmlfile/education/byzantium/byzhom.html
This well-designed website, produced by the Metropolitan Museum of Art in New York, contains beautiful graphics, textual material, a detailed timeline, glossary of terms, and educational resources.

Islam, Quran and Muhammad
http://www.lib.ox.ac.uk/internet/news/faq/archive/islam-faq.part5.html
A detailed discussion of Islam, its history, and the major tenets of the faith.

Medieval Sourcebook: Einhard, The Life of Charlemagne
http://www.fordham.edu/halsall/basis/einhard.html
An online edition of the complete text of the most readable contemporary account of the life and character of the Emperor Charlemagne.

Middle Ages: What Was It Really Like to Live in the Middle Ages?
http://www.learner.org/exhibits/middleages/
Produced by the Annenberg/CPB Project Exhibits Collection, this website examines feudal life, religion, homes, clothing, health, arts and entertainment, and town life.

Overview of Late Antiquity
http://www.unipissing.ca/department/history/orb/ovin/dex.html
This site, part of the "On-Line Reference Book for Medieval Studies," offers superb text and graphics on many aspects of history from the fall of Rome to the seventh century. Especially strong on religious developments.

Scrolls from the Dead Sea: The Ancient Library of Qumran and Modern Scholarship
http://sunsite.unc.edu/expo/deadsea.scrolls.exhibit/intro.html
This site provides extensive information about all aspects of the scrolls and the community of people that produced them. Superb text and graphics.

The Vikings
http://odin.dep.no/ud/nornytt/uda-302.html
This well-written account by a professor at the University of Oslo Museum treats the following topics: Overpopulation and Scarcity, The Tactical Advantage of the Viking Ships, Towns and Kingdoms, The Norse Gods, A Violent Society, 1000 Years of Development, and Christianity Takes Over.

Chapter
6

China in the Age of Disunity

MONGOLIA
GREAT WALL
TARTAR
KOREA
Yellow Sea
TIBET
Loyang
DISPUTED
Nanking
CHINESE
Yangtze R.
BURMA
ANNAM

0   250   500   750 Kilometers
0   250   500 Miles

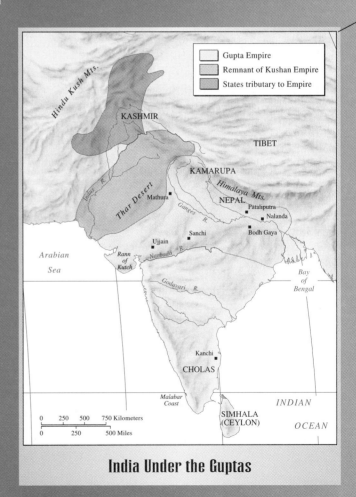

India Under the Guptas

Gupta Empire
Remnant of Kushan Empire
States tributary to Empire

Hindu Kush Mts.
KASHMIR
TIBET
KAMARUPA
Indus R.
Thar Desert
Mathura
Himalaya Mts.
NEPAL
Pataliputra
Ganges R.
Nalanda
Ujjain
Sanchi
Bodh Gaya
Arabian Sea
Rann of Kutch
Narbada R.
Godavari R.
Bay of Bengal
Kanchi
CHOLAS
Malabar Coast
INDIAN OCEAN
SIMHALA (CEYLON)

0   250   500   750 Kilometers
0   250   500 Miles

Disruption and Renewal in South and East Asia

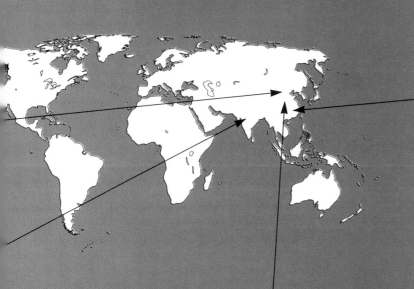

The Southern Sung

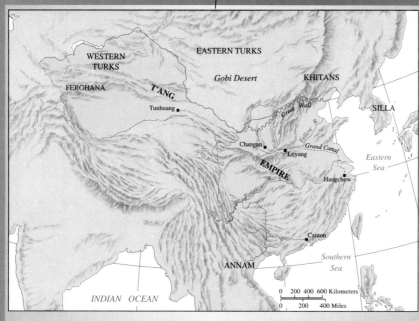

The T'ang Empire

In both India and China, the first great imperial age was followed by a period of disruption, invasions, and upheaval. As in western Europe after the Roman Empire collapsed, when imperial restraints crumbled and new peoples arrived, India experienced a new age of innovation and creativity.

Except for northern India, which was ruled by the Kushan kings for over a century, the Indian subcontinent remained fragmented for about 600 years after the fall of the Mauryan Empire. The Gupta dynasty reunified northern India in the fourth century C.E., and during the next two centuries, Indian culture enjoyed its golden age under their rule. During this era Hinduism began to assume the form that would continue until the present day. Buddhism, in the meantime, began to decline. Islam became a force on the Indian subcontinent at the beginning of the eighth century, and by 1000 Muslims from central Asia had gained control of all northern India. Although India was unable to ward off the invaders, Hinduism and Hindu culture survived. Buddhism, however, vanished from the subcontinent.

China's first imperial age ended with the fall of the Han dynasty in 220 C.E. China became fragmented, and northern China was ruled by nomadic invaders during the next 300 years. Buddhism became the dominant religion in China during these centuries of turmoil. It enriched the Chinese civilization with its teachings and the Greco-Roman-Indian artistic traditions it brought with it. Eventually, Buddhism provided a focus for the reunification of North and South China.

China was reunified in 581 and entered a grand second imperial age under the T'ang dynasty. Under the T'ang, China was powerful and cosmopolitan, absorbing elements from other cultures and passing on its great achievements. The following Sung dynasty refined many earlier traditions but was unable to continue the diplomatic and military successes of its predecessor. Though cultured, urban, and refined, the Sung suffered repeated military reverses until it was completely conquered by the Mongols in the thirteenth century.

The second imperial age in both lands is important because cultures in both India and China down to the present owe more to this era than to the first imperial age. Moreover, during the second imperial age both cultures exerted a lasting influence on neighboring lands. This chapter will explore the forces of disruption and renewal that shaped India and China during this period and examine the lasting legacies of these centuries.

India from the Guptas to the Muslim Dynasties

*The people are numerous and happy; they have not to register their households, or attend to any magistrates or their rules; only those who cultivate the royal land have to pay a portion of the gain from it. . . . Throughout the country the people do not kill any living creature, nor eat onion or garlic.**

* * * * *

He caused distress to no man in the city, but he chastised the wicked.
   Even in this mean age he did not fail the trust of the people.

1 C.E.	Ajanta and other cave excavations begin in India
	Buddhism arrives in China
	King Kanishka calls Fourth Buddhist Council
	Gandharan and Mathuran art styles
	Paper invented
	Three Kingdoms and era of disunity in China
	Spread of Buddhism
	The Gupta dynasty
	Revival of Hinduism in India
	Buddhist cave temples begin in China
500	
	Yang Chien reunifies China, Sui dynasty
	Grand Canal in China
	Harsha rules in India
	Hsuan-tsang goes to India
	Founding of T'ang dynasty
	Confucian revival
750	
	Golden age of Chinese poetry: Li Po
	Muslims invade India
	Printing invented
	Northern Sung dynasty
	Liao, Chin, Hsi Hsia states in North China
	Neo-Confucianism gains; Buddhism declines in China
	Chinese examination system fully developed
1000	Turkish Muslims conquer North India; Rajput resistance
	Porcelain manufacture perfected
	Gunpowder invented
	Southern Sung dynasty
	Mongols conquer the Southern Sung
1300	

He cherished the citizens as his own children and he put down crime.

*He delighted the inhabitants with gifts and honours, and smiling conversation, and he increased their love with informal visits and friendly receptions.***

*H. H. Gowen, *History of Indian Literature* (New York: Appleton, 1931), p. 336.

**A. L. Basham, *The Wonder That Was India* (New York: Grove Press, 1954), p. 104.

The first passage was written by Fa-hsien, a famous Chinese pilgrim who traveled and studied in India during the Gupta period. The second, which comes from a contemporary rock inscription, describes provincial administration under an early Gupta king. Later kings were encouraged to look to it as a model for their conduct. Both accounts describe a well-governed land under the Gupta dynasty, which had succeeded in uniting most of India. The Guptas and Harsha were the last of the Hindu/Buddhist monarchs to rule over a largely united and flourishing India. Soon after Harsha's death, India became fragmented again and was also subjected to centuries of Muslim invasions that permanently changed the religious composition of the subcontinent.

The Gupta Empire, Harsha, and the Rajputs

With the breakup of the Kushan Empire, northern India was once again fragmented politically, and little information about the petty successor states has survived. Early in the fourth century, a minor prince named Chandra Gupta rose to power in the Delhi region where the Jumna and Ganges Rivers converge. Around 320, after victories in war and marriage to the princess of a powerful tribe, he crowned himself "Great King of Kings," an act that inaugurated the Gupta era. By the time Chandra Gupta died in 335, the Gupta dynasty ruled the Ganges River valley, the heartland of the earlier Mauryan Empire.

In several respects the early reigns of the Gupta dynasty seemed to reenact the Mauryan era. Chandra Gupta I was followed by his son, Samudra Gupta (reigned 335–376). Much is known about him from a eulogy inscribed on an Asokan pillar. This eulogy praised him as a great warrior who had "violently uprooted" nine kings in northern India, an act that won him the title "exterminator of all other kings." Samudra Gupta brought much of northern India under his direct rule and made vassals of the remaining rulers. He was also a capable administrator, tolerant of different religions, cultured, and a patron of the arts. The reign of his son, Chandra Gupta II (reigned 376–415), was the high-water mark of the Gupta Empire, and some say of ancient India. Although southern India remained independent, Chandra Gupta II added the Deccan region to the Gupta Empire.

The early Gupta dynasty is India's classical age because it established the standards in culture and the arts that later eras looked to for inspiration and example. Just as the Greek ambassador Megasthenes' observations provided insights into the Mauryan Empire, another foreigner, the Chinese Buddhist pilgrim Fa-hsien supplied information about life in the reign of Chandra Gupta II. Fa-hsien traveled widely in India between 405 and 411 and spoke glowingly of the efficient and benevolent government, the merciful justice system, the rarity of crime, and the generally peaceful state of the land. Coming from a land that still suffered from internal divisions, he marveled that one could travel from one end of India to the other without fear of molestation and without need of passports. On social customs and mores Fa-hsien said: "In this country they do not keep swine or fowls, and do not deal in cattle; they have no shambles [butcher shops] or wine-shops in their market places. In commerce they use cowrie-shells. The Pariahs alone hunt and sell flesh." He also recorded the grandeur of Pataliputra, the capital city, its great religious processions, and the charitable institutions maintained by people of means. Considering conditions in divided China and the problems besetting the contemporary late Roman Empire, India under the early Guptas was without doubt the best-governed and most prosperous empire in the world.

The later Guptas, who reigned after 415, were mostly undistinguished rulers, and India once again came under attack by invaders. The White Huns, called Huna in India, were nomads from central Asia, who may have been related to the Huns who threatened Europe in the same period. The Huna invaded India repeatedly in the

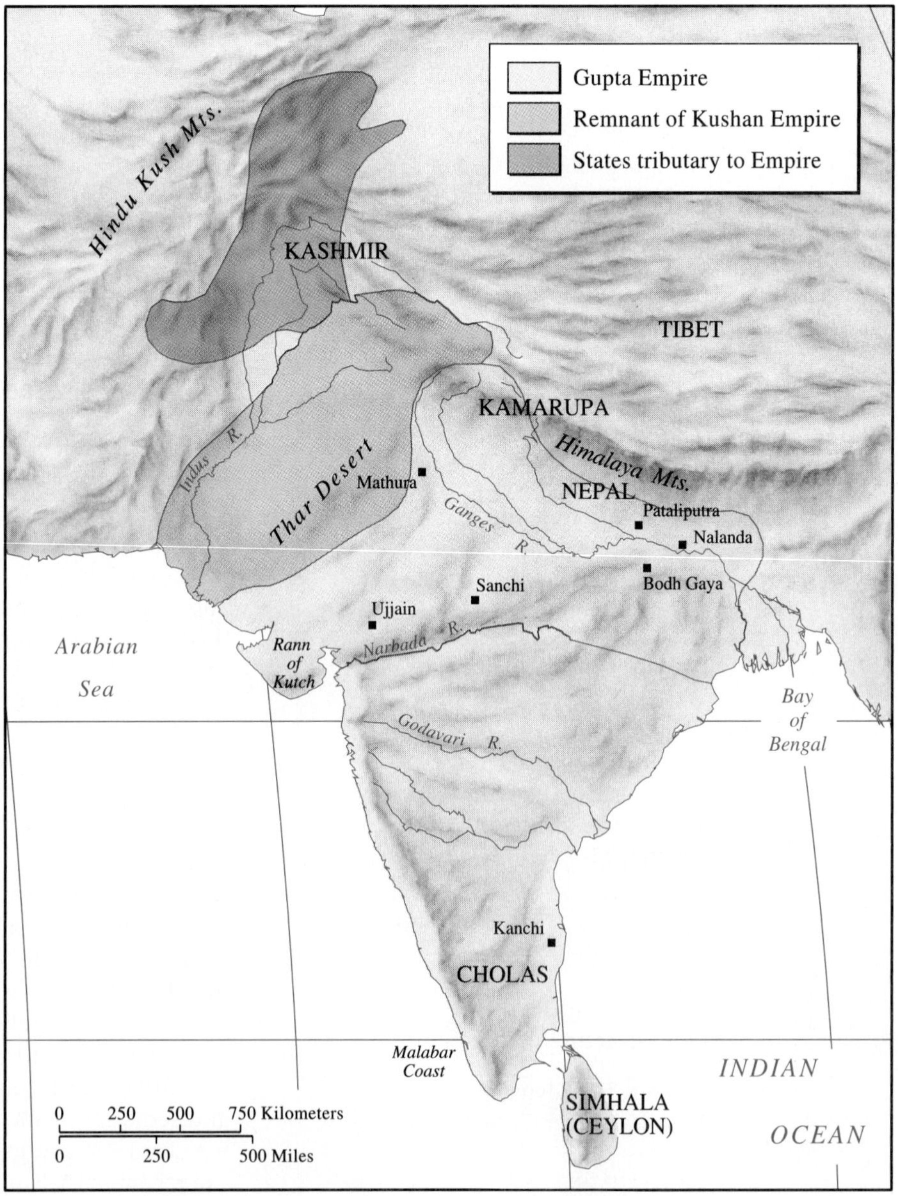
Gupta Empire
Remnant of Kushan Empire
States tributary to Empire
Hindu Kush Mts.
KASHMIR
TIBET
KAMARUPA
Himalaya Mts.
NEPAL
Indus R.
Thar Desert
Mathura
Ganges R.
Pataliputra
Nalanda
Bodh Gaya
Sanchi
Ujjain
Narbada R.
Rann of Kutch
Arabian Sea
Bay of Bengal
Godavari R.
Kanchi
CHOLAS
Malabar Coast
SIMHALA (CEYLON)
INDIAN OCEAN
0 250 500 750 Kilometers
0 250 500 Miles

MAP 6.1 The Gupta Empire. The great early Gupta rulers conquered most of northern India and gave that area an extended period of peace and prosperity. But even at its height, the Gupta Empire did not control southern India.

fifth century; much of northwestern India, especially Buddhist establishments in the region, suffered enormous damage from their depredations. The repeated invasions dealt the death blow to the already weakened Gupta Empire, which disappeared by 550. It was replaced by minor rulers who had once been Gupta vassals and by Hunnish and related tribal states.

In 606 a young man named Harsha, just sixteen years old, ascended the throne of a petty state in the Jumna-Ganges valley. He ruled for the next forty-one years and nearly succeeded in restoring the glory days of the Guptas. Two contemporary sources provide information about Harsha (reigned 606–648): one is the *Life of Harsha,* a biography by a protégé named Bana; the other is the journal of Hsuan-tsang, a celebrated Chinese pilgrim who spent fifteen years on the subcontinent, eight of them in Harsha's dominions, and kept a voluminous account. According to Bana, upon becoming king Harsha "went from east to west, subduing all who were not obedient." He was so busy that "the elephants were not unharnessed, nor the soldiers unhelmeted." In six years he had subdued all northern India but was unable to gain control of the Deccan and the south. He then reigned in peace for thirty-five years.

Harsha was a gifted and energetic ruler. He traveled constantly to render justice and to supervise the government. Although inclined toward Buddhism, he nevertheless patronized all religions. A distinguished scholar and patron of learning, he was also the author of three plays. Harsha was a lavish sponsor of charities and built many hospitals to dispense free medical care to the poor and to travelers. According to Hsuan-tsang, on one occasion for seventy-five days Harsha and his retinue distributed the wealth of the treasury and his personal possessions to half a million people, until "except for the horses, elephants and military accouterments, which were necessary for maintaining order and protecting the royal estate, nothing remained."

Soon after witnessing Harsha's remarkable largess, Hsuan-tsang, who had been away from home for sixteen years, decided to return to China. He refused all Harsha's gifts except for a fur cloak and money for his traveling expenses. Nevertheless, he was laden with the treasures for which he had come to India. They included 651 manuscripts and numerous relics and images of the Buddha and Buddhist saints. Harsha's escort accompanied the Chinese pilgrim to the frontier of his realm. When Hsuan-tsang arrived at Changan, the Chinese capital, in 646, he was welcomed as a great celebrity. The Chinese emperor, his court, and thousands of ordinary citizens went outside the city to greet him.

Thanks to the bond established by Hsuan-tsang, Harsha exchanged ambassadors with the Chinese emperor T'ai-tsung. When T'ai-tsung's third envoy arrived in India, however, he found that Harsha had been assassi-

Life during Harsha's Reign

With respect to the ordinary people, although they are naturally light-minded, yet they are upright and honourable. In money matters they are without craft, and in administering justice they are considerate. They dread the retribution of another state of existence, and make light of the things of the present world. They are not deceitful in their conduct, and are faithful to their oaths and promises. In the rules of government there is remarkable rectitude, whilst in their behaviour there is much gentleness and sweetness. With respect to criminals and rebels, these are few in number, and only occasionally troublesome. . . . As the administration of the government is founded on benign principles, the executive is simple. The families are not entered on registers, and the people are not subject to forced labour. The private [holdings] of the crown are divided into four principal parts; the first is for carrying out affairs of state and providing sacrificial offerings; the second is for providing subsidies for the ministers and chief officers of state; the third is for rewarding men of distinguished ability; and the fourth is for charity to religious bodies, whereby the field of merit is cultivated. In this way the taxes on the people are light, and the personal service required of them is moderate.[*]

These comments about India by the Chinese Buddhist pilgrim Hsuan-tsang paint a picture of good government and contented people under Harsha. They agree with observations of other Chinese pilgrims who had visited India somewhat earlier during the Gupta dynasty. In this sense, Harsha's reign forms the finale of the Gupta era.

[*]*Si-Yu-Ki Buddhist Records of the Western World,* trans. Samuel Beal (London: Truther, 1884), pp. 83, 87.

nated and his throne usurped. In a remarkable demonstration of Chinese power, the ambassador rushed to Tibet where T'ai-tsung's son-in-law was king, raised an army, and returned to defeat the usurper, who was arrested and taken to China as a prisoner. Nevertheless, Chinese intervention could not save Harsha's kingdom from disintegration.

Superficially, there were many similarities between the Gupta administration and that of the Mauryans. The great accomplishment of the Mauryans had been the creation of a highly centralized empire of continental proportions. The Guptas, however, failed to reduce their local administrators to total obedience. The town and village councils and the professional guilds also remained largely autonomous. Inadequate revenue compelled the Guptas to pay official salaries partly in land grants; unlike most feudal arrangements, however, the recipients of the land grants were not obliged to provide the king with revenue or military assistance. Thus the king's authority was limited to those areas under his direct control.

With the decline of the Mauryan Empire after Asoka, the peoples in the Deccan and southern India had freed themselves and established independent kingdoms. The inscriptions that have survived, the remains of cave temples, and the records of Chinese pilgrims agree that Buddhism flourished throughout the region in the post-Mauryan centuries. South India was prosperous because it produced spices and precious stones desired by other peoples. Since the first century C.E., increased knowledge of the winds and currents had led to a flourishing sea trade between South Indian ports and the Persian Gulf, the Red Sea, Southeast Asia, and China.

Harsha was assassinated in 648. Amidst the ensuing political anarchy in northern India, the first of many Muslim armies crossed the mountains in the northwest and appeared on the plains of the Indus in 712. While some Muslims raided and then retreated, others came to stay. In this sense they were no different from earlier invaders, but, whereas the Greeks and central Asian tribal raiders had been rapidly assimilated, the Muslims, with their rigidly defined religion, largely retained their separate identities.

Religious Developments: Hinduism and Buddhism

Modern Hinduism gradually emerged during and after the Gupta era. The intellectual basis of Hinduism was revitalized as the brahmans expounded the philosophy of the *Upanishads* and debated Buddhist theologians. At the same time, in response to the challenge of Buddhist and Jain teachings, ways of life for the ordinary Hindu also began to evolve. They were called the Way of Worship and the Way of Works. All Hindus believed in the law of karma, that deeds had their consequences; they hoped that by following dharma, or the sacred law, they could finally attain *moksha* (release from the round of reincarnations). While some brahmans and ascetics studied the philosophy of the *Upanishads* and thus followed the Way of Wisdom, most men and women followed the more attainable Way of Worship or the Way of Works.

In the Way of Worship, a devotee chose a personal deity and did his or her bidding, attended temple ceremonies, and went on pilgrimages. While the Vedic gods receded in importance, three earlier obscure gods came to the forefront. One was Brahma, the creator god and the personified universal spirit of the *Upanishads*. The primary objects of worship, however, were Vishnu (patron god to many Gupta rulers), the benevolent preserver god, and Shiva, the fearsome god of death and fertility. Myths about the gods were collected in the Pu-

✤ Krisha Dancing with the Gopis. This manuscript page shows Krishna playing the flute, surrounded by his maiden admirers, the gopis, each of whom imagines he is dancing only with her. T. Richard Burton, *Hindu Art* (Cambridge: Harvard University Press, 1993), fig. 82; courtesy of the Trustees of the British Museum

ranas, the equivalent of the Bible in popular Hinduism. As the Puranas told believers, Vishnu has been reincarnated nine times, and each time he saved the world from demons and evil forces. His early incarnations, or *avatars,* were in animal form; for example, the Fish, who saved Manu, the father of the human race, from the Cosmic Flood. The seventh incarnation was Rama, the perfect man, the deified hero of the epic *Ramayana,* who is worshiped together with his faithful wife, Sita, the ideal woman. The eighth incarnation was Krishna the "dark [skinned]," probably originally a non-Aryan god of the south. Stories about Krishna's pranks as a youth, his popularity with ladies as a young man, and his championship of moral duty as a mature man are known and loved by all Hindus. His ninth incarnation was Gautama Buddha. The admission of Gautama into the Hindu pantheon blurred the differences between Hindus and Buddhists and hastened the absorption of Buddhists into the orthodox Hindu fold. After the twelfth century, with the destruction of the remnants of the great Buddhist establishments in northern India by the Muslim conquerors, Buddhism finally vanished from the land of its birth. The tenth reincarnation of Vishnu is yet to come. Vishnu was worshpped with his wife, Lakshmi, the goddess of good luck; the two are frequently depicted together in affectionate poses.

While millions worshiped Vishnu, other millions called themselves devotees of Shiva. In addition to death and fertility, Shiva was identified with the Vedic storm god, Rudra, and was also patron god of ascetics, lord of the dance, and the embodiment of cosmic energy. Shiva's wife manifested herself in different forms, often as a fertility goddess, perhaps the mother goddess of the Indus civilization. As Durga and Kali, she was bloody and terrible and demanded sacrifices. (Among those who worshiped Kali were the members of a small sect called Thuggees, from which the English word *thug* derives. Thuggees specialized in robbing and killing travelers as acts of devotion to Kali.) Shiva and Kali's pot-bellied and elephant-headed son Ganesha was the patron god of learning.

Most Hindus to the present count themselves as devotees of either Vishnu or Shiva. The gods and goddesses are represented by idols and worshiped at home, in temples, and at special ceremonies with offerings of flowers, food, dance, and incense. Sites associated with them are also the destinations of pilgrims.

While worshiping their personal deities, Hindus were also encouraged to follow the Way of Works. It taught that all persons were born and reared in their respective castes and must follow caste rules, which became more firmly entrenched during the Gupta period than before. As an inscription of the Gupta dynasty says, good rulers should "keep the castes confined to their respective spheres of duty." In addition, all must repay their debts to parents and ancestors through the proper discharge of duty and responsibility to family, to seers through diligent study and proper respect, to the gods through worship, and to humanity through charity and kindness. In living up to the demands of the Ways of Worship and Works, Hindu men and women hoped to acquire good karma and either in this life or in future incarnations be able to follow the Way of Wisdom. These essential teachings and practices of Hinduism persist to the present.

The Guptas and Harsha patronized both Hinduism and Buddhism. Leaders of the two religions held frequent theological debates. Jewish and Christian communities also appeared in India during this era. Some Jews came

Shiva and Parvati. Millions of Hindus worship Shiva and his consort, Parvati, as their primary deities. The twelfth-century sculpture on the left shows the divine couple seated lovingly together. The eighteenth-century painting on the right shows the male and female aspects of the god of destruction with the Bull of Nandi, Shiva's mount and a fertility symbol, below them. Both pictures from T. Richard Burton, *Hindu Art* (Cambridge: Harvard University Press, 1993), fig. 58; courtesy of the Trustees of the British Museum

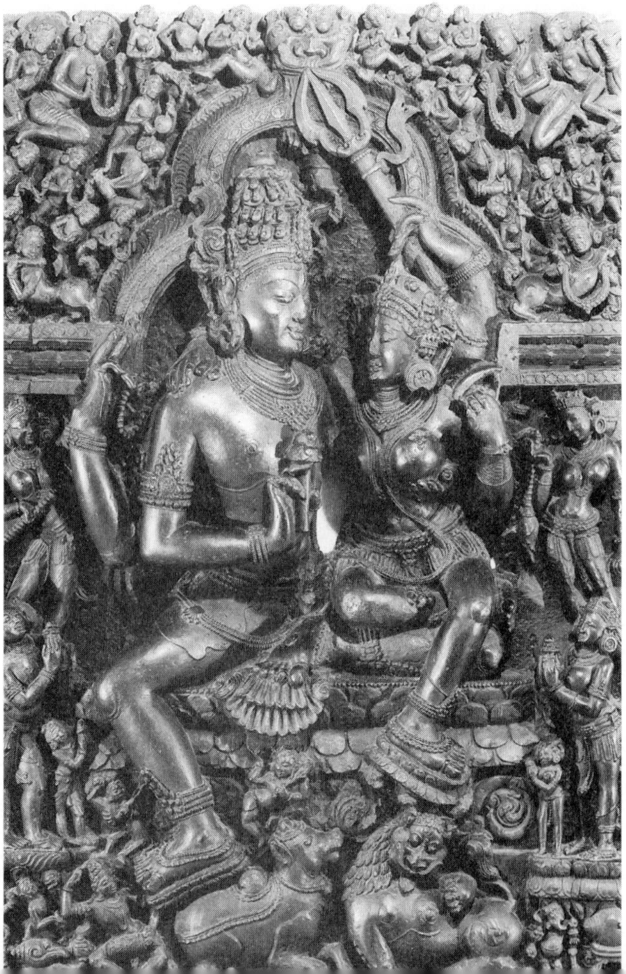

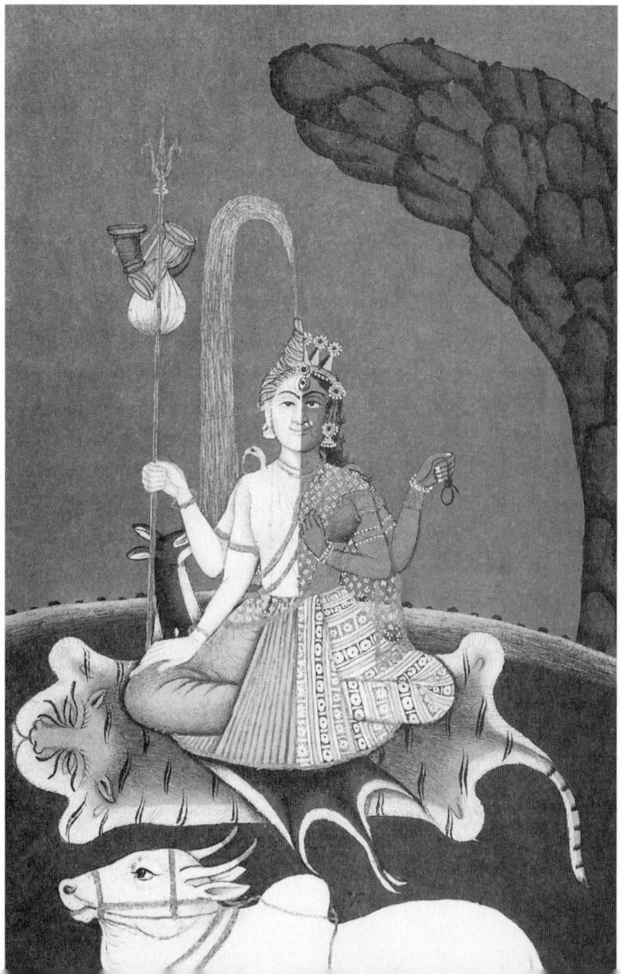

to India as refugees after the Diaspora of 70 C.E. Their descendants still live in Kerala on the southwestern coast of India and are divided into two groups: the "white Jews," who claim to have retained their Semitic racial identity, and the "black Jews," who have intermarried with Indians. Most Indian Christians also lived in Kerala. They claimed descent from converts of the apostle Thomas, who had reputedly come to proselytize in India. They professed the Syrian branch of Christianity; many are prominent in modern India.

A Vibrant Art, Architecture, and Culture

Indian art is inextricably linked with Indian religions. Both Buddhist and classical Hindu art reached their peaks during the Gupta era. This period saw the synthesis and climax of previous tendencies and produced the classical style that inspired much of the art of the entire Buddhist and Hindu world throughout Asia.

The goal of religious art, in India as elsewhere, was not only to reach the educated, but to make religious and philosophical ideals intelligible to ordinary people. The greatest contributions of the Gupta artists are their classical representations of the divinities of India. These works combine vigor, refinement, and sublime idealism with a sense of rhythm and movement. In sculptures of the Buddha, the ideal of serenity found its noblest expression and became the standard.

The most impressive surviving Buddhist sites are the cave temples. The grandest is Ajanta, located in the Dec-can in an isolated hillside by a river valley. Although the caves were excavated over a thousand years between the first century B.C.E. and the ninth century C.E., most were built during a great burst of artistic activity in the mid-fifth century. Each of the twenty-nine cave temples is entered through a portal into the main hall where two rows of columns divide the interior into a central nave and side aisles, in much the same way that the interior of Christian basilica churches is divided. At the far end of the hall is either a giant image of the Buddha or a stupa that commemorates his nirvana. A typical hall is sixty-five feet square with a fourteen-foot-high ceiling. Beyond the halls and cut still deeper into the cliffs are the monks' quarters. Intricately carved columns and capitals, sculptures in the round, and friezes decorate the caves. The Ajanta caves can be compared with the Acropolis, built in Athens a thousand years earlier. Both exemplify the highest artistic accomplishments of their respective cultures' classical periods, and both were built to honor the gods and the achievements of the people.

A remarkable number of fresco paintings have survived in Ajanta; the pictures are hailed as among the greatest wall paintings anywhere in the world. Although the subject matter is Buddhist, many scenes are drawn from contemporary life. The depictions of voluptuous ladies and sumptuous scenes demonstrate how Indians have reconciled the sensuous and worldly with the spiritual and religious.

Revitalized Hinduism, already strong in the Gupta period, was represented in cave and free-standing temples.

Ajanta Cave Temples. The rock temples were excavated in cliffs 250 feet high, standing above a river valley, and date from the first century B.C.E. to the ninth century C.E. This picture shows the façade (or entrance) of a Gupta-era cave temple at Ajanta.
Scala/Art Resource

Leisure Pursuits for Gentlemen in India and China

Life for upper-class men in India and China offered many refined pleasures. As always, books were written that purported to teach young gentlemen how to live. The first excerpt is from a fifth-century Indian work entitled *Kama Sutra* (Aphorisms on Love). The second is from the diary of an early fourteenth-century Chinese scholar-painter and describes his leisure pursuits.

He [a cultured gentleman] must get up early in the morning . . . wash his teeth, smear his body with just a little fragrant paste, inhale fragrant smoke, wear some flower, just give the lips a rub with wax and red juice, look at his face in the mirror, chew betel leaves along with some mouth deodorants, and then attend to his work. . . . In the forenoon still, he dresses and goes out for social calls and for enjoyment of the company of others. In the evening he enjoys music and dance. At the end of it, in his own apartments, decorated and fragrant with smoke, he awaits, along with his companions, his beloved who has given him an engagement, or else sends her a message and himself goes out to meet her. . . . Such is the daily routine.*

* * * * *

Liu Chu-ch'uan's newly made wine has just matured; its taste was pure and its flavor unique. In the morning he brought over a pot, and we enjoyed several cups with Mr. Chan. At noon Mr. Liu barbecued two birds, and we drank some wine together. . . . After the wine [another friend] . . . hired two small boats and invited me [and others] . . . to visit the Lotus Flower Swamp. . . . After lingering for some time, we went to Righteous Road Monastery. The master in the monastery prepared wine for us, but I cannot say very much for its taste. Next we went back to the boats and picked lotus seeds. By this time the sun was setting and a breeze began to blow. We made cups out of the lotus leaves and drank wine from them. Those who could not hold their liquor all got drunk. Not until the moon had risen on the horizon did we return. It was a very merry day.**

**William T. de Bary, ed., *Sources of Indian Tradition,* vol. 1 (New York: Columbia University Press, 1958), pp. 255–256.*

***Patricia B. Ebrey, ed., *Chinese Civilization and Society: A Source Book* (New York: Free Press, 1981), pp. 118–119.*

In addition to several Ajanta caves that were Hindu, other contemporary cave temples were dedicated exclusively to Hindu deities. Shiva and Vishnu were most often represented in these Hindu shrines. In contrast to the serenity exhibited by Buddha statues, Vishnu and Shiva are often shown in poses full of dynamic energy; they frequently appear in association with their female counterparts. A remarkable eighth-century Hindu temple dedicated to Shiva is located near Ajanta. The immense structure is actually not a building in the conventional sense. It was literally carved out of the rock of the hillside, a rare technical feat.

Metal casting also reached its apogee during the Gupta period. The castings range from fine miniature statues in bronze to an eighty-foot-tall copper image of the Buddha at Nalanda and the huge wrought iron Iron Pillar of Delhi, which would have been a feat for even the best foundries of the modern age. The rich variety of gold coins minted by the Guptas also showed artistic excellence. The highly developed aesthetic sense and superb execution of Gupta sculptors made them the ideal and despair of artists of later generations.

Literature and scholarship in India always depended in part on court patronage. The Guptas patronized many genres of the arts. Literature ranged from refined court poetry to popular fairy tales and fables. "Sinbad the Sailor" and several other stories popularized in *A Thousand and One Nights* originated in India.

Whereas the Egyptians wrote on papyrus and the Chinese invented paper, the first surviving Indian books date to the fifth century and were written on birch bark and specially prepared leaves. The resurgence of Hinduism resulted in a revival of Sanskrit, now used in Hindu as well as Buddhist and Jain writings. Other works from this period dealt with law, medicine, and the sciences. Indian scholars devised a sign for zero and worked out a decimal number system, knowledge that was transmitted to the Arabs and later adopted by the rest of the world, which called it the Arabic numeral system. India also led other cultures in knowledge of algebra and is largely credited with founding modern mathematics. Astronomers found out that the earth was round and rotated on its axis, but since this information had been known to Greek astronomers since the Hellenistic Age, Indians probably learned it from the Greeks. Universities for secular and religious studies flourished; the famous university at Nalanda had an international student body that included men from China and Ceylon.

Popular culture also flourished. Frequent religious festivals lent color to daily life. People participated in processions and elaborate religious festivals at richly decorated temples, the dwelling places of gods and goddesses. Like European Christians, they also watched drama and dances with religious themes.

The family was patriarchal; women were subordinate to men, but children were taught to obey both parents.

Marriages were arranged by parents and, except for princes, were monogamous. Because of the hot climate, clothing tended to be scanty and loose-fitting, except in the cold north, where people wore close-fitting jackets. Men often wore only a loincloth, sometimes with another piece of fabric thrown over the body. Women wore a *sari,* a long piece of cloth wound around the waist in folds, falling to the feet and draped across the shoulder. Both sexes wore long hair, loose or braided, and both, especially women, adorned themselves with jewelry and flowers.

Hsuan-tsang described the Indians as clean and fastidious. He said of their eating habits:

> Before every meal they must have a wash; the fragments and remains are not served up again; the food utensils are not passed on; those which are of pottery or of wood must be thrown away after use, and those which are of gold, silver, copper or iron get another polishing. As soon as a meal is over they chew the tooth-stick and make themselves clean. Before they have finished ablutions they do not come in contact with each other.

At death the mighty and humble alike were cremated. The virtuous widow committed *suttee,* or suicide by immolation on the funeral pyre of her husband.

India under the Impact of Islam

In 712, two generations after the death of Harsha, an Arab army conquered Sind in northwestern India, an event that heralded the powerful role that Islam would soon play in the history of India. Earlier attackers had been assimilated over time, but these Muslim invaders would not be, because their iconoclastic monotheism was incompatible with Hinduism and Buddhism. Although the zeal of some early Muslim conquerors embittered relations with many Hindus, some lower-caste Hindus found dignity in the religious equality that Islam accorded to all believers and converted voluntarily.

The Arab invaders of 712 did not penetrate beyond Sind and generally lived in amity with their neighbors. Meanwhile, the Arabs conquered and converted the Turks of central Asia. Ferocious warriors, now on behalf of Islam, the Turks at first served as bodyguards of their Arab rulers but in time asserted their independence and established their own states. One of these states was Ghazni, in present-day Afghanistan. In 1023 Mahmud of Ghazni rode into India with 30,000 mounted warriors, pillaging and killing as they went. Mahmud called himself the "image-breaker," because he delighted in destroying Hindu and Buddhist places of worship and killing "non-believers." His soldiers boasted that they massacred 50,000 Hindus in one Hindu shrine city alone.

Other Turkish conquerors after Mahmud ruled northern India with conquering armies of occupation and continued to wreak havoc on Buddhist and Hindu institutions and places of worship. Countless Hindu, Buddhist, and Jain shrines were demolished; some of their stones were recycled to build mosques and monuments to commemorate Muslim power. For example, the Kutb Minar (victory tower) in Delhi was partly built with stones from demolished Hindu and Jain temples. The great Buddhist university at Nalanda, including its library filled with priceless manuscripts, was destroyed. Buddhism never recovered from those blows. Hinduism survived in northern India, but without the state patronage that had allowed it to blossom intellectually, it turned inward. The caste system became more rigid, and in compliance with Muslim standards, women became more secluded and wore the veil in public.

Some Indians, most notably the Rajputs of northern India, fought the invaders bravely. *Rajput* means son of a king. Rajputs were kshatriyas (warrior caste), and according to their genealogies, they belonged to thirty-two clans that descended from the sun, moon, and stars. Modern scholars say instead that many probably were descendants of the Huna and other previous invaders who had become assimilated and had created fake genealogies to lend themselves greater dignity. Like the knights of medieval Europe and the *samurai* of Japan, they were fiercely proud hereditary warriors. Young Rajputs were brought up on epic stories of old. On reaching puberty, boys went through an initiation ceremony called the binding of the sword, which bound them to a code of honor that included respect for women. The men disdained manual labor; they either fought or hunted and played manly sports. Women enjoyed considerable freedom; they hunted and even went to war with their husbands. When her husband died in battle, a Rajput woman was expected to mount his funeral pyre and proudly commit suicide. When not fighting Muslim invaders, Rajputs often fought among themselves. Indian bards composed and recited epic poems that celebrated the brave deeds of Rajput lords and ladies, just as similar epics hailed the deeds of ancient Macedonian chieftains and medieval European knights.

Although the Rajputs performed many deeds of bravery and chivalry, they never became a united force and were defeated by the conquering Muslims. The caste system may have contributed to Hindu defeat. Since Hindu society clearly demarcated functions, only the kshatriyas had a duty to fight. On the other hand, during the next millennium, when the Muslims subjugated ever larger territories, the social cohesiveness of the caste system enabled the Hindus to persevere and thus preserve their way of life.

During these centuries politically divided southern India escaped Muslim conquest and the ravages suffered by the north. Temple building and religious art flourished in the south, and, with northern India under Turkish Muslim rule, it was here that Indian styles and trends

A Rajput Lady's Creed

"Boy, tell me, ere I go, how bore himself my lord?"

"As a reaper of the harvest of battle! I followed his steps as the humble gleaner of his sword. On the bed of honour he spread a carpet of the slain, whereon, a barbarian his pillow, he sleeps ringed by his foes."

"Yet once again, oh boy, tell me how my lord bore himself?"

"Oh mother, who can tell his deeds. He left no foe to dread or to admire him." She smiled farewell to the boy, and adding, "My lord will chide my delay," sprang into the flame.*

The Rajputs loved epics about heroic deeds in battle and the hunt. The stories, sung by bards, celebrated the heroism of both men and women. In this tale, the widow asks her fallen husband's page about his death at the Muslim siege of Chitor; then she sacrifices her life to honor him. Other tales told of Rajput ladies committing mass suicide at the news of their husbands' deaths in battle, rather than surrendering to the Muslims. They built a huge funeral pyre and leapt into the flames. This practice and the attitude toward women that it implies are still major barriers to the achievement of equal status for the women of contemporary India.

*H. G. Rawlinson, *India: A Short Cultural History*, p. 202, quoted in James Tod, *Annals and Antiquities of Rajasthan*, vol. 1 (London: H. Mitford, 1920), p. 246.

in art and architecture persisted. Southern Indian culture also inspired and influenced the Indianized states of Southeast Asia (see Chapter 7). In the north, Muslim rulers considered it their religious duty to build mosques and other monuments; they employed Hindu craftsmen to work on these constructions. In time an Indo-Islamic style developed from the blending of the Indian and Muslim traditions, but that style did not reach maturity until a later era.

The Age of Disunity in China

I climb to the ridge of Pei Mang Mountain
And look down on the city of Lo-yang.
In Lo-yang how still it is!
Palaces and houses all burnt to ashes.
Walls and fences all broken and gaping,
Thorns and brambles shooting up to the sky.
I do not see the old old-men:

I only see the new young men.
I turn aside, for the straight road is lost:
The fields are overgrown and will never be ploughed again.
I have been away such a long time
That I do not know which street is which.
How sad and ugly the empty moors are!
A thousand miles without the smoke of a chimney.
I think of the house I lived in all those years:
I am heart-tied and cannot speak.*

* * * * *

At this time in the city of Ch'ang-an there were not more than one hundred families. Weeds and thorns grew thickly as if in a forest. Only four carts could be found in the city. The officials had neither robes of ceremony nor seals. Instead they used tablets of mulberry wood on which their names and rank were inscribed.**

*Arthur Waley, *Translations from the Chinese* (New York: Knopf, 1941), p. 64.

**Charles P. Fitzgerald, *China: A Short Cultural History* (New York, Praeger, 1961), p. 260.

The first passage, a poem written in the early third century, describes Loyang after it had been sacked by a rebellious general at the end of the Han dynasty. The second passage describes Changan during the fourth century. Both cities, once proud metropolises and capitals of the great Han Empire, had been sacked and plundered by Chinese in civil wars and by nomadic invaders. Their desolate state was symptomatic of the ruin of northern China during the age of disunity.

As after the end of the Roman Empire, the dissolution of the Han dynasty was followed by several centuries of disruption, wars, and invasions. Although the age of disunity (220–581) was a period of political instability, the collapse of central authority also exposed people to new and enriching ideas. Just as Christianity and the Latin language eventually built bridges between conquerors and conquered in western Europe and became the basis of a common culture, Buddhism and the Chinese language ultimately united the Chinese and their nomadic rulers. By the end of the era, Buddhism had become the faith of the overwhelming majority of Chinese. It was also instrumental in bringing the artistic forms and ideals of the Greco-Roman-Indian traditions to China. In time these became Sinicized into a truly international art form and spread to Korea and Japan (see Chapter 7).

Political Turmoil: Division and Disunity

The age of disunity began in 220 when the ineffectual last emperor of the Han was forced to give two of his daughters in marriage to a powerful general and then to abdicate in favor of his son-in-law. Two rival claimants challenged the usurper's authority, and civil wars ensued. The usurper's heirs soon met the same fate he had meted out to the emperor. The chaos in the Chinese world allowed the regrouped Hsiung-nu to renew their attack. They destroyed Loyang in 311 and burned the imperial library, causing irreparable loss; in 316 they also laid waste to Changan. North China would be ruled by nomadic conquerors until the end of the sixth century. The Chinese peasants were reduced to serfdom or to slavery, working for a tiny class of alien rulers.

Some of the elite fled to southern China and established a new capital at Nanking in the lower Yangtze valley. The mountain range that divided the Yellow and the Yangtze drainage basins became the boundary between the northern and southern kingdoms. Although short-lived dynasties followed one another in the south, it did not suffer the massive destruction experienced by the north. Powerless to reconquer the north, the southern governments nevertheless claimed to be the true heirs of the Han civilization. By the time China was once more reunified, southern China had built up its population and was fully acculturated. The refugee governments in southern China claimed, with some legitimacy, to be the true successors of the Han and attempted to keep alive ancient traditions. The shift of the center of gravity from North to South China would continue after the end of the age of disunity.

Given their small numbers and lack of experience in administering a sedentary people, the conquering rulers of northern China were forced to employ the remaining Confucian officials in their government. The new mas-ters found themselves in a dilemma. To exercise effective control and fully enjoy their new power, they needed to be located in the Chinese heartland. Therefore, in 494 the T'o-pa king of the most successful and long-lived nomadic dynasty in North China moved his capital from Tatung, in the frontier region between agricultural China and the steppe grasslands, to the former Han capital of Loyang. In moving into China, however, the nomads risked losing their ethnic and cultural identity. This happened to the T'o-pa who became so Sinicized that their government even banned continued use of their tribal names, clothes, and customs. They soon also lost their martial ardor. Since their rule was based on conquest, the softened T'o-pa were soon ousted by other nomads and became merged into the general population. Thus, even in northern China, Chinese culture survived to triumph, assimilating and absorbing the conquerors.

Buddhism and Buddhist Art Arrive in China

Ages of bloodshed are often ages of faith; so it was during the age of disunity in China. The most important intellectual trend in China during this period was the growth of Buddhism and its adaptation to Chinese conditions. Buddhism followed different patterns in North and South China because of the different conditions that prevailed in each part of the country.

Most of the upper class in southern China initially came from the north, and while cherishing dreams of returning, they knew that in fact they had little chance of doing so. Thus some sought consolation in religion.

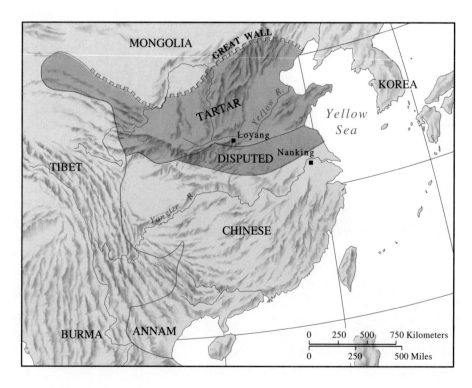

✣ MAP 6.2 China in the Age of Disunity. China was partitioned between 317 and 580 C.E. While Hunnish and other nomadic groups called Tartars ruled North China, Chinese dynasties controlled the Yangtze valley and lands to the south, with a disputed area between. While repeated invasions devastated North China, the south became developed for the first time.

"Though the Wei [T'o-pa] Dynasty [that ruled North China] is indeed prosperous, it is still one of the Five Barbarians. The correct New Year's Day [i.e., the calendar] has been passed down from one generation to the next, and this surely exists only south of the Yangtze. The jade seal of the First Sovereign Ch'in Emperor [seal of legitimate rule] now belongs to the Liang Dynasty [that ruled South China]."

So said the rather drunken guest of honor at a banquet. He was from the southern court, sent to the northern capital on a diplomatic mission. To this a northern nobleman replied:

"You are only using the area of the lower Yangtze as a temporary refuge, and there you live meanly in a corner of the empire. . . . Among your close-cropped gentry, there are none with strong and healthy looks, and your tattooed people [the aborigines] are endowed with bodies that are small and weak. They float about on your three rivers, row about on your five lakes—unaffected by ritual or music, not to be improved by laws and ordinance. Although the prisoners transported to the South under the Ch'in and Han dynasties brought in and intermixed the true Chinese speech [of the north], still the difficult southern languages of Min and Ch'u were not changed for the better. . . . You are steeped in these inherited ways; you have never felt the transforming effects of proper ritual; you are like the people of Yang-t'i [a notorious goiter area] of whom it is said that they don't know that a tumor is a deformity."*

This exchange of insults is interesting for several reasons. First, it shows that the northern nobleman, a man of nomadic roots, had become entirely Sinicized by the sixth century. By then intermarriage between Chinese and nomads had become so common that few purebloods could be found anymore. Second, it shows that after several centuries of partition, distinct cultures had developed with different dialects and ways of life that distinguished northerners from southerners. Third, it reveals the chauvinistic attitude northerners and southerners had toward each other. Each group claimed superiority, regarded themselves as the true heirs of the Han, and accused the other of being tainted by lower cultures, whether that of the nomads of the north or that of the aborigines of the south. China would eventually be reunited by a northern nobleman of mixed Chinese and nomadic descent.

*Arthur Wright, *The Sui Dynasty: The Unification of China*, A.D. 581–617 (New York: Knopf, 1978), pp. 32–33.

Being literary men, they discussed and studied Buddhism, contacting Buddhist centers in India and Ceylon by sea to obtain original texts. Buddhism reached its height under Emperor Wu (reigned 502–549) of the southern state of Liang, who called himself the Imperial Bodhisattva and compared himself with Asoka. Like Asoka, he gave up eating meat, forbade animal sacrifices, convened religious assemblies, and built temples. To honor his father, he built a monastic complex of thirty-six buildings that stretched for more than two miles and housed a thousand monks. He encouraged people to join the *sangha* (Buddhist religious community) and did so himself several times. He did return to his secular duties after each stint in the sangha, but only after the government paid huge "ransoms" to the monastery. Also reminiscent of Asoka, Wu lost control over the government in his later years, and his dynasty quickly declined after his death. Not surprisingly, Wu's blatant favoritism toward Buddhism led to criticism from Taoists and Confucians. It is a credit to the spirit of moderation typical of Confucian scholars that their opposition took the form of verbal warfare rather than persecution.

In North China, where chaos frequently prevailed, Buddhist missionaries attached themselves to the ruling princes, who exercised control over the church and sought the monks' advice in return for protecting them. Missionaries from India and central Asia were welcomed in the courts of the nomadic rulers, who found the universalist teachings of Buddhism more congenial than the ideals of Confucianism. Buddhism exerted a civilizing influence on the nomads and also offered consolation to the oppressed peasantry

Until the end of the fourth century, religious movements had gone one way, as missionaries traveled from India and central Asia to China. Fa-hsien was the first recorded Chinese Buddhist monk to travel to India to study and collect the canons and then return to China. He set off for India by the overland route in 399, studied at all the sites holy to Buddhism, and finally returned to China via Ceylon and the sea route, arriving in 413. He spent his remaining years translating the sutras (scriptural writings) that he had brought back from India into Chinese. Fa-hsien's journals provide valuable information on the history and geography of India and other lands where he traveled and lived.

Fa-hsien's pathfinding journey started a movement that would continue for three centuries. Pilgrims who traveled to India and the lands in between brought back information and ideas that made Buddhism a vital intellectual force. It was a perilous journey; a passage from

Fa-hsien's journal describes the real and imagined terrors of crossing the desert:

> In the desert were numerous evil spirits and scorching winds, causing death to anyone who would meet them. Above there were no birds, while on the ground there were no animals. One looked as far as one could in all directions for a path to cross, but there was none to choose. Only the dried bones of the dead served as indication.

Dedicated Buddhist missionaries and translators made their religion dominant throughout China; even sporadic persecution in North China by rulers who either did not believe in Buddhist doctrines or were jealous of Buddhism's influence did little to hinder it. Similarly, Christianity had triumphed in the Roman Empire despite periodic persecution. Nevertheless, it would be misleading to equate the triumph of Buddhism in China with that of Christianity in the Roman Empire because, unlike Western monotheistic religions (Judaism, Christianity, and Islam), Buddhism, Taoism, and Confucianism did not demand total loyalty from their believers. Most Chinese found no incompatibility in simultaneously honoring Confucius, worshiping Buddha, and practicing Taoist rites. To express this ideal, the Chinese coined the phrase "Three ways to one goal," which reflects both Chinese religious tolerance and Buddhism's adaptability.

Classical Greco-Roman-Indian art entered China with Buddhism. Its progress eastward can be easily traced from surviving Buddhist monuments and works of art. The oases of central Asia were the furthest outposts of the classical Greco-Roman world and were also the melting pot where several cultures and peoples met and where merchants, missionaries, pilgrims, and local peoples mingled. Buddhist sculptors were at work at the oasis at Miran on the southern branch of the Silk Road in the third century, and their art, preserved by the dry desert air, shows a definite classical inspiration. On the corner of one fresco in Miran, one can still see the decipherable signature of the artist. He was called Tita, perhaps the Prakrit form of the Latin name Titus, which suggests that he may have come from a province of the Roman Empire. The name explains the late Greco-Roman classical style of this and other frescoes in Miran and the similarity between the faces seen here and those at Fayum in Egypt of the same period.

East of Miran, images of Buddha turn up next at Tunhuang, the westernmost Chinese settlement on the Silk Road. Beginning in the fourth century, pious Buddhists excavated cave temples in the cliffs at Tunhuang. Over several hundred years, they honeycombed a whole mountainside with the "Caves of the Thousand Buddhas," decorating them with frescoes that show the gradual fusion of Chinese and imported styles.

By the late fifth century, Buddhist art had arrived in western China. Returning Buddhist pilgrims brought both small icons and memories of Indian religious art to China. Local artisans made copies of the former, and the colossal images of the Buddha at Bamiyan inspired similar efforts. Between 460 and 494, an escarpment near the Great Wall at the northern capital at Tatung was carved with twenty caves and adorned with Buddhist frescoes and sculptures. The largest image of the Buddha is seventy feet high. The concept of the cave temples was Indian in origin. Stylistically, the works were Greco-Roman-Gandharan, modified to suit Chinese ideals of formalism and stylization.

When the capital of the T'o-pa dynasty was moved east to Loyang, a new series of cave temples was begun outside that city at a site called Lungmen, where work continued with interruptions until the eighth century. According to a recent count, 142,289 Buddhist sculptures still survive at Lungmen. The Lungmen sculptures show a fusion and synthesis of Greco-Roman, Indian, central Asian, and Chinese styles. The often lengthy carved inscriptions that accompany them also tell of the Sinicization of Buddhism. For example, many of the statues were

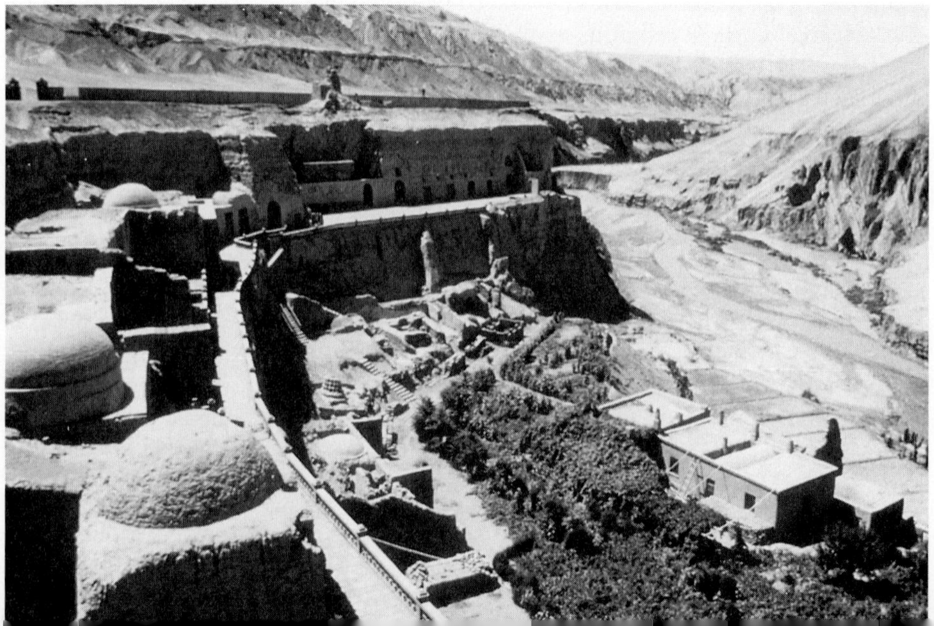

The Caves of the Thousand Buddhas. Situated along the Silk Road in northwestern China, these cave temples at Bizaklik were excavated after the third century. The site flourished during the centuries when it became a stop for missionaries, pilgrims, and merchants on an international highway. Courtesy of Dolkun Kamberi

✿ Buddhism Becomes Sinicized. When the T'o-pa dynasty moved its capital to Loyang, a new series of cave temples was excavated. Many sculptures from this era show Chinese facial characteristics. Courtesy of Jiu-Hwa Upshur

commissioned by monks and nuns, who dedicated them to benefit the souls of their parents and ancestors; this shows that even in joining the sangha, Chinese monks and nuns retained their family loyalty. People from all social classes participated in commissioning statues and other works of art at Lungmen; they even formed societies that collected donations in order to accumulate funds for that purpose. Many inscriptions expressed the hope that all living things will attain salvation, a clearly Mahayana message.

According to one account, Loyang around the year 500 had a population of 500,000 to 600,000 people and 1,367 temples. Built of wood, they have all perished. The cave temples at Tatung, Loyang, Tunhuang, and other sites, however, have survived to testify to the religious fervor of the period and the cosmopolitan nature of its art.

Despite Buddhism's dominance, nonreligious art, heavily influenced by philosophical Taoism's interest in nature, also thrived. The luxuriant and soft natural surroundings of the Yangtze valley, which were in sharp contrast to the landscape of the harsh north, inspired the northern refugees to develop landscape paintings in ink and colors. Although few have survived, several essays on paintings by masters of the day have. They discuss how landscape painting can serve as a mirror of the quest

for harmony of the human spirit and nature, which from this time on has been accepted as the goal of Chinese art. Ceramics and metalworks excavated from tombs show the persistence of ancient traditions alongside innovations, especially in ceramic forms and glazes.

China's Second Empire: The Sui and T'ang Dynasties, 581–907

Outside the inner doors, the two court ladies with
flowing purple sleeves,
Now turn to the throne to lead the procession from
the audience chamber.
The spring wind blows the swirling smoke of incense
in the hall,
The sunlight plays across the dazzling robes of the
thousand officials.
We hear the striking of the hour from the clepsydra
in the high tower,
As a servitor standing near, I note that the Heavenly
Countenance is joyful.

* * * * *

At Changan—a full foot of snow;
A levée at dawn—to bestow congratulations on the Emperor.
Just as I was nearing the Gate of the Silver Terrace,
After I had left the suburb of Hsin-ch'ang
On the high causeway my horse's foot slipped;
In the middle of the journey my lantern suddenly went out.
Ten leagues riding, always facing to the North;
The cold wind almost blew off my ears.
I waited for the summons within the Triple Hall.
My hair and beard were frozen and covered with icicles;
My coat and robe—chilled like water. . . .*

*Poems by Tu Fu and Po Chu-i, quoted in Cities of Destiny, *ed. Arnold Toynbee (New York: McGraw-Hill, 1967), pp. 147–148.*

These poems by two famous T'ang poets and officials describe court functions at the palace in the capital city from different perspectives. The first poem describes the grandeur and stateliness of a court ceremony in which thousands of officials took part. But an official's life was also hard. He had to get up long before dawn and ride long distances even in terrible weather to go to work.

Changan, cosmopolitan capital of the T'ang and largest city in the world, was also the commercial hub of the empire and the eastern terminus of the Silk Road. About 2 million people lived inside its thirty-mile-long wall or in the immediate neighborhood. In the sumptuous palaces at the northern end of the city, the emperor received tribute-bearing ambassadors from much of Asia. Aided by officials, he also conducted the business of a great empire. In other parts of the city, merchants from many lands traded their wares in the large markets. The 91 Buddhist temples, 16 Taoist temples, 4 Zoroastrian temples, and 2 Nestorian Christian churches provided places of worship for Chinese and foreigners, dispensed charities, and organized festive celebrations.

History of the Sui and T'ang Dynasties

The year 581 was a decisive one in Chinese history: in that year a northern nobleman named Yang Chien proclaimed himself emperor and established the Sui dynasty. Although it perished after only four decades, the Sui dynasty laid the foundation for the great and long-lived T'ang dynasty that followed. Lasting for three centuries, this second imperial age would prove more durable and successful than the Gupta Empire in India that had come into existence some 200 years earlier and the Carolingian Empire of western Europe that emerged 200 years later.

Yang Chien was a wily man. Empress Tu-ku, his strong and able wife, assisted him throughout his life and reign. Like many other aristocrats in northern China at the time, both were of mixed Chinese and nomadic ancestry. Yang used everything at his disposal—military force, diplomacy, religion (Buddhism and Taoism), and philosophy (Confucianism)—to forge an empire of continental proportions. He succeeded more completely than the Guptas and Charlemagne because China more than India and western Europe enjoyed the legacy of a unified language, written literary and historical traditions that extolled the ideal of unity, and an experienced bureaucracy that was shaped in Confucian learning and dedicated to public service.

The Sui dynasty did not long survive its frugal and wise founder because Yang Chien's son and heir was an unstable megalomaniac who reputedly murdered his father to gain the throne. He alienated everyone by his failed foreign military campaigns, overly ambitious public works projects, and luxurious court life. Revolts broke out everywhere, and chaos reminiscent of conditions at the end of the Ch'in again threatened to overtake China.

The chaos was short-lived, however, because one rebel named Li Yuan (as the Duke of T'ang, he was a high official in the Sui government; as first emperor of the T'ang, he is also known by his reign name of Kao-tsu or High

MAP 6.3 T'ang China. The T'ang Empire at its height was more extensive and populous than the Han. The Pax Sinica, maintained by T'ang armies, allowed merchants, missionaries, and pilgrims to travel freely across central Asia to India, Persia, and points west.

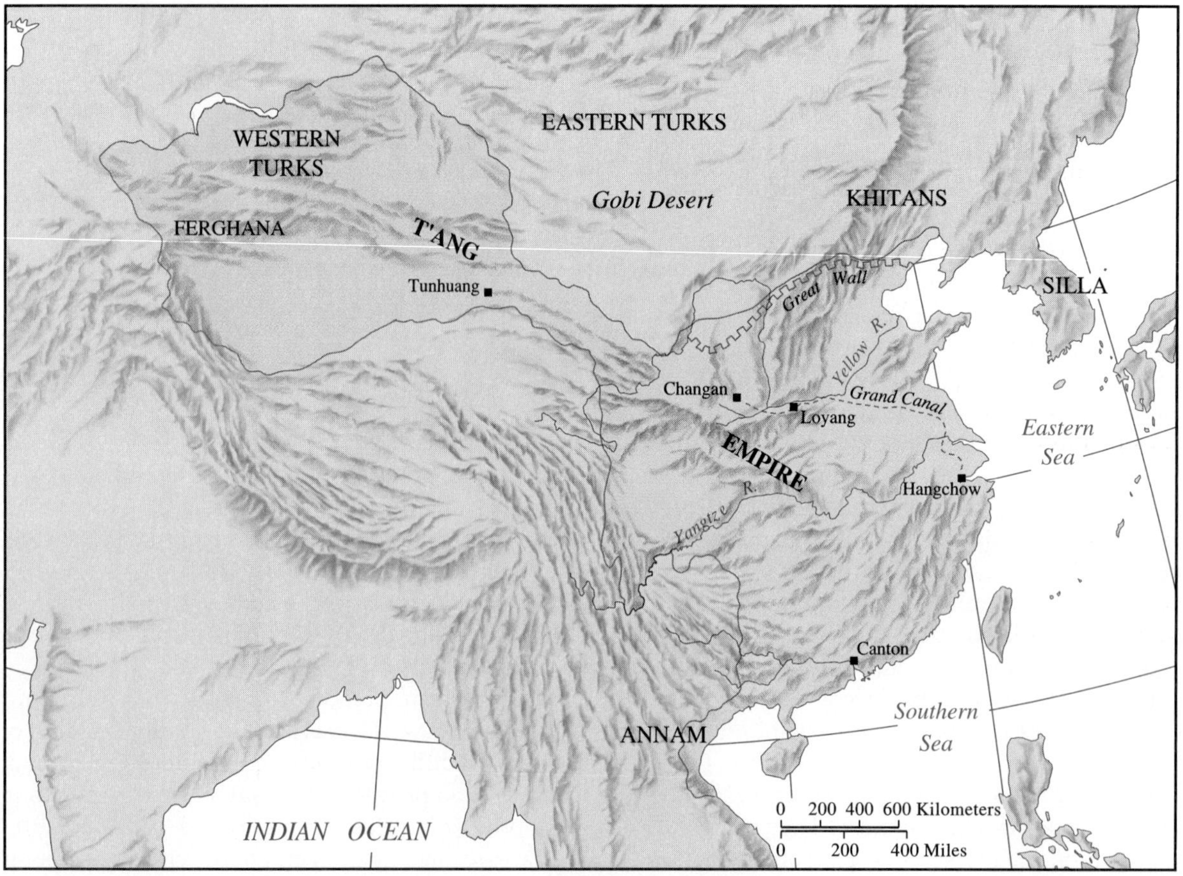

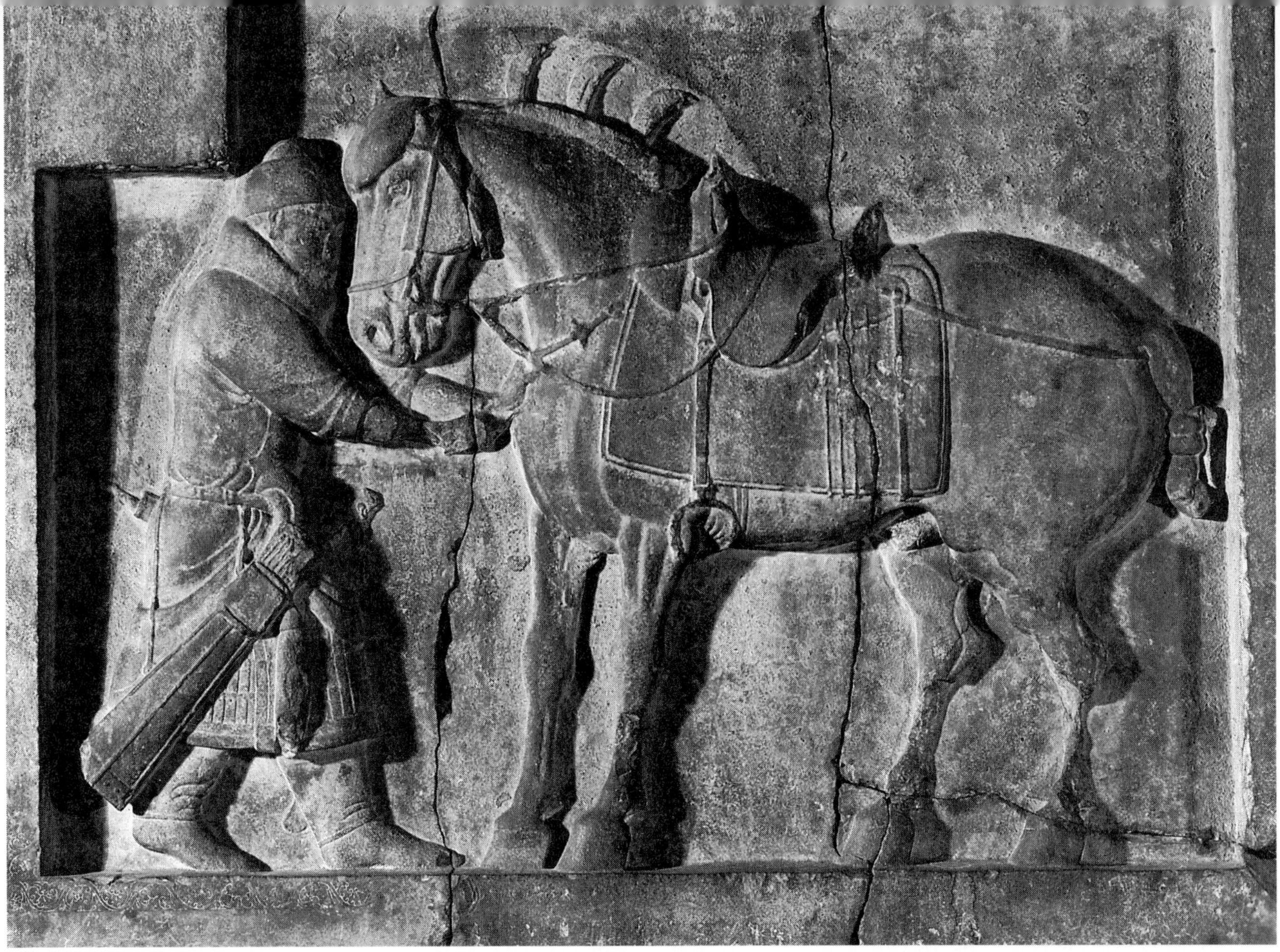

A Famous Battle Charger. The six horses that the T'ang emperor T'ai-tsung rode to his victories are commemorated in relief sculptures. They guard his tomb outside Changan. The University Art Museum, University of Pennsylvania, neg. #58-62844

Ancestor) quickly established a new dynasty. The Li family traced its genealogy to a famous Han general, and more fancifully to the mythical Lao Tzu (to whom later Taoist followers had given the surname Li). Most of the credit for Li Yuan's success is due to his second son, Li Shih-min. Then aged seventeen, he persuaded his timid father to revolt, fought to make his cause triumphant, and later succeeded him as emperor T'ai-tsung (the same ruler who sent his ambassador to the court of Harsha). The T'ang dynasty ruled from 618 to 907, a period that is remembered as one of the most brilliant epochs in Chinese history. T'ai-tsung is revered as the most heroic ruler of all Chinese history. His generals were deified in popular lore; statues of the six horses he rode in campaigns guard his tomb and were remembered in ballads composed by bards. Unlike Alexander the Great, however, T'ai-tsung did not name cities after his horses.

T'ai-tsung (reigned 626–649) established Chinese authority across Mongolia, Tibet, Afghanistan, and central Asia. In submitting, the Turks and Mongols acknowledged him as their Grand Khan, the first Chinese ruler to be so honored. He was also an able administrator and valued the advice of honest critics. At the death of an outspoken critic, Wei Cheng, he said: "With bronze as a mirror, one can correct his improper appearance; with history as a mirror, one can understand the rise and fall of nations; with good men as a mirror, one can distinguish right from wrong. I lost one mirror with the passing of Wei Cheng." He tolerated all religions, promoted Confucianism in government and education, patronized Buddhism, and welcomed Nestorian Christians.

T'ai-tsung's son and successor, Kao-tsung (reigned 649–683), was best remembered for his infatuation with Lady Wu, his father's young concubine. At T'ai-tsung's death, she was sent to a Buddhist convent. Kao-tsung paid a visit to the convent on the first anniversary of his father's death; when he left, he took Lady Wu with him. She later became her stepson's empress and then killed and deposed her own sons to become China's only woman "emperor." Empress Wu ruled until she was eighty. Old and ill, she was forced to abdicate in favor of one of her surviving sons. Confucian scholars had few good things to say about her because of the means she used to gain and maintain power (she killed and imprisoned many of her own children, stepchildren, in-laws, and officials who opposed her usurpation) and her scandalous private life. Just as aging male rulers took young concubines, she took numerous young lovers, as did the eighteenth-century Russian empress Catherine the Great. When in her seventies she heard reports that her grandson and granddaughter had laughed at her affairs, she ordered them to commit suicide. Nevertheless, she was a capable ruler, just as Empress Catherine was. Under Empress Wu Manchuria was brought under Chinese rule and the kings of Korea were compelled to acknowledge Chinese overlordship. This relationship between China and Korea continued until the late nineteenth century. She was also a devout Buddhist and endowed many temples.

T'ang prestige and prosperity reached their peak during the reign of Ming-huang, the Brilliant Emperor (reigned 712–756). Ming-huang worked hard for most of his reign and was also a patron of the arts. The most celebrated poets of the age lived at his court and immortalized his reign with their unsurpassed poetry. But Ming-huang lived too long for his own and China's good. At age sixty he fell under the spell of Lady Yang, a young concubine of one of his sons. He ordered his son to divorce her, took her into his own harem, and abandoned himself to the pursuit of pleasure. She was famous for her plumpness and briefly made obesity fashionable; she was also noted for her extravagance, which the doting and aged emperor indulged. Ming-huang's neglect of his duties and his elevation of Lady Yang's greedy and incompetent relatives and favorites to power had disastrous results: defeat by a Muslim army, which ended Chinese control of central Asia and destroyed Buddhism in that region, and a major rebellion led by Lady Yang's favorite, a general of Turkic origins and commander of "barbarian" mercenary soldiers. Ming-huang had to sacrifice Lady Yang to appease his angry loyal troops, who blamed her for the rebellion and would not fight for him until she had been killed. Her death and his subsequent abdication in humiliation became the subject of a famous romantic poem. Although the rebellion was put down, the central government never fully recovered its authority, nor the dynasty its prestige and vitality. Slow decline set in; the final end came in 907.

An Enlightened Government and a Prosperous Economy

The key to the T'ang dynasty's success was the restoration of a stable central government, aided by the revival of schools and the examination system. The T'ang rulers reinstated and expanded the Han system of examinations based on Confucian classics as the basis for selecting government officials. The government established a system of schools from the countryside up to the imperial university that were open to most young men of talent. It administered examinations at regular intervals on several levels and recruited successful candidates into the civil service. It also adopted a civil service rating system to determine promotions and dismissals.

Since bright young men studied the same curriculum in order to qualify for the examinations and public service, a uniform educational system emerged. Because Confucian ideology was the basis of the examinations, the schools produced a ruling class imbued with the same ethical principles and values. Even Buddhist schools offered a Confucian curriculum that helped poor boys realize their potential. The widespread use of paper, invented in the first century, made books cheaper. Although printing was invented during the T'ang period, it did not come into widespread use until a later era, at which time books became still cheaper and more widely available.

The competitive examination system strengthened the T'ang state by turning men of intellectual ability into strong supporters of the government. It created an elite dedicated to government service and to the consensus that the learned and morally worthy should lead and represent public opinion. The perfection of the examination system and the bureaucracy of merit that it produced in T'ang and later eras was one of the greatest achievements of Chinese civilization and a major reason for its stability and endurance.

The T'ang era was one of great economic prosperity. International trade flourished, and more caravans plied the Silk Road than during the best Han days. In post-Han centuries, the Yangtze valley had experienced enormous growth and development and was now the breadbasket (or rice bowl) of China. Realizing this, the Sui rulers had constructed an extensive system of waterways, called the Grand Canal, to link the Yangtze and lands further south with the Yellow River valley. The enormous drain of manpower and resources required by this project contributed to the popular discontent that ended the Sui dynasty. The Sui's expenditures benefited the T'ang rulers, however, because the system they inherited enabled them to tap the abundant resources of the south and helped them maintain their power.

T'ang prosperity was also based on a contented peasantry. Early in the dynasty the government undertook an ambitious land policy called the "equal field" system. It was an adaptation of the well-field system, supposedly instituted by the Duke of Chou, that had helped make the early Chou a golden age. Under the equal field system, all land theoretically belonged to the emperor or the state, which distributed about eighteen acres to every able-bodied man between twenty-one and fifty-nine years of age. Other categories of people—for example, widows who headed families and the elderly—received somewhat smaller allotments. The government then assessed taxes as well as labor on public works projects on the basis of the land allotment. It exempted certain able-bodied males from taxes in return for military service. This complex and largely equitable land and tax policy worked well for over a century. It was possible because the government was served by an able bureaucracy that kept careful census and detailed land survey records.

China and the World Beyond

China was at its most cosmopolitan during the T'ang dynasty. Not until modern times would it again be so open to foreign influences. About 2 million people lived in Changan and its environs, making it the most populous city in the world (for comparison, Constantinople around 600 had a population of about 1 million). The marketplaces of Changan and other large cities bustled with life; Chinese mingled with people from Japan, Korea, Southeast Asia, India, and the many lands of central and western Asia. Some had come freely to trade, settle, or offer their services; others were brought as slaves. The rich vied with one another to include foreign grooms, entertainers, dancers, and musicians in their entourages. Foreign fashions became fads, and foreign ways such as drinking grape wines and playing polo became fashionable.

Much of T'ang life can be reconstructed from the numerous pottery replicas of people, animals, and objects and other artifacts buried to serve the dead in the next world. In time, a burgeoning middle class competed with the court and nobility for luxury goods, both imported and domestic. Central Asian horses were great status symbols. Judging from the numerous examples of horses found in tombs, many people owned them. People loved expensive and exotic items, such as jewelry and gems from India and gold and silverware from western Asia, for their non-Chinese shapes and decorative motifs, their foreign ideas, and the foreign persons represented on them.

T'ang cosmopolitanism hinged on the dynasty's military power and the increase in international trade. Skillful military strategists, the early T'ang generals subdued the nomads from Manchuria westward to central Asia and posted garrisons at important strategic points to maintain peace and secure trade. A strong martial spirit drew recruits to the army. Besides able men, the T'ang produced several famous female warriors. T'ai-tsung's sister commanded troops and campaigned alongside him. Another young woman, Hua Mu-lan, disguised herself as a man and answered the call to arms for her aged father. According to tradition, she only revealed her identity years later at an audience before the emperor. A famous ballad celebrated her going off to war:

> In the eastern market she bought a fine horse,
> In the western market she bought saddle and blanket,
> In the southern market she bought bridle and reins,
> In the northern market she bought a long whip.
> At dawn she set out from her parents' house,
> At dusk she camped at the Yellow River shore.
> She did not hear her father and mother calling to their
>   daughter;
> She only heard the hissing voice of the Yellow River's
>   flowing waves.
> At sunrise they set off and left the Yellow River,
> At dusk they camped beside the Black Water.
> She did not hear her father and mother calling to their
>   daughter;
> She only heard the Hunnish horsemen shout across the
>   hills of Yen.
> Ten thousand li she rode on many duties,
> Borders and mountains crossed as swift as flight.
> Through the northern night there sounded out the
>   kettle-drum,
> In the winter daylight soldiers' armour gleaming. . . .

The flourishing international trade also contributed to the prevailing cosmopolitanism. The increased volume of trade and the need for a more efficient medium of exchange than metal coins led to the use of money drafts, the precursor of paper money. Invented in 811, the drafts had the picturesque name of "flying cash."

T'ang international relations took two forms. One was between powerful China, under the Son of Heaven, and

✸ Polo Players. A game that originated in Persia, polo became a fashionable sport among aristocratic men and women. The potter captured these two vigorous players and their fine horses at the gallop. Jiu-Hwa Upshur Collection; photo by John Nystuen

its dependent and subservient vassal states, particularly the various kingdoms of Korea, the many tribal states of the north and northwest, and Tibet. The presence of Chinese garrisons and the advantages of trade no doubt helped to maintain the overlord-vassal relationship between China and its small neighbors. The other kind was between peers, such as India, Persia, and the Byzantine Empire. For example, T'ai-tsung and Harsha exchanged ambassadors, and China had had ongoing diplomatic relations with the Sassanid dynasty of Persia for several centuries. The western limit of the Chinese world was the Byzantine Empire—Fu Lin to the Chinese. T'ang histories recorded four embassies from Byzantium, probably sent to enlist Chinese military aid against rising Muslim power. Nothing came of these missions, however, and no Chinese embassies were sent to Byzantium.

The Chinese government first heard about Islam in 638, when T'ai-tsung received an appeal for help from the king of Persia, then desperately trying to hold off the advancing Arab Muslims. T'ai-tsung did not deliver military assistance, because of the distance and because at the time he had barely consolidated his own empire. Early in the eighth century, as Muslim armies advanced on central Asia and Afghanistan, the Buddhist states, which were sometimes Chinese vassals, sent urgent appeals to China for help. From the Muslim side, Caliph Walid also sent an ambassador to the T'ang court to urge against intervention. China decided to do nothing to hinder the Arab advance. In 751 a Chinese garrison was routed by the army of Caliph Abul Abbas of the Abbasid caliphate in a battle near Tashkent, the only time the Chinese and the Arabs engaged in hostilities. Soon afterward, Lady Yang's favorite began his rebellion, and the remaining T'ang garrisons were recalled from central Asia. The caliph even sent an army to help the Chinese defeat the rebels. Although the rebellion was crushed, the weakened T'ang government could not reassert its power in central Asia, and Muslim rule was established there.

The Apogee of Buddhism and the Confucian Revival

Buddhism came of age in China during the early T'ang. Patronized by the court and supported by all elements of society, it served the ordinary people with festivals, lectures, and charitable activities. After the greatest Buddhist pilgrim, Hsuan-tsang, returned to China from India laden with precious manuscripts, he spent his remaining years translating them into Chinese. He was an indefatigable worker, who alone was responsible for translating works equivalent to twenty times the volume of the Bible. As a result of the outpouring of religious works, scholars stopped scorning Buddhism as the religion of barbarians. Hsuan-tsang also brought back many "genuine relics" of the Buddha, which became objects of veneration for mil-

lions of the faithful, in the same way that "relics" associated with Jesus, the prophets, and the saints were venerated by Christians.

As Chinese Buddhist leaders studied the voluminous religious writings, several distinctively Chinese Buddhist schools, all Mahayana, emerged. Three were especially important. T'ien-t'ai, begun about 600 and named after a famous monastery, reflected the Chinese tendency toward synthesis and harmony in the way it organized the vast body of Buddhist literature and recognized the validity of each sutra in its place. In this way T'ien-t'ai muted the conflicts that had risen between different Indian schools of interpretation. This sect appealed primarily to the educated.

The Pure Land sect was named after the "Pure Land" or Western Paradise that the masses of Mahayana believers strove to achieve. It taught that salvation, or rebirth in the Pure Land, could be attained by faith, expressed by calling the Buddha's name. The Pure Land appealed primarily to the common people and therefore had the most followers.

The Ch'an (or Zen in Japan) sect began in China in the sixth century. It was introduced by a semilegendary Indian missionary, Bodhidharma, who reputedly meditated for nine years facing a blank wall before he achieved enlightenment. The Ch'an's antischolastic emphasis and stress on meditation and intuitive enlightenment derived at least in part from philosophical Taoism, as did its love of nature and simplicity. Together with Taoism, Ch'an Buddhism was a major inspiration to artists and poets.

Buddhism reached its high-water mark in the early T'ang. Persecution in the mid-ninth century marked the beginning of its decline. Confucians criticized Buddhism on several scores: it promised people what they could not have; it encouraged people to make donations they could ill afford; and its encouragement of celibacy undermined the social order and teachings of filial piety. Confucians also attacked the Buddhist church for its wealth, its tax-exempt status, and the unproductive lives of its monks and nuns. Some of the criticisms were justified, but some were also xenophobic and nationalistic, as Han Yu's memorial showed.

Rivalry between Buddhism and Taoism on occasion led to persecution of one faith or the other, although in one instance, both religions were targeted at the same time. The most severe persecution of Buddhism occurred between 841 and 845 under a pro-Taoist emperor. The persecutions, however, were aimed chiefly at religious property and members of the clergy, and unlike religious persecutions in Christian Europe, they seldom bothered individual believers.

Buddhism's decline during the later T'ang was also attributable to competition from revitalized Confucianism. International developments played a role too. After the eighth century, Muslim armies seized territories from northwest India through Afghanistan and central Asia—

Now Buddha was a man of the barbarians who did not speak the language of China and wore clothes of a different fashion. His sayings did not concern the ways of our ancient kings, nor did his manner of dress conform to their laws. He understood neither the duties that bind sovereign and subject, nor the affections of father and son. If he were still alive today and came to our court by order of his ruler, Your Majesty might condescend to receive him, but it would amount to no more than one audience in the Hsuan-cheng Hall, a banquet by the Office for Receiving Guests, the presentation of a suit of clothes, and he would then be escorted to the borders of the nation, dismissed, and not allowed to delude the masses. How then, when he had long been dead, could his rotten bones, the foul and unlucky remains of his body, be rightly admitted to the palace? Confucius said: "Respect ghosts and spirits, but keep them at a distance!"*

Han Yu (786–824) was the author of this diatribe. A famous scholar and official, he was a staunch defender of Confucianism. He vehemently opposed Buddhism as an alien faith inimical to both Confucianism and Chinese society. This passage was part of a memorial he presented to the emperor to oppose a planned ceremony in the palace to honor a supposed relic of the Buddha. Han Yu's rhetoric shows that he was opposed to Buddhism both because it was superstitious and because it originated outside China (he also opposed Taoism). The emperor, who was a devout Buddhist, was so enraged by the memorial that he exiled the author. Later Chinese hailed Han Yu as the early leader of the Confucian revival and regarded this memorial as the opening salvo of that movement.

*William T. de Bary, ed., *Sources of Chinese Tradition*, vol. 1 (New York: Columbia University Press, 1960), p. 373.

---

lands that had hitherto been Buddhist. As a result, Chinese Buddhists were no longer able to maintain their contacts with their fellow religionists in India. Intellectually isolated, Chinese Buddhism ceased to be a vital religion.

In restoring the examination system, the T'ang monarchs gave emphasis to Confucian political ideology at the expense of Buddhism. Despite their personal commitments to Buddhism and/or Taoism, they realized that neither offered political theories and rules of organization upon which they could build a great centralized empire. Confucianism alone answered that need, as it had earlier for the Han dynasty. Thus Confucianism became the basis of education and once again began to dominate intellectual life. As first-rate minds were channeled to Confucian learning, Buddhism lost some of its intellectual vitality. Ironically, Buddhism contributed to its own intellectual decline by endowing Confucian schools to educate poor boys.

Zoroastrianism and Islam also entered China during this period; the former came through Persian refugees from Muslim invaders. The son of the last Sassanian king was given a commission in the T'ang army. However, unlike the larger Persian refugee community in India, whose members retained their faith and remained a distinct group called the Parsees, the Persians in China were soon assimilated. Reputedly, many Muslim troops sent by the caliph to assist in putting down the rebellion against Ming-huang did not return home. They married local women and settled down in northwest China, founding the Muslim community there. Similarly, in the Roman Empire soldiers stationed in such far-off provinces as Dacia (Romania) and North Africa had settled and intermarried with local women. Before the end of the T'ang, sizable settlements of Muslim traders had also been established in southern Chinese ports, most notably Canton. The Chinese government allowed them to elect their own leaders and to live by their religious laws.

The Golden Age of the Poet and the Sculptor

The T'ang was a great creative epoch. Many fields of art flourished, but above all it was a golden age of poetry. About 3,000 poets from this period are known to us, and several of them are considered unsurpassed. One of the best loved was the romantic Li Po, who relished good wine with or without company, as he wrote in "Drinking Alone by Moonlight":

> A cup of wine, under the flowering trees;
> I drink alone, for no friend was near.
> Raising my cup I beckon the bright moon
> For he, with my shadow, will make three men.
> The moon, alas, was no drinker of wine;
> Listless, my shadow creeps about at my side.
> Yet with the moon as friend and the shadow as my slave
> I must make merry before the Spring was spent.
>
> To the songs I sing the moon flickers her beams;
> In the dance I weave my shadow tangles and breaks.
> While we were sober, three shared the fun;
> Now we are drunk, each goes his way.
> May we long share our odd, inanimate feast,
> And meet at last on the Cloudy river of the sky
> [the Milky Way].

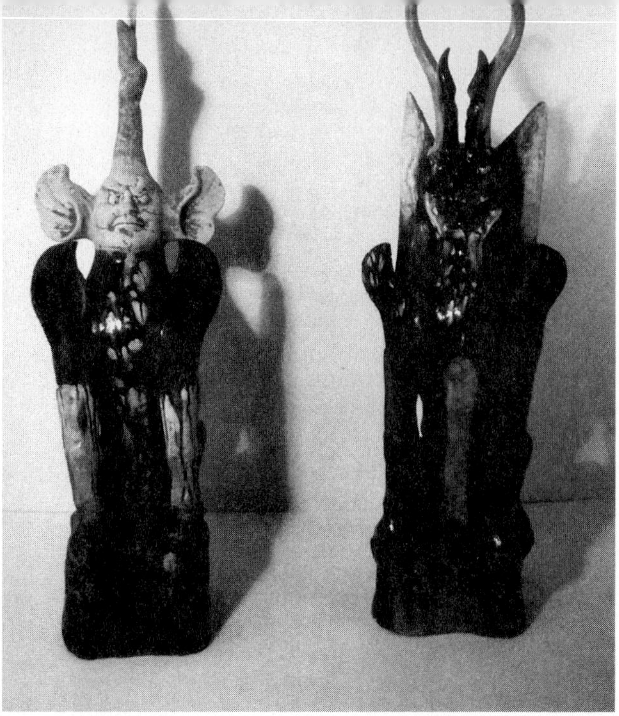

Tomb Guardians. Since Han times guardians were placed in pairs at tomb entrances. From the fifth century on, as a result of influence from West Asia, where lions were royal and sacred beasts, these guardians took the form of ferocious lions and man-lions, as this pair shows. Jiu-Hwa Upshur Collection; photo by John Nystuen

According to popular legend, Li drowned as he leaned out of a boat to embrace the moon during a drinking party with his friends. Great portraitists and painters of landscapes also distinguished the age, but few of these works on paper and silk have survived.

Buddhist art and sculpture also reached maturity under the T'ang. Many consider this the great age of sculpture, which until the flourishing of Buddhism had been a relatively minor art form in China. In addition to monumental sculptures preserved in the rock cave temples, artisans also produced small metal images of the Buddha and bodhisattvas, thousands of which survive. The T'ang Buddha images reflect Chinese humanistic interests—they are lifelike and intimate and mirror contemporary concepts of beauty.

Because of the power and prestige of the T'ang, their artistic forms became an international style that spread to Korea, Japan, and other lands. The imperial ambitions of the early T'ang, which led to Chinese control of central Asia, also caused Chinese Buddhist art to move westward, back along the same routes into central Asia. In the early twentieth century, at Tunhuang and further west, Western scholar-explorers discovered long-sealed Buddhist cave temples that had been forgotten or buried for centuries in sand. The paintings and sculptures show that for a thousand years this area was a melting pot where Gandharan, Indian, central Asian, and Chinese styles met and synthesized. Archaeologists have coined the name Serindia for this now desolate area.

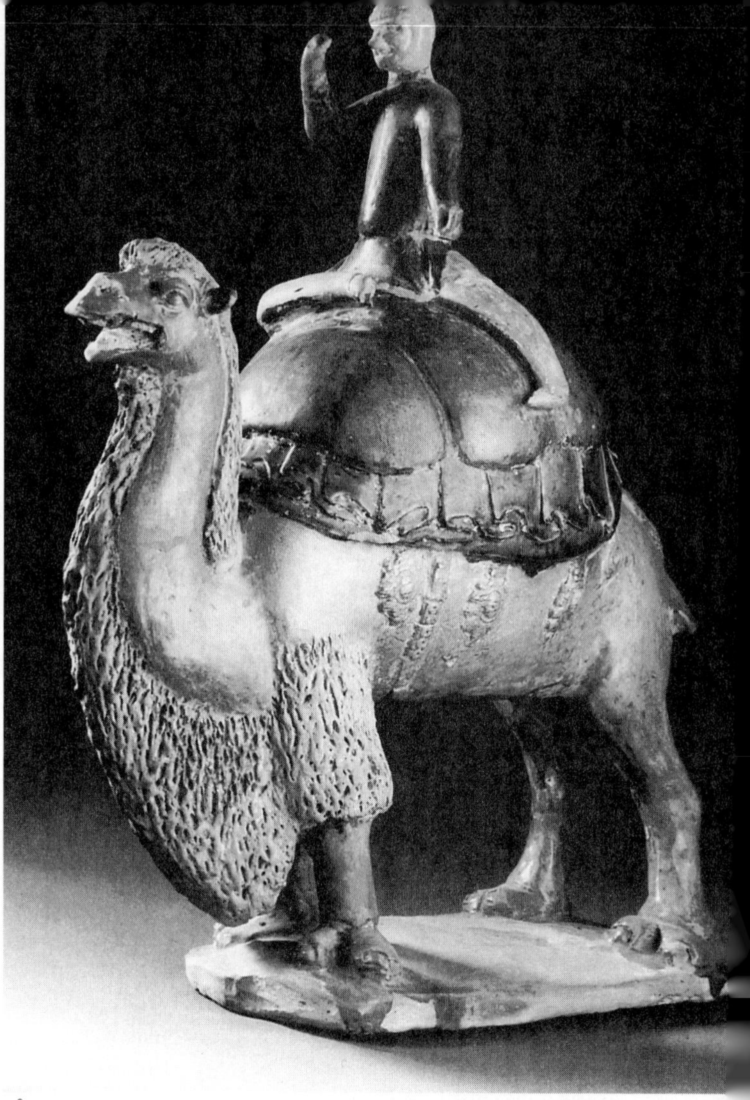

A T'ang-Era Camel. Believing that the dead would need the same things in the world beyond as they had while living, the Chinese made models of houses, animals, and utensils and buried them with the dead. Camels were the chief means of overland long-distance travel, and pottery models of camels are frequently found in T'ang-era graves. Courtesy of the Royal Ontario Museum, Toronto, Canada

Secular sculpture also flourished. The most spectacular are the monumental human and animal figures that lined the path to the artificial earthern mounds that covered the imperial tombs. More than a thousand years later, they are vivid reminders of the power of the ruling house. The six relief sculptures of T'ai-tsung's battle chargers that guarded his tomb, with inscriptions that recount their deeds and wounds, tell poignantly of the close relationship between the man and his horses. T'ang tombs have yielded tens of thousands of ceramic sculptures of horses, camels, grooms, officials, and entertainers that are minor masterpieces of the anonymous sculptors of the age. The countless other artifacts excavated from tombs, made of silk, jade, bronze, and other metals and materials, all testify to the great prosperity and high artistic standards of the era.

China Partitioned: The Sung and Nomadic Dynasties, 960–1279

*The [enemy's] heavy soldiery is entirely concentrated in the eastern capital. Having repeatedly suffered severe defeat, their morale has been destroyed. Within and without they are shaken and in alarm. According to intelligence reports I have heard, the enemy intends to abandon his baggage and hastily flee across the river. Moreover, now the loyalist guerrillas are responding to the changed situation. The officers and men are obeying orders. Heaven determines the course of human affairs in its own time . . . success is within our grasp. [Such] a time will not come again. The opportunity was hard [to come by] and can be lightly lost. . . . It is only for Your Majesty to desire it.**

*Edward Kaplan, "Yueh Fei and the Founding of the Southern Sung" (Ph.D. diss., University of Iowa, 1970), pp. 434–435.

So urged Yueh Fei, the most successful general of the Sung dynasty and one whose memory as a great patriot is revered by Chinese to the present. Yueh was hoping to stiffen the ruler's resolve and win support for his ongoing campaign to oust nomadic invaders from North China and regain lost lands. The emperor responded as follows:

> From the moment military operations began, We knew things must end with peace negotiations. . . . Military force was unavoidable, [but] how could We gain pleasure from offensive warfare? During this dynasty, [Emperor] Chen Tsung kept the peace with the Khitan for over one hundred years and the people did not know soldiers. Though [Emperor] Shen Tsung talked of war and trained soldiers, actually he never used them. From the beginning until the present, We have thought only of peace. As We loved the people of north and south equally, We have taken the road of accommodation to defend them. (Kaplan, pp. 557–558.)

Yueh Fei failed to win his emperor's support, and all the military advantage his army had gained was lost. The emperor's speech characterized the policy of the entire Sung dynasty toward the nomadic invaders from the north—avoid war almost at any cost and buy peace whenever possible. The Sung was the most pacifist dynasty in Chinese history. Its love of peace and abhorrence of war were in part responsible for the loss of North China to several nomadic groups and of South China to the Mongols.

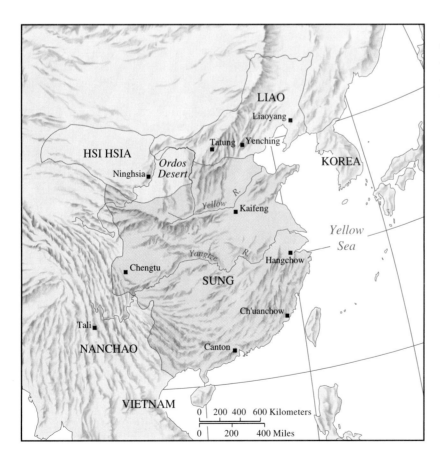

✺ MAP 6.4 The Sung and Its Neighbors. The Sung dynasty never ruled the entire Chinese world. During the first part of the dynasty (960–1125), called the Northern Sung in retrospect, powerful nomadic states, the Liao and the Hsi Hsia, constantly menaced China.

A Checkered History

The closing decades of the T'ang dynasty were wracked by civil wars brought on by ambitious generals and mutinous troops, who continued their power struggles for half a century after the T'ang ended in 907. While China was fragmented, much as it had been after the fall of the Han, the nomads once again began moving southward and attacking Chinese lands.

The Sung dynasty was born out of a mutiny. In 960 an adventurer who had recently proclaimed himself emperor in North China appointed a capable young general named Chao K'uang-yin commander-in-chief of an expedition against the nomads. His officers and men did not like their assignment and felt no loyalty toward the government, particularly after the emperor died and left an infant on the throne. They mutinied and hailed Chao as their emperor; thus a new dynasty, the Sung, was born. Such "elections" of emperors by rebellious troops had been frequent in the Roman Empire and in post–T'ang China; they had usually led to more violence and bloodshed. The Sung was an exception, for soon after unifying the country the new emperor removed the officers who had raised him to the throne from their military commands. He did it, however, with tact and generosity, rewarding them with titles and pensions.

Domestically, the Northern Sung enjoyed peace and prosperity. Even in its smaller territory, the population, more than 100 million in 1114, surpassed peak Han and T'ang figures. Cities grew, as did an urban middle class. The printing press, now in wide use, made books cheap and readily available, and literacy became widespread. For

Chao K'uang-yin, Founder of the Sung Dynasty. Although this portrait shows him wearing civilian clothes, the general who founded the Sung dynasty still looks to be a powerful man. Most of his successors, however, showed no military aptitude and let the army decline. National Palace Museum, Taiwan, Republic of China

How to Prevent Coups d'État

In the first year of his reign [960] the new Emperor summoned all his military officers—the men responsible for the mutiny to which he owed his throne—to a banquet. When the company had drunk deeply and were in a cheerful mood, the Emperor said:

"I do not sleep peacefully at night."

"For what reason?" inquired the generals.

"It is not hard to understand," replied the Emperor. "Which of you is there who does not covet my throne?"

The generals made a bow and all protested:

"Why does Your Majesty speak thus? The Mandate of Heaven is now established; who still has treacherous aims?"

The Emperor replied: "I do not doubt your loyalty, but if one day one of you is suddenly roused at dawn and forced to don a yellow robe [official robe of an emperor], even if unwilling, how should he avoid rebellion?"

The officers all declared that not one of them was sufficiently renowned or beloved for such a thing to happen, and begged the Emperor to take such measures as he thought wise to guard against any such possibility. The Emperor, having brought them to this point, promptly made his proposal known:

"Life is short. Happiness is to have the wealth and means to enjoy life, and then to be able to leave the same prosperity to one's descendants. If you, my officers, will renounce your military authority, retire to the provinces, and choose there the best lands and most delightful dwelling places, there to pass the rest of your lives in pleasure and peace until you die of old age, would this not be better than to live a life of peril and uncertainty? So that no shadow of suspicion shall remain between prince and ministers, we will ally our families with marriages, thus, ruler and subject linked in friendship and amity, we will enjoy tranquility."*

All parties carried out their parts of the bargain. No mutinies occurred during the Sung dynasty.

*Charles P. Fitzgerald, *China: A Short Cultural History,* 3d. ed. (New York: Praeger, 1976), p. 382.

the first time, many men of middle class or humbler origins passed the examinations and joined the civil service.

The Sung government was run by civilians. It was a pacifist and humane regime. Two dominant political parties, called the Conservatives and the Innovators, settled their differences on social and economic policies through political and philosophical debates. The losers lost their jobs but never their heads. Kaifeng, a city south of the Yellow River, became the Northern Sung capital. Changan and Loyang, despite their fine strategic locations, would never be capitals of China again. Centuries of wars and invasions had so depleted the economy in their vicinities that they could no longer support a central government, and lack of good water transportation made it too difficult and expensive to provision those cities. In contrast, Kaifeng was located in a rich agricultural plain and was easily reachable by canal from the south. However, it lacked natural defenses and was vulnerable to cavalry attacks from the north.

Although the dynasty was founded by a general, it produced no distinguished warrior rulers. Sung emperors were instead known for their patronage of the arts and connoisseurship, and several were accomplished artists. The cultured and art-loving Sung rulers were ill equipped to answer the military and diplomatic needs of the time. In 1127 nomads captured Kaifeng and carried the artist emperor, his heir, and 3,000 members of his court into

captivity in the steppes, where they were subjected to numerous indignities, as this victor's account relates:

> The two commoners [of the Sung, former Emperor Hui-tsung and his son Emperor Ch'in-tsung] were presented [to the Court of the nomadic Chin state, whose emperor] bestowed the title of Duke of Stupid Virtue to the father and the title of the Marquis of Double Stupidity to his son. . . . On the xxx day of the sixth month of the eighth year [1134] . . . the Imperial Decree ordered the six daughters of the Duke of Stupid Virtue to be the wives of members of the Imperial Household.

In 1127 Sung loyalists put another son of the captive emperor on the throne in South China and set up the Southern Sung (1127–1279) in Hangchow south of the mouth of the Yangtze River, a port Marco Polo later described as far superior to Venice. The new Sung emperor abandoned his captive relatives, made peace with the northern invaders, and agreed to establish the watershed of the mountains dividing the Yellow and Yangtze Rivers as the boundary. Everyone then settled down to enjoy the pleasures of peace, and culture flourished as never before.

Soon the fearsome Mongols rose from the steppes and began to cast a dark shadow over the Southern Sung. It was only a matter of time before the Sung, along with everyone else in the way, were swept away by Mongol power. Sung strategists even invented a new weapon—gunpowder-filled bamboo tubes launched in

✣ MAP 6.5 The Southern Sung. After the loss of North China, the Sung government moved its capital to Hangchow, south of the Yangtze River. It was pushed ever southward and destroyed by the Mongols in 1279. The period between 1127 and 1279 is called the Southern Sung.

rocket fashion—to defend against Mongol attacks. The Mongols proved to be good students of military science, however, and soon incorporated the gunpowder rockets into their own arsenal. The Sung were pushed ever southward, until the last emperor drowned off the coast of Canton in 1279 as his few remaining ships were being overwhelmed. By this time Kubilai Khan, grandson of the feared conqueror Genghis Khan and himself a great warrior, was well established in Peking as emperor of the new Yuan dynasty.

Difficulties in the Pursuit of Peace and War

Since antiquity Chinese statesman had learned that the best defense against the nomads was a good offense; that is, military initiatives were preferable to a defensive strategy. The Sung, however, opted for defense for two reasons. First, the Chinese people had by that time lost the will to fight. The great aristocratic families of the Han and T'ang eras who were noted for their martial spirit and love of hunting and sports had been decimated by the wars of the later T'ang period. By contrast, Sung leaders were literati with distinctly unmartial tastes and interests. Whereas T'ang ladies rode, hunted, and played polo, Sung court ladies began to bind their feet as small, dainty feet became fashionable.

The second reason for the Sung's defensive stance was the ruling house's deliberate strategy of subordinating the military to civilian control and reducing the esprit de corps among the soldiers. Thus officers and their troops were kept apart to prevent them from developing a sense of camaraderie. The Sung rulers also had little respect for military service. Their disdain was evident in a saying coined at that time: "You don't use good iron to make nails, you don't use good men to make soldiers." Indeed, soldiers were often used like prisoners to perform manual labor and were sometimes tattooed on the face to prevent desertion. The objective of the Sung's military policies was to prevent mutinies, and in that sense the policies were successful. No mutinies or revolts occurred under the Sung, but their army was also too weak to protect the empire.

Not surprisingly, the Sung produced few great generals. The most famous general was Yueh Fei, who lived in the twelfth century. Operating mainly on his own, Yueh achieved some impressive successes in recovering recent territorial losses to the nomadic Chin dynasty in North China. The peace party at court, however, fearful and jealous of his popularity, had Yueh arrested and then murdered in prison. The court quickly concluded a treaty with the Chin, conceding the entire Yellow River valley.

The Sung strategy for survival was to rely on diplomacy. International relations in East Asia had developed along quite different lines from those in Europe, where nation-states, equals in international status, had developed after Charlemagne. No similar evolution had taken

An Artist Emperor. Hui-tsung, last emperor of the Northern Sung, was a patron of the arts and a noted painter. This painting on silk is one of his works. His reign ended in disaster as he and most of his court were taken captive by nomadic invaders.
The Metropolitan Museum of Art, John M. Crawford, Jr. Collection, Purchase, Douglas Dillon Gift, 1981 (1981.278)

❖ Ceramics for Export. Chinese ceramics were widely exported during the Sung and were treasured from Japan to Egypt. Green glazed wares, called celadon, were especially treasured in the Middle East, where people believed that poisoned food could be detected if served on them. Courtesy of the Minneapolis Institute of Arts

place in East Asia. The diplomatic tradition of a single powerful state surrounded by satellites did not work during the Sung period, because the Sung rulers were compelled to share with other states territories that had formerly been part of the Han and T'ang Empires. After failed efforts to recover sections of North China from a nomadic state called the Liao, the Northern Sung government concluded a peace treaty that not only acknowledged loss of territory by the Sung, but also agreed to pay the Liao an annual tribute or "brotherly gift" of 100,000 ounces of silver and 200,000 bolts of silk. After several decades, the Liao demanded an increase of 100,000 units in each category, and the Sung government gave in rather than risk a military confrontation.

Anxious to share such good fortune, the Tibetan rulers of Hsi Hsia, another border state, also threatened war and ended up getting annual gifts of 200,000 units each of silver and silk from the Sung. These agreements left no doubt who was the "younger brother" or the lesser nation in the relationships. Likewise, the Southern Sung paid a tribute in silver and silk to the Chin, successors of the Liao in North China, and formally acknowledged the Chin's

status as overlord; the Sung emperor even addressed the nomad ruler as his "uncle." By accepting such treaties, the Sung rulers had submitted to terms that Han and T'ang emperors would have regarded as shameful and intolerable. Yet the Sung considered the payment of tribute or bribes a lesser evil than war. Thus they were in no position to help in the last decades of the eleventh century when three embassies arrived from the Byzantine Empire asking for military help against the invading Turks.

Because of its constant need to raise money to pay tribute and maintain the army, the Sung government encouraged international trade and taxed it for revenue. Chinese ceramics, desired everywhere from Japan to Egypt, were exported in large quantities. Assembly-line techniques were developed to speed up ceramic production, different types of wares were produced to suit the tastes of various customers, as determined by market research. Since hostile nomadic states blocked access to the west by land, Chinese traders worked to develop sea trade with Japan and Southeast Asia. Trade with western Asia was conducted through the Arabs, who dominated the Indian Ocean.

Cultural Borrowing and Adaptation—The Chair

Although the chair was a part of life in ancient Egypt, Greece, and Rome, where it was depicted in frescoes, paintings, and models, it did not exist in East Asia in antiquity. Until 1,000 years ago, the Chinese sat on mats on the floor, as do many Japanese even now. Their nomadic neighbors and the Persians and Arabs with whom the Chinese established contact about 2,000 years ago also sat on rugs or mats placed on the floor. By the eleventh century, however, the Chinese had changed entirely to sitting on chairs and had altered their domestic architecture, the interior arrangements of rooms, and their clothing styles to suit the new furniture.

Historian Charles P. Fitzgerald has studied the introduction of chairs to China and their adoption by the Chinese. He established that a large folding camp stool, which the Chinese called a *hu-ch'uang* (barbarian bed), was introduced to China in the second century from the eastern provinces of the Roman Empire. It became popular for informal seating because it elevated the sitter above the sometimes damp and drafty floor, but he still curled his legs on the seat. Fitzgerald further established

that by the mid-T'ang dynasty, around 800, the frame chair had been introduced to China, probably from the Byzantine Empire. The T'ang dynasty was a cosmopolitan period in China when many foreign customs were tried and adopted. The Japanese monk Ennin noted that T'ang officials sat on chairs, but with their legs curled on the seat. Fitzgerald concluded:

> In the more sophisticated Sung period which soon followed, the break with the old tradition gathered swift momentum. In A.D. 960 the great officials were furnishing their houses with chairs and tables; in the next century they were even designing their own furniture; by the dawn of the twelfth century the whole nation had given up on the floor and taken to chairs and benches.*

Interestingly, the Koreans and Japanese, who had always modeled their cultures on China, did not follow it in this important transformation.

*Charles P. Fitzgerald, *Barbarian Beds: The Origin of the Chair in China* (Canberra: Australian National University, 1965), pp. 49–50.

Dynamic Neo-Confucianism and Stagnant Buddhism

Buddhism, already in decline during the late T'ang, continued to wane as an intellectual force among the ruling classes of China. A reason for its decline was the collapse of Buddhism in India during the eleventh century, owing to the Muslim invasions. Denied intellectual stimulus from India, Chinese Buddhists created no new schools and produced no additional translations of the scriptures.

Sung governmental policy also contributed to the decline of Buddhism. To address the perennial budget crunch caused by tribute payments and the cost of maintaining a large standing army, the government raised revenue by selling ordination and other priestly certificates. Prior to this, governments had insisted that the sangha (monastic community) maintain its standards by examining candidate monks on their understanding of the scriptures before issuing them ordination certificates. The end of the religious exams and the sale of ordination certificates not only corrupted the priesthood, but also contributed to a decline in the doctrinal vitality of Buddhism. Although the Ch'an sect, which emphasized intuitive enlightenment, and the Pure Land sect, which stressed faith and prayer, remained popular, neither was interested in points of doctrine. Thus neither offered an intellectual counterpoint to revived Confucianism.

The only noteworthy development in this period was the metamorphosis of Maitreya, the Buddha of the Future, into the fat Laughing Buddha, surrounded by many children, that is commonly found in temples and domestic shrines. He came to embody all that was to be desired—prosperity (represented by the fat belly), many children, and contentment. As a poem commonly associated with him says:

> The big belly is capable to contain, it contains all
> the things under Heaven which are difficult to contain.
> The broad face is inclined to laugh, to laugh at the
> laughable men on earth.

The Confucian revival that had begun in the late T'ang reached its high point during the Sung period, when the best minds turned to the classical literature of antiquity. Although several Confucian schools emerged, the Neo-Confucian school led by Chu Hsi (1130–1200) eventually prevailed and was acknowledged as orthodox. Neo-Confucianism remained the official interpretation of the master's philosophy until the twentieth century. Chu Hsi and his followers claimed that earlier Confucians had misunderstood the real meaning of the master, which they had rediscovered.

Neo-Confucianism was the great intellectual contribution of the Sung. Its distinctive feature was its ethical character. It condemned the otherworldliness of Buddhism and insisted that human fulfillment in this life is possible through self-cultivation. It accepted a supreme controlling force in the universe and believed that this force is expressed through the five chief virtues, namely, benevolence, righteousness, reverence, wisdom, and sincerity. It accepted the goodness of human nature and explained that evil resulted from the neglect of this nature. Neo-Confucianism failed to provide an answer to the problems of injustice, however, nor did it explain why humans were born with varying fortunes. This is perhaps why Buddhism, which did explain such matters, continued to have a mass following.

Since Chu Hsi and other Neo-Confucians came from the ranks of scholar-officials, it is not surprising that much of their writing dealt with political philosophy and with policies intended to bring about the well-being and moral betterment of the people. As one famous Sung scholar-official put it: "The true scholar should be the first to become anxious about the world's troubles and the last to enjoy its happiness." Neo-Confucians advocated a benevolent and paternalistic government where morally upright officials advised the hereditary monarch. From the late Sung to the end of the nineteenth century, the school curriculum and examinations were based on Chu Hsi's interpretation of Confucianism. The triumph of Neo-Confucian orthodoxy during the last 700 years of imperial China largely explains the stability and conservatism of Chinese society until the present century.

Age of Refinement in Culture and the Arts

The Sung period was noted for its cultural refinement. From the emperor down, great and powerful men patronized the arts. The Sung ideal gentleman was a scholar-statesman, and most distinguished scholars and artists were also officials. Their output of historical, literary, and philosophical writing was prodigious. The printing press made their works, along with encyclopedias and other multivolume books, widely available.

Religion no longer dominated art in Sung China. No new monumental Buddhist shrines comparable to those undertaken during the T'ang and earlier eras were constructed during the Sung. Artworks were enjoyed for their aesthetic appeal, not their religious worth. Some of the greatest painters in Chinese history worked during the Sung period. Landscape painting flourished, and while some artists represented nature as a whole, others made intimate studies of a spray of flowers, a bird, or a branch of bamboo to depict nature in microcosm. Ceramics ranked highest among the minor arts. The technique of high-fired, hard-glazed porcelain was fully developed, and the words *porcelain* and *china* became synonymous. From this time ceramic wares replaced lacquer and metal articles for daily household utensils. New glazes and forms were invented, ranging from the refined and sophisticated pieces produced for the court to various folkware pieces for ordinary use. Potters also turned out sturdy items that would withstand the sea or land journey to Japan, Southeast Asia, the Middle East, or North Africa.

In the daily life of all classes, tea drinking, which had begun in the T'ang, became more common. The tea bush grows in the temperate climate of southern China, and the development of that region resulted in the spread of tea cultivation and drinking. With the completion of the

An Early Book. This Buddhist text, printed during the late T'ang dynasty, was among the earliest books. The easy availability of printed books from the Sung dynasty on allowed men from even humble families to pass the examinations and join the bureaucracy. By permission of the British Library, Or 8210/P2

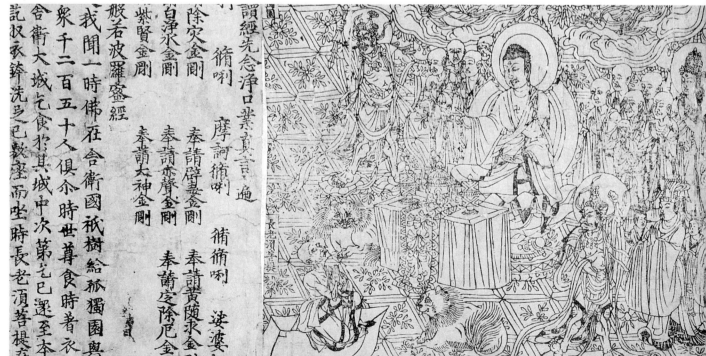

Grand Canal during the Sui dynasty, cheap waterborne transportation brought tea and other southern commodities to the north. Teahouses sprang up in all towns and cities and became social gathering places. The Sung court consumed 60,000 pounds of tea annually for various purposes, including official gifts. Tea often replaced alcoholic drinks at social occasions, and the well-to-do vied with one another to serve tea in the most attractive porcelain cups.

The peace of the Sung period was purchased at a high price, and this perhaps explains why so many people were determined to enjoy it at all levels. Hangchow and other cities were famous for their restaurants, tea and wine houses, and pleasure quarters. There was a mood of resignation even as people pursued their pleasures. As a poet of the Southern Sung wrote:

> Beyond the hills, more blue hills; tall buildings are backed by taller.
> When, here on the West Lake, does singing and dancing cease?
> So heady is the warm breeze that pleasure-seekers, quite drunk,
> Forget their southern exile, and take Hangchow for Kaifeng.
> [Hangchow, capital of the Southern Sung, was built around the shores of the scenic West Lake.]

As the Mongol forces advanced inexorably southward during the thirteenth century, the impending end must have been apparent. As a T'ang poet had written:

> The last glow of sunset, for all its boundless beauty,
> Portends the fast approach of darkness.

Summary and Comparisons

In 320 Chandra Gupta proclaimed himself king and founded the Gupta Empire in northern India, which lasted for over 300 years and brought great cultural advances and prosperity to much of the subcontinent. Half a century after the fall of the Gupta dynasty, another outstanding ruler emerged; he was called Harsha (reigned 606–648), and his reign briefly revived hopes that India would be united and great once again. But the unity failed to last, and divided India could not resist the Muslim invaders who appeared in 712 along the Indus. Successive waves of Arab and later Turkic Muslims gained control of all northern India by about 1000, despite the heroic resistance of the Rajputs. Islam became a permanent political and religious force in India. South India, however, remained under Hindu control. Unlike previous invaders, the strictly monotheistic Muslims resisted absorption into the Hindu culture and therefore remained largely apart. Buddhism was wiped out in the land of its origin, but despite the onslaughts of Islam, Hinduism endured due to the coherence and community of its caste system. During this era Hinduism took the form that has remained essentially unchanged to modern times. It evolved a Way of Wisdom for the philosophically inclined and the Ways of Worship and Works for the majority of its followers.

The golden age of Indian culture under the Guptas and Harsha was comparable to the Periclean Age in Athens and the Augustan Age in Rome. Buddhist art reached its apogee and became the standard for an international Buddhist style. Hindu art also attained great beauty and expressive power that would influence later styles of Indian and Southeast Asian art.

The nomads who invaded North China after the third century brought no high cultures with them. During the centuries of disunity, Buddhism took firm root in China. Buddhism brought both new religious beliefs and Indo-Hellenic art forms to China and eventually acted as a bridge that helped to reunite North and South China.

China's second imperial age was dominated by the cosmopolitan T'ang dynasty (618–907), which rivaled the Han in achievement. The T'ang produced two of the most celebrated rulers of Chinese history: T'ai-tsung, the warrior-statesman founder of the dynasty, and Ming-huang, under whom poetry and art reached their zenith. In Empress Wu, the dynasty produced the only woman in Chinese history who ruled in her own right. T'ang military power brought the Pax Sinica from Korea to central Asia and allowed commodities, people, and ideas to move freely among China, India, Persia, and the Byzantine Empire.

Chinese Buddhism reached its highest point in the early T'ang as pilgrims returned from India with precious manuscripts that were translated into Chinese. But soon after its prestige reached its peak, Buddhism began to decline in China. The Confucian revival, the decline of Buddhism in India, and the Muslim conquest of central Asia brought about this descent. China also came into contact with Christianity, Zoroastrianism, and Islam, but only Islam, which struck roots in northwestern China, persisted as a significant minority and regional religion.

In contrast to the expansive mood of the Han and T'ang, the Sung period (960–1279) was one of refined introspection. Militarily unsuccessful against its warlike nomadic neighbors, the Sung government pursued peace through diplomacy and appeasement. Led by pacifist civilians and never in control of all lands inhabited by Chinese, the Northern Sung gave way to the Southern Sung, which ruled only the Yangtze valley and lands to the south. Intellectually, the Chinese found in reinterpreted Confucianism, called Neo-Confucianism, an effective counter to Buddhism, which continued to decline. The Sung was also an age of increased urbanism, literacy, and artistic refinement. It was totally destroyed by the Mongols in the thirteenth century.

The fall of the great Mauryan and Kushan Empires in India and the Han Empire in China plunged both countries into centuries of tumult marked by civil wars and outside invasions. However, whereas the Greeks, Scythians, and Iranian invaders of India were not barbarians, the Hsiung-nu and other nomads who plundered and dominated northern China had neither written language nor high culture. As a result, while Indian culture was stimulated and enriched by the art and learning that the invaders introduced, China received minimal intellectual or material benefits from its invaders. The contrast is clear in the rich flowering of Indian art and architecture under the Guptas that blended and integrated the Greco-Roman and central Asian styles with indigenous Indian traditions. The mature artistic forms that emerged would later have an enormous influence on East Asian art and an even greater impact on Southeast Asian art.

China's cultural heritage suffered serious blows from the invaders who burnt libraries and destroyed schools. At the same time, however, the nomadic invasions did enrich China's civilization both directly and indirectly. The direct enrichment occurred because the nomadic rulers of northern China, awed by the grandeur of Buddhism, a much higher religion than their own crude systems, welcomed Buddhist missionaries and converted to Buddhism. Indirectly, they caused Buddhism to prosper because the disturbed and bloody times drove the Chinese people to seek consolation in salvation, and they saw in Buddhism hopes for a better world to come. Thus Buddhism, an exotic foreign religion during the Han dynasty, put down deep roots during the age of disunity and gradually became Sinicized.

Conversely, Indians did not take up the religion of the early invaders; rather, the deities of the invaders became absorbed into Hinduism-Buddhism and eventually disappeared. India's religious equation was dramatically changed by its Muslim invaders after the eighth century. Both the Arab Muslims and later the Turkic Muslims entered India in possession of advanced cultures as well as a strict monotheistic religion that would not compromise with Hinduism and Buddhism.

Although the Chinese state did not clash in force with the Muslim powers, the Muslim conquest of central Asia and northwestern India, which had once been mostly Buddhist, cut off the significant cultural and religious contacts between China and the original centers of Buddhism. In this way the Muslims contributed to Chinese Buddhism's loss of vitality.

Because invaders occupied and repeatedly ravaged the northern portions of India and China, the spared southern parts of both countries enjoyed accelerated development. Many lands in Southeast Asia would continue to advance because of inspirations from southern India. Similarly, the Yangtze valley in China developed so rapidly during the age of disunity that by the time of the second imperial age, the south had already surpassed the north in many areas. The continued prosperity of southern China was even more prominent during the subsequent Sung dynasty, which was forced to cede ever more territory in northern China to the barbarian states.

Selected Sources

Carter, T. F. *The Invention of Printing in China and Its Spread Westward.* Rev. ed. 1955. Chronicle of an event of vast world importance.

*Chang, K. C. *Food in Chinese Culture: Anthropological and Historical Perspectives.* 1977. Fascinating and entertaining account of Chinese food and eating habits from antiquity to the present.

*Ch'en, Kenneth. *Buddhism in China: A Historical Survey,* 1964. A comprehensive and readable survey of the evolution of Buddhism in China to the twentieth century.

China Central T.V. and Central Park Media. *The Silk Road.* 1982. A series of 55-minute films devoted to the Chinese portions of the ancient Silk Road.

Devahuti, D. *Harsha: A Political Study.* 1970. A detailed study of India in the sixth and seventh centuries and of Harsha's accomplishments.

*Ebrey, Patricia B. *The Inner Quarters: Marriage and the Lives of Chinese Women in the Sung Period.* 1994. A recent study of women and domestic life.

Ebrey, Patricia B., and Peter N. Buckley, eds. *Religion and Society in T'ang and Sung China.* 1993. A useful collection of articles by nine experts on this period of Chinese history.

Gernet, Jacques. *Daily Life in China on the Eve of the Mongol Invasions, 1250–1276.* Trans. H. M. Wright. 1962. A good book on an often overlooked subject.

Jaschid, Sechin, and Van Jay Symond. *Peace, War, and Trade along the Great Wall: Nomadic-Chinese Interaction through Two Millennia.* 1989. A pathbreaking study of interactions between China and inner Asia.

Lane-Poole, Stanley. *Medieval India under Mohammedan Rule (A.D. 712–1764).* Reprinted 1979. A comprehensive account of Muslim conquerors and rulers.

Lo, Kuan-chung. *Romance of the Three Kingdoms.* Trans. C. H. Brewitt-Taylor. 2 vols. 1925. This is one of China's best-loved, romanticized historical novels about events of the third century, written in the fourteenth century.

———, or Shih Nai-an. *All Men Are Brothers.* Trans. Pearl S. Buck. 1933. A popular Chinese novel about a band of men and women during the Sung dynasty who took the law into their own hands for just causes, much as Robin Hood did.

Puri, B. N. *India under the Kushanas.* 1965. A good survey of the Kushan era.

Reischauer, Edwin O. *Ennin's Travels in T'ang China.* 1955. T'ang China as observed by a Japanese Buddhist monk.

*Schafer, Edward H. *The Vermilion Bird: T'ang Images of the South.* 1967. An interesting account of southern China and Southeast Asia.

*——. *The Golden Peaches of Samarkand: A Study of T'ang Exotics.* 1983. An interesting book about the unusual things most history books leave out.

Sinor, Denis, ed. *The Cambridge History of Early Inner Asia.* 1990. This work by a number of specialists includes several chapters on China's nomadic neighbors.

Smith, Vincent A. *The Oxford History of India.* 4th ed. Ed. Percival Spear. 1981. Part of this authoritative book deals with the period this chapter discusses.

Steinhardt, Nancy C. *Chinese Imperial City Planning.* 1990. A comprehensive survey through the ages.

Tokyo Metropolitan Art Museum. *Grand Exhibition of Silk Road Buddhist Art.* 1996. Through art and artifacts, this book shows how Buddhism spread to East Asia and how it was transformed.

Twitchett, Denis, and John K. Fairbanks, eds. *The Cambridge History of China.* Vol. 3, *Sui and T'ang China, 586–906.* Part 1. 1979. Many experts contributed to this authoritative volume.

Waley, Arthur. *The Poetry and Career of Li Po.* 1958. Waley brings to life a wonderfully eccentric man and his great work.

Wright, Arthur F. *Buddhism in Chinese History.* 1959. A good book for both students and specialists.

———. *The Sui Dynasty: The Unification of China,* A.D. *581–617.* 1978. Excellent portraits of two men who ruled China around 600 C.E.

*Wu, Cheng-en. *Monkey.* Trans. Arthur Waley. A sixteenth-century novel that tells the story of how a supernatural monkey and other beasts helped Hsuan-tsang get Buddhist scriptures from India. Chinese children love it as fairy tale and adults as satire.

———————

*Available in paperback.

Internet Links

Gupta Dynasty: Golden Age of India

http://www.med.unc.edu/~nupam/Sgupta1.html
  This site offers excellent short texts on the kings of the Gupta dynasty, keyed to illustrations of contemporary coins.

History of Asia to 1500 A.D.: Religion and Culture

http://www.interchg.ubc.ca/arbgary/11.html
  This webpage gives a succinct discussion of the arrival and evolution of the Buddhist religion in China.

Li Po [Selected Poems]

http://www.physics.wisc.edu/~shalizi/Poetry/Li_Po/
  A collection of eighteen poems literally translated, plus three free evocations by Ezra Pound.

The Sung Dynasty (A.D. 960–1279)

http://www.cohums.ohio-state.edu/deall/jin.3/c231/handouts/h11.html
  An outline indicating general characteristics, governmental change, literary and artistic trends, and the emergence of Neo-Confucianism.

The T'ang Dynasty (A.D. 618–907)

http://www.cohums.ohio-state.edu/deall/jin.3/c231/handouts/h9.html
  A handy outline of political, economic, and cultural developments in the era.

Cultural Borrowing and Cultural Isolation

There are three religious groups here, the *panc-h'i* [pandits or brahmans] or learned men, the Buddhist monks or *ch'u-ku*, and the Taoists or *pa-ss'u*. (James P. Holoka and Jiu-Hwa L. Upshur, eds., *Lives and Times: A World History Reader,* vol. 1 [St. Paul: West Publishing, 1995], p. 278)

* * * * *

Cavalry warfare in Eurasia came about through a long process of historical evolution. . . . Horsemanship was practiced by Indo-European peoples of the Ukrainian steppes as early as 4000 B.C. . . . It is likely that the horse had been domesticated in China during the Neolithic era (circa third millennium B.C.) when it was harnessed to the chariot as well as used as a draft animal. . . . Chinese records indicate that the Di [a nomadic people living to the northwest of China] rode horses as early as the Spring and Autumn era (722 to 481 B.C.). By the time of the Warring States (403 to 221 B.C.), the nomadic use of mounted men had become a form of warfare so powerful as to inspire emulation. (Adam T. Kessler, *Empires beyond the Great Wall: The Heritage of Genghis Khan* [Los Angeles: Natural History Museum of Los Angeles County, 1993], pp. 17–18)

The first cultures evolved in isolation and advanced mainly through independent invention. For example, agriculture appeared at about the same time in three widely separated parts of the world (West Asia, China, and the Western Hemisphere); in each area it was based on different crops (grain/rice, maize/potatoes). Likewise many early cultures independently invented the technique of firing utensils made of clay to make pottery.

Travel, trade, and warfare brought peoples of different cultures together with the passage of time. Diffusion—the passing of ideas, technologies, and languages from one culture to another—became increasingly frequent. The two passages quoted above prove this point. The first was written by a twelfth-century Chinese visitor to Angkor, capital of ancient Cambodia. Situated in Southeast Asia, ancient Cambodia (also called the Khmer state) was ideally located to benefit from traders, missionaries, and settlers from China to the north and India to the west. Although the writer remarked on the presence of Taoist priests from China, Hinduism and Buddhism became the primary religions of that land, with Buddhism finally triumphing. The second passage shows the importantce of warfare in affecting technology transfers. When the Di, a nomadic neighbor of the Chinese, learned to ride horses, they posed a greater menace, compelling the Chinese to adopt the use of cavalry in warfare in self-defense.

Another example of war as an important catalyst of diffusion can be seen in the spread of iron weapons. The Hittites were the first people to use iron weapons and became widely feared as a result. In self-defense their neighbors and victims hastened to learn the new technology and make their own iron weapons. Eventually, the technology of making weapons and agricultural implements from iron spread throughout Europe, Asia, and Africa, and iron replaced bronze as the primary metal.

Wars and conquest also spread cultures and ideas. For example, through conquest the more advanced Chinese spread their culture to Korea and Vietnam. On the other hand, the less cultured Roman conquerors became admiring students of the sophisticated Greeks they subjugated. The Mongols eventually adopted the religions, written languages, and technologies of their various victims and, as a result, lost their homogeneity and unity.

Commerce has also been an important vehicle for the spread and diffusion of cultures. Greeks trading with the Phoenicians in the eastern Mediterranean adopted the Phoenician alphabet. Chinese traders and Buddhist teachers brought the Chinese writing system to Japan. The Silk Road, a major commercial route across Eurasia, introduced new religions, crops, technologies, art forms, raw materials, and finished products to different cultures across two continents. Indian merchants and other travelers by sea brought the science, mathematics, and writing of India's ancient civilization to the peoples of Southeast Asia. Oceans prevented dissemination from Eurasia to the Amerindian civilizations until the end of the fifteenth century. Iron-working was not independently invented in the Americas.

Group migration is another important means of diffusion. From earliest times, people have moved from one region to another in search of land and resources, as conquerors, or in flight from enemies. The immigration of the Etruscans from Asia Minor to Italy around 900 B.C.E. and of the Greeks after 700 resulted in rapid advances in technology and art throughout the Italian Peninsula. In Africa, when the Bantu migrated into the central and southern part of the continent, they brought their own language and customs, which in time were adopted by local peoples. The spread of the Indo-European languages is another example of this type of diffusion. This language system originated in the steppe heartland of Eurasia; the migrating tribes who moved into other parts of Europe and Asia spread their language. As a result, nearly all the languages from northern India to Ireland belong to the Indo-European family and are related.

In studying world history, it is important to understand that most civilizations were the amalgamation of indigenous and borrowed elements. Chapter 7 shows how true this was throughout classic Mesoamerica, the Amerindian empires, the early African kingdoms, Southeast Asia, and Japan. During more recent centuries, as means of transportation and communication have expedited contact between societies, diffusion has increasingly become the predominant mode of cultural change. As the world becomes more interconnected, the speed and extent of cultural borrowings and exhanges will also increase.

Chapter 7

Early Korea and Japan

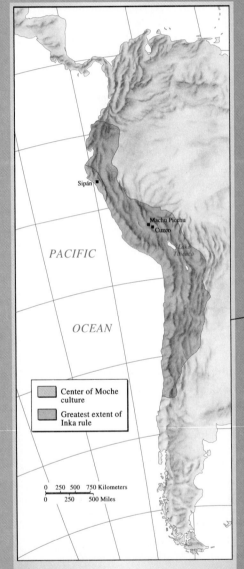

The Development of
Andean Civilization

Center of Moche
culture

Greatest extent of
Inka rule

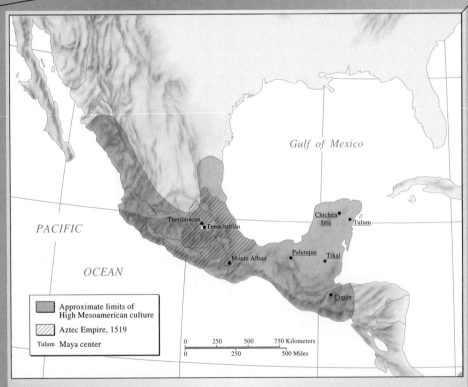

The Development of Mesoamerican Civilization

Approximate limits of
High Mesoamerican culture

Aztec Empire, 1519

Tulum Maya center

Developing Civilizations

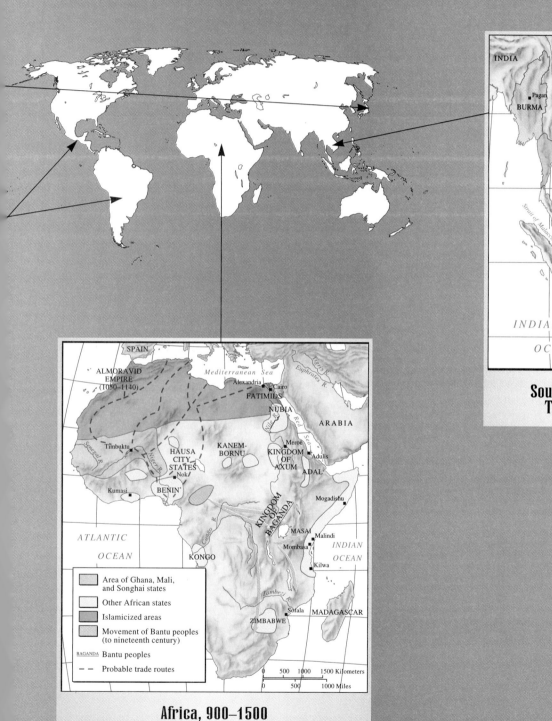

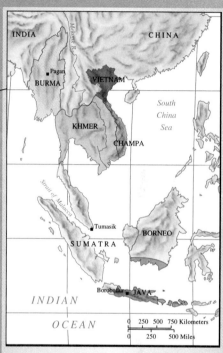

Southeast Asia in the Twelfth Century

(Southeast Asia map labels)

INDIA

CHINA

Mekong R.

Pagan

BURMA

VIETNAM

KHMER

South China Sea

CHAMPA

Strait of Malacca

Tumasik

BORNEO

SUMATRA

Borobudur · JAVA

INDIAN

OCEAN

0 250 500 750 Kilometers

0 250 500 Miles

Africa, 900–1500

(Africa map labels)

SPAIN

ALMORAVID EMPIRE (1050–1140)

Mediterranean Sea

Tigris R.

Euphrates R.

Alexandria · Cairo

FATIMIDS

NUBIA

Nile R.

Red Sea

ARABIA

Senegal R.

Timbuktu

Niger R.

HAUSA CITY STATES

KANEM-BORNU

Meroë

KINGDOM OF AXUM

Adulis

ADAL

Nok

Kumasi

BENIN

KINGDOM OF BAGANDA

Congo R.

Mogadishu

ATLANTIC OCEAN

KONGO

MASAI

Malindi

Mombasa

INDIAN OCEAN

Kilwa

Zambezi R.

Sofala

MADAGASCAR

ZIMBABWE

Area of Ghana, Mali, and Songhai states

Other African states

Islamicized areas

Movement of Bantu peoples (to nineteenth century)

BAGANDA Bantu peoples

- - - Probable trade routes

0 500 1000 1500 Kilometers

0 500 1000 Miles

This chapter looks at cultures located outside the crescent of civilizations stretching across Eurasia from Europe to China. It returns to Amerindian civilizations and African cultures taken up in Chapter 1 and brings in cultures in Southeast and East Asia not previously discussed. In looking at this gamut of civilizations, it is instructive to consider the concepts of cultural isolation and cultural borrowing discussed in the previous comparative essay. The chapter begins with the cultures that were completely separate from Eurasian civilization and proceeds across the spectrum, ending with those that are the most derivative.

The Amerindian civilizations that had already been established in Mesoamerica and the Andes continued to develop on an increasingly sophisticated course, particularly in engineering, mathematics, astronomy, and the decorative arts. Down through the years some have claimed that Egyptians or Phoenicians or early Japanese or Chinese or some other Eurasian group somehow crossed the ocean and created these civilizations. A few even professed to find evidence of extraterrestrials landing in Peru. Most scholars, however, view the Amerindian civilizations as completely indigenous.

Unlike the Amerindian civilizations, the cultures of sub-Saharan Africa, although separated from Eurasia by an ocean of sand, showed some signs of Eurasian influence. East Africa had close relations with Egypt because of the Nile, and proximity to commercial traffic on the perimeter of the Indian Ocean meant more substantial contacts in general with Eurasia. On the other hand, cultural diffusion into western Africa before the advent of

Islam was slight. The Bantu culture that spread into southern Africa showed the least evidence of diffusion.

Compared to the new civilizations that arose in the Americas and sub-Saharan Africa, the late-flowering societies of Southeast and East Asia were heavily influenced from the first by the great cultures in neighboring India and China. Indian influence was dominant from Burma to Indonesia and came to the area entirely by peaceful means, through traders and Hindu and Buddhist missionaries. Chinese cultural influence on Southeast Asia was limited to trade and technology, except for Vietnam, which was under Chinese rule for a thousand years and developed a variant form of Chinese culture. Everywhere in Southeast Asia, however, the foreign mixed with the indigenous to create unique cultures.

Korea and Japan in East Asia were exclusively influenced by Chinese civilization until recent centuries. Like Vietnam, Korea was under China's political dominance for many centuries. Though never controlled by China politically, Japan enthusiastically adopted key aspects of the Chinese civilization, which blended with the indigenous to form the Japanese culture.

Mesoamerican Civilization

Our first father-mothers . . . were simply made and modeled, it is said; they had no mother and no father. . . . No woman gave birth to them, nor were they begotten by the builder,

200 B.C.E. 1 C.E.	Indians sail to Southeast Asia

	Indian influence in Java, Sumatra,
	    Malaya, Burma
	Bantu migrations
	Moche culture rises in Peru
	Teotihuacán begins era of full
	    flowering in Mesoamerica

500	Indian influence in Burma,
	    Thailand, Malaya
	Chinese trade in Southeast Asia
	Maya civilization at its height
	Prince Shotoku's regency in Japan
	Japanese embassy to China
	Kingdom of Axum begins
	Silla unifies Korea
	Spread of Islam in North and East
	    Africa
	Khmer Empire
	Angkor Wat, Borobodur, Pagan
	    built
	Koryo dynasty in Korea
	Feudal Japan, code of Bushido

1000	Lady Murasaki, *The Tale of Genji* Thais form a state Shogunate in Japan Maya revival in Yucatán

	Kingdoms of Salt and Gold
	    predominant in West Africa
	Mongols conquer Korea, Southern
	    Sung, Pagan
	East African city-states
	Stone complexes in Zimbabwe

	Mansa Kankan Musa leader of Mali

1350	Rise of the Aztecs
	Inka Empire expands under Thupa
	    Yupanki
	Moctezuma II becomes ruler of
	    Aztec Empire

1500	

sculptor, Bearer, Begetter. By sacrifice alone, by genius alone they were made, they were modeled by the Maker, Modeler, Bearer, Begetter, Sovereign Plumed Serpent. And when they came to fruition, they came out human:

They talked and they made words.
They looked and they listened.
They walked, they worked.

They were good people, handsome. . . . Thoughts came into existence and they gazed; their vision came all at once. Perfectly they saw, perfectly they knew everything under the sky, whenever they looked. The moment they turned around and looked around in the sky, on the earth, everything was seen without any obstruction. . . .

They understood everything perfectly, they sighted the four sides, the four corners of the sky, on the earth, and this didn't sound good to the builder and sculptor. . . .

And so the Bearer, Begetter took back their knowledge: . . . They were blinded as the face of a mirror is breathed upon. Their eyes were weakened. Now it was only when they looked nearby that things were clear.

And such was the loss of the means of understanding, along with the means of knowing everything. . . .*

*Popol Vuh, trans. Dennis Tedlock (New York: Simon & Schuster, 1985), pp. 165–167.

This Maya creation story resembles explanations of the origins of humankind in other cultures. Unlike many of these other accounts, however, it has no "fall," as in the Judeo-Christian tradition, nor are men and women created as limited toys for the gods to enjoy, as in several Asian traditions. In the Maya version, human beings are made perfect and through no lapse of their own are later made imperfect. The stress on knowledge and perception is also notable and well suits a people who made great innovations in mathematics, astronomy, and engineering.

In Chapter 1 we discussed the Olmec, the parent culture of Mesoamerican civilization. After 400 B.C.E., Olmec society began to lose its vigor, and other cultures arose. The three most notable were the large urban culture centered on Teotihuacán, the mathematically and astronomically sophisticated Maya culture, which lasted almost 2,000 years, and the Aztec state, Mesoamerica's culminating Amerindian empire.

Urban Grandeur: Teotihuacán

Teotihuacán arose in an arid valley approximately thirty miles northeast of present-day Mexico City. In 100 B.C.E., the area was a cluster of villages; by 200 C.E., massive public buildings were under construction. Centuries of prosperity followed, and by 500 Teotihuacán, now a metropolis of 200,000 laid out on a grid, had become one of the largest urban centers of the world. One reason for Teotihuacán's preeminence was its reliable water supply. Although located in an arid climate, the city was centered on a dozen large, permanent springs in an area of rich volcanic soil. Like the inhabitants of the Tigris-Euphrates valley earlier, the Teotihuacános used terracing, canals, and other water-saving methods to produce abundant food crops that supported a large population.

The reconstructed center of the city gives some idea of its size and shape. Ceremonial buildings, ball courts, and two great pyramids, the largest almost 600 feet square, sit along a central avenue extending almost three miles. Less dramatic, but equally important to archaeologists, are the remains of some 3,000 other structures within the city. Most of these were multifamily dwellings; typically, each structure featured a patio, a cement foundation, and an elaborate drainage system.

Another factor in Teotihuacán's rise to prominence was its control of the obsidian trade between highland Mexico and the gulf coast. Teotihuacán built up a substantial industry for producing obsidian tools, and its artisans also manufactured pottery and other items for large-scale export.

It is unclear how far the Teotihuacános extended their rule from their valley. Some authorities claim that they expanded into Maya territory hundreds of miles to the east; others maintain that Teotihuacán's influence was commercial and cultural, but that political control reached only into neighboring valleys.

For many Mesoamericans, Teotihuacán was a focus of pilgrimage and worship, for it was there that their ancestors had emerged from the underworld. Much of Teotihuacán religion was directed to worship of a "Great Goddess," a female divinity who provided the springs of water. Her images depict her gesturing outward, with water, seeds, and flowers issuing from her body and her clothing. Another powerful symbol of water and fertility was the Feathered (or Plumed) Serpent, the fanged, feather-collared serpent who is depicted undulating on seashell beaches. The serpent was also a manifestation of the planet Venus, the Teotihuacán deity of warfare and blood sacrifice.

Living in a generally barren wasteland, Teotihuacános were undoubtedly anxious about the permanence of their existence and devised practices to help the Great Goddess keep Teotihuacán well watered. Mesoamerican astronomers had carefully recorded the appearance of Venus as the morning and evening star for many centuries. Calculating that Venus had a 584-day cycle and that five of these cycles corresponded to eight 365-day years, they devised an almanac of 2,920 days. Apparently, a warrior cult in Teotihuacán and in other Mesoamerican

Panorama of Teotihuacán. The city of Teotihuacán flourished in the central highlands of Mexico about 500 C.E. In the background is the enormous Temple of the Sun, larger than any pyramid at Giza. Jim Fox/Photo Researchers

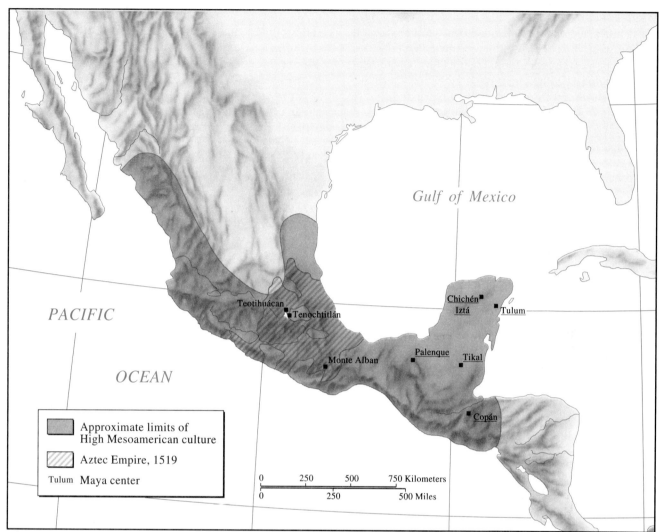

✳ MAP 7.1 The Development of Mesoamerican Civilization. A succession of advanced literate civilizations rose in present-day Mexico and Central America. The monumental architecture, art forms, and religious ideas of the urban center of Teotihuacán (100 C.E.–750 C.E.) influenced the region for centuries. The Maya civilization (100 C.E.–1400 C.E.) brought the architecture, mathematics, astronomy, and calendar of Mesoamerica to high levels of sophistication. The Aztecs built up a centralized empire surrounded by tributary states during the fifteenth century from their enormous capital, Tenochtitlán, on the site of present-day Mexico City.

cultures used the phases of Venus to find the most propitious times to undertake what some modern investigators have termed "star wars," campaigns conducted to secure sacrificial prisoners. These prisoners were executed in great public ceremonies, providing the blood "soul" that turned into water, thus sustaining Teotihuacán; Teotihuacán paintings depict red drops of blood from dead and dying prisoners literally turning into blue drops of water.

Although early Teotihuacán art rarely depicted military themes, after 500 C.E. more and more allusions to warfare appear, and archaeologists have found the remains of a great wall built at this time. At this same time, too, Teotihuacán's trading area began to contract. The population of Teotihuacán declined dramatically, and by 800 C.E. its inhabitants had abandoned the city and settled in outlying villages. Scholars have proposed many

reasons for the end of the Teotihuacán civilization, including environmental degradation, revolt, and invasion. When the Mexica (Aztecs) came wandering into the valley centuries later, only the crumbling ruins of the great city remained; so impressive were the ruins, however, that the awed visitors said it must be Teotihuacán, in their language "the Abode of the Gods."

The Integration of Mesoamerican Civilization: The Maya

More is known about Maya civilization than about either the Olmec or the Teotihuacán culture. Maya culture survived, even if somewhat transformed, until after the Spanish conquest, and 4 million people still speak Maya today. Although scholars have deciphered early Maya writing, overzealous Catholic missionaries, trying to annihilate the pagan past of the Maya, left only three preconquest Maya books intact, together with fragments of a fourth. Several postconquest Maya books, among them the *Popol Vuh,* are also of great value in understanding the Maya. Glyphs (inscriptions on rocks) have survived in great numbers. Archaeologists at first thought that most of them did little more than depict stylized human figures, list names and dates, and refer briefly to some important event. New discoveries, especially tombs containing murals, pottery, and jewelry, now make it clear that the Maya artisans often portrayed individual Maya rulers realistically.

The Maya lived in dense rain forest lowlands in present-day northern Guatemala and in neighboring Belize, Mexico, and Honduras. Their staple food was maize, and it was long thought that they practiced exclusively slash-and-burn agriculture. This technique wastes land and produces a relatively low yield and thus could have supported only a small population. Aerial surveys, however, revealed "unnatural" tracts of land under the jungle canopy. On-site investigation proved that the Maya had in fact employed a second type of agriculture. They built canals in swampy areas alongside raised plots of earth, which drew moisture from the canals by capillary action. The maize and vegetables were fertilized with swamp lilies (depicted on many Maya statues and monuments) dredged from the drainage ditches. The high yield of the raised-field system could support a population of millions.

By 700–800 C.E.—approximately the era of Muhammad, Charlemagne, and the T'ang dynasts—Mayan civilization was at its height. It was composed of about twenty-five independent city-states, of which the largest were Tikal and Copán with perhaps 30,000 inhabitants apiece. Each city had a number of satellite towns and villages. These city-states traded with—and made war on—each other via a complex river system supplemented by roads built by forced labor. The city-states were characterized by a highly stratified society in which royal dynasties supported by priests and warrior nobles ruled over farmers, artisans, and traders.

More than their Mesoamerican predecessors, the Maya had easy access to an enduring building material—limestone. They built colossal tomb-pyramids, some 250 feet high, topped by temples and palaces made of limestone. In the larger Maya cities, these impressive buildings, interspersed with walled ball courts, were surrounded by hundreds of smaller mounds supporting thatched private dwellings. The tops of the great pyramids were often connected by wide causeways, over which marched sumptuous royal and religious processions, while the massed populace watched from far below. The huge city of Tikal spread out from six temple complexes to cover thirty-two square miles; nevertheless, only 30,000 people lived there.

Unlike their Olmec predecessors and the Andean cultures, the Maya developed a written language, but it proved so difficult to translate that it eluded experts for generations. Some have claimed that the decipherment

of Maya writing is a feat that ranks with the unraveling of the "double helix," the DNA code. Steles recording the triumphs of Harvest Mountain Lord between 143 and 156 C.E. are the earliest dated writing so far deciphered in the Western Hemisphere. Unfortunately, surviving Maya writing is predominantly limited to astronomical almanacs and to glyphs on steles proclaiming genealogical and political propaganda about each city's royal dynasty. The bark books that might have furnished information about the economic, legal, and literary aspects of Maya civilization have perished through natural decay or destruction by European invaders.

The crowning glory of Maya civilization was the development of a mathematics-calendar complex that was among the most advanced in the world at that time. This system was initially devised about 600 B.C.E. by the Zapotecan and Olmec cultures in south-central Mexico and spread across the region. The mathematics system employed a base of 20, with a dot for units and a bar for fives. It included a sign for zero, a mathematical tool of enormous power. Chinese, Indian, and Muslim mathematics all made use of the zero, whereas the Romans, in contrast, had no zero.

The Mesoamerican calendar, as the Maya fully developed it, was extremely complicated: a 260-day year (thirteen 20-day units) ran parallel to a solar year (eighteen 20-day units plus 5 days that were considered ill-omened). Once every 18,980 days, almost exactly fifty-two years, the 260-day year and the solar year coincided, and the cycle began again; that date was one of great ceremony. Of greater significance in dating and understanding Mesoamerican civilization is the Long Count, a Maya linear calendar. The Maya believed that after several earlier creations and destructions, a new creation had occurred on August 13, 3114 B.C.E. It was to end no earlier than 4772 C.E. and, according to some extremely advanced Maya calculations, perhaps not for 142,000,000,000,000,000,000,000,000,000,000,000,000 (nonillion) years.

The Maya needed an elaborate calendar because the extensive astrological observations and mathematical calculations on which it was based helped them propitiate the gods, who demanded appropriate recognition every day of the year. The Maya pantheon contained a host of gods, many of whose functions are not well understood at present. Each day had a name associated with two gods, one from the 260-day ritual calendar and one from the 365-day solar calendar. The pairings of these gods changed daily throughout the fifty-two years it took the two calendars to come back to their starting point. The attributes of each god determined the characteristics of the day. It was no simple matter for an individual to get safely through a given day. He had to know not only the names of the two gods controlling the day but also the relations between the gods and thus what had to be done to placate them. The Maya were obsessed with "good"

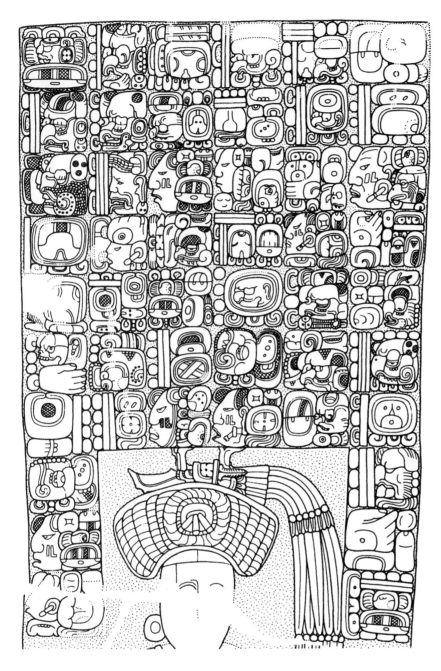

The Biography of a Maya Queen. This stela depicts the written language and calendar of the Maya, which is composed of carvings combining human figures, symbols, and numerals. It tells the story of Lady Katun Ahua, who was born July 7, 674 C.E. She was married at twelve to the future king of Piedras Negras, Yo'Acnal. On March 22, 708, she gave birth to a daughter, Lady Kin Ahua. The queen sits on a throne holding her daughter. (Based on a translation by Linda Schele, drawing by John Montgomery.)

and "bad" days; according to one of the surviving guides to good and bad days, the bad far outnumbered the good, and on those bad days, daily labors had to be performed with special care.

The religious mainstay of the Maya was the ruler, who performed the key ceremonies that perpetuated the order of the universe, visible and invisible. The lord, usually male but occasionally female, was divine, or descended from gods. The lord, especially in the role of chief priest, bound together the nine levels of the underworld, the earth, and the three levels of heaven and made it possible for the people to communicate with their ancestors and the gods. Upon the lord's death, elaborate state ceremonies prepared for his journey into the underworld. At the same time, other, equally intense ceremonies marked the ascension of the new lord, because the people of the city-state were in terrible danger until a lord was in place to maintain the universal order.

Like many premodern cultures, the Maya believed that their gods required humans to practice ritual sacrifices, thereby feeding the gods and recognizing their role in maintaining the universal order. A key sacrifice was human blood. In many cultures, such as the ancient Hebrew and Greco-Roman worlds, the gods were perceived to be satisfied by the blood of animals.

In Mesoamerican civilization the key sacrificial act of Maya culture was the frequent shedding of royal blood to properly connect the people of the state with the gods. In public ceremonies the lord pushed a stingray spine through his penis or scrotum, while his consort pulled a

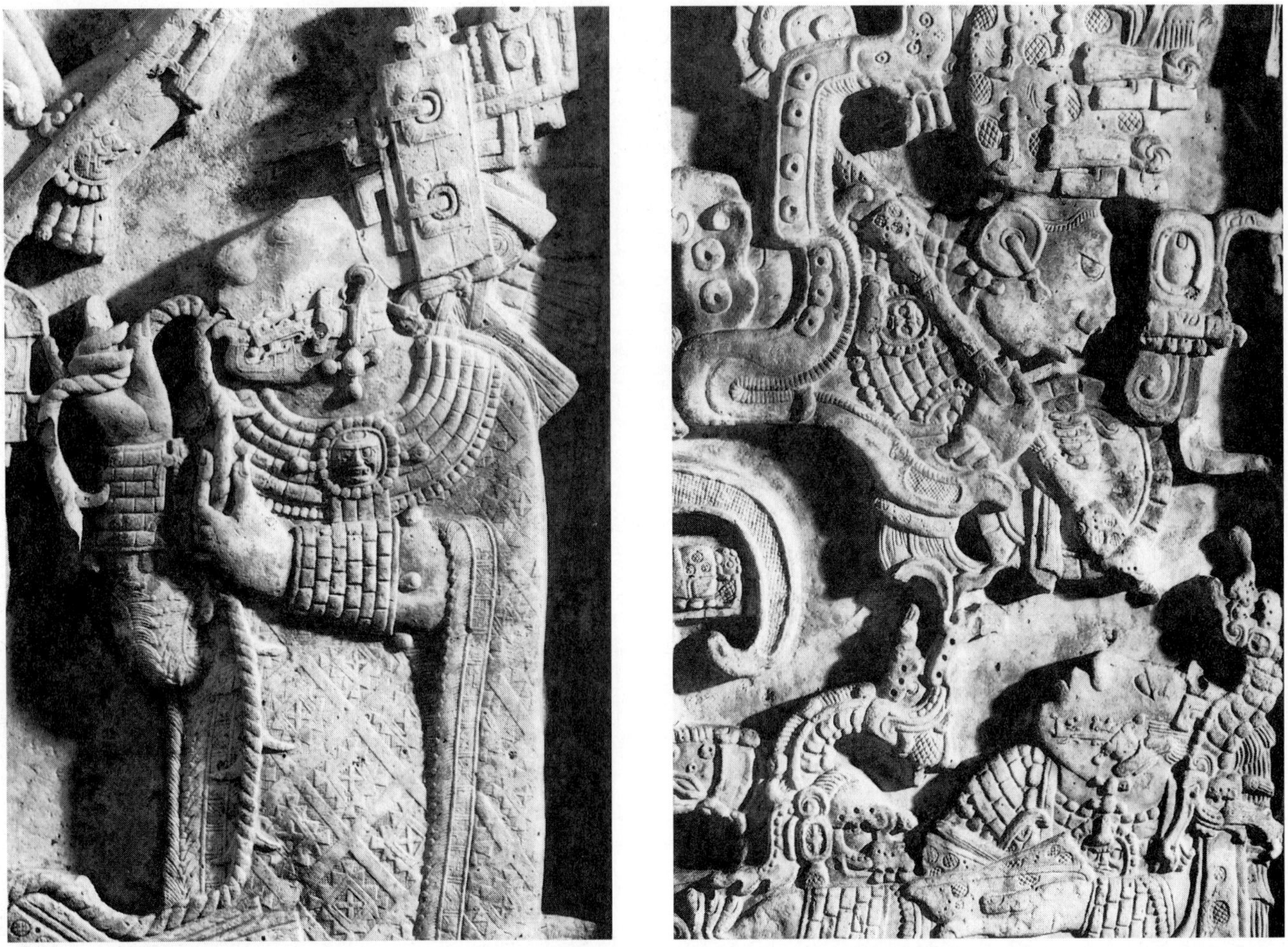

The Life-Giving Blood of Monarchs. This double panel of Maya carvings depicts a typical ceremony in which Maya rulers gave their blood so that the gods would bring prosperity to their realm and subjects. In the left panel, the queen consort of the Maya state pulls a rope braided with thorns through a hole in her tongue. In the right panel, the queen hallucinates, seeing the Vision Serpent, from whose mouth a warrior of the Venus cult begins to emerge. (Based on an interpretation by Linda Schele.) Both © British Museum

thorn-embedded rope through a hole in her tongue. Maya nobility also shed their blood. This bloodletting not only fed the gods but enabled the practitioner to hallucinate, bringing forth the Vision Serpent. The serpent in turn brought forth such images as Venus warriors and ancestors, who answered questions about the future. Hallucinogenic enemas were another way to contact one's ancestors.

Although Maya city-states waged wars of conquest against each other at times, often Maya wars were ritualistic, designed to capture the rulers of another state rather than destroy the adversary's city. From Teotihuacán the Maya had adopted the Venus warrior cult, which specialized in securing captives for sacrifice in Maya religious and political rituals. The blood of these captives apparently played a supplemental role in the rituals of the Maya. Some were tortured for years to give blood at many ceremonies, and a captive of high standing, perhaps a ruler, was killed at the accession ceremonies of the Maya monarchs. The number of victims was quite low, however, compared to the mass butchery of the Aztecs (see the next section).

The Maya version of the sacred ball game appears to have been more complex and deadly than the Olmec practice, although the rules are still not known. Clad in protective padding, Maya rulers are often depicted playing ball against a captive leader in a T-shaped court flanked by steep temple walls or stone bleachers. Apparently, after losing the ritual ball game, the captive leader was bound into a rubber ball and dropped from the high temple walls or bounced down the stone steps.

The Maya looked on the afterlife as a dangerous, but survivable, experience. The souls of living humans, lords and commoners alike, were portrayed as being transported across the water of life in huge dugout canoes paddled by the gods. As death approached, the dugout slowly sank, dropping the souls into Xibalba, a fearsome underground realm permeated by the overwhelming stench of rotting corpses and disease. Xibalba was peopled by death gods, creatures with overpowering bad breath and stupendous farts, who were out to kill human souls. Most souls never returned from that dread place, but the Maya had hope. Previously, ball-playing hero twins had fooled the not-too-bright death gods and had been reborn and returned as ancestors. Reigning monarchs claimed their predecessors had returned; ordinary Maya hoped their souls, too, would outwit the demons and return as ancestor spirits to advise their descendants.

Between 800 and 900, the canoe of Maya civilization in the Maya heartland of Guatemala began to sink. About 1100 a revival of Maya culture occurred, though mixed with outside influences; centered at Chichén Itzá and Uxmal in the drier climate of northern Yucatán, it reached its peak about 1300. After 1400 decline again set in, hastened by plagues, disastrous weather, recurrent warfare, and the lack of an effective central authority. When the Spanish arrived in 1517, Maya civilization, now almost 2,000 years old, was in a state of collapse.

Mesoamerican Imperialism: The Aztecs

As Maya civilization was fading in Guatemala and the Yucatán, a new Mesoamerican group, the Aztecs, became dominant in the highlands of central Mexico, scene of the Teotihuacán culture and later of a powerful Toltec state. The Aztecs, who usually called themselves Tenocha or Mexica, were a nomadic tribe from the north that straggled into the Valley of Mexico and tried to find a place to settle on the shore of Lake Texcoco. For several generations the Aztecs led miserable lives as mercenaries or cheap labor for the settled tribes. Then, in 1345, fleeing from an enemy, the Aztecs took refuge on several marshy islands in the lake. According to their legends, when they arrived on the largest island, they saw an eagle perched on a cactus with a serpent in its mouth. The eagle commanded the Aztecs to build temples and to feed the sun with the blood of sacrificed victims.

From their island base, the Aztecs created a formidable empire. At first they continued to serve as mercenaries, but in 1428, allied with two other towns, they destroyed their former employers and seized a base on the mainland to supplement their main island, Tenochtitlán. The Aztecs soon dominated their allies and moved into the areas that offered the greatest economic rewards.

By 1500 the Aztec Empire stretched from the Pacific Ocean to the Gulf of Mexico, controlling 28 million people. By then Tenochtitlán and other nearby islands had fused into one great capital city, with an estimated population of 200,000. Another million Amerindians lived in fifty or more city-states in the surrounding Valley of Mexico.

Tenochtitlán was an engineering marvel. The Aztecs built a dam to control the lake level and constructed two aqueducts to bring fresh water from the mainland to supplement the springs on the islands. To supply food for Tenochtitlán, the Aztecs expanded upon the Maya system of hydraulic agriculture, draining swamp land and creating artificial islands to grow food for the city. Three great

✳ Reconstructed View of the Aztec Capital City of Tenochtitlán. Built on islands in a lake, Tenochtitlán was surrounded by water. The area is now in the heart of Mexico City. © Sergio Dorantes

causeways, one of them more than five miles long, linked Tenochtitlán to the mainland. The city itself had wide avenues, imposing temples, and other public buildings.

Tenochtitlán could not be fed from its agricultural islands alone, so the Aztecs waged war to secure tribute in both food and luxury goods, as well as to obtain victims for their sacrificial rites. They carried on substantial trade with states that were still independent; merchants were an essential part of the Mesoamerican economy, as they had been since Olmec times. Probably as a matter of commercial convenience, the Aztec language, Nahuatl, became the standard language of the area they controlled.

Despite their economic needs, the Aztecs never completely centralized their government. The Aztecs combined direct control over Aztec areas with indirect control over nearby vassal states. At the center was the emperor, a reincarnation of the sun god. He lived in opulence, surrounded by a harem of concubines, a bevy of servants, and a battery of state officials. His governors, who administered the city of Tenochtitlán and the incorporated provinces, acted as rulers themselves as they held court, conducted religious ceremonies, collected taxes, and imposed regulations.

The rest of the empire was essentially a league of tribute-paying city-states. Although the Aztecs built strong fortresses here and there, they generally did not maintain garrisons in the conquered territories. If the flow of tribute required from a particular subject state diminished, the Aztecs sent out an army composed of imperial troops and allied forces, sometimes accompanied by local militia, and subdued the territory again.

In its exploitative aspects, the Aztec Empire resembled the Roman Empire; but whereas the Roman Empire provided its subject people with many benefits, the Aztecs gave their subjects few benefits and many burdens. Consequently, Aztec subject states were constantly looking for a way to topple their overlords.

With such restless subjects, and since war was essential to their economic system and religion, Aztec society stressed the virtues of the warrior, and the Aztec nobility was one of military service. Although the son of a noble had many advantages and certainly found it easier to rise in society than did the son of a commoner, he did not inherit his father's position or distinctions, which had to be earned. As in republican Rome and imperial China, but unlike most premodern cultures, it was possible for commoners, too, to earn distinction in war and rise to power.

Aztec society was not entirely organized on a military basis. Priests, who could be female as well as male, had a separate hierarchy, as did the merchants who engaged in long-range trade. The commoners, of course, formed the bulk of the population, and they owned only their personal possessions, not the land they worked. Beneath them was a large group whose legal status was about halfway between indentured servitude and slavery. For some, this status was temporary, until some debt was paid or some criminal punishment worked off; for others, it might be permanent. In either case, children born to members of this class were free commoners.

Women traditionally held a respected position in Aztec society. The early Aztecs had stressed matrilineal descent, and women could own and inherit property, make contracts, sue in court, divorce their husbands, and, under certain circumstances, remarry. Motherhood was honored.

As the Aztecs became more imperialistic, however, patrilineal concepts began to emerge, and female roles began to alter. The Aztecs introduced polygamy among the upper classes to balance out the excessive male mortality brought about by war. Aztec women were encouraged to bestow sexual favors on warriors, and women captured on campaign were given to the victorious soldiers.

Aztec religion focused on nourishing the sun, which in return furnished the light necessary for life. The food for the sun god was human hearts, extracted from the living chests of sacrificial victims. As was true at Teotihuacán and in the Maya culture, the Aztecs waged war in order to obtain captives for sacrifice, but the Aztecs took this practice much farther than their predecessors. They gathered not only captives from war, but also forced vassal states to pay tribute in the form of human beings. Precise numbers of those sacrificed are unreliable, but evidence indicates that the Aztecs sacrificed as many as 20,000 victims in one celebration, and Moctezuma II stated that when he came to the throne (reigned 1502–1520), he sacrificed 40,000 persons. Other gods, hundreds of them, controlled other facets of the world and received a diversity of offerings. To honor the god of planting and springtime, for example, the priests flayed sacrificial victims and then wore the newly removed skins for their rituals. Other offerings, however, might include flowers, music, and dancing.

Like the Maya, the Aztecs, who used the same Mesoamerican calendar, were obsessed with good and bad days, signs, portents, and divination. In their mind, the world was in delicate balance, and only continual human sacrifices at their religious rites and ceremonies kept the universe operating and prevented the dark forces from destroying nature.

The Aztecs rewrote history to mask their barbarian origins and their ignominious first century in the Valley of Mexico. They claimed kinship to the most celebrated recent culture, the Toltec.

Aztec metalwork was primarily artistic, not utilitarian. Aztec artisans employed gold, copper, silver, tin, and various alloys to create superb pieces based on Toltec models. Aztec art focused on the carving of massive stone statues, bigger than those of their predecessors and intended to last for eternity. Their literature, too, mostly in the form of poetry, was extraordinarily rich.

An Aztec Poet Sings

I, the singer, I make a poem
That shines like an emerald,
A brilliant, precious and splendid emerald.
I suit myself to the inflexions
Of the tuneful voice of the *tzinitzcan*. . . .
Like the ring of little bells,
Little golden bells. . . .
A scented song like a shining jewel,
A shining turquoise and a blazing emerald,
My flowering hymn to the spring.*

This poem not only provides a great deal of information about Aztec technology, but it also suggests the continuing fascination with colors that is a mark of modern Mexican esthetics. On the technological side it shows the use of metals to make bells, and even more, it shows that the Aztecs knew how to make an alloy that would produce a bright, cheerful sound, which is far more difficult that simply casting the metal. A *tzinitzcan* was probably some sort of xylophone.

*John H. Cornyn, "Aztec Literature," in *XXVIIe Congrès international des Americanistes* (Mexico, D.F., 1939), vol. 2: pp. 328–331.

Andean Civilization

In districts where the quantity of water for irrigation was small, they [the Inka] divided it proportionately (as they did with everything they shared out) so that there would be no dispute among the Indians about obtaining it. This was only done in years of scanty rainfall when the need was greatest. The water was measured, and as it was known from experience how long it took to irrigate a fanega *[1.6 acres] of land, each Indian was accordingly granted the number of hours he needed for the amount of land he had, with plenty to spare. Water was taken by turns, according to the order of the plots of land, one after another. No preference was given to the rich or the nobles, or to favorites, . . . or to royal officials or governors.**

*Garcilaso de la Vega, *Royal Commentaries of the Incas, and General History of Peru*, trans. Harold V. Livermore (Austin: University of Texas Press, 1966), vol. 1, p. 248.

This passage is by Garcilaso de la Vega, a second cousin of the last two Inka rulers. Here he depicts the essential justice of Inka rule in the Andes and Peru.

The Inka Empire was the last, and by far the greatest, of a series of Amerindian cultures that had flourished in Peru and the Andes for more than 3,000 years. In Chapter 1 we discussed the Chavin culture, the first civilization to appear in this area. Several cultures followed the Chavin in this area in the centuries after 200 B.C.E. In this section we will discuss the Moche, a culture just now coming to the attention of the world through a number of archaeological projects, but already renowned for its art. We will then turn to the Inka themselves and examine their engineering skills and thoroughgoing economic and political restructuring programs, which were unique to Amerindian experience.

The Artistry of the Moche Culture

The coastal Chavin culture that faded out in the last centuries B.C.E. was succeeded by the Moche society, which dominated the Peruvian coast and the nearby hill country between 100 and 700 C.E., the same time as Teotihuacán flourished and the Maya culture reached its apex in Mesoamerica. In Eurasian terms, the Moche were active from the height of the Roman Empire to the height of the Carolingian Empire and from the end of the Han to the beginning of the Tang dynasty. Scholars knew little about the Moche until the last decade, when archaeologists made a series of important discoveries, especially at a major new excavation site at Sipán, Peru, that bear on this major Amerindian group.

Like the peoples of Mesopotamia, the Moche maintained their population in an arid coastal climate by inheriting and expanding an elaborate irrigation system that provided sufficient food to support cities of more than 50,000. Their diet consisted of maize, beans, avocados, squash, peppers, potatoes, and peanuts, along with llamas, guinea pigs, and fish, a diet more nutritious than that of many modern South Americans. Moche society, like most of the others in Andean and Mesoamerican civilization, was rigidly hierarchical: warrior-priest kings, a warrior-priest nobility, and male and female priests lived in splendor while the masses worked. The newly discovered tombs of the elite are crammed with splendid artifacts demonstrating advanced techniques in textiles, pottery, and jewelry and depicting elaborate religious ceremonies. No examples of writing have come to light; it appears that the Moche, like the other Andean civilizations and the early Mesoamerican cultures, did not have a written language.

As in Mesoamerica, Moche art and architecture centered on religion. Like the religions of Mesoamerica, Moche religion was based on waging war to obtain prisoners whose blood sacrifice was needed to ensure fertility of the land. Warrior-priests, assisted by other priests, conducted these rituals on immense pyramids and platforms that were the center of urban complexes. The Pyramid of the Sun was among the world's largest buildings; built from over 100 million adobe bricks, it was 135 feet high and covered 12.5 acres. It served as an administration building and a mausoleum as well as a temple.

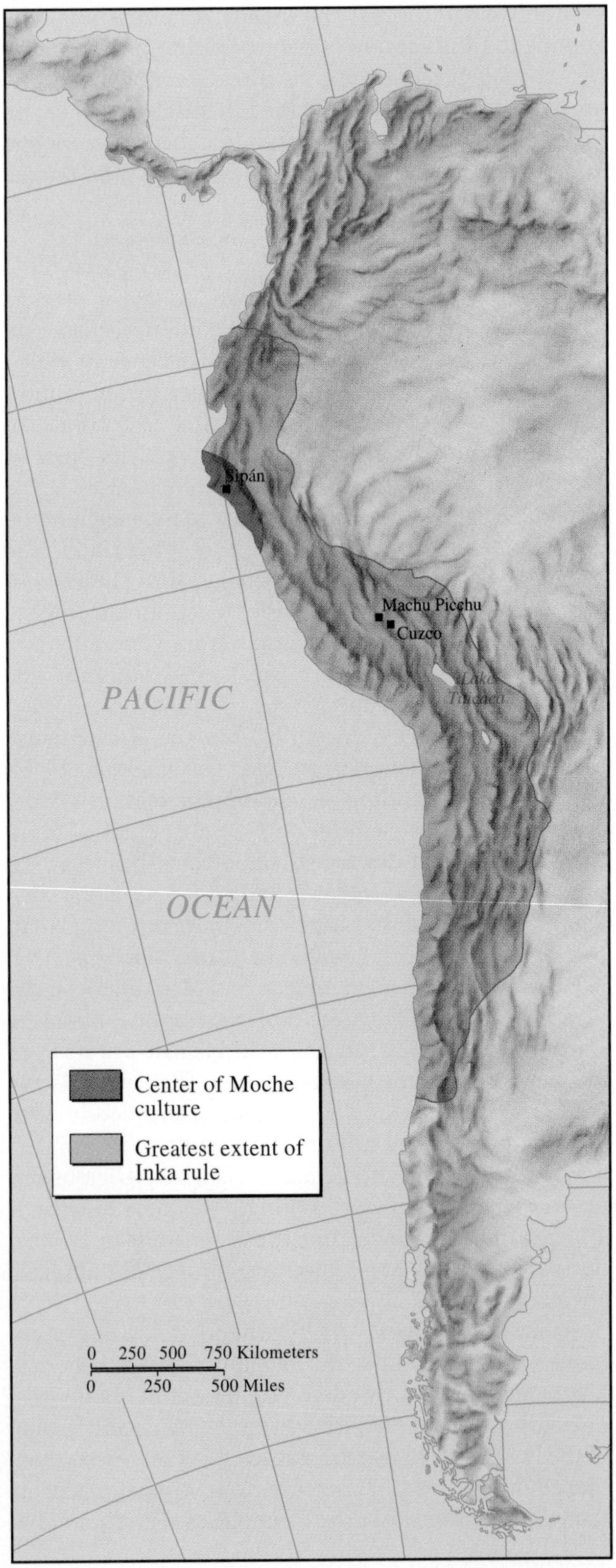

Sipán
Machu Picchu
Cuzco
PACIFIC
OCEAN
Center of Moche culture
Greatest extent of Inka rule
0 250 500 750 Kilometers
0 250 500 Miles

Moche culture is notable for the skills of its artists. The few surviving textiles are of high quality. Moche potters produced a variety of ceramics, including ritual goblets for religious ceremonies. They created pottery and three-dimensional clay sculptures that depict the lives of commoners as well as kings; one can see the misery of tortured captives and the joys of sex and chewing coca leaves. The potters also worked with low-relief designs and painted complex scenes of important rituals on their pottery.

The Moche were especially skilled and imaginative jewelers, working with smelted gold, silver, and platinum and with jade and turquoise. They used the lost-wax method to create three-dimensional metal castings with interchangeable parts. The artists also employed imaginative gilding techniques to make nonprecious metals, especially copper, look like gold. To adorn the bodies of the elite, Moche artisans created necklaces of gold and silver beads shaped like human heads with inlaid mother-of-pearl jaguar teeth, gold ear and nose plugs, gold protective plates for buttocks and chest, ritual masks made of a silver-copper alloy, and hammered gilded copper masks and helmets. Many other objects such as scepters and spearheads were also cast in precious metals or copper.

Moche political power faded about 700, and for several hundred years afterward, various empires dominated sections of the Andean uplands, extending their power down to the adjacent coast. Meanwhile, urban states continued to flourish on the north coast of Peru. Chan Chan, the capital of a secondary state, had more than 50,000 inhabitants. Its wide, straight streets divided the city into ten districts, each of which had massive protective walls thirty to forty feet high and ten feet thick and its own ceremonial center, an unusual and unexplained design for a city. The era of political fragmentation ended abruptly in the fifteenth century, however, when a highland people, the Inka, burst upon Peruvian-Andean civilization and transformed it.

Amerindian Social Engineering: The Inka

The Inka came late to the Peruvian scene. Because they, like their predecessors, were nonliterate, little is known

MAP 7.2 The Development of Andean Civilization. Over the centuries the coastal area of present-day Peru, followed by the Andean highlands from Ecuador to Bolivia and Chile, was the center of highly developed but nonliterate cultures. The Moche culture (900 B.C.E.–700 C.E.) featured monumental architecture and intricate work in precious metals. After 1200 the Andes began to fall under the domination of the Inka, operating from their capital at Cuzco. By the early sixteenth century, the Inka had conquered a vast domain. It was held together by a centralized administration, state socialism, and an extensive, well-engineered highway network.

of them before the Spanish came, and what is known generally concerns the period after 1438. Inka oral tradition, which the Spanish recorded, went back to a king who ruled about 1200. All that is certain is that the Inka started their rise to power from the city of Cuzco, in the Andean highlands northwest of Lake Titicaca. For 200 years, they expanded slowly at the expense of their neighbors.

Then, under their Inka (ruler) Pachacutec (reigned 1438–1473) the Inka flashed like a meteor across Andean civilization. Within two decades Pachacutec and his son, Thupa Yupanki (reigned 1471–1493) conquered dozens of other peoples in the Titicaca Basin and along the adjacent highland river systems. The more the Inka prevailed, the more human resources and supplies became available to them. The Inka conquered to the north as far as present-day Quito (Ecuador) and took control of the older cultures on the Peruvian coast. When Thupa Yupanki came to the throne, he smashed uprisings in some of the newly acquired territory and then moved south, adding much of present-day Bolivia and the northern part of Chile to the empire. Wayna Qhapaq (reigned 1493–1525) spent much of his reign consolidating the empire. He marched from Chile to the rain forests of the upper Amazon and on to Ecuador to put down rebellions, extending the northern limits of the empire slightly in the process.

The new empire, essentially acquired in fifty-five years, dwarfed any state hitherto created in Andean civilization. Inka emperors ruled some 12 million people scattered across a domain stretching some 3,000 miles from north to south. They had done this without wheeled transport, draft animals, or a system of writing and with only occasional use of copper tools and weapons. Ruling from the highland capital at Cuzco, the Inka called their empire *Tawantinsuyu,* the Land of the Four Quarters, referring to the four major divisions of their realm.

The Inka had an empire, but with it came a major problem. How could a tiny minority of perhaps 70,000 rule millions of recently conquered subject peoples scattered across a difficult terrain? To accomplish this task, Inka authorities carried out a remarkable, comprehensive restructuring of much of Andean civilization. They relocated populations, reordered the economy, constructed a huge transportation network, and inculcated a state religion. This program was carried out most thoroughly in the older parts of the empire in the central Andes; it was much modified on the Ecuadorian and Chilean frontiers and in the areas where it came into contact with the sophisticated cultures along the Peruvian coast.

Inka planning began with their campaigns of conquest. Inka leaders saw to it that ethnic Inka males were not wasted in nonmilitary tasks or unnecessary combat. In the early days, llamas and Inka women carried much of the military supplies; later, members of conquered groups hauled the goods. As much as possible, the Inka took over

other peoples by negotiation and bravado; they would mass their men in a show of force to overawe their opponents and obtain their peaceful submission. If a group fought back or held out in a siege, the Inka, like the Mongols or Alexander the Great, would massacre the population or deport them as a warning to others. To garrison the frontiers and to watch areas considered likely to rebel, the Inka settled groups of soldiers conscripted from other parts of their empire to remain as alien watchdogs.

The Inka needed reliable stocks of food and other materials to supply their armies, a difficult proposition considering the patchy pattern of settlement and production in their empire. Upon conquering a territory, the state took control over all resources, including human labor. In each locality, Inka authorities divided the land into portions for the sun (the state religion), the state, and the community. Laborers from the community worked Inka state and sun agricultural land as they had worked the lands of their former rulers. With many construction projects on its agenda, the state wanted the mass of families to be well fed and self-supporting so they could produce healthy youngsters for the labor force; accordingly, the Inka sometimes gave back part of their land to the community in exchange for *mit'a,* a special labor levy for road building and other state projects.

To build up food production the Inka, combining economic sophistication with military prudence, carried out a massive resettlement program. Before the Inka conquest, local feuds in many areas had forced the local populations to stay out of the more fertile, but more dangerous, valleys where maize could be grown. They lived in fortified towns on the more defensible ridges, raising potatoes. Having brought peace along with their conquest, Inka authorities moved families from the fortified ridge-top towns—thus reducing the chance of effective revolt—and resettled them in new, smaller villages in the nearby valleys. As a result, the production of maize expanded. The great mass of agricultural families retained their households and remained in a familiar neighborhood near their old town, yet they now had a much better diet. Some women in the agricultural communities wove common cloth from wool supplied by the state; other individuals made rope or utilitarian pottery or collected honey and feathers.

With staple food production stabilized and even increasing, the Inka then designated certain families or groups in every locality to specialize in producing sumptuary products such as fine textiles, elaborate metalwork, and imperial Inka pottery. Some groups were relocated to the eastern slopes to raise more cotton, cacao, and coca. The alien military colonies that watched the unreliable groups and garrisoned the frontiers were usually held responsible for producing special products. Some young women were selected to reside at the ceremonial centers in the new Inka towns in segregated quarters out of public sight. They wove cloth and brewed beer for religious ceremonies and were later married to men designated by the state. Other individuals were taken to Cuzco to be servants or concubines for the royal and noble families; some of these individuals rose to positions of prominence.

Like the Persians and the Romans, the Inka developed an elaborate road system so they could move military forces quickly around the empire, transport food supplies where needed, and, in general, tie their widespread domains together. Using the forced labor of their subject peoples, the Inka supervised the construction of two main roads, one on the coast and one in the highlands, that ran the length of their empire. With only humans and llamas to traverse them, the roads were only twenty-five feet wide, but well engineered. Built upon strong foundations and laid along efficient gradients, they passed across suspension bridges, through tunnels, and over mountains. These north-south trunk roads were connected with lateral east-west main roads at major cities; a network of secondary roads tied many villages in the empire to the system. Forced labor gangs built almost 20,000 miles of roads and thousands of rest stations a day's walk apart. Runners stationed at convenient intervals carried government messages throughout the breadth of the empire. In their engineering prowess, the Inka were typical of Andean culture, which had already developed an elaborate system of irrigation canals along the coast.

To tie supplies and the road network together, the Inka, directing masses of special mit'a labor, built a series of new towns on the new transportation grid and constructed hundreds of warehouses outside each town. They reserved the land nearest to each town for the production of state-owned food, which was stored in the warehouses. These storehouses did much more than feed the armies. The Inka used the stored food to support local officials, mit'a laborers, persons traveling on government business, those attending state ceremonies, special craft workers, areas suffering from crop failures, and other projects. Although Inka storage facilities were built along the highways, they were intended mostly for local or regional use. With transport limited to humans and llamas, it was impossible to carry a steady supply of goods over long distances to Inka armies in garrison or on campaign. The Inka could only hope that if they were efficient in producing supplies and storing them in large amounts throughout the realm, their armies could be fed and their empire preserved.

As might be expected, the elaborate Inka system of economic and social controls was administered by an extremely hierarchic and bureaucratic government. The hierarchy experienced trouble at the top, however, for choosing a new Inka was not an easy matter. For a number of cultural reasons, each reigning Inka had several wives and a number of concubines. The throne was sometimes disputed by rival claimants, and according to oral tradition, crimes and civil wars had plagued the succession over the years. Once in power the now divine Inka,

Son of the Sun, did rule, but in a way so did his immediate predecessor, as well as all previous Inkas. The deceased were believed to be intermediaries with the gods, and their mummified remains were brought forward to partake in religious ceremonies and be consulted by priests on important matters. The male relatives of each departed Inka were entitled to all the wealth that ruler had accumulated during his reign, in part to support the royal corpse in imperial style for eternity. As time went by, the number of royal households supporting imperial mummies had, naturally, increased, and each new Inka was faced with a need to accrue riches during his reign so that his descendants could maintain his corpse with becoming splendor. This need for each Inka to find "burial money" was one of the motives for Inka expansion.

Beneath the eccentric world of the Inka royalty, the machinery of government ran fairly smoothly. The upper nobility, composed of the Inka's relatives and various adopted persons, administered the four quarters and the provincial subdivisions of the empire. In much of the Inka domain, the local bureaucracy was organized on a numerical rather than a geographical basis. The top local official administered 10,000 families; under him ten officials administered 1,000 families, and so on down to the most minor official, who administered five families. To supply the huge number of officials necessary to run such an elaborate governmental system, the state employed some lesser Inka nobility, but it drew most of these officials (as had ancient Rome) from the traditional leaders of the group to be governed. The cooperating elite received honors and valuable state goods from the Inka. If the Inka found them sufficiently efficient and trustworthy, they could pass their office and status on to their children. This practice of having the local elite carry out Inka authority among their people was another means of holding the loyalty of conquered peoples and their leaders.

Inka local authorities strictly regulated the private lives of their subjects. They tried to impose their language, Quechua, on their subjects and did not allow individuals to travel far from their homes. Even marriage, which was obligatory, was, in theory, arranged by the government.

The lack of a written language did not handicap the government because the census and storehouse records vital to proper administration were kept on *khipus*. A khipu was a rope from which hung a collection of strings with knots tied into them to record numbers. Different knots and different textures and colors of strings were used to indicate various subjects and purposes; one khipu could very well have recorded as much information as a modern ledger.

The Inka used religion as another means of unifying the state. Although the subject peoples were allowed to worship their traditional gods, Cuzco and the new towns built by the Inka were used to stage elaborate ceremonies that indoctrinated their subjects in the state religion. The

DEPOCITODELIИGA
COLL CA

topaynga
yupanqui.

ayuin ri̇ɪ Hados
guɪyo yoc
dpo po macḩaʊ̆a

depocitos ntl ynga

co mo

❈ Inka Record Keeping. Inside a government storage complex, the Inka (emperor) Thupa Yupanki receives a report from a *khipu kamayog* (records keeper) holding his knotted rope ledger. Page 335 of *Nueva Coronica y Buen Gobierno* by Guaman Poma de Ayala, courtesy of l'Institut d'Ethnologie du Musée de l'Homme, © 1936, renewed 1989

Inka encouraged, perhaps required, the people of the nearby communities to come to the new towns for religious ceremonies that sometimes lasted for days. While in town the attendees were housed, fed, and provided with beer and sometimes given clothing and sandals—all at state expense.

The Inka religion contained a creator god, but the primary focus of public worship was the sun god, along with the god of rain and thunder. Inka religion included animism as well: practically every geographical feature had resident spirits, and each family and each individual had a guardian spirit. The religion had doctrines of sin and confession and taught a belief in personal immortality. The Inka had oracles, looked for omens, and practiced divination, but unlike the Maya, they were not obsessed with lucky and unlucky days. The wealthy sacrificed grain or killed llamas in the rituals, and the poor sacrificed guinea pigs. Human sacrifice took place at times, although the Inka never attained anything like the volume of victims killed by the Aztecs.

Despite their elaborate administrative and engineering systems, the Inka had major problems. Given the primitive level of transport and communication available to them, Inka rulers, when in their capital, Cuzco, were too far from the extremities of the empire to rule effectively. Some scholars maintain that the cumbersome bureaucracy of the Inka retarded economic development; others disagree.

Perhaps the greatest problem in the Inka state was the capricious system of attaining imperial power. Under the rule of the three great Inka monarchs, the empire was spared strife over the succession, but in 1525, when Wayna Qhapaq died, two of his sons claimed the throne. For seven years, civil war ravaged the empire, while a plague caught from the Europeans prowling the coast spread throughout the Inka world, killing many. When the Spanish emerged on the scene in 1532, Tawantinsuyu was a gravely weakened state.

African Cultures

The king . . . was naked, wearing only a garment of linen embroidered with gold from which hung four fillets on either side; around his neck was a golden collar. He stood on a four-wheeled chariot drawn by four elephants; the body of the chariot was high and covered with gold plates. The king stood on top carrying a small gilded shield and holding in his hands two small gilded spears. His council stood around similarly armed and flutes played.

I, 'Ezana, king of Axum . . . made war upon Noba [Nubia], for the peoples had rebelled and had boasted of it. Twice and thrice they had broken their solemn oaths, and had killed their neighbors. And as I had warned them, and they would not listen, I made war on them. They fled without making a stand, and I pursued them for 23 days, killing some and capturing others . . . burnt their towns, both those built of bricks and those built of reeds, and my army carried off their food and copper and iron . . . and destroyed the statues in their temples, their granaries, and cotton trees and cast them into the Seda [Nile]. And I planted a throne at the place where the rivers Sada and Takkaze join.

*Robert W. July, *A History of the African People* (New York: Scribner's, 1970), p. 48.
**The Horizon History of Africa* (New York: American Heritage, 1971), p. 80.

T he preceding passages offer glimpses into the wealth and power of the king of Axum (in present-day northern Ethiopia) who ruled a large empire of enormous military and commercial power that flourished contemporaneously with the Roman Empire around 350 C.E. The account of King 'Ezana's military victory over

Nubia was inscribed on a stele (carved stone pillar) at his capital in Axum. Axum was one of many empires that emerged in Africa, some of which dated from early historical times. These states were as varied in organization as the landscape from which they arose.

Geographical and Social Diversity in Africa

The continent of Africa, an area more than three times larger than the continental United States, exhibits enormous geographical and cultural diversity. Scholars estimate that there may be as many as 1,000 different ethnic groups speaking almost as many languages in Africa. Linguists have classified this multitude of languages into four major phyla or categories. Although human life probably first emerged in Africa, climatic extremes and infertile soil have kept human societies from prospering in much of the land area. Sitting directly on the equator, much of central Africa is subtropical, and there are vast arid areas in the north and in the south. Sparse rainfall, droughts, and resulting famines have been common in Africa since the beginning of recorded history. For example, along the 1,200-mile Niger River in West Africa rainfall averages between eight and twenty inches in a good year; the lack of rain has impeded population growth in many areas. Deforestation and overuse of the soil since ancient times have contributed to making much of the terrain inhospitable.

Save for the tropical rain forests, the central sections of the continent receive the most rainfall and are therefore the most conducive to agricultural development; however, these areas are infested with the tsetse fly. The fly carries the trypanosomiasis parasite, which is deadly to both humans and cattle, the main source of livelihood for many African societies. Humans, especially those living along fertile river banks, must also cope with other debilitating and often deadly diseases, including river blindness, malaria, and bilharzia (a parasitic disease transmitted to humans by river snails). African societies have generally adjusted to these diseases and climatic conditions by living within the constraints imposed by nature; or as one Swahili proverb put it, "Do not borrow off the earth, for the earth will require its own back with interest."

Owing to these basic ecological problems, some African peoples led a nomadic existence based on herding sheep, goats, or cattle. In many herding societies, including the Masai in present-day Kenya, a man's status within the community was judged by the number of cattle he owned. Cattle were also used as a medium of trade and given as a "bride price" to a young woman's family upon her marriage. Although herding societies often looked down upon the settled, farming communities, economic exchanges of goods (animals, hides, or ivory for sugar and other commodities) between the two were nevertheless commonplace.

In some areas, economic professions were monopolized by specific ethnic groups; for example, in landlocked present-day Mali, the Fulani, who are herders, use the banks of the Pondo River as pasture, while the Bambara farm along the river and still others are fisherfolk. Most African peoples, however, worked in mixed economies as both farmers and herders. As in Central and South America, traditional farmers in Africa frequently used the slash-and-burn technique to clear plots of land. They then cultivated the plots for several years; after the soil ceased to be productive, they abandoned the fields and repeated the entire cycle elsewhere. The slash-and-burn technique contributed to the nomadic existence of many African peoples and also led to further degradation of the soil.

Although the organization of living space, building materials, and architectural styles found in Africa were as diverse as its climate, African villages and homes tended to reflect the high value and emphasis placed on communal relationships. In contrast to the rather private closed-in buildings and rooms found in much of West Asia or Europe, many African homes and public buildings were tightly grouped in circular or irregular patterns and were circular in shape. Circular, communal storage granaries were often clustered around the villages and were frequently built beside or on top of homes or on stilts to protect them and to keep out the damp, insects, and vermin. Whereas the centralized governments of ancient Egypt and many Asian empires controlled the collection and storage of basic foodstuffs, in most of sub-Saharan Africa food storage was organized on a local level. The villagers constructed and maintained collectively owned granaries; in some areas separate granaries were built for men and women.

Most Africans used mud bricks, straw, clay, and wood to build their homes; stone construction was generally reserved for public or monumental buildings. Clay gave artists more freedom for artistic expression and greater ease in constructing contoured, free-form designs than did stone or brick; clay was also resistant to the extremes of temperatures, particularly heat, found in much of Africa. Great care was lavished on the upkeep of the clay walls. As early as the fourteenth century, the famous traveler Ibn Battuta remarked on the beauty of the decorative ornaments on the buildings of African towns and villages. Decorative shapes and designs varied tremendously. The one-story, one-room circular homes grouped around larger communal buildings in much of Mali were fairly typical, but homes with straw roofs and monumental entrances were also found in Mali and the Cameroons. In Mauritania and East Africa, stone buildings with elaborate interior designs were common.

Historically, the region north of the Sahara, extending from present-day Morocco in the west to Egypt in the east, was Mediterranean in orientation. The great

Carthaginian Empire flourished in present-day Tunisia, and much of North Africa had been part of the empire of Egypt and later of Rome. Farther south, however, the historical ties with Mediterranean cultures became tenuous.

Western and northern Africa and Egypt, however, had also been connected by trade routes with Saharan and central African societies. These caravan trails were generally controlled by the Berbers, who since ancient times have lived in large areas of North Africa. Their origin is unknown, and they speak their own distinct language. Thus, despite its ties with the Mediterranean world, North Africa had also been linked with central and southern portions of the continent by exchanges of goods, peoples, and ideas. As described in the following section, similar interrelationships existed between the great kingdoms in Egypt, the Sudan, and Ethiopia.

Ethiopian Kingdoms

In keeping with the patterns noted in the comparative essay on empires, the most sedentary populations, and ultimately the most highly advanced empires in Africa, tended to develop around the major rivers that provided consistent sources of water and fertile land. As noted in Chapter 1, the early empires of Egypt and the Kushites in the Sudan both arose along the banks of the Nile.

From 300 B.C.E., however, the Kushite kingdom with its capital at Meroë (in present-day Sudan) began to decline. As Egypt declined in military and economic importance under Roman rule, the demand for iron ore from the Kushite kingdom dropped, and its economy suffered. The Kushite kingdom was also weakened by attacks from surrounding desert tribes and, most crucially, by Axum, a new rival economic and military power based in Ethiopia.

In 700 B.C.E., Semitic tribespeople from Yemen, in the southern Arabian Peninsula, moved across the Red Sea to the eastern coastal regions of Africa. They gradually migrated to the Ethiopian highlands, possibly to escape the malaria-infested coast. The new immigrants intermarried with the indigenous population and transmitted their skills in dry stone building and hillside terracing.

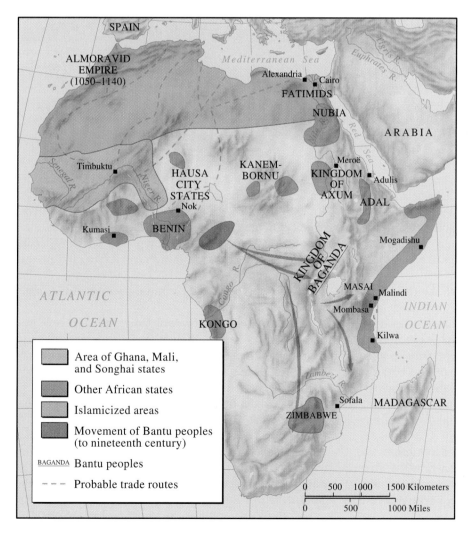

❋ Map 7.3 Africa, 900–1500. Many great empires or kingdoms, such as Ghana in West Africa, Axum in the east, and Zimbabwe in the south, flourished throughout the African continent from 900 to 1500. In North Africa the majority of the population converted to Islam.

Map labels:
SPAIN
ALMORAVID EMPIRE (1050–1140)
Mediterranean Sea
Alexandria
Cairo
FATIMIDS
NUBIA
ARABIA
Euphrates R.
Niger R.
Senegal R.
Red Sea
Timbuktu
HAUSA CITY STATES
Nok
KANEM-BORNU
Meroë
KINGDOM OF AXUM
Adulis
ADAL
Kumasi
BENIN
Congo R.
KINGDOM OF BAGANDA
Mogadishu
MASAI
Malindi
Mombasa
INDIAN OCEAN
ATLANTIC OCEAN
KONGO
Kilwa
Zambezi R.
Sofala
MADAGASCAR
ZIMBABWE

Legend:
Area of Ghana, Mali, and Songhai states
Other African states
Islamicized areas
Movement of Bantu peoples (to nineteenth century)
BAGANDA Bantu peoples
- - - Probable trade routes

0   500   1000   1500 Kilometers
0   500   1000 Miles

✻ Axum Stelae in Ethiopia. These are only a few of the more than 1,300 stelae found in Axum in Ethiopia. Although most of the inscriptions have not yet been translated, the monoliths indicate that the Axum architects were well advanced and that the city must have had elaborate stone palaces and public buildings. Photos (left) courtesy of Janice Terry; (right) Werner Forman Archive/Art Resource

From the assimilation of the Semitic and indigenous populations came a unique society with its own language, Ge'ez, though Ethiopians issued documents in Greek as well. The synthesis of African and Arabian peoples in Ethiopia is analogous to the assimilation of peoples in the Hellenistic world and the emergence of Swahili culture along the coast of East Africa.

The new Ethiopian kingdom, with its capital, Axum, in the highlands, and a port, Adulis, on the Red Sea, was in an advantageous position to benefit from increased sea trade in the region. As trade along the Red Sea prospered, Axum emerged as a major trading center for eastern Africa, the Nile, and southern Arabia. To protect both the sea and land trading routes, Axumite kings conquered large sections of Ethiopia, and by the fourth century C.E., they had overwhelmed the Kushite kingdom's capital city of Meroë.

Although the early rulers of Axum were animists, the empire became Christian in the fourth century, after decades of contact with the Christian world through Byzantium and the Coptic Christians in Egypt. A Syrian Christian was instrumental in converting King 'Ezana,

who, like other imperial rulers in Rome and Asia, encouraged or forced the religious conversion of his subjects. Thus the empire became predominantly Christian many years before much of Europe. The decline of Byzantium and the Muslim conquest of Egypt and North Africa in the mid-seventh century, however, cut Axum off from the Mediterranean world, and the Christian kingdom gradually lost its importance as a trading center and became increasingly isolated.

As the commercial power of Axum faded, people migrated to the nearby high plateaus intersected with mountains and deep gorges, which provided ideal terrain for well-defended fortresses. Here in Ethiopia they created a Christian kingdom under the *negus* or emperor, and Ge'ez remained the language of the Coptic (Christian) Ethiopian church.

The series of spectacular churches carved into solid rock at Lalibela are monuments to the artistic energy and religious fervor of the people. Constructed about 1181 by King Lalibela, the churches attest to his deep-seated religious devotion. Ethiopian tradition holds that one of the most remarkable of these churches was built in one day by fervent believers assisted by angels. In many ways these monuments are reminiscent of the Gothic cathedrals produced during an era of similar fusion of church and state in Europe. The development of the Ethiopian Christian kingdom in relative isolation from outside forces was made possible by its unique terrain and was in marked contrast to the extensive exchanges and assimilation of peoples in central and southern Africa.

The Bantu

As early as 200 B.C.E., peoples from the present-day Nigeria-Cameroon border began a migration that was to change central and southern Africa. Like other groups around the world, these people called themselves simply "the people," or Bantu. Although scholars disagree as to the exact size and chronology of the Bantu migrations, they followed the northern and eastern edges of the tropical forest and then turned south along the western coast. Future linguistic and anthropological studies will provide additional information about the Bantu origins.

Originally fisherfolk, the Bantu also grew crops such as yams and sorghum and hunted small game. In East Africa cattle were and, in many regions, still are the basis of the social-economic organization. Some Bantu groups like the Tutsi adopted cattle as the basis of their economic livelihood but did not worship the cattle or consider them sacred. While many Bantu peoples specialized as either agriculturalists or pastoralists, most practiced a mixed economy based on agriculture and herding.

Churches at Lalibela in Present-Day Ethiopia. Some of the many churches at Lalibela are freestanding, while others are carved into the sides of cliffs, as shown on the right. Haroldo and Flavia de Faria Castro/FPG International

In spite of the enormous diversity of the Bantu peoples throughout central and southern Africa, Bantu societies manifested certain common characteristics. Along with languages based on common linguistic roots, they shared folklore and oral historical traditions and similar pottery-making techniques. Lacking a written language, Bantu elders, like Greek epic poets before Homer, passed on long, involved stories of the history and culture from generation to generation.

Iron implements had come into use among the Bantu by 300 B.C.E. The Nok, who lived in the region between the Benue and Niger Rivers in present-day Nigeria, were apparently the first people in West Africa to use iron-making technology. As noted in Chapter 1, the Bantu peoples may have gained their knowledge of iron working and the lost-wax process for bronze casting from the Kushites, who migrated west from the Nile valley as their empire declined. It is also possible that ironworking developed spontaneously among the Bantu through independent invention; archaeological exploration in western Africa may yield more answers to these questions in the future.

As the Bantu put iron spears and hoes to use, they increased their food supply, thereby creating larger, healthier populations. The increase in population undoubtedly put additional strain on the available arable land, which was quickly exhausted by the slash-and-burn technique of the Bantu farmers. In addition, an influx of migrants seeking relief from the growing aridity of the Saharan regions also put pressure on the Bantu. With plenty of available land to the south, they began to migrate into central Africa along the Congo River. From there they apparently moved along the Zambezi and ultimately reached the eastern African coast and southern Africa, perhaps as early as the third or fourth century C.E.

These migrations, each of which may originally have numbered only a few hundred people, continued over hundreds of years. A superior iron technology enabled the Bantu to dominate groups in central and southern Africa. Temperatures above 1,500 degrees centigrade are needed to melt iron ore, and the Congo, with hardwoods that burned very hot, allowed for the production of particularly fine, high-grade iron. The Congo became a leading center for iron production. Numerous smelting furnaces remain scattered throughout central and southern Africa, but as caches of iron ingots have not been found, it appears that the crude iron metal was immediately made into hoes, other implements, and weapons.

With a few exceptions, such as the Pygmies in the equatorial forest, the Bantu successfully assimilated with other indigenous peoples. As a result, the Bantu language, like Indo-European in Eurasia or Nahuatl in Mexico, became the prototype of hundreds of central and southern African languages. Similarly, Bantu cultural and social mores spread throughout the territories, much as

Olmec cultural innovations spread throughout Mesoamerica. The Bantu diffusion was based not so much on military or even technological superiority as on their creation of settled agricultural communities, which attracted and culturally overwhelmed the nomads and hunters of central and southern Africa. These numerous Bantu societies were the direct ancestors of the multitudinous ethnic groups the Europeans encountered in the nineteenth century and are scattered from Nigeria in West Africa, north into the forest and south to the Congo, and to the Indian Ocean in East Africa.

Bantu societies had a complex system of belief in the supernatural and an extremely wide range of means of worship and of ways of dealing with the supernatural. Many believed in nature spirits and in the power of ancestors, who gave identity and onward movement to life. The ancestors were believed to be responsible for transmitting the accumulated wisdom of the society; for example, passing on the knowledge of iron smelting.

Many Bantu societies, as well as other West African ethnic groups, had a belief system based on a supreme god or higher deity. Some in West Africa, such as the Yoruba, who belong to a Bantu-related linguistic group, had an extremely complex cosmology with a pantheon of gods and goddesses. The Yoruba believed that the god Oduduwa sprinkled sand on water and then released a chicken that scratched the sand, thereby creating the first land on earth; the Yoruba city of Ife, founded about 850 C.E., was believed to have been built on the site of creation. According to Yoruba history, Oduduwa had sixteen sons from whom the Yoruba royalty and *oni* (king) were descended. Building on the Nok knowledge of carving, Yoruba artists at Ife created elaborate bronzes and carved stone sculptures of the royal rulers.

In many Bantu societies, worship involved the use of highly sophisticated and finely wrought carved masks or fetishes, used in a complex system of rituals that often included dance. Just as some Christians considered icons to be aids for spiritual devotion, so, too, did many Bantu peoples regard masks and other carved objects as a means of approaching the supernatural. Specialized experts, or medicine men and women, and diviners often assisted in these rituals and were viewed as intermediaries between the supernatural and the physical world. Many Amerindians had similarly complex cosmologies and ceremonial rites.

The family was the basis of Bantu societies and economies. As one proverb taught, "A man outside his clan is like a grasshopper without wings." Nuclear clusters of related families formed villages and clans. Much as Amerindian societies did, Bantu societies lived in balance with nature; when the population grew too large or the arable land was exhausted, Bantu clans had to migrate elsewhere. Most Bantu societies were organized

Folk Wisdom

Throughout history, riddles and proverbs have been popular forms of "folk wisdom" in Africa and the rest of the world. Folk wisdom amuses, teaches moral lessons, and tests mental quickness. Among the Yoruba of West Africa, storytellers often asked riddles to attract the attention of the audience before a performance. For example, a storyteller might pose the following riddle:

Question: We call the dead—they answer.
We call the living—they do not answer.

Answer: Dry, dead leaves; fresh tree leaves.

Proverbs are also popular in most African societies. As the wisdom of proverbs is often universal, it is not surprising that many African proverbs have equivalents in the Arab and Western worlds. The following are some examples of African proverbs and their equivalents from other cultures:

Mouth not keeping to mouth, and lip not keeping to lip, bring trouble to the jaws. (*Yoruba–West Africa*)
Talk is silver, silence is gold. (*Western*)

He fled from the sword and hid in the scabbard. (*Yoruba*)
Out of the frying pan, into the fire. (*Western*)

The tar of my country is better than the honey of others. (*Moroccan–North Africa*)
There is no place like home. (*Western*)

An old cat will not learn how to dance. (*Moroccan*)
You can't teach an old dog new tricks. (*Western*)

If music changes, so does the dance. (*Hausa–Central Sudan*)
What is written on the forehead, the eye must see. (*Arabic*)
Keep up with the times, or what must be, must be. (*Western*)

around the village and were patriarchal and polygamous, although a few were matriarchal.

Many Bantu societies were organized along age sets or age grades in which work, social life, and political responsibility were meted out on the basis of age. Age grades were divided along gender lines from the youngest boys and girls, to those who had reached puberty, to the elders, who had the most responsibilities and authority. When they reached puberty, young boys and girls often underwent extensive rites of initiation to mark their membership in the adult community. The Kikuyu in Kenya divided the male population among boys, warriors, and elders. Work was strictly defined along gender lines, with farming and cooking often considered to be "women's work" and hunting and martial arts "men's work." The elders in Bantu societies were highly respected for their knowledge and experience.

Bantu societies were often extremely democratic in that adult men had rights of full participation in the governing of the societies. Bantu governmental systems lacked uniformity and ranged from the highly organized monarchy of the Baganda to the decentralized system of the Kikuyu. The non-Bantu-speaking Igbo in southern Nigeria were organized into councils that conducted affairs of state and made political and economic decisions on the basis of consensus. The Igbo placed high value on the work ethic, rewarding those who prospered and contributed to the society. The Ganda had a highly institutionalized monarchy in which the kings were viewed as divine in the same way that the ancient Egyptians and

Romans, among others, had deified their rulers. Many of the centralized monarchies established a feudal system of patron-client relationships with other groups who paid tribute or were treated as vassals or held as slaves. In contrast, the Kikuyu never had kings or even chieftains, but lived in scattered homesteads in the Kenyan highlands and relied upon the extended family to act as the major governing force.

As in India, the extremely damp and humid climate conditions of central Africa has militated against the preservation of wood and straw architecture and carvings, and the lack of good building stone limited stone architecture. Nevertheless, some stone constructions do remain as evidence of the Bantu achievements. The great complexes of Zimbabwe will be described later in this section.

Kingdoms of Gold and Salt

Less accessible to the Mediterranean civilizations were the states of Ghana, Mali, and Songhai. These wealthy and elaborately organized kingdoms emerged in West Africa. They are are often referred to as successor states because each built on the ruins and contributions of its predecessor. Located on savannas (grassy plains with scattered trees), these states were originally based on wealth secured from the trade of salt and gold. Scholars do not know how much, if any, contact these states had in their early years with the empires along the Nile.

Muslim traders referred to ancient Ghana as the Land of Gold. The gold was mined in Upper Volta and in parts

A man came who was wearing beautiful clothes.
He was a real man, he was tall, someone who looked good in white clothes, his clothes were really beautiful.
One could smell perfume everywhere.
He came in to sit down next to Kassaye.
They chatted with each other, they chatted, they chatted.
He said to her, "It is really true.
"Kassaye, I would like to make love with you.
"Once we make love together,
"You will give birth to a boy,
"Whom Si will not be able to kill.
"It is he who will kill Si and will become the ruler."
Kassaye said to him, "What?"
He said, "By Allah."
She said, "Good, in the name of Allah."
Each night the man came.
It is during the late hours that he came,
Each time during the coolness of the late evening,
Until Kassaye became pregnant by him.
Kassaye carried her pregnancy.
Kassaye had a Bargantche captive.
It is the Bargantche woman who is her captive, she lives in her house, and she too is pregnant.

They remained like that,
Kassaye kneeled down to give birth.
The captive kneeled down to give birth.
So Kassaye, Kassaye gave birth to a boy.
The captive gave birth to a girl.
Then Kassaye took the daughter of the captive, she took her home with her.
She took her son and gave it to the captive.
So the people left for the palace.
They said to Si:
"The Bargantche captive has given birth."
He said, "What did she get?"
They said, "A boy."
He said, "May Allah be praised, may our Lord give him a long life and may he be useful."
Then they were thoughtful for a moment.
They got up and informed him that Kassaye had given birth.
They asked, "What did she get?"
They answered, "A girl."
He said, "Have them bring it to me."
They brought it to him, he killed it.
It is the boy who remained with the captive and Kassaye.*

The above is a portion of the long, oral epic tracing the history of the great Songhai ruler, Askia Muhammad Touré. By the trick described here, Askia Muhammad was saved from death; he ultimately surmounted his humble upbringing, defeated his family's enemies, and became the ruler of a vast empire in West Africa. At its zenith, this kingdom covered more than 154,000 square miles of territory.

*The Epic of Askia Mohammed, narrated by Nouhou Malio, in John W. Johnson, Thomas A. Hale, and Stephen Belcher, eds., Oral Epics from Africa: Vibrant Voices from a Vast Continent (Bloomington: Indiana University Press, 1997), pp. 127–128.

of present-day Guinea and Mali; the salt came from remote regions of the Sahara, where in some places it was so common that it was used as building blocks for houses. The rulers of Ghana, Mali, and Songhai became rich as the middlemen in this vast trade. They had the valuable gold and salt brought to central depots where the goods were loaded on camels in huge Berber-run caravans that traversed the Sahara to the Mediterranean coast. The salt was then sold around the Mediterranean.

The Ghanaian kingdom rose to power by 500 C.E., reaching its peak in 1050. Its founders were the Soninke people, but because all Ghanaian kings took the name Ghana, little has been ascertained about individual leaders. Oral traditions held that there had been twenty-two kings before the rise of Islam in 622, and by the eighth century Muslim writers were already describing the richness of the kingdom. By 1000 the Ghanaian kings ruled over extensive vassal states that paid tribute and were controlled by an army at least 200,000 strong, recruited from among those same vassal states. Ghana was a classic trad-

ing state, and its cities, including Kumbi Saleh, Gao, and the fabled Timbuktu, became exceedingly rich. As in similar feudal kingdoms elsewhere, internal strife and uprisings by vassal states undermined the central authority of the Ghanaian rulers, who by 1250 succumbed to the kingdom of Mali founded by Sundiata (reigned 1234–1255).

By this time, Islam had already begun to make a profound impact on the West African kingdoms. As Islam had spread across North Africa during the eighth century, traders and nomads had brought the new religion with them to West Africa. In general, throughout Africa, Islam made the greatest impact in urban areas, where Muslim traders often resided. Islam had a wide appeal because of its relatively direct theological precepts and its openness to all converts. There were also undeniable commercial benefits to be derived from alliances with the rest of the Muslim world. As a result, the ruling black aristocracy often converted to Islam, while the people in rural areas generally remained committed to the religions of their ancestors. However, converts to Islam often main-

Nok Terra Cotta Sculpted Head. This highly stylized sculpture, typical of the Nok civilization, was found at a tin mine in northern Nigeria; the Nok flourished from 500 to 200 B.C.E. Centuries later, African art would have a profound influence on twentieth-century abstract artists. © Dirk Bakker/National Museum Logos; courtesy of Detroit Institute of Arts

Ife Bronze Figure of an Oni. The Ife, from what is now Nigeria, were renowned for their finely wrought bronzes; the detail on many of the pieces is so precise that experts believe the work may depict actual historic figures. Artistic renditions of real people are relatively rare in African art, which tends to be more abstract or symbolic in nature. The Oni was the leader of the Ife; this piece shows the leader in all his regal splendor. Note the elaborate jewelry, royal insignia, and highly detailed headdress. This figure dates from the fifteenth or sixteenth century. © Dirk Bakker/Museum of Ife Antiquities; courtesy of Detroit Institute of Arts

tained many of their old religious and cultural practices along with their Islamic beliefs.

With the conversion of the ruling elites, Islamic and Arabic cultural and religious beliefs gradually merged with the indigenous cultures of West Africa. The ties with Islam provided the elites with further commercial and intellectual contacts with the vast and, at that time, powerful Islamic world. As in Europe, the conversion of a feudal leader often meant the ultimate conversion of the people under his rule; as Christianity spread through the conversion of key leaders, so did Islam and Islamic culture in Africa.

Mansa Kankan Musa (reigned 1312–1337) was the best known of the powerful leaders of Mali; Muslim historians were lavish in their praise of his leadership. In 1324–1325, he made a famous pilgrimage to Mecca with an entourage of 500 slaves, each with a golden staff; the slaves drove hundreds of camels loaded with some four tons of gold. According to contemporaries, Musa and his entourage spent gold so freely that they depressed the price of gold on the Cairo exchange for decades. Mali, however, soon fell to the same sorts of internal rivalries

and uprisings that had destroyed the Ghanaian kingdom. The nomadic Tuareg attacked and finally occupied Timbuktu in 1433–1434.

By the mid-fifteenth century, the growing Songhai kingdom, founded by Sunni Ali (reigned 1469–1492), had largely supplanted Mali. Ruling from the city-state of Gao, in present-day Mali, the Songhai spread their authority far across western Africa and into the Sahara. Sunni Ali extended and consolidated the empire, dividing it into

✵ Ivory Mask of a Benin Queen. Such sculptures were elaborately carved and symbolized the power and glory of the royal families. The carved heads on the crown depict Portuguese invaders. Werner Forman Archive, British Museum/Art Resource

the people remained pastoralists or small farmers. Vassal states were forced to pay tribute and to provide "volunteers" for the army upon demand. The rich elites and rulers held slaves, but in contrast to slavery elsewhere, the numbers were small and slaves were regarded as humans, not merely as property. Especially in Muslim areas, they often worked as household servants, not as field laborers.

As in China and the Muslim world, the ruling aristocracy patronized the arts. As previously noted, African artists excelled in sculpture, and many brilliant examples in stone, wood, and bronze survive. The Nok in northern Nigeria and the Ife and Benin, both forest peoples, were expert artisans. The Nok were known for their finely wrought terra cotta sculptures and beadwork. Nok terra cotta humans tend to be highly stylized, while their sculptures of animals are highly realistic; Nok sculptures, some of which are almost life size, are finely detailed and often show elaborate hairstyles and beaded jewelry. Many Benin bronzes utilizing the lost-wax method still exist; it is not known whether this technique was indigenous, the product of independent invention, or a cultural exchange from the Nile where the technique was also employed.

Both Mansa Musa and Muhammad the Great brought scholars from Mecca to encourage science and education. Their actions demonstrate how the annual pilgrimages to Mecca facilitated the assimilation and spread of arts and sciences throughout the Islamic world; the annual pilgrimage was undoubtedly a major contributor to the strength of Muslim societies. In addition, Muslim pilgrims brought back goods and ideas that were fused with indigenous cultures when the pilgrims returned home, and both ideas and cultures were assimilated and transmuted. Hence, Arabic language words and expressions and Islamic practices are still common in many contemporary West African societies.

Commercial Wealth in East Africa

The fusion of cultures was perhaps nowhere more apparent than in East Africa. Along the coastal regions of Ethiopia and Somalia (the Horn of Africa), and southward along the Kenyan and Tanzanian coasts, city-states based on commerce and trade evolved as the dominant political and economic structures. Owing to their proximity to the Arabian Peninsula, East African coastal towns had ancient trading ties with Yemen, Persia, and other parts of the Middle East; later they developed commercial contacts with the Greeks and the Roman Empire. Animal skins, ivory, gold from Zimbabwe, and slaves were traded for spears, porcelain, and beads.

By the eighth century, Muslim traders had begun trading with these coastal cities. Although the Christian kingdoms in Nubia and Ethiopia fought tenaciously against the Muslims, the expansion of Islam along the coastal re-

provinces under appointed officials and creating a navy to patrol the Niger River. The empire reached its zenith under Askia Muhammad Touré, known as Muhammad the Great (reigned 1493–1528). Like his predecessors, however, Muhammad failed to solve the problem of succession and internal rivalries. Threatened by military attacks from Morocco in the late sixteenth century and weakened by internal rivalries, the Songhai kingdom collapsed. With the arrival of Western explorers, slave traders, and merchants, the great savanna empires were supplanted by African peoples from the coast and forest regions or by Europeans.

As in the European feudal kingdoms, society in these savanna kingdoms was strictly regulated according to class. As in most preindustrial societies, the ruling monarchs controlled much of the wealth, and the majority of

Good Eating in Mogadishu

We sailed fifteen nights and arrived at Mogadishu, which is a very large town. The people have very many camels. The merchants are wealthy . . . the Sultan of Mogadishu is called Shaikh by his subjects . . . by race he is a Berber. He talks in the dialect of Mogadishu, but knows Arabic. When a ship arrives, it is the custom for it to be boarded by the Sultan's sanbuq [little boat] to inquire whence it has come; they also inquire the nature of the cargo. . . . The food of these people is rice cooked with butter . . . with it they serve side-dishes, stews of chicken, meat, fish, and vegetables. They cook unripe bananas in fresh milk, and serve them with a sauce. They put curdled milk in another vessel with peppercorns, vinegar, and saffron, green ginger and mangoes, which look like apples but have a nut inside. Ripe mangoes are very sweet.*

This passage is from a firsthand account of Mogadishu, written in 1331 by Ibn Battuta, the famous fourteenth-century traveler from Morocco Over thirty years, Ibn Battuta traveled some 75,000 miles—more than three times the distance covered by Marco Polo—visiting China, Ceylon, Turkey, North and East Africa, and Mecca in Arabia. Ibn Battuta had a keen eye for the smallest detail, and his diaries are full of colorful information about the diet, dress, habits, and culture of the peoples he observed.

*The Horizon History of Africa (New York: American Heritage, 1971), pp. 161–162.

gions was essentially peaceful. Muslim traders from Arabia and Persia began to settle in the port cities of East Africa, known to the Arabs as the Land of Zanj. Not surprisingly, Muslim sources tend to emphasize the role of Muslim culture and governors in these city-states. Because the indigenous Bantu peoples lacked a written tradition, sources dealing with their economic and political organization are far fewer than Muslim ones. Information comes from either oral traditions or written accounts by outsiders.

It is apparent, though, that the Muslim/Arab migrants assimilated with the Bantu majority. As these traders intermarried with the indigenous African population, a unique culture was created through assimilation and diffusion. Swahili, an African language infused with many Arabic and Persian words, became the language of trade and intercommunication, and Islam became the dominant religion. It is not always clear from the available sources whether these city-states were governed by migrants from Arabia or the Persian Gulf or by indigenous Muslim ruling dynasties.

This new culture prevailed along the coast from present-day Somalia to Tanzania in the cities of Mogadishu, Merca, Brava, and many others, which enjoyed the economic wealth brought by trade. Ivory, gold, and slaves were the primary commodities. By the tenth century, merchants from the Persian Gulf and Oman dominated economic life, extending their trading empire to include the large island of Madagascar and the Comoro Islands. From 1095 to 1291, the Christian crusaders, avid for riches to take back to Europe, increased the demand for gold and ivory, which came from central Africa through eastern Africa to the eastern Mediterranean, where the crusaders had established independent feudal kingdoms. Gold was brought from Zimbabwe through the port of Sofala to Kilwa in present-day Tanzania. Muslim sources refer to Sofala as the capital of Zanj, or "land of the Bantu," which indicates that Bantu peoples from central Africa had already settled along the southern coast by 900.

Numerous mosques and public buildings along the East African coast attest to the wealth of these city-states. Dating from the thirteenth century, the great mosque in Kilwa clearly demonstrates the preeminence of Islamic architectural forms and designs. Many of the mosques and public buildings that remain are remarkably similar to those constructed by the Umayyads and Abbasids in earlier centuries.

Inland Cities in Southern Africa

The commercial cities of the coastal regions were linked economically and socially with a series of inland cities ruled by various Bantu societies. Iron production and copper and gold mining provided the economic basis of these cities. They had a flourishing trade with the coastal regions, but it is not yet known whether the merchants who conducted this trade came from the inland cities or the coast.

The massive complex at Zimbabwe is one of the most extensive of these Bantu cities and served as the capital of several Bantu rulers. It includes a hill complex with a huge granite hall, a great enclosure with thirty-foot-high walls, and a valley complex. The great enclosure may have housed the rulers' wives, but the purpose of the conical stone tower in its center is unknown. These enormous ruins attest to the architectural skills of the Bantu people. Carbon dating of materials from Zimbabwe reveals that construction probably began around 200 C.E., but most of the surviving buildings date from after 1000. Although Europeans originally thought the stone walls were fortresses, these massive complexes were actually built as displays of wealth and power, not for military purposes.

Although the Zimbabwe complex is the most impressive of these Bantu constructions, more than 150 similar ones are scattered along the Zimbabwe-Mozambique border, but only about a dozen have been excavated. The gold

Zimbabwe. This photograph shows part of the high circular walls enclosing parts of the vast complex and a round tower. The fine granite surface covering the walls was probably added by Bantu builders after 1000. Much of the surrounding district remains to be excavated by archaeologists. © Jason Laure/Woodfin Camp

jewelry and carved objects found in the Mapungubwe burial mound in northern Transvaal (South Africa) indicate the wealth of the society and demonstrate the skill of its artisans. As archaeological research continues in Zimbabwe, more details about the economy, culture, and political and social life of the society will be revealed.

Indianized Southeast Asia

The city is twenty li *[three li equal a mile] in circumference and is pierced by five gates, each with two portals. . . . A huge moat protects the wall spanned by massive bridges. Fifty-four stone carved warrior deities stand guard on either side of each bridge, looking huge and fierce. All five gates are similar. . . .*

The city wall is twenty feet tall and made of stone, so well fitted together that grass cannot grow in the crevices. There are no crenellations. . . . On the inside of the wall there is a sloping earthen rampart over a hundred feet wide, pierced by gates that are open during day hours and closed at night, and watched by guards. . . .

In this country most trading is done by women; that is why as soon as a Chinese man arrives in the country he marries a local woman, to help him in business. Every day the market opens at six and continues until noon. Trading is not done in shops, but by displaying the goods on a mat spread on the ground. Each merchant has an allotted space. . . .

*I do not think gold and silver are found in this country, and that is why they desire above all gold and silver from China. Next in demand are lightweight and heavyweight textiles, tin wares, lacquered dishes, celadon glazed ceramics, and mercury, vermilion, paper, sulphur, saltpeter . . . linen, yellow grass cloth, umbrellas, iron pots, copper trays, freshwater pearls, tung oil, bamboo nets, baskets, wooden combs and needles. . . .**

*James P. Holoka, and Jiu-Hwa L. Upshur, eds., *Lives and Times: A World History Reader*, vol. 1 (St. Paul: West Publishing, 1995), pp. 278–280.

This description of Angkor Thom, the splendid capital city of the Khmer kingdom (present-day Cambodia), was written by Chou Ta-kuan, a Chinese member of the embassy sent by the Mongol ruler Kubilai Khan to demand Khmer's submission to the Mongol Yuan dynasty in 1296. Chou also described the desirability of many types of Chinese goods and the important role of Khmer women in local commerce, which made them useful brides to Chinese merchants who wished to succeed in business locally.

Contact with the older civilization of India had begun a thousand years previous to Chou's journey to Cambodia. It had led to the flowering of the brilliant Khmer culture during the centuries before and after 1000. The story of Khmer culture was typical of most of Southeast Asia, where Indian civilization made a significant impression. Indian traders and colonists began to trade and settle in Southeast Asia in the first century C.E. They brought their religions—Hinduism and Buddhism—and the art, architecture, science, and technology of India. Local rulers avidly accepted all they could learn from India and incorporated these ideas into their traditional cultures. As a result, highly sophisticated societies developed throughout much of Southeast Asia.

Indian Economic and Cultural Expansion

Although the nature and extent varied from region to region, Indian influence assumed a major role in the development of Southeast Asia during the first millennium C.E. For this reason Southeast Asia is often referred to as Greater India or Indianized Asia. Similarly, Asia Minor, southern Italy, and Sicily were called Magna Graecia or Greater Greece because the ancient Greeks immigrated to those areas and introduced important elements of Greek culture. Since the beginning of history, Southeast Asia's natural resources had been a magnet for international trade. Indian traders were the first to come; along with brahmans and Buddhist monks, they settled throughout Southeast Asia. No one knows for certain whether people from Southeast Asia also traveled to India and returned with new products and ideas. In any event, trade and settlement were vehicles for the spread of Indian culture, especially among the elite. Local chiefs modeled themselves on Indian rajas and invited brahmans to perform their court rituals in accordance with the Vedic traditions.

Once the resources of Southeast Asia became known, trade developed on a large scale. Skilled Indian mariners developed seaborne trade routes that carried exotic

goods throughout much of Asia and as far west as the eastern provinces of the Roman Empire. The early Indian traders who ventured to Southeast Asia bought spices and scented woods to sell to the Romans and to the people of West Asia and received gold in return. When the Parthians (Iranians) cut off the gold supply from Siberia and declining trade with Rome deprived India of the gold of the Roman Empire, Indians sought an alternate source in Southeast Asia. Some Buddhist Jataka stories told of princes and nobles sailing abroad to make their fortunes; others mention the Island of Gold to the east of India.

India's cultural influence in Southeast Asia was achieved entirely by peaceful means and continued for over a millennium. No military expeditions were launched from India to maintain Indian power in the lands where its cultural influence held sway. This influence waned after the thirteenth century, however, when Hindu and Buddhist Indian merchants and missionaries were replaced by Indian and Arab merchants of Muslim faith, who also spread Islam.

Except for northern Vietnam, which was a Chinese cultural and political satellite, Chinese contacts with Southeast Asia were mainly mercantile and technical. The Chinese treasured the ivory, pearls, hardwoods, and other products of Southeast Asia, and a small number of Chinese merchants settled in the region. China also adopted a strain of early-ripening rice from Champa in present-day southern Vietnam. Although most of the merchandise brought by Chinese traders to Southeast

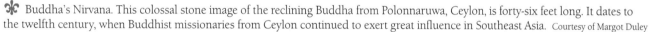
Buddha's Nirvana. This colossal stone image of the reclining Buddha from Polonnaruwa, Ceylon, is forty-six feet long. It dates to the twelfth century, when Buddhist missionaries from Ceylon continued to exert great influence in Southeast Asia.   Courtesy of Margot Duley

Asia has perished, large quantities of Chinese ceramics dating from the Han dynasty and later have survived. Some local peoples called porcelain pots "singing jars" because they made a resonant sound when struck . The ceramics were buried in graves or handed down and preserved as treasured heirlooms. Local potters in Thailand, Vietnam, and other lands learned the technology and art of ceramic making from Chinese potters. Some of their products were modeled after Chinese originals, whereas others reflected local taste. Other Chinese inventions and innovations in agriculture and metallurgy were also passed along to Southeast Asian lands.

Mainland Southeast Asia

Although geographically closest to India, Burma (recently renamed Myanmar) did not come under Indian cultural influence until the Gupta period. Around 500, Theravada Buddhist missionaries arrived from Ceylon and converted the people of Burma to Theravada Buddhism, to which they have remained faithful to the present.

Abundant rice grown with irrigation made Burma prosperous. Pious rulers and people contributed lavishly to build thousands of Buddhist shrines at Pagan on the Irrawaddy River, the political and cultural center of Burma. Many Burmese monks went to Ceylon for study and ordination. Just as in Ceylon, Pagan shrines were usually stupas, which stood on stepped terraces that symbolized the sacred mountain of the Buddhist cosmos. The Pagan stupa was tall and highly ornate, with a bell-shaped dome.

By the late thirteenth century, the dynasty that ruled from Pagan was in decline. At the same time, the expanding Mongol dynasty in China was seeking to subjugate Southeast Asia. In 1271 Kubilai Khan sent envoys to Pagan demanding submission and tribute. The Burmese king refused to receive them. Two years later, when another mission from Kubilai made the same demands, the Burmese king had the Mongol ambassadors executed. This meant war; the victorious Mongols annexed north and central Burma and devastated Pagan. Eventually, the Burmese king acknowledged Mongol overlordship, but shortly after these events, Mongol power began to wane and Burma regained its independence. After a period of civil wars, Burma was reunified in the second half of the fourteenth century, but Pagan never regained its ancient glory and did not become the capital again.

At the same time that the Buddhist religion and culture were flourishing in Burma, Indian influence inspired the Khmer people to build magnificent monuments and to decorate them with beautiful sculptures and friezes. A Chinese chronicle of the third century told of a kingdom called Fu-nan in the Mekong delta in present-day South Vietnam, which had been founded in the first century by an Indian brahman who married a local princess. Indian culture was thus introduced to southern Indochina. In the seventh century, Fu-nan was conquered by its vassal state, Cambodia, which gave its name to the region.

The full flowering of classic Cambodian (Khmer) civilization between the ninth and the fifteenth centuries was the result of the blending of Indian civilization with Khmer ideas and ideals. At its height, the kingdom of Cambodia ruled present-day Cambodia, Laos, Thailand, and parts of Burma, Vietnam, and the Malay Peninsula. Numerous Sanskrit inscriptions engraved in stone give many details of these centuries.

Hinduism and Buddhism came to Cambodia at the same time; Hinduism was preeminent until the twelfth century, Buddhism thereafter. Both Indian religions merged with local beliefs to form a state cult of the god-king. Thus, although temples and statues were dedicated to Vishnu, Shiva, or Buddha, they were really funerary shrines for the divine king who commissioned them and believed himself to be the earthly incarnation of that god. The art of Cambodia blended and integrated Indian concepts with local elements. The facial and physical features depicted in the statues and friezes are Cambodian. Using a unique style that incorporated many local folk elements, Cambodian artists not only integrated Hindu and Buddhist themes but also depicted stories that celebrate Cambodian history and the glory of Khmer rule.

Between the tenth and twelfth centuries, the kings of Cambodia built a capital at Angkor Wat, which even in ruin is one of the architectural wonders of the world. For more than two centuries, each god-king built temples and decorated them with statues and reliefs to outshine those of his predecessors, just as Egyptian pharaohs had done in ancient times.

The most magnificent monument in Angkor Wat was built in the twelfth century as a temple for Vishnu and as a sanctuary of the divine king who identified with him. Here a series of terraced structures culminates in the central shrine 213 feet above the ground. The walls and galleries are decorated with narrative relief carvings of Hindu legends and Khmer history. They depict dancing angels and stories of Vishnu's different incarnations, together with military and other scenes that celebrate the power of the Khmer kings.

In 1177 Angkor Wat was sacked by the forces of Champa, another Indianized state located in present-day southern Vietnam. After repelling the attackers, the Khmer rulers built a new capital nearby called Angkor Thom, a magnificent square city surrounded by an eight-mile-long stone wall and a wide moat (described by the Chinese ambassador in the passage at the beginning of this section) and provided with a remarkably complex drainage and irrigation system. The greatest monument in Angkor Thom is the Bayan, a Buddhist shrine dedicated to a popular bodhisattva and the king who identified with him. The Bayan is a shrine with a forest of

✴ Angkor Wat. Built in the early part of the twelfth century, Angkor Wat was dedicated to the god Vishnu and the king who identified with him. The monument shows the influence of South Indian tradition. Khmer civilization was at its height during this period.
Ray Garner/FPG International

towers; the central one, which dominates the rest, is 150 feet high. All the towers are decorated with giant heads of the bodhisattva-god-king. Miles of friezes portray religious and secular scenes, among them the Khmer army and navy in action against the forces of Champa. The huge expense of building Angkor Wat and Angkor Thom and monuments at sites still unexcavated sapped the Khmer state's economy, however, and contributed to its eventual decline.

Starting in the fourteenth century, the Khmer kingdom was increasingly threatened by Thai invaders from the west. In 1431 the Thai captured and looted Angkor Thom and carried off many prisoners. Without the bureaucracy to supervise and maintain the complex irrigation system, Cambodia's political power, art, and culture went into a long decline after this disaster. Those Khmer leaders who survived fled south and established themselves in a new capital called Phnom-Penh, which is still the capital of Cambodia.

The Thai, or "free people," came from the borderlands of Burma, Tibet, and southwestern China. The advancing Chinese, and later the Mongols, had gradually pushed them south. By the twelfth century, the Thai had formed a united government. They were Buddhist converts, having established close ties with Ceylon and Burma and accepted Theravada Buddhism before arriving in Thailand around the twelfth century. Ayuthia, Thailand's first capi-

tal, was named after Ayodhia, capital of the legendary kingdom of Rama in the Indian epic *Ramayana*. Although the Thai were Buddhist, they were also influenced by Hinduism, as evidenced by their decision to name their capital after a legendary city in a Hindu epic. Even today, Shiva and other Hindu deities are honored in Thai Buddhist temples, and stories from the *Ramayana* are popular in Thai art and theater.

Pali, the language of Buddhist scriptures, became Thailand's sacred language, and an alphabet based on Sanskrit became the writing system and remains so today. The Khmer prisoners who settled in Thailand ultimately influenced their captors. After the destruction of the Khmer state, Thai art and culture continued to flourish but showed a heavy debt to Khmer models. Although the iconography of Thai art, like that of most of Southeast Asia, derived from Indian sources, in time it became uniquely Thai and no longer dependent on Gupta or Khmer models. Buddhist art continued to develop in Thailand long after it had ceased to play a significant role in the rest of the Indian world.

Island Southeast Asia

In the Gupta and post-Gupta periods, Indians brought Mahayana Buddhism to Sumatra, Java, and Malaya. Indian writing systems, art, and architectural styles prevailed

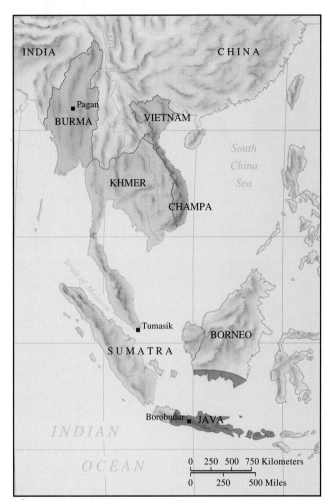

🎏 MAP 7.4 Southeast Asia in the Twelfth Century. No one empire dominated either mainland or island Southeast Asia. On the mainland, the Khmer state was at its height; on island Southeast Asia, various Indianized states warred against each other.

throughout the region. When the Chinese Buddhist pilgrim Fa-hsien returned to China from Ceylon by sea in 410 C.E., he sailed on a ship that carried more than 200 passengers. Such ships regularly plied the route between Ceylon and the islands in Indonesia where Buddhism had become a thriving religion. In the seventh century, another Chinese pilgrim studied Sanskrit in a monastery with more than 1,000 monks on Sumatra (an island of present-day Indonesia) and wrote that "many kings and chieftains of the Southern Ocean admired and believed in Buddhism."

Java, Sumatra, and other islands attracted traders from China and India, because such items as gold, tin, ivory, camphorwood, and, above all, spices, were much in demand not only in China and India, but also in West Asia and Europe.

The growing world demand for spices, especially pepper, which was used for preserving meat, had a powerful influence on the history of all Southeast Asia, especially the islands. Two factors outside Southeast Asia also played key roles in the economic development of the region: the Crusades and the policies of the Chinese government. The Crusades aroused demand for Asian products in Europe and thus stimulated trade between the two continents, much of which either originated in, or passed through, Southeast Asia. Indian Muslims became middlemen in the trade between East Asia, island Southeast Asia, and West Asia, from which the goods were transshipped to the Mediterranean. These merchants were also instrumental in the Islamization of Malaya and the Indonesian islands after the thirteenth century.

The trade policy of Southern Sung China also contributed to Indonesia's economic development. Always in need of revenue to appease or fight its northern nomadic neighbors, the Chinese government encouraged the export of porcelains and other products to Southeast Asia, which stimulated the economic development of the region.

The Sung government lacked the power and the desire to dominate Southeast Asia politically, but the next dynasty, the Yuan, under Kubilai Khan, demanded submission of not only the mainland states, but also the petty states on the island of Java. When some Javanese states refused, Kubilai sent a large naval expedition of 1,000 ships and 20,000 men in 1292 to conquer the island. It was a costly failure.

The art of the islands of Indonesia is heavily indebted to India. Some of the greatest examples of Buddhist art are, in fact, found on Java. Around 800, Mahayana Buddhists at Borobodur on Java built the single largest Buddhist monument. Conceived as a representation of Mount Meru, the World Mountain, it is a succession of terraces. As pious pilgrims climb the terraces, they are symbolically leaving behind the world of desire and moving upward toward spiritual perfection and ultimate union with the cosmic Buddha who dominates the central stupa that crowns the whole edifice. Although the sculpture closely follows the Gupta style, it also shows characteristics that are uniquely Javanese. The racial type portrayed is Malay rather than Indian, the figural style is softer than that of India, and the scenes depicted are uniquely Javanese. Moreover, the ten miles of relief sculptures of *Jataka* stories and scenes from the life of the Buddha show a narrative tradition that was more developed than in India. Many Hindu temples contemporary with Borobodur have also survived on Java. They show the wide range of Indian cultural influences that prevailed on the island.

From the ninth century until the final triumph of Islam after the fourteenth, Hinduism replaced Buddhism as the predominant cultural force on Java and Sumatra. Great shrines were built to worship Shiva, Vishnu, and other deities of the Hindu pantheon. Ganesha, Shiva's son, the elephant-headed and potbellied god of learning, was especially popular. He was represented in two aspects, as the benevolent and protective deity and as a fierce god whose throne is ornamented with human skulls.

An extensive literature, written in a Sanskrit-derived alphabet, also dates to the Hindu period. The *Ramayana* and *Mahabharata* epics were widely loved throughout the islands. To this day, their stories are told in the popular shadow-puppet plays called *wanyang* and in dance and theatrical performances. Thus, although Hinduism survived only on the island of Bali, the influence of Hindu India remains strong in the culture and language of Indonesia to the present day.

Although the Philippine Islands had been visited by Chinese ships since the first century C.E., as Chinese coins and pottery excavated there prove, the islands remained

Great Stupa at Borobodur. The greatest single monument of Buddhist art was built in the eighth century at Borobodur, in Java. This photograph of the Great Stupa shows how the Javanese made this monument a combination of the Buddhist stupa and the ideal of the World Mountain. Ann and Myron Sutton/FPG International

largely isolated and politically fragmented. No stable states emerged, and despite the introduction of Indian writing, few written materials survive. Thus the Philippines did not enter the historic era until their conquest by Spain in the sixteenth century. Four centuries of Spanish rule made the Philippines culturally, politically, and socially closer to Latin America than to Asia.

Two Sinicized States

At daybreak each morning, with the beating of a drum, the headmaster and the instructors of the academy assemble the students in the courtyard. After making a bow to the instructors, the students enter the hall, where lectures and discussions on the classics take place. They study, deliberate, and counsel and assist one another to reach a full understanding of the relationships between ruler and minister, father and son, husband and wife, elder brother and younger brother, and friend and friend. For days and months, they work and rest together as one body to train themselves until they become new men. It is from these students that the future loyal ministers and the future filial sons are produced in prolific number to serve the state and their families. Indeed, never before in the history of our country have we witnessed such a splendid success in nurturing loyal officials and filial sons as we see now.*

*Peter H. Lee and William T. de Bary, eds., *Sources of Korean Tradition*, vol. 1, *From Early Times through the Sixteenth Century* (New York: Columbia University Press, 1997), p. 298.

This passage, written in the early fifteenth century, describes the curriculum of young men studying at the Royal Confucian Academy, which the Korean government established adjacent to the shrine of Confucius in the capital city, Seoul. Like the state university established by the Han Chinese government in the second century B.C.E., the academy trained civil servants by teaching them the Confucian classics, with emphasis on moral teachings, especially the five cardinal human relationships.

Korean culture fused Chinese learning with its own native traditions, however. This is apparent even in Korea's founding myths. According to one myth, Kija (Chi-tzu in Chinese), a relative of the last king of the Shang dynasty, fled his native land with 5,000 followers in the twelfth century B.C.E. when the Shang ended; he then founded a new state in Korea. This story parallels Aeneas's flight from burning Troy and later founding of Rome. A second influx from China came during the end of the Chou dynasty in the wars that preceded unification by the Ch'in. The first Korean state was established

in the second century B.C.E., in northwestern Korea where Chinese influence was strongest. It was called Chosen, the name still often used for present-day Korea. According to the second founding myth, the mating of a tiger and a bear produced a human son called Tan'gun, who founded the Korean state and taught the people the arts of civilization.

The dichotomy between Chinese influence and indigenous Korean traditions persists. Despite Korea's transformation into a Sinicized state, it retained distinctive cultural characteristics, and Koreans resisted Chinese political domination. For example, written Chinese was the only script used in Korea up to the thirteenth century, even though spoken Korean belongs to the Altaic linguistic group, which is related to Japanese but not to spoken Chinese. A phonetic alphabet suitable for transcribing spoken Korean was invented in the thirteenth century; yet such was the prestige of written Chinese that the Korean alphabet was not adopted officially until the mid-twentieth century. Chinese vocabulary is so integral a part of Korean that even now Koreans must learn written Chinese. The number of Chinese characters Koreans know remains the measure of the level of their education. It is not possible to distinguish Koreans from Chinese by their personal names.

Korea

Situated on a peninsula on the northeastern tip of mainland China adjacent to Manchuria but separated from China by a mountain range and the Yalu River, Korea is about the size of Minnesota. The ancestors of Koreans migrated to the peninsula from Manchuria and North Asia starting around 2000 B.C.E.; the migration of peo-

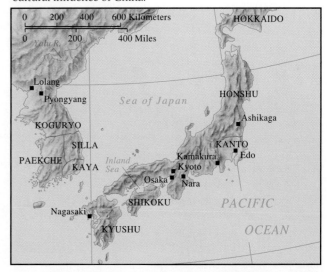
MAP 7.5 Early Korea and Japan. Both came under the cultural influence of China.

ples continued well into historic times. A wave of Chinese immigrants, fleeing the wars of the late Chou era, brought knowledge of bronze and iron making and other advanced technologies to the peninsula. By the third century, a northern Chinese state had extended some control over northern Korea. In 194 B.C.E., Koreans under Chinese influence established the first Sinicized state, called Chosen, in northern Korea, with its capital near modern Pyongyang.

Northern Korea was conquered by Emperor Wu of the Han dynasty in 108 B.C.E. and was organized into four commandaries (provinces) within the Han Empire. By 75, however, only one commandary, called Lolang, remained under Han control. Lolang prospered as a flourishing outpost of Han civilization and remained a part of the Han and its successor states until 313 C.E.

The Han conquest was important to Korea for both cultural and political reasons. Many Han-era tombs excavated near Pyongyang (then capital of Lolang, now the capital of North Korea) show strong Chinese influence. The Han conquest also stimulated the Koreans to organize regional states, which emerged during the first century B.C.E. The three largest contended for mastery until one unified the entire peninsula in the seventh century.

Sinicization in all three states had proceeded rapidly, as all adopted Chinese-style governments, legal codes, tax systems, state universities to teach Confucianism and Chinese history, and Buddhism as the officially favored religion. All three kingdoms also became tributary states of China. Nevertheless, Korea was a replica of China more on paper than in reality. Because Korean society was more tribal and aristocratic than Chinese, government positions were determined by one's "bone rank," or birth. Thus schools and examinations were limited to the elite few.

The reunification of China in the sixth century had a strong impact on Korea. The confident founders of the Sui and T'ang dynasties, hoping to emulate their illustrious Han predecessors, attempted to reconquer Korea. Control of Korea was also strategically important to the Chinese, because it would enable them to outflank the nomads to the north. For these reasons the Chinese governments launched successive campaigns to conquer Korea between 589 and 659. The Chinese threats speeded Korean unification under the Silla dynasty, which offered determined resistance to China and compelled the Chinese to withdraw in 668. Although the Silla kings accepted the status of vassals to the T'ang empire, they nevertheless enjoyed autonomy in their government.

The Silla dynasty was overthrown by the Koryo dynasty (918–1392), from which the name *Korea* derives. The Koryo remained vassals to the Sung and to the nomadic dynasties that ruled North China. The same nomadic groups who raided and conquered China raided and made vassals of Korea, the most ferocious of these

❉ Buddhist Pagoda. Buddhism became pervasive in Korea and was indistinguishable from Chinese Buddhism. This small pagoda, built during the Koryo dynasty, follows Chinese architectural style. Courtesy of Jiu-Hwa Upshur

groups being the Mongols. In one raid alone in 1254, the Mongols reportedly carried off 206,800 male Korean captives. In 1258 Korea surrendered completely to Mongol rule. The Mongol overlords retained the Koryo kings as puppets, married them to Mongol princesses, and frequently required them to live in Tatu (Peking), the Mongol capital established by Kubilai Khan. Mongol exactions in wealth and human resources, including the Korean lives lost when they were forced to serve militarily in Kubilai Khan's two failed attempts to conquer Japan, took a cruel toll on the population. It is no wonder then that when the Mongols were driven out of China, their Koryo henchmen were ousted from Korea as well.

From the seventh to the seventeenth century, unified Korea increasingly resembled China. Korean governmental, legal, financial, and educational systems were all modeled after the Chinese. Thousands of Koreans continued to study in China, so intellectual trends and styles in the two countries remained indistinguishable. Thus, of all the neighboring peoples who emulated China, the Koreans came closest to their model. In contrast to China, however, Korean society continued to be sharply stratified, with rank being determined by heredity. The Korean aristocracy constituted a close-knit ruling group and monopolized power.

Movable Type: Korea's Contribution to the World

In the third year [1403], King T'aejong remarked to the courtiers around him: "If the country is to be governed well, it is essential that books be read widely. But because our country is located east of China beyond the sea, not many books from China are readily available. Moreover woodblock prints are easily defaced, and it is impossible to print all the books in the world by using woodblock prints. It is my desire to cast copper type so that we can print as many books as possible and have them made available widely. This will truly bring infinite benefit to us." In the end, the king was successful in having copper type cast with the graphs modeled after those of the *Old Commentary on the Book of Odes* [one of the Confucian classics] and the *Tso Commentary* [a book explaining one of the classics], and that is how the typecasting foundry became established in our country.*

Movable metallic type was first developed in Korea in the thirteenth century. It was a great improvement on the woodblock method of printing developed earlier by the Chinese. The fifteenth-century Korean king described here is sponsoring book printing because a Confucian state had an obligation to promote scholarship and, concomitantly, good government. Movable type spread from Korea to Japan and China, and thence westward from China.

*Peter H. Lee and William T. de Bary, eds., *Sources of Korean Tradition*, vol. 1, *From Early Times through the Sixteenth Century* (New York: Columbia University Press, 1997), pp. 305–306.

Vietnam

Like Korea, Vietnam is a close neighbor of China. It is separated from the southern Chinese province of Kwangsi only by low mountains and jungles. Because the earliest Vietnamese histories were written by Chinese and because China influenced the making of Vietnamese civilization from early times, Vietnamese history and culture must be viewed against a Chinese background.

As in Korea, the historic period for Vietnam began toward the end of the first millennium B.C.E. At that time a people called the Yueh lived in coastal China from the southern bank of the Yangtze River southward to the Red River valley of northern Vietnam. They practiced slash-and-burn agriculture and made bronze artifacts. Toward the end of the third century B.C.E., the newly unified China under the Ch'in dynasty conquered and annexed what is now South China and the Red River valley in northern Vietnam. The Chinese called the Red River re-

gion Nan-Yueh (South Yueh) and governed it from Hanoi. Turned around and pronounced in the local manner, Nan-Yueh became Vietnam.

When the Ch'in dynasty fell, northern Vietnam came under a secessionist Chinese state centered at Canton. In 111 B.C.E., shortly before conquering Korea, Emperor Wu of the Han dynasty reconquered and annexed northern Vietnam to roughly the seventeenth parallel and organized the region into three commandaries (provinces). They remained part of China until 939 C.E.

Although upper-class Vietnamese assimilated Chinese culture, some resisted Chinese rule. When the Chinese governor killed a troublesome lord as an example to others in 39 C.E., his widow and her sister (called the Trung sisters) took up his cause, proclaiming themselves queens and leading a revolt that lasted for three years. Later Vietnamese honored them as national heroes. Before the tenth century, twelve separate Vietnamese uprisings against China occurred, propelled by nationalistic or anti-Chinese feelings and fueled by local grievances. During the T'ang dynasty, China renamed Nan-Yueh as Annan, meaning the "pacified south." Pronounced An-nam in the local dialect, this remains the name for northern Vietnam.

In 939 Vietnamese forces defeated the Chinese army and established an independent dynasty. Except for short intervals of Mongol invasions in the thirteenth century and Chinese control for several decades in the early fifteenth century, Vietnam has retained its own government since that time, although like Korea it acknowledged China as overlord until 1885. At home the Vietnamese ruler called himself emperor, but when he addressed the Chinese ruler, whom he called lord, he referred to himself as subject and vassal king.

Under Chinese rule, Vietnam benefited from rapid progress and technological innovation. Chinese-designed irrigation works made possible intensive rice culture in the Red River valley. China also introduced efficient bureaucratic administrative machinery that replaced the rule of old feudal chieftains. Confucianism became the foundation of the governmental, educational, and moral systems, and Mahayana Buddhism became the influential religion. The Chinese administrators collected taxes, demanded corvée labor from Vietnamese males, and drafted them for the military.

Upper-class Vietnamese, like their Korean counterparts, meticulously copied Chinese social customs and cultural norms. The Vietnamese adopted the same surnames and given names as the Chinese and wrote in the same language, although in time they created new words that were different from Chinese. They wore similarly styled clothing, used chopsticks to eat food of a cuisine closely related to that of southern China, made ceramic wares similar to those of China, and built and decorated their houses in a Chinese manner.

Despite Chinese cultural influence, a Vietnamese self-consciousness and national identity emerged due to several factors. Ancient cultural patterns from prehistoric times linked Vietnam to Southeast Asia. Vietnam's distance from the center of China's political power and its strategic insignificance to China made Chinese intervention less likely than in the case of Korea. Vietnam's frontier location between the Chinese world to its north and the Indianized states to its south and southwest allowed it to draw from two major cultures and sharpened its self-consciousness. This national consciousness was strengthened by the struggles against Chinese domination and by Vietnam's southward expansion against the Indianized Champa and Khmer states.

Japan: The Merging of Chinese and Native Cultures

Then Amaterasu . . . commanded the heir apparent . . . saying:

"Now it is reported that the pacification of the Central Land of the Reed Plains has been finished. Therefore, descend and rule it, as you have been entrusted with it."

Then the heir apparent . . . replied saying:

"As I was preparing to descend, a child was born; his name is . . . Ninigi. . . . This child should descend." . . .

Whereupon, in accordance with his words, they imposed the command upon . . . Ninigi. . . .

Hereupon, she [Amaterasu] imparted [unto him] the myriad MAGA-TAMA beads and the mirror which had been used to lure, as well as the sword Kusa-nagi; and also . . . [sent] along [two other deities] and said:

"This mirror—have [it with you] as my spirit, and worship it just as you would worship in my very presence."*

*Kojiki, trans. Donald L. Philippi (Princeton: Princeton University Press; Tokyo: University of Tokyo Press, 1969), pp. 137–140.

The *Kojiki* (Records of Ancient Matters), which was compiled in 712, is the earliest account of ancient Japan. Though reasonably reliable on later years, its early chapters are myths and traditions about creation and early Japan designed to glorify the ruling clan. The lines quoted here tell how Amaterasu, the sun goddess, sent her grandson Ninigi to earth in 660 B.C.E. and gave him the "three imperial regalia": the bronze mirror (her symbol), the iron sword, and the necklace of curved jewels, which remain symbols of imperial authority. This myth was designed to glorify the newly centralized Japanese government and to give the ruling Yamato clan, which claimed descent from Amaterasu, dignity above

other Japanese aristocratic clans. Like Korea, Japan's cultural heritage was a combination of native beginnings and borrowings from China.

Japanese Geography and Early History

The four main islands of Japan and the many smaller islands are located in northeastern Asia, separated from the mainland by the Sea of Japan and the East China Sea. Japan is roughly the size of California. Though dwarfed in size by its continental neighbor, China, it is larger than Great Britain and only slightly smaller than France.

There are several similarities between the British Isles and Japan. Both are separated from the continent by water, which gave them comparative freedom from the wars and invasions periodically sweeping the mainland. Compared with the English Channel that separates Britain from France, the seas that separate Japan from China and Korea are much more formidable, being 250 miles wide at the narrowest crossing point. Thus historically the Japanese were more isolated from Asia than the British were from Europe.

The topography of Japan does not favor agriculture. Only about 20 percent of the land surface, mostly along the coast and river valleys, is level enough for cultivation. The rest of the land consists of mountains covered with forests. Scenes of natural beauty abound; one of the most beautiful is Mount Fuji, whose peak is a perfectly shaped, snow-covered volcanic cone more than 12,000 feet high. Although arable land is scarce, Japan has temperate weather and abundant rainfall, allowing intensive agriculture, with frequent double-cropping. The main cereal crop is rice, grown in irrigated fields. The surrounding seas are rich in fish, shellfish, and edible seaweed, which provide protein for the diet.

Japanese written records date from about 500 C.E., but archaeological evidence and Chinese written records indicate that Japanese culture had been evolving for several millennia prior to that time. By the third century C.E., the Japanese were building huge earthen mounds up to 120 feet high, surrounded by moats and guarded by clay figures of animals and warriors, some riding horses. Those mounds were burial places for important people. We can infer from the size of the mounds and the artifacts they contain that society was highly aristocratic and that mounted aristocrats wielding iron weapons could mobilize the large workforce that was necessary for building the impressive mound tombs. The people of this tomb culture, in increasing contact with peoples of mainland Asia, would last into the seventh century and develop into the fully historic civilization of Japan.

The earliest Japanese written records pertaining to its origins are two works called the *Kojiki* and *Nihonji* (Chronicles of Japan), written in 712 and 720 C.E., respectively. Both open with the mythological "age of the gods,"

✻ Haniwa. Pottery warriors and horses are frequently found guarding the grave mounds of Japanese rulers that date to the early centuries C.E. Tokyo National Museum

a dimly remembered past reshaped to glorify the ruling family and to create a false picture of long-centralized rule and antiquity so the Japanese might enhance their self-image vis-à-vis China and its much older culture. As described at the beginning of this section, they recount how Amaterasu, the sun goddess and founder of the sun line, sent her grandson, Ninigi, from heaven to the southern island of Kyushu with the imperial regalia. All three items in the regalia had special significance in early Japan. The bronze mirror was a symbol of Amaterasu, but in general mirrors, often imported from China, were treasured and are frequently found in the burial mounds. The iron sword was a symbol of power to the warrior aristocrats, and swords are also found in the burial mounds. The curved jewels probably derived from the shape of bear and other animal claws and were used as amulets; such jewels have also been found in burial mounds in Japan and Korea.

According to the same creation myth, Ninigi's great-grandson overcame other deities and founded the Japanese state in Yamato around the Nara plain, not far from present-day Osaka, in 660 B.C.E. This part of the myth is probably a glorified account of how the Yamato sun-worshiping clan fought and defeated other clans and their patron deities and expanded its power. If so, the early

Japanese rulers are similar to the Greek heroes of the Trojan War and the chiefs of the Aryan invaders of India, who were also deified by posterity. Chinese records indicate that the Yamato state subdued areas hitherto dominated by "hairy men" (presumably, the proto-Caucasian first inhabitants of the islands called Ainu) and became increasingly powerful. Although the Yamato clan dominated Japan at the beginning of its historic period, the islands were actually ruled by semiautonomous clans, each worshiping its own deified ancestors but acknowledging the supremacy of the sun goddess and her descendants.

This body of myths was later given the name of Shintoism (Way of the Gods) to distinguish it from Buddhism and Confucianism. Shinto myths thus reflected the political supremacy of the sun goddess clan and the subordination of other local cults. The deified ancestors of the subordinate clans were given less important places in the pantheon. Ancestors, awe-inspiring objects, and emperors, called *kami,* were all considered superior and were objects of reverence and worship.

Primitive Shinto emphasized harmony with nature, but had no philosophy, theology, or clear moral code. Most rites involved reverence to the memory of dead family members and clan ancestors. Shrines were simple structures made of wood and frequently rebuilt. Worshipers who attended rites at the shrines bowed, clapped their hands to arouse the spirits' attention, and joined in processions. They also offered wine, food, the first catch or fruit of the season, and the firstborn child (symbolically). Shintoism had no notion of guilt or sin, but stressed ritual purity. Association with birth, death, sickness, and the like brought on ritual impurity, which could be removed with exorcism and cleansing ceremonies. Ritual cleansing involved bathing, which might explain the Japanese preoccupation with bathing and physical cleanliness since early times. Similarly, the official religion of ancient Rome stressed the observance of rituals such as purification and expiation and offered little ethical instruction.

The Adoption of Chinese Civilization

Japanese life was greatly altered by Chinese culture between the sixth and ninth centuries. Much impressed by the might of the Sui and T'ang dynasties, Japanese aristocrats cultivated a strongly Chinese style of life, built a powerful Chinese-style state, and absorbed Chinese art and learning. The year 552 is the traditional date for the formal introduction of Buddhism and the start of the heavy influx of Chinese culture into Japan. Buddhism, then at its height in China and already Sinicized, served as the vehicle for the introduction of many aspects of both Indian and Chinese culture that would transform Japan. Chinese influence continued at a rapid pace for the next three centuries and transformed Japan from a primitive to a sophisticated culture.

Three factors explain the great eagerness of the Japanese to learn from the continent beginning in the sixth century. First, the Yamato rulers had found the existing hereditary clan government, which resembled that of the Germanic tribes of Roman times, inadequate for their needs. They were therefore anxious to learn about more advanced concepts and methods from the continent. Second, by the sixth century the Japanese had attained a cultural level that enabled them to appreciate what China had to offer. Third, by the latter part of the century, China was again unified and entering a great era under the Sui and T'ang dynasties; thus it offered a successful model worthy of emulation.

Although an empress occupied the Japanese throne at this important time, the actual ruler was her nephew and regent, Prince Shotoku (ruled 573–621). This remarkable man was the chief architect of the great changes that would transform Japan. Legend says that Shotoku was born holding a statuette of the Buddha. He was not only a devout Buddhist, but also a learned theologian. By the time he came to office, many Chinese and Korean Buddhist missionaries were already at work in Japan, and their activities had provoked a heated controversy among the ruling aristocrats. Some were faithful to the traditional Shinto beliefs, whereas others enthusiastically converted to Buddhism. In 592 Prince

❉ Prince Shotoku and His Two Sons. This posthumous portrait shows Japan's revered ruler and his sons in Chinese-style court robes.
Imperial Household Agency, Tokyo

Shotoku's pro-Buddhist faction won control of the court, and with their victory, Buddhism was established as the official faith.

Buddhism was an attractive new force in Japan. Some, like Prince Shotoku, studied its teachings, but most early converts were attracted more by Buddhism's elaborate rituals and ceremonies and its magnificent art and architecture than by its theology. They were also impressed with the supposed magical powers of the new religion, or the prospect of gaining personal salvation. The eagerness of many to embrace Buddhism must have been inspired, at least in part, by the desire to partake in the material benefits it brought to Japan.

Early Japanese Buddhism was an extension of T'ang Chinese Buddhism. This was evident in temple and monastic architecture (the best extant examples of the T'ang style are found in Japan) and in the early Japanese Buddhist sects. The architects and artisans who built the early temples were probably Chinese and Korean immigrants, and some of the sculptures and decorations with which they adorned the temples were imported from China or Korea. In time Japanese artisans would imbue their works with a uniquely Japanese spirit. All six Buddhist sects in early Japan were Chinese in origin. The most popular, the Tendai sect (T'ien-t'ai in China), appealed to well-educated upper-class Japanese, just as it had to scholars in China. Buddhism ended the ancient Japanese custom of burying the dead. No more mound tombs were built after Buddhism prevailed; cremation became the norm.

Though a devout Buddhist, Shotoku turned to Confucianism for organizing the government. In 604 he issued a document called the Seventeen Article Constitution, which contained guidelines on morals and ethics for the government and society. An important goal of the constitution was to transform Japanese government into a centralized monarchy by stripping power from the hereditary clans. Except for Article 2, which enjoined all to respect the Three Jewels of Buddhism, the articles embraced Confucian principles and Chinese governmental practices. Article 16 enjoined in part:

> Let the people be employed [in forced labor] at seasonable times. This is an ancient and excellent rule. Let them be employed, therefore, in the winter months, when they are at leisure. But from Spring to Autumn, when they are engaged in agriculture or with the mulberry trees, the people should not be so employed.

This passage refers to the ancient Chinese practice of levying able-bodied male citizens to labor on government projects. The implementation of such a practice on a national level was new to Japan (no one knows precisely how labor was recruited and organized to build the mound tombs).

Prince Shotoku also adopted the Chinese calendar. In doing so he was also embracing the Confucian world order and indicating his acceptance of Confucian ideas about the relationship between heaven, earth, and humans. China required all vassal states to accept its calendar, but Japan did so voluntarily, without becoming a Chinese vassal state. Shotoku also copied the Chinese court rank system and established Chinese-style government offices.

Shotoku also broke ground in another area. In 607 he sent an embassy to China to learn from the Chinese; later he sent two more. Thirteen more embassies were sent after Shotoku's death, making a grand total of sixteen between 607 and 838. These embassies were major undertakings; each consisted of four ships carrying between 500 and 600 promising and eager young men from good families. They included junior government officers, Buddhist monks, scholars of Chinese literature, painters, and musicians, among others. These youths remained in China, some for ten years or more, to learn as much as they could in their chosen fields. After returning to Japan, they worked in important positions or taught their skills to others. The voyages were hazardous because the sailing ships had to cross open seas with no compasses. (The Chinese had invented the first magnetic compass in the fourth century B.C.E., but did not use it in navigation until sometime between 850 and 1050; subsequently, the instrument was widely adopted by other peoples.) The sustained commitment to send numerous embassies showed remarkable farsightedness on the part of Japan's government leaders. The embassies were remarkably successful and helped to bring about one of the greatest technology transfers in premodern times. In addition to the officially sponsored students, others were sent by Buddhist monasteries or went under private auspices with trading ships.

In 645 Chinese-trained officials with the goal of transforming Japan into a miniature T'ang China pushed Prince Shotoku's policy to its logical conclusion. A new set of laws, called the *Taika* (Great) Reform, made the ruler, now titled *tenno* (meaning heavenly emperor, a Chinese-sounding title), head of a theoretically centralized empire. The Taika Reform abolished private land ownership, made the emperor the theoretical owner of all land as in T'ang China, and instituted a Chinese-style tax system. Officials with Chinese titles assisted the emperor in administration, using Chinese bureaucratic practices, rituals, and ceremonies. Like China, the country was divided into provinces and counties, which were given Chinese-sounding names. The officials also promulgated a law code, sections of which were copied verbatim from the T'ang code.

Japanese women lost ground as a result of the Taika Reform. In compliance with Chinese notions of propriety, women were gradually barred from the imperial succession. As a result, Japan was transformed from a society based on a mixture of matrilineal and patrilineal principles, in which both men and women could succeed to political power (Amaterasu, a goddess, was the founder of the sun clan), to an exclusively patriarchal society. Between 592 and 770 half of the rulers were women, but after 770 women were excluded from the succession. A desire to conform to Chinese standards was one reason for the change. Another was the behavior of the last reigning empress, who virtually handed over the reins of government to her favorite, a Buddhist monk, rumored also to be her lover. He became so powerful that people feared he planned to usurp the throne. After she died, government leaders determined to forestall a repetition of her disastrous reign by barring women from the succession.

Until 710 Japan did not have a permanent capital city. This was due both to the rudimentary nature of the government and to Shinto notions of purity. According to Shinto belief, death was defiling; at the death of an emperor, his residence was abandoned or destroyed, and the residence of his successor became the new seat of government. Thus buildings, including Shinto shrines, were simple and impermanent. These ideas did not apply to Buddhist temples and monasteries. Early Buddhist buildings were grand and beautiful and dazzled the Japanese.

To symbolize the adoption of T'ang-style centralized government and display the grandeur of the court, a capital city was laid out at Nara in 710. A number of beautiful Buddhist temples already stood in the vicinity. Two and a half by three miles square, Nara was conceived as a scaled-down Changan, capital of T'ang China; its streets were laid out in a grid pattern with a magnificent palace at the northern end and many temples scattered throughout. The most spectacular temple in the city was called the Todai-ji (Great Eastern Temple); its main hall, built in the eighth century, was the largest wooden building in the world. It housed a fifty-three-foot bronze statue of the Buddha that weighed over a million pounds. In 752, when the temple was formally dedicated, 10,000 monks, including some from China, Korea, and India, attended the celebration. Neither the grand hall nor the great Buddha statue has survived. Many other great temples were built in the eighth and ninth centuries with the support of the court and aristocratic families.

Nara ceased to be the capital after 794; as a result, few buildings were added after that date. Thus it remains a T'ang period city, unique in the world. The emperor built a new capital called Heian some distance away in order to escape the domination of the powerful Buddhist monasteries at Nara. Heian was later called Kyoto (which means capital city) and remained the imperial capital until 1867. Somewhat larger than Nara, it, too, was planned as a scaled-down version of Changan. The four centuries between 794 and 1185 are called the Heian Age, which was characterized by refined and sophisticated culture.

Departures from Chinese Models

Even as the Japanese struggled to duplicate Chinese culture, many things remained different. The Japanese econ-

Prince Shotoku Sends an Embassy to China

Because We had heard of the great Sui empire of propriety and justice located in the west, We send tribute. As barbarians living in an isolated place beyond the sea, We do not know propriety and justice, are shut up within Our borders, and do not see others. . . .

Our queen has heard that beyond the ocean to the west there is a Bodhisattva sovereign who reveres and promotes Buddhism. For that reason, we have been sent to pay her respects. Accompanying us are several tens of monks who have come to study Buddhist teachings.

* * * * *

The emperor of China greets the Wo (another name for Japan) empress.

Your envoys . . . have arrived and made their report.

Having been pleased to receive the command of Heaven to become emperor, We have endeavored to extend virtue everywhere, irrespective of distance.

We are deeply grateful that the Wo empress—residing in the seas beyond—bestows blessings on her people, maintains peace and prosperity within her borders, and softens manners and customs with harmony.*

In 607 Prince Shotoku, acting for the Empress Suiko, sent the first Japanese embassy to China. It was the first of sixteen official embassies to China during the next two and a half centuries. The knowledge that the men brought back after studying in China would profoundly change Japan. The first passage presented here is from the *History of the Sui Dynasty:* the first paragraph is from the document sent by the empress, and the second paragraph is how the Japanese chief of mission explained the purpose of the embassy. In both, the Japanese mission is viewed from a Chinese perspective. The second passage, from the *Nihonji,* is written from the Japanese perspective.

*Delmer M. Brown, ed., *The Cambridge History of Japan,* vol. 1, *Ancient Japan* (Cambridge: Cambridge University Press, 1993), pp. 182–183.

omy was less developed than that of China. Shintoism continued to be important despite the popularity of Buddhism, because even a devoutly Buddhist emperor remained a Shinto high priest and carried out a heavy schedule of Shinto rituals, assisted by the Office of (Shinto) Deities.

Japanese society also remained sharply differentiated according to hereditary class. Thus, while Japan duplicated China's state university and examination system, both institutions were reserved for the sons of the aristocracy. Government posts remained hereditary, despite their Chinese-sounding titles. Thus some of the copying was in form only and without the substance that had made the institutions successful in China.

Some of the ambitious measures of the Taika Reform were abandoned or modified after a trial period, because conditions in Japan did not allow their operation. The most drastic reforms had involved land ownership and taxation. The reformers had attempted to adopt the T'ang "equal-field" system. Judging by surviving records, Japanese leaders during the Nara and early Heian periods made heroic efforts to carry it out, with considerable success in some areas. Even in T'ang China, with its considerable bureaucratic machinery and experience, the equal-field system had broken down after a hundred years; small wonder it could not be sustained in Japan.

The Heian period was one of general economic expansion, but the central government did not benefit. Aristocratic families evaded taxes and Buddhist institutions did not pay them. Possessing the capital and labor to bring new lands into cultivation, the aristocrats gradually gained control over larger and larger tracts of land. While they thrived and grew rich, the revenue-starved central government became steadily poorer, and its remaining officers had less and less work to do. Meanwhile the remaining small landowners and free peasantry were saddled with the entire burden of the land tax. To escape the crushing taxation, many peasants placed themselves and their land under the protection of a lord or monastery, working for their patrons for a fee less than the tax bite.

By about the tenth century, all that were left for the emperor and atrophied central government were ceremonial duties. But whereas a Chinese royal house that had become irrelevant would be overthrown, such were the prestige of the imperial line and respect for hereditary rights in Japan that no one attempted to replace the dynasty.

Instead of supplanting the imperial family, the most powerful and wealthy court family in Heian, the Fujiwara, simply married into it. The period between the ninth and twelfth centuries is called the Fujiwara centuries because that clan dominated the government through having a monopoly of supplying empresses and consorts to the emperors and princes. In this way, the imperial government became a sham headed by emperors who were puppets of the Fujiwara family. When a child emperor ascended the throne, his maternal uncle or grandfather, a Fujiwara, naturally became regent. When the emperor grew up and married, his empress and concubines were also Fujiwara women, perhaps the daughters of his mother's brother, the regent. Thus there was no reason for the regent to give up his power, even after the emperor became an adult. As soon as the son of a Fujiwara empress was old enough to sit through state ceremonies, the emperor was prevailed upon to retire so that the regency cycle could begin once again.

The Fujiwara were very wealthy because they owned numerous tax-free estates, but by the twelfth century, they had become decadent and their power faded. Other clans rose to power, but they left the Fujiwara to continue dominating the imperial family through their marriage games in Heian.

Language and the Arts in the Nara and Heian Periods

The court and nobility dominated culture and the arts during the Nara and Heian periods. Since the early Japanese had developed no written language, they borrowed the Chinese writing system. This posed problems because Chinese and Japanese belong to separate linguistic families, Sinitic and Altaic, respectively, with quite different grammar and syntax. Eventually, the Japanese incorporated Chinese words into their vocabulary and invented a system of syllables that enabled them to reflect the Japanese grammatical structure and to write Japanese words that had no Chinese equivalents. Initially, however, the Japanese were forced to read, write, and compose entirely in Chinese, and Chinese was used exclusively in all early books by Japanese authors, as well as in all government records and documents. The mastery of written Chinese gave educated Japanese a distinct advantage, for it enabled them to draw on the entire corpus of Chinese literature, the treasures of a 2,000-year-old civilization. Similarly, educated Romans' knowledge of Greek gave them access to the literature of ancient Greece.

Since the Chinese were keenly conscious of the importance of history, the Japanese naturally adopted the same attitude; like the Chinese, they preserved historical records and composed dynastic histories. The Japanese also honored the Confucian moral code, looked up to Chinese sages and heroes as role models, and revered learning.

After the ninth century, the Japanese were mature enough to innovate and depart from Chinese models. At this time a distinctly Japanese style began to emerge. A phonetic script, *kana,* was developed for writing Japanese. While men of the upper classes continued to write in Chinese according to Chinese conventions, noble ladies, who did not have to pursue an equally strict educational curriculum, learned to write in Japanese, using kana. The result was a flowering of Japanese literature written by women. Lady Sei Shonagon's *Pillow Book* was a journal of court life that painted a picture of sophisticated people preoccupied with good taste and manners even in religion. The outstanding work of the period was Lady Murasaki's *Tale of Genji.* It portrayed a decadent court society of cultivated but effete men and women from the emperor down who valued the ability to compose and write poetry more than government and form more than substance.

Such literary works indicate the growth of a native culture. They suggest a parallel with medieval Europe, where the clergy and government officials wrote in Latin, while popular literature was written in vernacular tongues. While Heian Japan and medieval Europe owed their cultural heritage to China and Rome, respectively, each developed distinctive characteristics. In its gradual development of feudalism, Japan was definitely departing from the contemporary Chinese model of the Sung dynasty and evolving its own unique culture.

Early Feudal Japan

In contrast to Europe, where feudalism declined with the rise of national monarchies, in Japan feudal institutions replaced national institutions after the eleventh century. The emperors continued to reign in Heian (Kyoto) but no longer ruled. They were replaced by the provincial lords, some of whom were descended from the old clan aristocrats, while others came from court families who had earlier left the capital. These lords managed the estates, supervised the peasants, and fought local wars against one another or the retreating Ainu. Some still acknowledged vassalage to great court families such as the Fujiwara and remitted part of their income to them, but less so with time since they no longer needed protection from the imperial government.

Mounted warriors dominated Japan's feudal society. Each aristocratic warrior was attended by a small retinue of squires, clad in light armor made of metal, fabric, and leather, which was superior to that worn by contemporary European knights. Armed with bows and arrows and curved swords made of the finest tempered steel in the world by Japanese smiths, they resembled the knights of medieval Europe. A Japanese knight was called either a *samurai*, which means "servant" (to a lord), or a *bushi*, which means "noble warrior." A feudal relationship, also resembling that in Europe, existed between lord and samurai and often continued for generations. The lord provided his knight with income derived from his agricultural estates. In return, the samurai was expected to serve his lord with absolute loyalty and die in his cause.

The samurai code of conduct, called *bushido* (way of the warrior), was unique. It did not idealize samurai women, who were expected to be brave and to die rather than submit to shame, but they could inherit property, and some were quite successful in managing estates. Samurai also took pride in living a hard, Spartan life.

Palace Scene. This thirteenth-century painting of the emperor, in flowing robes, playing a game of *go* is an illustration from *The Tale of Genji*, Japan's most famous novel. Picture Scroll of *The Tale of Genji: Yadorigi I* courtesy of the Tokugawa Art Museum, Nagoya, Japan

A preacher ought to be a good-looking man. It is then easier to keep your eyes fixed on his face, without which it is impossible to benefit by his discourse. Otherwise the eyes wander and you forget to listen. Ugly preachers have therefore a grave responsibility. . . . If preachers were of a more suitable age I should have pleasure in giving a more favorable judgement. As matters actually stand, their sins are too fearful to think of.*

About the twentieth day of the second month the Emperor gave a Chinese banquet under the great cherry-tree of the Southern Court. . . . The guests [royal princes, noblemen, and professional poets alike] were handed the rhyme words which the Emperor had drawn by lot, and set to work to compose their poems. It was with a clear and ringing voice that Genji read out the word "Spring" which he had received as the rhyme-sound of his poem. [After the party Genji spent the night with a lady of the court.] Suddenly they saw to their discomfiture that dawn was creeping into the sky. . . . "Tell me your name" he said. "How can I write to you unless you do? Surely this is not going to be our only meeting?" She answered with a poem in which she said that names are of this world only and he would not care to know hers if he were resolved that their love should last till worlds to come. It was a mere quip and Genji, amused at her quickness, answered, "You are quite right. It was a mistake on my part to ask." And he recited the poem: "While I still seek to find on which blade dwells the dew, a great wind shakes the grasses of the level land."**

$\sim$

Lady Sei Shonagon and Lady Murasaki were contemporaries who lived around 1000; both came from the Fujiwara clan and moved in court circles. The former wrote a book of sketches about court life, manners, and morals, and the latter a novel about the romantic life of a prince. Both works are masterpieces of prose written in kana, and both paint clear, wonderful pictures of the refined and effete life of the court in Heian.

*Lady Sei Shonagan, *The Pillow Book,* quoted from W. G. Aston, *History of Japanese Literature* (New York: D. Appleton, 1899), p. 116.

**Lady Murasaki, *The Tale of Genji* (New York: Modern Library, 1956), pp. 210–214.

They shunned luxury and were expected to face pain and death with indifference.

The feudal period in Japan was punctuated by many small conflicts between competing warrior cliques. In the twelfth century, these culminated in two major wars between rival clans, both descended from junior branches of the imperial line. They had early left Kyoto to make their fortunes in the provinces. Tales from these wars have provided material for countless plays and stories popular with later generations.

The final victor was a lord named Minamoto. He had the emperor appoint him "Barbarian-Quelling Generalissimo" and delegate to him all military authority. In Japanese, the shortened version of the title was *shogun,* a title the hereditary military dictators used until the mid-nineteenth century. Minamoto chose Kamakura, a seaside town near present-day Tokyo, as the seat of the shogunate. Kamakura was located in the productive Kanto plain, where many Minamoto estates were located. The shogunal dynasty called its government the *bakufu,* which means "tent government," that is, a military administration in contrast to the civil government in Kyoto and theoretically subordinate to it.

The Kamakura shogunate lasted for a century and half, outlasting the Minamoto line that had established it. In a typically Japanese fashion, another feudal clan, the Hojo, married a daughter to the Minamoto shogun and then eliminated the Minamoto line. The Hojo then installed a nonentity as shogun and ruled the country as shogunal regents. By the thirteenth century, Japan had an emperor, who was the puppet of the Fujiwara clan. That clan supervised a sham government in Kyoto, while in Kamakura a puppet shogun presided over the bakufu, which was really ruled by the hereditary shogunal regent, a man of the Hojo clan.

In the mid-thirteenth century, for the first time in its history, Japan faced a terrifying foreign threat: the Mongols who had conquered much of Asia and Europe and intimidated the rest. In 1266 Kubilai Khan sent envoys to Japan demanding submission. The bakufu refused, knowing that refusal meant war. In 1274 an invasion force of 25,000 Mongols and their Korean subjects landed at Hakata Bay in northern Kyushu. The Mongols were accustomed to massed cavalry tactics, while the samurai fought in individual combat. After an inconclusive battle, the Mongols returned to their ships in the face of a coming storm and sailed back to Korea, suffering heavy storm-inflicted losses en route. Their total casualties amounted to a third of the invading force.

Certain that the Mongols would return, the bakufu assembled a large force and erected a wall around Hakata Bay. When the Mongols returned in 1281 with 140,000 men and a huge armada, the wall restricted the Mongol cavalry, while small, and easily maneuvered Japanese crafts inflicted heavy damage on the large Mongol ships in the confined space of the bay. In the same way, Athenian ships had the advantage over the invading Persians in the Bay of Salamis in 480 B.C.E. Then a devastating typhoon struck, wrecking the Mongol fleet and marooning their soldiers. The invaders lost between 60 and 90 per-

Japanese Adaptations

Japan owed many of its cultural developments to China and to India via China. The transformation of the Indian Dhyana school of Buddhism to Ch'an in China, then to Zen in Japan is a good example. Tradition says that in 520 C.E. the Indian master Bodhidharma came to China to preach a religious discipline aimed at tranquilizing the mind of the practitioner so that he can devote himself to exploring his own inner consciousness. The goal is to attain serenity and peace amid a turbulent world. As it developed in China, Ch'an was influenced by philosophical Taoism, with its emphasis on spontaneity and naturalness.

Ch'an's introduction to Japan coincided with the establishment of a military-dominated regime called the shogunate. In Japan the sect became known as Zen, a variant pronunciation of the Chinese word. The shoguns patronized Zen in part because it was not dominated by the old court aristocrats as were the other Buddhist schools. In addition, its teachings could be adapted to the culture and code of conduct of the warriors who formed the backbone of the shogunate. Its close association with the military class infused Zen with a martial spirit, and it became especially influential with the Japanese military. During the strife-filled feudal period of Japanese history, however, people in many walks of life—not just the military—were attracted to Zen.

The rise of Japanese feudalism was also associated with increasing segregation of the sexes and sequestration of women. Thus the easy social intermingling between men and women described in Lady Murasaki and Sei Shonagan's books became history. With the seclusion of respectable women, men could only socialize freely with entertainers and courtesans. This situation had a parallel in ancient Athens, where respectable women were practically cloistered in their own homes, and professional "companions" (*hetairai*) provided physical and intellectual stimulation for males at dinner parties.

Like everyone else in hierarchically structured Japan, the courtesans were segregated in the *Yoshiwara* or "Flower District" of town and were strictly ranked. The *geisha,* which means "art person," stood on top. Like an Athenian hetaira, a geisha spent a long apprenticeship learning literature, song, dance, conversation, and the art of pleasing men. She was a fashion setter in her gorgeous clothes and jewelry and was waited on by maids. She entertained at lavish parties for her male customers, rarely granting her sexual favors except by arrangement. Some eventually became concubines to important men, while others retired to teach young aspirants.

cent of their men. The Japanese attributed their salvation to divine intervention in the form of *kamikaze,* or "divine wind," just as the English later thanked God for the storm that destroyed the Spanish Armada. The Mongols never returned, although the bakufu continued the mobilization for two decades just in case.

The strain of the Mongol invasion and the cost of constant mobilization sapped the strength of the bakufu. The joy of deliverance soon evaporated, and since there were no spoils to share, many of the samurai faced financial hardship. In any case, after several generations the personal bonds that had tied the samurai to the bakufu were wearing thin. The end came in 1333, with the extermination of the Hojo family by a rebel force. With that also came the end of the first phase of feudalism in Japan.

Religious and Social Life during the Early Feudal Era

During the twelfth and thirteenth centuries, cultural changes were also reshaping Japan. The Japanese began to alter Buddhism to reflect the outlook of their feudal society. While the Buddhist sects of the Nara and Heian eras survived and continued to serve the elite, new sects

imported from China or formed in Japan better served the needs of the warriors and the ordinary people. One new sect was the Pure Land, introduced from China in the twelfth century. By offering salvation to the faithful in the blissful Pure Land of Amida Buddha (the Japanese shortened form of Amitabha Buddha), Pure Land Buddhism gave hope to the masses and became immensely popular among them. It allowed the faithful to acquire salvation simply by repeating Amida Buddha's name in faith and sincerity. In the thirteenth century, a Japanese priest founded an offshoot called the True Pure Land, which discarded most of the scriptures and appealed to ordinary people by repudiating clerical celibacy and encouraging priests to live among the congregation. The True Pure Land went so far as to assert that a single sincere act of calling the Buddha's name was sufficient for salvation. Its simplicity contributed to its popularity, making the True Pure Land the largest branch of Japanese Buddhism, followed by the Pure Land sect.

The Zen sect, which is the Japanese pronunciation of the Chinese word *Ch'an* (meditation), was introduced to Japan at the end of the twelfth century. It especially suited the needs of the samurai because it emphasized simplicity and discipline, rather than scholastic studies, and reinforced the idea of physical discipline and mental toughness extolled by the bushido code. Thus Zen became the sect of the warrior caste of feudal Japan; and with their support, it achieved great prestige and influence.

Zen also helped shape the Japanese aesthetic sense by encouraging a synthesis of the refined artistic vision of Sung China with the Japanese love of the simple and tranquil. Tea drinking, newly popular in China, was introduced to Japan at this time, at first for medicinal use. As in China, tea soon became a national drink, and in the hands of Zen aesthetes, it evolved into the tea ceremony, which became an art and a unique style of social intercourse. Imported Sung ceramic ware was favored for the tea ceremony; surviving specimens are among Japan's loveliest cultural treasures.

A monk named Nicheren (1222–1282) founded a popular Buddhist sect named after himself. A fiery street preacher who militantly opposed the other Buddhist sects, he chauvinistically insisted that Japan was the land of the gods and that Japanese Buddhism was the only true Buddhism. Nicheren's sectarianism and nationalism, as well as his emphasis on congregational worship and reading the scriptures in Japanese translation, in some ways resembled Protestant Christianity that later developed in Europe.

Buddhist religious fervor, so strong at this time, was reflected in many new temple buildings and religious sculptures; the most famous is the monumental bronze Kamakura Buddha, cast in the mid-thirteenth century.

The temples that still stand show strong Sung influence, a reflection of the pervasive cultural contacts that continued between China and Japan. Many translations of Buddhist works were written in kana, reflecting the popularizing of Buddhism.

Japanese peasants lived in simple two-room huts, clustered in villages. A few could afford wooden floors, but most simply covered the dirt floor with straw mats. They usually wore clothes made from the fiber of a perennial hemp plant called ramie; less frequently, they wore clothes made of silk. Cotton cloths were first imported from Korea in the fifteenth century. By the sixteenth century, cotton was grown, spun, and woven in Japan. Although rice cultivation was widespread, most of the crop was turned over to the lord. Peasants ate inferior grains such as millet, roots, and wild grass seeds.

Although medieval peasants were largely self-sufficient, they did trade their surplus and items they made, such as vinegar and wines, for salt, pottery, and iron tools in the local markets, usually held three times a month. Peasants with the same skills formed guilds. Metal coins, mostly minted in China, were increasingly used in trade; in time peasants began to commute their dues in cash also.

Farm women did most of the planting, threshing, and milling and took goods for sale in the markets. They also formed guilds for recreation and for work associated with festivals. Religious festivals, organized around local shrines, provided villagers with plays and dance performances.

Summary and Comparisons

The cultures examined in this chapter range from completely indigenous to mostly derivative in relation to Eurasia. In Mesoamerica, the Teotihuacanos, Maya, and Aztecs were the cultural descendants of the Olmec, just as the Babylonians, Assyrians, and Chaldeans had followed the Sumerians. In a larger context, however, Mesoamerican culture as a whole derived little from the Amerindian culture in Peru and the Andes. Contact with Eurasia, if it occurred at all, was insignificant before the end of the fifteenth century.

The Mesoamerican cultures that developed after the first century C.E. were essentially clusters of city-states. These states were sometimes aggregated by conquest into larger entities, the largest and most complex was the Aztec Empire of the early sixteenth century. Although the major cities of Mesoamerica varied widely in population, most centered on monumental religious buildings shaped like flattened pyramids and flanked by sacred ball courts. Governmental systems in general had a strong religious element, headed by a ruler supported by a military elite and a priestly caste. The rulers of the peoples of Mesoamerica were obsessed with the capriciousness of good and evil. Increasingly, they

turned to massive sacrifices of human blood to preserve the universal order and a sense of security.

The development of Mesoamerican culture is a paradox. On the one hand, it became quite sophisticated intellectually, with an advanced mathematics and a complex calendar. On the other hand, it was technologically backward. Mesoamericans did not produce metal weapons and, since they lacked the wheel and large draft animals, failed to develop heavy-duty transportation. Invading Europeans would later take full advantage of these deficiencies.

The Inka Empire in the Andean highlands that extended from Ecuador to Chile was quite unlike other Mesoamerican states. A descendant of earlier affluent cultures on the coast of Peru, the Inka Empire developed the most centralized state in the Americas. A divine emperor presided over a highly structured socioeconomic and political system, controlling and allocating all land, resources, and labor.

Although facing the same problems as the Mesoamericans, the Inka built a remarkable network of roads and supply stations that helped to keep the far-flung empire together. Inka agents collected food in public warehouses and dispensed it, along with clothing and beer, at holidays, religious ceremonies, and other state occasions. In worshiping the sun, the Inka did not indulge in the blood-soaked religious practices found in Mesoamerica.

The young cultures of sub-Saharan Africa represent various mixes of indigenous and borrowed elements. Before its penetration by Islam after the seventh century, sub-Saharan Africa had largely indigenous cultures generally unaffected by the great Mediterranean civilizations. Ethiopia, in the mountains of the eastern sub-Sahara, saw early development because of its access to the Mediterranean via the Nile River. The Axum-Kushite trading empire that rose in this region was culturally based on the Coptic Christian faith. However, the culture of this area was cut off from the rest of the Christian world when the Muslims conquered North Africa.

In the sub-Saharan savanna of West Africa, an essentially indigenous culture arose. A succession of powerful kingdoms—especially Ghana, Mali, and Songhai—emerged between the fourth and sixteenth centuries. Based on the salt and gold trade, they enjoyed an urban existence supported by a firm agricultural base. Although illiterate, they were strong politically and militarily. Their ironworking was either a product of independent invention or an import from the Mediterranean. Islam was an increasing presence in the region after the seventh century.

A third cultural center was the east coast of Africa, where a number of city-states had profited from trade around the Indian Ocean since Greek and Roman times. In this area the Muslim/Arab culture mixed with the indigenous Bantu culture: one major example of the mixture was the evolution of the Swahili language.

Central and southern Africa saw the advent of the Bantu peoples, whose culture and language pervaded the lower third of the African continent as Indo-European had Eurasia. The Bantu were generally metal-working farmers and herders. By about 1000, they had developed at least one (as yet only partially excavated) major urban center (with monumental architecture) in the Zimbabwe area.

The societies of peripheral Asia that developed in the shadow of the rich and sophisticated civilizations of India and China adopted and/or adapted most of their culture. Indian culture, transported by Indian traders and colonists, was adopted throughout Southeast Asia. From present-day Burma to the islands of Indonesia, Indian religion, art, and architecture were omnipresent. Hinduism and Buddhism competed for supremacy throughout the region, with the latter usually victorious. The magnificent Buddhist temple complex at Angkor Wat in Cambodia is a good illustration of the expression of Buddhist devotion in a Cambodian idiom.

Like India, China had its cultural satellites. Though neighboring Koreans and Vietnamese resisted Chinese political domination, the language, bureaucracy, technology, education, philosophy, and religion of China exerted an irresistible attraction, especially on the upper classes.

China's largest cultural satellite, however, was Japan. Japan's island location, coupled with military preparedness and a "divine wind," enabled the Japanese to remain politically independent from China. But, like the Koreans and the Vietnamese, the Japanese willingly submitted to the prestige of Chinese culture. In the sixth century, the arrival of Buddhism ushered in a new era in Japanese history. These new elements melded with Shintoism, the indigenous state religion, to produce a unique cultural amalgam in Japan.

Prince Shotoku was a key agent in the calculated adoption of Chinese political and cultural elements, making Confucianism the basis for Japan's governmental system. The Japanese capital of Nara was built in direct imitation of Changan, the T'ang capital. Many aspects of Chinese culture, from the writing system to technology, followed religion and philosophy to Japan's shores. Politically, the power of the emperor and his hereditary chief subordinate, the shogun, was eclipsed and replaced by a feudal system in which provincial clan overlords supported by the samurai military class held sway.

Selected Sources

Arthaud, J., and Groslier, B. *Angkor.* 1957. A richly illustrated book on Angkor, with good text.

Bauer, Brian S. *The Development of the Inca State.* 1992. A standard treatment.

Bovill, Edward W. *The Golden Trade of the Moors: West African Kingdoms in the Fourteenth Century.* 2d ed. 1995. A lively account of Saharan trade routes and the Sudanic kingdoms of West Africa.

"Buddha in the Land of Kami." Films for the Humanities. Video on interactions between Buddhism and Shintoism in Japan between the seventh and twelfth centuries.

Carlson, John B. "Rise and Fall of the City of the Gods." *Archaeology* 16, no. 6 (1993): 58. A look at the Venus warrior cult that provided captives for religious rituals at Teotihuacán.

Carrasco, David. *Moctezuma's Mexico: Visions of the Aztec World.* 1992. A look at Aztec society and culture.

Coe, Michael D. *Maya.* 3d ed. 1985. The standard work on Maya historical development.

———. *Breaking the Maya Code.* 1992. The story of the century-long struggle to decipher the meaning of the Maya glyphs.

*Collins, Robert O., ed. *Problems in African History: The Precolonial Centuries.* Vol. 1. 1992. Includes many subjects for classroom discussion: Bantu origins, slavery, women, and trade, among others.

D'Altroy, Terence N. *Provincial Power in the Inka Empire.* 1992. Reveals the inner political, social, and economic workings of the Inka Empire by studying their operation in a key province.

Davies, Nigel. *The Toltecs.* 1977. A study of the civilization that linked Teotihuacán with the post-classic Maya and the Aztecs.

Deuchler, Martina. *The Confucian Transformation of Korea.* 1992. Deals with Korea between the tenth and fourteenth centuries.

Fairbank, John K., et al. *East Asia: Tradition and Transformation.* Reprinted 1978. A concise but comprehensive account of the histories of China, Japan, Korea, and Vietnam by three authorities on the fields.

Farris, William W. *Heavenly Warriors: The Evolution of Japan's Military, 500–1300.* 1991. Examines the early phase of Japan's warrior culture.

Fash, William L. *Scribes, Warriors, and Kings: The City of Copán and the Ancient Maya.* 1991. A comprehensive view of one of the great Maya cities and a general survey of current scholarship on the Maya.

Hall, D. G. E. *A History of South-East Asia.* 2d ed. 1964. A comprehensive and authoritative book.

Hamdun, Said, and Noel King, eds. *Ibn Battuta in Black Africa.* Rev. ed. 1994. Ibn Battuta's fascinating firsthand narrative of his travels in West and East Africa.

Henderson, John S. *The World of the Ancient Maya.* 1981. Profusely illustrated, focuses on the arts.

The Horizon History of Africa. 1971. A lavishly illustrated account of Africa with many excerpts from primary sources.

Inca. 1995. An informative Time-Life videocassette.

July, Robert W. *A History of the African People.* 4th ed. 1992. A good survey of historical developments throughout Africa.

Kellogg, Susan. *Law and the Transformation of the Aztec Empire.* 1995. Discusses the interface of two legal systems.

"The Lost City of Zimbabwe." Films for the Humanities. Video on the continuing restoration of this great African city.

Malpass, Michael. *Daily Life in the Inca Empire.* 1996. A comprehensive account.

Markman, Roberta H., and Peter T. *The Flayed God: The Mythology of Mesoamerica.* 1992. A combination of original text and contemporary commentary that leads the reader into the mythology of the Mesoamerican cultures.

"Maya Lords of the Jungle." British Broadcasting Corporation/Public Broadcasting Associates. 1980. This installment of the *Odyssey* program concentrates on agriculture and trade patterns.

Meyer, Karl E. *Teotihuacán.* 1980. An overview of the culture.

Munro-Hay, Stuart. *Aksum: An African Civilization of Late Antiquity.* 1992. Recent, scholarly account of the ancient kingdom in present-day Ethiopia.

Munsterberg, Hugo. *Art of India and Southeast Asia.* 1970. The short text and good illustrations show the links between India and Southeast Asia.

Lady Murasaki. *The Tale of Genji.* Trans. A. Waley. 1935. Japan's greatest novel on courtly life.

Packard, Jerrold M. *Son of Heaven: A Portrait of the Japanese Monarchy.* 1987. Traces the world's longest reigning royal house from its beginning to the present.

Patterson, Thomas Carl. *The Inca Empire: The Formation and Disintegration of a Pre-Capitalist State.* 1991. A special point of view.

Pearson, Richard. *Ancient Japan.* 1992. Incorporates the latest scholarship.

Prospouriakoff, Tatiana. *Maya History.* 1993. A well-written alternative to Michael Coe's standard account.

Quaritch Wales, H. G. *The Making of Greater India.* 1951. A concise but comprehensive treatment of the spread of Indian culture throughout Southeast Asia.

Schele, Linda, and Mary Ellen Miller. *The Blood of Kings: Dynasty and Ritual in Maya Art.* 1986. Text and pictures combine to give the reader insight into Maya religious and dynastic beliefs.

*Samson, George. *A History of Japan to 1334.* 1954. The first volume of a three-volume work on Japan by a recognized authority.

Sharer, Robert J. *Daily Life in Maya Civilization.* 1996. A comprehensive discussion of the topic.

Stierlin, Henri. *The Cultural History of Angkor.* 1979. Profusely illustrated, this short but interesting text deals not only with the Khmer culture, but also with those of Burma, Thailand, and Champa.

Swann, Peter. *Art of China, Korea, and Japan.* 1963. A good, short, well-illustrated book that integrates history and art.

*Tinker, Hugh. *Southeast Asia: A Short History.* 2d ed. 1990. A good, short introduction.

The World Atlas of Architecture. 1984. Lavishly illustrated and fascinating descriptions of building techniques and styles around the world from earliest times to the twentieth century. Includes chapters on African and Mesoamerican civilizations.

---

*Available in paperback.

Internet Links

Ancient African Empires and States

http://www.artsedge.kennedy-center.org/aoi/html/ancient.html
    Includes helpful, succinct discussions of "Western Sudanic Empires": Ghana, Mali, and Songhai.

Ancient Japan

http://www.wsu.edu:8080/~dee/ANCJAPAN/ANCJAPAN.HTML
    This site includes material on all aspects of ancient Japan, including the influence of Chinese culture, the role of Buddhism, the Nara and Heian periods, and cultural and social history generally.

Civilizations in Africa

http://www.wsu.edu:8080/~dee/CIVAFRCA/CIVAFRCA.HTML
    This homepage contains links to information on many African cultures, their literature, art, religion, and language. Provides excellent chronological and geographical aids as well.

History of Korea

http://www.violet.berkeley.edu/~korea/history.html
    This homepage contains links to additional pages pertinent to all eras of Korean history. See especially Ancient History (pre-918 C.E.) and the Koryo Dynasty (918–1392).

Lords of the Earth

http://www.realtime.net/maya/index.html

> This homepage contains links to extensive pages on Maya, Aztec, and Inka civilizations. Excellent photographs and text.

Mystery of the Maya

http://www.civilization.ca/membrs/civiliz/maya/mminteng.html

> This site, superbly produced by the Canadian Museum of Civilization, offers readable text, helpful "Slide Shows," a timeline, hyperlinks, and other aids for the study of Maya civilization.

Vietnam History

http://www.viettouch.com/vietnam_history.html

> This very informative site offers an objective survey of Vietnamese history and culture from ancient times to the present. Good graphics, including an elaborate timeline with hyperlinks to more detailed discussions of specific eras.

The Development of International Trade

An old merchant said to a person who wanted to find out the truth about commerce: . . . "Buy cheap and sell dear."

The merchant who knows his business will travel only with such goods as are generally needed by rich and poor. . . . Likewise, it is more advantageous and more profitable for the merchant's enterprise, if he brings goods from a country that is far away and where there is danger on the road. . . . They get rich quickly. (Ibn Khaldun, *The Muqaddimah: An Introduction to History,* trans. Franz Rosenthal [Princeton: Princeton University Press, 1967], pp. 310–311)

The business of America is business. (Calvin Coolidge)

What's good for General Motors is good for America; What's good for America is good for General Motors. (Attributed to Charlie "Engine" Wilson, General Motors Corporation, though his actual words were slightly different)

Ibn Khaldun's observations about commerce and trade are as true today as when he wrote in the fourteenth century—a time when international commerce was beginning to flourish. In the twentieth century, industrialists and leaders (like U.S. president Calvin Coolidge and Charlie Wilson of General Motors) have also recognized the important relationship between economic prosperity and national well-being. For centuries, rulers have sought to increase the wealth of their realms; commerce and trade have frequently made major contributions to the growing power of empires and nation-states.

By 1500 a well-developed international trade was being carried on among the major civilizations of Africa, Europe, and Asia. From that time to the present, international trade has been a crucial global driving force. Trade among diverse and far-flung parts of the world was made possible by revolutionary advances in the sciences, technology, transportation, and finance that began about 500 years ago. Since then advances in transportation and communications have shrunk the world to a global village.

It was not always the case. Although international trade had been important for several thousand years before 1500, trade volume grew slowly and was often subject to interruptions and disruptions caused by wars and politics. Viewing history over the span of several thousand years, we can discern three broad cycles in the rise and fall of trade among civilizations: the first cycle occurred between approximately 500 B.C.E. and 400 C.E., the second cycle took place between around 600 and 1200, and the third and most recent cycle began around 1500 and continues to the present.

Cycle 1: International trade in luxury goods or essential raw materials evidently began earlier than 500 B.C.E. In very ancient times, intricate, interlocking trade routes connected civilizations in Eurasia and Africa. For example, a semiprecious stone called lapis lazuli mined in high altitudes in Afghanistan has been found in tombs of ancient Egyptian rulers. During the Bronze Age, tin from Cornwall in Britain may have been carried as far as the eastern Mediterranean. Recent X rays and other tests suggest that Chinese silk fibers were used in the cloth that wrapped ancient Egyptian mummies over 3,000 years ago. Similarly, when a Chinese general arrived in northwestern India in the second century B.C.E., he found that Chinese silks were already available in India. They evidently had reached India via southwestern China and Burma.

These trade routes were regularized and expanded by the Hellenistic kingdoms in Egypt and western Asia, the Roman Empire, the Mauryan Empire in India, and the Han Empire in China. Along these routes people, goods, and ideas intermingled, and cosmopolitan towns grew up to provide housing, food, places of worship, and recreation for the merchants.

By 400 C.E. violent invasions had disrupted much of this Eurasian trade. The collapse of the Roman and Han Empires had by then reduced the Pax Romana and Pax Sinica to mere memories.

Available technology determined the mode of long-distance trade. Goods were hauled by carts where roads permitted and on pack animals such as oxen, mules, horses, and camels where roads were poor. The animals' carrying capacity severely restricted the quantity of goods that could be carried, so trade was often limited to luxury items. Water transport was always more efficient and much cheaper than land transport. For example, a ten-foot boat could carry as much weight as thirty pack horses. However, the vagaries of wind, storms, pirates, and the lack of navigational charts and compasses hampered shipping. Therefore most ancient sailing ships avoided open seas and hugged the coasts; long-distance sea voyages were undertaken in stages. Hull, mast, and sail designs were primitive compared to those of later sailing vessels and limited the size of waterborne cargoes. As a result, boats, too, tended to carry luxury items.

The high cost of transportation ensured that the most costly goods—silk, spices, precious metals, and gems—traveled the longest distances. Most of the cargo carried in ancient trade, both overland and seaborne, went from Asia to Europe. In exchange, Asian producers received silver and gold from Europeans. Large quantities of Roman coins have been discovered in many Indian towns, suggesting that the coins may have been so common that they circulated as the local currency. European rulers from the Roman emperor Augustus on bemoaned the loss of precious metals to Asian lands for ephemeral luxuries such as silk fabrics.

The Western Hemisphere was not involved in the intercontinental trade until the arrival of Europeans at the end of the fifteenth century. Within the region, the lack of any pack animals other than llamas, which could only carry small loads, and the absence of suitable water routes limited commerce. Thus trade between cultures in the Americas was limited to what could be borne on the backs of the porters and by canoes along river routes.

Throughout the ages, the wealthy have been major consumers of the goods obtained by long-distance trade. Governments fostered trade by building and maintaining roads and ports and by suppressing piracy; they also derived revenues by taxing commerce. Some governments, most notably some of the Islamic dynasties of West Asia, including the later Ottoman and Safavid Empires, encouraged trade through tax incentives and by inviting outside traders into their realms. In China the Han and T'ang governments encouraged foreign traders to settle in their empire by providing them with residential quarters and places of worship. Successive Chinese dynasties also established markets with the nomads beyond their borders, on the correct assuption that trade was preferable to war.

Cycle 2: The reestablishment of a unified govenrment in China in the sixth century and the gradual restoration of peace and order in Europe following the "dark age" of the barbarian invasions at the fall of the Roman Empire led to a revival of international trade. By the twelfth century, a new cycle of trade had peaked. Land and water routes extended from China to western Europe and North Africa, connecting eight overlapping trade zones. The linchpins of these zones were Changan in northern China and Canton on the South China coast, Calicut in India, Samarkand in central Asia, Baghdad in West Asia, Cairo (then called Fustat) in North Africa, Constantinople at the entrance of the Bosporus in the eastern Mediterranean, and Venice in Italy.

Although governments were more fragmented during the second cycle than the first, international trade flourished perhaps even more than during the previous cycle. Improved transportation technology was the reason for this increase. The increased volume of trade satisfied the demands for Asian goods that the Crusaders had stimulated among Europeans since the twelfth century. In East Asia after about 1000, economic advances in Japan and the Sung dynasty's encouragement of exports to raise revenue for defense against Mongols led to a vibrant international trade in that region.

The second golden age of trade was disrupted in the thirteenth century when nomadic people called the Mongols rudely erupted across Eurasia, causing enormous havoc to lives and material culture. However, Mongol rulers later promoted commerce, especially in luxury goods. Thus the devastation of the Mongol conquests was followed by the Pax Tartarica, or Mongol peace.

In the fourteenth century, a plague or "Black Death" swept across Europe and West Asia and also devastated China and India. It wiped out as much as a third of Europe's population and perhaps as much as half of the population of India. Recurrent warfare in western Asia and the high taxes exacted on transit trade by the newly established Ottoman Empire further disrupted trade between western Europe and India and China. As a result, supplies became irregular and prices rose.

Cycle 3: The third era of intercontinental trade began in the fifteenth century. The impetus came from the newly centralized European states, which adopted policies that led to the development of a new international trading pattern. As a result of advances in science and technology, Europe was propelled to the forefront of world trade. Portugal and Spain developed new trade routes that bypassed the old land and water routes and in the process opened up a new era of world trade.

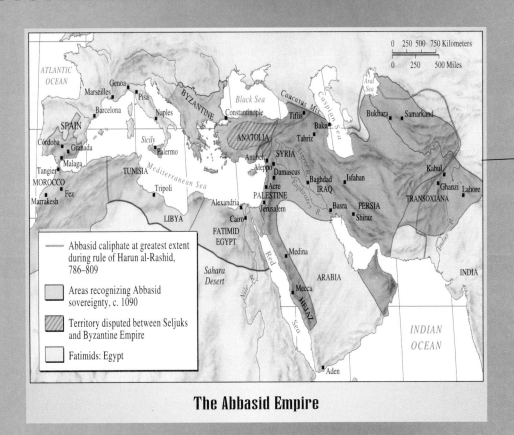

The Abbasid Empire

Legend:
- Abbasid caliphate at greatest extent during rule of Harun al-Rashid, 786–809
- Areas recognizing Abbasid sovereignty, c. 1090
- Territory disputed between Seljuks and Byzantine Empire
- Fatimids: Egypt

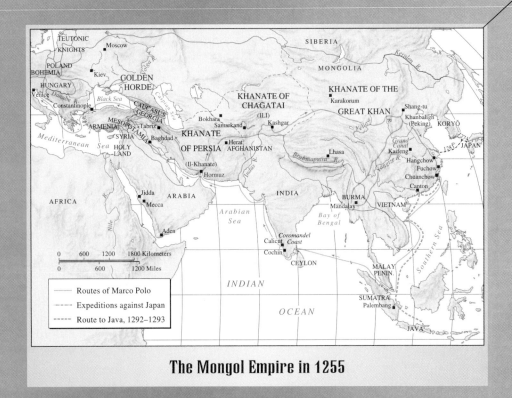

The Mongol Empire in 1255

Legend:
- Routes of Marco Polo
- Expeditions against Japan
- Route to Java, 1292–1293

Three Continents: Conflict and Commerce

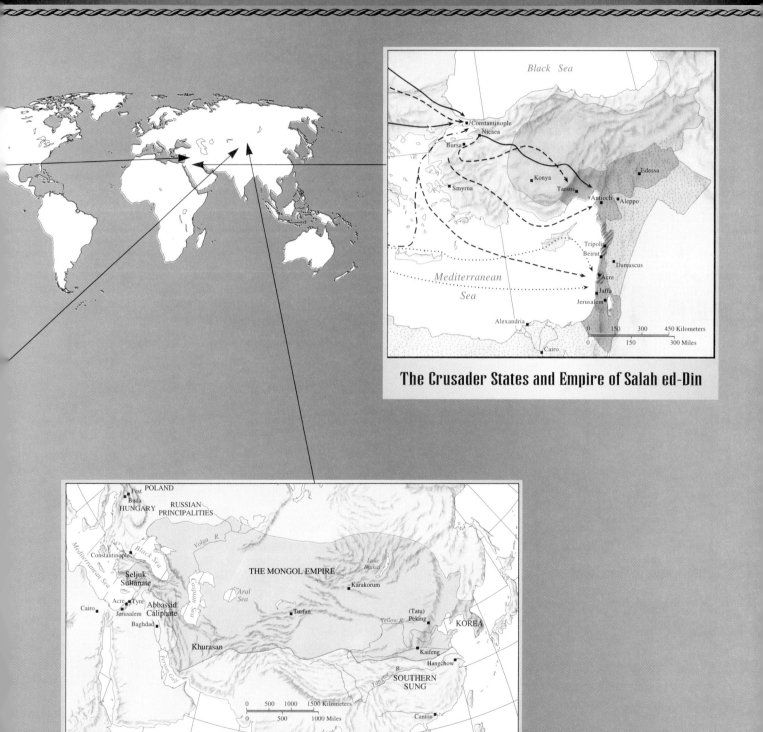

The Crusader States and Empire of Salah ed-Din

Black Sea

Constantinople
Nicaea
Bursa
Smyrna
Konya
Tarsus
Edessa
Antioch
Aleppo
Tripoli
Beirut
Damascus
Acre
Jaffa
Jerusalem

Mediterranean
Sea

Alexandria

0   150   300   450 Kilometers
0   150   300 Miles

Cairo

The Mongol Empire under Genghis Khan

Pest   POLAND
Buda
HUNGARY   RUSSIAN
PRINCIPALITIES

Mediterranean Sea
Constantinople
Black Sea
Seljuk
Sultanate
Cairo
Acre   Tyre
Jerusalem   Abbassid
Caliphate
Baghdad

Volga R.

Caspian Sea

Aral
Sea

THE MONGOL EMPIRE

Lake
Baikal

Karakorum

Turfan

Yellow R.
(Tatu)
Peking

KOREA

Khurasan

Persian Gulf

Kaifeng
Hangchow

Yangtze R.

SOUTHERN
SUNG

0   500   1000   1500 Kilometers
0   500   1000 Miles

Canton

In the period 1100–1500–the second cycle of flourishing and then disruption of trade–war and commerce brought the large populations of Europe and Asia into direct contact with one another. At the beginning of this period, trade between the West and the East flourished amid general prosperity. In West Asia, the Abbasid caliphate ruled over a vast and powerful Islamic state that enjoyed enormous economic wealth. This golden age of Islam marked a high-water point for Islamic sciences, arts, and literature. Commercial contacts across Eurasia were maintained in spite of the Crusades; and a larger number of Europeans than ever before acquired a taste for manufactured goods from Asia.

This period was also one of great disruption in the eastern Mediterranean and West Asia. The turbulence of the Crusades, extending intermittently over several centuries, pales into insignificance compared with the disorder caused by Mongol and Turkish onslaughts across Eurasia in the thirteenth and fourteenth centuries. The Mongol invasions had a devastating effect on central and West Asian societies; in the aftermath, many never recovered their former glory or power. The consolidation of Mongol rule in Asia, however, restored trade relations between that continent and Europe. Another important event during this convulsive period was the creation of the Ottoman state by the Turks of the Anatolian Peninsula. Making effective use of artillery in sieges and infantry carrying guns, the Ottomans, like the Mongols before them and others after them, created "gunpowder empires" that altered the course of history. With their technological military superiority, the Ottomans conquered the Balkans and captured Constantinople, thus ending the 1,000-year-old Byzantine Empire.

The Golden Age of Islam

The Caliph himself, surrounded by his chief ministers and favorite slaves covered with gold and jewels, resembled a planet amidst a galaxy of stars.

Eunuchs, black and white, with inferior officers of the number of eight thousand, served as a foil to these gems. Silk and gold-embroidered tapestries, numbering thirty-eight thousand pieces, ornamented the palace walls, and on a curious tree of gold and silver were perched a variety of birds whose movements and notes were regulated by machinery.

Twenty-two thousand carpets covered the floor, and there floated on the broad stream of the Tigris, before the windows of the palace, thousands of vessels, each splendidly decorated; while a hundred lions, in charge of their keepers, lent a contrast to the glittering scene.*

*Abufelda, "The Caliph of Baghdad Receives an Ambassador from Greece," in Rhoda Hoff, *The Arabs: Their Heritage and Their Way of Life* (New York: Henry Z. Walck, 1979), pp. 19–20.

This description gives some indication of the richness and splendor of the Abbasid court in Baghdad during what has become known as the golden age of Islam in the eighth and ninth centuries. During the golden age, Islamic society, which was known for its tolerance and intellectual dynamism, achieved a high level of cultural and artistic production. Many Islamic scientific, philosophic, architectural, and artistic creations sub-

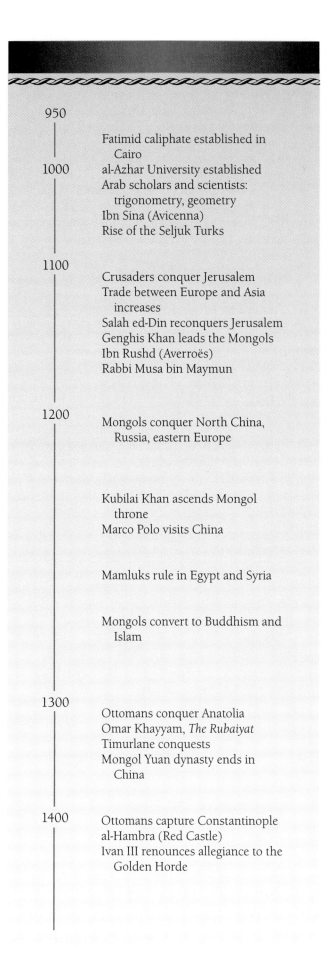

950

Fatimid caliphate established in
Cairo

1000 al-Azhar University established
Arab scholars and scientists:
trigonometry, geometry
Ibn Sina (Avicenna)
Rise of the Seljuk Turks

1100

Crusaders conquer Jerusalem
Trade between Europe and Asia
increases
Salah ed-Din reconquers Jerusalem
Genghis Khan leads the Mongols
Ibn Rushd (Averroës)
Rabbi Musa bin Maymun

1200

Mongols conquer North China,
Russia, eastern Europe

Kubilai Khan ascends Mongol
throne
Marco Polo visits China

Mamluks rule in Egypt and Syria

Mongols convert to Buddhism and
Islam

1300

Ottomans conquer Anatolia
Omar Khayyam, *The Rubaiyat*
Timurlane conquests
Mongol Yuan dynasty ends in
China

1400

Ottomans capture Constantinople
al-Hambra (Red Castle)
Ivan III renounces allegiance to the
Golden Horde

sequently formed the basis for scientific and artistic developments in surrounding societies and in the Western world. This section will describe the achievements of the golden age, both in the Abbasid caliphate and in Spain, where Muslim rulers created a vibrant, long-lived culture that had lasting influence. It will also examine the political and economic institutions created by the Abbasids and the political problems that weakened and ultimately destroyed their government.

Life under the Abbasids

The second Abbasid caliph, Abu Jafar (reigned 754–775) better known as al-Mansur, established a new fortress capital on the Tigris River, at the site of the village of Baghdad. This circular, walled complex took some 100,000 workers more than four years to construct. At its zenith in the ninth century, Baghdad, with a population variously estimated at 800,000 to 2 million, rivaled Constantinople as the largest city of the age. Officially known as Madinat al-Salam (City of Peace), Baghdad became the fabled city of *The Tales of the Arabian Nights,* a collection of highly romanticized and exaggerated stories based on court life under the Abbasids.

Baghdad was dominated by a massive palace that housed the caliph and the administrative complex. With its advantageous location on the Tigris, the capital dominated the trade routes and was a major entrepôt for commerce from the West and the East. Thus under the Abbasids the center of Islamic power shifted eastward from Damascus to Baghdad in present-day Iraq.

Under Caliph Harun al-Rashid (reigned 786–809) and his son Mamun (reigned 813–833), the Abbasid Empire reached its zenith of power and wealth. As in the Chinese empires, the government was highly centralized. The extensive Abbasid Empire was administered by a grand vizier and an advisory council. Taxes were collected for different categories of landowners, and a separate tax was levied on non-Muslims, who did not pay the *zakat,* or Islamic alms, or serve in the army. During the long reign of Harun al-Rashid, the Arabs began to tire of military service, and Turkish forces began to command the military. As the empire declined, they became the masters where once they had been slaves. Similar takeovers by mercenary forces contributed to the downfall of the Roman Empire.

Abbasid wealth rested primarily upon agriculture and trade efficiently administered by a series of able, dynamic caliphs and their advisers. An extensive highway network expedited trade, while a well-organized postal system enhanced communications and also facilitated intelligence gathering; reportedly, old women were particularly able agents. Most of the international trade was with China and India; Muslim traders brought textiles, paper, and porcelains from China and other parts of Asia along overland routes through Samarkand.

Because the Abbasids had the political and social support of the Iranian provinces, Persian influences were particularly strong, and Abbasid rulers often sought to copy the habits and cultural tastes of the old Persian Empire. Under the Abbasids, expert artisans, both from local areas and from other parts of Asia, produced finely decorated porcelains, carpets, jewelry, metal and inlaid wood products, and innumerable luxury items. Court life under the Abbasids was so lavish that Harun al-Rashid's wife, Zubayda, reputedly wore shoes studded with jewels and hosted feasts where the food was served on golden plates.

With enormous power and wealth at their disposal, the Abbasid caliphs also became famous patrons of intellectuals and artists. Under Abbasid rule, Baghdad became a center for learning and the arts. Although Muslim sources make little mention of the event, Charlemagne sent a mission in 797 to secure safe passage for Christian pilgrims to Jerusalem. After his delegates returned with stories about the untold wealth of Baghdad, the city became a symbol of the glories of the Muslim dominions.

Abbasid Decline

By the ninth and tenth centuries, the once mighty Abbasid caliphate was showing signs of decay. A major problem was that its rulers were constantly threatened by rival dynasties within the empire, as governors appointed from Baghdad sought to establish their own dynasties. In general, the more distant a province was from Baghdad, the more likely it was to become independent. In the future, the vast Ottoman Empire would have similar problems controlling its provincial governors.

Weakened by the growing economic strength of rival Muslim rulers in North and West Africa, the rulers in Baghdad turned increasingly to Persian and Turkish leaders for military and political support. The power of Baghdad was also undermined by religious schisms and the weakness of the caliphs, who preferred the pleasures of the court to administrative or military duties. Empires before and after the Abbasids have been weakened by rulers who have preferred lives of luxury to the hard work of administering vast territories or the rigors and perils of the battlefield. The actual collapse of the Abbasid Empire will be described later in the chapter.

The Umayyads: Rivals to the Abbasids

Even in its glory days, the Abbasids had been rivaled by another Muslim dynasty, the Umayyads. As early as 710 the Umayyads had crossed the Strait of Gibraltar into the Iberian Peninsula. After losing Damascus to the Abbasids in 750, they had established a rival caliphate in 756; the new Umayyad Empire included Spain and the western section of North Africa (present-day Morocco and Algeria). Under Caliph Abd al-Rahman I (reigned 756–788), who had escaped the Abbasid takeover in Damascus, the Umayyads based their rule in al-Andalusia in southern

�֍ MAP 8.1   The Abbasid Empire. At the zenith of its power, the Abbasid caliphate based in Baghdad included much of Arabia, present-day Iran, and Afghanistan. Rival Islamic regimes ruled Egypt and North Africa.

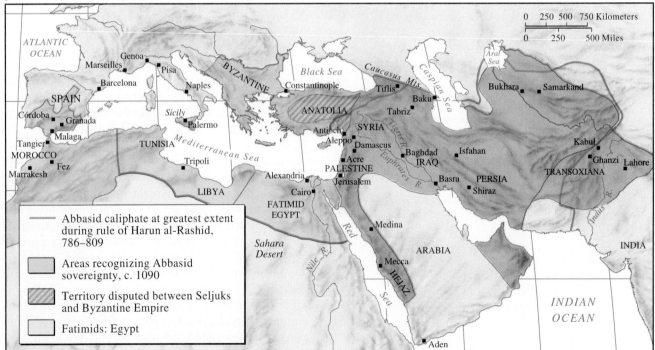

Spain, from which they governed until 976. Subsequent Muslim rulers continued to govern parts of Spain until their final defeat by Christian forces led by King Ferdinand and Queen Isabella in 1492.

Córdoba, the capital of the Umayyad Empire in the west, became one of the richest cities in Europe and exported goods to both the East and the West. Education was highly valued, and Abd al-Rahman III (reigned 912–961) established dozens of free schools and libraries. He also encouraged Jewish scholarship at a time when minorities were vigorously persecuted in the rest of Europe. Thus Muslim Spain became a dynamic center for the arts and sciences.

While Jews were suffering persecution at the hands of Christians in most of Europe, Spanish Jews lived in relative harmony with Muslims; many adopted Arab names and spoke Arabic. A noteworthy Spanish Jew who made valuable cultural contributions was Rabbi Musa bin Maymun, also known as Moses Maimonides (1135–1204), who spent most of his adult life in Egypt. As court physician to the Egyptian sultan Salah ed-Din (reigned 1174–1193), Rabbi bin Maymun wrote treatises based on empirical methods that criticized the still authoritative opinions of classical Greece. Subsequently, he wrote *The Guide for the Perplexed*, a philosophical interpretation of Judaism for those seeking a rational basis for their faith. His openness to Aristotle antagonized more traditional Jews, but his analysis of the connection between revelation and reason was soon adopted by Christian thinkers such as Thomas Aquinas.

Unfortunately, the Umayyads' political and military power did not match their cultural renown. The Muslim territories under Umayyad authority were continually plagued by civil wars in which local provincial governors or military commanders established rival governments. To save the empire, successive caliphs recruited outside forces, many from Africa; however, these mercenaries founded their own rival kingdoms in Africa, which frequently threatened Umayyad domination in Muslim Spain. To protect the empire from rival Muslim forces and from attacks from hostile Christian armies, fortified towns were built along the coastal areas. These ruins may still be seen along the coastal areas of Spain and Portugal.

By the end of the eleventh century, the Islamic Empire in Spain was clearly on the retreat in the face of military advances by the famous Spanish Christian hero, al-Cid, who also fought as a mercenary with Muslims. By the fifteenth century, Muslims in Spain held only the small kingdom around Granada, where the highly secular Nasrid rulers built lavish pleasure palaces that remain the epitome of "Moorish" (Moroccan) architecture in the

West. After years of fierce fighting, the forces of Queen Isabella and King Ferdinand defeated the Nasrids and entered Granada in January 1492. As Boabdil, the last Muslim monarch in Spain, looked down on his lost capital and wept, his mother allegedly said, "You weep like a woman for what you could not hold as a man." Boabdil escaped into exile, and several centuries of Muslim rule in Spain came to an end. For Christendom, the conquest of Grenada with its great al-Hambra palace in some ways compensated for the earlier loss of Constantinople to the Ottomans in 1453.

In the face of massive persecutions by the Spanish monarchy and Catholic church, Muslims and Jews either converted or fled to the relative safety of Muslim-dominated territories in Africa or the eastern Mediterranean. Many of those immigrants were merchants or highly skilled artisans whose exodus promoted the cultural and economic development of the Ottoman Empire. Their departure also impoverished Spain, hereafter the home of a small, wealthy elite and a large, poor peasantry. Although the Spanish monarchs swiftly moved to eradicate all traces of Muslim domination, the centuries of Muslim presence had made an indelible mark on the culture of the Iberian Peninsula, and Muslim/Arab artistic styles are still readily recognizable in the music and much of the architecture and language of Spain and Portugal.

Islamic Theology, Philosophy, and Science

Abbasid and Umayyad rulers actively supported philosophers and theologians. Islamic intellectuals were particularly instrumental in preserving and subsequently translating Greek works into Arabic. Had Islamic writers and thinkers not recognized the importance of keeping classical thought alive, many of the books and writings of Greek philosophers that were to form the basis of much subsequent European intellectual development might well have been lost forever. Since Islam had not separated the functions of government and religion, Islamic philosophers were also keenly interested in exploring the relationship between the spiritual and the so-called rational worlds.

Influenced by Plato and Aristotle, Ibn Sina (Avicenna, 980–1037) emphasized that prophecy could be based upon the intellect as well as upon the emotions. Another renowned philosopher, Ibn Rushd (Averroës, 1126–1198), also argued for the necessity of harmonizing revelation and reason. Ibn Rushd, known as the "prince of the learned," was an Islamic judge who served in Córdoba and Seville and for a short time also acted as court physician. As a Muslim renaissance man, Ibn Rushd wrote on subjects as diverse as Aristotle, medicine, and astronomy.

By contrast, Muhammad al-Ghazali (1058–1111) argued that the spiritual, even mystical, qualities of revelation were far more important. Orthodox Muslim

The Better Half

Women are superior to men in certain respects: it is they that are asked in marriage, desired, loved and courted, and they that inspire self-sacrifice. . . . An indication of the high esteem in which women are held is that if a man be asked to swear by God to distribute his possessions all that comes easily to him, but let him be asked to swear to put away his wife, and he grows pale, is overcome with rage, protests, expostulates, gets angry and refuses—God created a child out of a woman without the intervention of any man, but He has never created a child out of a man without a woman.*

This passage is from an *adab,* or graceful, sophisticated essay, by Abu Uthman 'Amer ibn Bahr al-Faqaimi al-Basri al-Jahiz (d. 869). Al-Jahiz, the grandson of a black slave, lived from the gifts of rich patrons in the Abbasid caliphate; he is reputed to have written more than 200 books.

*Al-Jahiz, "Women's Superiority to Men," trans. D. M. Hawkes, in *The Islamic World,* ed. William H. McNeill and Marilyn Robinson Waldman (New York: Oxford University Press, 1973; reprint, Chicago: University of Chicago Press, 1983), p. 131.

theologians generally agreed with al-Ghazali's approach, and Ibn Rushd's works were eventually labeled heretical. Indeed, al-Ghazali became one of the most widely read and cited philosophers in the Islamic/Arab world.

Islamic rulers were also eager patrons of scientific endeavors. Under the Abbasids, Baghdad became a major scientific center, much as Alexandria had been under the patronage of the Ptolemaic rulers. Translating voluminous materials into Arabic, Islamic scientists preserved both Greek traditions and Persian and Indian texts. Arab mathematicians studied and enlarged upon Indian traditions of numerical reckoning, including the concept of zero. Arab scholars were particularly interested in geometry and astronomy and were especially advanced in the development of navigational devices such as the astrolabe. They also made substantial progress in the study of optics.

Arab astronomers were familiar with the works of Indian and Persian scientists as well as treatises from the Greek. They were particularly influenced by the Ptolemaic (earth-centered) system and were keen observers of the heavens and climactic changes. New tables were developed on the basis of observations, particularly of solar and lunar eclipses. By 1259, in the reign of Hulagu, Muslim scientists had established what was perhaps the first professional observatory, with over a dozen full-time astronomers. Many stars are still known by their Arabic names, and remains of the Muslim observatory built at Samarkand by the grandson of Timurlane still exist.

In the field of medicine, Muslim doctors not only translated Greek medical writings, but wrote treatises on problems as diverse as kidney stones, smallpox, nutrition, and the relationship between the psyche and the body. In the eleventh century, Ibn Sina, a prolific writer on scientific subjects as well as philosophy, wrote a fourteen-volume work, *The Canon of Medicine,* and a twelve-volume one, *The Book of Healing.* In Seville the doctor Abu L-Ala Ibn Zuhr, or Avenzoar (d. 1130), was known for his clinical diagnoses and was far ahead of his time in advocating medical experimentation. The ibn Zuhr family carried on the tradition of medicine for five generations. A son, Abu Marwan (d. 1161), a friend of Averroës, wrote a manual of medical techniques.

Writing in both Hebrew and Arabic, Rabbi bin Maymun (Maimonides) became so famous that reputedly an Iraqi doctor traveled to Egypt to hear him lecture. The scientific achievements of Rabbi bin Maymun show the relatively open nature of Muslim society during this golden age. Likewise, the ease with which many Muslim intellectuals and scientists moved from place to place attests to the overall unity of culture, language, and society even in the far reaches of the Muslim world.

Hospitals also flourished under Islamic rule; Arabic-speaking doctors became renowned for their work in ophthalmology, surgery, pharmacology, and human anatomy. Islamic inventors were also fascinated with mechanical devices. In the book *Automata,* or *The Book of Knowledge of Ingenious Mechanical Devices,* written about 1206, the inventor Ibn al-Razzaz al-Jaziri drew designs for dozens of whimsical contraptions. His inventions, reminiscent of Archimedes' creations in Hellenistic times, range from devices for pumping water to automatic wash basins. As none of these devices is extant, it is not known whether the designs were actually constructed or were merely the fantasies of a creative mind.

Islamic scientists also devoted considerable efforts to trying to turn base metals into valuable gold or silver (alchemy), just as did many in medieval Europe. Alchemy proved to be a scientific dead-end, but in the process of experimenting, Islamic scientists gained some valuable skills.

Major Architectural Achievements

Although early Islamic architects quite literally built on the foundations of Byzantine or Persian edifices, they rapidly altered these earlier forms into a unique style. Mosques were initially constructed around a large open courtyard with a fountain where the faithful could wash before prayers. Simple, unadorned loggias and halls, used for community gatherings that helped bond the society together, surrounded the courtyard. In the central hall, a *mihrab* (prayer niche) pointed east toward Mecca, the direction for the faithful to pray. Minarets, or towers, for calling the faithful to prayer were constructed above the roof of the main hall.

As the Islamic communities grew richer, they ornamented their mosques and public buildings with elaborate designs, often based on various calligraphic renditions of verses from the Qur'an. The Great Mosque at Damascus and the Dome of the Rock and the al-Aqsa Mosque in Jerusalem are among the most important of the surviving early Islamic monuments. Built over an earlier Christian basilica, the Great Mosque in Damascus had a huge great hall and splendid mosaics depicting forest and village scenes. The Dome of the Rock in Jerusalem, completed in 691, is octagonal in plan and is decorated in sumptuous blue-glazed tiles and topped with a dome that was later covered in gold. Owing to decay caused by climactic extremes and destruction by conquest, few of the great architectural monuments built by the Abbasids in Baghdad remain.

Illustration from a Manuscript of al-Jaziri's *Automata.* This ingenious mechanical device measured the amount of blood lost by a patient during bloodletting. As the blood flowed into the bowl, the weight caused the pulley to move the two scribes, who then noted the amount on the tablet. Freer Gallery of Art, Smithsonian Institution, Washington, D.C. 30.75

The Ibn Tulun Mosque. This mosque in Cairo (built 876–879) typifies early mosques that had large open courtyards where the faithful could gather. The small building in the center of the courtyard contains the fountain used for ablutions before prayer. The square minaret is similar to brick towers found in pre-Islamic Mesopotamia. Today the Ibn Tulun Mosque is a quiet oasis in Cairo, one of the largest and busiest cities in the world. (Left) Ted H. Funk/FPG International; (right) courtesy of Janice Terry

The Ibn Tulun Mosque in Cairo is an outstanding example of Mesopotamian work. Ibn Tulun was appointed governor of Egypt in the mid-ninth century by the Abbasid caliph, but he soon established an independent regime. A great patron of the arts, Ibn Tulun financed numerous buildings and developments in Cairo. The mosque bearing his name was built between 876 and 879 and is noted for the huge central courtyard, for centuries second in size only to the courtyard surrounding the Ka'bah in Mecca, and for its simplicity of design. The minaret of Ibn Tulun is unusual because it is square and has an outside staircase, recalling the ancient ziggurats of Mesopotamia.

The caliphs of Muslim Spain were also determined builders. Begun in 785, the mosque at Córdoba has undergone numerous alterations and additions, including having a Christian church built in its center following the Christian conquests of the fifteenth century. The Holy Roman Emperor Charles V, generally no lover of the Muslim world, is reputed to have said of this addition, "They have taken something extraordinary and made it ordinary." The Córdoba mosque has a huge central dome with a "forest" of horseshoe arches in two tiers in what was an original development in Islamic architecture. The Great Mosque at Qairawan (Kairouan) in Tunisia has a similar "forest" of marble columns within the main hall.

In Spain, the al-Hambra, or Red Castle, and the summer palace, the Generalife, are the most elaborate and best known of the Muslim monuments that still survive. Built during the fourteenth century, these pleasure palaces have highly sophisticated systems of water fountains, gardens, and ornately decorated and ornamented salons. They are indicative of the secular nature of the Nasrid regime; mosques were added almost as afterthoughts. Sporting lavish stucco decorations throughout and an outstanding "court of the lions," the al-Hambra, in particular, remains among the most famous and best-preserved examples of secular Islamic architecture.

Islamic Literature and the "Lively Arts"

In addition to their work in philosophy and theology, Muslim writers developed a lively literary tradition. Muslims universally regarded the Qur'an as the highest achievement in the Arabic language. Hence, early Arabic writers used the flowing cadences and style of the Qur'an as their model for both prose and poetry.

In pre-Islamic Arabia, poetry had long been regarded as the ultimate literary form, and long narrative poems were passed down through the generations by oral transmission. After the advent of Islam, a strong written tradition developed, and poets enjoyed lavish court patronage under both the Umayyads and the Abbasids. Thus poetry continued to be the most highly esteemed creative form in Islamic societies.

Political and historical events were popular subjects for early Muslim writers. Poets were often employed to glorify conquests or to vilify political opponents of particular rulers. For example, the renowned classical Arabic poet, known by the irreverent pen name al-Mutanabbi, or "The Pretender to Be a Prophet" (915–965), wrote in praise of one ruler:

> Whither do you intend, great prince? We are the
> herbs of the hills, and you are the clouds:
> We are the ones time has been miserly towards
> respecting you, and the days cheated of your
> presence.
> Whether at war or at peace, you aim at the heights,
> whether you tarry or hasten.
> Would that we were your steeds when you ride forth,
> and your tents when you alight!

Al-Mutanabbi's motto was, "Live honorably or die heroically."

Often written in the vernacular, love poems were also extremely popular. For example, the twelfth-century Cordoban poet Ibn Quzman, who came from a noble Arab family, was noted for mixing colloquial Andalusian language with classical Arabic. Ibn Quzman was a master storyteller who successfully blended irony, cynicism, and dramatic language in a manner similar to European writers such as Dante and Boccaccio.

In the Arab world, music was closely linked to poetic traditions, and under the court influences of the Umayyads and Abbasids, Arabic music gradually fused with the musical traditions of the Byzantines, Syrians, and other Eastern empires. Caliphs patronized musicians and the very popular poet-singers. In Baghdad, Caliph Mamun had many Greek classical essays on music translated into Arabic; these formed the foundation for scholarly works on nomenclature and musical modes.

Based largely on quarter tones, Arabic music stressed melodies with complex nuances and ornamentation. A number of Arabic instruments influenced Western instruments. The lute was derived from the *'ud,* a pear-shaped stringed instrument, various percussion instruments from the drums, and the medieval rebec from the *rababah,* a single-stringed instrument played with a bow. Arabic musicians also played a wide variety of flutes and the *ganun,* a trapezoid-shaped stringed instrument similar to the zither. Musicians in Spain incorporated both Arabic and Western musical forms into their work; later, returning crusaders also brought Arabic musical instruments and songs back to Europe.

In the Spanish courts of Córdoba and Granada, singers elaborated romantic themes, which were then copied and expanded by the romantic troubadours in Europe. "Moorish" traditions or musical traditions

Interior of the Great Mosque, Córdoba. The Great Mosque was begun by the Umayyad prince Abd al-Rahman I. The horseshoe pillars form a forest of marble and decorated stucco. By placing the arches in two layers, one above the other, the architects achieved the illusion of greater height. The mosque has been enlarged several times and remains one of the outstanding architectural achievements of the Islamic world.
Jean Kugler/FPG International

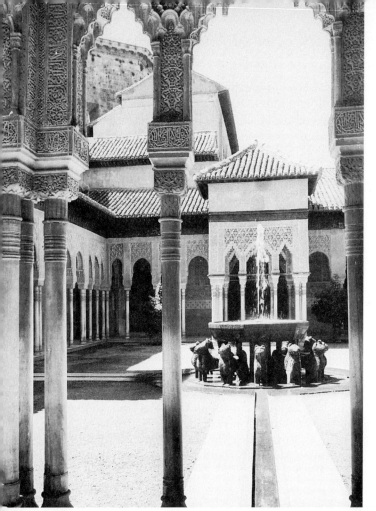

🔆 The Court of the Lions at the al-Hambra. This courtyard is a cool, shady spot that reverberates with the sound of falling water from the fountain. The al-Hambra complex is the epitome of lavish court architecture in Islamic Spain.

Josip Ciganovic/FPG International

transferred from Morocco, are still found in the popular flamenco music of Spanish Gypsies. Depictions of musicians and dancing groups were also popular subjects for artists and potters.

During the Islamic golden age, potters were well known for their sophisticated glazes, particularly the lusterware technique. Because Muslim tenets forbade the depiction of the human form as encouraging idolatry, Muslim artists became experts in the application of geometric patterns and "arabesques," ornate designs of plant forms in interlaced patterns, and in the use of Qur'anic inscriptions or other written forms to decorate their creations. The beautiful and elaborate penned writing called calligraphy was a highly prized skill that was amply rewarded by court patrons. Persian influences during the Abbasid caliphate prompted depictions of human forms in manuscripts and in painted miniatures portraying court life or favorite legends and stories. Poetry and architecture, however, remained the most esteemed artistic endeavors.

The Crusades

O race of Franks . . . race chosen and beloved by God! From the confines of Jerusalem and from Constantinople a grievous report has gone forth . . . that a race from the kingdom of Persians, an accursed race, a race utterly alienated from God . . . has invaded the lands of [Eastern] Christians and has depopulated them by the sword, pillage, and fire. . . . The labor of avenging these wrongs [is placed] . . . upon you. . . . Enter upon the road to the Holy Sepulchre; wrest that land from the wicked race, and subject it to yourselves. . . .*

*Robert the Monk, "The Speech of Pope Urban II at Clermont," trans. by D.C. Munro, *Translations and Reprints from the Original Sources of European History*, rev. ed. series 1, vol. 1, no. 2 (Philadelphia: University of Pennsylvania Press, 1902), pp. 5–8.

As Pope Urban II gave his rousing speech in the city of Clermont, France, in 1095, the crowd shouted, "It is the will of God! It is the will of God!" Much to Urban's surprise, his call for the Christian world to unite and attack the Muslim "infidel" in the Holy Land aroused a tremendous response. Many devoted believers were deeply committed to securing the holy sites for the Christian world. Urban's speech, which was given in response to an appeal from the Byzantine emperor for troops to assist him against the Muslims, helped initiate the Crusades, a series of Christian military expeditions against the Muslims in the eastern Mediterranean. The Crusades worsened European-Muslim relations by intensifying religious fanaticism and fostering long-lasting, deep-seated cultural prejudices. They also had a profound effect on East-West commerce. They initially disrupted trade patterns, but eventually boosted Western desire for Eastern commodities, a desire that would strongly affect the history of the world in the centuries to come.

Crusading Zeal

There were four main reasons for the Crusades. First, the pope hoped to unite the entire eastern Mediterranean and the divided Christian faith under the banner of the Latin church. Second, the Italian city-states, with their large navies, hoped for commercial gains and were therefore keen supporters of the Crusades. Third, the Byzantine Empire was in a severe decline and could no longer act as a buffer between the Muslim East and the Catholic West. Finally, the Seljuk Turks, declining in military power, were no longer able to ensure the safety of the Christian pilgrims visiting the holy sites.

By 1097 some 30,000 knights, primarily Frankish and German, were ready to conquer the "infidel" and secure the Holy Land for Christendom, while reaping their share

Pope Urban II Proclaims the First Crusade. Using the occasion of a church council, the pope appealed for a military expedition to take Jerusalem. Nobles and the clergy—and many pious poor people—responded enthusiastically.
Bibliothèque Nationale de France, Paris

of booty and glory. They were preceded by a Peasants' Crusade, a band of land-hungry peasants who journeyed east, only to have their hopes deflated in an alien land; the survivors quickly returned home.

The Divided Muslim World

Initially, the crusaders met with military success largely because of the political weakness of the Muslim/Arab world at the end of the eleventh century. The pressures of the religio-political schisms that had arisen within the Abbasid Empire in the tenth and eleventh centuries had undermined the ability of the Muslims to resist outside attacks. Local rulers in North Africa and central Asia at one time or another all pulled free of Abbasid control while the power of the Abbasid caliphs was usurped by rival Turkish and Iranian forces. Under the *atabeg* system, slaves (atabegs) acted as tutors to the royal princes and subsequently rose to key positions; often, however, the onetime slaves overthrew their former masters. The atabegs then hired new slaves as tutors for their sons, and the entire process repeated itself. The atabegs and Turkish mercenaries often joined forces to take control from the Abbasid rulers. In 861 Caliph Mutawakkil (reigned 847–861) was assassinated by Turkish mercenaries, who continued to put puppet caliphs in power. At one time, three blind former Abbasid caliphs were reduced to begging on the streets of Baghdad.

By 945, following the takeover of Baghdad by the Iran-based Buyids in 932, the Abbasid caliphate had effectively ceased to exist. Although Baghdad technically remained the center of the caliphate, the empire was increasingly ruled by various Persian and Turkish forces. Just as strong rulers in European nations competed for control or dominance over the papacy, so, too, did regional rivals within West Asia and North Africa compete for control over the caliphate.

Ultimately, the preeminence of the caliphate in Baghdad was challenged by the rival Fatimid caliphate in Cairo. The Fatimids, adherents of the Shi'i branch of Islam, claimed descent from the seventh imam and Fatima, the Prophet's daughter and wife of Ali. After becoming the dominant military force in North Africa, the Fatimids conquered Egypt in the second half of the tenth century. They moved their capital to the newly built city of Cairo and from there proceeded to take southern Syria by 969, thereby gaining control over two of the key trading routes in the Muslim world. They then established bases in northern Syria and Damascus and subsequently posed a serious economic and military threat to Baghdad. Thus two rival caliphates existed, one in Cairo and one in Baghdad, each dedicated to the eradication of the other.

Fatimid economic strength was based primarily on the sale of agricultural products and gold to European merchants. Under the Fatimids, Cairo became an economic and cultural center. Great builders, the Fatimids used the money from agriculture and commerce to construct numerous mosques and public buildings, most notably, al-Azhar University. Established in 972, al-Azhar is the oldest active university in the world and has been a major center for training Islamic theologians until the present.

When the Seljuk Turks began to expland out of Anatolia (present-day Turkey) in 1037, the fragmented political situation in West Asia became even more complex. The Seljuks replaced the old order in Baghdad with their own system of loosely associated kingdoms, each allied to a specific family. This governmental structure contributed to further political disarray. After conquering most of Persia and Mesopotamia between 1084 and 1117, the Seljuks moved into Syria, where they clashed with the Fatimids.

Schools and Universities

In early societies, education was the responsibility of parents, who generally trained their children from very early ages in the skills and crafts that they themselves used and followed. As societies evolved, the education of youth became more systematized and formalized. Ruling families and wealthy elites often hired private tutors to teach their children, particularly sons, reading, writing, mathematics, martial arts, and other skills needed by future leaders. In the Roman Empire, Pliny the Younger put up "matching funds" for a school in his hometown so that students would not have to travel far from home. Corporeal punishment was common; flogging was the traditional means of punishment in Europe, and the bastino, a whip cracked over the bare feet of students, was used in much of Africa and western Asia.

In ancient Egypt and in the Christian and Islamic worlds as well, temples, churches, or mosques were centers for formalized education. The curriculum stressed theology, religious law, and spiritual matters. In Islamic societies students memorized the entire Qur'an, often at a very early age. One of the first universities in the world, al-Azhar, was established by Islamic rulers of Egypt in the 900s. Its original goal was to train young men in theology and legal studies. Over the centuries, al-Azhar has remained one of the preeminent universities in the Islamic world, and its curriculum has been expanded to educate present-day students, including women, in a broad range of skills, including engineering and medicine.

Formal education was generally reserved for boys. In most societies, formal education of girls was limited to the home or, as in ancient Greece, actively discouraged. In most societies, only girls from privileged families were formally educated at home, and the curriculum often focused on the so-called feminine skills of weaving, music, and household management.

Acting out of self-preservation, the local rulers aligned with whatever side appeared the stronger at the time. To add to their difficulties, the Fatimids were plagued by the same problems the Abbasid Empire had faced; namely, numerous mercenary elements, particularly Berbers, within the army and a firmly entrenched atabeg system. A war against Byzantium in 1055 further weakened the Fatimids.

In 1060 the Mamluks, former Turkish slaves from central Asia, rebelled in Cairo, hastening the collapse of the Fatimid dynasty. That rebellion provided the signal for separatist movements throughout the empire. Syria became the battleground of local rival forces. Leaders in Damascus played off Berber forces within the army who, in turn, threatened the Fatimid rulers. Religious minorities, including the Druze, Maronites, and Alawites, proceeded to set up their own governments in Syria. In present-day Lebanon and Syria, these minorities continue to be political forces and sometimes rivals for power. Local emirs, whose feudal domains resembled those in Europe, also sought to expand at each other's expense.

The Seljuks sometimes persecuted and extracted heavy taxes from Christian Arab minorities—a reason why some Arab Christians initially were eager to assist the crusaders. European Christian pilgrims to the holy places in Palestine were also poorly treated by the Seljuks, who charged high tariffs and made it difficult for the pilgrims to enter. Under the Seljuks, merchants also found it increasingly difficult to conduct business. Torn by civil strife, the area became unsafe for travelers and merchants. Those who were brave enough to attempt the journey inland were often heavily taxed in every village. Each emir wanted to obtain his share of the wealth that passed through his area. Lacking any central control, each local ruler was free to do as he pleased.

By the late eleventh century, on the eve of the Crusades, Syria was in the throes of political collapse and economic stagnation. The Byzantine Empire and the ambitious mercantile Italian city-states had already taken advantage of this political weakness to attack along the frontiers of the Islamic Empire. Thus, when the call for the Crusades went out and it became obvious that the crusaders had a good chance of acquiring footholds along the eastern Mediterranean, the Italian city-states were prepared—for a price—to offer their services to the crusaders. The knights were soon followed by Italian merchants, ready to deal with Christians or Muslims.

The Crusader States

Moving into Asia, the heavily armed crusaders met little unified opposition. Wearing red crosses on their chests, they assembled in Constantinople, crossed Anatolia, and reached Antioch in the fall of 1097. In June 1098, with the aid of the large Christian Armenian population, they captured the city. After a brief respite they moved quickly down the coast and took Jerusalem in 1099. The crusaders massacred the civilian population—mostly eastern Christians and Jews—of Jerusalem; it was reported that human blood ran knee-deep. Many Jews were herded into the central synagogue, which was then burned to the ground. Following this massacre, the knights gathered at the Church of the Holy Sepulchre where, after some debate, they proclaimed Godfrey of Bouillon, a French nobleman, as king. Godfrey continued the war against the Muslims and extended Christian-held territory. About 3,000 knights remained around Jerusalem, more settled in Antioch, and a small group in Edessa. Successive European rulers continued to enlarge their territory. By 1123, the crusader states reached their zenith, controlling the Syrian coastal regions and Palestine. However, people in the nearby predominantly Muslim and Arab provinces in Arabia and Iraq were not greatly affected by the Crusades and viewed the wars as frontier skirmishes along the fringes of the Islamic world.

In the areas controlled by the crusaders, the ruling barons organized their states into feudal domains based on familiar European patterns. Each fief, granted to favorites and to those knights who had rendered particular service to the crown, became more or less an independent entity. The controlling barons were only loosely tied to each other by the common threat of attack by the Mus-

lims. Each lord was responsible for the defense of his own land, but in the event of a severe attack, the lords united forces. To protect their territories, the crusaders built imposing fortresses or castles, which were imitations of those in Europe. Scattered on hilltops in West Asia, many of these still survive as the main physical remains of the Crusades.

The European feudal system was superimposed upon the existing Arab village system. Because the two structures closely resembled each other, the native population was little affected. Under both methods, the people rendered tribute to a lord or emir; they also had specific military obligations to fulfill in time of war.

Under the crusaders, agriculture remained the backbone of the economy; cereals and fruits were the main crops. The crusaders attempted to enlarge the already existing industries such as sugar refining, soap making, and glassblowing. Jewelry making continued to flourish in Jerusalem.

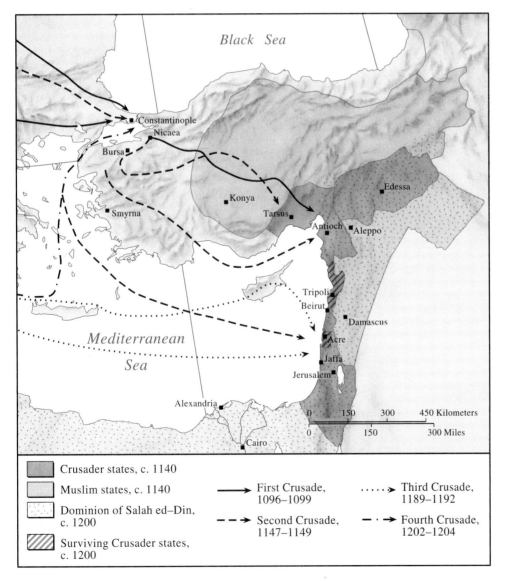

❊ Map 8.2 The Crusader States and Empire of Salah ed-Din. Although the first two Crusades relied on overland routes, later crusaders traveled east primarily by sea. At their greatest extent, the crusaders' holdings formed only a small coastal strip amid extensive Islamic territories, and by 1190 they were rather easily retaken by Salah ed-Din.

Crusader states, c. 1140

Muslim states, c. 1140

Dominion of Salah ed–Din, c. 1200

Surviving Crusader states, c. 1200

First Crusade, 1096–1099

Second Crusade, 1147–1149

Third Crusade, 1189–1192

Fourth Crusade, 1202–1204

Despite their apparently sound economy, the crusader states were in a precarious position. Both the church and the military orders, such as the Templars, were exempt from taxation. In addition, the various Italian city-states, which often provided both financial backing and sea transport for the crusaders, enjoyed special extraterritorial rights. The small crusader states were dependent upon these Italian city-states for protection and for banking and finance. Indeed, the Italians were the major financial beneficiaries of the Crusades. Finally, the crusaders expended considerable energy and money on fighting one another and in repelling attacks from Muslim/Arab forces. The pressures of internal divisions, coupled with external threats from the surrounding Muslim territories, made it impossible for the Frankish crusader states, hemmed in by their geographical position, to have either security or a sound economy.

Muslim Counterattacks

The Muslim community did not sit back and let the crusaders have free political and commercial movement. Each petty emir fought tenaciously to keep his sovereignty. Strong warriors, often of Turkish origins, emerged to counterattack the crusader kingdom. Zengi (reigned 1127–1146), the Turkish emir of Mosul (in present-day Iraq), and his son Nur ed-Din (reigned 1146–1174) were the first great challengers to the crusaders. Faced by a Muslim threat from the north, the crusaders, recognizing the internal divisions within the Muslim world, appealed to the Fatimid kingdom in Egypt for assistance. However, Nur ed-Din managed to outmaneuver both the Fatimids and the crusaders and succeeded in placing one of his own supporters, Salah ed-Din (Saladin, reigned 1174–1193), in charge of Egypt. Salah ed-Din, of Kurdish origins, moved swiftly to unite the Muslims and to lead the attack against the crusaders. His actions ended the Fatimid Shi'i domination and returned Egypt and the surrounding territory to Sunni rule. The battle of Hittin on July 4, 1187, ended any chance of crusader expansion into the heartland of the Arab world. On the offensive, Salah ed-Din continued to attack the crusaders' strongholds and eventually took Jerusalem in 1187.

The loss of Jerusalem provoked the Third Crusade, which attracted the flower of European knighthood, including King Richard the Lionhearted of England, Holy Roman Emperor Frederick I (Barbarossa), and Philip II of France. After Frederick drowned in Asia Minor in 1190, the other two kings quarreled, and Philip returned to France. Although Richard secured a truce that allowed Christians access to Jerusalem, the Third Crusade failed to defeat Salah ed-Din militarily. Salah ed-Din often par-

Quala'at al-Husn (Krak des Chevaliers). When the crusaders captured this old Arab fortress in present-day Syria, they enlarged it along the model of European military buildings. The vast outer wall protected the castle and numerous other buildings, including a church. Situated on high ground above the valleys around, the castle can be seen from miles away and was in an ideal defensive position. A. F. Kersting

Coping with Rude Franks

Everyone who is a fresh emigrant from the Frankish lands is ruder in character than those who have become acclimatized and have held long association with the Moslems. Whenever I visited Jerusalem I always entered the Aqsa Mosque, beside which stood a small mosque which the Franks had converted into a church. When I used to enter the Aqsa Mosque, which was occupied by the Templars, who were my friends, the Templars would evacuate the little adjoining mosque so that I might pray in it. One day I entered this mosque, repeated the first formula, "Allah is great," and stood up in the act of praying, upon which one of the Franks rushed on me, got hold of me and turned my face eastward saying, "This is the way thou shouldst pray!"

A group of Templars hastened to him, seized him and repelled him from me. I resumed my prayer. The same man, while the others were otherwise busy, rushed once more on me. The Templars again came in to him and expelled him. They apologized to me, saying, "This is a stranger who has only recently arrived from the land of the Franks and he has never before seen anyone praying except eastward." Thereupon I said to myself, "I have had enough prayer." So I went out and have ever been surprised at the conduct of this devil of a man, at the change in the color of his face, his trembling and his sentiment at the sight of one praying toward the qibla [toward Mecca].*

Muslims called the crusaders "Franks," or those from the west or foreigners. To the average Muslim, the Franks seemed remote and even barbarous. The Templars were a Christian religious and military order created to protect visiting pilgrims. In his autobiography (published as *Memoirs of an Arab-Syrian Gentleman*) Usamah Ibn-Munquidh wrote a highly personal account of his relations with the crusader knights; his memoirs are an insightful look at the clash of two cultures. In this excerpt, Usamah Ibn Munqidh describes his encounter with some knights when he attempted to pray at the al-Aqsa Mosque in Jerusalem.

*William H. McNeill and Marilyn Robinson Waldman, eds., *The Islamic World* (New York: Oxford University Press, 1973; reprint, Chicago: University of Chicago Press, 1983), p. 188.

---

doned his enemies, let captured prisoners go free, and provided lavish hospitality for Christian leaders. His honesty and chivalry earned him the respect of both Muslims and Christian crusaders.

The failure of the Third Crusade foreshadowed the demise of the crusader states. As Christian control over the Holy Land lessened, Pope Innocent III called for new attacks on Egypt, the Muslim power base since Salah ed-Din. The pope hoped to regain the holy places and to reunite Eastern Orthodox and Roman Catholic Christians. When the Venetians demanded exorbitant fares for transporting the Christian armies, however, the crusader knights agreed to conquer Zara, a city on the Adriatic coast, for the Venetians. In spite of the pope's arguments that Christians should not attack other Christians, the crusaders took Zara in 1202. In 1204, when a deposed and disgruntled Byzantine emperor promised them enormous payments if they would restore him to his throne in Constantinople, the crusaders seized the Byzantine capital. When the emperor failed to deliver on his promises, the crusaders looted the city and established the short-lived Latin Empire of Constantinople (1204–1261).

Although the crusaders ostensibly reunified the Christian world, in fact they embittered the Eastern Orthodox Christians. The schism, or division, between the Eastern Orthodox church and the Roman Catholic church widened and persists today, despite twentieth-century attempts by the Roman Catholic popes and eastern patriarchs to heal the wounds.

The attack on Constantinople discredited both the papacy and the crusading enterprise. It also crippled the Byzantine Empire so badly that the Byzantines proved unable to withstand later Ottoman Turkish expansion into southeastern Europe.

Renewed political divisions in the Muslim world after Salah ed-Din's death in 1193 enabled the crusaders to reestablish control over much of the territory they had lost. By the mid-thirteenth century, however, continued attacks by the Mamluk rulers from Egypt placed the crusader states once again on the defensive. After a protracted defense, the last crusader territory, Acre, fell in 1291.

Cultural and Commercial Exchanges

Although the Crusades were aggressive militaristic ventures, they produced a number of long-lasting cultural exchanges. The Muslim world introduced the crusaders to a wide range of new foods and luxury items, including silks and brocades, perfumes, and soaps. Some crusaders were so attracted to the different way of life that they joined it, intermarrying and becoming assimilated with the indigenous populations. Those who returned to Europe introduced the new commodities, particularly textiles, to their homelands. In a comparable fashion, republican Roman soldiers who had served in the Hellenistic east brought aspects of that life home.

Seeing the demand for these items, the Italian traders were not content to confine their activities to simply

Mosul and Cairo. Damascus was a key center for industry and commerce and profited as a stopping point for pilgrims on their way to Mecca. Jerusalem remained important solely for its religious monuments and as a seat of government.

On the negative side, the era of the Crusades intensified religious animosities between the Christian and Muslim worlds; to some extent these have persisted until the present. The Crusades also fostered further religious disputes between Roman Catholic and Eastern Orthodox Christians. As previously noted, many indigenous eastern Christians suffered persecutions at the hands of both Latin Christians and the previously usually tolerant Muslims, who came to view them as collaborators with the crusaders. In actuality, in spite of having been under Muslim control for over 400 years, nearly half the Arab population along the eastern Mediterranean was Christian when the crusaders arrived. Outraged by the excesses and massacres committed by the crusaders, many eastern Christians subsequently converted to Islam; still others converted to avoid persecution by zealous Muslim leaders. As a consequence, the Crusades ironically proved instrumental in making the eastern Mediterranean predominantly Muslim.

The Mongol Conquest of Eurasia

supplying the crusader states; instead, they sought to establish direct trade with the whole Muslim world. Such contacts with the Muslims gave the Italians a chance to tap into the land and sea trade routes to India, central Asia, and East Asia.

Eyewitnesses related with some surprise that trade continued across the frontiers even in times of open warfare. Salah ed-Din encouraged this trade, and various treaties between the Muslim state and the crusaders ensured free passage of goods. Even after the crusaders were ousted from the region, the Italian merchants continued their lucrative trade, which profited the Italian city-states and provided the economic basis for the artistic achievements of the Italian Renaissance.

The most important items of trade between East and West were spices, especially cinnamon from India, cardamon from Aden, and ginger and pepper from Indonesia. Although the crusader states raised cotton for export, Egyptian cotton was also in high demand, as were Egyptian linen and dates. Precious stones, particularly coral from Ceylon and pearls from the Persian Gulf, were desirable luxury items. Porcelain from China was shipped to Egypt via Aden. Silks and brocades manufactured in Syria were major trading items, as were metal goods from

T his passage recounts how Genghis Khan became ruler of all the Mongols in 1206, organized his men into thousand-man units, and rewarded his faithful lieutenants and relatives with commands and the promise of a share of his conquests. Genghis Khan was one of history's most feared conquerors—his name still conjures up terror through much of Europe and Asia. The path of the Mongol army in the thirteenth century was strewn with unprecedented death, devastation, and suffering. Erupting out of the North Asian steppes, the Mongols conquered China, central Asia, Persia, and Russia, creating the largest land empire in Eurasian history. Since Genghis Khan led his people out of obscurity to world dominion, to this day Mongols hold him in the deepest reverence. Mongol legend says that he will return and once again lead them to greatness.

Genghis Khan, the World Conqueror, 1155–1227

The Mongols originally roamed the steppes south of Lake Baikal in present-day Russia. They hunted and herded and, when possible, raided the settled peoples nearby for loot. Mongol custom dictated that men obtain wives from outside their own tribe. A man could have as many wives as he could afford but accorded preeminence to the first wife. Custom prescribed that the heir marry all his late father's wives except his own mother and that brothers marry their widowed sisters-in-law. Tribal wars to gain territory, seize cattle and horses, and capture slaves and wives were endemic. Mongols worshiped a great god and various spirits; shamans or priests interpreted the spirit world for them. Until the thirteenth century, the Mongols had no written language.

Genghis's given name was Temuchin, and he was the oldest son of a minor Mongol chief. At age nine, his father took him to the camp of his mother's tribe to arrange a marriage with the chief's daughter, named Borte, then ten years old. En route home, his father was poisoned by an enemy and died. The next few years were full of hardships for Temuchin, his mother, and his brothers, because they were cast out by his father's clan. He was hardened by the struggle of these years, claimed his bride, and, with his father-in-law's support, began to rebuild his tribe.

Soon after his marriage, an enemy raided Temuchin's camp and captured his wife and animals. By the time he rescued her from her abductor, she was the mother of an infant boy. Temuchin named him Juji, which means "guest" in Mongol, an indication of his doubtful paternity. Borte bore him three more sons. They and Juji would be their father's principal heirs. Temuchin so distinguished himself as a leader in war and in organization

✳ MAP 8.3 The Mongol Empire under Genghis Khan. Genghis Khan and his immediate successors conquered a huge empire that stretched from Korea to the shores of the Black Sea. The conquests brought the Mongols unprecedented wealth, but at the expense of millions of lives of their victims and terrible destruction.

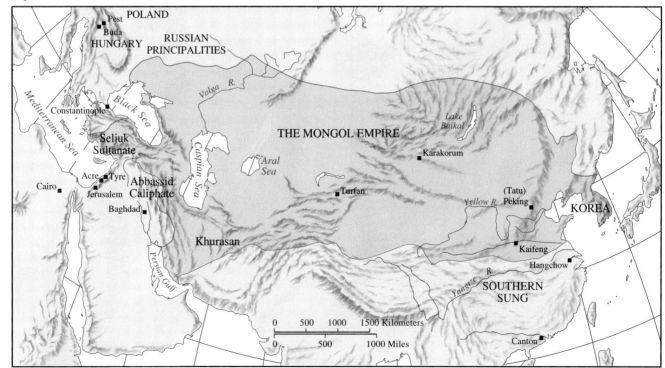

that he was acclaimed Genghis Khan (Universal Ruler) by the Mongol tribes in 1203.

It was Genghis's good fortune that the traditionally powerful Asian states that surrounded Mongol territory were suffering from internal divisions at the time of his rise. The Chin Empire, to which Genghis was initially vassal, was situated to the south of the Mongols. Since its victory against the Sung in the mid-twelfth century, the Chin dynasty had ruled all North China. Chin prosperity peaked in the late twelfth century, the result of a succession of good harvests and the heavy tribute in silks and silver that it received from the Southern Sung government annually. Its decline began in 1194 when the Yellow River burst its dikes, flooded large areas, and then changed its channel to the sea. Years of famine followed. Government currency manipulations added to the economic chaos. By the thirteenth century, the Chin dynasty was in irreversible decline. Because the Chin were conquering nomads themselves, they had no deep roots in China. Even though they had become partially Sinicized, they did not enjoy the full support of their Chinese subjects. Even in decline, however, the Chin remained a major power. According to the census of 1195, the Chin Empire had a taxpaying population of 48.5 million and an army of more than 500,000, including 120,000 cavalry. In addition, the Chin possessed impressive defenses in the Great Wall and numerous heavily fortified cities.

Portrait of Genghis Khan. Genghis Khan was described as tall with alert eyes and a luxuriant beard. This is an idealized portrait by a Chinese artist. The Hulton/Deutsch Collection

Two other states bordered Mongol lands, the Kara-Khitai to the west and the Hsi Hsia to the southwest. The Persian Empire and the Abbasid caliphate were located further west. Both had been weakened by domestic dissent and by the schism and struggles between the Sunni and the Shi'i branches of Islam.

Fired by ambition to rule the world and backed by his Mongol warriors, Genghis began his conquests. Even though the Mongol population was minuscule compared with that of the opposing states, the Mongols' control of the interior line of communications prevented their enemies from coordinating their defenses or forming alliances with one another. Nevertheless, Genghis Khan's victories over all his enemies were spectacular feats of generalship.

Genghis began by attacking the Hsi Hsia, a Buddhist nation situated in northwestern China next to the borders of Tibet, and the weakest of his three neighbors. Its people were proto-Tibetans called Tanguts. He had little difficulty ravaging the Hsi Hsia countryside, but suffered considerable losses at first because his soldiers had no experience storming walled towns. Accounts say that Genghis took his first walled town by cunning and ruse. He sent a message to the defending commander that he would lift the siege and retire in return for a ransom of 1,000 cats and 10,000 swallows. The astonished defenders complied. Then Genghis ordered his men to tie tufts of cotton wool to the tails of the animals, set the tufts afire, and release the animals. The frightened birds flew to their nests, and the cats ran back to their lairs, and in so doing, they set innumerable blazes in the town. Amidst the resulting confusion, the Mongols stormed the walls and captured the town. Later Genghis used more traditional methods to take walled towns by employing siege engineers whom he had captured. In 1209 the Hsi Hsia surrendered, acknowledged Genghis as overlord, and agreed to pay him tribute.

In 1211 Genghis Khan declared war on his next enemy, the Chin. His army of 150,000 ravaged the northern Chinese countryside, leaving famine and pestilence in its wake. Only the few towns that surrendered without resistance were spared. Captured civilians were driven in front of Mongol troops as cannon fodder or as filling for moats. Any town that resisted was razed and its people put to the sword. In six months, ninety towns lay in ruins. The Chin capital, located near present-day Beijing, fell in 1215 and was systematically looted and then torched. It burned for a month and then lay in complete ruin. The booty was sent to Mongolia by caravan. "Useful" men such as artists, craftsmen, engineers, astrologers, and philosophers were spared but taken captive. Some women became slaves or concubines; all others were massacred.

One of the captives from the Chin court who was spared was the scholarly Yelu Ch'u-ts'ai. He was a nomad by descent but a fervent admirer of Chinese culture. A professional astrologer, he became a powerful adviser to the Mongol court. He had the unique distinction of successfully dissuading Genghis from committing some of his worst atrocities. A typical nomad, Genghis hated and despised sedentary people and decided to order the extermination of all people in conquered North China so that their farmland could be turned into pasture for Mongol horses. Ch'u-ts'ai calculated the annual taxes the victims paid and noted that that sum was greater than could be produced by using the same land for grazing. The appeal to Genghis's greed succeeded and the people were spared.

The remnant Chin government entrenched itself in the well-defended city of Kaifeng, and the war dragged on. After conquering Manchuria in 1216 and Korea in 1218, Genghis put deputies in charge of the Chin campaign and turned west. In 1218 he destroyed the Kara-Khitai (in extreme northwestern China, peopled by remnants of the Liao, who were Buddhist by faith), an old enemy that blocked his route west. After annexing the territory of the Kara-Khitai, Genghis's empire touched the Khorezim Empire, which included modern Persia and part of Afghanistan and central Asia and was populated by Christians and Muslims. Between 1219 and 1221, he attacked the Khorezim with an army of 200,000 soldiers. The Khorezim, however, had a much larger force. As in China, the Mongols committed wholesale butcheries, sparing no civilians except those useful to them, whom they deported to Mongolia. Much of central Asia and northern Persia was systematically laid waste and depopulated. For example, Genghis reputedly massacred 700,000 people at Merv, sparing only 80 craftsmen. A small group of Turkic tribesmen nearby, the ancestors of the Ottoman Turks, were among the few who escaped. They fled westward to Asia Minor, where they were given asylum by the Seljuk Turks. Mongol armies advanced as far west as the Christian kingdom of Georgia in the Caucasus and to the Crimean Peninsula on the Black Sea, but did not consolidate these far-flung conquests until a later time.

In 1223 Genghis turned homeward. He was furious that the Chin still resisted and that the Hsi Hsia were in revolt. In 1226 he once again took the field against the Hsi Hsia, repeating atrocities against them. Their capital city, Ninghsia, did not fall until 1227 after Genghis's death. According to his wish, the entire population of the city and most of the people of the kingdom were put to the sword. According to Chinese records, only 1 percent of the people survived. The Hsi Hsia written language was lost, and their irrigation works were wrecked or abandoned because not enough people were left to work them. The fields were choked by sand and the land became desert. The region never regained its population or prosperity.

Genghis Khan's Heritage

Genghis died in 1227 at the age of seventy-two, as a result of falling from a horse while hunting. The guards who escorted his cortege back to Mongolia left nothing but death behind, for any living thing unlucky enough to have encountered the procession was slaughtered. Finally, at home in Mongolia, he was buried on top of Mount Burkan-Kaldun, a site he had loved since his youth. He is still revered by his people as Genghis the Heaven-Sent, and many Mongols hold the messianic hope that one day he will rise again and lead them to new glory.

To his immediate successors, Genghis left two main legacies, as a conqueror and as a law-giving administrator.

✵ Mongol Captives. These prisoners are placed in cangues (neck pillories) as they are led off by their captors. Mongols massacred millions of their captives, drove them in front of their assault troops as moat fillers and cannon fodder, or enslaved them.
Staatsbibliothek, Berlin. Photo © Bildarchiv Preussischer Kulturbesitz

As a conqueror, he had no peer and laid the groundwork for the largest land empire in the world. Like Alexander the Great, he was a military genius. However, unlike Alexander, who neglected to consolidate his conquests, Genghis and his successors were superb adapters and improvers of existing governmental and military practices. For example, centuries earlier the Chinese had packed gunpowder in bamboo tubes and propelled them as missiles. In resisting the Mongols, the Southern Sung replaced the bamboo tubes with cast-iron barrels, thereby introducing the first cannon used in warfare. Mongols quickly adopted the use of cannons in besieging walled cities, with devastating effect. Cannons quickly spread to Europe and were in use there by the early fourteenth century.

Genghis was also a master of other aspects of warfare. He inspired fanatical devotion and loyal service from a group of outstanding generals. His Mongol cavalry were the most skilled horsemen in the world. He was meticulous in doing all the necessary groundwork before embarking on a campaign. Well served by spies, he gathered information about his enemies. He also accumulated needed supplies and provisions and protected his lines of communication. Genghis was also a master of psychological warfare. To inspire terror and demoralize his enemies into surrender without resistance, he deliberately committed acts of cruelty of the greatest magnitude and spread tales of the bloody orgies his men had reveled in

during previous campaigns. He made terror a system of government and a method of diplomacy. Any foe that dared resist him found no mercy; any city that loosed one arrow against his forces could expect all its inhabitants (except those whose skills he could use) to be massacred. Thus he ensured success. His career brought glory to the Mongols but slavery and ruin to millions of others. As a Muslim poet lamented, no survivors were left to weep for the dead in his path. The devastation caused by his campaigns disrupted the economies and the trade routes across Asia for a generation.

Genghis looked on the empire he conquered as clan property, so clan members and his supporters formed the ruling class. To improve communications and administration, he supervised the invention of an alphabet for the Mongol language, based on the Turkic Uighur script. He also set up an efficient postal system that sped information and government business across the far-flung empire.

To facilitate the carrying out of law and order, Genghis promulgated a code called the Yasa. In it he decreed religious toleration, exempted the clergy from taxation, forbade washing and urinating in running water (an indication of how precious water was to nomads), and prescribed the death penalty for spying, desertion, theft, adultery, and butchering animals in the Muslim manner. He further ordered that no future decrees of Mongols could conflict with the Yasa.

Genghis also created an administrative structure to rule his empire, and since few Mongols had the requisite skills or inclination for the undertaking, he employed conquered peoples, such as Yelu Ch'u-ts'ai. After an area was fully subdued, Genghis would even permit the remaining population to return and rebuild their cities so that they could begin paying taxes to him. To his subjugated populace, Genghis was surely the most frightful and monstrous curse imaginable. The Chinese had never suffered such barbarities; few of the Buddhist Hsi Hsia people survived, and the Muslim and Christian peoples were cruelly battered. It is no wonder that the Christian Europeans called him the Scourge of God.

Genghis Khan's measures succeeded in the short term, and his heirs continued to expand the empire he created for half a century. In the long term, his plans failed because his people could not combine their pastoral way of life with the needs of governing sedentary populations. Most opted to change, became sedentary, were corrupted by the luxuries they enjoyed, and adopted the religions of their conquered subjects.

Mongol Domains under Genghis Khan's Heirs

Near death, Genghis Khan assembled his sons and grandsons. His eldest son, Juji, had predeceased him. The sons of Juji and the surviving three sons of Genghis and Borte were his heirs. Juji's sons received the westernmost of the conquered lands—Russia—and became the khans of the Golden Horde. This area was the least well defined; its western limit was described as the point "as far as the soil has been trodden by the hooves of Mongol horses." The second son, Chagatai, received central Asia; Ogotai, the third son, received Chinese Turkestan, while Tului, the youngest son, received the homeland, in accordance with Mongol custom, as well as North China. Genghis designated Ogotai to succeed him as grand khan, subject to confirmation by an assembly of Mongol leaders.

Two years after Genghis's death, the assembly met in Karakorum in Mongolia and formally elected Ogotai the second grand khan. After forming an alliance with the Southern Sung, Ogotai and Tului then resumed the war against the Chin. When Kaifeng, the Chin capital, was captured in 1233, the last ruler committed suicide and all North China fell under Mongol rule. The Mongols and the Southern Sung soon quarreled over the division of spoils. In 1235 Ogotai declared war against the Southern Sung, which was not totally subdued until 1279.

Earlier the Mongols had conquered Manchuria and forced the submission of Korea. The Koreans were assessed an annual tribute of 10,000 pounds of cotton, 3,000 bolts of silk, 2,000 pieces of gauze, and 100,000 large sheets of paper. Otter skins were later added to the list. Between 1217 and 1258, the Mongols repeatedly invaded and ravaged Korea, carrying off prisoners and looting the land. For a time the Korean kings of the Koryo dynasty sought safety on an offshore island, but eventually they had to submit. Many Koreans were later impressed to serve in Kubilai Khan's forces that invaded Japan.

In 1237 a major force set out to conquer Europe to secure the patrimony of Juji's sons. Led by another of Genghis's grandsons, Batu, the army swept across Russia and captured Moscow, Kiev, and other principal cities. The fall of Kiev ended the Kievan (or Ukrainian) phase of Russian history. The Mongol juggernaut then advanced through Poland, East Prussia, and Bohemia and swept into Hungary, seizing the cities of Buda and Pest on the Danube River. By the end of 1241, Mongol forces had advanced to the border of the Holy Roman Empire and were at the northern coast of the Adriatic Sea.

Unable to unite against the mighty foe, the rest of Europe was saved by Ogotai's death in 1241. The Mongol princes and generals rushed back to their homeland to elect a new grand khan, and the threat to Europe ended. Batu withdrew his forces to the lower Volga valley, where they remained and created the khanate called the Golden Horde. Europeans had ruefully learned that Mongols were not the people of Prester John, the legendary Christian king of the east, in whom they had hoped to find an ally against the Muslims.

Ogotai's early death and the lack of an obvious leader and heir almost caused a civil war among the Mongols. His widow temporarily assumed the regency while various factions of Genghis's family vied for power. Not until 1246 did the assembly elect Ogotai's son the third grand khan, but he was immediately challenged by rival claimants. Civil war was averted only because the new grand khan died within two years of his election.

To ensure a peaceful succession, the assembly now turned to the house of Tului, Genghis's youngest son. The assembly elected Mongke, Tului's eldest son, the fourth grand khan. Mongke was an able general and made the conquest of the Southern Sung his first priority. He personally directed the campaign and took his younger brother, Kubilai, with him. He appointed another younger brother, Hulagu, to conquer West Asia, while leaving the youngest, Arik-Boke, in charge of Mongolia.

Mongke's death in China brought about civil war. He had intended Arik-Boke to succeed him as grand khan, but Kubilai disagreed. In 1260 he convened an assembly in China and had himself elected the fifth grand khan. Contending that an assembly convened outside the Mongol homeland was invalid, Arik-Boke called a rival assembly at Karakorum, the capital of the whole empire, which elected him grand khan. In the civil war that followed, the descendants of Ogotai and Chagatai supported Arik-Boke while Hulagu declared for Kubilai. The fighting lasted for four years, and Kubilai emerged the victor. He pardoned his brother, but hostile feelings between the various branches of the family survived the protagonists,

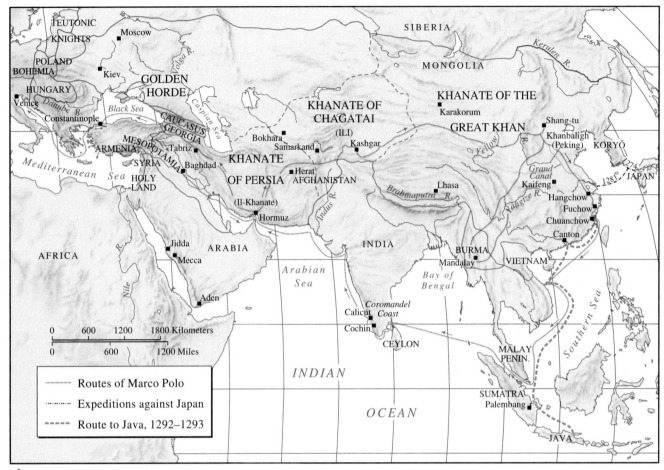

�֍ MAP 8.4. The Mongol Empire in 1255. Genghis Khan's successors added to his extensive conquests to create the largest land empire the world had seen. It stretched from Korea in the east to the heart of Europe. Mongol military force held the empire together under a great khan from the house of Genghis.

and some Mongols never recognized Kubilai as the legitimate grand khan. With Kubilai's election, the unity of the Mongol Empire ended forever.

Kubilai Khan's Empire

In 1260 Kubilai Khan established his capital at Peking, the former Chin capital that his grandfather had destroyed. He selected Peking because Karakorum in Mongolia was too far from major population centers and was no longer feasible as the capital of the empire. He called the grandly rebuilt city Tatu, or Great Capital, in Chinese. In Mongolian it was called Khanbalik, city of the khan.

Kubilai Khan resumed the conquest of the Southern Sung for several reasons. In Mongol eyes the success of a ruler was measured by how much new territory and wealth he could bring to his people, and by now southern China had definitely become the most prosperous part of the land. For decades the Southern Sung government had assiduously developed trade with Southeast Asia, another source of wealth that the Mongols would be happy to tap. Conquest of the south would also bring

valuable political benefits, for although Kubilai ruled North China, the traditional heartland of Chinese civilization, control of all Chinese territories would confer legitimacy and remove a possible source of danger.

Conquest of the south proved to be a slow and arduous process. The terrain was unsuited to Mongol cavalry operations, so Kubilai was forced to develop an infantry force, employ new weapons and tactics, and create a navy to counter the Sung navy. Hulagu helped by sending several Arab engineers, who devised powerful catapults capable of throwing huge rocks over long distances, flamethrowers, fragmentation bombs, and other war machines that could breach the formidable defenses of Sung fortress cities.

The Southern Sung resisted with determination. One strategic city in central China withstood a Mongol siege for five years before it finally fell. Fear and hatred of the Mongols also served to rally the people around the Sung government, which enjoyed wide support as the legitimate dynasty. Despite its resistance, the end of the Southern Sung was only a matter of time. In 1259 the Mongols captured the southwestern kingdom of Tali, in present-day Yunnan province. The Mongol conquest of Tali sent many of its inhabitants fleeing southward, where they found a home in modern Thailand, calling themselves the Thai, or free people. Control of Tali allowed the Mongols to attack the Southern Sung with two pincers. The capital city of Hangchow surrendered in 1276 without the slaughter that had been the fate of many other cities that had resisted the Mongol.

Sung loyalists continued to resist while retreating ever southward. During the dynasty's last decades, the throne was occupied by young boys, hardly the dynamic leaders that were needed if the fortunes of the dynasty were to be revived. The last Sung emperor drowned in 1279, as his last ships were overwhelmed. A few loyalists fled to Annam, Champa, and Thailand. In 1271 Kubilai Khan had already adopted a Chinese dynastic name, which he called Yuan, meaning the first. The Yuan dynasty ruled China until 1368.

Kubilai also consolidated Mongol dominion in Korea. The heir to the Korean throne became a hostage at his court; later this Korean prince was married to one of Kubilai's daughters. The practice of arranging marriages between Korean kings and Mongol princesses was continued by Kubilai's successors. In time the Korean royal family became a mere branch of the Mongol ruling house.

At least once a year, a Korean tribute mission would travel to Tatu, and a Mongol garrison was stationed in Korea, controlling it with an iron hand.

In his last years, Kubilai attempted to establish control over the many states of Southeast Asia. He first sent envoys to the states to demand submission and tribute. If a state refused, he would declare war to force it to submit. Annam (present-day northern Vietnam) submitted voluntarily in 1265, sending tribute and receiving in return a calendar from Kubilai (from early times a symbol of political submission to Chinese overlordship). Later, when the king of Champa (present-day central and southern Vietnam) refused to become the great khan's vassal, Kubilai decided to punish him. To do so, he demanded that Annam cooperate with him and allow Mongol troops passage on the route south. When the king of Annam refused that demand, he too found himself the target of Mongol attack. When the Mongol forces arrived at Hanoi, they found that the Annamese king had fled. Mongol troops soon bogged down in Annam and Champa. The terrain was unsuitable for cavalry action, and the Mongol warriors fell prey to tropical heat and diseases, while their morale plummeted in the face of guerrilla attacks.

Despite the difficulties the Mongols experienced in securing and holding Annam and Champa, the govern-

Mongol Forces Using a Siege Engine. Quick to learn about new military technology, Mongols effectively used siege engines to attack the walled cities of their enemies. Staatsbibliothek, Berlin. Photo © Bildarchiv Preussischer Kulturbesitz

ments of these states also realized the high cost of resistance. In compromise, they submitted to Mongol overlordship and agreed to send tribute regularly; in return, the Mongol forces withdrew from their territories. After the Mongols ravaged Pagan in present-day Burma (Myanmar), the Burmese also accepted Mongol overlordship. Next Mongol envoys were dispatched to Ceylon and Malabar to demand tribute. In the case of Ceylon, they were also in search of Buddha's relics, for by now Kubilai and many of his followers had converted to Buddhism. Kubilai's last costly tribute-enrolling expedition was dispatched to Java in 1292. It consisted of 1,000 ships, a 20,000-man army, one year's provisions, and 40,000 ounces of silver for expenses. Nevertheless, it was a failure.

Kubilai's inconclusive and stalemated campaigns against his cousin Khaidu Khan in central Asia ultimately brought a mutual recognition of the legitimacy of each other's dominion. Kubilai conceded he could not control central Asia, while Kaidu agreed not to make incursions into China. Kubilai's house had now become primarily a Chinese dynasty, identifying with some aspects of China's distinctive history and traditions. Other branches of Genghis's family went their separate ways.

The Last Mongol Conquests in West Asia and Russia

In 1255 Mongke had sent his brother Hulagu with a large army to West Asia to destroy the fortress of the Assassins and to bring about the submission of the caliph. Entrenched in their almost impregnable fortress of Alamut and other strongholds south of the Caspian Sea for over a century, the Assassins, members of a heretical Muslim sect, had been a great menace to both Muslim rulers and the crusaders. (They were called the Hashishans, because they used hashish in their rituals; the word assassin is a corruption of hashishan.) It took the Mongol army three years to wipe out the Assassin forts and to kill their leader, the "Old Man of the Mountain."

The caliph was the next target. Hulagu demanded that he submit to Mongol overlordship, and when the caliph refused, the Mongols besieged Baghdad. The fall of Baghdad in 1258 was followed by six days of pillage and massacre. The Caliph Musta'sim was captured, forced to reveal where his treasures were hidden, and then killed. Then the Mongols overran Mesopotamia and Syria up to the Mediterranean coast, completing the conquest of West Asia begun by Genghis Khan.

Hulagu was poised to attack Egypt in 1259 when he received news of Mongke's death. He left the command of his front forces to a general and returned to participate in the succession struggle. The battle at the Spring of Goliath (A'in Jalut) in present-day Israel in 1260 was a turning point in the history of Mongol conquests. Here, in Hulagu's absence, the Mamluk rulers of Egypt decisively defeated the Mongol forces and shattered the myth of their invincibility. When Hulagu was ready for another test, he found out too late that Mongol instructors sent by the khans of the Golden Horde (who had turned Muslim) had taught the Mamluks Mongol cavalry tactics. Thus ended Mongol dreams of further westward conquest.

Egypt and North Africa were thus saved from Mongol invasion. Egypt would continue to be a powerful bastion against the Mongols, and because Baghdad was under Mongol control, Egypt also became the political center of Islam. Hulagu supported Kubilai, acknowledged the latter as great khan, and was in turn recognized as the il-khan, or regional ruler, of western Asia from Persia westward.

From the middle of the thirteenth century to its end, the rulers of the Golden Horde, already masters of a realm that extended from the steppes of southern Russia to central Asia, launched great drives to conquer Poland and Lithuania. Although they failed, the region was widely devastated and depopulated. Afterward the Polish government invited German settlers to the area; their descendants accounted for the ethnic German minority in the region to the twentieth century.

By the late thirteenth century, the conquests of the Mongol people were over, and Genghis Khan's realm had lost its unity in the civil wars among his descendants. The next phase of Mongol rule would be consolidation, followed by rapid decline. These topics will be discussed in the next section.

The Mongol Legacy

Within the bounds of this royal Park there are rich and beautiful meadows, watered by many rivulets, where a variety of animals of the deer and goat kind are pastured, to serve as food for the hawks and other birds employed in the chase, whose pens are also in the grounds. . . . Frequently, when he [Kubilai Khan] rides about this enclosed forest, he has one or more small leopards carried on horseback, behind their keepers; and when he pleases to give direction for their being slipped, they instantly seize a stag, goat, or fallow deer, which he gives to his hawks, and in this manner he amuses himself.

In the centre of these grounds, where there is a beautiful grove of trees, he has built a Royal Pavilion, supported upon a colonnade of handsome pillars, gilt and varnished. . . . The roof, like the rest, is of bamboo cane, and so well varnished that no wet can injure it. . . . The building is supported on every side like a tent by more than two hundred very strong silken cords. . . . The whole is constructed with so much ingenuity of contrivance that all the parts may be taken apart, removed, and again set up, at his Majesty's pleasure.*

*Marco Polo, The Travels of Marco Polo, ed. Manuel Komroff (New York: Boni and Liveright, 1928), pp. 106–107.

arco Polo's description of Kubilai Khan's pavilion and hunting park at his summer capital, Shangtu (the Xanadu of Samuel Coleridge's poem), is quite revealing about the grandson of Genghis Khan. On the one hand, he remained true to his nomadic heritage, living in a pavilion that was a glorified tent and going hunting. On the other hand, his lifestyle had clearly been modified by contact with the settled civilization of his Chinese subjects. Genghis Khan had moved from one encampment to another; Kubilai Khan traveled among several capital cities. Whereas his grandfather had hunted in the wild, Kubilai sometimes hunted in an enclosed artificial game park. And whereas his forefathers had lived in tents made of felt and animal hide, his tent was made of fine fabric, and its opening was fastened by silken cords. The rapid assimilation by some Mongols of the life modes of their sedentary subjects became a source of tension between them and their compatriots who kept up the nomadic way of life, and ultimately it contributed to the speedy collapse of their empires.

After the heroic phase of conquest was over, Genghis Khan's grandsons were faced with ruling large agricultural and urban populations of many different cultural backgrounds. Since the Mongol rulers were warriors inexperienced in the complex tasks of government, they needed to enlist the aid of their non-Mongol subjects in order to govern. In time, each ruler inevitably identified with the interests and needs of the people he ruled. Additionally, the center of the empire, present-day Mongolia, was economically and culturally insignificant compared with several of the conquered parts. Thus, when Mongol rulers were pulled several ways by the competing interests of their different subjects, the Mongol way often lost. Nevertheless, the heirs of Genghis who ruled large parts of Europe and Asia left a lasting impact. The four Mongol states were:

1. The Yuan dynasty (1279–1368), ruled by Kubilai Khan and his descendants, controlled China, Mongolia, and peripheral lands.
2. The Il-Khanate of Persia (1256–1349) was built by Hulagu Khan and his descendants.
3. The Khanate of the Golden Horde on the lower Volga River was created by the house of Juji; it broke up in the fifteenth century, and remnants were completely subjugated by the Russian state in the sixteenth century.
4. The Khanate of Chagatai in central Asia was controlled by the family of Chagatai; its western part was incorporated into Timurlane's empire after 1370.

The Yuan Dynasty

Kubilai Khan (1260–1294) was the first Yuan emperor of China and Mongolia and overlord of Korea and much of Southeast Asia. He was also the first great khan who was

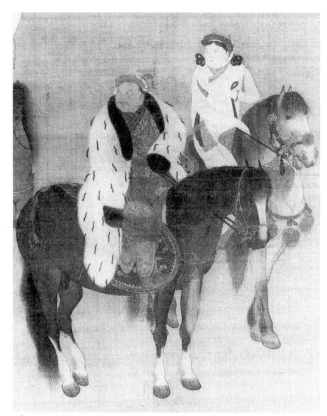

❉ Kubilai Khan Hunting. This detail of a large painting shows Kubilai Khan, clad in a dragon robe and ermine coat, and mounted on horseback, with a female companion. It was painted in 1280 before he became too obese to ride.
National Palace Museum, Taiwan, Republic of China

not acknowledged by all Mongols. As the fifth great khan, he claimed to be ruler of the whole Mongol world and overlord of the other khanates. He was in reality the emperor of China, the largest and wealthiest part of Genghis Khan's empire, but nevertheless not the khan of the entire Mongol world. In crowning himself emperor of China, Kubilai can be compared with Charlemagne, who had been crowned in 800 by the pope as emperor of the Romans of the West. As emperor of the Yuan dynasty, Kubilai ruled from his capital Tatu (Peking), shifting the axis of the Mongol Empire. As a result, Mongolia became a mere province of his expanded Chinese empire.

When conquering the Southern Sung, Kubilai's legions did not pillage and massacre to the same extent that the warriors of Genghis had done earlier. Nevertheless, it was as conquerors that the Mongols ruled reunified China. The people of the Yuan Empire were divided into four hierarchic classes. On top were Mongols, followed by Persians, Arabs, Turks, and other non-Chinese minorities (called light-color-eyed people). Then came the northern Chinese, including the assimilated nomads who had earlier settled in the region. The southern Chinese, the most recently conquered, came last.

Since most Mongols had neither the inclination nor training to staff and maintain an administration, Kubilai relied heavily on non-Mongols to run the imperial bureaucracy. He and his heirs never trusted the Chinese, however, so they turned to Persians, Arabs, and other central Asians of the Muslim faith. Muslims usually served as "tax farmers" (people who collected taxes in return for a percentage of the total amount collected) and finance administrators for the Yuan rulers and enriched themselves in the process. Ahmad, Kubilai's long-time minister of finance, was a central Asian Muslim. He was notoriously corrupt and was hated for the merciless way he collected taxes for his master. Kubilai also hired a few Europeans, of whom Marco Polo is the best known.

Kubilai favored Muslims and other non-Chinese for several reasons. As a small minority of foreigners, they were easy to control and utterly dependent on their Mongol masters. Muslims also were active in the international trade, both overland with West Asia and by sea with Southeast Asia and India. Since Mongols benefited from international trade, they rewarded the Muslims who were active in it. Finally, whether consciously or not, the Mongols used the Muslims as scapegoats to divert Chinese anger from themselves—an endeavor that was partially successful. Chinese writings of this period complain bitterly about the excesses and financial manipulations of the Muslim officials and merchants.

The non-Chinese officials were still too few to administer all China, so Chinese recruits filled numerous subordinate positions, where they were carefully watched by their Mongol supervisors. All state documents had to be written in Mongol, a language the Chinese were not allowed to learn. When the Confucian civil service examinations were finally reinstituted, half the top degrees had to be awarded to Mongols, regardless of qualification.

Yuan economic policy was designed to produce revenue for the Mongol ruling class and not to promote general well-being. It favored trade, since trade brought revenue and rare luxuries for the rulers and their allies. The Yuan government made sure that the roads were kept open and safe for travelers so that international trade flourished and luxury goods were traded among the Mongol realms. To the extent that agricultural prosperity underpinned international commerce and increased tax revenue, the Mongol government fostered agricultural recovery, but it did not allow the peasants to benefit. Thus the prosperity observed by Marco Polo was superficial and enjoyed only by the ruling groups, merchants, and privileged foreigners. To most Chinese the Yuan era was a period of unparalleled degradation. Millions were pauperized and an unprecedented number of people became slaves. Northern China was especially devastated and depopulated; even in southern China, which escaped the worst Mongol depredations, vast acreages were turned into pasture and parkland for the Mongol lords.

Kubilai, like his forebears, was tolerant of other religions if they helped promote obedience and stability. He protected Christians, befriended Muslims and Taoists, and above all paid honor to Buddha. He particularly favored Tibetan Buddhism, partly because the Tibetan Buddhist clergy identified him with the Boddhisatva of Wisdom and portrayed him as a universal Buddhist emperor that all must obey. The magic and rites of Tibetan Buddhism, which somewhat resembled the Mongols' traditional shamanism (animism and belief in magic), were easy for Mongols to relate to. Thus the Mongols of the homeland became Buddhists of the Tibetan church.

Kubilai Khan died in his eightieth year. In death as in life, he was pulled between the two worlds he dominated. He was not buried in a sumptuous mausoleum in the manner of Chinese rulers. Rather, his remains were returned to Mongolia and laid to rest near those of his grandfather and father. A Mongol assembly in Tatu ratified his appointment of a grandson (since his favorite son and heir had predeceased him) as next emperor and great khan.

Kubilai ruled long and accomplished much. He maintained the Mongolian Peace (Pax Mongolica), under which his realm began to recover. His cosmopolitan court opened up East and West to each other, and his lavish patronage of the arts led to wide interchanges of ideas. These positive achievements must be weighed against the misery of the great mass of his subjects. His successors were lesser men who did not share his vision. Thus the Pax Mongolica did not measure up to the sustained and genuine accomplishments of either the Pax Romana or the Pax Sinica, which more than a thousand years earlier had given the world so much.

The Yuan dynasty did not long survive Kubilai's death. Power struggles quickly divided the royal family. In the twenty-six years between 1307 and 1333, seven rulers occupied the throne, none surviving beyond age thirty-five. Many of the early deaths were due to palace coups and murderous intrigues, but some can be attributed to diseases caused by excessive indulgence. Mongols loved a strong drink called *koumiss* made of fermented mare's milk. Kubilai's father and other kinsmen had died early from alcohol-related causes. Kubilai himself drank heavily and excessively in his old age and suffered from diseases associated with alcoholism. In their love of strong alcoholic drink, the Mongols were akin to the ancient Macedonians; Philip II and Alexander the Great both loved strong drink and feasting and were likely alcoholics.

Other factors also contributed to the downfall of the Mongols. The government became increasingly extortionate and inefficient, and natural disasters contributed to a worsening economic situation. As famines spread, so did peasant revolts. South China led in uprisings against Mongol rule. In 1368 troops of a southern-led rebel movement captured Tatu. The remaining Mongols fled northward back to the steppes.

The Il-Khanate of Persia

Hulagu was invested by his elder brother, Kubilai Khan, as il-khan, or regional ruler, and settled down to rule Persia and part of Mesopotamia. In the continuing power struggle between Genghis's descendants, the brothers who ruled empires with sedentary populations, Hulagu and Kubilai, were allied against the Golden Horde of southern Russia and the Chagatai khans of Turkestan, who upheld the traditional nomadic Mongol way of life. The Golden Horde, now Muslim, was also allied with the Egyptian Mamluks. Thus the il-khan's lands were ringed by hostile neighbors.

Persian Muslims were most numerous among Hulagu's subjects. Just as Kubilai favored foreigners and minorities to staff his administration, Hulagu employed Jews, Christians, and Buddhists to run his government and had many Chinese soldiers in his army. Hulagu died in 1265 at age forty-eight. He had held to his Mongol faith, although his principal wife was a Christian and his son and successor was married to a daughter of the Byzantine emperor.

Hulagu's son was confirmed by Kubilai as il-khan of Persia, but Kubilai could not provide effective military support for his nephew and his successors because their territories were separated by the hostile Chagatai khanate. Faced with the Mamluks, the il-khan turned to the non-Muslim West for assistance. He sent ambassadors to the pope and to European monarchs to offer alliances against the Mamluks and even promised to support the return of Jerusalem to Christian rule should the allies succeed in ousting the Mamluks from Palestine. But by now crusading zeal had gone out of the Europeans, who moreover remembered earlier Mongol savageries. The proffered alliance was declined.

Around 1300 the il-khan announced his conversion to Islam and changed his title to sultan in the Muslim fashion. In so doing he also renounced his vassalage to the great khan (ruler of Yuan China), because he was not a Muslim. The conversion showed a growing identification with the il-khan's subject Persians and was also a political tactic aimed at weakening the alliance between the Golden Horde and the Mamluks by depriving them of a religious reason to oppose the Il-Khanate of Persia. The conversion also ended the favored status of the minority religious groups. The Buddhists in the Il-Khanate fared worst as a result of their ruler's conversion; as polytheists, many were persecuted or forcibly converted to Islam. Civil wars between members of the ruling house ended the dynasty in 1349.

Like Yuan China, Persia under the il-khans was superficially prosperous. Merchants benefited from the international trade that passed through their land. A luxury-loving court and aristocracy encouraged crafts

❊ A Mongol Feast. Hulagu Khan, younger brother and ally of Kubilai Khan in the succession struggle, was rewarded by Kubilai with the appointment as il-khan or regional ruler of Persia and western Asia. In this picture Hulagu is seated with another Mongol potentate at a feast before a battle against the Mamluks of Egypt. They are surrounded by standing and kneeling servants.
Warburg Institute, University of London

Mongol Rule through Victims' Eyes

The Mongols rank high among the most ruthless conquerors and exploitative rulers the world has seen. They used armies of occupation to rule and mercilessly exploit conquered lands. The following quotation is from the *Chronicle of Novgorod, 1016–1471*, written by monks of that Russian city, which was spared because it paid human and material tribute to the Mongol rulers. The *Chronicle* recounts the terror tactics the Mongols used to conquer their enemies, putting to death the inhabitants of whole towns that dared resist.

> [In 1238] foreigners called Tartars came in countless numbers, like locusts, into the land of Ryazan . . . and thence they sent their emissaries to the Knyazes [leaders] of Ryazan . . . demanding from them one-tenth of everything: of men and Knyazes and horses—of everything one-tenth. And the Knyazes of Ryazan . . . without letting them into their towns, went out to meet them. And the Knyazes said to them: "Only when none of us remain then all will be yours." . . . The Tartars took the town on December 21 . . . and they killed the Knyaz and Knyaginya, and men, women, and children, monks, nuns and priests, some by fire, some by the sword, and violated the nuns, priests' wives, good women and girls in the presence of their mothers and sisters.*

In the following quotation, a Chinese subject of the Mongol Yuan dynasty bemoans the especially pitiful condition of scholars under Mongol rule:

> According to the Great Yuan system, people are reckoned in ten classes. First, officials; second, clerks . . . seventh, craftsmen; eighth, "entertainers" [actors and prostitutes]; ninth, Confucian scholars; tenth, paupers. . . . Ah, how low! Those who are sandwiched under the "entertainers" and above the "paupers" are the Confucian scholars of today! The Emperor, feeling sorry for these people, ordered that two school professors be installed for each circuit and district in the Chiangnan provinces. . . . These school officials look noble but are actually debased. Their salaries are not even sufficient to save them from cold and hunger. The worst among them have sunken faces, needle-sharp Adam's apples, and firewood-like bones.**

*Robert Michell and Nevil Forbes, trans., *The Chronicle of Novgorod, 1016–1471*, vol. 5 (London: Offices of the Society, 1914), pp. 81–84.

**Sherman E. Lee and Wai-kam Ho, *Chinese Art under the Mongols: The Yuan Dynasty (1279–1368)* (Cleveland: Cleveland Museum of Art, 1968), p. 77.

and certain cultural activities, especially painting and architecture. Meanwhile the peasants and ordinary people were burdened with crushing taxation and financial mismanagement. Many peasants, in addition, had their fields and crops regularly destroyed by the Mongols, as the nomad lords made their annual migration north and south through the countryside. Finally, the il-khans resorted to printing paper money with no backing (as the Yuan government had also done with similar results) and brought on financial ruin.

The Golden Horde

The westernmost part of Genghis's empire, ruled by the descendants of Juji and called the Khanate of the Golden Horde, stretched from the Carpathian Mountains and the northern shores of the Black Sea across the Caspian Sea to the Aral Sea. Unlike the Mongol rulers of China and Persia who adopted some of the sedentary ways of their subjects, the Mongols on the Eurasian steppes maintained their ancestral nomadic habits, assimilating the indigenous nomads.

The khans of the Golden Horde ruled southern Russia from Sarai, their capital city on the lower Volga River. Because they were furthest from the Mongol homeland, they were the first to go their own way. After successful campaigns to the north and west from 1240 to 1242, they received the submission of all Russian princes, who were required to go to Sarai to tender personal homage and to offer tribute in gold, silver, fur, cattle, and young men and women slaves.

The khans found indirect rule lucrative and effective. They appointed one Russian ruler grand prince and authorized him to keep the other rulers in line. The position of grand prince was not hereditary, however, and since the khan could invest any Russian prince with the position, he was able to sow dissension among the Russian princes and promote loyalty and subservience to himself. The princes of Moscow gradually proved their loyalty to the Golden Horde and therefore won continued confirmation as grand princes. In this way Moscow became second only to Sarai in importance during the Mongol period. Mongol expeditions periodically burned towns and ravaged crops to punish disobedience and to instill fear.

Mongol power lasted in Russia without effective challenge until 1380, when the prince of Moscow defeated the Mongols in the major battle of Kulikovo. Although weakened, Mongol authority continued for another hundred years. Finally, in 1480, Ivan III, prince of Moscow, renounced his and Russia's allegiance to the khan. The Golden Horde split up, and after the sixteenth century, in a reversal of events, the rulers of Russia absorbed the

Golden Horde's successor states one after another into the Russian Empire. Russians called the descendants of the Mongols Tartars.

Two major factors account for the longevity of Mongol power over Russia. One was the disunity among the Russian princes, who succumbed to the Mongol policy of divide and rule. Since Russia was simultaneously threatened by Lithuanians and Germans to the west, Mongol overlordship even afforded some Russians a measure of protection against their western enemies. Another reason was Russia's relative cultural backwardness compared with China and Persia. The Russian way of life was less a model for Mongol emulation than Chinese and Persian ways, so Mongols in Russia remained distinct and did not assimilate.

In the fourteenth century, the Golden Horde converted to Islam. This act placed an insurmountable barrier between the Mongols and their Christian subjects. It turned the Russian struggle for independence into a crusade for Orthodox Christianity and encouraged Russians to turn to their religion for identification and consolation. This religious difference continued to accentuate the division between Russian and Mongol and later prevented the full integration of Mongols into Russian life.

The Khanate of Chagatai

The region including present-day Chinese Turkestan and the central Asian republics of the former Soviet Union was assigned to Chagatai, Genghis's second son. It con-

sisted of landlocked steppe grasslands and was home to mostly Turkish-speaking nomads. There were few cities to provide wealth, but the khans were able to draw substantial revenues from the international luxury trade, since the famed Silk Road passed through their territory.

The Chagatai Khanate was surrounded by the three empires ruled by other branches of the Genghis clan: Yuan China, the Il-Khanate of Persia, and the Golden Horde of Russia. Since it could not expand outward, its leaders turned their energies inward, concentrating on destructive and complicated dynastic struggles and civil wars. Because the civil wars concerned the descendants of Genghis Khan, they often drew in other branches of the clan, and because its geographical position was central to the whole Mongol imperial structure, politics in the Chagatai Khanate came to have consequences for the Mongol Empire as a whole. The bitter internecine wars, especially those against Kubilai Khan, helped destroy the already shaky structure of the Mongol Empire.

The Chagatai Khanate broke up in the fourteenth century. The peoples in the western portion embraced Islam. Mongols from the eastern part allied with the remnant Yuan Mongols who had been expelled from China. They reverted to the ways of their ancestors, staging raids against the Chinese for plunder. This was a fatal mistake: whereas China had been weak and divided at the time of the first Mongol incursions, it was now united and strong under the new Ming dynasty. In revenge, a Chinese army hammered into Karakorum in 1388 and burned to the ground what remained of the once grand capital. The

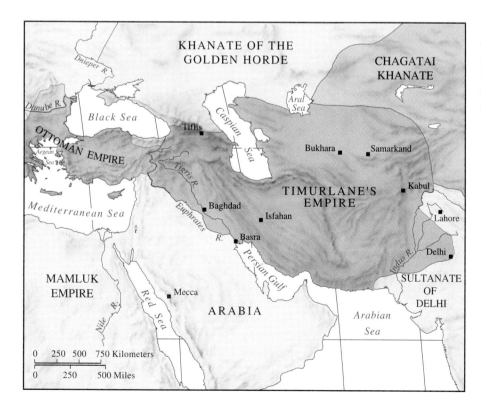

✤ MAP 8.5 Timurlane's Empire. Timurlane subjugated twenty-seven states, and his empire stretched from India to Anatolia. His dream of creating a lasting empire was not realized, however, because he left no capable heir.

Chinese then chased the Mongols further northward and smashed their last pretense of power. By the fifteenth century, only memories and legends remained.

The Empire of Timurlane

In 1369, as the Chagatai Khanate was breaking up, a Turkish leader established himself in Samarkand and began a career of conquest as remarkable and terrible as that of his ancestor Genghis Khan. Known in the West as Timurlane or Tamerlane (Timur the Lame), he first consolidated his power over central Asia and conquered Persia and Mesopotamia. He next defeated and captured the Ottoman sultan (descended from the Turks who fled Genghis Khan and finally settled in Anatolia), invaded the realm of the Golden Horde, and turned north, briefly occupying Moscow. He next proceeded southward and eastward, marched through Afghanistan, and descended on India, where his forces progressed as far as the Ganges

✳ Timurlane's Tomb. Timurlane was buried in his capital, Samarkand. Although he spent little time there, the city benefited enormously from the loot he sent back from all the lands he conquered and ravaged. Paolo Koch/Photo Researchers

valley. He was planning to attack China when he died in 1405 at the age of seventy.

Although a devout Muslim, Timurlane was regarded as another Scourge of God by Christians and Muslims alike, because he plundered and slaughtered his way across Eurasia, massacring Muslims, Christians, and Hindus indiscriminately. His men relished cruelty and reenacted some of the worst atrocities committed by Genghis Khan, such as building pyramids from the severed heads of captives. He left depopulated lands in his wake. Some, such as Mesopotamia, would never recover fully, for his men irrevocably wrecked the irrigation system that had sustained the population. At the same time, he was the lavish benefactor of Samarkand, capital of his short-lived empire. Here he brought the loot of continents and the captives of many lands—to build and decorate a city he never found time to live in.

Unlike Genghis, who had consolidated his conquests and left an empire to his heirs, Timurlane moved too quickly to forge an enduring empire. His empire split up and collapsed after his death. His was the last assault of the Mongol era.

The Legacy of Mongol Imperialism

The Mongol invasions had both negative and positive long-term results. In the short term, destruction and devastation were the result wherever Mongol armies had swept through. The population of China was reduced by half as a result of the massacres and other horrors that the invaders inflicted. Similar drastic population declines took place in Persia and other lands the Mongols conquered and ravaged.

Everywhere Mongol rule contributed to the brutalizing of society; some of the barbarous practices they introduced persisted after their collapse. For example, when the first Chinese emperor of the succeeding Ming dynasty died, a large retinue of his concubines was killed to serve him in the next world. Since such inhuman practices had died out in China more than 2,000 years earlier, their revival can be attributed to precedents recently introduced by the Mongols.

Mongol rule was blatantly racial and helped define Chinese national consciousness. Mongol discrimination against Chinese was especially humiliating to the scholar-gentry. The memory of the foreigners who had collaborated in the Mongol rule of China contributed to the isolationist and antiforeign policies of the succeeding dynasty. Such policies were in marked contrast to the confident cosmopolitanism of the earlier Han and T'ang eras. In Persia the rule of the il-khans helped solidify modern Persian boundaries and sense of identity.

In Russia, where overthrow of the Mongol yoke resurrected an independent nation, the centuries of humiliation served to forge a national, religious, and racial consciousness among the Russian people. Mongol domination cut

The richness and abundance of this great capital and its district is such as is indeed a wonder to behold: and it is for this reason that it bears the name of Samarqand [which means] "Rich Town." This land of Samarqand is not alone rich in food stuffs but also in manufactures, such as factories in silk. Further they make up special fur linings for silk garments, and manufacture stuffs in gold and blue with other colours of divers tints dyed, and besides all these kinds of stuffs there are the spiceries. During all his conquests wheresoever he came he carried off the best men of the population to people Samarqand, bringing thither together the master-craftsmen of all nations. Thus from Damascus he carried away with him all the weavers of that city. Further the bow-makers who produced those crossbows which are so famous; likewise armourers; also the craftsmen in glass and porcelain who are known to be the best in all the world. From Turkey he had brought their gun-smiths who make the arquebus, and all men of other crafts wheresoever he found them, such as the silversmiths and the masons.*

The victories of the Ottoman Turks and the imminent fall of the Byzantine Empire at their hands terrified much of Europe during the fourteenth century. When Timurlane inflicted a crushing defeat on the Ottoman Turks and captured their emperor in 1402, European monarchs wanted to find out more about him. Thus King John of Castile and León in Spain sent Gonzalez de Clavijo as an ambassador to Timurlane's court to learn about the mighty warrior. Arriving at Samarkand in 1404, Clavijo was lavishly entertained by Timerlane, then seventy years old, nearly blind, and in poor health from age and overindulgence. Nothing came of the embassy because Timurlane was preparing for war against Ming China and died soon after Clavijo's departure before completing his plans. Clavijo left a full account of his journey, including a description of life in Samarkand, much like Marco Polo's *Travels* a century earlier. The passage quoted here describes the riches of Samarkand and rightly attributes them to the labors of the captive workers.

*Gonzalez de Clavijo, *Embassy to Tamerlane, 1401–1406*, trans. from the Spanish by Guyles Strange with an introduction (New York: Harper & Brothers, 1928), pp. 287–288.

Russia off from Europe, turned it inward, and isolated it from the advances brought about by the Renaissance. Subsequent Russian fear of the "yellow peril" can be traced to Mongol rule. Mongol destruction of the Grand Duchy of Kiev and their occupation of southern Russia shifted Russia's power center northward to Moscow, whose rulers rose to power as servants of the khans and then led the way in liberating Russia from the Mongol yoke.

The Mongol conquest brought about the spread of the Turkish ethnic/linguistic group throughout West Asia. Turks had played a role in West Asia since the ninth century, but Mongol rule gave them an unprecedented opportunity to expand. The first people conquered by Genghis, the Turks far outnumbered the Mongols and were more advanced than their conquerors; they were as a result co-opted into Mongol armies and administration. The Turkish Uighur script was adopted to make Mongol a written language. Later, most Mongols began to speak Turkish, which became the dominant language across the Eurasian steppes. By the fourteenth century the peoples of the Chagatai Khanate and the Golden Horde thought of themselves as Turks rather than Mongols. Only the small remnants who were chased back to Mongolia by the Chinese retained their Mongol identity, although that was also altered by conversion to Tibetan Buddhism. In Mongolia a modified Tibetan script was adopted for the alphabet, replacing the Uighur one.

The Mongol conquests also reshaped religious patterns in Asia. Though they initially put Islam on the defensive, Mongols in western Asia soon embraced the religion of their subjects, with several important consequences. One was the end of Arab dominance of the Muslim world. Arab leadership was replaced by that of the Turks. Another was the collapse of Asian Christianity, both Nestorian and Catholic. The Nestorian Christian church, found across Asia from Syria to China, had roots that went back for centuries. Both Kubilai's and Hulagu's chief wives were Nestorian Christians, as were many other Mongols and Turks. Their faith did not survive the tumult of events, except in small pockets. The Catholic West's rejection of the alliance proffered by the il-khans resulted in the collapse of a Western Christian bridgehead in the Holy Land, which was conquered by Muslim Mamluks. Buddhism was wiped out in central Asia, but the Tibetan branch of Buddhism was accepted by Mongols in the homeland when Kubilai patronized that church. Mahayana Buddhism remained dominant in China.

The postconquest Pax Mongolica revived commercial and cultural exchange across Eurasia; travelers and their goods moved in safety as never before. Europeans, who had become accustomed to the luxury products of Asia long before the Mongol invasions, were again able to acquire such products.

The demand for luxury goods stimulated the creativity of artisans. For example, the best cobalt was mined in Persia, and the best porcelain was made in China. During the Yuan, Persian cobalt was brought to China and used by Chinese potters to decorate ceramics. The result was the blue and white china of that era that is still considered unsurpassed in the world. Chinese called the cobalt-decorated porcelains "Mohammedan blue wares." Turks, Egyptians, and Europeans marveled at the thin, translucent Chinese porcelains. They snapped up these Chinese exports and later learned to make porcelains themselves. Early Turkish porcelains made in Isnik and European porcelains such as Delft ware showed distinct Chinese influence. Persians adapted Chinese portrait painting techniques to produce miniature paintings.

New Dynasties in West Asia

History makes us acquainted with the conditions of past nations as they are reflected in their national character. The writing of history requires numerous sources and much varied knowledge. Historians . . . have committed frequent errors in the stories and events they reported. This is especially the case with figures, either of sums of money or of soldiers. . . . They offer good opportunity for false information. A hidden pitfall in historiography is disregard for the fact that conditions within nations and races change with the change of periods and the passage of time. When politically ambitious men overcome the ruling dynasty and seize power, they inevitably have recourse to the customs of their predecessors and adopt most of them. At the same time, they do not neglect the customs of their own race. This leads to some discrepancies between the customs of the new ruling dynasty and the customs of the old race.*

*Ibn Khaldun, *The Muqaddimah* (Introduction to History), trans. Franz Rosenthal (Princeton: Princeton University Press, 1969), pp. 11, 24–25.

Born in Tunisia in 1332, Ibn Khaldun, who studied the patterns of change in civilizations over long spans of time, was a pioneer in the study of the philosophy of history. His analytical yet encyclopedic studies are early examples of rational attempts to trace patterns of change while centering on human beings as the main instruments of change. In the passage quoted here, Ibn Khaldun could well have been describing the world in which he lived. During Ibn Khaldun's lifetime, sweeping changes and military upheavals transformed the old Islamic/Arab empires and brought about the emergence of several new competing centers of power.

After the disruptions caused by the Crusades and the Mongol invasions, West Asia split into three rival political entities: the Persians in present-day Iran; the Mamluks in Egypt, who had repelled the invading Mongols and thereby fell heir to a major portion of the old Islamic Empire; and the Ottomans in present-day Turkey. With some variations, these divisions have persisted until the present.

The Flowering of Islamic Culture in Persia

In Persia and Iraq, the Mongol ruler Hulagu had established the Il-Khanate dynasty, which had practiced religious toleration. Although the early il-khans had favored Buddhism, the majority of their subjects remained Muslim. In hopes of converting the il-khanids to Christianity, several popes sent missions to the capital of Tabriz, but these attempts failed. Over successive decades, il-khans intermarried with Persian or Turkish Muslims, converted to Islam, and adopted the Persian language, known as Farsi (the Persian word for "Persian").

During the Arab conquests, Persian culture and language had been preserved and, as noted in the discussion of the early Islamic empires, had influenced many Islamic/Arab cultural forms, including art, architecture, and literature. Persian writers, particularly Firdawsi (c. 920–1020) in the *Shahnama* (Book of Shahs), helped to glorify and popularize Persian history. Just as Homer's *Iliad* and the Chinese Book of History relate tales from the mythological and ancient past, so, too, does the exceedingly long, 120,000-line *Shahnama* chronicle Persian history. The hero, Rustam, with his trusty horse Rakhsh, slays enemies, falls in love, mistakenly kills his own son, and lives over 500 years. This massive epic remains one of the greatest Persian cultural achievements.

As a result of the Mongol conquest, Persia had been freed from Arab domination, and it subsequently continued to develop along separate linguistic, political, and cultural lines. Persian became the language of the court and later heavily influenced literary Turkish. The il-khanids introduced Chinese and Indian cultural influences and thereby freed Persian artists and scholars from some of the more puritanical constraints of Islamic/Arab culture. For example, the depiction of the human form, discouraged by strict adherents to Islam, became fairly commonplace among Persian artists. The vibrant Persian literary tradition, which developed separately from the Arabic tradition, furthered the division between the two societies, as did the continued predominance of Shi'i practices and interpretations of Islam among most Persians.

Persian poetry exemplifies these new influences. Persian poetry had already been heavily influenced by Sufism, or Islamic mysticism, which was generally frowned upon by Sunni Muslim communities. Sufis advocated using a variety of modes, including dance, music, poetry, and song, to attain unity with God.

Under the il-khans, Persian poetry developed in several innovative ways. New meters and subject matter were introduced, as were rhyming couplets. As a result, Persian poetry—and, for that matter, other cultural fields—became more varied than the Arabic forms, which tended to remain static and traditional. Persian poets composed long epic and lyrical poems celebrating love, wine, women, and song. Rhyming quatrains such as the following from *The Rubaiyat* by Omar Khayyam, who was also a noted astronomer, remain among the most widely read and quoted poetical works in the world:

> Here with a little Bread beneath the Bough,
> A Flask of Wine, a Book of Verse– and Thou,
> Beside me singing in the Wilderness–
> Oh, Wilderness were Paradise enow!
>
> . . . .
>
> The moving finger writes; and, having writ,
> Moves on: nor all your piety nor wit
>   Shall lure it back to cancel half a line,
> Nor all your tears wash out a word of it.

Following the collapse of the Il-Khanate and the chaos of Timurlane's invasions, a powerful new dynasty, the Safavids, emerged in Persia. The Safavids perpetuated and augmented the Persian cultural identity. The dichotomy between Persian and Arab societies–although both remained Islamic–has persisted until the present.

Mamluk Dynasties

With the destruction of the Islamic state in Baghdad, Egypt became another center for Muslim cultural expression under the patronage of the new Mamluk dynasties. The first Mamluks, mostly of Turkish and Mongol origin, were former slaves and professional soldiers. These slaves were brought from outside Muslim territory to huge slave markets in Syria and Egypt where they were purchased by rulers who had themselves been slaves. The new owners educated the Mamluks (literally, those possessed or owned) and then freed them in a formal ceremony. The newly freed slaves were given a state subsidy and entered the service of the ruling households. The slaves became the masters following the collapse of the Ayyubids, the descendants of Salah ed-Din's dynasty.

The Mamluks did not follow the principle of hereditary succession. A son did not inherit his father's position; instead, power was passed on to new slaves who had been raised to become generals or administrators. Although this process ensured a degree of upward mobility and a constant infusion of new, ambitious leaders, it also frequently led to bloody struggles for power. Indeed, the average reign of a Mamluk sultan was only six years. Throughout history, dynasties and governments have struggled with the problems posed by rules of succession and the passing on of leadership (see Comparative Essays 4 and 5).

The first twenty-four Mamluk rulers were known as the Bahri (river rulers); they were followed by a succession of so-called Burji (tower Mamluks), who took their name from having been quartered in the towers of the Citadel fortress, overlooking the city of Cairo. The Burji Mamluks were predominantly Circassian (a region in the Caucasus) in origin. The Mamluks successfully maintained Egyptian control over the Syrian provinces and,

under Baybars (reigned 1260–1277), succeeded in driving the crusaders out of the region. Crucially, they also succeeded in repelling four major invasions by the Mongols. Unable to extend his authority over North Africa, and with a keen sense of power politics, Baybars established alliances with potential enemies, including Sicily, Seville, and the Turks.

Mamluk government was based on a strictly hierarchical, feudal system of allegiance of vassals to higher-ranking officials. In addition to their obvious military prowess, the Mamluks were also known for their cruelty and corruption, and as zealous converts to Islam, they were not as tolerant of minorities as their predecessors. Essentially foreign rulers, the Mamluks excluded most Egyptians from positions of authority, and many never learned Arabic.

The Mamluks sought to legitimize their rule by fervent support of Islamic institutions. Although many of them

Mausoleum of Qait Bey (reigned 1468–1495). The mausoleum includes a fountain and a monastery, as well as the tomb chamber. Like many Mamluks, Qait Bey was a great builder, and more than a dozen monuments by his architects remain in present-day Cairo. Qait Bey had been a slave purchased for about $130; an outstanding soldier, he worked his way to the commanding position and ultimately became a renowned Mamluk sultan. A. F. Kersting

✳ Mamluk Painted Manuscript. This painting depicts the fable of the clever hare and the foolish lion. The lion is deceived by his reflection in the water and is about to leap in after his "enemy." Meanwhile, the hare remains securely seated. The rocks are painted in tones of pink and orange, and the water is a vivid blue. Bodleian Library

were not personally religious, the Mamluks gave sanctuary to the exiled Abbasid caliph (Islam's spiritual leader) from Baghdad. Successive caliphs had no real power, but the presence of the caliphate in Cairo gave the Mamluks legal authority throughout much of the Islamic world. The acceptance of Mamluk authority by the holy cities of Mecca and Medina provided a further stamp of legitimacy.

By protecting the trade routes and encouraging commercial activities, the Mamluks made Egypt the most prosperous Islamic state during much of the fourteenth and fifteenth centuries. Because the Mamluks were keen patrons of the arts, they encouraged artisans, particularly metalworkers and textile manufacturers, to settle in their territories, often providing them with substantial financial rewards. However, Mamluk attempts to monopolize the trade in luxury goods and heavy taxation ultimately caused many merchants to shift their activities away from Egypt.

The Mamluks also supported building trades and social welfare projects. Many of the medieval monuments remaining in the modern city of Cairo date from the period of Mamluk rule. In addition to huge complexes of hospitals, schools, and mosques, they erected massive mausoleums for themselves and their wives and children. The great Islamic university, al-Azhar, and other Islamic schools, prospered under Mamluk patronage. Scholars from throughout the Islamic world flocked to Egypt, which became a center of intellectual activity.

The life of Ibn Khaldun, the best known of these scholars, demonstrates the overriding cultural unity of the Islamic world, a unity that persisted despite continual political upheavals and divisions. At various times in his life, Ibn Khaldun worked in his native Tunisia and in Morocco, Granada (the last Muslim stronghold in Spain), and Egypt. He was sent as an emissary to negotiate with the king of Castille in Spain, and he even met with Timurlane after the fall of Damascus. Not surprisingly, Ibn Khaldun's historical studies deal extensively with the problems of establishing good government and the negative effects created by political rivalries.

Despite the insights of Ibn Khaldun, the Mamluks continued their perpetual infighting, which seriously undermined their power and made them increasingly vulnerable to outside threats. Failing to forge a united front, the Mamluks fell in 1517 to the superior political and military organization of the Ottoman Turks.

The House of Osman

When the nomadic Turkish tribes converted to Islam, they devoted their traditional warrior way of life to protecting their new religion from internal and external threats. Turkish warriors, adherents to Sunni Islam, viewed themselves as the "guardians" of Islam and fought tenaciously along the religious frontier between Islam and Christianity, particularly against the Byzantine Empire. Known as *ghazis,* these warriors amassed booty and slaves in their fights against the enemies of Islam, and many of their leaders established separate emirates (principalities). One of the Turkish emirs, Osman (reigned 1299–1326), was the founder of one of the greatest world empires, the Ottoman Empire (*Ottoman* is an Italian corruption of Osman). Between 1300 and 1320, Osman, leading his ghazi warriors personally into battle, began to extend his authority from his capital at Bursa out into the Anatolian Peninsula.

Clearly, the army was a key institution in the creation of the Ottoman Empire. Originally, the army was composed mostly of volunteers from the nomadic Turkish tribes, but as it grew, recruitment and organization were formalized. As Osman's power increased, other ghazis, attracted by the promise of wealth, joined him. These Islamic warriors were guided by a strict code of behavior, similar to the European knights' code of chivalry.

The creation of the *janissary corps* (from the Turkish term *yeni cheri,* or new soldiers) was a uniquely Ottoman military innovation. Male child slaves taken from predominantly Christian communities under Ottoman control became janissaries, trained from childhood to become professional soldiers. The janissaries learned Turkish, became Muslims, and owed loyalty only to their immediate superiors and to the Ottoman rulers. Like the professional warriors in ancient Sparta and the samurai warriors in Japan, the janissaries became known for their fighting zeal and professionalism. They lived, ate, and fought together and became a highly cohesive force. Janissaries did not marry until they retired from active military service, and even after marriage, they often continued to take their meals with their colleagues.

When the empire was at its zenith, the janissaries were a key force in the expansion and power of the state. As the sultans became weaker and less dynamic, however, the janissaries often revolted against them. Not infrequently, the sultans, like Roman emperors under the control of their personal bodyguards, ruled only at the pleasure of the janissaries, who had the power to oust or even to assassinate them. But the potential threat of the janissary forces was not evident during the early centuries of Ottoman rule. Wisely, Osman and his son Orhan (reigned 1326–1360) willingly accepted outside recruits and formed alliances with Greeks in the captured territories. Such alliances, often reinforced through marriage (for example, Orhan married the daughter of a Greek noble), helped the Ottomans to consolidate their conquered territories.

Ottoman rulers gave land to soldiers as a reward for bravery and success on the battlefield; as a result, some soldiers held huge fiefs and retired as wealthy landown-ers who frequently hired overseers to manage their holdings. Similarly, the collection of taxes was often "farmed out" to professional tax collectors, a system that resulted in pervasive abuses and corruption. Booty from war and revenues from the tax on land remained the two major sources of income for the Ottoman Turks, who generally looked down on business and trade. Although the Ottoman government encouraged trade and kept the trade routes in good repair, the commercial life of the empire was in the hands of non-Muslim and non-Turkish merchants and artisans, who often amassed large fortunes from the lucrative trade with Europeans.

The whole Ottoman economy was strengthened by the booty gained in warfare. Merchants and artisans joined together in *akhis,* which were similar to the European guild. Often members of the guilds were also members of the same *sufi,* or mystical Islamic order. Hence, the religious and economic institutions were highly cohesive. The Ottomans followed the Islamic precept of allowing freedom of worship for all "people of the Book." Through the "millet" system (the Islamic system for governing religious minorities), they granted considerable autonomy to the many heterogeneous religious and ethnic groups under their control. For example, the large Jewish community in Ottoman-controlled lands enjoyed considerable prosperity under Ottoman rulers.

The Ottoman sultans rapidly expanded their empire at the expense of Byzantium. By 1362 Murad I, Orhan's young warrior son, successfully led his forces into Thrace (in present-day Greece and Turkey) and took Adrianople, which became the new Ottoman capital of Edirne. Taking the title of sultan, Murad (reigned 1360–1389) pushed his army further into the Balkans. At Kossovo in 1389 Murad decisively defeated the Serbian rulers, but lost his life in the process. The military defeat at Kossovo is still remembered by the people of contemporary Balkan nations. Through the marriage of his son Bayezid to the daughter of a leading emir in Anatolia, Murad nearly doubled Ottoman holdings in Asia.

Bayezid (reigned 1389–1402) immediately sought to consolidate his own position. He had his only brother—a possible rival—killed, thereby establishing a tradition. For the next several hundred years, new Ottoman sultans had their siblings assassinated or imprisoned within the imperial palaces. Having secured sole possession of the leadership, Bayezid then moved to avenge his father's death with further victories in Europe. He surrounded Constantinople and closed the Bosporus and the Dardanelles.

In the face of this renewed threat to Christian authority over Constantinople, rulers in Europe, particularly Sigismund, the king of Hungary and later Holy Roman Emperor, were roused to action. Bayezid forsook the siege of Constantinople to meet the crusading Christian forces at Nicopolis in 1396. Attacking directly into the center of the Ottoman forces, the Europeans were routed, and many were taken as slaves or held for ransom. Enjoying the fruits of victory, Bayezid was the first Ottoman sultan to establish the trappings of a royal court.

Had Bayezid concentrated on the Balkan territories, he might have continued to enjoy unparalleled military success; however, he aimed to extend Ottoman control over all of Asia Minor, and this led to disaster. As his forces began attacking rival Turkish emirates in Asia, he aroused the anger of Timurlane. At the battle of Ankara in 1402, Bayezid's army was defeated, and he was taken prisoner. Placed in a cage as a prize of war, Bayezid probably died en route to Timurlane's capital of Samarkand. The Balkans were lost, but Timurlane turned over the Anatolian territories to Bayezid's sons. After swearing allegiance to Timurlane as his vassals, the sons promptly began fighting among themselves. When Timurlane died in 1405, his loosely fashioned empire dissolved into competing, rival local emirates.

The Conquest of Constantinople

The restoration of the Ottoman Empire was a long and complicated process. After a decade of internecine fighting, Mehmed I (reigned 1413–1421) became sultan. He created a fleet to challenge Venetian dominance over the Aegean islands, the Anatolian coast, and other coastal regions of the eastern Mediterranean. After several confrontations, Mehmed and the Venetians negotiated an uneasy peace. He and his successor, his son Murad II (reigned 1421–1451), fought tenaciously to restore Ottoman control over most of the Balkans and even raided into Hungary. Known for his piety and adherence to the ghazi warrior traditions, Murad attracted a loyal following of old Ottoman families. He resumed the siege of Constantinople, but renewed revolts in Asia Minor forced him to lift it.

Under Murad's patronage, Turkish arts flourished. A new literary tradition glorifying the warrior ethos of the early Ottomans developed and gained popularity. Murad

✳ MAP 8.6 Ottoman Empire in 1461. From its small territory in central Anatolia, the Ottoman Empire had defeated the old Byzantine Empire, making Istanbul its new capital. From there the Ottomans conquered much of the rest of the Anatolian Peninsula and the Balkans, known as Rumeli.

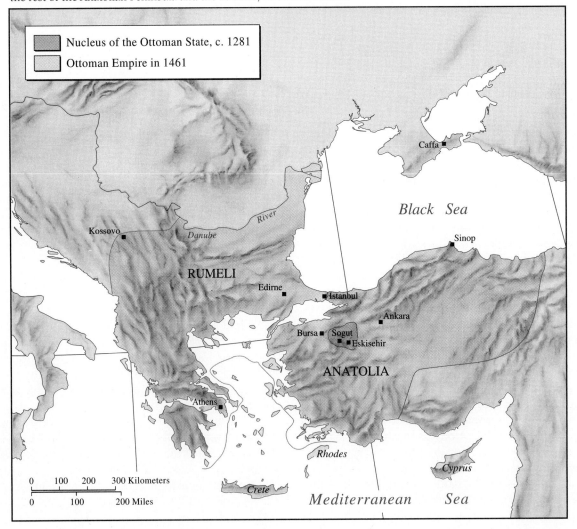

The Last Day of the Roman Empire

Sultan Mehmed . . . saw that the palisade and the other part of the wall that had been destroyed were now empty of men. Realizing from this that the defenders had fled and that the wall was deserted, he shouted out: "Friends, we have the City!" . . . So saying, he led them himself. . . . Then a great slaughter occurred . . . men, women, and children, everyone, for there was no quarter given. When they had enough of murder . . . some of the troops turned to the mansions of the mighty for plunder and spoil . . . and the desecrating and plundering and robbing of the churches. After this the Sultan entered the City and looked about to see its great size, its situation, its grandeur and beauty. . . . When he saw what a large number had been killed, and the ruin of the buildings . . . he was filled with compassion and repented not a little at the destruction and plundering. Tears fell from his eyes as he groaned deeply and passionately: "What a city we have given over to plunder and destruction!"

Then, with the notable men, and his courtiers, he went through the City. First he planned how to repopulate it . . . so that it should be a worthy capital for him, situated, as it was, most favorably by land and by sea.*

Kritovoulos, a Greek who became a government official under Mehmed "the Conqueror," thus describes in vivid prose the fall of the great city of Constantinople after a siege of over seven weeks. He also is careful to paint, by the standards of the time, a flattering portrait of Sultan Mehmed II, his benefactor.

*From Kritovoulos, "History of Mehmed the Conqueror," in *The Islamic World*, ed. William H. McNeill and Marilyn Robinson Waldman (New York: Oxford University Press, 1973; reprint, Chicago: University of Chicago Press, 1983), pp. 330–336.

---

also paid close attention to the education of his sons. Like the Roman Emperor Diocletian and the later Holy Roman Emperor Charles V, Murad twice announced his retirement for a life of study and contemplation, but attacks by Hungarian and Balkan leaders, who apparently thought the empire would collapse with Murad's departure, impelled his return to the battlefield.

Under Murad's leadership, Ottoman forces easily conquered Serbia, Bosnia, and parts of Greece. Many Eastern Orthodox Christians willingly aligned with the Ottomans who, unlike the Roman Catholic Hungarian leaders, were relatively tolerant of adherents to the Eastern Christian rites; some even sent their sons as hostages to the sultan, and others willingly converted to Islam.

When Murad II died in 1451, his son, Mehmed II (reigned 1451–1481), became the new sultan. Competent and well educated, Mehmed knew several languages and was a student of philosophy. All Ottoman rulers were skilled in a trade, and Mehmed was an accomplished gardener who worked in the royal gardens for relaxation between battles. He was also an efficient administrator who established highly centralized systems of taxation and bureaucracy.

Upon accession to the throne, Mehmed II immediately launched his plans for a total assault on Constantinople. He assembled a fleet at Gallipoli and amassed a huge supply of armaments, including cannon, gunpowder, timbers, and bows and arrows. Although the Mongols, as previously mentioned, had primitive cannon, the Ottomans effectively utilized forged metal cannon to gain strategic advantages over their enemies and thereby became one of the first "gunpowder empires."

To assist in taking Constantinople, Mehmed II constructed Rumeli Hisar, a massive fortress on the European shore of the Bosporus opposite the fortifications built by his great-grandfather. He then had siege cannon moved into position, and when all the preparations were in order, the actual siege began in April 1453. It lasted fifty-four days. Mehmed even had ships hauled up a wooden ramp to the Golden Horn so that he could bombard the city

❁ Mehmed II. In this portrait by the Turkish artist Sinan Bey, Mehmed II is depicted not as an able military commander but as a cultured gentleman. An expert gardener, Mehmed was known for his love of flowers; here he enjoys the aroma of a favorite rose blossom. Topkapi Palace Museum, Istanbul. Photo © Giraudon/Art Resource

from all directions. With the city completely surrounded, Emperor Constantine called for help from Rome, but by this time most Byzantine citizens preferred the toleration of the Ottoman Muslims to the noted intolerance of the Roman papacy.

Finally, on May 29, 1453, the walls were breached, and the Ottoman forces entered the fabled city. After three days of pillage, Mehmed entered the city and proclaimed Istanbul (the Turkish name for the city) the new Ottoman capital. Eyewitness accounts relate that Mehmed was much taken with the glory of the city and was determined to create an even more glorious capital for himself.

Mehmed II, now "the Conqueror," encouraged artisans and merchants from around the world to settle and work in Istanbul and embarked on an ambitious program to make the city a capital worthy of the new Ottoman Empire. For the Christian world, the fall of Constantinople marked the end of the old Roman Empire and the beginning of an era of Ottoman Muslim control over the eastern Mediterranean.

Summary and Comparisons

The spectacular military and political success of the Muslims from the seventh century onward produced an era of affluence and cultural achievement known as the golden age of Islam. It reached its zenith under the Abbasid caliphs in Baghdad contemporaneously with the early medieval period in western Europe. Assimilating many diverse peoples, a new Islamic/Arabic amalgam developed in culture and the arts. Muslims acted as a conduit for the transmission of the classical contributions of the Greeks and Romans to later generations. Similar contributions to culture and the arts were fostered by the T'ang dynasty in China, the Guptas in India, and the Ghanaian kingdoms in West Africa.

Schisms, both religious and political, especially between Turks and Persians, finally fragmented the Abbasid Empire into rival components. Earlier empires in the region had been weakened and torn apart by similar problems. Weakened by internal divisions, the coastal areas along the eastern Mediterranean fell to a small army of Christian crusaders from Europe.

The Crusades were launched by European Christians of the Roman Catholic church with the goal of ending Muslim control of the Holy Land and establishing European-style feudal kingdoms in the eastern Mediterranean region. Ultimately, the Crusades failed to keep the Holy Land from Muslim control, but they contributed to the rising prosperity of the Italian city-states by stimulating European demand for Asian goods and thus the growth of international trade. On the negative side, the Crusades also contributed to tension between Christianity and Islam and to mutual intolerance.

In the early thirteenth century, Genghis Khan led the Mongol nomads out of the grasslands north of China to begin the conquest that created the largest land empire in history. For millions of people in Korea, China, Persia, the Arab world, Russia, and eastern Europe, the Mongol conquest was a cataclysmic event that brought death and destruction; it also cut Russia off from the rest of Europe.

The empire of Genghis Khan remained essentially united until his grandsons' generation, when, as in so many earlier empires, civil wars led to its collapse. With no tradition of settled government, the Mongol rulers recruited foreigners to rule their empires. As had occurred in Rome and other earlier empires, when the Mongol rulers became corrupt and decadent, their subject peoples rose up and overthrew them. The Mongols of the heartland and those who ruled China became Buddhists; the others converted to Islam.

Mongol rule did have some beneficial effects. The Mongol rulers fostered international trade in luxury items and provided safety for merchants under the Pax Mongolica. The prosperity mainly benefited the rulers, but the new order imposed by the Mongols also stimulated the transfer of ideas and artistic techniques across Eurasia. Nevertheless, slavery and oppression remained the lot of the Mongol subjects; unlike the Roman and Islamic Empires, the Mongols did not grant citizenship to conquered peoples or generally assimilate them. In marked contrast to earlier empires in Egypt, Mesopotamia, India, and the Western Hemisphere, the Mongol Empire did not leave many monuments or long-lasting cultural achievements for future generations.

The Mongol invasions did not destroy the culture or religious zeal of the Muslims. With the decline of the Abbasid caliphate in Baghdad, three new ruling dynasties emerged. Under Mongol and Safavid rule, the Persians increasingly established their own linguistic and cultural traditions, some aspects of which were heavily influenced by the Chinese, Indian, and Sufi (Islamic mysticism) traditions.

The Mamluks, former slaves, established their own dynasties in Egypt and greater Syria. They helped to preserve Islamic traditions and encouraged architecture and the arts, but political disunity led to their defeat.

Beginning in the thirteenth century, the Turkish leader Osman and his successors extended Ottoman control into Europe and across Anatolia, forming a frontier society based on a strict code of conduct and adherence to Islam. Despite a temporary setback at the hands of Timurlane in Asia, by the mid-fifteenth century the Ottomans were in control of most of the Balkans and Anatolia. In 1453 Mehmed II took Constantinople, destroying the last vestiges of the Byzantine Empire. The city, known to the Turks as Istanbul, became the new capital of the Ottoman Empire. As in China under the Sui and T'ang dynasties, the Ottomans established a highly centralized government with rule emanating from the top down and following a dynastic line through the ruling family. Earlier empires in the ancient world had been organized along similar principles.

Selected Sources

Allen, T. T. *Mongol Imperialism.* 1987. A study of the overall effects of Mongol rule.

*Babinger, Franz. *Mehmed the Conqueror and His Time.* 1978. A colorful account of the outstanding Ottoman leader.

Chambers, James. *The Devil's Horsemen: The Mongol Invasion of Europe.* 1979. A good, short account of the origins and results of the Mongol incursion into Europe in 1241.

De Hartog, Leo. *Russia and the Mongol Yoke: The History of the Russian Principalities and the Golden Horde.* 1996. A good, new book on how the Mongols dominated Russia.

*Fletcher, Richard. *Moorish Spain.* 1993. A short introductory text with emphasis on cultural and social life.

*Grousset, René. *The Empire of the Steppes: A History of Central Asia.* 1970. Trans. Naomi Walford. A classic study of nomadic peoples and empires from the ancient Huns on.

*Hart, Henry. *Venetian Adventurer.* 1956. A good biography of Marco Polo.

Kwanten, Luc. *Imperial Nomads: A History of Central Asia 500–1500.* 1979. A study of the influence of nomads, especially the Turks and Mongols, on the civilizations of China, Persia, and Russia.

Langolois, John D., Jr., ed. *China under Mongol Rule.* 1981. A collection of articles on many topics.

Lewis, Bernard, ed. *Islam and the Arab World: Faith, People, Culture.* 1976. An extremely well-illustrated and well-written survey of Islamic civilization.

*Maalouf, Amin. *The Crusades through Arab Eyes.* 1987. A highly readable account of Arab/Islamic reaction to the crusaders, with descriptions of how the Arabs overcame political divisions to oppose the European invaders.

Martin, H. Desmond. *The Rise of Chingis Khan and His Conquest of North China.* 1971. A good biography of the feared conqueror and an assessment of his place in history.

Nicolle, David. *The Mongol Warlords.* 1990. Discusses the rise and rule of the Mongols.

Ratchnevsky, Paul. *Genghis Khan: His LIfe and Legacy.* 1991. A well-written study, based on the latest scholarship.

*Riley-Smith, Jonathan, ed. *The Oxford Illustrated History of the Crusades.* 1995. An excellent, recent account, with superb photographs, maps, and chronologies.

*Rossabi, Morris. *Khubilai Khan: His Life and Times.* 1988. The only biography of the first Mongol ruler of China and a good one. It brings to life the man and his times.

———. *Voyage from Xanadu: Rabban Souma and the First Journey from China to the West.* 1992. This is a tale of a trip that was the reverse of Marco Polo's journey.

Twitchett, Denis, and John K. Fairbanks, eds. *The Cambridge History of China.* Vol. 6: *Alien Regimes and Border States, 907–1368.* 1994. This comprehensive and authoritative book is written by many experts.

*Wibke, Walther. *Women in Islam.* 1993. Short, readable accounts of notable Muslim women from early Islam to the modern era.

*Available in paperback.

Internet Links

Abbasid Caliphate (Baghdad): 750–1258
http://www.northpark.edu/acad/history/WebChron/Islam/Abbasid.html
A helpful chronology of political and cultural events and trends; part of the online "WebChronology project."

Chronology of the Crusades
http://www.wcslc.edu/pers_pages/m-markow/sscle/ssclechr.html
A quite detailed listing of the year, season, month, and often day of important events. "While by no means complete, this list of significant dates can serve those who start a quest for understanding the crusades."

Empires beyond the Great Wall: The Heritage of Genghis Khan
http://www.com/khan/
Based on a special exhibit at the Royal British Columbia Museum in 1995, this website features concise texts and some graphics "representative of the rich cultural heritage of Inner Mongolia." Includes biographical information about Genghis Khan.

The Fall of Constantinople, 1453
http://www.greece.org/Romiosini/fall.html
An excellent, accurate, and lively account by Dionysios Hatzopoulos, professor of Classical and Byzantine Studies at the University of Montreal.

Medieval Sourcebook: Al-Makrisi: Account of the Crusade of St. Louis
http://www.fordham.edu/halsall/source/makrisi.html
A lengthy extract from an important early Arab source for this crusade.

The Mongol World Empire
http://www.mongoliaonline.mn/english/history/empire.html
This site outlines the following subjects: "Genghis Khan," "The Campaign in the West," "The Army," "Organization of the Empire," "Ogodai Khan," and "Guyuk Khan."

The Umayyad Palaces
http://www.jeru.huji.ac.il/ee23.html
This site informs about archaeological excavations that have revealed remains of five Umayyad palaces below the Temple Mount in Jerusalem. Contains links to general information about the period and a helpful map.

European Imperialism through the End of the Seventeenth Century

I came to get gold, not to till the soil, like a peasant.
   Hernán Cortés (William Prescott, *The History of the
   Conquest of Mexico* [Chicago: University of Chicago Press,
   1966], p. 47)

Tell me, by what right or justice do you hold these Indians in such a cruel and horrible servitude? On what authority have you waged such detestable wars against these peoples, who dwelt quietly and peacefully on their own land? Wars in which you have destroyed such infinite numbers of them by homicide and slaughter never before heard of? Why do you keep them so oppressed and exhausted, without giving them enough to eat or curing them of their sicknesses from the excessive labor you give them, and they die, or rather, you kill them, in order to extract and acquire gold every day?
   Fray Antonio de Montesinos (George Sanderlin, ed., *Bartolomé de Las Casas: A Selection of His Writings* [New York: Knopf, 1971], p. 81)

Not only have [the Indians] shown themselves to be very wise people and possessed of lively and marked understanding, prudently governing and providing for their nations . . . and making them prosper in justice; but they have equalled many diverse nations of the world, past and present, that have been praised for their governance, politics and customs, and exceed by no small measure the wisest of all of these, such as the Greeks and the Romans, in adherence to the rules of natural reason.
   Bartolomé de Las Casas (Lewis Hankey, *All Mankind Is One* [Northern Illinois Press, 1959], p. 77)

Cortés's statement, made to the secretary of the governor of Hispaniola, aptly describes the motive that drove him and other Spanish adventurers beyond the coast into uncharted territory, risking their lives and doing battle with Amerindian forces many times larger than their own. The conquistadors not only seized the treasures they found, but enslaved the Amerindians and compelled them to work in the mines for the conquistadors' further enrichment and that of their masters. Fray Antonio de Montesinos's sermon, part of which is quoted above, initiated the Dominican campaign against slavery. Influenced by what he heard, Las Casas joined the order in 1511 and took the lead in the effort to arouse the conscience of Spain. In his many writings, he attempted to refute the argument that the Amerindians were inferior and should be considered the natural slaves of the Spaniards. Las Casas's plea before the king was so eloquent that new laws were passed in 1542, resulting in the amelioration of the lot of the Amerindians.

The urge of strong and dynamic states to subjugate weaker ones dates back to the earliest civilizations. The word *imperialism,* which is used to designate this drive, suggests the use of force to establish and maintain domination. The forms of imperialism varied from region to region, depending on the nature of the governments involved and the level of civilization of the conquered population. In some instances foreign rule was exercised through local tribal chiefs. In others it was administered directly through colonial administrators. The motives for expansion were mixed, but political, economic, religious, and strategic reasons were the most important.

During the early modern period, imperialism was largely, but not exclusively, a European phenomenon. Prior to the eighteenth century, several major Asiatic states also dominated weaker neighbors. In 1453 the Ottoman Turks breached the walls of Constantinople, completing their conquest of the 1,000-year-old Byzantine Empire. Early in the sixteenth century, they conquered Syria, Palestine, and Egypt, creating a state that stretched from the Danube to the Nile and posed a major threat to western Europe. In China the Ming emperors' expansion to the northwest was primarily defensive in nature, designed to forestall renewed Mongol invasion. More impressive were their great maritime expeditions that ventured thousands of miles south and west into the Indian Ocean, the Persian Gulf, and the Red Sea. These voyages, however, were intended essentially to proclaim the resurgence of China, to promote commerce, and to gain geographic knowledge. Because the Chinese established no overseas naval bases and planted no colonies, these early expeditions had no lasting effect. Issuing from central Asia, the Moghuls embraced the Islamic religion and invaded India, uniting the country's many petty principalities. Babur, the founder of the Moghul dynasty, and his descendants established an empire that, at its peak, embraced almost the entire subcontinent.

In the late fifteenth century, Europeans embarked on an exploratory burst that changed the course of history. By then, improvements in navigational techniques and ship designs had made possible long ocean voyages. Then, too, the centralized monarchies could look outward, having attained relative internal peace and stability and possessing the material resources to carry out large-scale enterprises. Portugal, a seafaring nation with a long Atlantic coastline, began the process of opening new worlds to Western peoples. A series of Portuguese expeditions slowly inched along the west coast of Africa and rounded the Cape of Good Hope before a fleet captained by the intrepid Vasco da Gama reached India in 1498. The fear that Portugal would dominate the sea lanes spurred Spain to underwrite Columbus's famous journey to find a new route to East Asia. By the seventeenth century, other nations, notably England, France, and the Netherlands, had entered the scramble for overseas empires, establishing footholds in Africa and parts of Asia and annexing large territories in the Western Hemisphere.

The desire for profit was the dominant motive for overseas exploration. Hoping to find new sources of gold and silver, monarchs funded exploratory voyages. Merchants and traders also had reason to look abroad. For centuries Asia had supplied Europe with luxury goods and spices, essential for the preservation of food and in pharmaceutical products. The cost of Asian goods was exorbitant because each intermediary who handled them took huge profits. Thus western European commercial interests were anxious to bypass the middlemen and go directly to the source.

Competing European powers tried, usually unsuccessfully, to gain effective control over high-priced commodities. For example, the Dutch jealously guarded their monopoly over nutmeg from the Dutch Indies, even going so far as to treat the seeds with lime to prevent their propagation elsewhere. Ultimately, however, the English were able to break the monopoly and established nutmeg plantations in the Caribbean.

Although the importance of religious zeal has probably been exaggerated by historians, it certainly ranks high among the reasons that drove Europeans across the seas. The crusading impulse against non-Christians was still very much alive in the fifteenth century, particularly among the Spanish and Portuguese, whose commitment to Catholicism had been reinforced during the reconquest of the Iberian Peninsula. The Iberian nations spearheaded the movement to convert heathens and to identify supposedly lost Christians in the East who might serve as allies against Islam. Christian missionaries had little success in Asia because the adherents of Hinduism, Buddhism, Islam, and Confucianism resisted conversion. Spanish and Portuguese missionaries were much more successful in the Western Hemisphere, where they compelled the surviving indigenous Amerindians to abandon their traditional faiths. France, regarding itself as the "eldest daughter of the Catholic church," sent missionaries to Indochina and other areas of the world. Although not as zealous to win converts, the Protestant Netherlands and England used their colonies to rid themselves of religious dissenters.

The lure of adventure was another factor prompting Europeans to probe the unknown. They yearned to see for themselves the distant lands and cultures that were so different from their own. Stories about exotic lands in Asia had been popularized by early travelers like Marco Polo, and many other tales told of the mythical Christian kingdom of Prester John in Africa.

Finally, national rivalry also stimulated imperialism. In the seventeenth century, the English, Dutch, and French governments joined in the search for trade and empire partly because of nationalistic hostility toward Spain and Portugal. Not only did they compete against one another for new lands, but they frequently intruded into the overseas colonial possessions of Spain and Portugal.

Several different patterns of European colonization emerged during this period. The first and oldest form was the fortified trading post, initially established by the Portuguese and later emulated by other European powers in Africa and East Asia. As European states expanded, they often conquered territories possessing the desired commodities. For example, Spain seized control of the gold and silver supplies of Mexico and Peru; the Dutch took over much of the spice trade by conquering most of the East Indian islands; and many of the imperialist European nations annexed sugar-producing regions in the Caribbean and Brazil. When there were not enough indigenous laborers to work the sugar plantations, black slaves were imported in large numbers from Africa, thereby altering the racial composition of many parts of the Western Hemisphere.

Beginning in the seventeenth century, the English and the French, in particular, created "new Europes," or areas in which a flood of European immigrants replaced the small local populations. Colonies of settlements were established for various economic, political, and religious reasons. The English, Dutch, and French created such colonies on the eastern coast of North America. Spanish and Portuguese settlers had come a century earlier and, in spite of their scant numbers, had succeeded in transplanting key aspects of European culture to Latin America. Western Europeans did not attempt to form settlements in Asia, where the dense population provided sufficient labor for their economic exploitation.

Chapter
9

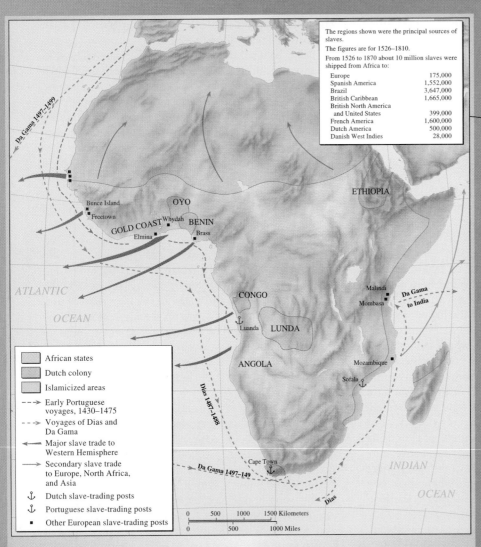

The regions shown were the principal sources of slaves.

The figures are for 1526–1810.

From 1526 to 1870 about 10 million slaves were shipped from Africa to:

Europe	175,000
Spanish America	1,552,000
Brazil	3,647,000
British Caribbean	1,665,000
British North America and United States	399,000
French America	1,600,000
Dutch America	500,000
Danish West Indies	28,000

Legend:
- African states
- Dutch colony
- Islamicized areas
- ---→ Early Portuguese voyages, 1430–1475
- --→ Voyages of Dias and Da Gama
- ←— Major slave trade to Western Hemisphere
- → Secondary slave trade to Europe, North Africa, and Asia
- ⚓ Dutch slave-trading posts
- ⚓ Portuguese slave-trading posts
- ■ Other European slave-trading posts

Labels on map: Da Gama 1497–1499, Bunce Island, Freetown, GOLD COAST, OYO, Whydah, BENIN, Elmina, Brass, ETHIOPIA, ATLANTIC OCEAN, CONGO, Luanda, LUNDA, Malindi, Mombasa, Da Gama to India, ANGOLA, Mozambique, Sofala, Dias 1487–1488, Cape Town, Da Gama 1497–149, Dias, INDIAN OCEAN

0 500 1000 1500 Kilometers
0 500 1000 Miles

Africa and the Slave Trade

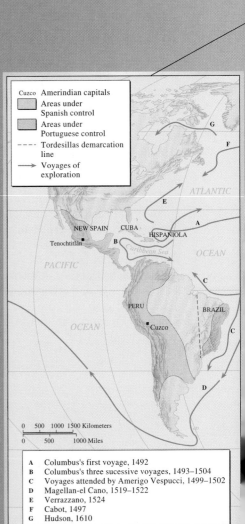

Legend:
- Cuzco Amerindian capitals
- Areas under Spanish control
- Areas under Portuguese control
- --- Tordesillas demarcation line
- → Voyages of exploration

Labels on map: NEW SPAIN, CUBA, HISPANIOLA, Tenochtitlán, Caribbean Sea, ATLANTIC OCEAN, PACIFIC OCEAN, PERU, Cuzco, BRAZIL, OCEAN, A, B, C, D, E, F, G

0 500 1000 1500 Kilometers
0 500 1000 Miles

- A Columbus's first voyage, 1492
- B Columbus's three sucessive voyages, 1493–1504
- C Voyages attended by Amerigo Vespucci, 1499–1502
- D Magellan-el Cano, 1519–1522
- E Verrazzano, 1524
- F Cabot, 1497
- G Hudson, 1610

The Western Hemisphere, c. 1600

Emerging Global Interrelations

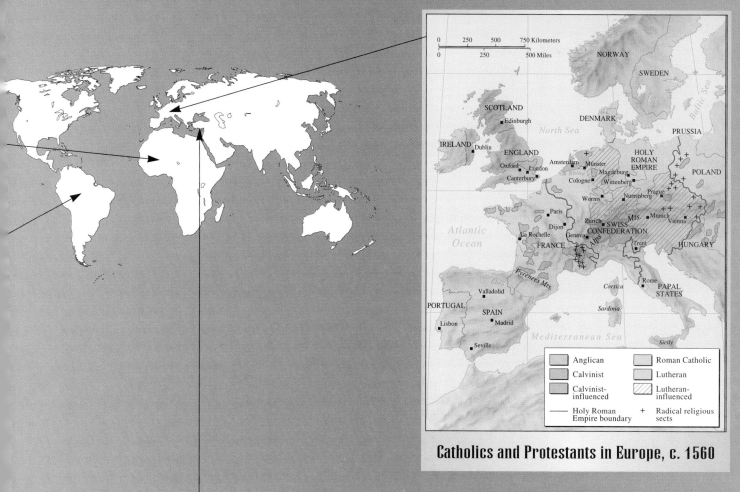

Catholics and Protestants in Europe, c. 1560

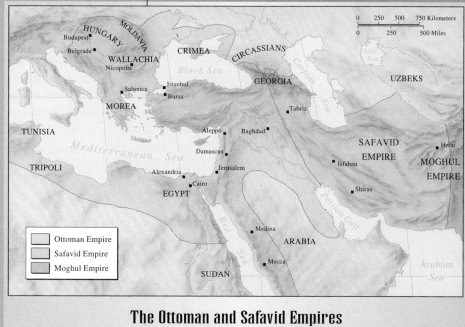

The Ottoman and Safavid Empires

Wednesday, November 28, 1520, we debouched from [the Strait of Magellan, at the tip of South America], engulfing ourselves in the Pacific Sea. We were three months and twenty days without getting any kind of fresh food. We ate bisquit, which was no longer bisquit, but powder of bisquit swarming with worms. . . . It stank strongly of the urine of rats. We drank yellow water that had been putrid for many days. We also ate oxhides . . . and sawdust from boards. Rats were sold for one-half ducados apiece, and even [then] we could not get them. [But the worst was that] the gums . . . of some of our men swelled [from scurvy], so that they could not eat under any circumstances and therefore died. . . . Had not God and His blessed mother given us . . . good weather we would have all died of hunger in that exceeding vast sea. Of a verity I believe no such voyage will ever be made again. . . .

On Monday, September eight [1522] we cast anchor near the quay of [Seville, Spain] . . . with only [twenty-one] men and the majority of them sick. . . . Some died of hunger; some deserted . . . and some were put to death for crimes. . . . We had sailed fourteen thousand, four hundred and sixty leguas [c. 40,000 miles] and furthermore completed the circumnavigation of the world from east to west. . . . Tuesday we all went in shirts and barefoot, each holding a candle, to visit [shrines]. . . .*

*Antonio Pigafetta, in Charles E. Nowell, ed., Magellan's Voyage around the World (Evanston, Ill.: Northwestern University Press, 1962), pp. 122–124, 259.

The (appropriately named) Portuguese ship *Victoria*, which limped into the harbor near Seville on 6 September 1522 with its sick and ragged surviving crew, had made history by circumnavigating the globe. Although the expedition's commander, Ferdinand Magellan, did not live to savor the triumph, his crew had done what no humans had done before.

Magellan's expedition was the culmination of a century of European voyages of discovery that had begun with Prince Henry the Navigator of Portugal. The European appetite for adventure and taste for the luxuries of Asia dated back to the First Crusade (1096–1099); Marco Polo's accounts of his travels in the thirteenth century had also created great interest in Asian lands far removed from Europe. But not until the fifteenth century did advances in shipbuilding and navigational knowledge permit oceangoing vessels to sail around the Cape of Good Hope and across the Indian Ocean to Asia. At the end of the century, Christopher Columbus sailed across the Atlantic and stumbled on a "New World" in the Western Hemisphere while seeking an alternate route to Asia. Magellan proved the existence of such a route by sailing around South America, past Cape Horn, and across the Pacific to Asia.

Whereas major civilizations had developed in relative isolation from each other in the preceding 5,000 years, the voyages of discovery of the fifteenth and sixteenth cen-

1300	Petrarch and the Italian Renaissance The Black Death Renaissance in northern Europe
1450	Johannes Gutenberg's printing press Benin kingdom in West Africa
1500	End of Muslim rule in Spain Centralization of western European monarchies Leonardo da Vinci Michelangelo Buonarroti Desiderius Erasmus Beginnings of the Safavid Empire Voyages of Balboa and Magellan Martin Luther's ninety-five theses
	Spain conquers Aztecs and Inkas
	Ottoman Turks conquer Arab territories Suleiman the Magnificent Suleimaniye complex in Istanbul
	John Calvin
	Afonso I, king of the Kongo
	Henry VIII
	Roman Catholic Reformation
	Slave trade in Africa
	Queen Elizabeth I

1600	Shah Abbas the Great
	William Shakespeare
	British and French establish
	  colonies in North America
	Miguel de Cervantes, Don Quixote
	The Thirty Years' War
	"King" Nzinga in Angola
	Ashanti kingdom
	Louis XIV, the Sun King
	Dutch make settlement in South
	  Africa

1700	English Bill of Rights

turies began to meld the world into an interrelated whole. The earth today is truly an interdependent "global village."

This chapter begins with a discussion of the highly centralized and powerful Ottoman and Safavid Empires and their interactions and confrontations with one another and with Europe. Commercial interactions between Asian empires and Europe had fueled Europeans' appetites for Asian luxury goods and commodities and also helped to foster the new intellectual and artistic climate of the Renaissance, which began in Italy and spread through the rest of Europe. Following a description of the Renaissance, this chapter will trace the development of centralized monarchies in Europe and the religious and political changes brought about by the Reformation.

A discussion of African states prior to the advent of European explorers and traders will follow with a description of the impacts of the slave trade on African societies and the Western Hemisphere. The chapter will conclude by examining how European horizons in the fifteenth century expanded to include the—for Europeans—newly discovered continents of Africa south of the Sahara and North and South America. The chapter closes with a discussion of the creation of colonial empires by Europeans in the Western Hemisphere.

The Rival Ottoman and Safavid Empires

The Sultan was seated on a rather low sofa, not more than a foot from the ground and spread with many costly coverlets and cushions embroidered with exquisite work. Near him were his bow and arrows. His expression . . . is anything but smiling, and has a sternness which, though sad, is full of majesty.

The Sultan's head-quarters were crowded by numerous attendants, including many high officials. All the cavalry of the guard were there . . . and a large number of Janissaries. . . . The Sultan himself assigns to all their duties and offices, and in doing so pays no attention to wealth or the empty claims of rank. . . . He only considers merit and scrutinizes the character, natural ability, and disposition of each.

The Turks were quite as much astonished at our manner of dress as we at theirs. They wear long robes which reach almost to their ankles, and are not only more imposing but seem to add to the stature; our dress, on the other hand, is so short and tight that it disclosed the forms of the body, which would be better hidden.

What struck me as particularly praiseworthy in that great multitude was the silence and good discipline. . . . Each man kept his appointed place. . . . The officers . . . were seated; the common soldiers stood up. The most remarkable body of men were several thousand Janissaries, who stood in a long *line apart and so motionless that . . . I was for a while doubtful whether they were living men or statues.**

*The Turkish Letters of Ogier Ghiselin De Busbecq, trans. Edward S. Forster (Oxford: Clarendon Press, 1927), pp. 58–62. Another brief excerpt of the letters can be found in Peter N. Stearns, ed., *Documents in World History,* vol. 2 (Oxford: Clarendon Press, 1988), pp. 73–77.

In these words, the imperial ambassador for the Holy Roman Empire described the court of Suleiman the Magnificent, the ruler of the Ottoman Empire. While Christian Europe was entering a period of religious turmoil (discussed later in the chapter), Suleiman's empire and its powerful rival, the Safavid state in Persia, were both on the ascendant. Indeed, the Ottoman Empire profited from Christian turmoil and dynastic rivalries, extending its rule into central Europe and advancing to the gates of Vienna. Religious differences also existed in the Islamic world, however; the Ottoman and Safavid states were sectarian as well as political rivals. Although Ottoman taxation of international trade helped to stimulate European interest in developing new trade routes to Asia, the two Muslim empires were far too strong in this period to feel adverse effects from European expansion.

Ottoman Territorial Expansion and Government

Immediately after the conquest of Constantinople in 1453, the Ottoman sultans moved to extend their control over the Balkans. Aided by the rugged terrain in the region, the predominantly Christian but politically divided Balkan peoples repelled Ottoman advances until late in the sixteenth century. Papal calls for crusades against the Ottomans were ignored as Europeans, more interested in economic gains than religious confrontations with the Muslim Ottoman government, sought to establish commercial and political relations.

Sultan Selim I (reigned 1512–1520) sought territorial gains in the east and south. After successfully thwarting

✿ MAP 9.1 Ottoman Expansion. The Ottomans expanded rapidly throughout the fifteenth and sixteenth centuries, conquering vast amounts of territory around the Black Sea, in the Balkans, and in the Arab provinces along the eastern Mediterranean and North Africa.

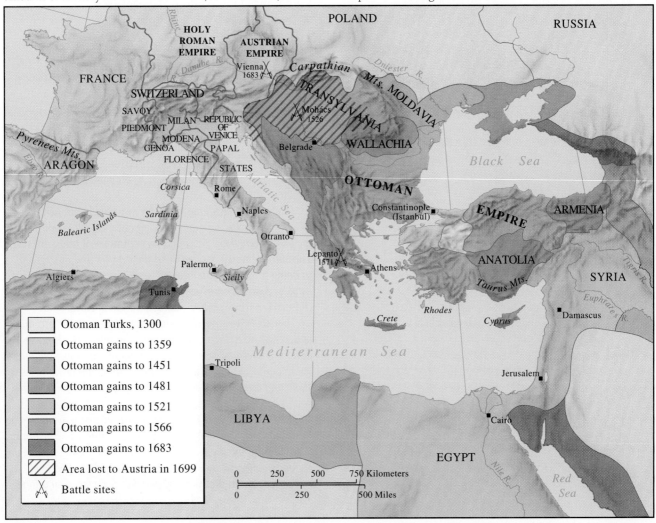

the threat of expansion by the Safavid emperors in Persia, in 1517 Selim routed the Mamluks in Egypt and gained control of Palestine and Syria. The defeat of the Mamluks gave the Ottomans control over most of the Arab world, including the key Muslim cities of Mecca, Medina, and Jerusalem. The Ottoman rulers moved the caliphate to Istanbul and assumed leadership over the Sunni Islamic world. They now viewed themselves as the guardians of Islam and the military might of their empire as the Sword of Islam. Later, the sultans also took the title of caliph.

Ottoman expansion continued during the reign of Suleiman the Magnificent (reigned 1520–1566), when the empire reached the apex of its power. Suleiman brilliantly led his armies against rulers in central Europe and in 1521 seized the Serbian capital of Belgrade. In an age of mighty kings, Suleiman was probably the most powerful and dynamic. He was a successful military commander and a clever diplomat; competing European powers, such as France, sought and secured his protection. By exploiting the rivalry between the Austrian Habsburg emperors and the French kings, Suleiman's forces conquered most of Hungary. His political alliance with the French soon expanded into mutually beneficial economic relations.

In 1529 Suleiman laid siege to Vienna, but due to overextended communication lines and heavy rainfall that made transporting heavy cannon difficult, the Ottoman forces failed to take the city before the onset of winter. Because the Janissaries (the elite, professional soldiers of the Ottoman army) and the cavalry refused to campaign during the winter months, Suleiman was forced to retreat without taking the Habsburg capital. Reportedly, the retreating Ottoman army left behind sacks of coffee, a new product that soon gained popularity among the Europeans.

At its height in 1566, Suleiman's empire included Hungary and the Balkan Peninsula; extensive territory around the Black Sea; the entire Anatolian Peninsula; Arab territories bordering the eastern Mediterranean and the Red Sea; Egypt and the northern Sudan; most islands in the eastern Mediterranean, including the strategic islands of Rhodes and Crete; and the coastal areas of North Africa east of Morocco. Imposing though the empire was, its golden age did not long survive Suleiman.

Like many emperors in other powerful empires before him, Suleiman failed to leave a worthy successor to his throne. Persuaded by his most beloved wife, Hurrem Haseki ("the Joyous One"), to make her son the successor, Suleiman had his favorite and more able son killed, just as rulers in China and the Roman Empire had killed members of their own families in order to ensure their own power or the succession of particular favorites. Following Suleiman's death in 1566, Hurrem Haseki's son succeeded to the throne as Selim II, but this alcoholic, nicknamed the Sot, proved unworthy of his capable and abstemious father. Ottoman military and naval supremacy waned under his rule, and at the battle of Lepanto in 1571, the navies of

✳ Suleiman the Magnificent. Here Suleiman, who wrote poetry under the pen name *muhibbi,* or beloved, is flanked by two guards. Suleiman is clad in a fur-trimmed ceremonial kaftan; the white turban was worn by all the early Ottoman sultans.
Topkapi Palace Museum, Istanbul; photo © Giraudon/Art Resource

the Habsburgs and the Italian city-states crushed the Ottoman fleet. This defeat marked the beginning of a military decline that lasted more than 200 years.

The administration of the Ottoman Empire, like that of the Safavid in Persia and the earlier T'ang in China, was highly centralized. The sultan acted as the supreme political, religious, and military ruler, subject only to divine law. Below him, the grand vizier and the divan (imperial council) were responsible for political and economic administration. Ottoman administration was highly complex and required a multitude of bureaucrats, drawn from an elite whose prestige was based on ownership of land and booty acquired in military campaigns. They were responsible for matters as diverse as the translation of documents and the supervision of the vast royal palace complex of Topkapi in Istanbul, where the sultan maintained his harem, with separate chambers for his mother, wives, children, and servants.

Without a firm tradition of primogeniture (succession of the eldest son), all the half-brothers in the harem were potential candidates for the throne. Consequently, wives, mothers, sisters, and sons often intrigued to gain the sultan's favor. As the example of Hurrem Haseki demonstrates, a sultan's mother and favorite wife could exercise considerable political power. When the sultans were

Elegy for Suleiman the Magnificent

That master-rider of the realm of bliss
For whose careering steed the field of the world was
    narrow.

The infidels of Hungary bowed their heads to the tem-
    per of his blade,
The Frank admired the grain of his sword.

He laid his face to the ground, graciously, like a fresh
    rose petal,
The treasurer of time put him in the coffer, like a jewel.

May the sun burn and blaze with fire of your parting;
In grief for you, let him dress in black weeds of cloud.

Weeping tears of blood as it recalls your skill,
May your sword plunge into the ground from its scab-
    bard.

May the pen tear its collar in grief for you,
The standard rend its shirt in affliction.*

This elegy was written by Muhammad Baki (1527–1600), one of the greatest Ottoman poets. It is a lyrical idealization of the imperial ruler, much in the vein of the celebrations of great rulers as mighty heroes in ancient Greek and Latin poetry.

*Wayne S. Vucinich, *The Ottoman Empire: Its Record and Legacy,* trans. Bernard Lewis (Princeton: Van Nostrand, 1965), pp. 146–147.

Founded by the military, the Ottoman Empire remained dependent upon the army, which, like the government, was rigidly structured. Along with the cavalry, the Janissaries were the backbone of the military. They quickly adapted to the use of European military technology, especially siege and field artillery, and became a major military force of the age.

In this Islamic empire, the Sheik al-Islam was responsible for religious life, and because there was no separation of civil and religious law, he served as supreme judge, handing down *fatwas* (legal opinions). In the provinces, *qadis* (judges) appointed by the central government in Istanbul joined with local experts in religious law to settle legal disputes. They also served as overseers of such charitable religious endowments as orphanages, soup kitchens, and hospitals.

Social and Economic Life in the Ottoman Empire

During the golden age of the empire under Suleiman, Ottoman society was remarkably open. The Ottomans did not see fit to settle Turkish tribes throughout their empire; most Turks remained peasants scattered in remote and poor agricultural villages throughout the Anatolian Peninsula. Ottoman rulers initially made no attempt to impose the Turkish language or customs on their subjects or to force non-Muslims to convert to Islam. On the contrary, Ottoman society allowed diversity, and considerable upward mobility occurred. Under the *millet* system, religious and ethnic minorities retained their own educational, religious, and judicial institutions and enjoyed considerable economic autonomy in return for paying an additional tax. Arabs, Armenians, Christians, and Jews were able to reach the highest levels of society, and some served as advisers and doctors to the sultan himself. Only the sultanate was denied them, for it was reserved solely for the heirs of the Osman rulers. This open society, remarkable for the age, was one of the sources of Ottoman strength.

The Ottoman Empire was at the center of a lively international trade from East to West and West to East that persisted despite rivalries among Western and Eastern monarchs. Istanbul and Cairo became major centers on the route between India and Europe. Slaves, gold, and ivory were transported from sub-Saharan Africa through Cairo to European markets. New foodstuffs like potatoes, tomatoes, and tobacco came from the Western Hemisphere into the Ottoman Empire and into Asia. Coffee from Ethiopia and Yemen were traded to Europe. Coffeehouses became major gathering spots for the elite in Ottoman, Safavid, and European cities. The use of tobacco quickly spread from Europe to the Ottoman Empire, where pipe smoking became a common practice among both men and women.

Despite the lucrative trade that passed through the empire, the Ottoman elite, reflecting the values of a still

---

strong rulers, the harem did not pose a threat to effective government. For example, the first ten sultans, from 1299 to 1566, all led their military forces directly into battle and were personally in charge of military strategy and governmental policy. Indeed, the personal dynamism and strength of the first Ottoman sultans were major factors in Ottoman expansion. However, the less able sultans who succeeded Suleiman frequently became virtual prisoners of the royal court, the harem, and the Janissaries.

Like the Safavids in Persia, Ottoman rulers placed the major provinces under appointed governors who ruled for about two years. As authorities in Istanbul correctly feared, provincial governors often tried to establish their own bases of authority. Generally, the central Ottoman government retained tight control over its Anatolian territories, which lay close to Istanbul. The more distant European and Arab territories tended to enjoy more autonomy.

The administration was financed through new wealth acquired from the expansion of the empire and from taxes. The collection of taxes was assigned to "tax farmers," who collected as much as possible from a given territory in return for a percentage of the total amount collected. As in Rome and China, tax farming became a source of abuse and corruption within the empire.

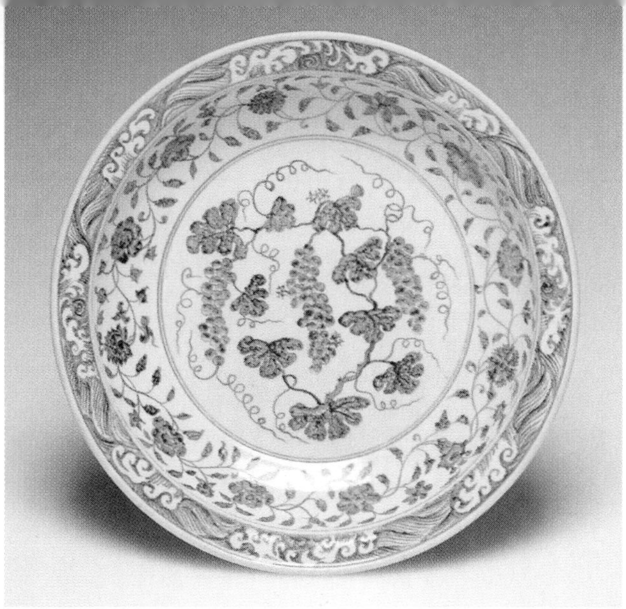
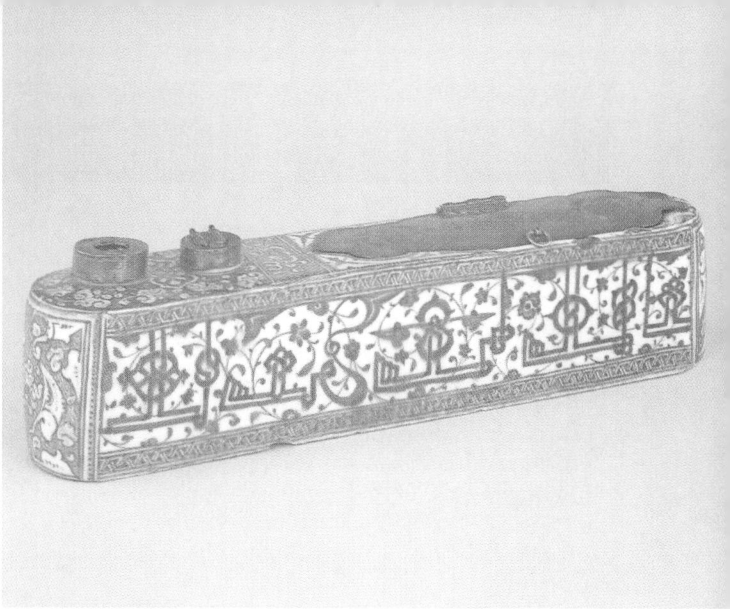

Chinese and Ottoman Blue and White Porcelain. Chinese blue and white decorated porcelains were widely exported to Moghul India and the Ottoman Empire. Pieces such as this large dish (left) influenced Ottoman artisans, who made this porcelain pen box (right) in the early sixteenth century. The Qur'anic verse along the sides reads, "Help from God and speedy victory." (Left) Asian Art Museum of San Francisco, Avery Brundage Collection B65P6; (right) © The British Museum

predominantly agrarian society, held commerce, banking, and most manufacturing businesses in low esteem. As a result, they permitted and encouraged subject peoples (such as Armenians) and foreigners to organize and maintain these economic activities. Under the system of capitulations, which had also been used by the Mamluks and the Safavids, foreign Christians living in the empire were allowed freedom of activity and were exempted from Ottoman taxes and laws. When the empire flourished, these special privileges fostered international trade and increased revenues, but as the empire declined and the European nations grew stronger, the capitulations enabled Europeans and minorities to dominate the empire's economic life.

Ottoman authorities encouraged international trade across their domains in part, of course, to benefit the imperial treasury. Taxes on trade had often gone uncollected in the Arab provinces in the period of political instability before they were conquered by the Ottomans. The Ottoman government began to collect these taxes with more efficiency and, in some cases, raised them. Traders in turn raised prices, which angered European consumers, especially those at the end of the line in western Europe. Consequently, the newly centralized and energetic nations of Europe became increasingly eager to find new trade routes to Asia.

Cultural and Artistic Achievements

The noteworthy cultural achievements of the Ottoman Empire began at the top. According to custom, Ottoman sultans were all trained in a craft, and some achieved considerable artistic and literary skill. Suleiman, for example, was an accomplished goldsmith. Ottoman sultans were also great patrons of the arts; and as in most Islamic societies, literary skills, especially the ability to write poetry, were much admired. An accomplished poet in his own right, Suleiman strongly supported the cultural life of Istanbul in an effort to make his court the most splendid of the age. The Turkish language continued to develop, borrowing many words from both Arabic and Persian. Some poets wrote in Turkish and Arabic. Turkish historians chronicled the development of the empire and the exploits of the military, and although most literature was highly derivative of Persian or Arab forms, a lively folk literature continued to flourish.

Like many imperial rulers, Suleiman was also a great builder. He financed the construction of monumental buildings, many designed by Sinan, one of the most prolific architects of all time. Originally a slave from the conquered Greek provinces, Sinan was recruited as a Janissary and became a military engineer. His skills attracted the attention of the sultan, who enlisted him as the royal architect. Living to the (at the time) incredibly advanced age of ninety-nine, Sinan designed buildings to commemorate Ottoman imperial power. His massive, interconnecting buildings surmounted by domes became the hallmark of Ottoman architecture throughout the empire. Although the Suleimaniye complex of mosque, schools, hospital, bath, shops, and cemetery in Istanbul is the largest of Sinan's creations, the Selimiye Mosque in Edirne, outside Istanbul, finished in 1575, is generally considered his masterpiece.

In the fine arts, Ottoman artisans synthesized earlier Islamic/Arab designs and techniques with Chinese and European motifs and crafts. They decorated Sinan's structures with Isnik (named after a Turkish city) tiles, whose glazed surfaces contained painted floral designs. Clearly an imitation of Chinese porcelains, these tiles still retain their crystal-clear colors. Such glazing techniques and designs were copied in much of Europe. Ottoman artisans also produced textiles, silver work, bookbindings, and calligraphy of remarkable beauty and luxury. The Ottomans were known for their woven textiles and carpets. "Oriental" carpets from Turkey and Persia became popular decorative items among wealthy classes around the world. Although Ottoman culture, like Roman culture, has been criticized for its lack of originality, the synthesis of disparate cultural ideas and motifs from West and East enabled Ottoman artisans to fashion unique objects of remarkable beauty.

The Imperial Safavids

During the sixteenth and seventeenth centuries, the Ottoman Empire's chief rival in the Muslim world was the neighboring Safavid Empire centered in Persia (present-day Iran). The Safavid realm differed from that of the Ottomans in two major respects. First, it was based upon Shi'i Islam rather than on orthodox Sunni Islam. Second, the Safavids maintained and reinforced the separate identity of Persian society and language. In contrast, the Ottoman Empire sought to assimilate many new cultural styles while retaining cultural pluralism. The Ottomans made no attempt to impose their language or values on the diverse peoples they ruled. In particular, the Arabs, the single largest linguistic and ethnic group within the empire, were allowed to retain their linguistic and cultural identity.

Founded by Shah Isma'il, who ruled from 1500 to 1524, the Safavid Empire reached its zenith under Shah Abbas the Great (reigned 1587–1629), an autocrat who ruled with an iron hand. He killed or blinded three of his five sons and, like Suleiman the Magnificent, left no able successor. In the Safavid Empire, as in most empires, whenever the central authority was strong, the local chieftains remained submissive, paid taxes, and rendered homage to the shah. Whenever the shah or central authority was weak, the local rulers assumed more power. One of Shah Abbas's first moves in consolidating his power was to curb the influence of the local chieftains.

The populace of Safavid Iran consisted largely of peasants who lived in small rural villages. There were a few nomadic pastoralists as well as a small urban middle class that engaged in cottage industries and trade. In this predominantly rural setting, the Safavid government was organized along feudal lines, and officials acquired fiefs from the shah in return for services to the central government. The Safavids divided their territories into provinces administered by appointed governors. The shahs also depended upon the *ghulams,* or slave elite. Obtained mainly from central Asia, these slaves were converts to Islam and gradually achieved prominent positions in the royal court, thereby following a tradition in other Muslim empires.

The mullahs, or Shi'i clergy, also exercised considerable power within the empire; like the feudal landowners, the mullahs tended to be more powerful whenever the shah was ineffective. Their authority was particularly strong in rural areas, where the peasants looked to them for both religious and political guidance.

Taxes, land, and commerce were the major sources of wealth in the Persian economy. Crown lands were owned directly by the royal court to use as it wished; as in the Ottoman Empire, state lands were given as payment or rewards to officials or army officers, generally for a specific time, after which the lands reverted to the crown to be parceled out again at the pleasure of the court. Some land was owned directly by the religious authorities; the revenues from these lands provided the mullahs with an independent source of income and also helped to finance mosques, religious schools, and welfare projects for the poor.

The manufacture and sale of textiles, particularly silk fabrics and carpets, became a major source of Safavid income. Soon after coming to power, Shah Abbas added the silk-producing areas in the north to his empire. Although Abbas did not directly confiscate the land, the sale of silk became a royal monopoly. Anxious to expand the silk industry, Abbas encouraged foreign traders and Christian communities, particularly the Armenians, who formerly had been silk producers, to settle in his domain. Although earlier Safavid rulers had persecuted religious minorities and forced conversion to Shi'i Islam by the sword, Abbas was known for his relative tolerance. To some extent, his more liberal policies regarding the Armenians and other Christian minorities, who dominated the silk manufacturing and commercial trade with the West, were motivated by economic considerations.

To strengthen the Persian economy, Shah Abbas established a new Safavid capital at Isfahan, situated at the intersection of key trade routes. He moved a number of Armenians into a new community on the outskirts of the city and provided interest-free loans for them to rebuild their houses and businesses. As a result of Shah Abbas's tolerance and patronage, Isfahan quickly became a world center for trade in luxury textiles.

In search of new markets, Shah Abbas sent emissaries with samples of luxurious silks to Venice, Spain, Portugal, Holland, Russia, and Poland. Foreign traders were encouraged to establish operations in Persia by special financial inducements, including tax breaks. These privileges contributed to an economic boom from which the

�֍ MAP 9.2 The Ottoman and Safavid Empires. By 1689 the Ottoman Empire had reached the zenith of its power and included most of the Arab provinces of the eastern Mediterranean, the holy cities of Mecca and Medina, and most of North Africa. However, the Safavid Empire in Persia continued to compete for control over the region; in spite of numerous wars, neither empire was able to conquer its rival. Isfahan was the glorious capital city of the Safavid court.

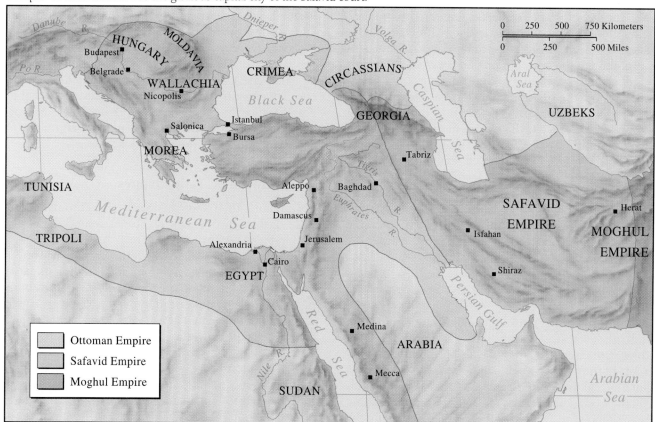

🏶 Persian Silk Robe. This elaborate brocaded taffeta robe in rich blues, oranges, and gold shows the floral designs and styles favored by the rich at the Safavid court. The Textile Museum, Washington, D.C., 1985.5.1, Ruth Lincoln Fisher Fund

important trading routes. His Shah Mosque in Isfahan with its ornate tiles, large entrance facades, and bulbous dome epitomizes Safavid architecture at its best. Safavid artists also continued to excel in painting complex miniatures on paper and ivory. Many such miniatures adorned and illustrated Persian manuscripts.

The Safavids and the Persian aristocrats were conspicuous in their love of luxury items. They lived lavishly and wore ornate silk robes adorned with gold brocade. Persian artisans were noted for their skill in weaving gold brocade and large, extremely fine carpets. Many carpet weavers were women and children. European traders often commented on the conspicuous consumption of Safavid lifestyles. Nevertheless, the Safavids were early believers in recycling. Every seven years the used clothes from the royal court were burned and the gold and silver threads collected for use in new garments. For relaxation, the upper class enjoyed games such as chess (a Persian invention) and polo. The entire population participated in religious festivals marking the Shi'i calendar. Services commemorating the death of Ali (the Shi'i believe that the ruling authority of the Muslim community should have passed through Ali's descendants) and the martyrdom of his son, Husayn, were particularly important; Husayn's death was reenacted in protracted and moving passion plays.

Indeed, much Safavid literature was devoted to religious themes, and the Safavids financed numerous religious schools that reinterpreted and reinforced Shi'i theological tenets. Religious differences between the Shi'i Safavids and Sunni Ottomans were one of the sources of conflict between the two empires. In contrast to the religious written works, romantic love poetry continued to be highly popular, and Persian poets and poetry dominated and influenced literary life in both the Ottoman and Moghul Empires. Like the Ottoman sultans, Safavid rulers encouraged writers to immortalize their military and political achievements in long histories and biographies.

royal court benefited. As early as 1617, agents from the English East India Company arrived along the Persian Gulf and petitioned the shah for permission to trade. By the middle of the seventeenth century, Bandar Abbas on the Persian Gulf had become a major seaport for trade with Europe. The Safavids also enjoyed a lively trade with Russia via northern routes. Trade often continued to move through the northern provinces even during periods of open warfare with the Ottoman Empire.

Control of the silk trade provided the Safavid rulers with the economic means to extend their control over all of Iran. As was true for the sultans in the Ottoman Empire, when the central authority of the shahs was strong, the special privileges for foreign communities were not a threat. As subsequent Safavid leaders became weaker, however, and the global power of the European nations strengthened, these privileges enabled foreign governments, acting in support of their subjects, to undermine the central government and to dominate Iran.

Architecture, the Fine Arts, and Literature in Persia

Literature, painting, music, and architecture flourished under the Safavids. Like imperial rulers in China, Egypt, Rome, and elsewhere, the Safavids encouraged and patronized the arts. The new capital of Isfahan became a glittering cultural center; as the Persians said, "Isfahan is half the world." Shah Abbas ordered numerous mosques, inns, schools, and baths built in Isfahan and along the

Wars between the Rival Empires

Throughout their long histories, the Ottomans and Safavids were rivals for the territories around the Tigris-Euphrates valley (present-day Iraq). As Sunni Muslims, the Ottomans also clashed with the Shi'i Safavids over domination of Islamic territories and interpretations of basic Islamic doctrines. The long struggle drained both of needed military power and resources. Neither was able to deliver a fatal military blow to the other, but the debilitating intermittent warfare made both increasingly vulnerable to other outside enemies.

The conflicts began when Suleiman's father, Selim I, initiated a "holy war" against the Shi'i and the Safavid dynasty. In 1514 Ottoman forces equipped with cannon decisively defeated the Safavids in the northern provinces of Iran, but Selim failed to follow through on his victory. Suleiman continued the struggle by launching several campaigns against the Safavid ruler, Shah Tahmasp I, who employed a "scorched earth" policy as a defensive measure, thereby forcing the Ottomans to bring all their supplies with them. Suleiman successfully conquered the major northern city of Tabriz, but found it costly to maintain control. In 1555 his difficulties holding the northern territories forced him to negotiate a treaty with the Safavids. Suleiman retained Iraq, with the major trading center of Baghdad and a port on the Persian Gulf, but had to withdraw from the northern Persian provinces.

The Safavids countered Ottoman power by allying with the Habsburgs, the major Ottoman enemy in eastern Europe. Taking advantage of the power vacuum following Suleiman's death, Shah Abbas occupied Iraq and parts of the Anatolian Peninsula. By 1623 the Ottomans, now strengthened by internal reforms, took advantage of Safavid weakness after Shah Abbas's death to oust the Safavids from these territories. A peace treaty between these two mighty empires in 1639 established boundaries that approximate those of present-day western Iran.

In spite of several attempts to implement internal reforms, the Safavid Empire never regained the power wielded by Shah Abbas. As a consequence, it was ill prepared to meet the challenges of its expansionist neighbors. By the eighteenth century, tribes from Afghanistan began to expand into Safavid territories, and by 1722, Afghan forces took Isfahan. Safavid weakness then allowed Ottoman forces to move into the northern Persian provinces. Under Shah Tahmasp II, the Safavids unsuccessfully counterattacked the Afghan forces. The assassination of Nader Shah in 1747 ended the Safavid dynasty. With the collapse of effective centralized government, numerous rival, local rulers vied for political and military control until the Qajar dynasty emerged as the dominant power in 1794.

The Culture of the Renaissance in Europe

If then we are to call any age golden, it is beyond doubt that age which brings forth golden talents in different places. That such is true of our age, he who wishes to consider the illustrious discoveries of this century will hardly doubt. For this century, like a golden age, has restored to light the liberal arts, which were almost extinct: grammar, poetry, rhetoric, painting, sculpture, architecture, music . . . and all this in Florence. Achieving what had been honored among the ancients, but almost forgotten since, the age has joined wisdom with eloquence, and produce with the military art . . . and in Florence it has recalled the Platonic teaching from darkness into light.*

*Letter of Marsilio Ficino to Paul of Middleburg, in M. M. McLaughlin, ed. and trans., *The Portable Renaissance Reader* (New York: Viking, 1953), p. 79.

In this excerpt, the Florentine philosopher Marsilio Ficino (1433–1499) expresses his joy at living in a time of intellectual revolution, sparked by a reawakened interest in the values and culture of ancient Greece and Rome. Ficino and his contemporaries scorned what they perceived as the ignorance and barbarism of the "dark ages," the thousand years between the collapse of the Roman Empire and their own era, to which they applied the term *Renaissance,* meaning "rebirth" in French. They believed that they were living in a golden age that had broken abruptly with the immediate past.

Although Renaissance thinkers were aware of the contrast between their own and the medieval world, they failed to appreciate the full dimensions of their age. To them, the revival of cultural antiquity was the outstanding characteristic of their progressive era. Yet artistic creativity was only one aspect of the Renaissance. In fact, changes affected every element of European society—political, so-

✵ Safavid Architecture. The Shah Mosque in Isfahan is one of the glories of Safavid architecture. The mosque is covered in elaborately decorated, vivid blue tiles. © Sue Pashko/Envision

cial, and religious as well as cultural. Nor did the Renaissance develop in complete isolation from the era that preceded it. The Renaissance continued many trends of medieval civilization. The difference lay in the faster pace of change, not in the creation of something entirely new.

This is not to say that there were no differences in attitude between the Middle Ages and the Renaissance. The medieval cultural perspective had centered on theology, with emphasis on God's will, human sinfulness, and a heavenly existence after this earthly life. That outlook permeated all intellectual life: education, philosophy, theology, art, and architecture. Medieval religion had firmly rejected life in this world as evil, useless, and perilous to the salvation of the soul. Abandoning secular culture in favor of a monastic life seemed to many the surest way to attain salvation and please God. During the Renaissance, however, thinkers, writers, and artists made man, not God, the chief center of interest. They glorified the human body as beautiful and the human intellect as capable of unlocking the deepest mysteries of nature by rational processes. Renaissance thinkers known as humanists argued that God in fact wanted men to engage in political and civic life, to create and discover, and to marry and have families. In short, fulfillment within the secular sphere was in accord with God's will. Thus a major innovation of the humanists was to reconcile the new urban culture and life with Christianity and the possibility of salvation.

The Origins of the Renaissance: Italian Literature and Humanism

The Renaissance was an age of rapid transition, linking medieval to early modern ways of life. It began in Italy in the early fourteenth century and had spread to the rest of Europe by its conclusion in the mid-sixteenth century.

There are many reasons why Italy was the birthplace of the Renaissance. For one thing, the survival of the Roman artistic and architectural heritage and the continued use of Latin had kept memories of classical civilization alive. Italy also had profited from both Islamic and Byzantine cultural influences. Trade remained important in Italy, which gave rise to early modern capitalism, and furnished the material resources for cultural development. Less feudal than northern Europe, Italy enjoyed renewed vigor in its urban centers in the wake of the Crusades. Political developments fostered the growth of independent city-states, and prominent commercial cities such as Genoa, Venice, and Milan competed in cultural as well as commercial affairs. These cities gave rise to an affluent middle/upper class with the leisure for education and a sense of political responsibility. Such individuals sought models of civic duty, social responsibility, and governmental values. The urbanized, sophisticated world of ancient Greece and Rome provided just such models

in an extensive body of literature and art. Thus the humanists returned to classical literature and found inspiration there for an active life of political involvement and reasoned analysis of morals and beliefs.

The early Renaissance in Italy during the fourteenth century centered on a few eloquent writers from Tuscany (the area around Florence) who stimulated interest and delight in the physical world. Francesco Petrarca, or Petrarch (1304–1374), sometimes called the father of humanism, idolized the ancient Roman authors and emulated their literary compositions and writing styles; he also adopted the ancient writers' secular outlook on life in his own works. Petrarch as a man of letters gained enduring fame from his poetry, written in the Tuscan vernacular. A keen observer of nature, he wrote tender sonnets and exquisite odes in celebration of his burning love for Laura, a married woman whom he adored at a distance. Although Petrarch expresses real love for a living woman and rhapsodizes over her physical features, his devotion to her is essentially spiritual, so a conflict between body and mind underlies his poems. Being ambitious and desiring fame and fortune, he struggled against the medieval notion that God wished men to renounce the things of this world. Petrarch's work thus exemplifies the typical Renaissance propensity to elevate the secular.

The new interest in worldly life that marks Petrarch's thought is also evident in the work of his friend, Giovanni Boccaccio (1313–1375), the first great Italian prose writer. His *Decameron* is concerned with everyday life, portraying people from all social classes, often with a strong satirical flavor. With Boccaccio, the lustfulness and earthy wit of the lower classes entered serious literature during the Renaissance. In contrast to Dante's *Divine Comedy,* the *Decameron* is sometimes called the "Human Comedy."

Although many humanist literary works were written in Italian, most writers maintained that the Latin of Cicero was the supreme literary language. Shunning "corrupt" medieval Latin, they found in classical literature a purity of style, form, and eloquence absent from most medieval literature, and they argued that to speak and write correctly one should imitate the ancients. Petrarch, for example, developed the finest Latin style of his age. Succeeding Renaissance writers and scholars, stimulated by the arrival of Byzantine scholars who had begun to flee Constantinople before its fall in 1453, promoted the study of Greek.

An important aspect of humanist activity was the recovery of manuscripts of classical literary, scientific, and historical works. Searchers discovered many Latin manuscripts in European monasteries and churches. Increasingly, during the fifteenth century, Greek history and literature became available to Western scholars as the humanists obtained copies of Greek manuscripts through

Racy Tales

Renaissance writers, with their interest in describing society as they observed it, tended to be tolerant of human behavior. The following racy passages illustrate how far Renaissance society had departed from Christian moral restraint.

The first excerpt centers around an adulterous relationship. A young wife, Petronella, tells her lover, Gianello, to get into a tub when her husband returns home unexpectedly. Petronella explains that she has sold the old tub to a man who is inspecting it from the inside. Gianello leaps out of the tub and expresses satisfaction with it, except for an area that is coated with a hard substance. The wife tells her husband to climb into the tub to scrape it off.

> While she was busy instructing and directing her husband in this fashion, Gianello, who had not fully gratified his desires that morning before the husband arrived, seeing that he couldn't do it in the way he wished, contributed to bringing it off as best he could. So he went up to Petronella, who was completely blocking up the mouth of the tub, and in the manner of a wild and hot-blooded stallion mounting a Parthian mare in the open fields, he satisfied his young man's passion, which no sooner reached fulfillment than the scraping of the tub was completed, whereupon he stood back, and Petronella withdrew her head from the tub and the husband clambered out.*

In this excerpt, a wife justifies her decision to take a lover:

> As you can see, Lusca [her maid], I am young and vigorous, and I am well supplied with all the things a woman could desire. In short, with one exception I have nothing to complain about, and the exception is this: that my husband is much older than myself, and consequently I am ill provided with the one thing that gives young women their great pleasure.**

The third excerpt describes a young man's clumsy and crude efforts to seduce a noble Parisian lady:

> "Would you like a bolt of bright crimson velvet, striped with green, or some embroidered satin, or maybe crimson? What would you like—necklaces, gold things, things for your hair, rings? All you have to do is say yes. Even fifty thousand gold pieces doesn't bother me. . . ."
>
> "No. Thank you, but I want nothing from you."
>
> "By God," said he "I damned well want something from you, and it's something that won't cost you a cent, and once you've given it you'll still have it, every bit of it. "Here"—and he showed her his long codpiece—"here is my John Thomas, who wants a place to jump into."***

*Giovanni Boccaccio, *The Decameron*, trans. G. H. McWilliam (London: Penguin, 1995), p. 494.
**Ibid., p. 534.
***François Rabelais, *Gargantua and Pantagruel*, trans. Burton Raffel (New York: Norton, 1990), p. 201.

contacts with Byzantine scholars. Manuel Chrysoloras, a Byzantine diplomat, began a regular course of lectures on Greek in Florence in 1397; his grammar textbook gained wide circulation (it was used by Erasmus, discussed later in this section) and in 1471 became the first Greek grammar to be printed.

The recovery of so many texts gave rise to modern textual criticism, including the disciplines of paleography (the analysis of manuscripts and the handwriting in which they are transcribed) and philology (the critical study of language and literature). Dictionaries, grammars, indexes, and commentaries were produced, and the texts of ancient authors were put on a sound footing by scholars who collected and compared manuscripts. From their careful textual studies, the humanists learned how to assess authenticity, showing, for example, that the "Donation of Constantine," used by the popes to support their territorial sovereignty over Rome and its environs, was in fact a forgery written 400 years after the Roman emperor's death.

The spread of classical learning was accelerated by print. The use of movable type to print books, a momentous innovation for Europe, though known earlier in China and Korea, is attributed to Johannes Gutenberg of Mainz about 1450. The mass production of texts that printing facilitated soon made the cultural heritage of the classical world and, with it, the Renaissance widely available in Europe.

Classical texts were the basis of humanist elementary and secondary education; the curricula included literature, mathematics, music, science, and athletics. In contrast to medieval scholars, teachers and students achieved a direct familiarity with classical Greek authorities in most subject areas. Students who received such classical training excelled in law and theology or became secretaries for princes, prelates, and town councils.

Renaissance historians modeled their work on the classical authors, producing histories of their city or state rather than the universal histories or annalistic accounts favored by medieval historians. They departed from medieval precedents in emphasizing politics and stressing the role of human motives over divine intervention. Renaissance historians were also more critical in their evaluation of source materials.

The philosophers of the Renaissance were proponents of the new humanist outlook. Unlike the Scholastics of the late Middle Ages, they tended to prefer Plato to Aristotle because of the former's superior literary style and the more mystical nature of his thought. Marsilio Ficino translated into Latin all the works of Plato as well as many commentaries on his philosophy. Renaissance Platonists drew on Plato's fascination with numbers and harmonies to promote interest in geometry and mathematics. Ficino and the brilliant young scholar, Giovanni Pico della Mirandola (1463–1494), also held that humans were free, perfectible individuals, with social responsibilities and a dignity derived from their position midway between the material world and the spiritual God. Pico's "Oration on the Dignity of Man," delivered in Rome in 1486, was a manifesto of humanism:

> Oh unsurpassed generosity of God the Father, Oh wondrous and unsurpassed felicity of man, to whom it is granted to have what he chooses, to be what he wills to be! The brutes, from the moment of their birth, bring with them . . . from their mother's womb all that they will ever possess. The highest spiritual beings [angels] were, from the very moment of creation, or soon thereafter, fixed in the mode of being which would be theirs through measureless eternities. But

upon man, at the moment of his creation, God bestowed seeds pregnant with all possibilities, the germs of every form of life. Whichever of these a man shall cultivate, the same will mature and bear fruit in him. If vegetative, he will become a plant; if sensual, he will become brutish; if rational, he will reveal himself a heavenly being; if intellectual, he will be an angel and the son of God. . . . Who then will not look with awe upon this our chameleon, or who, at least, will look with greater admiration on any other being? (A. R. Caponigri, trans., *Giovanni Pico della Mirandola: Oration on the Dignity of Man* (Chicago: Regnery, 1956), pp. 8–9.)

Women and the Renaissance

In the Renaissance, as in earlier periods of European history, education and the intellectual professions were accessible almost exclusively to males. Historians have identified fewer than 300 learned women in Europe prior to the eighteenth century. Despite their disadvantages, a few women did receive schooling in the revived classical learning during the Renaissance; they were typically daughters of aristocrats or royalty instructed by fathers or husbands or by private tutors hired for them. Even in such cases, women's intellectual pursuits were often restricted to their youth, cut short by wifely and maternal obligations of child bearing and rearing. They could avoid all-absorbing familial duties only by entering religious life and becoming a nun, but that choice meant living in cloistered seclusion and contemplation with slim chance of following a career in writing or art.

The problems faced by women who wished to follow intellectual pursuits are well illustrated by the experience of Isotta Nogarola (1418–1466), known as the most learned woman of her century. She and her sister were trained by a humanist tutor; at age eighteen she started a correspondence with male humanists in Verona. Though her letters show great promise and were praised by some, others advised her that she would have to "become a man" if she wished to continue her career as a writer. Isotta decided against both the alternatives of married life and the nunnery. Instead, she lived as a recluse in her mother's home, producing some fine Latin verse and an important theological tract but little else before she suffered a long series of illnesses. As the distinguished women's historian Gerda Lerner has put it, "there simply was no acceptable social role during the Renaissance for a thinking woman who did not renounce her sexuality." This was true of earlier eras as well. Sappho, for example, in ancient Greece, though a first-rate poet whose work was much admired, was something of an anomaly and was often vilified in later times for departing from traditional gender roles.

Despite the unenlightened attitudes about women's roles, the Renaissance did produce a number of accomplished women. Christine de Pizan (1365–c. 1430), for example, was the first woman known to have made her

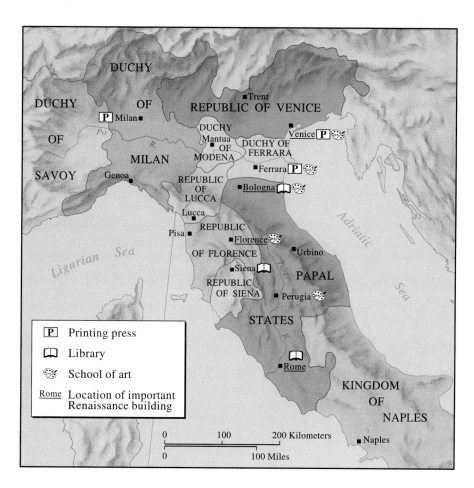

P Printing press

📖 Library

🎨 School of art

<u>Rome</u> Location of important
Renaissance building

0   100   200 Kilometers

0   100 Miles

�֎ MAP 9.3 Renaissance Italy. The commercial vitality and political disunity of northern Italy stimulated cultural creativity. Prosperous towns patronized and promoted artists and scholars. A remarkable number of Italian cities contributed significantly to Renaissance thought, literature, and art.

living as a professional writer. In 1390 the death of her husband, a secretary at the court of the French king (Charles V), left her with three children, her mother, and two brothers to support. To do so, she developed her skills in a variety of genres: love poetry, literary criticism, histories of eminent women, political theory, religious meditations, a biography of King Charles V, and poetry written for aristocratic patrons; her last work was a poem celebrating the victory of Joan of Arc at the siege of Orléans during the Hundred Years' War (see the next section). She also penned a fascinating autobiography entitled *Christine's Vision.*

A number of women artists also achieved some prominence during the Renaissance. The work of Sofonisba Anguissola (c. 1535–1625)—one of six sisters who were painters—drew praise from Michelangelo and won her commissions to do portraits at the court of King Philip II of Spain. During the Baroque phase of the Italian Renaissance, Artemisia Gentileschi (1593–c. 1652), trained by her father and other artists, achieved a reputation on a par with that of Leonardo da Vinci and Michelangelo. She often chose women for her subjects: for example, the biblical heroines Susannah and Judith beheading Holofernes. In another medium, Properzia de' Rossi (c. 1500–1530) was singled out by the biographer Vasari

for the excellence of her relief sculptures in the Church of St. Peter in Bologna and for her great versatility: "[she was] skilled not only in household matters . . . but in infinite fields of knowledge. . . . She was beautiful and played and sang better than any woman in the city." Few women of the Renaissance were able (or allowed) to be so multitalented.

Renaissance Art in Italy

During the fourteenth century, Renaissance painters and sculptors, like Italian writers, drew inspiration from classical models. They could do so because Roman antiquities (monuments and ruins) were so numerous and near at hand and also because Gothic art, so prominent elsewhere in Europe, had penetrated only slightly into Italy.

Art in the Middle Ages tended to be subservient to the church and its purposes. The object was to emphasize spiritual aspiration at the expense of physical beauty. Italian painting, usually religious figures against solid backgrounds, had been stiff and flat, with the human form covered almost entirely with clothing. In short, the art of the Middle Ages had tended to ignore nature and the physical features of the human figure, because these were thought to be sources of evil and corruption that distracted from

✤ Sofonisba Anguissola, *Self-Portrait*. Anguissola came from a noble Italian family in Cremona. Her father encouraged her to study painting, and her work for Philip II of Spain won her many honors and privileges, including the position of lady-in-waiting to the court. Uffizi Gallery/Art Resource

the contemplation of God. Renaissance artists, by contrast, following the lead of the humanists, depicted a world in which nature, human beauty, the family, and even fame were pleasing to God. Because human beings were to fulfill themselves as Christians in this world, the things of this world were now, in wonderful detail, suitable subjects for artists.

Artists faced a serious challenge in imitating nature in painting, however, because they did not know how to simulate movement and depth on a flat surface. A late medieval painter, the Florentine Giotto di Bondone (1266–1337), overcame this obstacle by discarding the flat forms, aloof figures, and formal compositions of the Byzantine style that had dominated Italian painting. Allegedly able to draw a fly so realistically that viewers attempted to brush it away, he skillfully contrasted light and shadow to create an illusion of depth that made his human figures look solid and round. Among the artists influenced by Giotto was Tomasso Guidi (1401–1428), better known as Masaccio. He employed the laws of atmospheric perspective to show objects receding into a background and to make figures appear round and truly three-dimensional. Although only twenty-seven when he died, Masaccio's innovations inspired succeeding genera-

tions of painters, including Michelangelo and the other giants of the High Renaissance.

The first of these was Leonardo da Vinci (1452–1519), who more than any other person of his age personified the Renaissance ideal of versatility. As an artist, he was keenly interested in the natural world and a masterly portrayer of human psychology and personality. *The Last Supper* is a careful study of the emotions that each of Jesus' disciples was likely to have expressed on that occasion. In the *Mona Lisa,* Leonardo skillfully employed light and shadow and perspective to make the figure fully human, enigmatic and mysterious, and forever fascinating.

The most popular of the Renaissance painters, Raphael Sanzio (1483–1520) excelled in composition and the use of soft colors. His *School of Athens* is a symbolic and allegorical portrayal of the classical philosophers Plato and Aristotle with their students. Raphael was best known for his many Madonnas, which are warm, pious, and graceful.

Michelangelo Buonarroti (1475–1564) considered himself a sculptor first of all, but as a painter he was unsurpassed in technical excellence and grandeur of conception. He painted with a sculptor's eye and made the muscular male figure his ideal of beauty. His most ambitious project, perhaps the greatest single achievement in Renaissance art, was the painting of the frescoes covering the ceiling of the Sistine Chapel in the Vatican. This masterpiece, which required four years to complete, often with the artist lying flat on his back on a scaffold, depicts nine scenes from the Old Testament, from the creation to the flood.

Sculpture followed a parallel course to painting in its development. The first major artist in this medium was Donato di Niccolò di Betto Bardi, known as Donatello (c. 1386–1466). He drew on models of classical antiquity for inspiration, traveling to Rome to study ancient art remains. His studies included anatomy and the human body, and he employed models. Donatello's *David,* the first nude statue of the Renaissance, is graceful, well proportioned, and superbly balanced.

Michelangelo brought to sculpture the same scientific accuracy, endowment of life, and deep emotion that distinguished his paintings. His statues, whether standing like *David* or seated like *Moses,* show dramatic and emotional postures and expressions. His absolute mastery of sculptural technique powerfully served the Renaissance glorification of man. Especially moving is his exquisite *Pietà,* which depicts a grief-stricken Mary looking at the dead body of Jesus lying across her lap.

Michelangelo's later works exemplify an important change that took place in the art of the sixteenth century. His later sculptures show an exaggeration, elongation, and distortion that heightens their emotional and religious qualities. For example, his crowded *Last Judgment* painting on the Sistine Chapel's end wall is full of violence, tragedy, and horror in contrast to the classical harmony and restraint of the ceiling figures.

Architects, though slower in exploring new directions, were still more strongly influenced by classical models. In his church designs, Filippo Brunelleschi (1377–1446) combined the Romanesque cruciform floor plan with such classical features as columns, rounded windows, and arches. His greatest triumph was the cupola (dome) atop the cathedral in Florence, which echoes both Rome's Pantheon and Constantinople's Hagia Sophia.

The Renaissance Outside Italy

A great watershed in western European literature and thought was the spread of the Renaissance outside Italy between 1490 and 1530. Italian humanists accepted positions as secretaries and diplomats with northern kings and princes. Scholars from the north studied in Italy and returned home to write and teach humanism. Northern universities incorporated humanist studies into their curricula, and humanist historians used their critical skills in writing the histories of northern lands.

Italian humanism, fostered in the republics and communes of Italy, had a strong civic strain that was believed to be acceptable to God and quite consistent with Christian life. In northern Europe, humanists wrote less about civic and political duty and more about personal morality, though they still drew heavily upon both Christian and pagan (that is, non-Christian Greek and Roman) authors. Although they stressed the Bible and the words of the church fathers over classical writings, northern humanists believed that by absorbing the wisdom of both, they could improve individual morality and revitalize and purify their contemporary social and religious life. Nevertheless, like their Italian predecessors, northern humanists also believed, as Thomas More (1478–1535) said, that education in Latin and Greek "doth train the soul in virtue." More, who was a lawyer and diplomat (even becoming lord

❧ *The School of Athens.* In this painting the Renaissance master Raphael presented his version of the humanist ideal of classical antiquity. Many Greek and Roman cultural heroes are depicted in the dress of sixteenth-century Italians in a setting of Renaissance architecture and sculpture. At the center of the composition, framed by the arch, Plato and Aristotle are deep in discussion. Vatican Museums

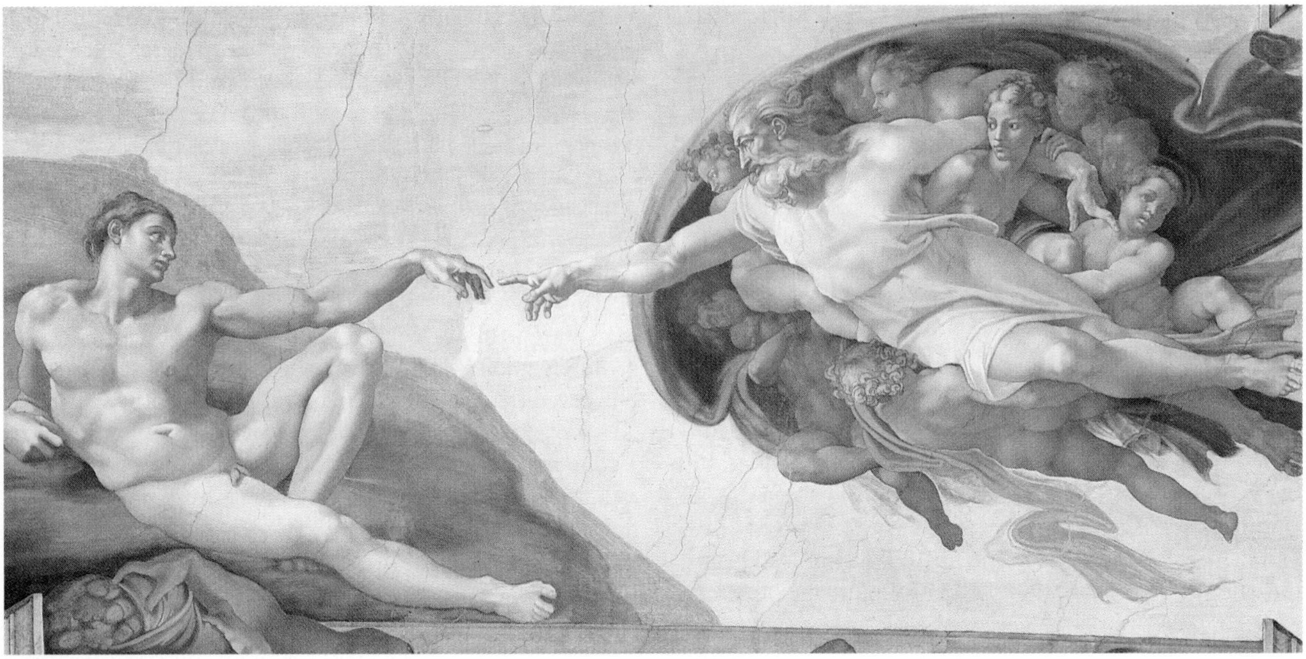

The Creation. In this scene from the Sistine Chapel ceiling, Michelangelo used the simple device of two fingers nearly touching to render dramatically the transmission of the spark of life. The woman and child behind God represent Eve, the first woman, and Christ, the second Adam. Vatican Museums

chancellor of England) as well as a humanist, is best known for his *Utopia.* The *Utopia* contrasted the evil conditions of sixteenth-century Europe with an idealized, peaceful, and prosperous society living communally in accord with reason and Christian values.

The foremost northern humanist was Desiderius Erasmus (c. 1466–1536), a native of Rotterdam. His wit, marvelous writing style, and extensive travels won him international renown and ensured that his works would be "best-sellers." Erasmus formulated a humanist religion of simple piety and noble conduct based on a belief in human dignity and free will. He embraced the naturalism, tolerance, and humanitarianism he found in classical writings and used his formidable satiric power to oppose war, violence, ignorance, and irrationality. His *Adages* collected apt sayings from classical Latin writers, and the *Praise of Folly* attacked the pedantic dogmatism of scholars and the ignorance of the masses. Erasmus's fresh edition of the Greek New Testament became the basis of various translations into the vernacular languages.

In areas of Europe outside Italy, vernacular literatures, already developing in the thirteenth century, now registered remarkable achievements. In England, Geoffrey Chaucer (1340–1400) made the East Midland dialect the ancestor of modern English. His highly entertaining *Canterbury Tales* are filled with realistic and humorous portrayals of men and women from various social classes and occupations.

By the fifteenth century, humanist stimulation had fostered a quickening of literary achievement in western Europe. In France, François Rabelais (1490–1553) produced a prose masterpiece, *Gargantua and Pantagruel,* that glorified the human and the natural, rejected Christian doctrine and morality, and satirized Scholasticism, bigotry, and church practices with bawdy humor. At the abbey where many of the book's episodes occur, the only rule is "do what you will." A little later Michel de Montaigne (1533–1592) introduced the essay as an important literary form. His great collection of *Essais* is a kind of extended intellectual autobiography, ranging over a wide variety of topics in an engaging conversational tone. Characteristic of Montaigne's essays is a healthy skepticism regarding human opinions, doctrines, institutions, and customs, as in the following passage from "On Cannibals":

> I am not so anxious that we should note the horrible savagery of these [cannibalistic] acts as concerned that, whilst judging their faults so correctly, we should be so blind to our own. I consider it more barbarous to eat a man alive than to eat him dead; to tear by rack and torture a body still full of feeling, to roast it by degrees, and then to give it to be trampled and eaten by dogs and swine—a practice which we have not only read about but seen within recent memory, not between ancient enemies, but between neighbors and fellow-citizens and, what is worse, under the cloak of piety and religion—than to roast and eat a man after he is dead. (J. M. Cohen, trans., *Michel de Montaigne: Essays* (Harmondsworth: Penguin, 1958), p. 113.)

For the most part, the golden age of Spanish literature came somewhat later than that of France. Miguel de Cervantes's (1547–1616) *Don Quixote,* sometimes regarded as the greatest novel ever written, is a rich depiction of human nobility and folly. Cervantes ridicules the nobles' pretensions to be champions of honor by recounting the adventures of a Spanish gentleman who, after reading too many chivalric romances, becomes a wandering knight. Imagining windmills to be giants and inns to be castles, the hero (mis)behaves in accord with those (mis)perceptions. His squire, Sancho Panza, is, by contrast, a practical man untroubled by romantic dreams and content with the simple creature comforts of eating, drinking, and sleeping.

England's literary developments were contemporary with those of Spain and were most impressive in drama. William Shakespeare (1564–1616) drew themes and story lines from Greek and Roman literature and English history. Extremely adept in the use of language and the analysis of character, he showed a deep understanding of human potential, both for good and for evil.

> What a piece of work is a man! How noble in reason! How infinite in faculty! In form and moving how express and admirable! In action how like an angel! In apprehension how like a god! The beauty of the world! The paragon of animals! (*Hamlet* 2.2.315–319)

In an ironic vein reminiscent of Greek tragedy, Shakespeare's heroes are responsible for their own dilemmas and suffer by their own sins and mistakes. His strongest plays express bitterness and overwhelming pathos, as the characters conduct a troubled search into life's mysteries. Of these plays, the later works present an overall view of the universe as benevolent and just, despite individual tragedy and grief.

Northern Renaissance art represented physical and emotional reality by use of detail, careful observation of nature, and skill in the technique of foreshortening. Jan van Eyck (1370–1440) capitalized on the advantages of oil paints, excelling in the painting of portraits, in which the subjects seem to live and breathe; each detail, from a blade of grass to the hair of a dog, is meticulously rendered. Albrecht Dürer (1471–1528) studied the human form carefully and gave attention to both detail and harmonious composition in woodcuts, engravings, and paintings. He admired Martin Luther (see the next section) and often chose biblical themes for his work. Many of his pieces have a pervasive somber and often gloomy quality. The great Spanish painter, Doménikos Theotokópoulos

❧ *Melancholia I.* The melancholy figure by Albrect Dürer sits amid symbols representing the new learning of the sixteenth century, suggesting that greater knowledge does not necessarily produce happiness. If Dürer meant this as a self-portrait, it is a very early example of the theme of the "tormented artist," so familiar in modern times. The work shows the extremely fine detail that a master engraver could achieve. Courtesy of the Board of Trustees of The Victoria and Albert Museum

(1541–1614), known as El Greco from his birth on the island of Crete, was an avid admirer of Michelangelo. He used severe colors and elongated features to express Spanish religious zeal in powerful and emotional paintings. His greatest work, *The Burial of Count Orgaz*, conveys the Catholic spirit of communion among God, saints, and humans.

Architects outside Italy continued to use Gothic techniques in building both churches and secular structures, but as they reached the structural and decorative limits of the Gothic, they began to employ the classical Greco-Roman style revived by fifteenth-century Italians. Those Italian influences are especially evident in central France's Loire Valley chateaux, country houses for French kings, nobles, and wealthy townspeople.

European Nation-States and the Reformation

[At the Diet of Worms in 1521, the spokesman said:] "Martin, how can you assume that you are the only one to understand the sense of Scripture? Would you put your judgment above that of so many famous men and claim that you know more than they all? You have no right to call into question the most holy orthodox faith, instituted by Christ the perfect lawgiver, proclaimed throughout the world by the apostles, sealed by the red blood of the martyrs, confirmed by the sacred councils, defined by the Church in which all our fathers believed until death and gave to us as an inheritance, and which now we are forbidden by the pope and the emperor to discuss lest there be no end of debate. I ask you, Martin—answer candidly and without horns—do you or do you not repudiate your books and the errors which they contain?"

*Luther replied, "Since then Your Majesty and your lordships desire a simple reply, I will answer without horns and without teeth. Unless I am convicted by Scripture and plain reason—I do not accept the authority of popes and councils, for they have contradicted each other—my conscience is captive to the Word of God. I cannot and I will not recant anything, for to go against conscience is neither right nor safe. God help me. Amen." [In the earliest printed version the words: "Here I stand. I cannot do otherwise," were added.]**

*Roland H. Bainton, *Here I Stand: A Life of Martin Luther* (New York: Mentor, 1958), p. 144.

This exchange was the culmination of a sequence of events that produced the Protestant Reformation, a broad revolt against the medieval church. Although religious dissent was the root of the problem, the Reformation was also intimately bound up with political, social, economic, and intellectual matters. Within a generation of Luther's defiant act, many Europeans had set up separate religious organizations outside the Catholic church, ending the centuries-long religious unity of western Europe. Although the various Protestant denominations disagreed among themselves on minor theological points, they were firmly united in their opposition to Catholicism. The confrontation inspired a long period of bloody strife that would profoundly affect Western civilization.

The Reformation was closely associated with the formation of powerful national states in western Europe, a process that had begun some two centuries earlier. The pride, power, and resources of these states found expression in various forms of political and commercial rivalry, including the developing trade overseas (see the following sections). The emergence of these nation-states of western Europe will open this section.

The Centralization of Western European Monarchies

The High Middle Ages had witnessed the resurgent power of the monarchy in Europe as the prelude to the development of the modern state. However, the troubles of fourteenth- and fifteenth-century Europe—civil and foreign wars, economic depression, and the plague—undid much of the earlier work of consolidation. The powers of government came to be divided between the king and his semiautonomous vassals, the great nobles of the realm. Royal vassals maintained private armies, dispensed justice in the courts, and served as advisers and royal officials. The nobles were monarchs in miniature, often having the power of life and death over the people in their territories. As a result, a country like France was not a single nation under one king; rather, it was a mosaic of principalities, each with its own ruler. At times of a major threat, the vassals would sometimes temporarily join forces under their king.

For the peasants or serfs, it made little difference whether they were exploited by king or duke, because life close to the soil was harsh in either case. For dwellers in manufacturing and trading towns, the situation was less clear. The city fathers longed to win self-rule and, to that end, liked to play one great lord off against another or against the king. At the same time, however, those who aspired to trade over larger areas found the political fragmentation of their country a hindrance.

The trend toward decentralization was dramatically reversed during the second half of the fifteenth century with the emergence of strong, ambitious kings in France, England, and Spain. They ended internal disorders in their lands, reduced the power of the nobility, and exerted greater control over their subjects. The achievements of these "New Monarchs" served as examples for lesser kings.

Several factors led to the recovery of the monarchy in western Europe. As in the centralized states around the world previously discussed, the European kings needed to generate an assured source of income sufficient to create an army and a bureaucracy under their control. The new towns provided a potential source of new money. In a mutually beneficial arrangement, the kings granted the towns privileges and rights in return for money payments to the royal treasury. In this way, towns and monarchs became allies against the great lords, who often sought to encroach on the independence of both. These arrangements not only reduced the kings' dependence on the great nobles but resulted in the growth of semiindependent towns in early modern Europe.

With the new revenue, the kings moved to abandon feudal levies and create a powerful army. In the traditional feudal levy, vassals supplied forces for temporary service, but so long as the great nobles controlled the military, the king's power was limited. Accordingly, the monarchs began to build up armies of paid soldiers commanded by loyal officers who were willing to follow orders and even make war on the nobles, if necessary.

The kings further strengthened their position through marriages calculated either to neutralize powerful antagonists or to add territory to their own realm. No less important was the development of bureaucracies. Civil servants attached to districts collected taxes and administered the districts in the king's name. Kings selected their officials from outside the nobility and paid them in money and in small, scattered estates instead of huge blocks of territory. In this way, the kings ensured that the officials would be dependent on them and thus loyal to the crown.

In France, the first of the New Monarchs, Louis XI (reigned 1461–1483), inherited a realm devastated by the Black Death and the Hundred Years' War (1337–1453). The latter was a debilitating struggle fought between the English and the French, and among the French, over a maze of feudal claims and commercial competition. At a dark moment for France, a young woman, later known as Joan of Arc (1412–1431), changed the course of the war. Believing herself to be acting at God's urging, she persuaded the heir to the French throne, the future Charles VII (reigned 1422–1461), to appoint her to a military command. Her prestige reached its height in 1429 when she succeeded in relieving the besieged city of Orléans and cutting a path for Charles to Rheims, where he was properly crowned in the place and manner of his ancestors. Joan, who was later captured and executed, came to symbolize the French national spirit.

Louis XI was nicknamed the "Spider," in part because his misshapen body appeared spiderlike, but more because he devised political traps and plots reminiscent of

a spiderweb. He attracted the loyalty of the lesser nobility and employed many of them as royal officials. Louis used the army to expand royal power within France, and in a series of adroit, if underhanded, moves, he suppressed the great nobles, already weakened by losses during the Hundred Years' War. At the same time, he curbed town autonomy and asserted administrative control over the provinces. He seldom convened the Estates General, France's rudimentary representative assembly. By the time of his death in 1483, Louis had united France, strengthened its economy, and laid the foundations for royal absolutism.

Like France, fifteenth-century England was wracked by factionalism, which culminated in a civil war (the War of the Roses, 1455–1485) between the great feudal families of Lancaster and York. The civil war ended in 1485 when Henry Tudor, the foremost surviving Lancastrian, seized the crown as Henry VII (reigned 1485–1509) and married Elizabeth of York, the leading Yorkist claimant, thereby uniting the two feuding groups. With peace temporarily assured, Henry set out to centralize his power. He drew his officials from the ranks of the lesser gentry and townsmen and seated many of his councilors in Parliament, where they could manipulate matters to the king's liking. Henry received such ample revenues from customs duties on increased international trade and from fines derived from active law enforcement that he needed to summon Parliament only once in the last twelve years of his reign. He supplemented traditional English law with Roman law for many purposes. Roman law, formulated to govern a far-flung empire, favored central authority over the rights of aristocrats and common people alike and helped Henry legally justify seizing the lands and revenues of "overmighty subjects." At his death in 1509, Henry left a powerful monarchy to his son, Henry VIII.

Events in the Iberian Peninsula paralleled those in France and England. Beginning in the eleventh century, the salient feature of Iberian history was the Christian *Reconquista* (Reconquest) against the Muslims, who controlled most of the peninsula. By the mid-fifteenth century, the three kingdoms of Aragon, Castile, and Portugal dominated the peninsula. Portugal was the first national state to emerge in Europe. There the house of Avis centralized royal administration by suppressing revolts of nobles and executing many of their leaders. Partly as a result of this centralization, Portugal was the first European nation to use its resources to expand overseas (discussed later in the chapter).

The marriage of Ferdinand, king of Aragon (reigned 1479–1516), to Isabella, queen of Castile (reigned 1474–1504), in 1469 united their two realms into the kingdom of Spain. Ferdinand and Isabella moved against the nobles, who objected to any increase in the crown's power and opposed the introduction of Roman law, which the royal couple supported. They forged alliances with the towns, ostensibly to combat bandits, but actually to counter the power of the feudal levies. The Cortes, the representative assembly dominated by the nobility, steadily lost power.

The desire to consolidate their strength led the Spanish rulers to establish the Inquisition, a tribunal for the detection and punishment of heresy. It operated as an agency of the state, free from papal or church control. Ferdinand, who was not religious, did not hesitate to use it as an instrument to enforce civil despotism; in particular, to suppress rebellious churchmen and nobles. Most of the Inquisition's fury, however, was aimed at achieving religious uniformity. Its officials energetically and carefully examined the religious purity of all, searching for blasphemers and heretics. The officials conducted trials and passed sentence, often gathering information and confessions through torture. The state then executed those found guilty. When Ferdinand and Isabella conquered Granada (1492), the last Muslim outpost on the peninsula, they ordered all unconverted Muslims and Jews to leave the country with only what they could carry. The confiscated property of the religious exiles, coupled with the profits from discoveries overseas, greatly enriched the crown.

The Background of the Protestant Reformation

The Reformation, the religious upheaval that splintered the Roman Catholic church, took place during the sixteenth and seventeenth centuries, at the same time that centralized monarchy was on the rise in western Europe. Earlier, in 1054, Christianity had split into two main branches, the Eastern or Orthodox church, which prevailed in the Byzantine Empire, and the Western or Roman Catholic church, which was dominant in central and western Europe. In the High Middle Ages, the popes had succeeded in centralizing the administration of the church under their control, enabling them to impose religious uniformity and to exercise a potent influence on European political life. The Catholic church reached the height of its power under Pope Innocent III (reigned 1198–1216). Laxity and worldliness characterized Innocent III's successors, however, weakening the papacy's moral authority and opening the way for defiance and contempt. Papal power eroded at the same time that the prestige of the new national states was on the rise.

Beginning in 1305, a series of religious and political intrigues brought about the Great Schism, a bizarre situation in which two rival popes—and at one point three popes—were presiding simultaneously. It was a distressful time for conscientious Christians, who had no sure way of knowing which pope to support. Bishops, professors, and powerful laymen concluded that a church council must be called to end the schism.

The Council of Constance (1414–1417) reunited the Catholic church. The delegates deposed the rival popes and elected a new pope, Martin V. Radical elements wanted to go further and strip away papal powers and have councils govern the church, but their efforts were thwarted by papal intransigence and by their own inability to agree. In the meantime Martin and his successors tried to win over the temporal rulers who had initially supported the conciliarists. The popes achieved their objective, but only after permitting the monarchs to assume more control over the church in their respective countries. Before the end of the fifteenth century, the papacy had once again asserted its dominance over the church, although it was unable to recapture the spiritual and moral leadership it had once enjoyed. The price for the papacy's triumph was high. Preoccupied for many years with combating the conciliarist movement and practicing power politics, the popes showed little interest in undertaking the reforms that sincere Christians were demanding.

A number of abuses had arisen in the church in the fourteenth and fifteenth centuries. Simony, the sale of church offices, was one such problem. Some 2,000 church offices were for sale, and the resulting revenues formed a significant part of papal income. A case in point was the archbishop of Mainz, who paid the astronomical sum of 30,000 ducats for his office—equivalent to fifteen years' salary for a mid-level functionary in the papal bureaucracy. Another serious problem was pluralism, where one individual held several church offices at the same time. Priests and bishops often hired stand-ins to fulfill their duties. In Germany in 1500 more than 90 percent of the parishes were served by part-time priests. The practice of nepotism, giving lucrative church offices to relatives of the higher clergy, was widespread. Churchmen, from the highest rank to the lowest, were frequently affected by the secular spirit of the Renaissance and showed more interest in worldly pleasures and pursuits than in attending to their spiritual responsibilities. Popes led a life of luxury rivaling that of the secular rulers of their time. The church's ever-growing fiscal demands, together with the immorality and secular interests of the clergy, aggravated the resentment and sense of alienation felt by many Christians.

When church leaders did not initiate reform, some priests and laity on the local level tried to make changes, while in other areas, secular princes led popular reform movements. Appealing to scriptural precedents, the life of Jesus, and the activities of the early church described in the Book of Acts, most reformers demanded back-to-basics change. Such was the general situation on All Saints' Eve in 1517, when Martin Luther made his famous demand for reform of church practice and doctrine.

Martin Luther Breaks with the Church

Martin Luther was born in 1483 at Eisleben in Saxony (central Germany), the second son of a moderately prosperous miner. To please his father, he went to the University of Erfurt in 1505 to study law. That same year, according to his account, he was caught in a fearsome thunderstorm and thrown to the ground by a flash of lightning. Following his miraculous survival, which affected him emotionally, he entered an Augustinian monastery at Erfurt, where he was ordained a priest in 1507. He returned to the university and became a doctor of theology. From 1511 until his death thirty-five years later, he served as professor of theology at the newly founded University of Wittenberg.

Luther's growing reputation as a biblical scholar masked his torment about gaining God's grace and his own salvation. Beyond scrupulous monastic observance, he had been diligent in confessing his sins, praying, and fasting. Yet performing good works, as commanded by the church, did not give him the comfort and spiritual peace he was seeking. Through the study of the Bible he found the answer to his dilemma in one of the apostle Paul's letters to the Romans, especially in the phrase "the just shall live by faith." It dawned on him that people could be saved only by repenting their sins and throwing themselves on God's mercy and accepting his grace. Salvation was a gift from God as a reward for faith in his mercy and could not be earned by doing good works. This doctrine struck at the heart of orthodox Catholic belief, which held that only through the sacraments of the church could sinners be redeemed and made worthy of salvation. Luther was at first unaware of the conflict. He thought he was simply giving more emphasis to the Bible in Christian education. Only after he was drawn into the indulgence controversy did he realize the revolutionary implications of his religious views.

According to Catholic teaching, an indulgence was supposed to remit punishment in purgatory for sins for which insufficient penance had been done while on earth. It was granted on condition that the sinner was repentant and was willing to perform some pious deed such as going on a crusade or a pilgrimage. By the sixteenth century, however, the practice had become perverted. Church agents made extravagant claims, implying that indulgences secured total remission of sins, on earth and in purgatory, without bothering to mention the acts of contrition and confession demanded of every sinner as a prerequisite for forgiveness. An indulgence, so it was advertised, guaranteed swift entry into heaven for the purchaser or for a loved one in purgatory. As one hawker put it: "As soon as the coin in the coffer rings, the soul from purgatory springs." Many flocked to buy indulgences; the huge sums collected went either into the pockets of leading political and church officials or to Rome to pay for such papal projects as Saint Peter's Basilica.

Luther was outraged to see poor people being deprived of their hard-earned money under false pretenses. He objected to the sale of indulgences on the grounds

Martin Luther and the Wittenberg Reformers. In this painting by Cranach the Younger in 1543, Luther is at the far left. The large figure in the center foreground is Elector John Frederick of Saxony, who gave Luther crucial protection and support against the Roman Catholic church. The Toledo Museum of Art, Toledo, Ohio; purchased with funds from the Libbey Endowment, gift of Edward Drummond Libbey

that the pope had no control over purgatory and, more importantly, that indulgences did not mandate repentance as a condition for forgiveness of sins. On October 31, 1517, Luther posted a list of ninety-five theses (statements of error) on the church door at Wittenberg. His purpose in doing so was to challenge the defenders of indulgences to a debate. Luther had expected reaction to be confined to the university community, but to his surprise printed copies of his theses circulated throughout Germany, arousing widespread public interest. To the consternation of church authorities, the sale of indulgences fell off sharply.

As Luther was forced by critics to define his theological position, it became increasingly apparent that his beliefs were sharply at odds with those of the Catholic church. In 1520 Pope Leo X (reigned 1513–1521) condemned Luther's teachings and ordered him to recant within two months or face excommunication. Luther responded by publicly burning the document. The pope then formally excommunicated Luther and called upon the Holy Roman Emperor, Charles V, to punish him as a heretic. But Luther had become a national figure, and the German princes did not feel he could be condemned without a hearing.

In the spring of 1521, Luther, under the protection of an imperial safe conduct, appeared before Charles V at a diet (meeting) at Worms. There he refused to recant unless it could be proved that his writings were contrary to Scripture. Branded an outlaw with a price on his head, he traveled home with the assistance of agents of Frederick, elector of Saxony, under whose protection he would remain for the rest of his life. In 1522 Luther returned to Wittenberg, where he gathered his supporters and established the first Protestant church.

The rapid spread of Lutheranism was in marked contrast to other reform movements, which had failed to divide the church. Luther was a brilliant theologian and possessed nearly every quality essential to a revolutionary leader. He also enjoyed advantages that had been denied to his predecessors. First, his revolt against Rome occurred when the church was in a state of decline and was being strongly criticized from within. The abuses resulting from the Great Schism and a series of worldly Renaissance popes had lowered public support for the church. Meanwhile, the writings of Erasmus and other humanists generated a critical spirit that challenged many accepted beliefs. Erasmus's scholarly edition of the New Testament (1516) and the publication of the writings of the church fathers, including all of Jerome's letters, in the vernacular, coupled with other humanist texts, revealed that some church doctrines had shaky foundations. Second, the invention of the printing press allowed for the mass production of books, including the Bible, at relatively low cost. Published materials became available to larger numbers of people, permitting the rapid spread of new ideas. Third, an unusual political situation existed in Germany. Charles V, the Holy Roman Emperor, was committed to maintaining an alliance with the papacy and also wanted to extend his authority over Germany. About half of the 300-odd German rulers supported Lutheranism as a way to resist Charles. Some among them may have been moved as much by material considerations as by religious concerns. By adopting Lutheranism, the princes could confiscate the rich and extensive Catholic holdings in their domains. Finally, the rising capitalistic

classes, finding Catholicism incompatible with the practice of trade and banking, were willing to push for a system that suited them better.

Many of Luther's early followers broke away from his guidance. The largest group to do so was the Anabaptists, a radical religious sect who refused to bear arms and advocated the abolition of private property, among other social ideas. Luther disavowed them for, apart from sharp religious differences, his views on the social order were extremely conservative. The humanists, who had scorned and ridiculed church practices, hailed Luther for his efforts to restore the purity of Christianity. But the humanists, placing unity ahead of doctrine, wanted to reform the church from within, not start a new religion. When Luther refused to patch up his differences with Rome, most of them, including Erasmus, decided to remain within the Catholic fold. In 1524–1525 the Peasants' Revolt had far more serious consequences. Thousands of downtrodden peasants in southwestern Germany, seeking relief from economic and manorial burdens, revolted against their landlords. At first Luther showed considerable sympathy for the commoners' cause, but when they resorted to violence, endangering the fabric of society and the structure of the state, he called for their suppression. The princes did so with unspeakable cruelty, causing Lutheranism to lose much of its appeal among the poor of southern Germany.

Luther saw himself not as a social and economic reformer but as a restorer of the true doctrine and practices of the early Christian church. In final form, Luther's religion differed from the Catholic church in a number of important ways. Luther believed that salvation came through faith in God rather than through good works, sacraments, and rituals. The true church, he contended, consisted of all believers and was not just an organization of ecclesiastics; thus he eliminated the hierarchy of pope, cardinals, and bishops and reduced the importance of the clergy. For Luther, ultimate authority rested with the Scriptures, not with church traditions and papal pronouncements. Of the seven Catholic sacraments, he retained only baptism and communion, the two found in the Bible. He abolished monasteries and the celibacy of the clergy. Luther himself married a former nun, by whom he had six children. He replaced the Latin liturgy with a German service that included Bible reading and the singing of hymns. So that the Bible would be available in German, Luther translated both the New and Old Testaments. Finally, unlike Catholicism, Luther gave the state supreme authority over his church except in matters of doctrine.

The spectacular progress of Lutheranism troubled Charles V, who sought to find an accommodation that would prevent Germany from being divided by religion. His political skirmishing with the Lutheran princes only intensified matters, however, and led to open war in 1546, the same year that Luther died. Although Charles was determined to crush the Lutheran states, he was unable to intervene forcefully because of his preoccupation with wars against the French and the Turks. With neither side able to gain a clear advantage, the Peace of Augsburg in 1555 ended the nine-year conflict. By this compromise sovereign German princes and cities were given the right to decide between Catholicism and Lutheranism; subjects who objected to their ruler's choice would be permitted to emigrate. The Peace of Augsburg left Lutheranism firmly entrenched in the northern half of Germany. From there it spread to Scandinavia and to the Baltic lands under the control of Sweden. Lutheranism would also have a great influence on all subsequent Protestant movements.

Protestant Reformers after Luther

Luther may have been the first to revolt against the established church, but others soon followed. Ulrich Zwingli (1484–1531) led a reform movement in Zurich, Switzerland, that incorporated many of Luther's teachings. Zwingli believed in the supreme authority of Scripture and simplified church services, taught justification by faith instead of good works, and opposed clerical celibacy. But he went beyond Luther in considering baptism and communion to be merely symbolic ceremonies. These doctrinal differences proved irreconcilable and marked the first in a long series of Protestant schisms. Zwingli also maintained that the church needed to take the lead in imposing Christian discipline on civil life. The Swiss confederation of cantons could not agree on which church to follow, so it allowed each canton to make its own decision.

The reform tradition that Zwingli started in Zurich was carried on by John Calvin (1509–1564) in Geneva a generation later. Calvin, who was the most celebrated Protestant leader of the sixteenth century next to Martin Luther, was born in the French town of Noyon, the son of a prosperous lawyer. His heart was set on becoming a priest, but at his father's insistence, he abandoned theology for law. Early in life he associated with followers of Luther and about 1534 converted to Protestantism. Forced into hiding to avoid persecution, Calvin fled to Switzerland and settled in Geneva, where, as a dynamic agent of change, he rose to become virtual dictator of the city.

Calvin outlined his religious views in *The Institutes of the Christian Religion,* published in 1536 when he was only twenty-six. The book was a clear, logical, superb synthesis of Protestant theology. On the surface Calvin's beliefs resembled those of Luther. He accepted the sinfulness of humans and their impotence to save themselves; denied the value of good works as a means of salvation; regarded the Bible as the sole authority in matters of faith; and rejected all the Catholic sacraments except baptism and communion. But Calvin's differences with Luther were significant enough to rule out collabo-

ration between the two. For Calvin, church and state were both divinely inspired institutions, but each was independent of the other. Luther subordinated the church to the state. Calvin favored suppressing anything that was not clearly sanctioned in the Bible, which he regarded as the supreme authority in every aspect of life. Luther, regarding the Bible as a vehicle for Christ's teachings, permitted anything that it did not specifically forbid.

Far more than Luther, Calvin stressed the omnipotence of God. Calvin accepted Luther's concept of salvation through God's grace, but believed more strongly than the latter that this priceless gift was granted only to some. According to Calvin, people were condemned to live in perpetual sin as punishment for Adam and Eve's fall from grace. But God through his infinite mercy had chosen some human beings to be saved and had damned all the rest to suffer in hell. Men and women could do nothing to change their fate, which was predestined before they were born. The doctrine of predestination was at the core of Calvin's theology. The doctrine itself was not new, but Calvin's emphasis on it was. Luther's belief in justification by faith implied divine predetermination, but he was too consumed with other matters to follow through. Calvin, with his rigorous logic, was driven to carry the doctrine to its ultimate conclusion.

Logically, one might think that if individuals could have no effect on their destiny, they would be indifferent about their personal conduct. Calvin took another position on that point, however: although people had no sure way of knowing who would be saved and who would be damned, those living in accordance with God's will could take it as a hopeful sign. Even if a pious life did not ensure salvation, an immoral life proved that one was not among the chosen. Calvin's doctrine had an enormous appeal. It gave believers a powerful motive to do God's work in order to convince themselves that they would be saved.

Calvinism was not confined to Switzerland. Geneva became a training center for Calvinist preachers who came from many parts of Europe. Impelled by a sense of militancy and dedication, they returned to promote Calvin's teachings in their homelands. Calvinism triumphed in Scotland under the leadership of John Knox (c. 1510–1572), in the German Palatinate, and in the Dutch Netherlands, where it played a major role in overthrowing Spanish tyranny. It gained many converts in England (Puritans) and a vigorous following in France (Huguenots), Bohemia, and Hungary. From Europe Calvinism made its way to America, where it contributed significantly to the growth of constitutional government.

The act that sparked the English Reformation had little to do with Calvinism or church doctrine, however. The king, Henry VIII, wanted to annul his marriage to his wife, Catherine of Aragon, by whom he had only a daughter, Mary. Although England had no law that barred a

Calvin on Divine Predestination

When we attribute foreknowledge to God, we mean that all things always were, and perpetually remain, under His eyes, so that to His knowledge there is nothing future or past, but all things are present. . . . And this foreknowledge is extended throughout the universe to every creature. We call predestination God's eternal decree, by which He determined with Himself what He wished to become of each man. For all are not created in equal condition; rather, eternal life is foreordained for some, eternal damnation for others. Therefore, as any man has been created to one or the other of these ends, we speak of him as predestined to life or to death.*

In these few words, John Calvin stated the doctrine of predestination, which became a distinguishing characteristic of Calvinist churches. The doctrine of predestination stimulated Calvinists to do God's work. Although absolute certainty was impossible, indications of election were a desire to live rightly, the practice of pious conduct, and the affirmation of a personal profession of faith.

*John Calvin, *The Institutes of the Christian Religion*, ed. John T. McNeill (Philadelphia: Westminster Press, 1960), bk. 3, chap. 21, p. 5.

woman from the throne, Henry and his advisers felt that the country should be ruled by a male. Though divorce was contrary to church law, ecclesiastical authorities sometimes allowed marriages to be annulled, especially when monarchs were involved. The problem in this case was that Catherine was the aunt of the Holy Roman Emperor, Charles V, whose troops were then in control of Rome. Henry was not a patient man; when the pope delayed acting on his request, he turned to the compliant archbishop of Canterbury, Thomas Cramner, who granted the annulment in 1533. The following year Parliament passed the Act of Supremacy, which repudiated papal primacy and declared the king head of an independent Anglican church. In this capacity, Henry subsequently dissolved the monasteries and enriched his treasury with their great wealth.

Despite his break with Rome, Henry continued to think of himself as a devout Catholic. The official theology of the Church of England made few departures from Catholicism. When Henry died in 1547, his nine-year-old son, Edward VI, ascended the throne. During the regency government of the youth, Protestants gradually moved Anglican doctrine closer to mainstream Protestant tenets through the Book of Common Prayer. When Edward died without an heir in 1553, the crown passed to Mary, a devout Catholic, who dedicated herself to restoring the Roman Catholic church in England. Persecution of Protestants during Mary's rule earned her the nickname "Bloody Mary." In 1558 the childless Mary died unexpectedly, and the crown went to her Protestant half-sister, Elizabeth, who quickly restored the Anglican church and declared herself its governor. During her long reign, Elizabeth successfully steered a middle course between Roman Catholicism and Calvinism. The Anglican church's beliefs were spelled out in a modified Book of Common Prayer and in the Thirty-nine Articles, published in 1563.

A great upheaval, such as the Protestant revolt, was bound to produce extremist groups. The most radical among the reformers were the Anabaptists, the ancestors of the modern Mennonites and Amish. They generally came from the lower classes and stressed a literal interpretation of Scripture, seeking a return to the simplicity of primitive Christianity. The name *Anabaptist* meant "baptize again" and came from their rejection of infant baptism and their belief that only adults capable of free choice should be baptized. Adults who had been baptized as children had to be rebaptized. Generally, the Anabaptists rejected any association between church and state, refused to recognize civil authority when it conflicted with their religious ideals, and favored the creation of egalitarian communities like those of the early Christians. Because the Anabaptists posed a religious and political threat to established society, they were intensively and cruelly persecuted by both Catholics and Protestants.

The aim of the early Protestant movements was to modify rather than reject the medieval church. All, to varying degrees, retained features of the old Roman church, but their sharp differences could not be harmonized. By the mid-sixteenth century, Protestantism had triumphed in nearly half of Europe, and the existence of the Catholic church itself seemed threatened.

Women and the Reformation

Women showed as much interest in the Reformation as did men. For most women exposure to Protestant doctrines came through their husbands or fathers. Some were even permitted to promote their new faith. Anabaptist women preached and administered baptism, and occasionally, zealous wives of evangelizers were active alongside their husbands from the pulpits. However, larger Protestant groups, as with Catholics, closed the ministry to women. John Calvin declared: "The custom of the church . . . may be elicited first of all from Tertullian [church father, c. 160–230] who held that no woman in church is allowed to speak, teach, baptize or make offerings; this in order that she may not usurp the functions of men." Apart from their lack of theological training, women serving conspicuously in nontraditional roles would have been objectionable to most men.

Life in Sixteenth-Century Geneva and Venice

Under a constitution Calvin helped to write, Geneva became a theocratic republic in which the administration of church and state were closely interwoven. Calvin's objective was to transform the city into his version of the ideal Christian community. Ruling with the assistance of a council known as the Consistory, he considered it his duty to supervise every aspect of the city's life and to enforce God's will. Guided by the Bible, the Consistory passed laws forbidding such things as idleness, dancing, frivolous pastimes, card playing, profanity, adultery, and marriage to Catholics. People were instructed on how they should dress, on how women should arrange their hair, and even on the names parents should select for their infants. Calvin demanded sobriety, regular church attendance, hard work, frugality, and pursuit of a trade. Secret agents were on the lookout for wrongdoing.

Calvin had no tolerance for human weaknesses, and even common sins were punished with unprecedented rigor. The most notorious example of Calvin's harshness was the execution of Michael Servetus, a Spanish refugee, for publicly denying the doctrine of the Trinity. Gradually, as the more liberal-minded people left the city and were replaced by zealots from all over Europe, the character of the city changed. In 1546 John Knox reported that Geneva was the most perfect community of Christ seen anywhere on earth since the days of the apostles.

In many ways unique among Italian cities, Venice stood in sharp contrast to Geneva. Built almost exclusively on trade and shipping, Venice was a rich, highly cultural, cosmopolitan city. It was governed by a hereditary oligarchy of wealthy merchants comprising only about 2 percent of the population. Although members of this aristocracy, as they styled themselves, tolerated no opposi-tion, they ruled wisely and did much to improve the economic welfare of the disenfranchised masses.

Venice was untroubled by internal disorder, social tensions, or party factionalism. Travelers were struck by the paradoxical nature of the city. On the one hand, they saw a city that projected a sober image of republican restraint and judicious modesty, founded on the principles of equality, magnanimity, domestic harmony, and justice for all of its citizens. On the other hand, they reported that Venice was a pleasure-seeking community—full of festive people and indulgent gambling, roisterous parties, the theater, and lax sexual mores. As early as the fourteenth century, Petrarch noted with disapproval his impression of the city: "Much freedom reigns there in every respect, and what I should call the only evil prevailing—but also the worst—far too much freedom." Freedom was possible because the government faced no opposition, but there were few grounds for criticism because the government had adopted progressive social policies and secured boundless wealth.

Laws in Venice were enacted without reference to God's will. In fact, the government was anticlerical and as a rule ignored interdicts issued by the papacy. During the Counter-Reformation, the papacy rejuvenated the Inquisition as a means of maintaining orthodoxy and effectively extending the church's power in the Catholic world. Most Catholic countries rallied behind this institution without reservation. However, Venice, long impervious to papal influence, adopted a middle position designed to contain heresy without compromising the authority of its secular government or severely restricting rights traditionally enjoyed by its citizens.

The venue in which women conveyed their views and feelings was the home. Here they discussed doctrinal matters and instructed occasional visitors and friends on the virtues of their new faith. Some educated women composed hymns and wrote devotional works. Married women taught their children the catechism, pronounced prayers, and sang hymns. There were even instances of noblewomen converting their husbands.

The Reformation affected women not only through new religious ideas but also through institutional and political changes. Protestant reformers stressed the value and sanctity of marriage, challenging the medieval tendency to denigrate women and encourage celibacy. Luther considered marriage a divinely ordained union and a natural vocation for women. Although he and other Protestant reformers exalted the state of marriage and urged husbands to treat their wives kindly and share authority with them within the household, they nevertheless insisted that women remain subject to men in that union. Convinced that women's primary duty was to obey their husbands and bear children, the reformers did not want women to serve as ministers or hold too many public responsibilities. A strong patriarchal family seemed indispensable to the social stability of the state.

Laws regulating marriage were quite equitable: if a marriage failed, women had the same right as men to divorce and remarry. Unlike Catholics, who permitted only separation from bed and board, Protestant reformers allowed divorce under circumstances such as abuse, abandonment, or adultery. Still, the various Protestant denominations discouraged the breakup of families, permitting divorce only after all efforts to reconcile had failed. Even "liberated" women rarely sought divorce, which was apt to leave them without financial support.

The closing of convents in Protestant territories imposed a cruel hardship on many nuns. Some married or returned to their paternal homes, but most were left alone to face the hazards of life. They took whatever employment was available; some found no work; others, in desperation, even turned to prostitution.

Protestant leaders, eager to increase biblical literacy and make individuals better Christians, encouraged education for women and men alike. They established schools for both sexes at the primary and secondary levels, as well as academies and colleges to train pastors and male lay church workers. Education gave women an opportunity to find employment as teachers or become authors. Although illiteracy remained pervasive in Europe, a base for expanding educational opportunity had been laid: it proved to be one of the most enduring legacies of the Reformation.

The Roman Catholic or Counter-Reformation

Rome responded slowly to the Protestant challenge and to calls for changes from within. Finally, however, as hopes for reconciliation dimmed and Protestantism continued to make gains, the Catholic church launched a vigorous counterattack on a number of fronts, a response termed variously the Catholic Reformation or Counter-Reformation. First and foremost, success in halting the spread of Protestantism and reclaiming lost lands depended on reform within the Roman Catholic church. Long before Luther acted at Wittenberg, many sincere and devout Catholics, disturbed at the deterioration of the church, had urged that a general council be held to carry through needed reforms. The popes had resisted summoning a church council, in part because they were mindful of the efforts of the conciliar movement in the fifteenth century to strip them of their authority. Ultimately, however, the pressure for reform became too great, and Pope Paul III (reigned 1534–1549) summoned a church council.

The most important work of the council, which met at Trent in northern Italy between 1545 and 1563, dealt with doctrinal matters. All doctrines, especially those under Protestant attack, were reaffirmed. They were set out in clear and precise terms, and the differences with Protestantism were specified. The council also outlined a comprehensive program of reform. It condemned such corrupt practices as simony, pluralism, and nepotism and made provisions for better discipline and higher educational standards among the clergy.

Besides reforming itself, the Catholic church took measures to halt the spread of Protestant beliefs. The council instituted the Index of Forbidden Books—a list of books, periodically revised, that Catholics were forbidden to read. The council also revived and extended the Inquisition to combat heresy and the practice of witchcraft. At least 110,000 persons were formally tried for witchcraft and about half were executed. The work of the Council of Trent created a foundation on which a new, more vibrant Catholic church could be built.

The most effective single weapon of the Catholic church in battling the Protestants was the Society of Jesus, popularly called the Jesuit order. Founded by Ignatius Loyola (1491–1556), a Basque noble and former soldier, the order was modeled on military lines, highly disciplined, and devoted to actively promoting and defending the teachings of the church. Applicants for membership were carefully screened, and those selected had to pass rigorous training and a long apprenticeship. When found ready, they were sent to whatever field seemed most in need of their services.

The Jesuits were effective missionaries, carrying the Gospels to lands as far away as China, Japan, and South America. Some became priests and from the pulpit preached simple sermons that stressed morality. As confessors and advisers to kings and princes, they were able to influence state policy to the benefit of Catholicism. They won their greatest fame, however, in the field of education. In Europe the Jesuits built schools or took over existing ones and in many areas were the dominant force in education. Their results were impressive. Through their dedication and zeal, they played a key role in holding southern Germany and France and in bringing Poland and much of Hungary back to Catholicism.

The zealous efforts of the Catholic church to stamp out Protestantism led to bitter religious wars in the late sixteenth century and the first half of the seventeenth. England experienced an attempted invasion in 1588, and heavy fighting occurred in the Netherlands, France, and elsewhere in Europe (see Chapter 11). In Germany the Peace of Augsburg proved to be only an uneasy truce. The growing tensions finally erupted into a destructive conflict known as the Thirty Years' War, which began in 1618 and continued until 1648. Over time, every major power became involved in the struggle, and the character of the war changed from religious to political. Protestant and Catholic armies, mostly composed of mercenaries, crisscrossed the German landscape, wreaking havoc.

The Thirty Years' War ended in 1648 with the Treaty of Westphalia, in part because of mutual exhaustion. Most of the contending major powers demanded and received grants of territory. Sweden secured western Pomerania and some neighboring territory on the Baltic. Brandenburg ended up with increased territory and was awarded western Pomerania as compensation for surrendering eastern Pomerania. France obtained much of Alsace and the fortress cities of Metz, Toul, and Verdun. In addition, the treaty recognized the independence of Protestant Switzerland and the Netherlands and gave Calvinist rulers the same right to determine the religion practiced in their territories that Catholic and Lutheran princes had enjoyed since 1555. Germany was the big loser. Perhaps 300,000 soldiers and civilians were killed during the campaigns, and several times that number died from malnutrition and disease. The damage wrecked the economy of the German states and caused many Germans to migrate to North America.

The Treaty of Westphalia, like the Peace of Augsburg, did not quell religious enmities. Religious strife continued to plague Europe, but on a much smaller scale than in the previous century. By regenerating itself and taking the offensive, the Catholic church had staged a strong comeback, stemming the Protestant tide and even winning back some lands that seemed irretrievably lost. But it could not regain domination over all of Western Christendom. After 1648 the religious map of Europe would not change appreciably.

European Expansion

Beginning in the fifteenth century, the new European monarchies, which, as discussed earlier in this chapter, had achieved a high degree of national unification, embarked on five centuries of expansion that brought European power to every continent on the globe. Most of the indigenous societies around the world felt the impact of this movement in one way or another. Some were relatively untouched; many were profoundly altered; some were destroyed. In the process Western society would itself feel the impact of other cultures.

European overseas expansion occurred for numerous reasons. The new national states of western Europe were now sufficiently centralized to support and finance exploration and expansion. Technological advances in

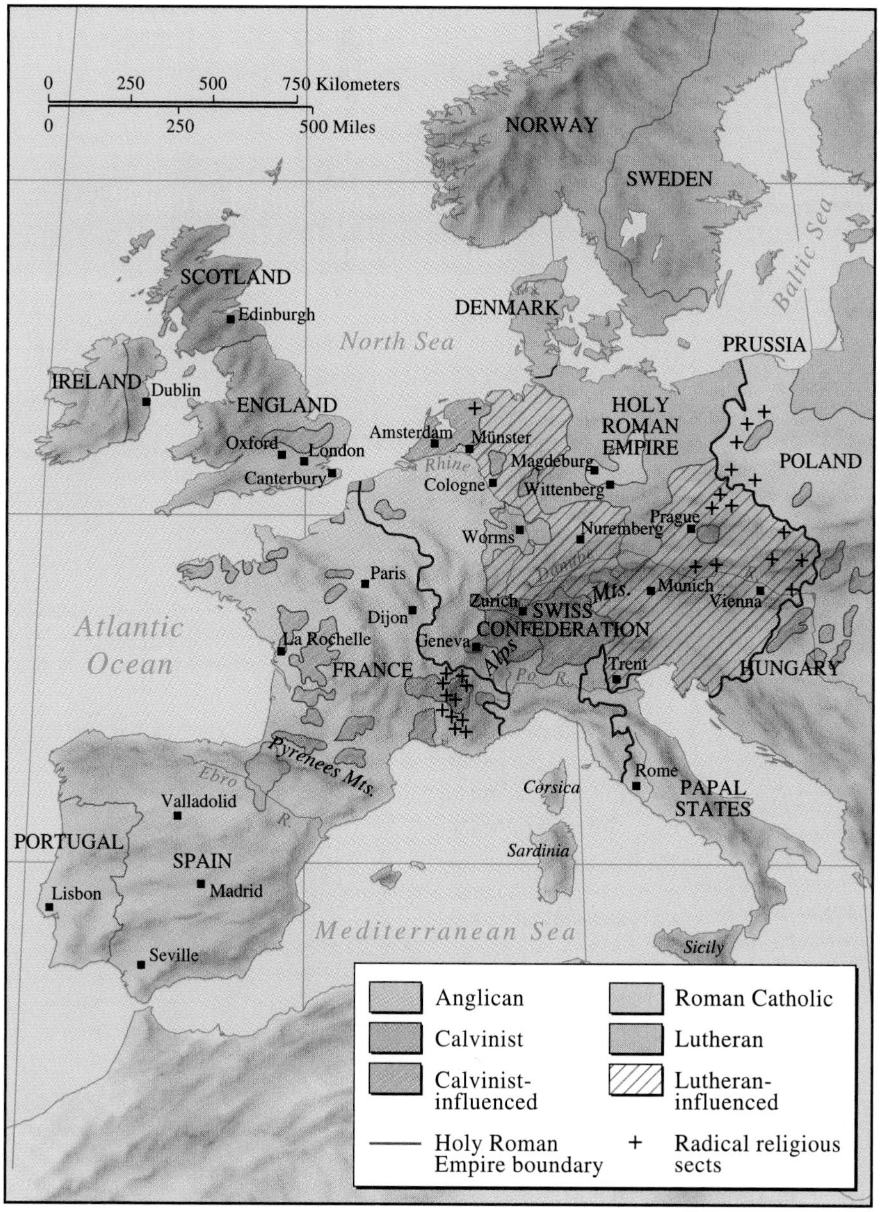

MAP 9.4 Catholics and Protestants in Europe by 1560. Reformation religious upheavals affected most of Europe, with Protestant faiths becoming dominant in northern Europe. Protestantism also made substantial headway in France, the Habsburg dominions, southern Germany, and Poland, but these areas were eventually won back to Roman Catholicism.

Jesuit Duty in a World of "Heathens" and "Heretics"

From your letter we learned of your . . . ardent desire for the salvation of the souls that are [ready for] the harvest in the Indies [Western Hemisphere]. Would that we were able to . . . appease our own desires, which are aflame with the same zeal! . . .

To be sure, we are not afraid of the great distance at which the missions lie nor of the labor involved. . . .

We have heard of the door which . . . has opened to the preaching of the gospel and the conversion of the people of Japan and China. . . .

You know how important [is] the preservation and increase of the faith in those lands, and in Guinea [Africa] and Brazil. . . .

We enjoin . . . prayers for the spiritual needs of England and Germany. . . and of all others that are infected with heresy so that at length the God of those nations shall have pity on them and of all others that are infected with heresy and deign to lead them back to the purity of the Christian faith and religion.

It is our desire that these prayers continue as long as these nations need our help, and that no provinces, even in the farthest Indies, be exempt from this duty of charity.*

These passages are excerpts from letters written by Ignatius Loyola, the founder and head of the Jesuit order, from the vantage point of his headquarters in Rome. Loyola's letters express, in microcosm, two of the main concerns of mid-sixteenth-century Europe: contact with strange new lands and peoples, and religious strife. Loyola's statements mirror the narrow intensity of his day. Protestants were equally convinced that they were the Christians and that the Catholics were "infected with heresy." Both factions would have been equally aghast at the notion that other peoples might have valid religions and not stand in need of conversion.

*The Letters of St. Ignatius of Loyola, trans. William J. Young (Chicago: Loyola University Press, 1959), pp. 35, 36, 298, 299, 301, 302.

navigational systems and ship design enabled sailors to undertake longer voyages. Moreover, Europeans had visions of wealth; gold, pepper, ivory, and slaves from Africa were all valued commodities on world markets. European governments and merchants were also eager to find alternative ocean routes so they could avoid the high import taxes imposed by the Ottoman Empire on goods coming overland from Asia by caravan. For Spain and Portugal, religion also played a role. After years of struggle against Muslim domination of the Iberian Peninsula during the *Reconquista,* the devoutly Christian rulers of Spain and Portugal were eager to dominate Muslim states in North Africa and to convert non-Christians. Some Europeans even dreamed of forging links with the legendary African kingdom of the Christian leader Prester John.

Portugal was the first to move. With a long maritime tradition and an advantageous geographical position on the Atlantic, Portugal was the first European nation to look for a seaborne route to tap the wealth of the Atlantic islands, Africa, and (hopefully) Asia. Beginning in the 1430s, Prince Henry (later called the "Navigator" by the English), the brother of the king of Portugal, used the royal treasury to finance voyages of discovery down the African coast; by 1498 the Portuguese were in Asia. In 1492, with the voyage of Columbus, Spain moved westward to the Americas. A century later, England, France, and the Netherlands joined in. The text will take up European expansion in the context of the cultures of each geographical area the Europeans entered; this chapter will discuss Africa and the Western Hemisphere, and Chapter 10 will deal with Asia.

African Kingdoms, European Contacts, and the Slave Trade

Your people . . . seize many of our people, freed and exempt men; and very often it happens that they kidnap even noblemen and the sons of noblemen, and our relatives, and take them to be sold to the white men. . . .

And as soon as they are taken by the white men they are immediately ironed and branded with fire, and when they are carried to be embarked, if they are caught by our guards' men the whites allege that they have bought them but they cannot say from whom. . . .

And so to avoid such a great evil we passed a law so that any white man living in our Kingdoms and wanting to purchase goods in any way should first inform three of our noblemen and officials of our court . . . who should investigate if the mentioned goods are captives or free men. . . . But if the white men do not comply with it they will lose the aforementioned goods.

*A letter from King Afonso of the Kongo to the king of Portugal, October 18, 1526, in *The Horizon History of Africa* (New York: American Heritage, 1971), p. 334.

In this letter in 1526, King Afonso, a convert to Christianity, complains of the excesses of European slave traders in his Kongo kingdom. The slave trade, however, was but one aspect of the dynamic and complex situation in Africa during the period from the fifteenth to the seventeenth century. Africa encompassed a wide variety of states and cultures. The North African states had been adherents to Islam for centuries and had strong contacts with the rest of the Muslim world and with Europe. Centrally organized states with dynastic rulers controlled much of central and western Africa, where Islam continued to spread. Many Africans along the eastern coast, in the Sudan, and in the northern regions of West Africa chose to embrace it. Meanwhile, the Portuguese were moving down the West African coast; eventually, they reached southern and eastern Africa and began to trade for the riches of those regions as well. In the fourteenth century, when Europeans first began to make extensive contact, many West African societies were not appreciably weaker in economic terms than most European societies. The slave trade substantially altered that balance. As it turned out, the greatest wealth for European traders was to be found in the labor of human beings. The slave trade devastated many regions of Africa; it also profoundly changed the Western Hemisphere (see the following section). The ensuing discussion will focus on a number of African societies beginning about the fifteenth century, when European explorers and traders began to have extensive contact with local African rulers and peoples.

Islamic North Africa and Christian Ethiopia

Except for Morocco, the Islamic societies that had been established in North Africa were all incorporated into the Ottoman Empire in the sixteenth century. These North African provinces were ruled by governors who were either appointed directly by the sultan or were local rulers who pledged their loyalty to Istanbul. Although trade with sub-Saharan states continued, the northern sectors of Africa remained tied culturally, religiously, and politically with the Arab world and the Ottoman Empire.

The Berber rulers in Morocco, meanwhile, resisted most Portuguese and Spanish territorial onslaughts and at the same time expanded southeastward. In 1590, under Sultan Mansur, Moroccan forces armed with cannon attacked the declining Songhai Empire (present-day Mali), whose soldiers were equipped only with spears and bows and arrows; the power and wealth of that once-great state came under direct Moroccan control.

By the sixteenth century, Muslim armies from Arabia, which already controlled most of the coastal regions of the Horn of Africa, began to attack Christian Ethiopia. Early in the sixteenth century, a local military ruler, Ahmad ibn Ghazi (reigned 1506–1543), threatened the very survival of Ethiopia. Known as Gran, or left-handed, Ahmad instilled his forces with a fervent belief in *jihad* (holy war) and brought most of Ethiopia under his control. To save his government, the Ethiopian emperor, Lebna Dengel (reigned 1508–1540), who claimed direct descent from King Solomon and the queen of Sheba some 2,500 years earlier, appealed to the Portuguese for assistance.

The emperor's appeal fell on receptive ears. The Portuguese and Ethiopian cultures were both headed by devoutly Christian absolute monarchs hostile to the Muslims. In addition, the Portuguese had long been fascinated with Ethiopia, which they believed might house the famed realm of Prester John. The myth of this fabled Christian kingdom and its exact location had created lively debate in Europe; Mongolia, China, and India had been suggested as possible locations. When these possibilities had been discarded, Portuguese adventurers began to search for Prester John's mythical kingdom in Ethiopia. Most were initially disappointed by the poverty of Ethiopia and dismayed by many of its religious customs. Nevertheless, the Portuguese missionary Father Alvarez was impressed by the riches of Ethiopian religious art and architecture. Alvarez's books on Ethiopia described these finds and aroused even more European interest in the remote African kingdom.

In response to Emperor Lebna Dengel's appeal, Portugal sent an expeditionary force under the command of Dom Christoval da Gama to rescue the Christian kingdom from its many enemies. In 1529, however, da Gama was surrounded by Muslim forces, taken captive, and decapitated. His death marked the apex of Muslim power in Ethiopia, which waned after the death of Ahmad the Gran. In the remote mountains of northern Ethiopia, the emperors attempted to continue their absolute rule, but their power was weakened by internal political rivalries, religious disputes, and Muslim opposition. Although Ethiopia's relative isolation prevented it from keeping pace with the commercial and political growth of other, wealthier kingdoms in central and western Africa, its difficult terrain made it almost impossible for outside forces to conquer it.

Life in Prosperous West African Kingdoms

Before the fifteenth century, three large, highly centralized empires had emerged across much of the Sudanic belt and forest regions of western and central Africa. These states (see Chapter 7) consisted of Ghana (500–1250), Mali (1250–1450), and Songhai (1450–1600). The economy of these kingdoms was largely based on the trade of salt and gold with the Islamic world; and as a result of extensive contacts with that world, most of the rulers and elite gradually embraced Islam.

Published memoirs in Arabic by Muslim travelers, various works by Europeans, oral traditions, and archaeological and anthropological studies have all contributed to our knowledge of these kingdoms. Firsthand written accounts by contemporaries tend to be more numerous in the kingdoms under Islamic rule, where literacy in Arabic was fairly widespread among the elite. Many of the non-Muslim kingdoms, lacking written languages, relied on oral traditions to transmit knowledge of historical and social events; recent scholarship indicates that many of

A Strong Muslim Kingdom in Africa

Our Sultan Haj Idris . . . sought to follow the example of our Lord and Master Muhammad.

So also his exploits when he fought the Barbara, till the earth in its fulness became too narrow for them and the desert too small for them.

So he made the pilgrimage and visited Medina. . . . He was enriched by visiting the tomb of the companions of the prophet Muhammad . . . and he bought in the noble city a house and date grove.

Among the most surprising of his acts was the stand he took against obscenity and adultery, so that no such thing took place openly in his time.

He built the big town near Damasak and made four gates in the town and placed a keeper in charge of each gate and quartered there a detachment of his army. He ordered all his chiefs who were powerful and possessed of a defense force, to build houses and leave part of their equipment there as for instance, the horses, and quilted-armor . . . and coats of mail.

Among the gifts with which God had endowed him, was an impressive appearance. All his followers, small or great, never felt contented except in his presence. Even though he sent large armies in one direction and went in some other direction with a small force himself, his captains were not content to go without him.

Such is the account we have given of the character of our Sultan and his wars in the time when he was king. We have written it after there has passed of his reign twelve years.*

⁓

Idris ibn Ali, or Idris Alooma, was the powerful African king of the Bornu kingdom from 1570 to 1602. He was a devout Muslim who extended the faith and his realm through negotiation and military conquest. At the peak of its power, Bornu centered on Lake Chad and stretched far into present-day Libya. Many of the exploits and extensive experiences of ibn Ali were recorded by Ahmad ibn Fartua in his *History of the First Twelve Years of Mai Idris Alooma.*

*The Horizon History of Africa (New York: American Heritage, 1971), pp. 236–238.

these oral traditions are as accurate and detailed as the written records. Like written accounts, oral renditions often exaggerated the glory and power of victorious, successful rulers.

These and subsequent centralized states in West Africa shared a number of political and cultural characteristics. The Oyo and Benin Empires were ruled by "divine kings" whose welfare was often thought to determine that of their kingdoms. The status of these kings was so high that their subjects sometimes feared that an ailing, sick

king meant that the state would weaken and probably die. The Oyo Empire prospered under a series of dynamic kings until the eighteenth century. In conquered areas, village chieftains reported to palace chiefs appointed by the king, who, together with other notables, assisted in his administration.

Benin, perhaps the most powerful of the centralized states, was already a powerful kingdom by 1300. Under Ewuare the Great (reigned c. 1440–1473), the prosperous kingdom extended from the port at Lagos to the Niger. Although the economies of the western and central African kingdoms had long been indirectly connected with Europe through trade with North Africa and the Muslim world, Benin, a center for overland and sea trade, was one of the first West African kingdoms to come into direct contact with European traders and explorers.

Portuguese traders described Benin city as a large fortified stronghold at least twenty-five miles in circumference. While the *oba* (king) of Benin and his court resided in a lavish palace decorated with bronze plaques, most of the populace lived in mud houses covered with palm leaves. The city was divided by broad streets and connected to the coast by a good road. Portuguese travelers reported that there were no beggars in Benin, as the king and government officials cared and provided for the poor.

Both the Oyo and Benin societies assimilated and extended the artistic traditions of the earlier Ife kingdoms of western Africa. Benin artists were particularly renowned for their highly realistic bronze sculptures made with the lost-wax process. They also excelled in wood, ivory, and terra cotta sculpture. The oba and notables adorned their dress with finely crafted gold and ivory ornaments. At ceremonial functions, the oba wore robes decorated with red coral beads and carved ivory masks attached to his belt; ivory had religious symbolism and indicated the ruler's divine aspects. Ivory carvings were often handed down to royal successors as a symbol of kingship. As in the Ottoman, Safavid, and Chinese empires, the rulers subsidized a lively court art. By controlling the craft guilds, Benin kings guaranteed that they would acquire the finest art works in bronze, gold, and ivory.

The Akan states, in present-day Ghana, were also led by strong kings, assisted by councils of notables. Some of these kings were advised by priests in a type of theocratic government. These states were all dependent upon agriculture for revenues, but they also engaged in trade; the most profitable items were gold and kola nuts. The Ashanti, who moved from the interior into the coastal area of present-day Ghana, were the most powerful of the Akan people. Leading strong military forces, the Ashanti kings soon subjugated the peoples living in the coastal regions; by gaining control over the trade routes for gold from the savanna regions, they became both rich and powerful.

The Ashanti excelled in making finely wrought and lavish gold objects. The kings held a monopoly over gold nuggets and crafted pieces; the people could only own gold dust. Ashanti kings appeared at state functions dressed in golden hats, bracelets, and necklaces and even gold-decorated sandals. Europeans were so impressed by these displays of wealth that they called the region the Gold Coast. The Ashanti were also known for handwoven cloth known as *kente*. Kente cloth is woven into long strips, which are then sewn together; originally, only chiefs and notables wore the kente. Much as clans in Scotland have their own tartans, Ashanti royal families had their own designs, usually in bright greens, reds, blues, and gold.

The States of Central Africa

Like many of the West African states, the Kongo kingdom along the Congo River and the Lunda state were well organized politically and economically. The Kongo capital was on high ground more than 100 miles inland from the coast. Following a matrilineal line, the Kongo kings were often succeeded by their sisters' sons. King Nzinga Nkuwu (1506–1543), baptized Afonso, was one of the first African monarchs converted to Christianity by Portuguese missionaries.

Afonso I learned to read and write Portuguese and sent a number of officials, including his son, Dom Henrique, to Portugal for education and religious training. As his numerous letters to the Portuguese king indicate (see the excerpt at the beginning of this section), Afonso considered himself an equal to European monarchs. Although he adopted Christianity and European dress and habits, Afonso was clearly not a puppet or vassal of the Portuguese. Indeed, the Kongo kingdom governed more people and territory than Portugal. Afonso's alliances and agreements with the Portuguese were made on the basis of equality, and he exercised strict administrative controls over both commerce and the slave trade.

As this description indicates, the societies of western and central Africa had developed their own unique and durable political organizations long before the advent of European exploration. Trade between African states and Europeans was initially established on an equal footing and for mutually beneficial economic reasons. During this era, most Africans, with some exceptions such as the king of the Kongo, retained their own unique traditional religious beliefs and effectively ignored or resisted attempts by European missionaries to gain converts for Christianity.

European Entry into Africa

In the early fifteenth century, the Portuguese began to move into Africa. Portugal's first target was Morocco, where it conquered small coastal areas. During the next half-century, the Portuguese worked down the West

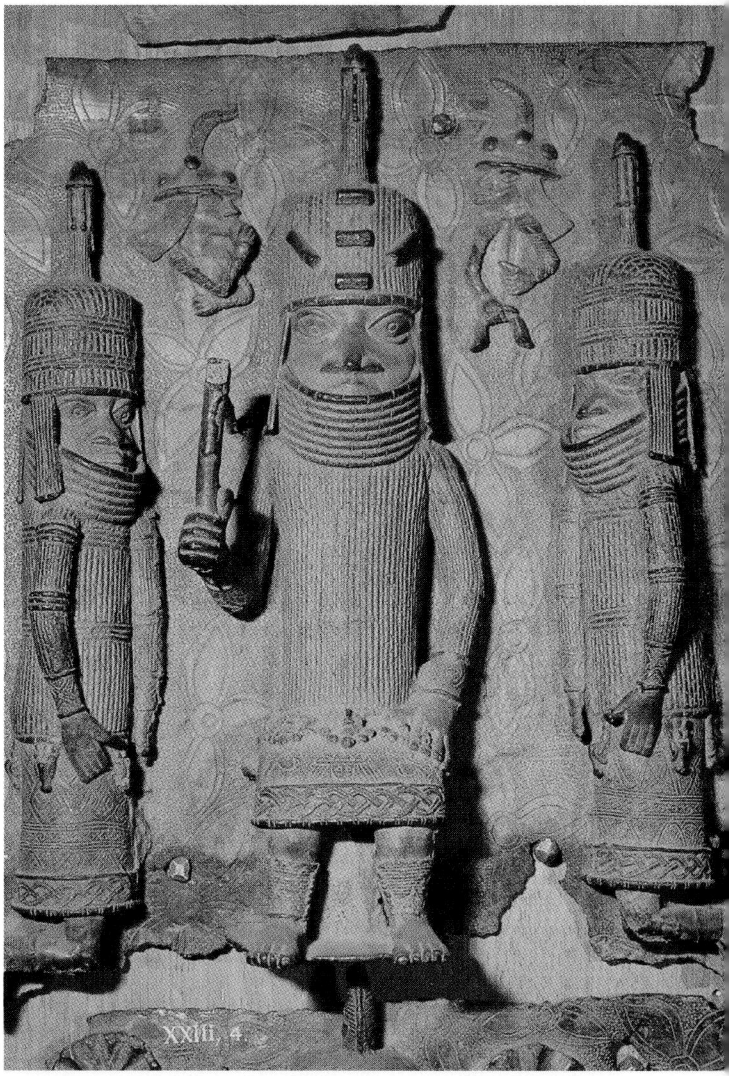

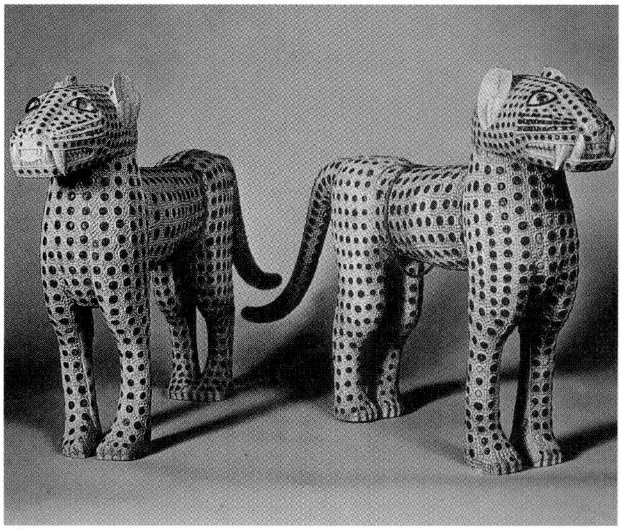

Benin Bronze. Above, the oba is flanked by two attendants. He is wearing the dress, collar, and anklets signifying his high position. Below, ivory and brass leopards were a symbol of royalty. Both photos: Bridgeman/Art Resource

African coast to Angola. The voyages of Bartholomeu Dias in 1487–1488 and Vasco da Gama in 1497–1499 opened up the Cape of Good Hope and East Africa to Portuguese traders and explorers; in 1498 da Gama arrived in India (see Chapter 10). At the East African city-state of Malindi, da Gama was greeted by a king seated on a bronze chair and wearing an ornate robe trimmed in green satin. The leaders of Malindi welcomed an alliance with the Portuguese as an aid in their commercial rivalry with traders in Mombasa.

Traders and adventurers, the Portuguese were not initially interested in founding colonies in Africa. However, they did establish fortified trading posts at strategic ports along the western and eastern coasts. Fort São Jorge was established at Elmina on the west coast in 1482. In 1576 it was followed by Luanda, which became a major center for the transport of slaves from Angola. Along the East African coast the Portuguese extracted tribute from the local rulers of Kilwa in 1502 and later extended their domination over the older commercial city-states of Malindi and Mombasa.

African forces from the interior frequently attacked the Portuguese enclaves, limiting Portuguese domination to the coastal regions. Mombasa resisted for so many decades that the Portuguese nicknamed it the Island of War. In 1592 the Portuguese finally seized Mombasa and largely destroyed the local opposition. Afterward they built a new outpost, called Fort Jesus, which still stands as evidence of Portuguese presence in Africa.

Although the Portuguese struggled to monopolize the African trade routes and the access to the Asian trade these routes provided, they were quickly challenged by the Spanish, Dutch, English, and other Europeans. By 1630 English traders were operating along West Africa; they were soon followed by the French and Dutch. The Swedes and Danes also competed for territorial footholds in Ghana, or the Gold Coast. The Dutch proved a particularly formidable rival, and by 1610 they had effectively ended Portuguese dominance in the Indian Ocean. These rival European powers built many forts and military installations along the West African coast; these installations were intended primarily to defend the nation's trading interests against competing Europeans, not as protection against the African states.

As Portuguese naval power waned in the seventeenth century, first Mombasa and then other East African city-states revolted. Mombasa requested aid from fellow Muslims, most notably from the *imam* (leader) of Oman on the Arabian coast. The Omanis, who had a long naval tradition, quickly responded and after several failures succeeded in ousting the Portuguese from Mombasa in 1698 and subsequently from neighboring East African city-states. The Omanis then established a Muslim empire in coastal East Africa that lasted into the nineteenth century.

Dutch Settlements in South Africa

In 1652, at Table Bay in South Africa the Dutch founded Africa's first European settlement. Originally, the settlement was intended as a reprovisioning station for ships of the Dutch East India Company undertaking the long voyage between Europe and Asia; it was not meant to be an outpost for further Dutch settlement or colonial expansion. However, the persistent need for fresh food supplies led the Dutch East India Company to bring in colonists to establish farms in South Africa in 1657. Slaves were then brought in as forced laborers.

As the colony expanded, the Dutch attacked the indigenous Khoi and forcibly dispersed them. The colonists recruited single Dutch women so that the predominantly male population of the colony could marry Europeans. The Dutch settlers were reinforced by French Huguenots who fled the persecution of Louis XIV. These frontier farmers, who called themselves both Boers (farmers) and Afrikaners, were strict Calvinists. Their descendants continued to dominate South Africa well into the twentieth century.

The Boers viewed black Africans as inferior human beings and used their strict Calvinist tenets to justify their attitude of racial superiority. They established a system of strict social and racial stratification in which the Dutch Boers were at the top, followed by later Asian immigrants and coloreds (people of mixed race), with blacks at the bottom. This racial hierarchy, based on white European domination, continued into the 1990s.

The Slave Trade in Africa

The slave trade was a key element of European expansion and had disastrous results for African peoples. As in many other societies and cultures, slavery had very deep roots in Africa and was known in antiquity. Africans had enslaved other Africans, and despite Qur'anic injunctions against such practices, Islamic societies in Africa had perpetuated the system. It persisted throughout Africa and especially in the Sudan in the ninth century; it was common in Islamic Africa and was practiced in Bornu in the fourteenth century. African slaves could be found throughout the Islamic world, in India, and perhaps also in China prior to European expansion into these areas. Slavery in Africa and the Islamic world was not based on race or religion, however. Animists, Christians, and Muslims in Africa and elsewhere had historically enslaved members of their own and other religions. As in most civilizations up to this time, Africans acquired slaves from raids or victories in wars. In African and Islamic cultures, slaves were generally treated as part of the family and were integrated into the larger society. Most such slaves in the Islamic world served as domestic servants, concubines, or slave-soldiers.

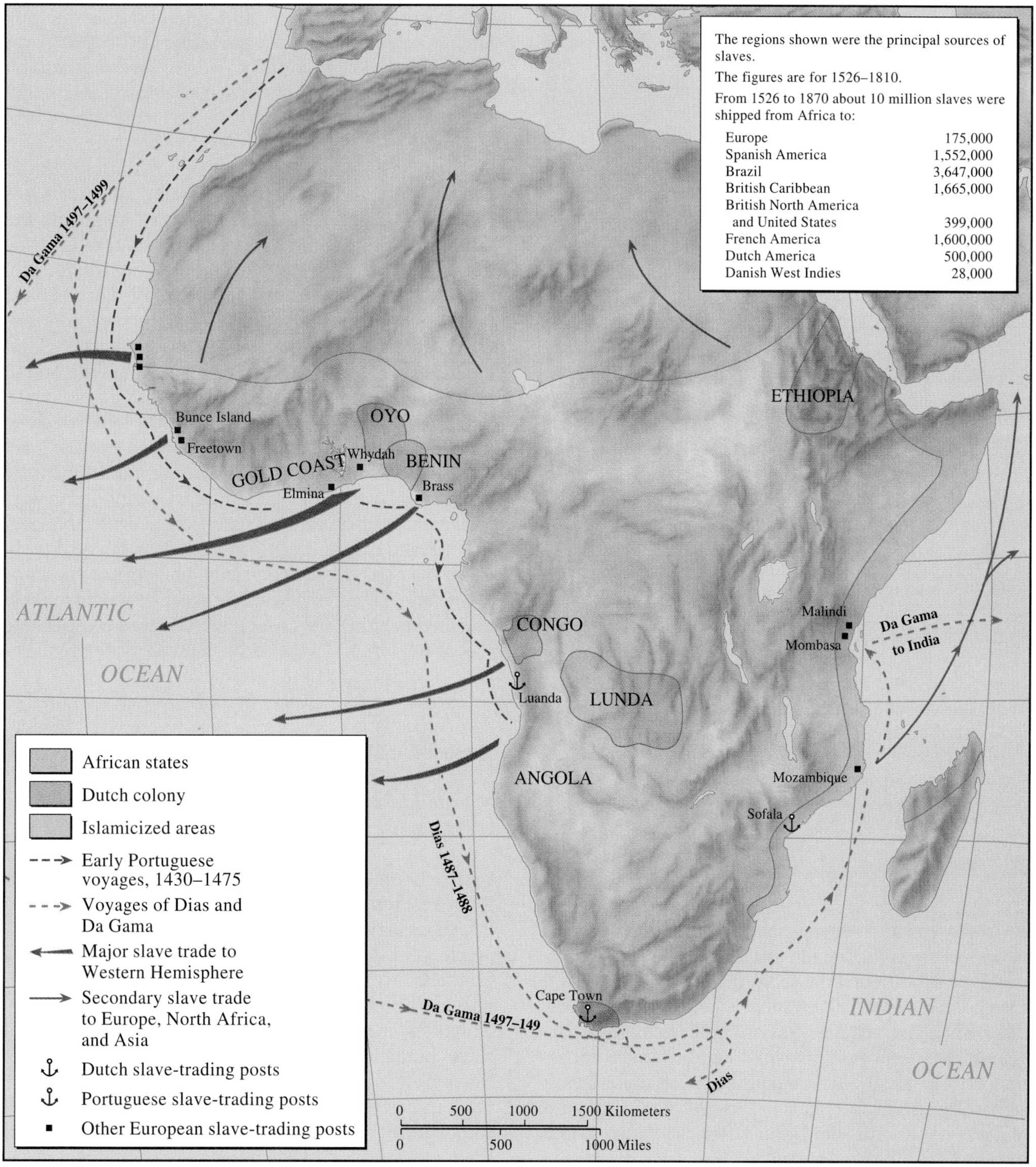
The regions shown were the principal sources of slaves.
The figures are for 1526–1810.
From 1526 to 1870 about 10 million slaves were shipped from Africa to:
Europe 175,000
Spanish America 1,552,000
Brazil 3,647,000
British Caribbean 1,665,000
British North America and United States 399,000
French America 1,600,000
Dutch America 500,000
Danish West Indies 28,000
Da Gama 1497–1499
ETHIOPIA
Bunce Island
Freetown
OYO
GOLD COAST
Whydah
BENIN
Elmina
Brass
ATLANTIC
OCEAN
CONGO
Luanda
LUNDA
ANGOLA
Malindi
Mombasa
Da Gama to India
Mozambique
Sofala
Dias 1487–1488
Cape Town
Da Gama 1497–149
Dias
INDIAN
OCEAN
African states
Dutch colony
Islamicized areas
Early Portuguese voyages, 1430–1475
Voyages of Dias and Da Gama
Major slave trade to Western Hemisphere
Secondary slave trade to Europe, North Africa, and Asia
Dutch slave-trading posts
Portuguese slave-trading posts
Other European slave-trading posts
0 500 1000 1500 Kilometers
0 500 1000 Miles

MAP 9.5 Africa, 1500–c. 1750, and the Slave Trade. By the sixteenth century, Islam had spread throughout much of North and East Africa, while many independent kingdoms and city-states continued to prosper. Along the African coasts, European explorers also founded small trading posts, where the slave trade flourished. The slave trade grew as increasing numbers of able-bodied African men and women were transported as slave labor for plantations in the Western Hemisphere.

Memoirs of a Slave

The first object which saluted my eyes when I arrived on the coast was the sea, and a slave ship which was then riding at anchor and waiting for its cargo. These filled me with astonishment, which was soon converted into terror when I was carried on board. I was immediately handled and tossed up to see if I were sound ... and I was now persuaded that I had gotten into a world of bad spirits and that they were going to kill me. Their complexions too differing so much from ours, their long hair and the language they spoke (which was very different from any I had ever heard) united to confirm me in this belief. ...

I now saw myself deprived of all chance of returning to my native country. ... I became so sick and low that I was not able to eat. ... In a little time after, amongst the poor chained men I found some of my own nation. ... I inquired of these what was to be done with us; they gave me to understand we were to be carried to these white people's country to work for them.*

The slave trade persisted for centuries. In this excerpt, Olaudah Equiano, from present-day Nigeria, describes his reactions to being captured and taken into slavery. Equiano was taken to the West Indies, Canada, England, and the United States; he was freed in 1766 and became a spokesperson for the antislavery movement. His memoirs offer a moving testimony to the human cost of slavery and its disruption of African society.*

*Olaudah Equiano, in *Modern Asia and Africa,* ed. William H. McNeill and Mitsuko Iriye (New York: Oxford University Press, 1971), pp. 82–84.

The extensive trade in African slaves by the Western nations between the late fifteenth and the nineteenth centuries severely affected the social, cultural, economic, and even political life of the African societies. Although experts disagree on how adversely this trade affected African development, none deny its social and economic consequences. Although Muslim and European traders took some African slaves for sale in Europe, the Canary and Madeira Islands, Muslim North Africa, the Ottoman Empire, and Asia, the vast majority of those taken by the Europeans and their African allies were sent to the Western Hemisphere for sale.

In contrast to slaves in other societies, the overwhelming majority of slaves in the Western Hemisphere was used as agricultural workers on vast cotton, tobacco, or sugar plantations or as laborers in copper and silver mines. Because only able-bodied men and women were suitable for such hard labor, most slaves taken from Africa were young males from fifteen to thirty years of age. Although experts disagree on the exact numbers, it appears that between 10 and 15 million Africans were forcibly removed from their homelands to become slaves in the Americas; in addition, possibly several million more were killed during the armed raids to secure the slaves or died as a result of the forced marches and brutal conditions to which the captives were subjected.

The first African slaves were shipped from Spain to Latin America in 1501. By 1518 Spanish slave traders had established direct trade routes between Africa and the Americas. Recognizing the enormous profits to be made in this human traffic, the Portuguese, English, French, and Dutch also engaged in the slave trade. For the most part, European slave traffickers did not capture the slaves, but paid professional African slave traders or local political leaders to secure slaves from the interior and to bring them to ports or marshaling yards on the coast. They were then herded into ships for the long voyage to the Western Hemisphere.

Although some slaves were sold as punishment by their African owners or rulers, most were captured in wars and raids. Slave hunting was a violent activity. Able-bodied men and women were torn from their villages, shackled in chains, and fastened together in long lines by strips of rawhide. These long human chains were then forcibly marched to either the East or West African coast, where they were purchased by European traders. Many slaves died of abuse or committed suicide before they ever reached the coast. Others (at least 15 percent) died of inadequate food or disease in the overcrowded, vermin-infested ships that transported the slaves to the Americas. Slave revolts were not uncommon, particularly among Muslim Africans, especially after they reached the Western Hemisphere.

African leaders who cooperated with European slave traders became rich from the slave trade. They coveted European armaments with which to extend their authority. The Songhai leaders in northwestern Africa, for example, sold slaves for horses and guns. On Goree Island off the coast of present-day Senegal, one of the major depots for the traffic in human beings, West African women, who often engaged in commerce, controlled the sale of slaves brought from the interior regions. Likewise, some Muslim African traders became wealthy from the slave trade in East Africa and the Sudan. On the other hand, some African leaders sought to stop or at least to contain the trade. The obas in Benin banned the export of males from their territories until the end of the seventeenth century. King Afonso I in the Kongo also protested the trade and made numerous attempts to control and curtail it.

In Angola, where the Portuguese were particularly active, Africans fiercely opposed the slave trade and foreign intervention. The Portuguese had made considerable inroads into Angola when the Africans were led by weak monarchs, but in 1623–1624 Nzinga Mbandi ascended to the throne. As strong a ruler as Cleopatra of Egypt or Catherine the Great of Russia, Nzinga was an astute

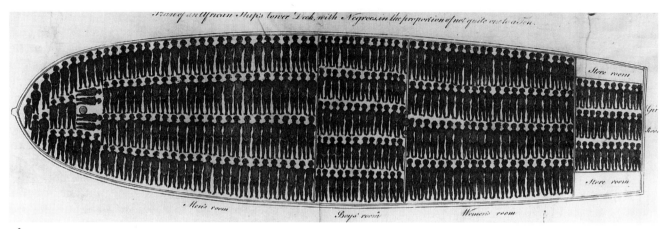

�֍ Slave Ship. This diagram shows how slaves were "packed" into ships for the long and often fatal journey to the Americas. Slaves were crowded onto all decks and all possible spaces and frequently died of asphyxiation, thirst, and disease during the long sea voyage. Historical Society of Pennsylvania, Pennsylvania Abolition Society Papers

diplomat and politician. Forbidding her subjects to call her queen, Nzinga took the title king and promptly launched a lifelong struggle against the Portuguese. She joined forces with the Dutch against the Portuguese and lured Portuguese slave-soldiers to desert by promising them freedom and land. In spite of several uneasy treaties with the Portuguese, she continued fighting them until her death in 1663. No strong ruler followed Nzinga. As a result, the Portuguese were able to prevail, and Angolan villages were increasingly decimated by slave raids.

While coastal areas of Africa frequently prospered because of the slave trade, many villages, farms, and political institutions in the interior were weakened or destroyed. Damage to the cultural and economic life of African societies varied greatly from region to region. The forced removal of vital segments of their populations had a lasting impact on some African societies. Many major states, however, particularly West African states like Benin, survived the attacks. Most African states remained independent of outside rule until the nineteenth century.

One of the most abusive and inhumane enterprises shared between Africa and the West, slavery spread throughout much of the Western Hemisphere in the following century. Slavery profoundly altered traditional social, economic, and political patterns in both Africa and the Western Hemisphere (as discussed in the next section).

European Colonial Empires in the Western Hemisphere

Strange people have come to the shores of the great sea [the Caribbean]. . . . Their trappings and arms are all made of iron; they dress in iron and wear iron casques on their heads.

Their swords are made of iron; their shields are iron; their spears are iron. Their deer carry them on their backs wherever they wish to go. Those deer, our lord, are as tall as the roof of a house. . . . The strangers' bodies are completely covered, so that only their faces can be seen. Their skin is white, as if it were made of lime. They have yellow hair, though some of them are black[-haired]. Their dogs are enormous, with flat ears and long dangling tongues. . . . Their eyes flash fire. [Referring to a gun:] a thing like a ball of stone comes out of its entrails; it comes out shooting sparks and raining fire. The smoke that comes out has a pestilent odor, like rotten mud. . . . If the cannon is aimed against a mountain, the mountain splits and cracks open.*

*Miguel Leon-Portilla, ed., The Broken Spears: The Aztec Account of the Conquest of Mexico, trans. A. M. Garibay and L. Kemp (Boston: Beacon Press, 1969), pp. 30–31.

This vivid description of the Spanish arrival in Mexico occurs in a report given to Moctezuma II, the Aztec ruler, by his spies, who observed the landing and advance of the Spaniards in 1519. The presence of the Spanish in the heartland of Mesoamerican civilization was but one aspect of a remarkable historical phenomenon—the expansion of European power around the globe during the sixteenth century. At the time the Spanish were confronting the Aztecs, Europeans were constructing fortified trading posts along the African coast and building up the slave trade. Europeans were also appearing on the shores of Asia (see Chapter 10).

Early European Exploration of the Western Hemisphere

Spanish and Portuguese explorers and settlers were the first Europeans to exploit the resources of the Western Hemisphere. Christopher Columbus, an Italian financed

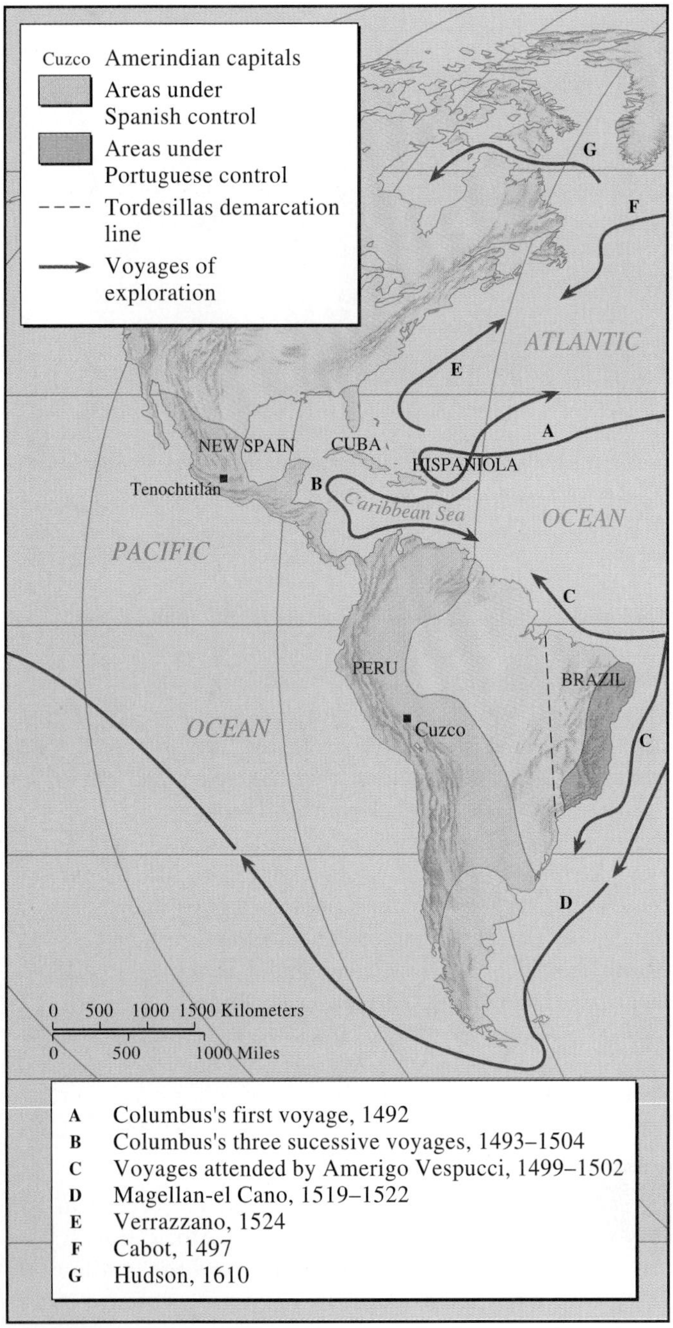

Cuzco Amerindian capitals
Areas under Spanish control
Areas under Portuguese control
Tordesillas demarcation line
Voyages of exploration
ATLANTIC
OCEAN
PACIFIC
OCEAN
NEW SPAIN
CUBA
HISPANIOLA
Tenochtitlán
Caribbean Sea
PERU
BRAZIL
Cuzco
A
B
C
D
E
F
G
0 500 1000 1500 Kilometers
0 500 1000 Miles
A Columbus's first voyage, 1492
B Columbus's three sucessive voyages, 1493–1504
C Voyages attended by Amerigo Vespucci, 1499–1502
D Magellan-el Cano, 1519–1522
E Verrazzano, 1524
F Cabot, 1497
G Hudson, 1610

MAP 9.6 The Western Hemisphere, c. 1600. After a century of exploration and conquest, Spain had created a huge colonial holding, based in large part on the ruins of the Aztec and Inka Empires. The Portuguese were beginning to create a major colony in Brazil.

by Queen Isabella of Castile, led the way. By sailing west, Columbus expected to find a shorter route to Asia than the one the Portuguese were pursuing around the African coast. He calculated that Japan was about 2,400 miles west of the Canary Islands (off the northwestern coast of Africa), putting Asia within range of the sailing ships of that day. On October 12, 1492, Columbus made landfall in the Bahamas, approximately where he had calculated Asia to be. Assuming that he was off the coast of Asia, he called the islands the "Indies" and their inhabitants "Indians" (in this text, Amerindians). In 1493 Columbus triumphantly returned to Spain.

In January 1492, just a few months before Columbus's first voyage, the Spanish had conquered Granada, the last Muslim enclave on the Iberian Peninsula. The victory was the culmination of seven centuries of the Reconquista, the reconquest of the peninsula from the Muslims–a crusade that had had a profound impact on Spanish institutions and practices. The struggle against the Muslims had forged a powerful partnership between church and state in Spanish society. The end of the Reconquista left a large number of men looking for new and profitable adventures and for new areas for Christianity to conquer.

During the quarter-century after Columbus's landing in the Bahamas, the Spanish occupied the major Caribbean islands. They found that European crops and domestic animals could thrive in the Western Hemisphere. Eventually, it became clear that the islands could produce valuable crops of sugar and tobacco. These products, however, required constant attention and thus a large labor force.

To get this labor, the Spanish instituted the *encomienda* system, in which the Spanish king gave individual Spaniards control over Amerindian lands and villages. The *encomiendero* had the right to force the Amerindians under his control to work in his mines and fields. This brutal labor system and the ravages of new diseases from Europe, along with secondary factors, killed nearly all of the Amerindians in the Caribbean. Deprived of a native workforce, the Spanish imported large numbers of black slaves from Africa.

To avoid confrontation, the Spanish and Portuguese negotiated a treaty to divide the Western Hemisphere between them. Under the Treaty of Tordesillas in 1494, the pope selected a line of longitude; Spain received everything west of the line and Portugal everything east of it. The treaty technically gave Asia, the East Indies, and Brazil to Portugal, while everything else in the Western Hemisphere went to Spain. In 1500 Pedro Cabral landed in Brazil and formally claimed the area for Portugal. Brazil eventually became a major sugar-producing area.

Meanwhile, Europeans were readjusting their thinking about the nature of the lands that Columbus had found. After two voyages to the Western Hemisphere in which he visited much of the eastern coast of South America, Amerigo Vespucci claimed in 1501 that he had seen a "new land . . . a continent." In 1507 cartographers putting out a new map labeled the area representing present-day Brazil "America" in his honor.

By the early sixteenth century it was becoming clear that Asia was far away from Europe and that America was in between. In 1513 Vasco Núñez de Balboa crossed the

Panamanian isthmus and saw what he called the South Sea (the present-day Pacific Ocean), a sea that ships might sail on to Asia if a way could be found to get through or around America. Various European expeditions searched for a "passage to India," a water route around or through America that led to Asia. They all failed; to the Europeans' dismay, America appeared to be an unbroken barrier extending northward and southward from the Caribbean to the stormy and icy waters of the Arctic and Antarctic Seas.

In 1519 the Spanish government dispatched an expedition under Ferdinand Magellan to find a passage to Asia that would justify a Spanish claim to some of the Southeast Asian Spice Islands held by the Portuguese. For thirty-eight days Magellan fought his way through a stormy water passage (later called the Strait of Magellan) at the tip of South America. Afterward, Magellan pushed across the enormous stretches of Balboa's South Sea, which Magellan termed the Pacific (from the Latin word for "calm") Ocean. His men died from lack of water and ate rats to survive. In 1521 he reached the Philippines, where he was killed in a skirmish. His navigator, Juan Sebastián del Cano, and one surviving ship pushed on across the Indian Ocean, reaching Spain in September 1522, three years after their departure. This first circum-navigation of the globe was one of the great epics of human courage and was the high mark of the age of European exploration. The discoveries of Magellan and del Cano demonstrated that Asia was too far away, and the trip too dangerous, for a successful westward trade route. Although it held on to the Philippine Islands, Spain would have to derive its main colonial wealth from the Western Hemisphere, not the Eastern.

Spanish Conquests in Mexico and South America

Great wealth was not long in coming to the Spanish. For years Spaniards had heard tales of Amerindian empires of gold and silver on the mainland of present-day Mexico. In 1519 Hernán Cortés organized an expedition of 11 vessels, 550 men, 16 horses, and 10 cannon, and sailed from Cuba to the Mexican coast. Marching inland, Cortés swiftly reached the outer fringes of the Aztec Empire.

Aided by large forces of Amerindian allies disaffected by the parasitic rule of the Aztecs, Cortés and his tiny band of Spaniards defeated the Aztecs and conquered Mexico. The key reasons for their victory were clear. Cortés himself gave much credit to his Amerindian allies, both as warriors and porters. The Tlaxcalans, armed with

✺ The Conquest of Mexico. This Amerindian painting depicts several of the techniques by which the Spaniards triumphed. Although the painting does not show the firearms of the Spanish, it pictures their horses, war dogs, and numerous Amerindian allies. The Amerindians on both sides are equipped with black, razor-sharp obsidian, whose lethal effects are apparent.

Stock Montage

razor-sharp obsidian weapons, were especially effective. The Spanish firearms and cannon, as well as their metal armor and weapons, totally outclassed the Aztecs' Stone Age weapons and cotton armor. In battle the Spanish horses and huge mastiffs, which were unknown to the Amerindians, often unnerved them. Cortés also capitalized on prophecies in Mexican folklore that seemed to foretell his coming.

Disease was perhaps the greatest ally Cortés had. An epidemic of smallpox saved him from an Amerindian revolt in 1520. Since Amerindians did not have natural immunities to the many diseases the Europeans carried, including smallpox, measles, and influenza, the ravages of these diseases continued unabated. When Cortés landed, about 28 million people were living in the Mexican heartland. Fifty years later the population had plummeted to 3 million. By 1620 only 1 million Amerindians lived in the area. As a result of the massive depopulation, Amerindian culture in the Western Hemisphere was substantially demolished.

In 1532 the Mexican story was repeated in Peru when Francisco Pizarro led a force of 170 men into the Andes, looking for the gold and silver of the Inka Empire. Inka rule centered in the mountains of present-day Peru, Ecuador, Bolivia, and northern Chile. Like the Aztecs, the Inkas had only lately come to power (see Chapter 7). By the time the Spanish arrived, the Inka ruled about 8 million people and an area about half the size of the Roman Empire at its height. The Inka state was a rigid autocracy in which all power focused on the person of the ruler, the

Inka; this proved to be a fatal weakness. Finding this highly structured civilization divided by civil war and wracked by an epidemic, Pizarro captured, imprisoned, and murdered the Inka ruler, Atahualpa, and destroyed every element of the Inka leadership; in a year he had gained control over the empire.

The *conquistadores* in Mexico and Peru were well rewarded for their ruthless daring. In both Mexico and the Andes, they found substantial reserves of gold and huge amounts of silver. Their search for precious metals and other opportunities for wealth took them into the southern third of the present-day United States, throughout Central America, and across much of South America outside Brazil. In 1545 a very rich lode was discovered at Cerro Potosí in Bolivia, which supplied enormous quantities of silver to the Spaniards. Potosí had a population of 160,000 persons in 1650 when the silver mine was at its most productive. By 1825 when the mine had been largely depleted, the city had shrunk to 8,000 persons.

To exploit the wealth of the Inka Empire, the Spanish instituted a forced labor regime that was, if anything, more brutal than those in Mexico and the Caribbean. Inka rulers had demanded *mit'a* (forced labor) from their subjects. The Spanish claimed that their own demand for forced labor was an extension of the mit'a; under the Inka, however, mit'a demands were harsh but could be met without starvation and other ills that became prevalent under the Spanish. The dangerous and arduous labor in the mines killed many Amerindians. Its effects, coupled with recurrent epidemics, caused the Andean population

❊ The Mountain of Silver at Potosí. This 1553 woodcut shows the main fruit of Pizarro's conquest of the Inka Empire. The silver mines and smelteries at Potosí (in present-day Bolivia) produced about $1 billion worth of silver for the Spanish during the colonial period. The woodcut omits the deaths of tens of thousands of Amerindian workers. Stock Montage

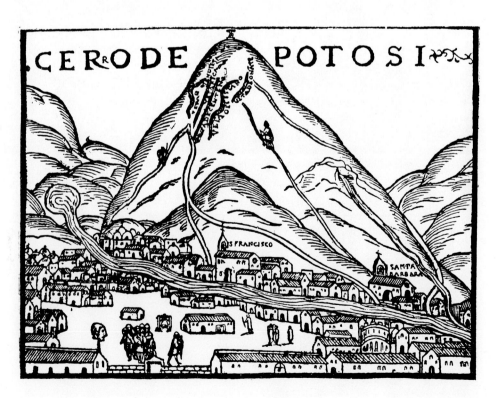

to decline in the same proportion as in Mexico, with the same devastating results on Amerindian culture.

It is likely that the Amerindians gave their conquerors syphilis in exchange for the terrible plagues that had been let loose among them. Syphilis raged for decades as an epidemic, mortal disease in Europe. Eventually, it became a slow-acting but still immensely dangerous disease.

In the middle of the sixteenth century, the Amerindians were proclaimed subjects of the Spanish crown and under its protection. As such they could no longer be legally enslaved, but many were still worked to death in the mines, businesses, and croplands of their Spanish overlords. Over time, racial interrelationships created many individuals of mixed ancestry called *mestizos,* who eventually formed a major element in the Latin American population.

Based on the toil of this Amerindian and mestizo workforce, Spanish fleets carried enormous wealth in silver, hides, gold, dyes, cacao, and quinine from the mainland of the Western Hemisphere to Spain. As its share of the precious metals and as taxes, the Spanish monarchy took 40 percent of the value of these shipments. Two fleets from Spain carrying food, clothing, wine, tools, household items, and a few settlers sailed to the Western Hemisphere annually, but the goods sent over were inadequate for the colonial population.

The Spanish and Portuguese made their colonies Roman Catholic, at least in name. In many areas church teachings mixed with indigenous Amerindian and African religious practices. Some of the Spanish religious leaders went to great lengths to destroy all remnants of the Amerindian heritage on the grounds that their preconquest cultures were based on devil worship, sodomy, and cannibalism. A Spanish bishop destroyed all the preconquest Maya books he could locate because they contained aspects of the old religion. Of the hundreds of Maya books that once existed, only four survived to modern times. In many areas Catholic clergy were responsible for exploration and settlement. Some priests also led the fight for more humane treatment for the Amerindians.

Several aspects of the Western Hemisphere were transmitted to Europe. Foods such as potatoes, maize, several varieties of peppers, tomatoes, chocolate, and many others became a part of the European diet; maize also became a staple in China and Africa.

Rival Empires in the Western Hemisphere

By the middle of the sixteenth century, the Spanish and Portuguese had used the Western Hemisphere as an arena to create enormous colonial empires. Unlike the collection of fortified coastal towns and trading depots set up by the Portuguese in Africa and Asia, the Spanish colonies constituted territories many times larger than

Forced Labor in Peru, 1652

According to His Majesty's warrant, the mine owners on this massive range have a right . . . to 13,300 Indians in working and exploitation of the mines. It is the duty of the Corregidor of Petosi [governor] to have them rounded up and to see that they come in from all the provinces. . . . These Indians are sent out every year under a captain. . . . This works very badly, with great losses and gaps in the quotas of Indians, the villages being depopulated. . . . After each has eaten his ration, they climb up the hill, each to his mine, and go in, staying there from that hour until Saturday evening without coming out of the mine; their wives bring them food, but they stay constantly underground, excavating and carrying out the ore from which they get the silver. They all have tallow candles, lighted day and night; that is the light they work with, for as they are underground, they have need of it all the time. The mere cost of these candles used in the mines . . . will amount every year to more than 300,000 pesos, even though tallow is cheap in that country, being abundant; but this is a very great expense, and it is almost incredible, how much is spent for candles in the operation of breaking down and getting out the ore.*

This description of forced Amerindian labor in silver mines provides insight into both the working conditions for the miners and the attitudes of the Spanish observers. This report seems more concerned about the cost of candles than about the health or well-being of the Amerindian workers.

*"The Petosi Mine and Indian Forced Labor in Peru," in Antonio Vasques de Espinosa, *Compendium and Description of the West Indies,* trans. C. U. Clark (Washington, D.C.: Smithsonian Institution, 1942), pp. 623–625, in Peter N. Stearns, ed., *Documents in World History,* vol. 2 (New York: Harper & Row, 1988), pp. 83–84.

Spain itself. Portugal created an equivalently huge colony in Brazil.

During most of the sixteenth century, while the Spanish and Portuguese exploited the riches of Latin America, the English, French, and Dutch, preoccupied with religious wars and other domestic problems, stayed home. Late in the century, however, these nations were ready to compete with the Spanish and Portuguese; in particular, they had devised effective economic incentives to foster their own colonialism. The Spanish and Portuguese had allowed a small percentage of their business community to monopolize opportunities abroad, thus limiting available investment resources. In contrast, the English, French, and Dutch governments encouraged merchants and bankers to invest in overseas commerce by granting

New Stuff on Your Plate

We have already seen two developments of interhemispheric consequence that occurred after invaders from Europe conquered much of the Western Hemisphere. One was the moving of millions of Europeans and Africans to the Americas. The second was the spread of diseases, especially smallpox, that killed millions of Amerindians, depopulating certain areas of the Western Hemisphere. European conquest also had a third effect: the reciprocal introduction of new foods. Europeans brought into the Western Hemisphere agricultural products, both field crops and livestock. Wheat introduced from Europe supplemented maize in some areas, and produce such as citrus fruit and grapes likewise enjoyed local success in the Americas. Cash crops such as sugar, rice, bananas, and tobacco (indigenous) brought substantial wealth to the landowning elite in the Americas.

The coming of European livestock had an enormous impact in the Americas. Before Columbus, the Amerindians had domesticated only dogs, turkeys, ducks, alpacas, and llamas—none of which provided much food or hauling power. Worst of all, the Amerindians had few animals that could turn grass into meat. The introduction of sheep, goats, swine, cattle, and horses varied the diet of many and provided powerful beasts of burden. Later, horses, cattle, and sheep became the basis of full-scale Amerindian herding and riding cultures among, for example, the Navaho and the Apache.

At the same time, the introduction of Amerindian field and tuber crops to Europe, Asia, and Africa had tremendous consequences after 1500. Two commodities, maize and potatoes, spread through the Eastern Hemisphere, where they superseded the indigenous staples because they provided more nutrients per hectare.

The potato, native to the cool valleys of the Andes, adapted very successfully to the temperate climate of northern Europe and became the dietary mainstay from Ireland to Russia. The Dutch peasant family depicted at supper in Van Gogh's *The Potato Eaters* could just as well have been Peruvian. Maize, native to the warm climate of Mesoamerica, was adopted in much of southern Europe; its cultivation in Africa steadily increased until by the 1990s it had become the number one consumer crop on that continent. Maize and sweet potatoes became major crops in Asia, surpassed only by rice and wheat. Other Amerindian foods that spread around the world were tomatoes, squash, certain beans, and peanuts. Manioc (cassava) was an important food crop, first in Brazil and later in Africa.

Enormous economic consequences flowed from the improvement in diet caused by the expansion of maize and especially potato cultivation. In the British Isles, for example, the new crops helped bring about a sharp increase in the population that provided both the labor and the consumer basis for the Industrial Revolution.

---

charters to new "joint stock" companies specializing in trading and colonization. For participants in joint stock companies, the risks were limited to the proportion of their investment; this restricted liability encouraged smaller investors to put their money in new overseas ventures. Investment was further encouraged by easier access to marine insurance. The wealth brought into Europe from the Western Hemisphere later helped to fuel further European expansion into Asia (see Chapter 10).

At first the northern European nations concentrated on finding a way to share the Asian trade. During the sixteenth century, despite the discouraging news of earlier explorers, many northern Europeans hoped that a water route to Asia might yet be found somewhere in the northern latitudes. Beginning in 1497, English, French, and Dutch expeditions hunted for a "Northwest Passage" around North America, but to their dismay the northern seas were clogged with impenetrable ice. However, the explorers did learn that the northern parts of North America contained valuable timber and furs and that the North Atlantic teemed with fish.

As hopes of finding a northern route to Asia faded, the northern European nations turned their attention to the Western Hemisphere. Since Spain and Portugal monopolized the wealth of the most valuable parts of the Americas, England, France, and the Netherlands had to fight their way in. In the beginning this meant smuggling goods and slaves into the Spanish colonies; the Dutch were particularly active in this endeavor. Soon the interlopers were attacking Spanish and Portuguese ships laden with wealth bound for Europe. Pirates, both freelance "buccaneers" and marauders secretly outfitted by European governments, pillaged the "Spanish Main," raiding Spanish silver fleets and attacking Caribbean ports.

By the mid-seventeenth century, the English, French, and Dutch were strong enough to attempt to conquer the Spanish and Portuguese colonies in the Western Hemisphere, as well as in Africa and Asia. The Spanish and Portuguese held on to their main possessions in the Americas, but the newcomers did capture a number of small islands in the West Indies, turning them into agricultural plantations for growing sugar and tobacco. To work the crops, the English, French, and Dutch shipped in slaves from their trading posts in West Africa. The constant importation of slaves to the European plantation colonies quickly transformed the racial composition of the eastern fringe of the Western Hemisphere, replacing the original Amerindian population with a few Europeans and masses of black slaves.

During the seventeenth century, the northern European states established new colonies on the east coast of North America. The Dutch, Swedes, and French were primarily interested in developing a lucrative fur trade with the Amerindians, but their colonies proved to be only modestly profitable, considering the cost of maintenance and defense. To cut down on costs, they brought over a few farmers to provide food.

In 1607 the English established a new kind of colony on the east coast of North America. In such colonies, often termed "New Europes," large numbers of European settlers landed, killed off or drove out the Amerindian inhabitants, and set up replicas of European society. The English authorities had originally hoped to trade with the Amerindians for skins and furs, as the French and Dutch were doing. Failing that, they wanted to find or grow the products that had made the Spanish and Portuguese rich: gold, silver, silk, spices, and tea. They had other motives as well: outflanking the Spanish, converting Amerindians to Christianity, and removing some of England's criminals, paupers, unemployed, religious dissenters, and political unreliables. English leaders believed that the work of these people would be profitable to the merchant trading companies. Encouraged by such boosters as Richard Hakluyt (see the box on colonization), and with varying degrees of pressure by the government and the trading companies, more

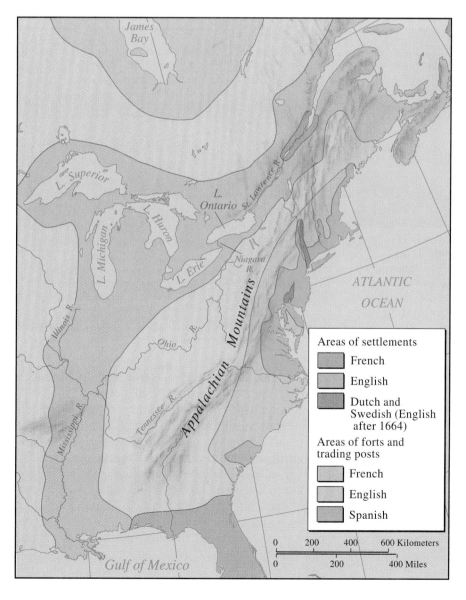

✤ MAP 9.7 European Holdings in North America, c. 1685. After nearly a century of activity in North America, the French and the English had built up very different colonial holdings. The French had a rapidly expanding domain of fur and deerskin trading posts based on a small French settlement in Quebec. The English controlled a smaller but much more populous area, dominated by family farms.

⚜ Slavery in Virginia. In 1619 at Jamestown, England's Virginia colony, a Dutch slave ship has landed with the first blacks offered for sale. The Virginians stare at the strangers, trying to gauge the economic and social consequences of purchasing them. Their decision to buy the blacks contributed to the radical transformation of the racial composition of the Western Hemisphere. Corbis-Bettmann

A Plea to Englishmen to Begin Colonization

The soil yields . . . all the several commodities of Europe . . . that England trades with. . . .

3. A safe passage, and not easy to be annoyed by prince or potentate whatsoever. . . .

6. This enterprise may keep the Spanish King from flowing over all the face of America, if we seat and plant there in time. . . . And England possessing the proposed place of planting, her Majesty [Queen Elizabeth] may . . . have plenty of excellent trees for masts, of good timber to build ships and to make great navies . . . and to spoil Philip's [King Philip II of Spain] . . . navy and to deprive him of yearly passage of his treasure into Europe and consequently to abate the pride of Spain . . . and pull him down in equality to his neighbor princes, and consequently to cut off the common mischief that comes to all Europe by the peculiar abundance of his Indian treasure. . . .

14. Salt, . . . wine, oils, oranges, lemons, figs, . . . iron, all with much more is hoped. . . .

16. We shall by planting there enlarge the glory of the gospel, and from England plant sincere religion, and provide a safe and a sure place to receive people from all parts of the world that are forced to flee for the truth of God's word.*

Richard Hakluyt's words, written in 1584, reflect the mixture of economic, political, strategic, and religious arguments for colonization that were advanced in England in the late sixteenth century. Shortly after Hakluyt wrote this tract, Sir Walter Raleigh and others attempted, unsuccessfully, to establish a settlement at Roanoke Island in present-day North Carolina.

*Richard Hakluyt, "A Discourse Concerning Western Planting," in *Documentary History of the State of Maine,* Maine Historical Collections, 2d ser., vol. 2 (Portland, Maine: 1869–1916), pp. 36–41.

than 100,000 settlers came to English North America by the middle of the seventeenth century.

To the disappointment of the English investors, many of the colonies produced little in the way of Asian and Latin American wealth. North of Chesapeake Bay, the natural products were timber, fish, grain, and meat; only the first was wanted in England. The foodstuffs, however, could be sent to the Caribbean, allowing the planters there to keep their slaves at work growing sugar and tobacco exclusively. From the Chesapeake southward, the English had more luck: Here settlers could grow tobacco and (later) rice, indigo, and cotton—all valuable products. Slave traders brought in slaves from the Caribbean and from Africa to raise these products; as a result, some areas from the Chesapeake southward rapidly took on the brutal economic and social characteristics of the plantation culture of the Caribbean and Brazil.

By the mid-seventeenth century, the center of economic power in Europe had shifted from the Iberian Peninsula to the northern European nations. Having sufficient power and economic stability, these nations created, enlarged, and protected their colonial empires. Increasingly efficient in mercantile and banking affairs, they augmented the profits obtained from their colonies and avoided dissipating their wealth in European wars. Many English and Dutch families became wealthy from overseas trade, and company investors plowed profits from their colonial enterprises into new manufacturing and trading projects in Europe (see Chapter 11).

Summary and Comparisons

The fifteenth, sixteenth, and seventeenth centuries were marked by the rise and fall of absolutist states. Several of the Atlantic-facing nations of Europe were building up centralized monarchies; the Ottoman and Safavid Empires were flourishing; the papacy was beleaguered; and the Aztec and Inka Empires were overthrown. The Renaissance reissue of classical histories and biographies gave some new perspective to this process.

Another major theme of this chapter concerns the beginning of a remarkable five-century period in which certain nations of Europe extended their power into four other continents. In the process they moved large numbers of persons of two races across the Atlantic. They also destroyed or profoundly altered many indigenous cultures in North and South America and in parts of Africa and Asia. As a result of these developments, the center of political power shifted from Mediterranean to Atlantic groups.

Authoritarian government was well established in the Ottoman and Safavid Empires. Although old enemies, these empires were remarkably similar. Each was highly centralized politically and economically, and their cultural and social life shared a common Islamic heritage. Differences did exist, however, because the Ottoman Empire adhered to Sunni Islam while the Safavids were ardent believers in Shi'i Islam.

As a leading military power in the eastern Mediterranean, the Ottomans successfully absorbed the Balkans, Hungary, and the Arab lands of the eastern Mediterranean and North Africa. Ottoman attempts to take Vienna and to destroy Safavid power failed, however. The Ottoman Empire reached its zenith under Suleiman the Magnificent, a great patron of the arts, but steadily declined in world status after his reign. Although Suleiman engaged in numerous battles against the European powers, particularly the Habsburgs, he encouraged trade with the Western world.

The Safavid Empire entered its golden age under Shah Abbas, who created a new, glorious capital at Isfahan and made Persia a cultural center. Control of the silk industry provided the Safavids with economic wealth and enabled them to become patrons of the arts. Like the Ottoman Empire, the Safavids encouraged trade with European nations and granted special privileges to European traders. Both the Safavids and the Ottomans also maintained economic links with Asia, where other centralized empires flourished during the sixteenth and seventeenth centuries.

During these centuries European societies also underwent profound changes. In Europe the otherworldly orientation of the Catholic church gave way to a secular outlook in thought and in art. Spurred on by refugee scholars who fled Ottoman advances in the eastern Mediterranean, Italy became the center of a remarkable intellectual, literary, and artistic reawakening called the Renaissance. Deriving inspiration from recently recovered manuscripts by classical Greek and Roman authors and from contacts with Islamic scholars, humanists produced superb works in history, phi-

losophy, and philology. Drawing from nature, painters and sculptors now concentrated on capturing and interpreting the world about them.

By the sixteenth and seventeenth centuries, the practices and perspectives of the Italian Renaissance had spread into western Europe. Vernacular literature flourished, and humanism became a strong force. France, England, and Spain enjoyed golden ages of literary productivity, particularly in drama. Artists represented nature by meticulous attention to detail and developed the techniques of oil painting, woodblock printing, and engraving, while architects followed Italian models.

During the fifteenth and sixteenth centuries, national monarchies also developed in western Europe. These national monarchies established territorial unity and centralized governmental functions, and their monarchs overcame the opposition of the nobles by allying with towns and relying on advisers and bureaucrats from outside the aristocracy. In England, Tudor monarchs, beginning with Henry VII, controlled Parliament to royal advantage. In France, the Estates General remained unimportant as kings brought the nobility under control and extended their authority over the provinces. In the Iberian Peninsula, Portugal and Spain also became strong national monarchies in the course of reconquering the peninsula from the Muslims. Spain was created by the marriage of Ferdinand of Aragon and Isabella of Castile, who curbed the nobles' power, controlled the church, and received the support of the towns. Expanding centralized monarchies also had impacts on the relationships of European governments with the Catholic church.

The Protestant Reformation of the sixteenth century had several causes. Popular support for the Catholic church had waned as the papacy weakened and abuses of simony, indulgences, and pluralism became rampant. The church's problems stirred reformers to action. Luther and Calvin led the movement to break with the Catholic church and establish Protestant Christianity. Luther's teaching of salvation by faith made the Catholic apparatus for earning salvation unnecessary. He recognized the Bible as the sole source of religious authority; Calvin stressed God's arbitrary sovereignty and the doctrine of predestination. Protestantism in England began as a result of Tudor dynastic difficulties; the Anglican church retained many Roman Catholic features. Within the Roman Catholic church, humanists and clergy led reforming activities, and Pope Paul III made reform a churchwide activity. The Council of Trent reaffirmed traditional Roman Catholic doctrines and sought to eliminate abuses. Religious wars disrupted European societies until 1648, when the Treaty of Westphalia recognized both Protestant and Catholic states in Europe.

The newly unified European states along the Atlantic Ocean had also amassed the economic resources and technology necessary to explore new trade routes. Spurred on by Ottoman taxes on goods from Asia, and to some degree by a desire to make converts to Christianity, they began to search for routes to Asia that they could control. In the process they explored much of the globe and brought European power not only to Asia, but to Africa and the Western Hemisphere as well.

In this period Africa saw both the spread of Islam and the appearance of Europeans. North Africa, with the exception of Morocco, which remained independent, was conquered by the Ottoman Empire during the sixteenth century. These territories were incorporated into the larger Islamic Ottoman society. Islam spread further into both East Africa and the area south of the Sahara. Simultaneously, numerous, vibrant independent kingdoms in western and central Africa developed along their own particular political, economic, and cultural lines. The Benin and Kongo kingdoms were two examples of African kingdoms that dealt as equals with early European explorers and traders.

The Portuguese, Dutch, French, and English all established trading routes along the coasts of Africa and gradually built ports and trading depots. The Portuguese were initially strongly entrenched in both West and East Africa, but they gradually lost their favored positions to the Dutch and English.

In East Africa, indigenous African and Arab opposition drove out the Portuguese, who had been weakened by Dutch naval victories in the Indian Ocean. In South Africa, the Dutch established a permanent colony based on the racial supremacy of the white Boers. This initially small colony would have many long-term ramifications for the history of South Africa.

Finally, the slave trade, which lasted some 400 years, affected all of Africa. Millions of Africans were shipped by force to the Americas. Although some Africans cooperated and benefited from this trade, many, like "King" Nzinga of Angola, fought against it. The slave trade had many disastrous results on individual African societies, particularly in the interior of the continent. In spite of the negative impacts of the slave trade, most of Africa remained independent and continued to develop under its own political and cultural institutions until the nineteenth century.

During this era, European powers, led by Spain, began to expand across the Atlantic. In Mexico and South America, the Spanish established vast empires rich in gold and silver; in the course of this conquest, the great majority of Amerindians died from European diseases. Europeans also transformed the Caribbean islands into sugar and tobacco plantations worked by black slaves who lived and died under brutal conditions. Portugal established a similar plantation-based economy in Brazil. Three key characteristics of Iberia—paternalistic government, aristocratic privilege, and mercantilist economics—were essentially replicated in Latin America, but in this case they were imposed on populations who were predominantly Amerindian and black. Amerindian and black culture—especially food, clothing, textiles, music, and speech—modified the lifestyles of Europeans, both in Latin America and elsewhere.

In the seventeenth century, the French, Dutch, and English also became active overseas. Although they failed to find passages to Asia through the Arctic ice, the northern European states did establish colonies on the Atlantic seaboard of North America and used the wealth from these colonies for financial and industrial developments in Europe. Thousands of Europeans settled in North America, displacing and often massacring the Amerindians. These colonies began to exhibit more liberal social, political, and religious values and practices than Europe.

Selected Sources

Adas, Michael, ed. *Technology and European Overseas Enterprise: Diffusion, Adaptation, and Adoption.* 1996. Presents ideological justification for colonization and imperialism.

*Atil, Esin. *The Age of Sultan Suleyman the Magnificent.* 1987. A lavishly illustrated discussion of art, crafts, and culture during the zenith of Ottoman power.

Augustijn, Cornelius. *Erasmus: His Life, Works and Influence.* Trans. J. C. Grayson. 1991. A balanced account of Erasmus's life and works.

*Bailyn, Bernard. *Origins of American Politics.* 1970. Examines colonial roots of American political theory and practice.

*Balewa, Abubakar Tafawa. *Shaihu Umar.* 1967. A novel about the life of a slave by a former prime minister of Nigeria.

Barber, Noel. *The Sultans.* 1973. A readable account of the Ottoman Empire, based on the lives of the sultans.

Benesch, Otto. *The Art of the Renaissance in Northern Europe.* 1965. A well-illustrated presentation relating northern European art to contemporary trends in thought and religion.

Bethell, Leslie, ed. *Colonial Spanish America.* 1987. *Colonial Brazil.* 1988. Both books contain essays concerning Latin America from the conquest to independence. Noted authorities write about rural society and the hacienda, urbanization, and Amerindian cultures.

*Bouwsma, William J. *John Calvin: A Sixteenth-Century Portrait.* 1988. An essential biography of Calvin.

Boxers, Charles R. *Four Centuries of Portuguese Expansion, 1415–1825.* 1969. Provides an overview of Brazil within the context of the Portuguese Empire.

Braudel, Fernand. *The Mediterranean and the Mediterranean World in the Age of Philip II.* Abridged 1992. Excellent background for understanding Spain and Spanish transplantations in the Americas.

*Cellini, Benvenuto. *Autobiography.* 1927. Cellini, a noted artist of the period, vividly depicts both art and life in Renaissance Italy.

*Costain, Thomas B. *The Moneyman.* 1947. A historical novel about the life of a French merchant.

Cutter, Donald C. *Quest for Empire: Spanish Settlement in the Southwest.* 1996. Details Spanish policies.

Ferro, Marc. *Colonization: A Global History.* 1997. A good overview.

Fuentes, Carlos. *The Buried Mirror: Reflections on Spain and the New World.* 1992. Excellent introduction to Spain and the Americas; beautifully crafted with prints, maps, and artwork.

"The Glories of Ancient Benin." Films for the Humanities. A short video on the founding of Benin in West Africa, with scenes from the museum and palace of Porto-Novo.

*Goodwin, Godfrey. *A History of Ottoman Architecture.* 1971; reprinted 1992. Includes hundreds of illustrations and dozens of floor plans for mosques, government complexes, and homes; also includes a particularly informative chapter on Sinan, the noted Ottoman architect.

"Gorée: Door of No Return." Films for the Humanities. A moving historical description of Gorée, a slave-trading center in West Africa.

Green, Guy, director. *Luther.* 1974. Stirring film interpretation of Luther's reforming activities.

Grimm, Harold J. *The Reformation Era: 1500–1650.* 2d ed. 1973. Focuses on the religious issues and personalities of the Reformation era.

*Haring, Clarence H. *The Spanish Empire in America.* 1975. An authoritative study that is sympathetic to the Spanish.

*Hodgson, Marshall G. S. *The Venture of Islam: The Gunpowder Empires and Modern Times.* Vol. 3. 1974. A scholarly analysis with a truly global approach to the confrontation of Islamic states, including the Ottoman and Persian Empires and Muslim India, with the West.

*Innes, Hammond. *The Conquistadors.* 1969. A lively, beautifully illustrated account.

"The Isfahan of Shah Abbas." 1987. This 28-minute film is a stunning visual presentation of Safavid culture with narration by art expert Oleg Grabar.

Jensen, De Lamar. *Reformation Europe.* 1992. The best one-volume account.

Joffe, Roland, director. *The Mission.* 1986. A visually spectacular film about a Jesuit mission in the jungles of Brazil and its destruction by the greed of merchants and factionalism within the church.

*Kinross, Patrick Balfour. *The Ottoman Centuries: The Rise and Fall of the Turkish Empire.* 1977. A well-written account of Ottoman history, with good analysis of the empire's strengths and weaknesses.

*Kristeller, Paul O. *Renaissance Thought: The Classic, Scholastic, and Humanistic Strains.* Rev. ed. 1961. The six concise essays in this book provide a very useful guide to Renaissance learning.

Labalm, Patricia, ed. *Beyond Their Sex: Learned Women of the European Past.* 1980. Contains a number of useful articles analyzing educational and scholarly roles open to females in Renaissance society.

*Leonard, Irving A. *Baroque Times in Old Mexico: Seventeenth-Century Persons, Places, and Practices.* 1959. A colorful insight into the society and culture of Latin America.

Leon-Portilla, Miguel. *The Broken Spears: Aztec Accounts of the Conquest.* 1962. An enduring classic, employing Amerindian accounts of the fall of the Aztecs.

———. *Pre-Columbian Literatures of Mexico.* 1992. An anthology of poetry and prose, including indigenous accounts of the conquest.

*Maalouf, Amin. *Leo Africanus.* 1986; reprinted 1992. A novel based on the celebrated traveler's life, with vivid, historically

accurate descriptions of Moorish Spain, Timbuktu, and Italy during the Renaissance.

Marks, Richard L. *Cortés: The Great Adventurer and the Fate of Aztec Mexico.* 1993. A biography of the Spanish conqueror against the backdrop of the clash between the Aztec and European civilizations.

Marshall, Sherrin, ed. *Women in Reformation and Counter-Reformation Europe.* 1989. Explores the role and status of women in the Reformation era and their contribution to spiritual renewal and reform.

*Morison, Samuel E. *Christopher Columbus, Mariner.* 1983. A lively, if traditional, introduction to Columbus.

Oberman, Heiko O. *Luther: Man between God and Devil.* Trans. E. Walliser-Schwarzbart. 1989. Examines Luther and his theology against the intellectual currents of the later medieval world.

*Pernoud, Regine. *Joan of Arc, by Herself and Her Witnesses.* Trans. Edward Hyams. 1969. A powerful biography; also the film *Joan of Arc,* director Victor Fleming, 1948, starring Ingrid Bergman.

*Perroy, Edouard. *The Hundred Years' War.* 1965. Combines social and political history with military events.

*Perry, Glenn E. *The Middle East: Fourteen Islamic Centuries.* 3d ed. 1997. A concise overview of the region from early times to the present day.

Rubin, Nancy. *Isabella of Castile: The First Renaissance Queen.* 1991. A lively biography of the strong-willed queen.

Sale, Kirkpatrick. *The Conquest of Paradise: Christopher Columbus and the Columbian Legacy.* 1990. A fervent exposition of the concept that a sickly, dispirited post–Black Death Europe essentially destroyed the environment, native population, and indigenous culture of the Americas.

Shaffer, Peter. *The Royal Hunt of the Sun.* 1981. A moving play depicting the story of the capture, imprisonment, and execution of the Inka emperor by Pizarro.

*Stone, Irving. *The Agony and the Ecstasy.* 1961. A historical novel based on Michelangelo's life; also the basis for a movie of the same title.

"Suleiman the Magnificent." 1987. This one-hour film, produced by the National Gallery of Art, is a colorful, historically accurate account of the Ottoman Empire at its zenith.

*Tawney, R. H. *Religion and the Rise of Capitalism.* 1926. A classic study that stimulated extensive controversy on a possible relationship between Protestantism and capitalism.

*Thompson, Vincent Bakpetu. *The Making of the African Diaspora in the Americas, 1441–1900.* 1988. A full account of the slave trade and its cultural impacts.

Williams, Selma. *Demeter's Daughters.* 1976. A survey of the various roles of women in British North America, stressing the stories of individuals.

Wölfflin, Heinrich. *Classic Art: An Introduction to the Italian Renaissance.* 3d ed. 1968. A brief, comprehensive, well-illustrated introduction to this large topic.

Zophy, Jonathan W. *A Short History of Reformation Europe.* 1997. A concise, readable overview of the period. Tailored for students who have not had much exposure to the subject.

———. *A Short History of Renaissance Europe.* 1997. Like its companion volume, a useful introduction for the beginning student.

*Available in paperback.

Internet Links

Art History: Renaissance Italy
http://www.scottlan.edu/academic/art/dsadler/203/main.html
  Hundreds of well-reproduced illustrations of Italian renaissance art works from the fourteenth through early sixteenth centuries.

The Art of Renaissance Science: Galileo and Perspective
http://www.bang.lanl.gov/video/stv/arshtml/arstoc.html
  Detailed discussion of renaissance artists' innovative use of new knowledge of proportion and perspective in depicting the human body, and applying mathematics in their painting and architecture. The graphics are plentiful and superb.

The Beginnings of European Slave Trade
http://www.wsu.edu/~dee/DIASPORA/SLAVE.HTML
  This concise account is one segment of the excellent "African Diaspora" website at Washington State University.

The Conquest of Mexico
http://www.wavenet.com/~prashkin/conquest.html
  One of the better history sites available on the internet: offers extensive text, with relevant quotations from Bernal Díaz and the letters of Hernán Cortés. Many excellent illustrations.

History of the Ottoman Empire
http://www.sscnet.ucla.edu/history/shaw/classes/111A/
  This site, constructed to accompany a course at UCLA, includes links to quite detailed lecture notes and cross-references to chapters in good textbooks.

Islamic Art, 1250–1723
http://www.home.eznet.net/~mcdonoug/gallery/Islamic/index.html
  A sampling of extremely well-reproduced art works from various periods, including the Mamluk Empire, the il-Khanate, and the eras of the Timurids and the Safavids.

National Museum of African Art Collections
http://www.si.edu/nmafa/collect/start.html
  Includes a section devoted to "The Ancient West African City of Benin, A.D. 1300–1897."

The Reformation
http://www.infinet.com/~obeng/reformation/reformationhistory.html
  This detailed and lucid account encompasses Causes of the Reformation, Original Ideas and Purposes of the Reformers, Methods of Spreading the Reformation, Spread of the Reformation in the Various Countries, Different Forms of the Reformation, and Results and Consequences of the Reformation.

Romanizing Chinese Words

There are two systems in current use for romanizing Chinese words. The Wade-Giles System has been in use longer than the Pinying System. Both are equally in use by scholars of China. Newspapers tend to use the Pinying system for the People's Republic and the Wade-Giles for the Republic of China. This book follows the Wade-Giles System for pre-1949 China and the Pinying System for the post-1949 era. The following table equates some of the Wade-Giles and other conventional spellings with the Pinying spelling used in this text. Since not all words differ in the two systems, only those words that do are included.

WADE-GILES	PINYING	WADE-GILES	PINYING
Canton	Guangzhou	Kwangsi	Guangxi
Ch'an	Chan	Kwangtung	Guangdong
Chao	Zhao	Lao Tzu	Laozi
Chekiang	Zhejiang	Li Po	Li Bo
Chengchow	Zhengzhou	Loyang	Luoyang
Ch'ien-lung	Qianlong	Mao Tse-tung	Mao Zedong
Ch'in	Qin	Nanking	Nanjing
Ching-te Cheng	Jingdezhen	Peking	Beijing
Ch'ing	Qing	Shang-ti	Shangdi
Chou	Zhou	Shantung	Shandong
Chu Hsi	Zhu Xi	Shansi	Shaanxi
Chu Yuan-chang	Zhu Yuanzhang	Shensi	Shanxi
Chungking	Chongqing	Sian	Xi'an
Fukien	Fujian	Sinkiang	Xinjiang
Hangchow	Hangzhou	Sung	Song
Honan	Henan	Szechuan	Sichuan
Hopei	Hebei	T'ang	Tang
Hsiung-nu	Xiongnu	T'ang T'ai-tsung	Tang Taizong
Hung-wu	Hongwu	Taoism	Daoism
K'ang-hsi	Kangxi	Tatung	Dadong
Kansu	Gansu	Tien	Tian
Kiangsi	Jiangxi	Tz'u-hsi	Cixi
Kiangsu	Jiangsu	Wu-ti	Wudi
K'ung Fu-tzu	Kong Fuzi	Yang-tze	Yangzi
Kuomintang	Guomindang	Yung-cheng	Yongzheng

Index